The Wiley Handbook on What Works for Offenders with Intellectual and Developmental Disabilities

An Evidence-Based Approach to Theory, Assessment, and Treatment

Edited by William R. Lindsay, Leam A. Craig, and Dorothy Griffiths

WILEY Blackwell

This edition first published 2020
© 2020 John Wiley & Sons Ltd

The right of William R. Lindsay, Leam A. Craig and Dorothy Griffiths to be identified as the authors of the editorial material in this work has been asserted in accordance with law.

Registered Offices
John Wiley & Sons, Inc., 111 River Street, Hoboken, NJ 07030, USA
John Wiley & Sons Ltd, The Atrium, Southern Gate, Chichester, West Sussex, PO19 8SQ, UK

Editorial Office
The Atrium, Southern Gate, Chichester, West Sussex, PO19 8SQ, UK

For details of our global editorial offices, customer services, and more information about Wiley products visit us at www.wiley.com.

Wiley also publishes its books in a variety of electronic formats and by print-on-demand. Some content that appears in standard print versions of this book may not be available in other formats.

Library of Congress Cataloging-in-Publication Data is Available:
9781119316251 (hardback), 9781119316237 (paperback), 9781119316275 (ePDF), 9781119316282 (epub)

Cover Design: Wiley
Cover Image: © yaibuabann/Shutterstock

Set in 10/12pt Warnock by SPi Global, Pondicherry, India
Printed and bound in Singapore by Markono Print Media Pte Ltd

10 9 8 7 6 5 4 3 2 1

In memory of the late William (Bill) Lindsay, his contribution to the field of intellectual disability research was immeasurable.

Contents

Acknowledgements

We are grateful to the contributors of this volume for sharing their experience and expertise and who have worked tirelessly on this project alongside their hectic schedules.

We would like to thank all those at Wiley-Blackwell for their patience and guidance in bringing this project together.

About the Editors

The Late **William R. Lindsay, PhD, FBPS, FIASSID, FAcSS,** was Consultant Forensic Clinical Psychologist and Head of Research for Danshell. He was previously Head of Psychology (LD) in NHS Tayside and Consultant Psychologist with the State Hospital. He was Professor of Learning Disabilities and Forensic Psychology at the University of Abertay, Dundee and Honorary Professor at Deakin University Melbourne. Professor Lindsay had published over 350 research articles and book chapters, published 5 books, held around 2 million pounds in research grants and given many presentations and workshops on cognitive therapy and the assessment and treatment of offenders with intellectual disability. His recent publications included a workbook entitled *The Treatment of Sex Offenders with Developmental Disabilities: A Practice Workbook* (2009), and co-edited books entitled *Offenders with Developmental Disabilities* (2004), *Assessment and Treatment of Sexual Offenders with Developmental Disabilities* (2010), and *Offenders with Developmental Disabilities: Second Edition* (2018) published by Wiley-Blackwell.

Leam A. Craig, CPsychol, CSci, MAE, FBPsS, FAcSS, EuroPsy, PhD, is a Consultant Forensic and Clinical Psychologist and Partner at Forensic Psychology Practice Ltd. He is Hon. Professor of Forensic Psychology at the Centre of Applied Psychology, University of Birmingham, Visiting Professor of Forensic Clinical Psychology at the School of Social Sciences, Birmingham City University, UK and Hon. Associate Professor of Forensic Psychology, University of Nottingham, UK. He is a Chartered and dual Registered (Forensic and Clinical) Psychologist, a Chartered Scientist, holder of the European Certificate in Psychology and a Full Member of the Academy of Experts. He was awarded Fellowship of the British Psychological Society and the Academy of Social Sciences for distinguished contributions to psychology and the social sciences. He has previously worked in forensic psychiatric secure services, learning disability hospitals, and consultancy to prison and probation services throughout England, Wales, and Northern Ireland, specializing in high-risk, complex cases. He was previously Consultant Lead to three community forensic psychiatric hospitals for people with personality disorders, learning disabilities, and challenging behaviour. He is currently a Consultant to the National Probation Service on working with offenders with personality disorders. He acts as an expert witness to civil and criminal courts in the assessment of sexual and violent offenders and in matters of child protection. He has previously been instructed by the Salvation Army, Catholic and Church of England Dioceses, South African Police Service, and currently receives instruction from the United States Air Force European

Defence Counsel. He has over 100 publications including 11 books. In 2013 he received the Senior Academic Award by the Division of Forensic Psychology for distinguished contributions to academic knowledge in forensic psychology and in 2018 won the Emerald Literati Award for a Highly Commended paper. In 2015 he co-authored a Ministry of Justice research funded report into the use of expert witnesses in family law and in 2016 he was appointed as Chair of the British Psychological Society, Expert Witness Advisory Group. His research interests include sexual and violent offenders, personality disorder and forensic risk assessment, and the use of expert witnesses in civil and criminal courts.

Dorothy Griffiths, CM, OOnt, PhD, is Professor Emerita at Brock University, St. Catharines, Ontario, Canada. Formerly Professor in the Department of Child and Youth Studies and Centre for Applied Disability Studies, Co-Director of the International Dual Diagnosis Certificate Programme, and Associate Dean, Faculty of Social Sciences, Dr Griffiths has extensive experience in working on clinical issues regarding dual diagnosis (persons who are developmentally disabled and have mental health issues). Her expertise more specifically is in the area of sexual abuse and offence, aggression and self-injury, and social skills training with persons with developmental disabilities. Her recent research interests have included Human Rights and Deinstitutionalization. She has written and speaks extensively on these topics. She is notably recognized for five books that she co-authored/co-edited called *Changing Sexually Inappropriate Behaviour, Dual Diagnosis, Demystifying Syndromes, Ethical Dilemmas of Sexuality and Developmental Disabilities*, and *The Human Rights Agenda*. Her most recent coauthored book is *Sex Offending Behavior of Persons with an Intellectual Disability: A Multi-Component Applied Behavior Analytic Approach*. She is a recipient of numerous teaching, research, and advocacy awards, including the Order of Ontario and the Order of Canada.

Notes on Contributors

Berindah Aicken, is the State-wide Manager of Specific Needs and has worked for Corrective Services New South Wales, Australia in the roles of Forensic, Senior, and Chief Psychologist. Her work and research interests include offenders with disability, mental health impairment, ageing offenders, female offenders with children, and those at risk of suicide/self-harm, particularly the intersection of these issues with broader systemic concerns and the implications for policy and practice.

Regi T. Alexander, MD, is a Consultant Psychiatrist at Hertfordshire Partnership University NHS Foundation Trust and Honorary Senior Lecturer, Department of Health Sciences, University of Leicester.

Nigel Beail, PhD, is a Consultant Clinical Psychologist and Professional Lead for Psychological Services for South West Yorkshire Partnership NHS Foundation Trust, and Professor of Psychology at the Clinical Psychology Unit, Department of Psychology at the University of Sheffield, UK. He is a Fellow of the British Psychological Society, a Trustee of the British Institute for Learning Disabilities, former President of the European Association for Mental Health in Intellectual Disability, and a founder and Fellow of the Institute for Psychotherapy and Disability. He has published extensively on practice-based research from his clinical work.

Astrid Birgden, PhD, is a Forensic and Clinical Psychologist with over 30 years experience working with serious offenders, including clients with intellectual disability. As a practitioner, Dr Birgden conducts assessments, designs programmes and training packages, and develops policy in correctional and human services systems. She is also an Adjunct Clinical Associate Professor at Deakin University and has published in the areas of offender rehabilitation, human rights, and therapeutic jurisprudence.

Peer Briken is a Professor of Sexual Research and Forensic Psychiatry and Director of the eponymous institute at the University Hospital Hamburg-Eppendorf. The Institute was the first institution of post-war university-sexology in Germany and is today the largest interdisciplinary institution of sexual science in Germany. His research focuses on the diagnosis and therapy of sexual disorders and sexual violence. He also works as a court expert and is co-editor of the *Journal of Sexual Research* and the journal *Personality Disorders: Theory and Therapy*. Until 2016 he was the first chairman of the German Society for Sexual Research. Since January 2016, he has been a member of the Independent Commission on the Treatment of Child Sexual Abuse.

Verity Chester is a PhD Candidate in the Norwich Medical School at the University of East Anglia, and a Research Associate at St Johns House, a forensic intellectual disability service in Norfolk.

Leam A. Craig, CPsychol, CSci, MAE, FBPsS, FAcSS, EuroPsy, PhD, is a Consultant Forensic Clinical Psychologist, a Chartered and Registered [Forensic and Clinical] Psychologist, and a Partner at Forensic Psychology Practice Ltd. He is the Hon. Professor of Forensic Psychology, Centre of Applied Psychology, University of Birmingham; Visiting Professor of Forensic Clinical Psychology, School of Social Sciences, Birmingham City University; and Hon. Associate Professor of Forensic Psychology, University of Nottingham, UK. He was awarded a Fellowship of the British Psychological Society and the Academy of Social Sciences for distinguished contributions to psychology and the social sciences. He has previously worked in forensic psychiatric secure services, learning disability hospitals, and consultancy to prison and probation services throughout England, Wales, and Northern Ireland, specializing in high-risk, complex cases. He is currently a Consultant to the National Probation Service on working with offenders with personality disorders. He has over 100 publications including 11 books. In 2013 he received the Senior Academic Award from the Division of Forensic Psychology for distinguished contributions to academic knowledge in forensic psychology and in 2018 won an Emerald Literati Award for a Highly Commended paper. In 2015 he co-authored a Ministry of Justice report into the use of expert witnesses in family law and in 2016 he was appointed as Chair of the British Psychological Society, Expert Witness Advisory Group. His research interests include sexual and violent offenders, personality disorder, and forensic risk assessment and the use of psychologists as expert witnesses in civil and criminal courts.

Danielle Davidson, PhD, is a lecturer in social work and human services in the School of Public Health and Social work, Queensland University of Technology. She has a multi-discipline background with degrees the areas of criminology, psychology, and counselling, and a PhD in social work and human services. She has extensive social research experience across these three disciplines and is passionate at teaching and carrying out applied research. Since completing her PhD on youth counsellors' experiences of telephone counselling she has continued her interest in exploring the experiences and well-being of human service practitioners, through the lenses of critical, complexity, and organizational theories. Her current publications include an evaluation report and journal article about a relational case management programme to assist those experiencing generational poverty, and a conference paper outlining the limitations of the existing employment service system in Australia and the need for more holistic service provision in this area of practice.

Monique Delforterie, PhD, is a senior researcher at Trajectum, a treatment facility for adults with mild intellectual disability and severe behavioural and mental health problems.

Michelle Denton, RN, MBA, PhD, has worked for over 30 years in a range of clinical, management, research, and policy roles in mental health as well as some involvement in the disability and refugee health sectors. She has worked in numerous senior policy and strategic planning roles such as managing The Queensland Forensic Mental Health

Service for 14 years including the development of mental health services in prisons across the state. After completing her PhD in 2014 on the prison-to community experience of men with co-occurring mental illness and substance use disorder she was awarded a postdoctoral research fellowship in the School of Nursing, Midwifery, and Social Work at The University of Queensland to teach mental health and undertake research on the health service user experience and experience-based co-design. She retains a strong commitment to collaboratively supporting the development of human service organizations, particularly for people with mental illness and disability.

Robert Didden, PhD, is a Professor of Intellectual Disability, Learning, and Behaviour at the Radboud University at Nijmegen. In addition he is a health care psychologist and senior researcher at Trajectum, a treatment facility for adults with mild intellectual disability and severe behavioural and mental health problems.

Stewart L. Einfeld is a child and Adolescent Psychiatrist, Emeritus Professor at the Faculty of Health Sciences, University of Sydney, and a Senior Scientist at the Brain and Mind Centre. Professor Einfeld has research interests in the area of child and adolescent psychiatry, developmental disabilities, including intellectual disability and its genetic causes, and autism. Professor Einfeld is co-developer of the Developmental Behaviour Checklist. This instrument is widely used in clinical and research settings both within Australia and internationally, and has been translated into 21 languages. Professor Einfeld was co-Chief Investigator of the Australian Child to Adult Development (ACAD) Study, funded by the National Health and Medical Research Council and National Institutes of Health. This study examined a broad range of biological, psychological, and social factors of potential protection and vulnerability in the development of behavioural and emotional problems in children and adolescents with intellectual handicap. Professor Einfeld has played a major role in promoting a re-emergence of interest in intellectual disability in the psychiatric profession in NSW in particular. Professor Einfeld's awards include the World Health Organisation Travelling Fellow, Australian Society for Psychiatric Research Junior Travel Award, National Research Prize from the Australian Society for Study of Intellectual Deficiency.

Kathy Ellem, **PhD** is a Senior Lecturer in social work at the School of Nursing, Midwifery, and Social Work, University of Queensland. She has many years of practice experience as a social worker in the disability sector in both government and non-government services and is currently a member of the Regional Disability Advisory Council for the Queensland government. Her research publications include qualitative life-story work with ex-offenders with intellectual disability, and practice research on working with people with a disability and their families. Her current research examines the experiences of young people with cognitive disabilities and the police, and the transition experiences of young people with complex needs (including intellectual and developmental disability) through multiple service systems, including youth justice, child protection, homelessness, and drug and alcohol services.

J. Paul Fedoroff, MD, is the Director of the Sexual Behaviors Clinic at the Royal Ottawa Mental Health Centre. His primary clinical and research interests are in the assessment and treatment of men and women with problematic sexual behaviours, especially those with intellectual disabilities. He is also a Professor of Psychiatry at the University of

Ottawa with cross-appointments to the Faculties of Criminology and the University of Ottawa Faculty of Law. He is Head of the Division of Forensic Psychiatry at the University of Ottawa. He has published over 100 papers and chapters. He has provided consultations and been an invited speaker locally, nationally, and internationally.

Emma Gardner, PhD, PGDipClinPsyc (Distinction), is a Consultant Clinical Psychologist and Clinical Leader at the Regional Intellectual Disability Secure Service (RIDSS) in Wellington, New Zealand. The RIDSS provides specialist secure care and rehabilitation for offenders with an intellectual disability. Emma has worked with mainstream offenders and offenders with intellectual disabilities and complex behavioural needs for over a decade. She has developed and implemented a variety of evidence-based clinical interventions for both individuals and groups. She enjoys working with teams and implementing service-wide initiatives that improve client care. Emma has published in a variety of scientific journals and has presented at forums in Australia and New Zealand.

Dorothy Griffiths, CM, OOnt., PhD, is Professor Emerita at Brock University, St. Catharines, Ontario, Canada. Formerly Professor in the Department of Child and Youth Studies and Centre for Applied Disability Studies, Co-Director of the International Dual Diagnosis Certificate Programme, and Associate Dean, Faculty of Social Sciences, Dr Griffiths has extensive experience in working on clinical issues regarding dual diagnosis (persons who are developmentally disabled and have mental health issues). Her expertise more specifically is in the area of sexual abuse and offence, aggression and self-injury, and social skills training with persons with developmental disabilities. Her recent research interests have included Human Rights and Deinstitutionalization. She has written and speaks extensively on these topics. She is notably recognized for five books that she co-authored/co-edited called *Changing Sexually Inappropriate Behaviour, Dual Diagnosis, Demystifying Syndromes, Ethical Dilemmas of Sexuality and Developmental Disabilities*, and *The Human Rights Agenda*. Her most recent coauthored book is *Sex Offending Behavior of Persons with an Intellectual Disability: A Multi-Component Applied Behavior Analytic Approach*. She is a recipient of numerous teaching, research, and advocacy awards, including the Order of Ontario and the Order of Canada.

Susan Hayes, PhD, is a forensic psychologist and Professor Emeritus at Sydney Medical School, University of Sydney, Officer of the Order of Australia (AO), Fellow of the International Society for the Scientific Study of Intellectual and Developmental Disability, and Fellow of the Australian Psychological Society's College of Forensic Psychology. She is recognized internationally for expertise with people with intellectual disability in the justice system, including the areas of criminal justice (offenders and victims of crime), family court, capacity for medical consent, guardianship, and child protection. She has authored over 120 publications and 100 conference presentations, and received 30 research grants; she teaches post-graduate students in the Sydney Medical School.

Patricia Howlin is Emeritus Professor of Clinical Child Psychology at the Institute of Psychiatry, Psychology, and Neuroscience, King's College London. Her principal research interests focus on the long-term prognosis for individuals with autism spectrum and other developmental disorders and on developing intervention programmes that may help to improve outcome. Professor Howlin is a Fellow of the British Psychological Society and Fellow of the International Society for Autism Research. She is President of the Society for the Study of Behavioural Phenotypes and past Chair of the UK Association of Child Psychology and Psychiatry. She is a founding editor of the journal *Autism* and author of over 200 research publications. Awards include the Autism Association of Western Australia – for Services to Autism; International Society for Autism Research (INSAR): Life-time Achievement Award; German, Austrian, Swiss Society for Research in Autism Spectrum Conditions: Kanner –Asperger medal; UK National Autistic Society: Life-time Achievement Award.

Stephanie Ioannou, is a Board Certified Behaviour Analyst who has provided assessment and treatment to persons with dual diagnosis and sexual offending behaviour in community settings. Within a biopsychosocial framework, she has worked with adults with dual diagnosis and challenging behaviours and provides clinical oversight of the delivery of ABA services to children/youth with autism and their families.

Andrew Jahoda, PhD, graduated from the University of Stirling in 1983, and then completed a PhD in 1989. After obtaining an MPhil in Clinical Psychology at the University of Edinburgh in 1993, he took up his first post as a Clinical Psychologist in the Learning Disability service in Dundee. He subsequently moved to the University of Glasgow where he is Professor of Learning Disabilities in the Institute of Health and Wellbeing. He also has a clinical role as an honorary Consultant Clinical Psychologist in NHS Greater Glasgow and Clyde. Andrew's research interests concern the mental health and wellbeing of people with learning disabilities, and the contribution made by a range of psychological and social factors. In recent years much of his work has focused on adapting psychotherapeutic approaches in a manner that is sensitive to the lived experience of people with learning disabilities.

Marije Keulen-De Vos, PhD, is a senior researcher at Forensic Psychiatric Center de Rooyse Wissel in Venray, the Netherlands. In addition, she is the president of the Dutch Chapter of the Association for the Treatment of Sexual Abusers (ATSA). Her research interests are forensic treatment, personality disorders, sex offenders, and intellectual disabilities.

Frank Lambrick, PhD, is a forensic psychologist with over 30 years' experience working within this field, most of which has been specifically within the disability area. He is the Academic Coordinator in the Specialist Certificate in Criminology (Forensic Disability) at the University of Melbourne. He also holds the position of Senior Practitioner (Disability) in the Department of Health and Human Services in Victoria.

Peter E. Langdon, DClinPsy, PhD, CPsychol, AFBPsS, is Professor of Clinical and Forensic Psychology at the Tizard Centre, University of Kent, as well as an Honorary Consultant Clinical and Forensic Psychologist and Approved Clinician working within the Broadland Clinic, Hertfordshire Partnership University NHS Foundation Trust, in Norfolk, United Kingdom. He was twice a Research Fellow with the National Institute for Health Research, and is Co-Editor of the *Journal of Applied Research in Intellectual Disabilities*. He has worked in forensic mental health care services for over 15 years and has a specific interest in developing clinical interventions for offenders with intellectual and other developmental disabilities.

The late **William [Bill] R. Lindsay** was a Consultant Forensic Clinical Psychologist and Head of Research for Danshell. He was previously Head of Psychology (LD) in NHS Tayside and Consultant Psychologist with the State Hospital. He was Professor of Learning Disabilities and Forensic Psychology at the University of Abertay, Dundee and Honorary Professor at Deakin University Melbourne. Professor Lindsay had published over 350 research articles and book chapters, published 5 books, held around 2 million pounds in research grants and given many presentations and workshops on cognitive therapy and the assessment and treatment of offenders with intellectual disability.

Ken MacMahon, PhD, graduated from Aberdeen University with a degree in Psychology in 1995. After completing a PhD on implicit learning, anxiety, and movement, he was subsequently involved in research studies on Parkinson's disease and sleep. He trained as a Clinical Psychologist at Glasgow University and has held a number of clinical posts within NHS intellectual disability services. He moved to the School of Health in Social Science at Edinburgh University in 2014, but continues to work clinically. His research interests focus on a number of areas across intellectual disability and autism, including offending behaviour.

Jane McGillivray, PhD, is Professor and Head of the School of Psychology and Director of the Post Graduate Professional Programmes at Deakin University, Victoria, Australia. She is a registered clinical and health psychologist who has longstanding practice, teaching, and research experience in the area of intellectual and developmental disabilities. Her research interests include the development and evaluation of screening, early intervention and treatment strategies that enhance the social and emotional development and well-being of people with disability and disadvantage, including those who come into contact with the forensic system. Her research is supported by grants and consultancies and she is well placed to enhance translation to practice through her role in developing professional training programmes in psychology and her well-established professional and community links.

Danielle McLeod, completed her Masters of Social Policy at the University of Melbourne and in partial fulfilment of the requirements for this degree, completed a placement with the Senior Practitioner (Disability), in the Department of Health and Human Services in Victoria, Australia.

Amanda M. Michie, MA, PhD, CPsychol, AFBPsS is a Consultant Clinical Psychologist and until recently was the Professional Lead for learning disability services in NHS Lothian. She has specialist expertise in the field of forensic ID and provided a clinical service to community and IP forensic settings across Lothian. She worked closely with criminal justice staff; providing training, consultancy, and clinical input. She is also an established researcher, publishing regularly, particularly in the area of assessment and treatment of offenders with ID. She currently works independently in her own private practice.

Danielle Newton, PhD, is a Research Fellow in the School of Psychology, Deakin University, Australia and the School of Social and Political Sciences, The University of Melbourne, Australia. She is a registered psychologist with the Australian Health Practitioner Regulation Agency and holds an endorsed health psychology specialization as recognized by the Psychology Board of Australia. She has over 14 years' experience as an academic researcher specializing in qualitative methods. She is primarily interested in how biological, environmental, psychological, and sociocultural factors shape and influence health and health service delivery particularly in relation to the experiences of people living with intellectual and developmental disabilities. Her research interests also include how forensic, justice, disability, and health systems can collectively work together to better support the reintegration of ex-offenders back into the community. Danielle has been involved in a broad range of projects including those funded by government grants and contracts. In addition, she also undertakes independent consultancy roles for Government, university, and community-based organizations.

Henk Nijman, PhD, is Professor of Forensic Psychology at Radboud University in Nijmegen, the Netherlands, and senior researcher at the forensic psychiatric institute Fivoor in the Netherlands.

Tyler Oswald, BSc, LLB, MD, FRCPC, completed law school in Victoria, British Columbia, medical training in Winnipeg, Manitoba, and forensic psychiatry in Hamilton, Ontario, Canada. His interests bridge the worlds of law and medicine. He works as a psychiatrist in correctional and forensic environments.

Paul Oxnam, MSc, PGDipClinPsyc, is a Consultant Clinical Psychologist and Clinical Leader at the Regional Intellectual Disability Secure Service (RIDSS) in Wellington, New Zealand. The RIDSS provides specialist secure care and rehabilitation for offenders with an intellectual disability. Paul has worked with mentally disordered offenders and offenders with intellectual disabilities and complex behavioural needs for over a decade. He has expertise in developing service-wide models of care and enjoys working with multidisciplinary teams to implement evidence-based interventions that improve client outcomes. Paul led the creation of the Stepping Stones emotion regulation group treatment programme and has overseen its implementation in forensic disability services internationally. He has presented at a variety of forums in New Zealand, Australia, and the United Kingdom and has published in a range of scientific journals.

Lauren J. Rice is a Postdoctoral Research Fellow at The University of Sydney Children's Hospital Westmead Clinical School and the Faculty of Health Sciences, University of Sydney. Her research focuses on understanding the mechanisms of emotion and behaviour disturbance in developmental disabilities. Lauren Rice completed her PhD in 2016 under the supervision of Professor Stewart Einfeld at the Brain and Mind Centre, University of Sydney. Her thesis explored the characteristics and causal mechanisms of temper outbursts in Prader Willi syndrome (PWS) and included the first study to identify a deficit in brain gamma-aminobutyric acid levels in PWS. Awards include the Foundation for Prader-Willi Research Trainee Publication Award, the Society of the Study of Behavioural Phenotypes Bursary Award and the Elide Editing Write-Up Scholarship.

Deborah Richards, MA, CHMH, RP, is a Registered Psychotherapist and Consultant in private practice in Ontario, Canada. Her expertise is in the area of sexuality, dual diagnosis, and forensics. She is the co-clinician of a Sexual Behaviours Clinic specific for people who have intellectual disabilities and problematic sexual behaviours. Deborah has an established career in determining risk and treatment of sex offenders with ID.

She has conducted research on abuse prevention and ID as well as problematic sexual behaviours, offenders and ID. She has presented nationally and internationally and published extensively in these areas.

Phillip Snoyman, PhD, is the Director State-wide Services, Offender Services & Programmes, Corrective Services New South Wales, Australia and has worked for Corrective Services New South Wales, Australia as a Senior Psychologist and Principal Advisor Disabilities. He has researched or worked with offenders for the past 17 years and has authored journal articles, book chapters, and presented at conferences on topics primarily relating to people with disability in contact with the criminal justice system.

Lesley R. Steptoe, PhD, CPsychol, FBPsS, is a Principal Forensic Psychologist, a Visiting Research Fellow at the University of Abertay, Dundee and a Fellow of the British Psychological Society. Within her work with Abertay University and also NHS Tayside she has carried out research on offenders with intellectual and developmental disability (IDD). She has extensive experience in the assessment and treatment of sex offenders with IDD and is the lead in the development and delivery of the Pathways to Progress adapted sex offender treatment programme in the NHS Tayside Forensic Service for offenders with IDD. Her particular research interests are attachment and past abuse in offenders with IDD, assessment and management of sex offenders with IDD in the secure and community settings, treatment efficacy for sex offenders with IDD, risk assessment and protective factors to relapse of sexual offending for this client group.

Peter Sturmey, PhD, is Professor of Psychology at The Graduate Center and the Department of Psychology, Queens College, City University of New York, where he is a member of the Behaviour Analysis Doctoral and Masters in Applied Behaviour Analysis programmes. He specialized in autism and other developmental disabilities, especially in the areas of applied behaviour analysis, dual diagnosis, evidence-based practice, and staff and parent training. He is the resident speaker at ABAC and Chief Scientific Officer at Long Island ABA. He gained his PhD at the University of Liverpool, United Kingdom and subsequently taught at the University of the South West (Plymouth) and University of Birmingham, United Kingdom. He then worked for the Texas Department of Mental Retardation from 1990 to 2000 as Chief Psychologist, first at Abilene then San Antonio State Schools during a Federal class action law. There he supervised behavioural services and Masters level psychologists providing behaviour support plans for severe behavioural and psychiatric disorders in adolescents and adults with developmental disabilities and implementing large-scale active treatment and restraint reduction programmes. Professor Sturmey has published 25 edited and authored books, over 210 peer reviewed papers, over 60 book chapters. He provides webinars on ABA to qualified professionals and others on a regular basis. He has made numerous presentations nationally and internationally, including recent presentations in Canada, Brazil, Belgium, Luxemburg, and Italy. He has an active lab of graduate and undergraduate students working on developing and evaluating effective and efficient ways of training caregivers using modelling and feedback to use applied behaviour analysis with children and adults with autism and other disabilities. He provides training and consultations widely.

Kendra Thomson is an Associate Professor in the Department of Applied Disability Studies at Brock University, and a Doctoral-level Board Certified Behavior Analyst

(BCBA-D). Dr Thomson's research focuses on investigating best practices for training others (parents, support staff, etc.) how to provide evidence-based support to individuals with intellectual and developmental disabilities, and the related impacts on individuals and their families.

Samuel J. Tromans, is an Honorary Academic Clinical Lecturer in the Social and Epidemiology Psychiatry Group, Department of Health Sciences, University of Leicester, and a Specialist Registrar in the Psychiatry of Intellectual Disability at Leicestershire Partnership NHS Trust.

Chelsea Troutman, is a Board Certified Behaviour Analyst with experience in America and Australia, working with people who engage in high risk and challenging behaviours across a range of settings. She previously managed the Compulsory Treatment team under the Senior Practitioner (Disability); and is currently the Principal Practitioner for children with a disability and children in the out-of-home-care system in the Department of Health and Human Services in Victoria, Australia.

Daniel Turner, PhD, achieved his master in psychology at the University of Frankfurt, Germany. Afterwards he completed his medical studies at the University of Hamburg, where he also achieved his PhD degrees in psychology and medical studies. He has worked as a PhD student at the institute for Sex Research and Forensic Psychiatry, at the University Medical Center Hamburg, Eppendorf and is now working as a post-doc and medical resident at the department of psychiatry and psychotherapy at the University Medical Center Mainz, Germany. His research interests are pharmacological offender treatment, neuropsychological assessment of sexual offenders, and sexuality education within medical studies.

Neomi van Duijvenbode, PhD, is a psychologist who specializes in clients with complex problems – clients with a triple diagnosis (an intellectual disability, substance use disorder, and psychiatric problems), often even with co-occurring psychosocial or forensic issues. She has completed her PhD on the neuropsychology of substance use disorders in individuals with an intellectual disability, is involved in several research projects and has written numerous book chapters and research articles on this topic. She is currently working as a psychologist in a forensic treatment centre of Tactus addiction medicine, as a researcher of the Centre for Intellectual Disability and Addiction at Tactus addiction medicine. In addition, she works as a researcher and lecturer at Radboud University Nijmegen.

Joanne E.L. VanDerNagel, MD, PhD, is a psychiatrist and head of the Centre for Intellectual Disability and Addiction at Tactus addiction medicine, and a consultant psychiatrist at Aveleijn Intellectual Disability Services. She is involved in several PhD projects into epidemiology and treatment of substance use disorders in individuals with intellectual disabilities, developed interventions (including a screening instrument, two CBT protocols, a preventative intervention, and a guideline for collaboration between services), and has written a book and numerous chapters on this topic.

Jayson Ware, PhD, is the Group Director, Offender Services & Programmes, Corrective Services New South Wales, Australia. He has researched or worked with offenders for the past 20 years and has authored over 40 journal articles or book chapters primarily relating to the treatment of sex and violent offenders. He has particular research interests in the enhancement of treatment effectiveness, group work, and sex offenders' denial.

Paul Willner, DPhil, graduated from Oxford University with a degree in PPP (psychology/physiology) in 1969 and a DPhil in 1974, followed later by the award of a DSc in 2004. He has held chairs in psychology at what is now London Metropolitan University and at Swansea University where he is now an Emeritus Professor; he was appointed to a Fellowship of the British Psychological Society in 1988. In the late 1990s he used a sabbatical to train clinically and subsequently worked in the NHS as a clinical psychologist (appointed Consultant in 2004). His major research interests in recent years have been in decision making and mental capacity, and evidence-based psychological interventions for people with intellectual disabilities.

Robin J. Wilson, PhD, is a board certified clinical psychologist with 30 years' experience in hospital, correctional, and private practice settings. He has published and presented internationally on topics related to sexual violence prevention. Dr Wilson is an Assistant Clinical Professor (adjunct) of Psychiatry at McMaster University in Canada and he maintains a clinical and consulting practice in Sarasota, Florida. His current interests centre on constructing safe and responsive models of skill development and restoration for individuals returning to the community after long-term hospitalization or incarceration.

Foreword

In late March 2017, an unexpected email from Scotland from an old friend announced that William R. 'Bill' Lindsay, in my memory as always fit and healthy, had tragically died in his sleep after a day of watching football (apparently after seeing his team win for a change) and playing with his grandkids. Whilst his team won that day, his family and friends suffered an unexpected huge loss and, of course, the rest of the world lost a champion in the field of forensic disability. Bill was probably the hardest working clinician I had ever met – the 'About the Editors' section of this book lists his academic achievements and appointments – his various cross-appointments and numerous publications are just simply amazing for a person who was very much a practitioner as well as a scientist. However, his editor bio doesn't mention that Bill was also just a great guy, down-to-earth, fond of a social beverage, and always up for good craic and a laugh (and then probably writing an article). For example, some years ago I was giving a workshop in Edinburgh and he hopped the train from Dundee just to meet up for lunch. Lovely guy, we all miss him.

This book is a typical Bill product. Along with two other outstanding persons in the forensic intellectual and developmental disability (IDD) field, Dorothy Griffiths and Leam Craig, this book includes a stellar list of contributors covering a broad range of topics. Having helped with a couple of edited books (two of which were with Leam) and several test manuals (two of which were with Bill), I have a good notion that this book would have been conceived several years ago in collaboration with Bill and is only now coming to fruition. The contents are testament to Bill's broad expertise and I couldn't be happier to write the foreword, partially to celebrate his memory, but also to celebrate his genius and collaborative nature.

The editorial group's expertise is complementary and extensive. Bill's expertise was primarily to do with the assessment and treatment of offenders (both sexually and non-sexually violent) with an IDD. Bill created tests, developed programmes, and meticulously collected data. His treatment programmes and tests were always well-grounded in empirical data. Leam's accomplishments are vast as well – with over 100 publications and 11 books to date. His many awards (as noted in the 'About the Editors' section of this book) show the progression of his career along with his eminent knowledge regarding the treatment of inappropriate sexual and other types of violent behaviour by persons with an IDD, but also with personality disorder more broadly, as well as the issue of expert witness testimony in both civil and criminal courts. Dorothy has had a very broad and eminent career which has been recognized nationally in Canada (e.g. she has received both the Order of Ontario and the Order of Canada for her work) and internationally as witnessed by her recent scholarship in terms of human rights and deinstitutionalization. Her clinical and published works have included issues regarding dual diagnosis (persons with an IDD and mental health issues), as well as sexual abuse and offending, aggression and self-injury, and social skills training for persons with an IDD.

This is a large book given that it is very focused on a relatively small subset of the offender population – those individuals with an IDD who have committed an offence. The title of the book truly speaks to the content: *The Wiley Handbook on What Works for Offenders with Intellectual and Developmental Disabilities: An Evidence-Based Approach to Theory, Assessment, and Treatment.* In my humble opinion, Wiley has become the pre-eminent publisher of the best collections of work to do with sexual and violent offenders (and correctional psychology in general) and this book, is perhaps one of the best collections to date regarding offenders with an IDD. Anyone working with offenders with an IDD needs this book on their shelf for constant reference.

The book contains 22 chapters and is structurally divided into 5 Parts: Introduction, Phenotypes and Genotypes and Offending Behaviour, Validated Assessments, Treatment, and Conclusions. As a practitioner would hope, the Validated Assessments and Treatment Parts contain most of the chapters (from Chapters 5 to 21), but the other three Parts provide essential context and meaningful counterpoint to the main body of the work.

The 'Introduction' Part contains three chapters that provide an overview of the book (and hence I won't repeat the overview here in detail – but I will include a brief summary by Part). The 'Introduction and Overview' chapter (Chapter 1) was written by the editors and reveals one of the strengths of the book: an empirical focus on proof of treatment effectiveness and validation of assessment methods. As a result, the book is less a collection of 'what we do' and rather a collection of 'what has been proven to work' (or at least aspirational criteria by which therapies can be judged in terms of efficacy). The second chapter (by Dorothy Griffiths) provides an overview of the ethical challenges and issues faced by those professionals doing the work with offenders with IDD. The third chapter (by Lambrick and colleagues) provides a complementary chapter to the ethics chapter by Griffiths and cover some of the major human rights issues relevant to persons with an IDD who have offended.

The chapter titled 'Behavioural and Cognitive Phenotypes in Genetic Disorders Associated with Offending' is the sole chapter in the 'Phenotypes and Genotypes and Offending Behaviour' Part. This is a fascinating chapter and explores the often-ignored area (in books focused on psychological assessment and treatment) of persons who have genetic syndromes associated with IDD who offend and how these persons may be similar or different from other persons with an IDD. The authors have produced an accessible chapter that is both scholarly and yet comprehensible to those persons without a background in the science of genetics.

The 'Validated Assessments' Part is so named (presumably) because of the rigorous focus on validated approaches to assessment. The scope of the eight chapters in this Part is broad and extensive. In general, each chapter provides the reader with a grounding in the issues under consideration (e.g. anger and violence or inappropriate sexual behaviour) and then examines the assessment tools relevant to the issue, both in terms of description of the tools and their psychometric properties. In my view, this is an unusually well-done Part on assessment practices – again, not just what sorts of tools people are using, but an evidence-based critique of assessment tools for possible use with offenders with an IDD.

The 'Treatment' Part is similar to the 'Validated Assessments' Part and it would have ideal if it could have been similarly titled (i.e. 'Validated Treatments'). I suspect the problem is that there are few actual validated treatments compared to actual validated assessment procedures. Nonetheless, there are nine chapters in the Part, some of which are complementary in content to several of the chapters in the preceding Part. For me, two of the highlights in this Part were the chapters by Susan Hayes (on the 'Treatment for Social Problem-Solving and Criminal Thinking') and Peter Sturmey (regarding the 'Treatment Outcomes for People with Autistic Spectrum Disorder in Forensic Settings'). Well-written and scholarly as always, these two authors are of major importance in their respective areas of research in my view and these chapters are testament to their expertise.

The 'Conclusions' chapter written by two of the Editors (i.e. Dorothy and Leam) high-lights that the book had an evaluative (evidence-based) focus, and notes that treatment of offenders with an IDD is often best done using a multimodal approach, with an emphasis on habilitation (not rehabilitation), along with recognizing the importance of comprehensive planning (including improving the offender's quality of life) to maxi-mize treatment outcomes.

I thoroughly recommend this book to anyone working with offenders with IDD. The book actually delivers on its title and provides the practitioner with valuable informa-tion on ethics and human rights issues regarding working with offenders with an IDD before going into depth on the evidence basis for assessment and treatment practices with these offenders. An important thread that goes through this book is that of how important it is to promote effective assessment and treatment if we, academics and practitioners alike, are to help our clients with an IDD most effectively in order to help these individuals live happier and safer lives. In my view, this book will be of immeasur-able assistance to everyone committed to such goals.

Professor Douglas P. Boer
University of Canberra
Australia
douglas.boer@canberra.edu.au

Part I

Introduction

1

What Works for Offenders with Intellectual and Developmental Disabilities

Systems for Evaluating Evidence and Book Overview

Leam A. Craig[1,2,3], William R. Lindsay, and Dorothy Griffiths[4]

[1] *Forensic Psychology Practice Ltd, Sutton Coldfield, UK*
[2] *Centre for Applied Psychology, University of Birmingham, UK*
[3] *School of Social Sciences, Birmingham City University, UK*
[4] *Brock University, St. Catharines, Ontario, Canada*

1.1   Introduction

For some years there have been systems for analysing the quality of studies in order to gauge the effectiveness of any assessment or intervention. For people with intellectual and developmental disabilities (IDD) this is especially important because it is a population that has traditionally been ignored on the one hand and on the other, grateful for any interest that professionals may show, whatever the evidence for effectiveness (Sturmey and Didden 2014). The evidence base is essential to any therapeutic investigation. However, looking across therapies for this client group, one quickly realizes that therapies spring up right, left, and centre and can be carried forward more effectively by evangelical zeal than they can by scientific rigour. Indeed, when dealing with a class of individuals who are generally devalued, as with those in the current volume, one becomes aware that they may be vulnerable to anyone who takes a genuine interest, however idiosyncratic. Therefore, it has become extremely important to review the evidence base for the range of assessment and therapeutic techniques that are currently used in the field of offenders with intellectual disabilities. The double-blind cross-over placebo trial is viewed by many as the sine qua non of experimental approaches to treatment evaluation. But it is not the only approach. Several sciences are not experimental: the sciences of astronomy and palaeontology have a hard time manipulating independent variables.

Single-subject research designs involve a different approach to science. Rather than pursuing statistical significance, single-subject research pursues demonstrating a replicable and consistent functional relationship between an independent variable and client behaviour. If a therapist or experimenter can turn a behaviour on and off by systematically applying and withdrawing an independent variable and observe a systematic change in the client's behaviour, then we can say that we have truly

*The Wiley Handbook on What Works for Offenders with Intellectual and Developmental Disabilities:
An Evidence-Based Approach to Theory, Assessment, and Treatment*, First Edition.
Edited by William R. Lindsay, Leam A. Craig, and Dorothy Griffiths.
© 2020 John Wiley & Sons Ltd. Published 2020 by John Wiley & Sons Ltd.

identified an independent variable (Baer et al. 1968). Hence, reversal, multiple baseline, and other single-subject designs can show causal relationships between independent and dependent variables. Single-subject experimental designs can be clearly differentiated from case studies, including case studies with data. Single-subject designs demonstrate a functional relationship between treatment and outcome, whereas case studies do not.

However, any experimental design by itself does not directly address the social significance of behaviour change: it would be possible to have experimental control over an effect of trivial magnitude. It would also possible to have huge changes in socially irrelevant variables. Study designs should address social significance by a variety of methods known as *social validity* (Wolf 1978). Social validity can be demonstrated using ratings of the importance of behaviour change from the client, and significant others, in the environment. This is especially true for offending since the effectiveness of interventions is so important to the public. It could be argued that there is little point of an intervention that is hugely successful for offenders' self-esteem but has no impact on rate of offending.

In this introduction we will review the principle methods for assessing the effectiveness of assessment and treatment techniques for all interventions, including those for offenders with IDD.

1.2 The Cochrane System

The Cochrane review system has been influential in categorizing evidence on the effectiveness of psychological and pharmaceutical interventions from different studies. In earlier iterations, the system evaluated the quality of evidence in five categories. The highest quality of evidence from clinical research was from systematic reviews including at least one randomized controlled trial (RCT) and high-quality meta-analyses that include controlled trials. The second level of acceptable evidence was one RCT. The next quality of evidence included cohort studies and waiting-list controlled trials and the quality below that included well designed observational studies and well controlled case studies. The final (5th) quality of evidence was based on expert opinion and influential reports.

In 2005 the Cochrane Collaboration (Higgins et al. 2011, 2016; Cochrane Library www.cochranelibrary.com) adopted an alternative strategy and rather than assessing studies for level of quality, they took the approach of assessing 'risk for bias'. Their considerations were now confined to assessment of studies and especially RCTs. The first recommendation was to avoid using scales to assess the quality of the study. The subsequent recommendations were concerned with focus on the internal validity and risk of bias of the study. Risks of bias indicate flaws in the study that are likely to undermine the reliability, validity, and integrity of the findings. These risks include incomplete outcome data, different aspect of blinding (e.g. participants, therapists, outcome assessments), the length of the 'washout' period in crossover trials and criteria for exclusion of participants.

One of the most prominently cited technical reviews was Guyatt et al. (1995) in which they outline a series of relative risks to the strength of evidence in a study. For example, the first risk is having heterogeneity of treatment effects in different studies. The greater the difference in treatment effects indicated greater heterogeneity in study outcomes which in turn indicated greater risk to the integrity of findings. Heterogeneity might indicate unexplained differences in results from study to study. Therefore, reviews with greater heterogeneity were ranked lower than those without significant heterogeneity. They also noted that the potential for bias was much greater in cohort and case studies (no matter how well controlled) than in RCTs and subsequently recommendations from these were much weaker. The Cochrane recommendations (Higgins et al. 2011, 2016; Sterne et al. 2016) are that the bases for bias assessments and judgements by the reviewer(s) should be explicit in the review. The Cochrane system remains the most exacting of review systems for clinical evidence.

1.3 What Works Levels System

In analysing the quality of studies on the treatment of offending behaviour, reviews have for some time employed the evaluation of evidence supporting particular therapeutic techniques and their use with particular types of offenders. The work has been subsumed under the category 'What Works' in the treatment and management of offenders to reduce crime. Sharman et al. (1997) developed a technique for reviewing the evidence in response to a request by the US Congress for an evaluation of the effectiveness of annual grants from the Department of Justice of more than $3 billion. Since then, there has been an accumulation of 'What Works' literature in mainstream criminal research, the focus of which has been on the evidence-based approach to assessment and treatment in offender rehabilitation (Craig et al. 2013).

The Sharman et al. (1997) system considered five levels relating to the quality of the evidence supporting any given intervention in the field of criminal behaviour. Level I studies indicated some correlation between the programme and measures of recidivism. Interventions would lack a comparison group. At this level, the evidence was not considered sufficiently robust to help assess effectiveness. Level II studies indicated some association between the programme and recidivism. However, given the research design, alternative explanations could not be ruled out. Level III studies compared two or more groups, one with the programme and one without the programme. The study design would allow a reasonable similarity between the two groups. Level IV studies included comparisons between a programme group and one or more control groups controlling for extraneous factors. Level V studies included randomized assignment and analysis of comparable programmes and comparison groups. This level of evidence would also control for attrition, a common problem in offenders' studies.

The literature on Evidence-Based Corrections has provided guidelines on 'What Works', 'What Does Not Work', and 'What Is Promising'. A number of studies supported the findings that effective programmes are structured and focused, use multiple treatment components, focus on developing skills including behavioural and cognitive skills, focus on clearly defined overt behaviour as opposed to non-directive counselling focusing on insight, self-esteem, or disclosure (e.g. Landenberger and Lipsey 2005). There should be meaningful contact between the treatment personnel and the participant. Crucially, they should focus on characteristics of the offenders that are associated with criminal activities and can be changed (criminogenic needs: Andrews and Bonta 2010; Bonta and Andrews 2017).

1.4   American Psychological Association (APA) System

There have been a number of other innovations to develop evaluation systems in psychological therapy, including the APA and their system for developing Empirically Supported Psychological Interventions. Chambless and colleagues (Chambless and Ollendick 2001; Chambless and Hollon 1998; Chambless et al. 1998) have described the way in which treatments for specific diagnostic groups are split into well-established treatments, possibly efficacious treatments, and experimental treatments. Well-established treatments are characterized as those that have at least two good between group design experiments that would usually be RCTs. These controlled trials should demonstrate the treatment's superiority to psychotherapy placebo or medication or to some other treatment. Alternatively, they may demonstrate that the treatment is of equivalent efficacy to an established treatment. A second way of demonstrating that the treatment has well-established efficacy is through a series of single case design experiments. These single case experiments should show good experimental design and may compare the intervention to another treatment. They should also be conducted in a standardized manner with a treatment manual, the characteristics of the sample should be specified and treatment effects should have been demonstrated by independent research teams.

Probably efficacious treatments have a lower standard of verification with two experiments that should show the treatment to be superior to a waiting list control. Alternatively, one RCT that demonstrates the treatment is superior to psychotherapy placebo or pill placebo, or a smaller series of single case design experiments meeting well-established treatment criteria would be sufficient. Experimental treatments are those which are not yet tested and do not meet the criteria for either well-established treatments or probably efficacious treatments. These three categories have been used to establish clinical research support for a number of treatments for specific diagnoses, e.g., exposure treatment for specific phobias, stress inoculation for stress disorder, and systematic desensitization for a specific phobia.

1.5   Applying What Works Principles to Offenders with IDD

These systems of evaluation are not without their difficulties and critics, particularly when considering that these systems of evaluation can be applied to the assessment and treatment of offenders with IDD. One particular criticism is that it is artificial to force diagnostic categories into such discrete divisions. In addition, critics have suggested that it is similarly artificial to categorize psychological treatments so tightly. This latter point is particularly relevant given one of the criteria for meeting both well-established, and probably efficacious categorization is that the treatment should be based on a manual or an equivalent clear description. This is often an artificial distinction in that therapists can be flexible in the way they employ the various tenets of treatment. This is particularly true when working with offenders with IDD where the intervention is more fluid and based on the individual's or group's progress (see Craig and Hutchinson 2005). It is, however, the case that many programmes for offence-related issues are manualized (e.g. sex offender treatment programmes, anger management, problem solving).

Two other criticisms are particularly important from the point of view of the current chapter. The APA task force required that reliable and valid methods for determining outcome were employed. A review of the outcome measures suggests that they were largely self-report assessments such as self-reported anxiety, self-reported depression, and self-reported confidence and self-esteem. With work on offenders, self-reported measures can only be considered proximal and the only evidence of interest from a social policy point of view is whether or not another offence has been committed. From a societal stance, it is of little value to know that an offender reports low levels of anger if he or she continues to commit an equivalent number of violent offences following treatment. Similarly, it is of little value if an offender reports low levels of cognitions related to sexual offending if he continues to commit offences at an equivalent rate. Therefore, the most valid outcome measure for offender treatment is the number of future incidents in comparison to the number of incidents prior to the commencement of treatment. It is an exacting standard, but it is the case.

Another relevant criticism has been the establishment of conditions during periods of follow up. For the APA task force, the follow-up period should be as uncontaminated by other variables as possible. This can be extremely difficult in intellectual disability services when a number of agencies may be involved with individuals in order to help them integrate with society. Following treatment, a housing agency may be involved to help establish residency, or criminal justice agencies may continue to monitor the individual as part of their conditions from court disposal. As we shall see, some of the evaluations of treatment programmes for offenders with IDD have been delivered within the context of forensic intellectual disability services that apply a holistic approach to individuals including psychiatric review, or occupational placement, nursing interventions, community management, criminal justice involvement, and even 24-hour supervision as well as the psychological therapy being evaluated. Typically, interventions for offenders with IDD, usually consist of small scale studies, single-subject research designs or bespoke case studies (Chapman et al. 2013; Cohen and Harvey 2016). This is clearly important for the evaluation of the particular therapy but is probably less important from a social policy point of view. If this amalgamation of intervention produces a lowering in the rate of offending, then, if it can be replicated, it is successful.

There are further crucial limitations in applying the APA criteria to offenders with IDD. The Chambless and Hollon (1998) criteria deemphasize the importance of long-term follow-up focusing, rather, on the efficacy of treatment compared to relevant control conditions. Long-term follow-up is crucial in work with offenders to the extent that a relapse after 15 years has been considered a failure. Cann et al. (2004) conducted a 21-year follow-up study of 419 sexual offenders discharged from prisons in England and Wales. They found that some individuals reoffended 15 years after they had been discharged from custody. Their conclusion, far from indicating the success of treatment with no 'relapse' up to 15 years after treatment was quite to the contrary. They concluded that these individuals were 'at risk' in the community for 15 years prior to reoffending. Therefore, treatment with sex offenders is considered with a different yardstick when compared to work with other groups. Any 'relapse' no matter how long after treatment it occurs is likely to be considered a treatment failure. Therefore, a behavioural treatment that has a short follow-up (which is often the case in follow-up studies on offenders with IDD) but has been shown to be consistently effective over three or four individual carefully controlled case studies, might be considered as a contribution towards effective treatment in other areas, but in sex offender treatment, the short follow-up is a huge limitation.

As we shall see if the coming chapters, the empirical evidence base for effective assessment and treatment of offenders with IDD is limited compared to their non-disabled counterparts. Applying the What Works systems of evaluation will likely limit the extent to which researchers can be confident of demonstrating repeatable treatment effects in this client group. Given the difficulties in attempting to apply What Works principles to the field of offenders with IDD, we propose that a wide range of evidence, not normally considered within the What Works framework, is drawn from criminology, sociology, and public health to understand what may work in transition support for people with intellectual disability. This approach provides a multidimensional understanding of evidence that includes consumer wisdom, professional experience and findings from qualitative research that can stand as equal partners with more traditional forms of evidence that have been developed from experimental research. Forensic intellectual disability services can delineate a clear role and level of expertise in the What Works paradigm through targeted goals and discrete measures of success. We propose that practitioners and researchers go beyond a purely psychological and clinical focus that is often found in the What Works literature, to a non-linear and non-reductionist way of understanding multiplicity of need. These can include addressing diversity of need; adopting appropriate assessment tools; determining if generic or specialist agency intervention is warranted; acquiring the necessary resources and funding; and determining what constitutes a good outcome from intervention. As a minimum, these studies should utilize a pre-post design, with appropriate and normed psychometric measures, specific evaluation outcomes, with follow-up evaluations to determine the longevity of attitude change.

1.6 Structure of the Book

The book is divided into five parts, each of which is described next.

1.6.1 Part I: Introduction

The first Part of this book provides some of the foundational issues that underlie the topic of What Works with offenders with IDD. In this first chapter we have introduced the importance and methods of analysis for determining empirically sound treatment and support for persons with IDD who have offended. This chapter provides the basis upon which other chapters are written and is the underpinning of current accepted practice.

This is followed by Chapter 2, where Dorothy Griffiths describes some of the pivotal yet complex ethical questions that emerge for researchers and clinicians in the application of treatment and support of persons with IDD who have offended. Griffiths provides a brief history of interventions for people with IDD before reviewing five key ethical areas of inquiry that highlight some of the ethical challenges that face science-practitioners in the treatment of persons with IDD who have offended, and which could serve as basic guidelines for clinical practice. Griffiths concludes that we should be seeking ways to gain a better understanding of this client group, to communicate with them, and to work with them towards achieving fulfilling lives.

In Chapter 3, Frank Lambrick, Astrid Birgden, Chelsea Troutmann and Danielle McLeod further this discussion with a detailed analysis of the rights of persons with IDD that are involved when they become entangled in correctional settings. They begin by reviewing the compulsory treatment (CT) framework in operation in Victoria, Australia, a unique legislative charter that allows treatment to be provided without consent as either a diversionary or a step-down alternative to prison. They review the characteristics of people who are likely to be subject to a CT before detailing the results of a study into detention histories and characteristics of people subject to a CT, the sample split between those admitted to a correctional facility versus those who were not admitted to a correctional facility. They report notable differences in mental distress and behavioural disorders diagnosed in childhood. They conclude by considering the human rights of recipients of CT who have engaged in offending behaviour and who can be considered both as an offender *and* a person with a disability.

1.6.2 Part II: Phenotypes and Genotypes and Offending Behaviour

This Part focuses on particular areas of assessment that have specific relevance to determining appropriate treatment and support. In Chapter 4, Lauren J. Rice, Stewart L. Einfeld, and Patricia Howlin, elaborate on an important but often unexplored area in both research and practice, that being the influence of genetics on the behavioural and cognitive phenotypes of persons with IDD and how this can influence the nature of offending behaviour as well as the implications it has for treatment and support.

1.6.3 Part III: Validated Assessments

The assessment Part begins with Chapter 5 by Nigel Beail who describes the nature of personality disorder (PD) and the presentation of personality disorders in people who have IDD and in offenders who have IDD. He begins by providing a detailed definition of personality disorder and considers the diagnostic criteria. He highlights the importance of considering a number of issues in relation to people with IDD when considering diagnoses of personality disorders including issues around emotional development, anger management, impulsivity, and co-morbidity, which all have relevance when making diagnostic considerations. He goes on to discuss approaches when assessing for personality disorder and implications for interventions (psychological and pharmacological). He concludes that diagnosis should be structured and made within a multidisciplinary context and judgments around interventions can only be based on the developing research on interventions with people who have PD in the general population.

This is followed by Chapter 6 by Paul Willner, Andrew Jahoda, and Ken McMahon on the assessment for anger and violence in people with IDD. They begin by providing useful definitions of anger before discussing how these definitions apply to people with IDD who experience anger-related difficulties. The chapter is divided into two main sections. The first section reviews current anger management assessments, with the second detailing the underpinning evidence for their use, and then measures of aggression will be outlined. The relevance of assessments of aggression to risk assessment and management for offenders with intellectual disabilities is discussed. In conclusion they highlight that aggressive acts can have complex contextual factors that may be idiosyncratic to the individual, which the existing measures may not be sufficient to tease-out, particularly in terms of information processing, attention, and encoding of cues within 'real-life' situations, and structured assessments of social goals.

In Chapter 7, Lesley R. Steptoe and Amanda M. Michie, discuss the assessment of sexual offenders with IDD and outline the psychometric principles underlying the assessment. They outline and evaluate the available psychometric assessments commonly used when assessing psychological constructs with sexual offenders with IDD. They caution that although there are similarities between sex offenders with IDD and non-IDD sexual offenders, methodological differences between studies of these two groups and the difficulties of standardization of normative data within assessment measures for sexual offenders with IDD challenges this assumption. Firstly, they considered the psychometric assessment of cognitive ability before exploring theories of sexual offending before considering psychometric assessments used with sexual offenders with IDD. Finally, they consider the merit of actuarial and structured risk assessment frameworks. They argue that assessment is the critical factor to inform risk, needs, and responsivity in respect of treatment and those individuals scoring on higher levels of deviancy should be prioritized for treatment and appropriate risk management whether within an institutional setting or community.

Chapter 8 by Peter E. Langdon considers models of social problem-solving and related theoretical perspectives, such as how social information processing has been augmented to incorporate developmental perspectives, mainly drawn from moral psychology. He reviews the literature on theoretical models of social problem-solving and argues that the Social Information Processing-Moral Decision Making (SIP-MDM) framework integrates several previous theoretical perspectives into a single framework which attempts to capture variables and constructs that develop over time, whilst also attempting to consider how real time decision making and social problem-solving occurs. He concludes that the methods of assessing social problem-solving and pro-offence distorted cognitions are limited to questionnaire-based or semi-structured interviews, and there are very few well developed and validated tools for use with this population. Using new technologies such as virtual immersion therapy (VIT) may help to enable more effective communication and participation, not only within assessment procedures, but eventually within interventions.

Chapter 9 by Joanne E.L. VanDerNagel, Neomi van Duijvenbode, and Robert Didden, continues the discussion of assessment by exploring assessment of alcohol use disorder (AUD) and alcohol-related offending behaviour in persons with IDD. They highlight that, due to several factors, individuals with IDD and substance use disorder seem to be less likely to receive treatment or to remain in addiction treatment. They begin by summarizing research on the prevalence of substance use disorder – particularly alcohol use disorder – amongst individuals with IDD in a forensic context and its relationship to offending behaviour. They then provide suggestions for the assessment of substance use in individuals with IDD in a forensic context. They conclude that systematic screening and assessment of alcohol use and AUD in individuals with IDD in forensic contexts is relevant and special attention should be paid to the possibility that alcohol use continues in prison and forensic treatment settings and the influence that intoxication can have on the assessments process.

In Chapter 10, Samuel J. Tromans, Verity Chester, and Regi T. Alexander highlight that fire-setting behaviours amongst individuals with IDD present numerous challenges for assessment and management by healthcare professionals, requiring coordinated multidisciplinary team input, and treatment programmes adapted for their level of intellectual functioning. They begin by clarifying definitions between fire-setting, arson, and pyromania and note that reliable prevalence estimates are lacking. They note that the risk factors for fire-setting in persons with IDD are complex and often interwoven, much like in the non-IDD population and summarize the key characteristics of fire setters. They argue that assessing fire setters with IDD should follow the same approach as those without an IDD, but with a number of additional considerations and they detail a number of specific fire-setting assessments with details of their use in persons with IDD. They highlight that assessing the future recidivism risk of those with histories of fire setting is challenging due to very low base rates. Helpfully, they provide areas of specific focus for a clinical interview in a patient with IDD whom has engaged in fire-setting behaviours as well as using collateral information before briefly highlighting treatment considerations.

This is followed by commentary on the biopsychosocial (BPS) assessment approach for offenders with IDD by Deborah Richards, Tyler Oswald, and J. Paul Fedoroff. They discuss the process of biological-medical assessments, including neurodevelopmental disorders, mental health, and personality disorder before considering psychological and emotional assessment approaches and understanding the person's development history and influences and finally the socio-environmental assessment. The importance of each section is highlighted by a case study of a young man with history of abuse and neglect and a suspected diagnosis of Fetal Alcohol Spectrum Disorder (FASD) and who has a history of violent and inappropriate sexual behaviour which is interwoven throughout the chapter. They argue that employing a systematic and comprehensive assessment approach to address the maladaptive problems experienced by offenders who have IDD is necessary in developing effective treatment strategies and that integrating clinical information from a multidisciplinary BPS framework can better support the whole person.

The assessment Part ends with a discussion on a multicomponent model of assessment of persons with IDD and problem sexual behaviours by Robin Wilson, Stephanie Ioannou, and Kendra Thomson. They begin by countering the argument that 'nothing works' and argue for rehabilitative processes over long-term incarceration as seen in the civil commitment of sexual offenders in some US states. They go on to outline the principles of effective interventions and describe an applied behaviour analytic framework, specifically, a multicomponent, function-based decision model that is a refinement of strategies that have empirical support with the neurotypical population, applied to people with intellectual disabilities and sexualized offending behaviour. The process begins with a functional behavioural assessment of the presenting problem, including a combination of indirect measures and descriptive/direct measures and experimental functional analysis. The assessment phase is followed by a treatment based on functional behaviour assessment where preventative coping skills and replacement behaviours should be taught including teaching individuals how to get their sexual needs met in a non-offending way. They suggest that all the environmental variables to which the individual is exposed should be considered and that treatment should attempt to begin with the least intrusive and/or reinforcement-based intervention strategies including alternative functional replacement behaviour in any behaviour reduction programme. The final stage of the process is the generalization and maintenance of treatment effects, which focuses on reductions in inappropriate behaviours and increases in alternative behaviours. They illustrate the approach by providing two case studies and conclude by arguing that an idiosyncratic approach is in order to gain a better understanding of the individual.

1.6.4 Part IV: Treatment

The first chapter (Chapter 13) in the treatment Part begins with a discussion on supporting people as they transition from secure custody settings to the community. Kathy Ellem, Michelle Denton, and Danielle Davidson highlight that prison-to-community transition is a complex psychosocial phenomenon that requires a broad interdisciplinary perspective beyond the important contribution of psychological treatment. They consider post-prison support needs within an adapted reintegration theory. They discuss the intrapersonal conditions (impact of impairment, physical and mental health, substance use and gambling), and subsistence conditions of people with IDD leaving prison, specific individual issues related to cognition and behaviour, as well as social influences regarding housing, income, and employment conditions. They review recent research in formal and informal supports for ex-prisoners with IDD and provide some insight into What Works in prison-to-community transition.

Continuing the discussion on prison progression, in Chapter 14, Philip Snoyman, Berindah Aicken, and Jayson Ware discuss prison-based programmes for people with IDD. They begin by exploring definitional and identification issues specific to prisons and consider what treatment for people with IDD in prison seeks to achieve. They go on to review the existing research specific to prison-based programmes for people with IDD, debating the issue of adapting mainstream programmes versus the design of specific programmes for people with IDD. They highlight that a number of specific programmes have been developed in Australia including the Self-Regulation Program (SRP) suite of programmes, including programmes for people with IDD who sexually offend (SRP-SO), who violently offend (SRP-VO), and those with general offending (SRP-GO). In considering the wider literature on treatment efficacy they note that only five articles appear to provide adequate, albeit limited, evidence regarding the effectiveness of programmes for people with IDD in prison, which they review. They conclude there are programmes that meet criminogenic need and/or disability need although a number of evaluation questions still need to be addressed including therapeutic alliance, nature of treatment, and models of treatment.

In Chapter 15, Robert Didden, Henk Nijman, Monique Delforterie, and Marije Keulen-De Vos discuss treatment for anger and violence for people with IDD. They review a number of published studies from the past two decades that have evaluated the effectiveness of cognitive behaviour therapy (CBT) and mindfulness for anger and violence (aggression) in individuals with intellectual disabilities and have provided recommendations for adaptations of CBT to persons with IDD. They conclude with recommendations, based on studies that have evaluated staff-training approaches for staff who work with persons with IDD who have problems with anger and violence.

Following on from Lesley R. Steptoe and Amanda M. Michie's chapter on assessing sexually harmful behaviour in people with IDD, in Chapter 16, Leam A. Craig considers meta-analytical reviews and individual treatment studies for sexual offenders with IDD within the What Works systems framework. He begins by discussing the What Works systems of review and considers how these can be applied to treatment studies of sexual offenders with IDD, many of which, at face-value, would fail to meet the empirical rigour of the What Works principles. He argues that treatment efficacy and therapeutic outcomes can also be demonstrated in other ways such as behavioural change, changes in attitudes towards offending, improvements in sexual knowledge and victim empathy, a reduction in cognitive distortions and problem sexual behaviours. He first considers the aetiological explanations of sexual offending behaviour for people with IDD before reviewing treatment efficacy. He concludes that although the findings from treatment studies may not necessarily meet the empirical rigour of the core What Works principles, there is consistent and emerging evidence of treatment efficacy and therapeutic outcomes demonstrated in other ways such as behavioural change, changes in attitudes towards offending, improvements in sexual knowledge and victim empathy, and self-regulation.

In Chapter 17, Susan Hayes, considers the treatment for social problem-solving and criminal thinking in people with IDD. She argues that social problem-solving and criminal thinking are two inter-related concepts that contribute to offending behaviour and recidivism. These concepts are particularly relevant to offenders with IDD owing to their deficits in adaptive behaviour, propensity to impulsivity, difficulties in foreseeing the long-term consequences of their actions, poor problem-solving skills, and the prevalence of dual diagnosis of a co-existing mental disorder. Hayes highlights that comparatively little clinical and evaluative research has been undertaken with this group, studying the most efficacious treatments regarding poor problem-solving and criminal-thinking styles consistent with offending behaviour. She concludes that CBTs and a range of manualized programmes appear to offer positive and effective solutions for assisting offenders with IDD to improve social problem-solving skills, adaptive skills, and criminal-thinking styles.

The next chapter (Chapter 18) by Danielle Newton and Jane McGillivary examines treatment approaches for substance misuse amongst offenders with IDD. They begin by providing a brief overview of substance use/misuse amongst people with IDD including the prevalence in community and prison-based samples, and the reasons and risk factors for their substance use. They go on to make the link between substance misuse and offending behaviour amongst this population and the few treatment programmes with evidence of effectiveness are discussed. They highlight that despite indications that the risks associated with substance misuse are elevated amongst people with IDD there are surprisingly few evidence-based substance use/misuse treatment programmes targeting this population, the majority of published treatment programmes being community-based programmes that do not specifically target offenders with IDD. They note that although the studies reviewed did provide some evidence of the effectiveness of treatment programmes for substance use/misuse amongst people with IDD, they all suffer from methodological limitations. The chapter concludes with a review of the barriers to effective assessment and treatment of substance misuse amongst people with IDD and provides a summary of further research needed in this area.

In Chapter 19, Paul Oxnam and Emma Gardner discuss treatment for emotional difficulties related to offending for people with IDD. They begin by discussing the high prevalence of co-morbid diagnoses of mental illness in people with IDD and possible explanations. Despite the increased awareness that people with an IDD are more vulnerable to emotional difficulties, the authors note practitioners can often fail to understand their distress and misattribute mental health symptoms (e.g. head banging, social withdrawal) to the person's IDD (i.e. challenging behaviour or poor social skills, respectively) in a phenomenon known as diagnostic overshadowing. In this chapter, they provide an overview of the three types of emotional difficulties that are most frequently encountered during the course of working with offenders with an IDD; depression, anxiety, and trauma. They describe the assessment processes involved in each condition and provide and illustrate their approach to working with people with IDD with mental health problems in the form of case studies. They briefly discuss the role of group therapy programmes in the treatment of these emotional difficulties. They emphasize that clinicians must work to understand what the person is attempting to communicate through behaviours that are often concerning and offensive to staff, and that utilizing assessment criteria specific to this population, collecting psychometric data, making behavioural observations, using collateral sources, and taking time to listen to those who work most closely with the person, will ensure a rich formulation that the multidisciplinary care team can invest in.

Next, Peter Sturmey considers treatment outcomes for people with Autistic Spectrum Disorder (ASD) in forensic settings. He begins Chapter 20 by describing in detail a case study of a young man who was diagnosed with ASD and who engaged in extreme violence. He highlights that at several critical points keys pieces of information were missed which may have later resulted in a different outcome. He considers prevalence studies and concludes there is no empirical support of large differences between individuals with ASD and those without in terms of offending behaviour. Of the small number of studies which have reported treatment of individuals, mostly in uncontrolled descriptive case studies, there is a growing literature on the use of CBT-type approaches, Mindfulness, and Applied Behaviour Analysis (ABA) in the assessment and treatment of offenders with ASD, with some pharmacological studies reporting results. Sturmey concludes by highlighting where lessons could have been learned, and warning signs identified, in preventing offending in people with ASD.

In Chapter 21, Daniel Turner and Peer Briken consider how pharmacological approaches can be used in supporting offenders with IDD. They highlight that there is no pharmacological treatment approach for offenders per se that prevents offenders from relapsing with criminal behaviours, but, as different mental health conditions deteriorate, which seems to increase the risk for offending, pharmacological agents can be used to tackle symptoms of underlying mental disorders. They note that there is almost no research on pharmacological interventions explicitly addressing offenders with IDD and thus most recommendations are based on findings with mentally disordered offenders without IDD. They consider mental disorders found most frequently in general or violent offenders; antisocial personality disorders, substance use disorders, and traumatic brain injury with commentary on treating psychotic disorders in offenders with IDD and those who engage in sexually harmful behaviour. Although the state of research concerning pharmacological interventions in offenders with IDD is limited, they provide suggestions on how pharmacological treatments might be used with people with IDD who display violent behaviours or co-morbid mental illness.

1.6.5 Part V: Conclusions

In the final chapter, we (Dorothy Griffiths and Leam Craig) examine the role of evidence-based practice (EBP) and summarize the key points of the chapters in this volume. Three major shifts appear to be emerging. First, there was a strong trend towards a holistic approach to the assessment and treatment of people with IDD who offend that is multi-modal. Second, there was prominent emphasis on habilitation directed at reducing vulnerabilities that put the offender at risk of future offences and that affect treatment outcomes. Third, there was recognition of the importance comprehensive planning and supports to achieve long-term effects and provide the offender with the elements of a quality of life that could prevent relapse. We highlight that the What Works systems of evaluation are not easily translated when considering the assessment and treatment of people with IDD who offend and that there are significant limitations in using rates of recidivism as the primary outcome measure of programme success. We have seen in this volume that practitioners and researchers have gone beyond a purely mechanical focus, emphasizing an understanding of multiplicity of need, incorporating comprehensive evaluative frameworks into programme designs and adopting controlled case studies to demonstrate psychological change and attitudinal shift in offenders with IDD. We end by offering some suggestions as to where the future direction of What Works research in this client group should go.

References

Andrews, D.A. and Bonta, J. (2010). *The Psychology of Criminal Conduct*, 5e. Cincinnati, OH: Anderson Publishing Co.

Baer, D.M., Wolf, M.M., and Risley, T.R. (1968). Some current dimensions of applied behavior analysis. *Journal of Applied Behavior Analysis* 1: 91–97.

Bonta, J. and Andrews, D.A. (2017). *The Psychology of Criminal Conduct*, 6e. New York: Routledge.

Cann, J., Falshaw, L., and Friendship, C. (2004). Sexual offenders discharged from prison in England and Wales: a 21-year reconviction study. *Legal and Criminological Psychology* 9: 1–10.

Chambless, D.L. and Hollon, S.D. (1998). Defining empirically supported therapies. *Journal of Consulting and Clinical Psychology* 66: 7–18.

Chambless, D.L. and Ollendick, T.H. (2001). Empirically supported psychological interventions: controversies and evidence. *Annual Review of Psychology* 52: 685–716.

Chambless, D.L., Baker, M., Baucom, D.H. et al. (1998). Update on empirically validated therapies, II. *The Clinical Psychologist* 51 (1): 3–16.

Chapman, M.J., Hare, D.J., Caton, S. et al. (2013). The use of mindfulness with people with intellectual disabilities: a systematic review and narrative analysis. *Mindfulness* 4 (2): 179–189.

Cohen, G. and Harvey, J. (2016). The use of psychological interventions for adult male sex offenders with a learning disability: a systematic review. *Journal of Sexual Aggression* 22 (2): 206–223.

Craig, L.A. and Hutchinson, R. (2005). Sexual offenders with learning disabilities: risk, recidivism and treatment. *Journal of Sexual Aggression* 11 (3): 289–304.

Craig, L.A., Dixon, L., and Gannon, T.A. (2013). *What Works in Offender Rehabilitation: An Evidenced Based Approach to Assessment and Treatment.* Chichester: Wiley-Blackwell.

Guyatt, G.H., Sackett, D.L., Sinclair, J.C. et al. (1995). Users' guides to the medical literature. IX. A method for grading health care recommendations. Evidence-Based Medicine Working Group. *Journal of the American Medical Association* 274 (22): 1800–1804.

Higgins, J.P.T., Altman, D.G., Gøtzsche, P.C. et al. (2011). The Cochrane Collaboration's tool for assessing risk of bias in randomised trials. *The British Medical Journal* 343: d5928.

Higgins, J.P.T., Sterne, J.A.C., Savović, J. et al., (2016). A revised tool for assessing risk of bias in randomized trials. In: *Cochrane Methods. Cochrane Database of Systematic Reviews*, 10 (Suppl 1) (ed. J. Chandler, J. McKenzie, I. Boutron et al.). https://sites.google.com/site/riskofbiastool/welcome/rob-2-0-tool (accessed 10 May 2019).

Landenberger, N.A. and Lipsey, M.W. (2005). The positive effects of cognitive–behavioral programs for offenders: a meta-analysis of factors associated with effective treatment. *Journal of Experimental Criminology* 1 (4): 451–476.

Sharman, L.W., Gottfredson, D., MacKenzie, D. et al. (1997). *Preventing crime: what works, what doesn't, what's promising.* Washington, DC: National Institute of Justice https://www.ncjrs.gov/pdffiles/171676.PDF (accessed 5 June 2018).

Sterne, J.A.C., Hernán, M.A., Reeves, B.C. et al. (2016). ROBINS-I: a tool for assessing risk of bias in non-randomised studies of interventions. *The BMJ* 355: i4919.

Sturmey, P. and Didden, R. (2014). *Evidence-Based Practice and Intellectual Disabilities.* Chichester: Wiley-Blackwell.

Wolf, M.M. (1978). Social validity: the case for subjective measurement or how applied behavior analysis is finding its heart. *Journal of Applied Behavior Analysis* 11: 203–214.

2

What Works

Ethical Considerations When Treating Offenders with Intellectual
and Developmental Disabilities

Dorothy Griffiths

Brock University, St. Catharines, Ontario, Canada

In this chapter, some of the ethical questions regarding the application of empirically based assessment and treatment for offenders with intellectual and developmental disabilities (IDD) will be discussed, with the intent of integrating standards of clinical practice for offenders within the emergent culture in the field of intellectual disabilities.

2.1   Introduction

> Ethics is a term bandied about with a sense of near abandon in the field of developmental disabilities. Broadly in this context, the term ethics or ethical is generally used to refer to a position, or rule stated in the form of a moral imperative, with the implication that if one's conduct is guided by this rule, one will be acting in an ethical manner. (Sturmey 2005, p. 435)

Sturmey (2005) who suggested that ethics includes concepts such as promotion of the greatest good as often preserved in law and professional practice, however noted that history has shown that many things that 'are or have been legal are not ethical' (p. 437) particularly regarding the treatment of persons with intellectual disabilities. This sentiment was echoed by Paul and Elder (2005), who suggested that 'What is illegal may or may not be a matter of ethics. What is ethically obligatory may be illegal. What is unethical may be legal. [In essence, t]here is no essential connection between ethics and the law' (p. 11). They went on to suggest that 'because we cannot assume that social conventions are ethical, we cannot assume that human laws are ethical. What is more, most laws are made by politicians, who routinely confuse social values with ethical principles .... their primary motivation is, except in special cases, power, vested interest or expediency' (p. 11). Sturmey noted (2005) noted that history has witnessed the legal sterilization, killing, and starvation of persons with intellectual and developmental

The Wiley Handbook on What Works for Offenders with Intellectual and Developmental Disabilities: An Evidence-Based Approach to Theory, Assessment, and Treatment, First Edition.
Edited by William R. Lindsay, Leam A. Craig, and Dorothy Griffiths.

disabilities (IDD) and current practice in the USA legally allows for the abortion of a foetus that has a developmental disability. He remarked that although these are legal, the ethics of these acts may be questionable. As O'Manique (2003) remarked, 'Law itself is relative and arbitrary, its origin and test being within the human community and with no necessary connection to morality' (p. 167).

Paul and Elder (2005) noted that ethical reasoning raises religious, social, legal, and ethical questions. They suggested that social questions involve group customs and taboos, whereas legal questions arise from aspects of behaviour that have been 'codified by a society into law' and as noted above 'may or may not have an ethical basis' (Paul and Elder 2005, p. 13).

Ethics has been described as consequentialist or theological (Thiroux 2001). Consequential ethics involve evaluation of the outcome based upon what benefits the greatest number in society. The foundation of this thinking is that what is being done should be based on what is for the good of the many, not the good of the few or the one. Whereas theological thinking is nonconsequential; ethical behaviour according to this theory is based on the idea that there is a set standard of doing what is right that can be followed. When applied to persons who have committed a crime against society, ethical treatment practice could therefore be judged from either the stance of what serves the greatest good (i.e. protects and benefits society) or from the stance that there should be a standard to which treatment decisions should be judged (i.e. protects and benefits the individual).

Treatment decisions regarding persons with IDD have ostensibly been based on both rationales, sometimes concurrently. Simpson and Hogg (2001, p. 384) stated that:

> Offending has variously served as an indicator of social menace, an expression of lack of social competence, and an effect of exclusionary social structures and practices. It has been used in arguments for the protection of society from people with ID, and for the care and protection of such individuals from a social order in which they cannot compete or conform.

In the early part of the last century, persons with IDD were deemed to represent a social risk to the moral fabric and financial viability of society (Scheerenberger 1983). Scientists claimed that persons with IDD were genetically determined to be allied to criminality (Goddard 1912). The emergent Eugenics Movement purported that criminal behaviour, mental disorders, intellectual disability, promiscuity, alcoholism, amongst other social ills, were all linked genetically and that to protect society from persons with intellectual disabilities and the resultant negative social impact, social isolation and sanctioning should follow. The movement was grounded in flawed scientific studies such as Goddard's genealogical trace of the Kallikak family amongst others. Nonetheless the research produced a social movement across North America and into Europe that attempted to control the financial and social burdens of society that they purported were the by-product of persons with IDD.

The Eugenics studies have long since been debunked (i.e. Fancher 1987) however their impact, such as institutionalization, sterilization, and even mass murder, the latter at the hands of the Nazis (Scheerenberger 1983), had greatly affected the field of IDD and steered much of the direction of the treatment and policy of persons with IDD until the past few decades. Even today a debate looms regarding the incidence of offending amongst the population of persons with IDD compared to the neuro-typical population. It is commonly written that persons with IDD are more likely than non-disabled persons to be involved with the criminal justice system. According to Petersilia (2000), persons with IDD represent only 2–3% of the population, yet they are over represented in the prison population at 4–10%, with an even greater percentage amongst juvenile offenders.

Others have questioned whether these data are accurate. For example, after analysis of multiple studies, Simpson and Hogg (2001) concluded that 'the prevalence of offending among people with ID compared with the general population is impossible to assess firmly on the available information' (p. 390). They noted that the challenges in making conclusive findings relates to the lack of uniformity between the studies that have been conducted, the lack of consistent definitions of IDD, some poor research methodology, and analyses conducted at different points in the justice process (Simpson and Hogg 2001). Similarly, Lindsay (2002), in his thoughtful review of the research on offenders with intellectual disabilities, concluded there is no clear evidence that there is either an over or under representation of people with intellectual disabilities amongst offenders. He suggested that the failure to produce an accurate prevalence rate of sexual offence amongst persons with intellectual disabilities is complicated by the differential sampling techniques employed. Further Griffiths et al. (2004) cautioned that because research is often based on prison data or arrest/conviction rates, the data may be less indicative of an over representation of higher rates of offending but an artefact of the criminal justice system, which witnesses a greater rate of arrest, confession, and conviction (Murphy et al. 1983; Santamour and West 1978).

A critical look at the presumed incidence of offending amongst persons with intellectual disabilities is important. There are ethical and treatment implications of making false assumptions about heritability or inherent offence propensity compared to examining factors that may have led an individual to offend.

2.2 Ethical Reasoning Regarding Offenders with Intellectual Disabilities

Paul and Elder (2005) noted that questions of ethics revolve around behaviour that is either helpful or harmful to others. Ethical reasoning is therefore undertaken for the purpose of helping others, thereby posing the question of how best to act in order to help rather than harm (Paul and Elder 2005). Fundamental to ethical reasoning is reliance on information that will aid in the achievement of the purpose. However, also involved is the matter of inference in judging what is helpful or harmful and what will lead to 'contributing to rather than undermining the well-being of others' (p. 15). Empirical research is often the basis for the information on which treatment ethics is shaped.

In recent decades, there has been increasing research published on the assessment, management, treatment, and support of offenders with IDD. The research has added a level of confidence in the field regarding appropriate and ethical practice regarding offenders with IDD and enabled the establishment of some basic ethical principles for assessment and treatment founded on the science that guides evidence-based practice.

Claude (2002) characterized science as devotion to truth, avoiding bias and assumptions, corroboration and replication of findings, and open communication and discourse.

Van Houten et al. (1988) advocated that persons with IDD should have the right to the most effective treatment. The concept of effective was based on science founded in replicated *research*. Green (1999) added to this argument stating that recipients should have the right to the most effective treatment that follows assessment with a goal of benefiting personal welfare, conducted in a therapeutic environment, and provided by a qualified professional who monitors the ongoing treatment effects and efficacy. The right to appropriate treatment brings into discussion the ethics of appropriate assessment and the determination of treatment that is least restrictive, least intrusive whilst being most-effective based upon empirical evidence that is scientifically grounded.

Sturmey (2005) suggested however that these supposed rights are not enshrined in law but in the aspirations for professional practice. He noted that 'consensus on professional practice does not necessarily mirror an appeal to authority rather, it reflects a social contract with society in which professionals are granted certain prerogatives in exchange for accountability, in a variety of forms, including ethics as principles or guidelines of conduct' (Sturmey 2005, p. 436).

Given the history and misunderstandings that have plagued persons with IDD regarding the issue of criminal behaviour, there has been a heightened awareness of the importance of empirically validated therapeutic approaches to the treatment of offending behaviour.

2.3   Ethics and Evidence-Based Practice

Evidence-based practice in psychology (EBPP) is the integration of the best available research with clinical expertise in the context of patient characteristics, culture, and preferences (American Psychological Association [APA] Presidential Task Force 2006). Empirically validated or supported treatment involves approaches that are well established through experimentation and found to produce significant and positive outcomes (Chamless et al. 1998). There is no one type of research design that constitutes the basis for evidence-based practice, although randomized control trial studies are often seen as the standard for empirically validated practice. Greenberg and Newman (1996) suggested that the research design should match the nature of the inquiry. For example, case study research is often the basis of innovative practice and hypothesis testing, qualitative research adds to knowledge of the experience of the subjects, aggregated case studies allow comparison across subjects, single-case studies permit causal relationships to be explored, intervention studies in natural settings provides the ecological validity to be addressed, and meta analyses allow for the synthesis of various studies (Greenberg and Newman 1996).

In examining a variety of challenging behaviours presented by persons with intellectual disabilities, the use of single-subject research has been an asset in guiding evidence-based practice, as long as strict criteria are met. Horner et al. (2005) identified the criteria for appropriate scientific merit of this type of research as: (i) using operationally defined criteria to allow replication, (ii) involving description of the methodology with sufficient precision so that individuals other than the developers can replicate it with fidelity, (iii) having a clearly defined population, method of practice, qualifications of personnel, and outcomes, (iv) having demonstrated fidelity, (v) being able to demonstrate a relationship functionally or causally to outcomes, and (vi) employing an experimental design repeatedly over multiple subjects and in different venues to produce a sample of at least 20 subjects over five different studies.

Psychology has long been a strong proponent of evidence-based practice (APA Presidential Task Force 2006). The APA has suggested that one method of evaluating evidence-based practice is through the development of guidelines for best practice. Some aligned fields, such as the Association for the Treatment of Sexual Abusers (ATSA), have developed practice guidelines for the assessment, treatment, and risk reduction and management of sexual abusers (ATSA 2014). Although not specific to persons with IDD, the ATSA standards provide important principles on which practice should be based. Similarly, the Behaviour Analysis Certification Board has produced similar guidelines calling for the use of evidence-based practice (Section 1 of the Code, BACB 2014). Newsom and Hovanitz (2005, p. 31) noted however that 'professional organizations typically avoid an explicit requirement that practitioners use *only* scientifically valid interventions'. Thus, in absence of a universally accepted scientific methodology, treatment acceptability is often weighted on variables such as cost-effectiveness and common practice (Newsom and Hovanitz 2005), neither of which consider the efficacy of the treatment.

2.4 Key Ethical Areas of Inquiry into Practice

For the purpose of this chapter on ethics and what works with offenders with intellectual disabilities, there are several questions that could serve as basic guidelines for clinical practice:

1) Has a comprehensive assessment of the individual and circumstances surrounding the offence been examined to distinguish if the offence is criminal behaviour or inappropriate behaviour, to determine what conditions led to or contributed to the commission of the offence, and lastly to identify the factors that may enhance or create challenges to treatment for this individual?
2) Has the assessment led to an individualized plan based on best-practice strategies that provides both habilitative and rehabilitative elements, as required?
3) Has a distinction between treatment and management been delineated?
4) Does the treatment and management approach recognize the rights of the offender with intellectual disabilities to consent or refuse treatment?
5) Is there a long-term plan based on person-centred planning to ensure generalization and transference of the treatment outcomes into the least-restrictive environment that can provide optimal quality of life whilst at the same time ensuring community safety?

Within the discussion of the above questions, both principles of good practice that have emerged in recent decades in both the forensic field and from the field of those supporting persons with intellectual disabilities will be discussed.

Question 1 on Ethical Practice: Has a comprehensive assessment of the individual and circumstances surrounding the offence been examined to understand if the offence is criminal behaviour or inappropriate behaviour, to determine what conditions led to or contributed to the commission of the offence, and lastly to identify the factors that may enhance or create challenges to treatment for this individual?

One of the first issues that must be addressed is whether the offending person with an IDD can be held criminally responsible for the commission of an offending act and as such is treatment for this behaviour as an offence appropriate or even possible. Determination of criminality and consequent treatment of persons with IDD in our societies occur within the context of intersecting social conditions including how IDD is socially constructed and defined in the criminal justice system.

> A historical perspective indicates that investigating the relationship between people with ID and offending is beset with difficulties. Valid interpretation of the findings requires considerable thought. First, what is meant by the term 'intellectual disability', and what methods have been used to establish whether a person does or does not fulfil the criteria for this condition? Secondly, how is 'offending' defined? Is being 'at risk' or 'suspected' of committing an offence sufficient, or is it necessary for a conviction through the criminal justice system to have taken place? (Holland et al. 2002, p. 7)

'There is a vast difference from stating that people with an intellectual disability are disproportionately represented in regard to the offender populations to the statement that people with intellectual disability are more likely to offend than other populations' (Griffiths et al. 2018, p. 6). People with IDD may have become embroiled in the legal system, not because of the volitional commitment of a crime but as a by-product of other factors. These factors may be related to the disability as mediating variables, be associated with circumstances of their life as a person with a disability that produced vulnerabilities for commission of a crime, and/or be the result of inequities within the criminal justice and judicial system that might criminalize behaviours or disadvantage persons with intellectual disabilities when involved in the justice system. For example, Petersilia (2000) has cautioned that:

> Many offenders with cognitive disabilities may not be so much 'lawbreakers' as they are low-functioning citizens who lack education on how to function responsibility in a complex society. Some research suggests that they are frequently used by other criminals to assist in law-breaking without understanding their involvement in the crime or its consequences (p. 5).

There are several factors related to the individual's disability that may have influenced the commission of the crime. Persons with IDD may be more susceptible to be lured by others into a criminal act because of naivety or because of a desire to be accepted by others. Hingsburger (2013) coined the phrase *counterfeit criminality* to refer to those individuals who have criminally offended because of a lack of social belonging, self-advocacy skills, or the inability to discriminate situations that are risky. Holland et al. (2002) cautioned that when reporting prevalence rates there is a need to distinguish between challenging behaviour that becomes misinterpreted as antisocial or criminal from behaviour that is clearly criminal. The idea of a behaviour appearing criminal, when it is not, was espoused earlier by Hingsburger et al. (1991) in the context of possible hypotheses for sexually inappropriate behaviour committed by persons with IDD. They noted that some of the reasons why persons with intellectual disabilities offended sexually were both clinically significant and criminal, whereas others who had offended fell into the category that would be deemed *counterfeit deviant.*

Persons with IDD may also be overrepresented in the criminal justice system because of a lack of knowledge about the law (ignorance of the law, lack of criminal intention) and the rules governing social mores. In many cases people with intellectual disabilities have been denied knowledge of their basic rights, including education regarding the law and social mores (Lindsay 2009). In such cases, it has been argued that such behaviours, albeit inappropriate or challenging, may fail to meet the definition of criminality (Emerson 1995). Holland et al. (2002) proposed that offenders with IDD represent two identifiable groups. The first group of offenders with intellectual disability was exemplified by issues of social disadvantage, substance abuse, and mental disorder. However, a second, but smaller group, were offenders with IDD whose behaviours they characterize as inappropriate rather than criminalized. In the latter case, these behaviours that lack criminal *mens rea* have often been criminalized by the criminal justice system, where *mens rea* refers to the intention of the criminal act. The ethical question that arises from this discourse is: Was a crime committed volitionally, or without knowledge that the behaviour was criminal, or as a product of duress or trickery? The importance of this determination lies in the fact that the consequent treatment should be determined by the circumstances.

Individuals with IDD do not represent a homogeneous group. An intellectual disability can result from genetic, traumatic, or environmental factors, each that present differently and pose unique strengths and challenges. Whilst many differences associated with an IDD may play mediating roles, such as impaired judgement or a lack of adaptive skills, some represent unique challenges. Such an example is an individual with Prader-Willi syndrome who was found guilty of stealing food. Whilst indeed a crime was committed, the lack of hunger cessation typically experienced after eating was not felt by the individual and as such foraging for food resulted. Although many people with Prader-Willi syndrome have been able to benefit from programmes to teach them to control their eating, this individual had not been given education and therefore had followed his natural yearnings. Knowledge of the influence of his syndrome would play an invaluable role in putting a plan in place to reduce a further occurrence that would be unique to other offenders.

Secondly, there may be factors relating to circumstances of the life of the person with an IDD that produce an increased vulnerability to offend. It has been reported that persons with intellectual disabilities are likely to experience more abuse of all types, than the nondisabled population (Sobsey 1994). Sexual abuse, in particular, has been estimated to be twice as likely amongst this population and the experience of abuse has been hypothesized as a factor in the later commission of a sexual offence amongst some persons with intellectual disabilities (Firth et al. 2001). This was demonstrated by Lindsay et al. (2001), who found that 38% of the sexual offenders with an IDD had been abused compared to 12.7% of the non-sexual offenders with an IDD. Their study added weight to the concept that some individuals may be re-enacting their own sexual abuse (traumagenic re-enactment) or may be an indication that they had not learned appropriate social mores to counteract their experiences.

Hingsburger (2013) also suggested that the social isolation of people with IDD increases their vulnerability to be used by others in the commission of a crime because the person exists in a void of social belonging. The importance of social isolation as it relates to offending and persons with intellectual disabilities was also addressed by other authors (Isherwood et al. 2007). Additionally, increased vulnerability may be associated with the IDD, or the risk factors potentially associated with the lifestyle of a person with an IDD including poverty, clustered living, lack of education, and abusive experiences (Griffiths 2002).

Some individuals, because of the vulnerabilities of their life experiences, combined with a lack of education or therapy, may have failed to learn that certain behaviours are inappropriate, a violation of the rights of others, and illegal, thereby leaving them in a moral vacuum. Given the social and psychological vulnerabilities in the life experiences of persons with intellectual disabilities, Holland et al. (2002) suggested the offence rates of persons with intellectual disabilities appear comparatively low.

Thirdly, persons with IDD often experience many inequities when becoming entangled within the criminal justice and judicial system. The typical path for a person with an IDD who engages with the legal system, as an accused, is fraught with challenges that may lead to an innocent person being convicted of a crime. There are cases dating back many years of persons with IDD being wrongly accused and convicted, such as the Timothy Evans case in 1939 in the UK (Taylor 2017). In recent years there has been an increased concern raised in the media about persons with IDD who have been apparently wrongly accused and convicted, the most recognized of which is Brenden Dassey, made famous in the Netflix docuseries The Making a Murderer (Ricciardi and Demos 2015). In Canada, there is the famous case of a 23-year-old man with IDD and behavioural challenges, named Simon Marshall. Marshall confessed to a series of sexual assaults and was convicted and imprisoned in 1997 for six years. In prison, he was abused by the other inmates. Later upon release he was arrested a second time and again confessed to another sexual assault, however at that time DNA evidence confirmed he was not guilty and a reconstruction of the original cases to which he had confessed revealed he had not committed the original offences either (CBC News 2005). The DNA evidence from the first offences had never been tested. The Quebec Court of Appeal ruled that Mr Marshall had been a victim of police misconduct (CBC News 2009).

Throughout every level of the justice system, offenders who have an IDD are disadvantaged. Marinos et al. (2014) noted that because of a lack of understanding regarding their rights and lack of affordable legal counsel, the accused with intellectual disabilities are more likely to incriminate themselves or confess, even if falsely, to seek approval from authority or because of leading interviewing. They are also more likely to be denied bail or personal recognizance and detained pre-trial. In courts, they often lack the means to attain or advise counsel and are unaware of how to interact in court. Seen often as unfit to stand trial, they are diverted to a psychiatric facility with the assumption that fitness can be achieved or to a treatment facility without due process having been followed. If they are deemed fit to engage in the court process, their disability is often unevaluated in terms of how the disabling condition might have been a mitigating factor in their commission of a crime or how accommodations might be provided to enable them to provide a voice in the court (Marinos et al. 2014).

This lengthy evaluation of the difference between criminal and inappropriate behaviour is an important distinction in assessment. Although many offenders may commit an offence for the same reasons as the neuro-typical population, it is important for effective treatment to identify variables that may relate to the person's disability or experiences that may be involved in either the commission of the crime or that should be considered in intervention. The events leading to the commission of the offence, the factors relating to the individual's disability as it may affect participation in treatment, and the motivating operations at work in setting the stage for the offence provide a strong foundation on which to provide treatment that is specifically designed to the needs of the individual. For example, the person who has been arrested for masturbating in public may need training in sexual education and discrimination of public and private, or may need to be provided a place to engage in this behaviour without punishment, rather than treatment for sexual offending. However, conversely the assessment may indicate that the individual displayed the behaviour for the same reasons that the neuro-typical offenders commit this crime, as such treatment should follow a path that include rehabilitation for the paraphilia (exhibitionism). In addition, the assessment can determine the vulnerabilities that the individual faces for re-offence because of possible social conditions or a lack of habilitative skills. These vulnerabilities provide the basis to build an effective habilitative plan.

Question 2 on Ethical Practice: Has the assessment led to an individualized plan based on best-practice strategies that provides both habilitative and rehabilitative elements, as required?

Much of the recommended practice for offenders with IDD is based on programmes developed for the neuro-typical population with adaptations (Lambrick and Glaser 2004; Wilcox 2004). This often involves simplification of the programme or the use of additional educative strategies. However, in the field of intellectual disabilities it is accepted that the key to effective and ethically based treatment hinges on designing a programme that is individualized for the person. Conversely, Newsom and Hovanitz (2005, p. 39) suggested that efficacy of any treatment method must be demonstrated by independent research teams who have utilized a 'written treatment manual'.

Following from some of the earlier behavioural work, treatment manuals were developed to ensure therapeutic integrity in the offender field (Laws and Marshall 2003). Without a manual, clinicians may run the risk of unspecified targets or procedures and the length of treatment or treatment approach may be unspecified (Marshall 2009). If the procedures are vague they do not allow for evaluation of outcomes, replication, or empirical investigation. However, Marshall (2009) argued that highly detailed procedures in the manualization of treatment produces generic fixed targets and procedures, including the nature of treatment and the number of sessions. He cautioned that this rigidity can result in the loss of therapeutic quality.

Whilst the use of manuals ensures that treatment over time and across settings is consistent, some have argued that they can be anti-therapeutic (Laws and Ward 2006; Marshall 2009), suggesting that many highly prescriptive manuals are designed as 'one size fits all' treatment approaches. In support, Marshall (2009) summarized the literature noting that critics of manuals suggest that manualization detracts from therapeutic rapport and fails to provide the flexibility to deal with unique individual variables. Moreover Marshall and Marshall (2007, 2008) suggested that given the nature of offending behaviour and duration of therapy, the use of fixed manuals that would not allow for variation, needed to sustain treatment integrity, may constrain the clinician from introducing new elements that may represent progress on behalf of the individual. Marshall (2009) further advised that prescriptive manuals can interfere with the therapeutic process that must emerge between clinician and the individual. He suggested that therapeutic style is a critical fact in work with offenders. He submitted that reinforcement, direction, warmth, and empathy, provided by the therapist, accounted for a significant amount of therapeutic improvement, concluding that the more one adhered to a rigid manual the less likely it would be that therapeutic rapport would be achieved. Marshall et al. (2006) further noted that therapy that employs empathy and warmth, rather than confrontation leads to better treatment compliance, outcomes, and satisfaction. Additionally, Silverman (1996) has cautioned that reliance on empirical researched approaches may lead to restrictive practices, possibly financed by third parties.

Secondly, Marshall and Marshall (2007) suggested that prescriptive manuals can interfere with the therapeutic process that must emerge between clinician and the individual who is receiving treatment. Marshall (2009) proposed that an important element of offender treatment lies in responsivity. As illustrated in the work of Andrews (2001), offender work must be allowed to adapt to the individual learning approaches and differences. Whilst this is true for all offenders, individuals with IDD pose unique issues. This point will be elaborated more fully in a later section.

It should be noted that guidelines, as suggested by various associations and in this chapter, should not be confused with the manualization of treatment of offenders (Marshall 2009). Marshall suggested that guidelines provide information to facilitate the implementation of effective treatment by informing clinicians about the details of a particular treatment approach with the freedom to provide choice in targets and procedures that are dependent on the needs of the individual. For example, Blasingame et al. (2014) developed an informational treatment package titled the 'Assessment, treatment, and supervision of individuals with intellectual disabilities and problematic sexual behaviors' for the Education and Training Committee Report for the ATSA. Lindsay (2009) created a workbook that provided guidance on assessment and treatment of offenders with intellectual disabilities; the workbook was not prescriptive, rather it afforded the reader with both the theoretical and research developments in the addition to possible intervention strategies that can be employed as assessment dictates.

More recently, the Risk, Need, Responsivity (RNR) model (Bonta and Andrews 2007) has gained increasing empirical support as a best practice approach for reducing re-offence. Their rehabilitation model is based on three principles of Risk, Need, and Responsivity that emphasize the importance of individualization of treatment. According to their model:

Risk involves matching the level of treatment intensity and supervision to the posed risk of offence. According to this principle, failing to match intervention and supervision to level of risk can have detrimental effects on offender outcomes (Andrews et al. 2011).

Need involves selecting targets for intervention to treat the risk and criminogenic factors that relate to the specific offender. Andrews et al. (2011) emphasized the importance of focusing on altering the lifestyle that precipitated the offence to enhance treatment effectiveness and reduce recidivism.

Responsivity includes matching the personal characteristics of the offender (i.e. learning approach, cognitive ability, assets, motivation) to the personal and interpersonal circumstances specific to the offender (Wilson and Yates 2009, p. 158).

For offenders with intellectual disabilities, treatment should be based upon a plan to provide habilitative opportunities to learn and exercise skills that represent vulnerabilities for the person, as well as to learn coping skills to reduce the behaviours and associated factors that led to the offence. These latter variables represent the dynamic risk factors that serve as contributing conditions to an offence for that individual; determination and intervention for those individual factors are critical factors for intervention. Dynamic factors, sometimes, referred to as criminogenic needs (see Andrews and Bonta 2010) represent potentially changeable factors that have been linked to the offending behaviour, such as lack of self-management or self-regulation strategies (see Hanson et al. 2007).

Question 3 on Ethical Practice: *Has a distinction between treatment and management been delineated?*

Management strategies are employed to stop the behaviour from occurring by use of external forces; treatment strategies are designed to enable the offender to not offend by providing the skills and opportunities to apply alternative behaviours to those that were previously offending. The former is used as short-term problem stopping; the latter is necessary to create long-term problem solving. Based on a survey administered to agencies that support offenders with IDD, it was reported that 73.8% of the agencies employed management strategies to reduce risk, however only 40.7% employed structured treatment (Ward et al. 2001).

Management strategies, some of which utilize various forms of restrictions and punishments, have been employed with offenders to reduce risk rather than to treat. The use of management strategies however should not be confused with the application of treatment. Although some individuals who pose high-risk offences may, even after treatment, require ongoing management strategies or scaffolding of their skills to ensure a non-offence, the use of management strategies should be phased out if and when treatment outcomes dictate. Unfortunately, there is often reluctance on the part of providers to reduce management approaches even following effective treatment or in lieu of treatment.

Glaser (2009, p. 248), in speaking about the general sex offender programmes, suggested that a central issue facing treatment providers is the 'conflict between the best interests of the offender and the protection of the community'. However, Glaser (2009) posed the question as to what happens when these humane approaches have not worked. At this point clinicians are faced with the critical ethical dilemma of creating ongoing management sanctions, which may include residential and supervision options that the person does not wish, in the name of community protection and safety.

Traditionally behaviours involving an offence were managed by environmental restrictions and punishments or through medications. Vause et al. (2009) noted that there was a proliferation of published research in the 1960s and 1970s on the use therapeutic punishment for persons with intellectual disabilities, who engaged in various inappropriate behaviours. Early treatment approaches for inappropriate sexual behaviours by persons with IDD included highly intrusive methods such as, 'facial screening, overcorrection, the use of contingent lemon juice, and time-out' (Griffiths et al. 1989, pp. 9–10). The research was based on the principles of operant conditioning. By the 1980s and 1990s an important shift began which saw a diminishing emphasis on punishment with the introduction of functional analysis as a precursor to all treatment and the emphasis on using this knowledge to reduce behaviour using non-aversive methods and provide the least intrusive method of intervention (Vause et al. 2009). Since the mid-1980s research has been conducted to move away from restrictive and intrusive interventions and towards an enhanced focus on positive reinforcement, environmental changes, planned natural consequences, and teaching functionally equivalent skills.

Recommended practice in mainstream offender work, has similarly moved from traditional punitive measures towards the application of educative services to reduce recidivism. McGuire (2001) noted that research clearly demonstrated that punishment and restrictive methods have not led offenders to a path that discourages reoffending. According to Ward and Salmon (2011), 'the ethics of care acknowledges the importance of establishing and maintaining practices that help people to meet their needs, develop and protect basic capabilities for problem-solving, emotional functioning, and social interaction, and avoid pain and suffering' (p. 397).

Glaser (2009) made the distinction between punishment and treatment. He noted that punishment is the intentional infliction of a consequence following a transgression; treatment should however be characterized by actions that benefit the individual, and at the very least do no harm (beneficence and non-maleficence). The offender may however perceive some treatment as punishing, despite the intention of beneficence (i.e. medication or restrictions access to certain items or people).

An additional ethical question, regarding the right to effective treatment, emerges when examining the inconsistency in the field regarding treatment availability for offenders with IDD. Treatment for this group requires specialized expertise that is not available in all areas. Professional ethics would deem it inappropriate for a clinician to undertake treatment for which they were not appropriately trained and supervised. Moreover, the financial cost of providing these services, particularly if there are issues of high risk may require specialized settings that are more secure. These issues have often resulted in persons with intellectual disabilities who have offended being warehoused in the criminal justice system or the developmental system, either institutional-based or community-based, rather than provided treatment; the consequent intervention often becomes only management, not treatment.

Question 4 on Ethical Practice: *Does the treatment and management approach recognize the rights of the offender with intellectual disabilities to consent or refuse treatment?*

In a chapter on ethics, it is imperative to discuss balancing the rights of the offender to the rights of the community. Fedoroff and Moran (1997) suggested that ethical issues in the treatment of offenders are controversial; the ethical dilemmas increase when faced when dealing with offenders with intellectual disabilities.

> There is little doubt that ethical considerations are of paramount importance in dealing with individuals with intellectual and developmental disabilities (IDD). This is no less important for those individuals entangled in the criminal justice system and the subsequent ethical aspects of working with people with IDD who have been labelled as an offender. (Griffiths et al. 2018, p. 1)

In the past few decades, the field of intellectual disabilities has witnessed major paradigm shifts in the support of persons with IDD to ensure that their rights as citizens are recognized and fully protected, including the right to justice and to effective treatment. In line with this, international conventions, such as the Convention on the Rights of Persons with Disabilities (United Nations 2006), have been ratified in many nations throughout the world. The field of IDD has shifted to focus on ensuring that people with intellectual disabilities are provided equitable treatment in all aspects of their lives. With this emergent recognition, services, and supports for persons with intellectual disabilities have been moving from institutionalization to community living, from other-directed determination and care to self-determination and person-centred approaches. The importance of this shift is apparent in all areas of service and treatment, but is of paramount importance when discussing the issue of treatment of offenders with intellectual disabilities.

When discussing rights and persons with intellectual disabilities, the fundamental question of autonomy and self-determination inevitably arises. In treatment, the most basic of these rights involves the right to consent or refuse treatment. Practitioners are expected to work within ethical principles that do not violate the autonomy of the individual, including those with intellectual disabilities (Wilson et al. 2008). Consent to treatment is a legal requirement governed in different countries and by different disciplines. All individuals, including those with IDD are presumed capable of consenting or refusing treatment unless otherwise demonstrated (Griffiths et al. 2002).

Glaser (2009) suggested that agreement to participate in various treatment programmes requires that consent be provided. Consent must be informed and free from duress. It must involve ensuring that the person understands the potential consequences of consenting or refusing to consent; 'informational poverty' needs to be addressed to ensure consent is given with knowledge (Dinerstein 1999, p. 3).

Szmukler (1999), however, has argued that offenders with a mental disorder, such as brain damage, IDD, or mental illness, may not understand that their condition requires a particular therapeutic support, thereby calling on the need for paternalistic decision making by others. Additionally, others have argued that some offenders with IDD may be well-aware of the unacceptability of their behaviour but still make an informed choice to not consent. This latter point was explored by Brown and Thompson (1997, p. 703) who argued that there must be 'recognition that men with learning disabilities may have, for whatever reason an element of "diminished responsibility" for their behaviour'. This led them 'to insist that agencies must be held accountable when their actions fail to prevent further incidents of abuse' (Brown and Thompson 1997, p. 703), thereby allowing agencies to control behaviour or to conduct research on the individual without their consent. The ethics of involvement of persons with IDD in research is often fraught with challenges; McDonald and Patka (2012) noted that researchers in the field hold various views regarding how best to conduct this research. Some researchers argue for participatory research with persons with IDD serving as collaborators (Malott 2002); others suggest that research should be shown to benefit persons with disabilities (Dalton and McVilly 2004). Decisions regarding the engagement of persons with IDD in research may stem partially on differential allegiance to the disability rights movement or to the pragmatics that stem from recruitment and consent issues (McDonald and Patka 2012).

Brown and Thompson (1997) argued that although the principles of traditional ethics would dictate that in the absence of informed consent that intervention, or research, would not be justified, the harm their actions produce, for persons with IDD who have offended and who lack of control over their behaviour, and their lack of decision making ability should justify acting in what they determine is best interest. 'When researchers believe that an individual cannot provide consent, some feel they should be excluded from research', whereas others report that this 'revokes their right to volunteer, marginalizes them, and inhibits their access to scientific advancement' (McDonald and Patka 2012, p. 207). Nonetheless, current research standards are still built on the foundations that were developed following the Nuremberg trials, such as informed voluntary consent, participation that is free from duress, and confidentiality (Claude 2002). The key to inclusive practices in research may lie in a more involved process of both recruitment and enhanced strategies to improve collaboration and comprehension of the particulars involved in consent, rather than to a dismissal of the fundamental principles.

A second ethical issue arising from the rights of the offender with IDD relates to confidentiality. Ethical codes for practitioners require confidentiality, except in situations where there is imminent harm posed to self or others (i.e. American Psychological Association 2002). These codes require practitioners to inform an individual that their confidentiality will not be upheld if there is a present threat to others or where the law requires disclosure. However, limited confidentiality for high-risk offenders is often routine practice. Salter (1988) cautioned that for offenders such as sex offenders, total confidentiality may be impossible if treatment or effective after care are to be achieved. The right to protect the public is a primary principle that has often been cited as the reason for limited confidentiality for high-risk offenders (Briggs et al. 1998). In such cases breach of confidentiality might not appear as an exceptional event, such as when there is pending risk, but a matter of routine protocol (Glaser 2009). However, breach of confidentiality must be made with full awareness of the offender. Prior to intervention, offenders must understand that confidentiality cannot be protected if they pose an imminent risk to others. As well, when individuals are entering into activities that might pose potential risks, such as getting a community job placement, discussions need to take place with the offender about who needs to know about their challenge and to what degree, in order to keep them safe and the community free of risk, if this opportunity is to be explored. Thus, level of rights must be balanced with community protection; this balance is determined by the level of risk.

A third ethical point relates to the values employed within the treatment of offenders with intellectual disabilities. Skinner (1971, p. 150) suggested that 'there is nothing in a methodology which determines the values governing its use'. Good clinical intervention would suggest that a fundamental right in treatment would be conducted in a way that demonstrates respect and dignity. By violating the right to respect and dignity of offenders with IDD, the system is failing to model that type of respect and dignity for others that would be a cornerstone of effective treatment. In contrast, by ensuring that the therapeutic milieu treats offenders with dignity and respects their goals establishes an atmosphere that will increase compliance and responsivity to treatment (Ward and Birgden 2007). Weiss and Knostor (2008) noted that:

> Because all people are to be valued and respected equally does not mean that all behaviors are acceptable in society. Some people exhibit behaviors that are dangerous or that interfere with the quality of their own lives and/or the lives of the people with whom they interact. Professionals who work with people with

behavioral challenges, family members, and other support providers have a responsibility to offer intervention and supports to people to help them change problem behavior. Our shared responsibility, however, is to do this in ways that value, enhance, and include people rather than through the use of methods that are coercive and controlling and on occasion can come dangerously close to manipulation (p. 72).

When respecting human rights, clinicians are placing value on allowing an offender the opportunity to work with the programme to enhance their own interests through the development of skills and opportunities to achieve their own goals. Ward and Maruna (2007) further suggested that by allowing the offender to reach personal goals, there is a likelihood that the offender will also learn to gain some appreciation that others also have rights, thereby assuming a reciprocity effect. Several researchers (Andrews and Bonta 2003; Marshall et al. 2003; Ward and Stewart 2003) have suggested that by ensuring that offenders are able to use their personal interest to develop areas of competence, increases motivation, cooperation, and therapeutic engagement, which in turn leads to greater treatment effects.

Thus, despite the challenges and distinctions made earlier, the rights of the offender to engage to consent to treatment, confidentiality, and respect of dignity in the therapeutic process cannot be eliminated on the basis of a person's disability. Although public opinion may differ, depriving offenders of their human rights is likely to lead to increased hostility and resistance (Matravers 2000).

Question 5 on Ethical Practice: *Is there long-term plan based on person-centred planning to ensure generalization and transference of the treatment outcomes into the least-restrictive environment that can provide optimal quality of life whilst at the same time protecting community safety?*

The goal of rehabilitation is to establish, for the offender, the opportunity to regain a life and self-esteem following *effective* treatment. The real value of empirically supported treatment lies in the potential of treatment to transfer and generalize outside of the treatment setting, where conditions are carefully controlled and well-trained staff are monitoring treatment adherence, to one in which the person is able to function with the least amount of intervention and supports that are needed. This suggests that there is an obligation to provide active generalization strategies embedded in a habilitative environment that can potentially allow the person to transfer treatment outcomes to the community and resume an offence-free life. In order for this to occur, there needs to be careful planning to ensure that all steps have been put in place to successfully reintegrate the person into a community, with whatever supports and protections required, and to further ensure that the strategies learned within the treatment setting can be transferred to the least restrictive and intrusive environment possible. As Ward and Stewart (2008, p. 306) asserted there is an 'obligation to provide the resources that will enable people with disabilities to either function as purposive agents on their own (with appropriate support and learning) or else continually scaffold their agency attempts'. In the case of offenders this means evaluating the needs relative to the potential risk to the community to ensure that safety is maintained.

Newsom and Hovanitz (2005) cautioned that there are some who believe the empirical evidence that shows treatment effectiveness in the treatment settings may be unable to be sustained in the natural environment. Behaviour analysts have long since been challenged by the need to implement strategies that will ensure generalization and maintenance, both within the treatment setting and within the transfer phase (Stokes and Baer 1977). In working with offenders with IDD, some of the early work on high-risk offenders in community settings provided anecdotal evidence of the integration of strategies within treatment programmes to ensure the long-term reintegration to whatever extent possible (i.e. Griffiths et al. 1989; Ward et al. 1992). The behavioural risk management strategies for offenders in the community were elaborated by Ward and Bosek in a 2007 article, extending Ward et al.'s (1992) earlier work. The consequent plan of risk management support is designed to establish an environment that will minimize the potential of risk in conjunction with teaching, promoting alternative and coping behaviours, and active monitoring (Ward and Bosek 2007). They noted that 'the plan delineates external controls with rationales for imposing them, with objective measures to justify withdrawal of these controls to provide accountability for programmatic decisions' (Ward and Bosek 2007, p. 53). Included in their approach was an emphasis on community safety and the use of supervision, environmental arrangements (i.e. electronic monitoring and control of potential inappropriate triggers or setting events), and ongoing monitoring. In particular, they noted the importance of inclusion of the offender in the planning process suggesting that the long-term success is inextricably linked to the person's ability to understand and self-manage the plan.

In the past decade, mainstream offender treatment programmes have also begun to emphasize the critical importance of building a life during and after therapy that can be successfully sustained. The Good Lives Model (Ward et al. 2007) has taken momentum within the offender field, establishing it as the gold standard for intervention. This model represents a significant shift in the approach and philosophy for offender treatment, by placing the needs and goals of the offender at the centre of the intervention strategies. Andrews et al. (2011) noted that crimes are committed to attain human goods; if human goods are available the need to offend is reduced and where there is a lack of human goods there is nothing to lose by not offending. With persons with IDD, this often occurs, where so many of the basic goods of life (relationships, activities, etc.) have been taken away there is no motivation to not offend.

The Good Lives approach has embedded into recommended practice the fundamental respect for the rights and dignity of the offender, not just as a philosophical or legal dimension, but as an essential element of therapeutic effectiveness. However, enhancing well-being without regard to a balancing of risk 'may result in a happy but dangerous individual' (Ward et al. 2007, pp. 92–93).

The Good Lives Model, designed for nondisabled offenders (Ward et al. 2007), interconnects well with the emergent use of Person-Centred Planning (Kincaid et al. 2005) in the developmental sector. Within services for persons with IDD, lifestyle planning, usually referred to as person-centred planning, has become the preferred approach for formulating goals, services, and supports for individuals. A person-centred approach is a set of values, and methods that aim to set the stage for the enhancement of the lives of persons with IDD through goal-directed support. There is a proliferation of terms used to refer to these approaches, generally founded on the Personal Futures Planning approach introduced by Mount (1994). The various methods and terminology on which this movement has developed has resulted in some criticism as the approaches can often be ambiguous (Schwartz et al. 2000). Unlike other approaches to support individuals, person-centred planning has been criticized because its inception was based on a desire to improve the lives of persons with IDD rather than on research. Osborne (1999) suggested that whilst the goal is worthy, the lack of research may in some cases lead to false assumptions that planning with and on behalf of the person to ensure their needs are met is sufficient, thereby superseding and potentially displacing the need for therapeutic interventions (Schwartz et al. 2000). However, within the field of IDD a research-based approach has emerged that integrates the values of person-centred planning with the framework of applied behaviour analysis; this approach is called Positive Behavioural Support (PBS) (Koegel et al. 1996; Reid and Parsons 2007). PBS interventions have resulted in significant decreases in self-injurious, aggressive, and destructive behaviours in adults and children with intellectual disabilities (Feldman et al. 2002).

In the PBS approach, problem behaviour is remediated based upon the outcome of a functional analysis; remediation occurs as a result of environmental changes and active habilitative training to treat the problem behaviour. The resultant goal is to not *only* reduce the problem behaviour but to enhance a positive lifestyle. Carr et al. (1999) wrote that the ultimate goal and an important index of effectiveness of PBS is the provision of a normalized life for the person with IDD. Although this approach has inherent logic, it has yet to be empirically validated to produce effective outcome results with offenders with intellectual disabilities. Yet, the emergent trends in the field of IDD are similar to the developments that have occurred in the offender prevention and treatment field, both which emphasize enhancement of the skills and experiences of the offenders as foundational to effective treatment.

The critical ethical factor involved in the above approaches is that they establish the groundwork for active strategies to be embedded in an environment during and following active treatment that can potentially allow the person to reach their personal goals for change and development and that can enhance the potential of generalizing treatment outcomes into the community to whatever extent is possible.

2.5 Conclusion

The chapter has been offered as a look at some of the ethical challenges that face science-practitioners in the treatment of persons with IDD who have offended. The key point has been well stated by Weiss and Knostor (2008) who note that '[r]ather than seeing ways to control people (in the name of treatment and/or intervention), we should be seeking ways to better understand them, to communicate with them, and to work with them toward achieving fulfilling lives' (p. 77). The points made are not exclusive of many other issues, however they pose areas of consideration that demonstrate the intersection of the criminal justice system and the developmental system in the treatment of offenders with intellectual disabilities as they exist in this point in time. Perhaps a note from B.F. Skinner provides an apt conclusion to this chapter to remind of us of the ever-changing landscape of the fields:

> We have no reason to suppose that any cultural practice is always right or wrong according to some principle or values regardless of the circumstances or that anyone can at any given time make an absolute evaluation of its survival value.

So long as this is recognized, we are less likely to seize upon the hard and fast answer as an escape from indecision, and we are more likely to continue to modify cultural design in order to test the consequences. (Skinner 1953, p. 436)

References

American Psychological Association (2002). *Ethical Principles of Psychologist and Code of Conduct*. Washington, DC: American Psychological Association.

Andrews, D.A. (2001). Principles of effective correctional programs. In: *Compendium 2000 on Effective Correctional Programming* (eds. L.L. Motiuk and R.C. Serin), 9–14. Ottawa: Correctional Service of Canada.

Andrews, D.A. and Bonta, J. (2003). *The Psychology of Criminal Conduct*, 3e. Cincinnati, OH: Anderson.

Andrews, D.A. and Bonta, J. (2010). *The Psychology of Criminal Conduct*, 5e. Cincinnati, OH: Anderson.

Andrews, D.A., Bonta, J., and Wormith, J.S. (2011). The risk-need-responsivity (RNR) model. Does adding the good lives model contribute to effective crime prevention? *Criminal Justice and Behavior* 38 (7): 735–755.

APA Presidential Task Force (2006). Evidence based practice in psychology. *American Psychologist* 61 (4): 271–285.

Association for the Treatment of Sexual Abusers (2014). *Practice Guidelines for the Assessment, Treatment, and Management of Male Adult Sexual Abusers*. Beaverton, OR: Association for the Treatment of Sexual Abusers.

Behavior Analyst Certification Board (BACB) (2014). Behavior analyst certification board professional and ethical compliance code for behavior analysts. http://bacb.com/ethics-code (accessed 1 June 2019).

Blasingame, G.D., Boer, D.P., Guidry, L. et al. (2014). *Assessment, Treatment, and Supervision of Individuals with Intellectual Disabilities and Problematic Sexual Behaviors: Informational Packet*. [Education and Training Committee Report]. Beaverton, OR: Association for the Treatment of Sexual Abusers.

Bonta, J. and Andrews, D.A. (2007). Risk-need-responsivity model for offender assessment and treatment (User Report No. 2007-06). Ottawa: Public Safety Canada.

Briggs, D., Doyle, P., Gooch, T. et al. (1998). *Assessing Men Who Sexually Abuse: A Practice Guide*. London: Jessica Kingsley.

Brown, H. and Thompson, D. (1997). The ethics of research with men who have learning disabilities and abusive sexual behaviour: a minefield in a vacuum. *Disability and Society* 12 (5): 695–707.

Carr, E.G., Horner, R.H., Turnbull, A.P. et al. (1999). *Positive Behavioral Support for People with Developmental Disabilities: A Research Synthesis*. Washington, DC: American Association for Mental Retardation.

CBC News Posted: Aug 10, 2005 Man confessed to sex crimes he didn't commit. CBC News (10 August). http://www.cbc.ca/news/canada/man-confessed-to-sex-crimes-he-didn-t-commit-1.536266 (accessed 10 May 2019).

CBC News (2009). Canada's wrongful convictions: Cases where the courts got it wrong. CBC News (6 August). http://www.cbc.ca/news/canada/canada-s-wrongful-convictions-1.783998#marshall (accessed 10 May 2019).

Chamless, D.L., Baker, M., Baucom, D.H. et al. (1998). Update on empirically validated therapies, II. *The Clinical Psychologist* 51: 3–16.

Claude, R.P. (2002). *Science in the Service of Human Rights*. Philadelphia, PA: University of Pennsylvania Press.

Dalton, A.J. and McVillly, K.R. (2004). Ethics guidelines for international multicenter research involving people with intellectual disabilities. *Journal of Policy and Practice in Intellectual Disabilities* 1: 57–70.

Dinerstein, R.D. (1999). Introduction. In: *A Guide to Consent* (eds. R.D. Dinerstein, S.S. Herr and J.L. O'Sullivan), 3–6. Washington, DC: American Association on Mental Retardation [AAIDD].

Emerson, E. (1995). *Challenging Behaviour: Analysis and Intervention in People with Learning Disabilities*. Cambridge, UK: Cambridge University Press.

Fancher, R.E. (1987). Henry Goddard and the Kallikak family photographs: 'conscious skullduggery' or 'Whig history'? *American Psychologist* 42: 585–590.

Fedoroff, J.P. and Moran, B. (1997). Myths and misconceptions about sex offenders. *The Canadian Journal of Human Sexuality* 6: 263–276.

Feldman, M.A., Condillac, R., Tough, S. et al. (2002). Effectiveness of community positive behavioral intervention for persons with developmental disabilities and severe behavior disorders. *Behavior Therapy* 33: 377–398.

Firth, H., Balogh, R., Berney, T. et al. (2001). Psychopathology of sexual abuse in young people with intellectual disability. *Journal of Intellectual Disability Research* 45 (3): 244–252.

Glaser, B. (2009). Treaters or punishers? The ethical role of mental health clinicians in sex offender programs. *Aggression and Violent Behaviour* 14: 248–255.

Goddard, H.H. (1912). *The Kallikak Family: A Study in the Heredity of Feeble-Mindedness*. New York: Macmillan.

Green, G. (1999). Science and ethics in early intervention for autism: what does research tell us? In: *Autism: Behavior Analytic Perspectives* (eds. P.M. Ghezzi, W. Williams and E. Carr), 11–28. Reno, NV: Context Press.

Greenberg, L.S. and Newman, F.L. (1996). An approach to psychotherapy change process research: introduction to the special section. *Journal of Consulting and Clinical Psychology* 64: 435–438.

Griffiths, D. (2002). Sexual aggression. In: *Aggression and Other Disruptive Behavioral Challenges: Biomedical and Psychosocial Assessment and Treatment* (ed. W.I. Gardner), 325–398. New York: National Association for Dual Diagnosis.

Griffiths, D., Hingsburger, D., Ioannou, S. et al. (2018). Ethical considerations in working with people with intellectual disabilities who have offended. In: *The Wiley Handbook on Offenders with Intellectual and Developmental Disabilities: Research, Training and Practice* (eds. W.L. Lindsay and J.L. Taylor), 105–122. Chichester, UK: Wiley.

Griffiths, D., Owen, F., and Arbus-Nevestuk, K. (2002). Sexual policies in agencies supporting persons who have developmental disabilities, part II: practical issues and procedures. In: *Ethical Dilemmas: Sexuality and Developmental Disabilities* (eds. D. Griffiths, D. Richards, P. Fedoroff, et al.), 77–132. Kingston, NY: NADD Press.

Griffiths, D., Quinsey, V.L., and Hingsburger, D. (1989). *Changing Sexually Inappropriate Behaviour*. Baltimore, MD: Paul H. Brookes Publishing.

Griffiths, D., Watson, S., Lewis, R. et al. (2004). Sexuality research and persons with intellectual disabilities. In: *International Handbook of Applied Research in Intellectual Disabilities* (eds. E. Emerson, C. Hatton, T. Thompson, et al.), 311–334. Oxford: Wiley.

Hanson, R.K., Harris, A.J.R., Scott, T. et al. (2007). Assessing the risk of sex offenders on community supervision: The Dynamic Supervision Project. (User Report 2007-05). Ottawa, ON: Public Safety Canada. https://www.publicsafety.gc.ca/cnt/rsrcs/pblctns/ssssng-rsk-sxl-ffndrs/index-en.aspx (accessed 10 May 2019)

Hingsburger, D. (2013). Counterfeit criminality: cautions in community living. *The Direct Support Worker Newsletter* 1 (6): 1–5.

Hingsburger, D., Griffiths, D., and Quinsey, V. (1991). Detecting counterfeit deviance. *Habilitative Mental Healthcare* 9: 51–54.

Holland, T., Clare, I.C.H., and Mukhopadhyay, T. (2002). Prevalence of 'criminal offending' by men and women with intellectual disability and the characteristics of 'offenders': implications for research and service development. *Journal of Intellectual Disability Research* 46 (1): 6–20.

Horner, R.H., Carr, E.G., Halle, J. et al. (2005). The use of single-subject research to identify evidence-based practice in special education. *Exceptional Children* 71 (2): 165–179.

Isherwood, T., Burns, M., Naylor, M. et al. (2007). 'Getting into trouble': a qualitative analysis of the onset of offending in the accounts of men with learning disabilities. *Journal of Forensic Psychiatry & Psychology* 18 (2): 221–234.

Kincaid, D., Knab, J.T., and Clark, H.B. (2005. *Person-centered Planning*. Mental Health Policy Law and Policy Faculty Publications, 702. https://www.scholarcommons.usf.edu/mhip_facpub/702(accessed 10 May 2019).

Koegel, L.K., Koegel, R.L., and Dunlap, G. (1996). *Positive Behavioral Support: Including People with Difficult Behavior in the Community*. Baltimore, MD: Brookes.

Lambrick, F. and Glaser, W. (2004). Sex offenders with an intellectual disability. *Sexual Abuse: A Journal of Research and Treatment* 16 (4): 381–392.

Laws, D.R. and Marshall, W.L. (2003). A brief history of behavioral and cognitive behavioral approaches to sexual offenders: part I. Early developments. *Sexual Abuse* 15 (2): 75–92.

Laws, D.R. and Ward, T. (2006). When one size does not fit all: the reformation of relapse prevention. In: *Sexual Offender Treatment: Controversial Issues* (eds. W.L. Marshall, Y.M. Fernandez, L.E. Marshall, et al.), 241–254. Chichester, UK: Wiley.

Lindsay, W.R. (2002). Research and literature on sex offenders with intellectual and developmental disabilities. *Journal of Intellectual Disability Research* 4 (1): 74–85.

Lindsay, W.R. (2009). *The Treatment of Sex Offenders with Developmental Disabilities: A Practice Workbook*. Chichester, UK: Wiley-Blackwell.

Lindsay, W.R., Law, J., Quinn, K. et al. (2001). A comparison of physical and sexual abuse: histories of sexual and non-sexual offenders with intellectual disability. *Child Abuse & Neglect* 25 (7): 989–995.

Malott, R.W. (2002). Notes from a radical behaviorist: is it morally defensible to use the developmentally disabled as Guinea pigs? *Behavior and Social Issues* 11: 105–106.

Marinos, V., Griffiths, D., Fergus, C. et al. (2014). Victims and witnesses with intellectual disability in the criminal justice system. *Criminal Justice Quarterly* 61 (4): 517–530.

Marshall, W.L. (2009). Manualization: blessing or a curse? *Journal of Sexual Aggression* 15 (2): 109–120.

Marshall, W.L. and Marshall, L.E. (2007). The utility of the Random Controlled Trial for evaluating sexual offender treatment: The gold standard or an inappropriate strategy? *Sexual Abuse: A Journal of Research and Treatment* 19: 175–191.

Marshall, W.L. and Marshall, L.E. (2008). Good clinical practice and the evaluation of treatment: a response to Seto et al. *Sexual Abuse: A Journal of Research and Practice* 20: 256–260.

Marshall, W.L., Marshall, L.E., and Serran, G.A. (2006). Strategies in the treatment of paraphilias: a critical review. *Annual Review of Sex Research* 17: 62–182.

Marshall, E.L., Serran, G.A., Fernadez, H.M. et al. (2003). Therapist characteristics in the treatment of sexual offenders: tentative data on their relationship with indices of behavior change. *Journal of Sexual Aggression* 9: 25–40.

Matravers, M. (2000). *Justice and Punishment: The Rationale of Coercion*. Oxford, UK: Oxford University Press.

McDonald, K. and Patka, M. (2012). 'There is no black or white': scientific community views on ethics in intellectual and developmental disability research. *Journal of Policy and Practice in Intellectual Disabilities* 9: 206–214.

McGuire, T. (2001). Sex offending: behavioral analysis perspective. *Advances in Psychology Research* 6: 129–155.

Mount, B. (1994). Benefits and limitations of personal futures planning. In: *Creating Individual Supports for People with Developmental Disabilities: A Mandate for Change at Many Levels* (eds. V.J. Bradley, J.W. Ashbauigh and B.C. Blaney), 97–108. Brookes: Baltimore, MD.

Murphy, W.D., Coleman, E.M., and Haynes, M. (1983). Treatment and evaluation issues with the mentally retarded sex offender. In: *The Sexual Aggressor: Current Perspectives on Treatment* (eds. J. Greer and I. Stuart), 22–41. New York: Van Nostrand Reinhold.

Newsom, C. and Hovanitz, C.A. (2005). The nature and value of empirically validated interventions. In: *Controversial Therapies for Developmental Disabilities: Fad, Fashion and Science in Professional Practice* (eds. J.W. Jacobson, R.M. Foxx and J.A. Mulick), 31–44. Mahwah, NJ: Lawrence Erlbaum Associates.

O'Manique, J. (2003). *The Origins of Justice: The Evolution of Morality, Human Rights and Law*. Philadelphia, PA: University of Pennsylvania Press.

Osborne, J.G. (1999). Renaissance or killer mutation? A response to Holburn. *The Behavior Analyst* 22: 47–52.

Paul, R. and Elder, L. (2005). *Ethical Reasoning*. Dillon Beach, CA: The Foundations for Critical Thinking.

Petersilia, J. (2000). *Doing Justice? Criminal Offenders with Developmental Disabilities. Detailed Research Findings*. (Policy Research Program). Berkley, CA: University of California.

Reid, D.H. and Parsons, M.B. (2007). *Positive Behavior Support Training Curriculum*, 2e. Washington, DC: American Association on Intellectual and Developmental Disabilities.

Ricciardi, L. and Demos, M. (2015). *Making a Murderer*. Netflix.

Salter, A.C. (1988). *Treating Child Sex Offenders and Victims*. London: Sage.

Santamour, W. and West, B. (1978). *The Mentally Retarded Offender and Corrections*. Washington, DC: US Department of Justice.

Scheerenberger, R.C. (1983). *A History of Mental Retardation*. Baltimore, MD: Brookes.

Schwartz, A.A., Jacobson, J.W., and Dunlap, S.C. (2000). Defining person centredness: results of two consensus methods. *Education and Training in Mental Retardation and Developmental Disabilities* 33: 235–249.

Silverman, W.H. (1996). Cookbooks, manuals and paint by numbers: psychotherapy in the 90s. *Psychotherapy* 33: 207–215.

Simpson, M.K. and Hogg, J. (2001). Patterns of offending among people with intellectual disability: a systematic review. Part I: methodology and prevalence data. *Journal of Intellectual Disability Research* 45 (5): 384–396.

Skinner, B.F. (1953). *Science and Human Behavior*. New York: Collier-Macmillan.

Skinner, B.F. (1971). *Beyond Freedom and Dignity*. New York: Knopf/Random House.

Sobsey, D. (1994). *Violence and Abuse of Persons with Intellectual Disabilities*. Baltimore, MD: Paul H. Brookes.

Stokes, T.F. and Baer, D.M. (1977). An implicit technology of generalization. *Journal of Applied Behavior Analysis* 10: 349–367.

Sturmey, P. (2005). Ethical dilemmas and the most effective therapies. In: *Controversial Therapies for Developmental Disabilities: Fad, Fashion and Science in Professional Practice* (eds. J.W. Jacobson, R.M. Foxx and J.A. Mulick), 435–449. Mahwah, NJ: Lawrence Erlbaum Associates.

Szmukler, G. (1999). Ethics in community psychiatry. *Australian and New Zealand Journal of Psychiatry* 33: 328–338.

Taylor, L. (2017). Timothy Evans: wrongfully executed. Owlcation. https://owlcation.com/humanities/Timothy-Evans-Wrongfully-Executed (accessed 10 May 2019).

Thiroux, J. (2001). *Ethics, Theory and Practice*. Upper Saddle River, NJ: Prentice Hall.

Van Houten, R., Axelrod, S., Bailey, J.S. et al. (1988). The right to effective behavioral treatment. *Journal of Applied Behavior Analysis* 21: 381–384.

Vause, T., Regehr, K., Feldman, M. et al. (2009). Right to evidence based treatment for individuals with developmental disabilities: issues of the use of therapeutic punishment. In: *Challenges to the Rights of Persons with Intellectual Disabilities: Historical, Legal, Policy and Theoretical Issues* (eds. F. Owen and D. Griffiths), 219–239. London: Jessica Kingsley Publishing.

United Nations (2006). Convention on the rights of people with disabilities. https://www.un.org/development/desa/disabilities/convention-on-the-rights-of-persons-with-disabilities.html (accessed 1 June 2019).

Ward, K.M. and Bosek, R.L. (2007). Behavioral risk management: strategies to support dually diagnosed men who exhibit sexually inappropriate behavior. *NADD Bulletin* 10 (3): 51–57.

Ward, K.M., Heffern, S.J., Wilcox, D.A. et al. (1992). *Managing Inappropriate Sexual Behavior: Supporting Individuals with Developmental Disabilities in the Community*. Anchorage: Alaska Specialized Education and Training Services, Inc.

Ward, K.M., Trigler, J.S., and Pfeiffer, K.T. (2001). Community services, issues, and service gaps for individuals with developmental disabilities who exhibit inappropriate sexual behaviors. *Mental Retardation* 39 (1): 11–19.

Ward, T. and Birgden, A. (2007). Human rights and correctional clinical practice. *Aggression and Violent Behavior* 12: 628–643.

Ward, T. and Maruna, S. (2007). *Rehabilitation: Beyond the Risk Paradigm*. London: Routledge.

Ward, T. and Salmon, K. (2011). The ethics of care and treatment of sex offenders. *Sexual Abuse: A Journal of Research and Treatment* 23: 397–413.

Ward, T. and Stewart, C. (2003). Criminogenic needs and human needs: a theoretical model. *Psychology, Crime & Law* 9: 125–143.

Ward, T. and Stewart, C. (2008). Putting human rights into practice with people with an intellectual disability. *Developmental and Physical Disabilities* 20 (3): 297–311.

Ward, T., Mann, R.E., and Gannon, T.A. (2007). The Good Lives Model of offender rehabilitation: clinical implications. *Aggression and Violent Behavior* 12: 87–107.

Weiss, N.R. and Knoster, T. (2008). It may be nonaversive, but is it a positive approach? *Journal of Positive Behavior Intervention* 10 (1): 72–78.

Wilcox, D.T. (2004). Treatment of intellectually disabled individuals who have committed sexual offences: a review of the literature. *Journal of Sexual Aggression* 10 (1): 85–100.

Wilson, N., Clegg, J., and Hardy, G. (2008). What informs and shapes ethical practice in intellectual disability services? *Journal of Intellectual Disability* 52 (7): 608–617.

Wilson, R.J. and Yates, P.M. (2009). Effective interventions and the Good Lives Model: maximizing treatment gains for sexual offenders. *Aggression and Violent Behavior* 14: 157–161.

3

Protecting the Rights of People with Intellectual Disabilities in Correctional Settings

Frank Lambrick[1,2], Astrid Birgden[3,4,5], Chelsea Troutman[2], and Danielle McLeod[1]

[1] *University of Melbourne, Victoria, Australia*
[2] *Department of Health and Human Services, Victoria, Australia*
[3] *Deakin University, Melbourne, Victoria, Australia*
[4] *Just Forensic, Melbourne, Victoria, Australia*
[5] *Griffith University, Brisbane, Queensland, Australia*

3.1   Introduction

A major concern for governments worldwide is to prevent crime, protect public safety, maintain universal human rights, and rehabilitate undesirable behaviours. The challenges to achieving these goals are most apparent when a society's most vulnerable individuals are involved, particularly those who have limited insight into the impact of their behaviour on others and are unwilling to comply with treatment.

This chapter will first provide an overview of the compulsory treatment (CT) framework operating under the Disability Act (Victorian Government 2006a). An in-depth analysis of a cohort of recipients of CT will then be described focusing on the socio-demographic, historical, and clinical characteristics of the men and women with intellectual disability (ID) who completed a term of CT between 2007 and 2014 in Victoria. Finally, a set of key principles based on human rights and key psychological theories will be discussed that have been designed to reduce the likelihood of discrimination against forensic disability clients in correctional service settings.

3.1.1   Compulsory Treatment Framework

A new system for the mandatory treatment of people with ID in Victoria came into effect in July 2007. This legal framework arose in response to significant legislative and administrative gaps between the criminal justice system (CJS) and the human services available to people with ID who present as being at significant risk of serious harm to others. In a systemic review, the Victorian Law Reform Commission (2003) found that

The Wiley Handbook on What Works for Offenders with Intellectual and Developmental Disabilities: An Evidence-Based Approach to Theory, Assessment, and Treatment, First Edition.
Edited by William R. Lindsay, Leam A. Craig, and Dorothy Griffiths.
© 2020 John Wiley & Sons Ltd. Published 2020 by John Wiley & Sons Ltd.

the detention of individuals without their consent for the purposes of providing services or programmes to reduce these risks was problematic. The Commission identified:

- A lack of power in some court jurisdictions to order supervision for people with ID who were found not guilty;
- A lack of power to sentence people with ID to an approved treatment facility as an alternative to prison;
- An insufficient length of community-based orders (two years) to provide the level of treatment and support required to reduce risk; and
- An ongoing need for care and treatment at the expiry of sentences/orders.

As a result of this review the role of the Senior Practitioner was established in 2007 by the Disability Act (Victorian Government 2006a) to protect the rights of people with a disability who are subject to restrictive interventions and CT, and to ensure that appropriate standards are complied with respect to these practices. Pursuant to the Disability Act (Victorian Government 2006a), the Senior Practitioner is required to evaluate the use of restrictive interventions, including CT, and subsequently develop guidelines and standards to improve these practices. A number of powers with respect to restrictive interventions and CT permit the Senior Practitioner or delegate to investigate, audit, and monitor disability services involved in the use of restrictive interventions and CT, request information from these services and direct them to cease, and alter or implement particular practices.

CT under the Disability Act (Victorian Government 2006a) occurs when a person with an ID is: (i) admitted to a secure residential treatment facility under the direction of specific criminal orders; or (ii) subjected to a civil order referred to as a Supervised Treatment Order (STO) which requires them to reside in an approved residential setting in order to be suitably supervised and treated. Detention for treatment is considered necessary when an individual presents with behaviour that places others at significant risk of serious harm and when all least-restrictive options have been considered to reduce this behaviour. Whilst under CT, an 'authorized program officer' is responsible for developing and implementing a 'treatment plan' which must be approved by the Senior Practitioner. This plan outlines; what treatment will be provided to the individual and the benefits to them; any restrictive interventions and the necessary supervision requirements; and details about the process of transition to a lower level of supervision and eventually life in the community without legal restriction. This individualized plan is subject to periodic review by the Victorian Civil and Administrative Tribunal (VCAT) to ensure the ongoing detention remains warranted.

The process of monitoring, oversight, and review of treatment plans developed for individuals subject to CT is overseen by VCAT with the Senior Practitioner being responsible for approving and supervising the implementation of the treatment plans. The person with an ID in most cases attends and participates in the VCAT hearing and has the right to apply to VCAT to review or vary their STO or treatment plan, or to revoke the Order. The residential service where the person is being detained appoints an authorized programme officer whose responsibility is to make applications to VCAT for the various CT processes and to develop and implement the treatment plan. The Victorian Office of the Public Advocate is also usually joined as a party to CT hearings, having an independent statutory role in promoting the rights and dignity of people with disabilities under the Guardianship and Administration Act (Victorian Government 1986a).

In 2010, the Senior Practitioner published a paper discussing the restraint and seclusion of people on CT orders (Webber et al. 2010). This initial investigation provided basic information about the characteristics of the then smaller sample of 27 recipients; however, the primary focus of the paper was upon restrictive interventions. This chapter reports on subsequent research conducted by the Senior Practitioner that provides a more detailed socio-demographic analysis, including historical factors and details of the behaviours and offences that lead to detention. The differences between recipients who were imprisoned during the study period, and those who were not, have also been quantified and compared.

A further focus of this research was on how the legal framework of CT has functioned for this particular group since its introduction. Given the CT framework primarily relates to detention in approved accommodation facilities, the research considered the movement of subjects between different accommodation settings before, during, and after CT. Visual data mapping was used to uncover patterns in these movements and basic quantitative statistics were used to analyse the characteristics of the sample, such as intelligence quotient (IQ), employment, early life experiences, schooling, substance use and gambling, convictions, and imprisonment history.

The following sections provide a brief literature review of what are the most likely characteristics associated with the CT population drawn from the broader research literature.

3.1.2 Socio-demographic, Historical, and Clinical Presentation

The CT sample does not represent an ideal population[1] therefore generalizations from broader research must be made very cautiously. Previous studies focusing on Victorian forensic disability services can, however, provide more accurate insight into the probable characteristics of this sample. When compared with a matched group not under CT,[2] subjects under CT in Victoria in 2008–2009 showed higher rates of psychiatric disorder but were less likely to be diagnosed with autism spectrum disorder or multiple disabilities (Webber et al. 2010). Between 1989 and 1994, offenders in the Intensive Residential Treatment Program (IRTP) (the secure residential treatment facility which currently accommodates the subset of the CT group on criminal orders) were likely to be young, single, indigenous, and previously imprisoned (Glaser and Deane 1999). Most of these offenders had lived in institutions as children, experienced disruptive family environments and had abused substances, although not at a significantly higher rate when compared against offenders in prison.

A common co-morbidity for people with ID with behaviours that are harmful to others is mental illness (Cooper et al. 2007; Allen 2008). A significant difference between subjects in the IRTP and those in prison was that IRTP residents were at least twice as likely to have had previous contact with mental health services (Glaser and Deane 1999). People with ID under the Norwegian mandatory detention system also presented

---

1 This primarily relates to the inclusion criteria being directly linked to a legal framework rather than a specific characteristic that is common to the population and uncommon to other populations. For example, the sample is not reflective of all people with ID in Victoria who exhibit behaviours that are harmful to others or all service users in receipt of a specific intervention.
2 The matched group consisted of people with ID under restrictive interventions in Victoria.

with significant rates of mental illness (Nøttestad and Linaker 2005). Psychosocial issues such as mental illness, substance misuse, and associated issues of homelessness are commonly referred to in the forensic disability literature and generally reflect the extreme disadvantage experienced by this group (Baldry et al. 2013). Like other offending populations, substance abuse is also associated with antisocial behaviours in people with ID (Winter et al. 1997; McGillivray and Moore 2001). For example, 35% of patients from a forensic disability service had used substances in the immediate lead-up to an offence and up to 50% had problematic substance use behaviours (Plant et al. 2011).

These experiences of disadvantage often begin at an early age for people with ID with antisocial behaviours, and are often typified by childhood abuse, neglect, and family dysfunction (Lindsay et al. 2010). Amongst offenders with ID, there is evidence of: low socio-economic background (Lund 1990; Farrington 1995); family involvement in the CJS (Farrington 1995; Winter et al. 1997; Nøttestad and Linaker 2005); behavioural dysfunction from an early age (Farrington 1995; Nøttestad and Linaker 2005); and interrupted learning (Winter et al. 1997). These apparent indictors for criminal behaviour have also been well documented amongst the general offending population (Holland et al. 2002).

3.1.3 The Prison Experience

Given that complex presentation is not unique to offenders with ID, of particular interest are the additional challenges facing people with ID within the CJS. Glaser and Deane (1999) were of the opinion that offenders with ID commit crimes because of 'poor socialisation, lack of social skills, history of institutionalisation, and poor anger management and impulse control' (p. 352). Others have also observed that this group tend to overestimate their ability to independently manage their care and behaviour in the community (Palucka et al. 2012). People with ID are more likely to have problems with communication, social skills, and adaptive behaviours (Emerson et al. 1999) and these often translate to difficulties negotiating the rules of prison. As a result they may be subject to further punishment and/or loss of opportunity (Hayes and McIlwain 1988; Glaser and Deane 1999). On release, at a time when they are facing the additional challenges of discrimination and the stigmatization of incarceration, prison leavers with ID are more likely to lack informal support (Borzycki and Baldrey 2003). Without the support to address these deficits in social networks and daily living skills people with ID are likely to reoffend (Borzycki and Baldrey 2003; Dinani et al. 2010; Palucka et al. 2012) and according to some Australian studies, they are also more likely to be re-imprisoned and to remain in prison longer (Holland and Persson 2011).

3.1.4 Accommodation and Treatment Alternatives

The social isolation of the prison environment presents impossible challenges for learning the basic skills required for life outside prison (Glaser and Deane 1999). Skill development programmes delivered in a community-based setting such as home or school are understood to be more effective at reducing antisocial behaviour than congregate settings such as the prison or other institutions (Hayes 2004; McGrath et al. 2007). This is because for people with an ID newly learned skills are often not generalisable to all settings and learning tends to be situation specific (Taylor 2002). As a result, Hayes (2007) contended that rehabilitation is best achieved in a supervised residential placement involving individualized planning and goal attainment, where residents work towards a gradual downgrade in restriction. There is some evidence that offenders with ID (as opposed to non-offenders with 'behaviours of concern') living in secure units do demonstrate more positive treatment outcomes (Reed et al. 2004). However, the literature in this area is limited because it tends to focus on specific treatment effectiveness rather than accommodation setting. However, two pertinent issues remain for both treatment and accommodation services that relate to the diversion of people with ID from the prison system, those of consent and compliance (Lindsay 2002; Hayes 2007). A legal framework for compulsory detention aiming for minimal restriction is partly justified by such considerations.

Suitable alternatives to prison in the community that support residents to reduce and prevent antisocial behaviours are paramount to reducing recidivism (Hayes 2004). These alternatives are crucial because an individual's accommodation at the time of police intervention is significantly associated with future forensic outcome and access to services (Raina et al. 2013). For example, people with ID who lived independently with no structured activity and who had experienced transient accommodation over the previous 10 years were more likely to have been involved in the CJS than those attending day services or living in a group home (Wheeler et al. 2009). A South Australian court diversion programme found that participants who had problems with accommodation at referral were almost twice as likely to reoffend within a year than those with stable accommodation (Skrzypiec et al. 2004). These preliminary studies suggest that outcomes are better where stable accommodation and specialized support are provided.

3.1.5 Disability and Forensic Service Pathways

Some researchers see value in determining the factors that predict the placement of people with ID with antisocial behaviour in certain accommodation and treatment services (Hogue et al. 2006; Wheeler et al. 2009; Lindsay et al. 2010; Raina et al. 2013). Using a regression model, Hogue et al. (2006) found that certain administrative variables, such as an individual's classification under the mental health act or previous imprisonment, probation, or civil detention, appeared to be related to residents in higher security settings (the higher of three levels of security). However, these factors were not as significantly associated with a higher security rating as a conviction for murder, criminal damage, or a diagnosed personality disorder. To the contrary, another study concluded that whether or not a person had been previously involved with the CJS was not related to whether they received support from a community-based disability team as opposed to being committed to a restrictive forensic facility (Wheeler et al. 2009).[3] Lindsay et al. (2010) agreed that few diagnostic variables are significant to an individual's accommodation setting but they disputed the significance of administrative variables (such as previous imprisonment),

---

3 This study examined the service-user pathways of people ID who engaged in antisocial and offending behaviour through various settings: prison, secure hospital, inpatient unit, community team, or no placement. They compared a group with prior contact with the CJS and a group with no prior contact, finding that over time, mostly service users who did not have contact with the CJS were being serviced by community disability teams. These results are gleaned from the diagrammatic presentation of service users' pathways, which mapped the number of people moving from one setting to another over various time periods: at behaviour, referral, one year and two years after referral.

placing more emphasis on the assessing clinicians' interpretation of the qualitative case information. In other words, the professional judgements of expert staff are probably based on a combination of many of the administrative and socio-demographic characteristics mentioned, and possibly other information that may not have been identified by these quantitative studies. Although there is conjecture about which factors have most influence, context-specific research will begin to identify determinants of the accommodation pathways of people with ID under CT.

Although there are no national or international case studies that are directly comparable with the CT legal framework, this review has found that people with ID who demonstrate behaviour that is harmful to others live with complex psychosocial circumstances with detrimental experiences beginning in childhood. These findings are not dissimilar to those concerning the general population of offenders. For this reason, the specific needs and experiences of people with ID who offend, or who exhibit offending-like behaviours within the mainstream CJS, are a key focus of disability rights advocates. It is within the prison environment where, without adequate intervention, disadvantage is compounded. Deficits in skill development, a lack of social support, and the impact of intellectual impairment on an individual's insight into their behaviour are key challenges to reducing criminal behaviour and the high rates of recidivism amongst this group. Although, supported accommodation appears to be related to improved rehabilitation outcomes for people with ID who offend, the research relating to people with ID exhibiting 'non-criminal' behaviours is more limited. It remains unclear whether accommodation access can be determined by a person's characteristics or administrative variables but it would seem that consent and compliance are certainly problematic to such service use. Context-specific research might uncover results that are more relevant to the specific sample and shed more light on how CT has functioned up until now.

3.2 Method

Initially it was proposed to compare subjects under CT who had been imprisoned at some time in their life with those who had never been to prison. Due to a lack of reliable evidence (the case file information in relation to imprisonment histories was often deficient) and uneven group sizes (significant because of the small sample) the study aims were adjusted. That is, after cross-referencing, it was evident that almost all subjects had experienced some form of imprisonment.

The research aims were to:

1) Describe patterns in the accommodation changes of the entire sample by examining accommodation over five periods in time: at the time of the index behaviour; immediately before, during, and immediately after CT; and at follow-up at March 2014;
2) Describe the characteristics of the sample including socio-demographic and historical factors, diagnoses, behaviours, and offences; and
3) Compare the characteristics of those admitted to a correctional facility (CF) during the study period with those not admitted to a correctional facility (NCF) (these groups arose from the analysis at point 1).

3.2.1 Hypothesis

There is evidence within the literature (Holland et al. 2002; Wheeler et al. 2009; Lindsay et al. 2010) as well as some anecdotal evidence to suggest that there are two observable groups of service users within the forensic disability field. The first group has a higher IQ and more significant levels of social disadvantage, including mental illness and substance misuse (Wheeler et al. 2009), more likely to be young and male (Wheeler et al. 2009) and have a history of impulsivity and behavioural disorders diagnosed in childhood (Holland et al. 2002) and are often difficult to engage in services (Wheeler et al. 2009) and therefore the age they are assessed for eligibility is more likely to be older. The second group is labelled a 'typical disability service user'. Holland et al. (2002) believed the process whereby the behaviours of concern of this group become 'offending' is far less understood. That is, their behaviour is more often described as an 'escalation', rather than 'illegal' or 'criminal'. This group is smaller, has a lower IQ and are better known to services, often being engaged in structured routine activities and supportive formal relationships (Wheeler et al. 2009).

It was hypothesized that the CF group would be more likely to fit the description of a more 'typical offender' and the NCF group would be more closely aligned with the 'typical disability service user' profile.

3.2.2 Subjects

The focus of the research was a group of 45 recipients of CT between 1 July 2007 (the introduction of CT) and 1 March 2014. All recipients were over 18 years old and eligible for disability services in Victoria.[4]

All individuals under CT are subject to one or more of the following legal orders:

- As resident in a secure treatment facility for people with ID (the IRTP), individuals are often subject to a Residential Treatment Order (RTO, Victorian Government 2006a), but may also be subject to another type of order such as a Parole Order (PO, Victorian Government 1986b) or a Supervision Order (SO, Victorian Government 2009).
- Subject to a STO, (Victorian Government 2006a), requiring they reside in an approved, disability residential service in the community.
- Subject to an Interim STO (Victorian Government 2006a), issued when it is necessary to detain a person before an application for an STO is determined.
- Subject to an Assessment Order (AO) (Victorian Government 2006a), issued when it is necessary to detain a person for an urgent assessment to determine whether an application for a STO is warranted.

3.2.3 Data Collection

Data were collected and managed in accordance with the Senior Practitioner's information management governance policies. All data analysed and disclosed by this research were

---

4 According to the Department of Health and Human Services, the eligibility criteria define an ID as significant sub-average intellectual functioning (an IQ more than two standard deviations below the population mean) together with significant deficits in adaptive behaviour, each of which became manifest before the age of 18 years.

non-identifiable. Recipients' initials were used during the data collection phase but all identifying information was removed when the data were analysed.

One researcher collected data from the following data sources:

Client information database: The Department of Health and Human Services' Client Relationship Information System contains important chronological information, especially in relation to eligibility and accommodation moves and addresses.

Restrictive intervention database: The Senior Practitioner's Restrictive Intervention Data System contains legal documents relating to CT matters, including dates for the start and end of CT and the reasons for certain decisions as required.

Paper case files: Clients of the Department of Health and Human Services may have a number of files containing data relevant to any given service area. The Senior Practitioner's case files hold information relevant to CT or restrictive interventions, such as clinical assessments, reports and reviews, records of court proceedings and court orders, correspondence relating to the work of the Senior Practitioner, and treatment and support plans. Only the Senior Practitioner client files were accessed in the formulation of this research.

Data were collected in relation to recipients' accommodation changes. These variables were categorized as either: CF, residential treatment facility, residential treatment facility (long term), institutional disability facility, shared supported accommodation (SSA), private residence, homeless/transient, or other. Accommodation changes were noted at time of the index behaviour, immediately before CT, during CT, immediately after CT, and at 1 March 2014 (follow-up). The living arrangement was also included (residing alone, alone in special support arrangements, family, homeless/transient, other offenders, other offenders with a disability/illness, others with a disability, other, or unknown).

Recipients' legal status was recorded including the reason that CT ended. These 'end reasons' were categorized as: completed term in treatment facility and planned transition, criteria never satisfied, criteria no longer satisfied, moved, no longer assessed as having ID, offended, order expired, removed because of behaviour, or under a new order.

Other data related to the recipients' socio-demographic and historical file information, including: IQ, employment history, early life experiences (in relation to child abuse and neglect, transience, transient foster care, institutional care, and significant loss), the type of schooling attended, substance use and gambling, and convictions and imprisonment history.

Where possible, the reliability of the data was tested by comparing data obtained from different data sources. Data tables were assessed by the Senior Practitioner's Senior Practice Advisors and any discrepancies were clarified by further cross-checking.

3.2.4   Data Analysis

Socio-demographic, historical, and clinical data were collated and analysed and are presented in Table 3.1. The accommodation data were primarily analysed using visual data mapping techniques. A similar approach was adopted by Wheeler et al. (2009) in their diagrammatic representation of people who engaged in antisocial and offending behaviour as they moved through a range of settings (prison, secure hospital, inpatient unit, community support, or no placement) over four different time periods. The rChart software package was used to generate the Sankey flow diagram, which distinguishes

Table 3.1 Socio-demographic, historical, and clinical characteristics associated with the NCF and correctional facility (CF) groups.

	NCF (N = 24)		CF (N = 21)		Total (N = 45)	
	N with NCF	% within NCF	N with CF	% within CF	Total N	% of Total
Gender						
Female	2	8.3	0	0	2	4.4
Male	22	91.6	43		95.5	
Age (at start of compulsory treatment [CT])	33		30			
Aboriginality	0	0	3	14.3	3	6.6
Level of intellectual disability (ID):						
Borderline (with low adaptive)	3	12.5	4	19	7	15.5
Mild	13	54.2	14	66.6	27	60
Moderate	6	25	3	14.3	9	20
Severe/Profound	2	8.3	0	0	2	4.4
Psychiatric diagnoses						
Suicidal ideation	5	20.8	9	42.9	14	31.1
Mood disorder	1	4.2	2	9.5	3	6.7
Adjustment disorder	0	0	3	14.3	3	6.7
Depressive disorder	8	33.3	7	33.3	15	33.3
Anxiety disorder	6	25	6	28.6	12	26.7
Sexual disorder	4	16.7	4	19	8	17.8
Psychotic disorder	5	20.8	5	20.8	10	22.2
Personality disorder	2	8.3	7	33.3	9	20
Autism or traits of autism	7	29.2	2	9.5	9	20

(Continued)

Table 3.1 (Continued)

	NCF (N = 24)		CF (N = 21)		Total (N = 45)	
	N with NCF	% within NCF	N with CF	% within CF	Total N	% of Total
Oppositional defiance disorder (ODD), Attention deficit and hyperactivity disorder (ADHD), conduct/behaviour disorder (in childhood)	3	12.5	6	28.6	9	20
Epilepsy	3	12.5	3	28.6	9	20
Acquired brain injury	2	8.3	1	4.8	3	6.7
Detrimental early life experiences						
Childhood abuse – all (physical, sexual, deprivation, neglect, etc.)	18	75	17	80.9	35	77.8
Childhood sexual abuse	10	41.7	11	52.4	21	46.7
Childhood physical abuse, neglect, deprivation	15	62.5	15	71.4	30	66.7
Institutional care (under 18)	5	20.8	4	19	9	20
Transient foster care (under 18)	5	20.8	6	28.6	11	24.4
Homelessness/transience (under 18)	2	8.3	4	19	6	28.6
Other significant trauma or loss	6	25	8	38.1	14	31.1
Index behaviours/harm caused to others						
Physical assault	7	29.2	2	9.5	9	20
Sexual assault	12	50	14	66.7	26	57.8
Physical and sexual	3	12.5	5	23.8	8	17.8
Arson	1	4.2	0	0	1	2.2
Physical, sexual and arson	1	4.2	0	0	1	2.2

Accommodation setting at index behaviour (NCF and CF)

	N of convictions	% of total
Residential treatment facility	1	2.2
Institutional disability facility	4	8.8
Shared supported accommodation (SSA)	10	22.2
Private residence	22	48.9
Homeless/transient	7	15.5
Other	1	4.4

Convictions by category	N of convictions	% of total	N of convictions	% of total	N of convictions	% of total
Intentional injury	8	18.6	12	12.8	20	14.6
Sexual assault and related	14	32.5	18	19.1	32	23.3
Negligent acts endangering life	1	2.3	1	1.1	2	1.5
Abduction, harassment, offences against the person	3	7	2	2.1	5	3.6
Robbery, extortion and related	1	2.3	3	3.2	4	2.9
Unlawful entry, burglary, break and enter	1	2.3	7	7.4	8	5.8
Theft and related	2	4.6	12	12.8	14	10.2
Fraud, deception and related	0	0	2	2.1	2	1.5
Illicit drug offences	1	2.3	3	3.2	4	2.9
Prohibited weapons	2	4.6	4	4.2	6	4.4
Property damage	5	11.6	12	12.8	17	12.4
Public order offences	2	4.6	6	6.4	8	5.8
Traffic and vehicle offences	0	0	5	5.3	5	3.6
Offences against government	3	7	7	7.4	10	7.3
Total convictions	43	100	94	100	137	100

between the number of subjects flowing in and out of an accommodation setting at each time period. The Gephi software package was also used to map the inward and outward flows as a network, highlighting the most popular pathways. Both the flow diagram and network analysis require colour coding for accurate review so were unable to be produced for this publication. These results can be made available by request to the primary author.

3.3 Results

Sankey diagrams and a network analysis showed two distinct patterns in recipients' movements between different accommodation settings: one dominated by standard disability residential group homes referred to as SSA and one involved a stay in a CF and the IRTP. However, recipients did not necessarily follow one of each of these pathways and there were certainly numerous less populated routes.

Many of the recipients who were part of the correctional pathway moved there from a private residence and after a stay in the CF, they were moved to the IRTP. There were also a number of people who were homeless or transient (at the time of the index behaviour) who were part of this correctional group.

Immediately after exiting the IRTP, this correctional group split into two; one group transitioned to a CF and the other group into private residence in the community. The group who ended up in a CF were very likely to remain there until the follow-up period.[5] There were also some recipients (who are considered part of this group) who moved into a CF from SSA or private residence sometime before follow-up. Private residence seemed to be more associated with movements to and from correctional facilities than with SSA. Recipients who were housed in SSA from the beginning (or at least immediately before CT) largely remained there until follow-up however there were some exceptions.[6] For example, after their CT ended, some recipients moved into private residence.

As a result of these findings, the CT group was split into the CF group and the NCF group and compared to see if there were any notable differences in characteristics. Table 3.1 outlines the key characteristics relating to the CF and NCF groups. Both groups differed slightly in the age they were assessed as being eligible for disability service provision. The average age of eligibility assessment for the NCF group was 16 years, which was lower than the CF group at 20 years. However, the range was very broad for the whole group, from 3 years to 43 years of age (median 17 and a standard deviation of 9.25).

The average length of CT was 28 months with the period of detention varying from under one month to the longest possible term of five years. The NCF group had an average of four months longer in treatment.

---

5 Apart from one person who moved from prison into a private residence and one who moved from prison to supported accommodation.

6 One particular exception is attributable to changes to the Disability Act (Victorian Government 2006a). This involved a small number of recipients who were transferred from the IRTP to SSA because to be detained legally they were required to be under certain orders. These moves were considered a once only administrative decision.

Seven of the 45 cases never satisfied the criteria for CT. All of these recipients were under an Assessment Order or an Interim STO. Of the sample, 20% concluded CT because they offended; all of these instances were in the CF group. However, most periods of CT came to an end because the recipient no longer met the legal criteria required for detention. Following CT there was a 157% increase in behaviour support plans for the NCF group and only a 25% increase for the CF group.[7]

Of the sample, 60% had a mild ID. Two recipients (one from each group) were assessed within the borderline range (above the eligible IQ range) but significant deficits in their adaptive functioning meant they were eligible for services.[8] The average IQ level was slightly lower for the NCF group than the CF group. Although the groups did not differ markedly for IQ categories in the higher range of intellectual functioning, in the moderate and the moderate to severe ranges the numbers from the NCF group were higher.

The average age of the total CT sample was 32 years. At the start of CT, the youngest person was 18 and the oldest was 59 years. The NCF group was slightly older (33 years) than the CF group (30 years) at the start of CT. The majority of the sample was born in rural and non-metropolitan areas (60%) as opposed to metropolitan Melbourne (40%) but the difference between groups was fairly small. Two of the 45 recipients (4.4%) were women and three (6.6%) identified as Aboriginal.

Low, unstable, and sporadic employment histories were common. Of the recipients, 60% had no employment history or minimal work experience but the remainder had experienced either stable (18%) or unstable work histories (16%). These work experiences were in both supported employment and unsupported employment situations. There were only slight differences between the two groups in this area.

In terms of detrimental early life experiences, for at least 77.8% of the sample there was evidence of childhood abuse, whether physical, sexual, or some other form of deprivation or neglect. The NCF group was slightly less likely to have experienced childhood abuse. This difference was also evident when abuse was separated into sexual and all other types of abuse. Of the total CT group, 52.4% had experienced sexual abuse and 71.4% other types of abuse. There was insufficient information for 6% of cases.

Of the CT group, 19% had lived in an institution for people with disabilities under 18 years of age and 28.6% had experienced transient foster care placements, primarily because of the inability of carers to manage their behaviour. The CF group were slightly more likely to experience transient foster care. They were also more likely to experience transience or homelessness (under 18), which was relevant for 19% of the sample, and to have had other significant trauma or loss in their lives (38.1% of the total group).

In terms of psychiatric diagnoses as adults, there were some notable differences between the two groups. Suicidal ideation was more common amongst the CF recipients, with 42.9% of the client files for this group showing a history as opposed to 20.8%.

---

7 Under the Disability Act (Victorian Government 2006a), treatment plans are required for people under CT and Behavioural Support Plans (BSPs) are required when any person with a disability is subject to a restrictive intervention. In effect, a BSP replaces a Treatment Plan at the conclusion of CT if the individual resides in accommodation delivered by Disability Services and the individual is subjected to a restrictive intervention. A Treatment Plan also replaces a BSP if the person is approved for CT.

8 One of these recipients was later assessed as ineligible, leading to the completion of the CT period for this individual.

Diagnoses of personality disorders were more likely to be given to recipients within the CF group (33.3% as opposed to 8.3%). There were only three cases of Adjustment Disorder and these were found within the CF group. Some of the biggest differences between the NCF and CF groups were in additional diagnoses they had been ascribed by treating professionals.[9] The NCF group was more likely to have been diagnosed with Autism Spectrum Disorder or be ascribed traits of Autism (29.2% as opposed to 9.5%). The CF group were more likely than the NCF group to have been diagnosed with a behavioural disorder in childhood such as Oppositional Defiance Disorder (ODD), Attention Deficit and Hyperactivity Disorder (ADHD) or a Conduct Disorder (CD).

The entire CF group had references to substance use or gambling in their file histories, whereas less than half of the NCF group had such references. Overall, 70% of the sample engaged in these activities in some form, however, whether or not the behaviours were 'problematic' was more difficult to ascertain. Thirty-one per cent of client files indicated that substance use or gambling was certainly problematic (NCF group 13% and CF group 18%).

The two groups differed in the type of harm their index behaviour caused to others. The NCF group were more likely to have caused physical harm (29.2% compared to 9.5%) but those in the CF group were more likely to have caused sexual harm (66.7% compared to 50%). These two categories of harm accounted for 95.6% of the total index behaviours (17.8% of subjects had both physically and sexually harmed their victim/s). There were two instances of arson (one in each group) and one case involving all three categories of harm.

The highest number of convictions was for sexual assault and related offences. Intentional injury and property damage were also highly represented. There was at least one case of homicide and possibly more, however the case-file evidence was inconsistent. The NCF group were slightly more likely to have been convicted of a sexual crime than the CF group and there were more cases of theft amongst the CF group.

Ten of the NCF group had not been to prison before the study period. Of this group seven had no convictions, with three having had formal convictions that did not result in a prison sentence. Nineteen out of 20 (95%) of the CF group had been in a CF at some point before the study period. Therefore, only one of the CF group was incarcerated for the first time during the study period.

3.4 Discussion

This study provides the first in-depth analysis of the characteristics and accommodation changes of the only group of individuals to have completed a term of CT under current legislation in Victoria. A major point of difference between the CT model and other service models is the unique legislative charter, which allows treatment to be provided without consent as either a diversionary or a step-down alternative to prison. Although the framework allows for individualized treatment in a diversity of settings, this study design did not capture these details, but instead, revealed overall patterns in

---

9 Diagnoses were not considered mutually exclusive and all diagnoses were listed even if they had been challenged.

the use of CT. In particular, CT was increasingly used to ensure ongoing treatment of individuals exiting prison rather than as a diversion from the mainstream CJS and a proportion of this offending group was returned to prison. However, these observations must be qualified by certain limitations on the study's findings. Specifically, legal standing appeared to be more influential to recipient accommodation than an individual's characteristics or group membership.

Comparing the CF and NCF groups revealed notable differences in mental distress and behavioural disorders diagnosed in childhood, which were both higher in the CF group. In relation to socio-demographic and historical factors, a typical individual in the sample could be described as having a mild ID, a history of underemployment, a diagnosed mental illness (and probably a behavioural disorder) and at least one experience of imprisonment. Most notably there were also very high rates of conviction for sexual assault and experiences of childhood abuse and neglect.

3.4.1 Limitations of the Study

Some of the accommodation variables were limited in how adequately they reflected the actual experience of the recipients of CT. This is because accommodation settings were categorized very generally. For example, the SSA consisted of group homes managed by a range of community service and Government organizations; some forensic-specific with high staff-to-resident ratios, and others with a mixed group of residents receiving varying levels of support. Similarly, 'private residence' varied from living alone with no formal or informal support to living with family and receiving intensive support from disability and correctional services. In spite of this simplification, the research depicted overall trends in the movement of subjects.

Other limitations to the accommodation variables related to their reliability and ability to draw comparisons between cases. Firstly, the researcher's judgement about the 'index behaviour' and when it occurred was less reliable as compared with other time periods that were legally defined (such as the start and end of CT). However more significantly, the follow-up time period did not allow comparison between cases because it was calculated from a specific date (1 March 2014) rather than a defined period of time (for example, one year).[10] These limitations could easily be rectified in further research where a longer time frame is available.

3.4.2 Patterns in the Use of CT

Although accommodation at follow-up could not be accurately compared between cases, it did indicate the length of time since CT ended. The NCF group completed CT on average of 38 months prior (just over 3 years) whereas the CF group only 25 months prior (just over 2 years). This reveals that the majority of most recent instances of CT were from the CF group, suggesting an increasing tendency of CT to service those who have had recent involvement in the correctional system over those who did not.

---

10 Those in correctional facility (at follow-up) had an average follow-up period of 28 months, whereas those in SSA and private residence had average follow-up periods of 36 months and 32 months respectively. Grouped differently, the CF group had an average follow-up period of 25 months, whereas the NCF group average was 38 months.

However, further investigation would be needed to ascertain exact numbers and whether the trend continues over time.

Recipients' legal orders also provided evidence as to how CT was applied during the study period. Apart from two recipients, all those who commenced CT after moving from a CF were subject to court orders other than RTOs (that is, orders not under the Disability Act [Victorian Government 2006a]). In fact, the number of RTOs (n = 6) remained low over the entire study period. This is significant because RTOs are more commonly requested by the courts as an alternative to a prison sentence (as a diversionary strategy). Therefore, it is almost certain that recipients who exited prison on a court order other than RTOs were doing so after a more lengthy stay than just remand. It is likely that that they left prison without having achieved sufficient behavioural change to live safely in the community and in this sense, CT provided a last resort for rehabilitation.

3.4.3 Prison as a post-CT Outcome

There were seven cases where a recipient exited prison to CT but later returned to prison and two cases where a recipient entered prison after being in SSA during CT. The data revealed that prison was a post-CT outcome because either certain behaviours could not be safely managed within the treatment environment or CT was no longer a legal option and the recipient was not able to manage in the community without reoffending. Interestingly, there were three known cases of recipients expressing a want to return to prison in preference to the less restrictive environment. This could be for a range of reasons including the institutionalizing effect of previous prison stays, a personal preference for or feeling of security/containment from the predictability, rigid structure, and strict authority provided by the prison, and/or a preference for a more diverse environment as opposed to one solely for people with ID. In any case, it is clear that not every environment meets the basic needs of every individual, and compliance certainly remains a complex challenge to providing effective treatment to some despite the legal structure designed to aid this process.

3.4.4 The Length of Legal Detention and Further Limitations of Accommodation Findings

Being imprisoned before the planned end of CT, which was only relevant to the CF group, was one of the reasons for the difference between groups in their average length of treatment. Assessment and Interim STOs also lowered the group average for the NCF group because these orders tended to be shorter due to their purpose. The tendency for some orders to be longer or shorter than others highlights an obvious and crucial limitation: a recipient's legal status is not only related to the length of an order but to whether or not a recipient was imprisoned immediately before CT.[11] In other words, legal orders were not truly independent of group membership and caused an

---

11 For example, court orders (such as, POs and SOs – Extended Supervision Order (ESO) SO, Non-Custodial Supervision Order (NCSO) – are only possible for those recipients who have entered a correctional facility and the IRTP is the only accommodation provider that can accept individuals under court orders (as determined by the Disability Act [Victorian Government 2006a]).

uncontrolled influence on the accommodation patterns of the sample. This is the most convincing explanation for the 'correctional' and 'shared supported accommodation' patterns in accommodation changes.

3.4.5 Testing the Hypothesis

In relation to the group's socio-demographic characteristics it was hypothesized that the NCF group would be more well-known to disability services. Assuming that an earlier eligibility assessment date was an indicator of being more well-known, and arguably it was not because eligibility did not necessarily indicate service access from that date, the CF group were slightly less well-known. Some recipients had been known to disability services since their early childhood, whereas others were first assessed at the time they were being considered for CT. The CF group were, on average, four years older when they were assessed for eligibility however the cases where recipients were assessed for eligibility whilst in prison (usually immediately before release) are most relevant to the less well-known hypothesis because it was certain that they had not accessed disability services before that time. Given there were few (4 of 45) of these cases, there was little support for this part of the hypothesis.

The hypothesis also proposed that the NCF would have a lower IQ. The NCF group did have a slightly lower average IQ and there were more instances of a lower range IQ. This may suggest that some recipients better fit the more typical disability service user profile however there were too few cases to confirm this. Drawing conclusions from IQ alone is not necessarily useful in terms of typifying the sample because, as one case illustrates, IQ can differ for one person over multiple assessments. One individual in the study was found to be ineligible after a significant term of CT when a retest showed his IQ was higher than first assessed (another convincing case for the impact of professional decision making on outcomes). This case is probably not completely uncommon considering that eligibility is decided via a legal process and many candidates have a mild ID in the upper range.

Despite these observations about the lack of differences in eligibility age and IQ, the groups did show differences in diagnoses and index behaviours. The NCF group members had higher instances of Autism Spectrum Disorder and were more likely to have behaviours that were physically harmful to others than the CF group. These two characteristics were not always attributed to the same individuals, nor to individuals who also had a mild ID (there were only three cases where individuals had all three characteristics). Therefore, support for the proposition that the NCF group better fits the 'typical disability service user' profile is weak.

Although the NCF and CF profiles were not so detailed as to specify clinical characteristics, the two groups did show notable difference in these areas. The number of diagnoses of behavioural disorders in childhood also varied between the two groups. Although emotional and behavioural problems in children with ID are more common than for those without ID (Alimovic 2013), the CF group were obviously more likely to be amongst the estimated 65% of people with ID whose behavioural issues do not decrease with age (Einfeld et al. 1999; Tonge and Einfeld 2003). Winter et al. (1997) believed their study showed that childhood behavioural problems (amongst other indicators related to socio-economic disadvantage) were one of the most important factors in trying to understand why one group of people with ID offended and another did not.

It would be interesting to further examine whether people with ID who are diagnosed with childhood behavioural disorders are more likely to have more frequent contact with the CJS than people with no ID and childhood behavioural disorders.

Other clinical characteristics that differed between the groups were personality disorders and suicidal ideation. The CF group experienced more instances of both. A study of offenders with ID in secure units in the UK by Alexander et al. (2010) found personality disorders were evident in about 50% of these cases. However, the authors also found no support for specialized treatment facilities for people with ID and personality disorders over general treatment facilities for the broader group of people with ID who have offended. Despite this conclusion, detailed information about the clinical presentation of people under CT is extremely useful to practitioners in other ways. It enables practitioners to provide targeted training to disability support workers as well as encouraging the development of more tailored treatment strategies that better respond to individual needs. These indicators of mental distress in the CF group may not fit the 'typical offender profile' but this is still an important finding.

3.4.6 Common Characteristics

Although the initial hypothesis cannot be confirmed in relation to the two small groups of recipients, the findings give some indication of some common characteristics within the CT sample. Overall, the following typical features were observed in the small sample. Recipients were most likely to be male with a mild ID, a history of underemployment, experiences of childhood abuse and neglect, a diagnosed mental illness (and probably a behavioural disorder), a conviction of sexual assault or a related offence, and at least one experience of imprisonment. Some recipients also had a history of substance abuse or gambling problems.

Although an experience of childhood abuse and neglect is common amongst other samples of offenders, there were higher rates amongst the CT sample than other studies of people with ID, even those within the CJS (see Lindsay et al. 2010). Amongst studies that cite some of the highest percentages, Lindsay et al. (2006) found that up to 40% of offenders with ID in their sample had experienced some form of abuse in their childhood. The rates within the CT sample were closer to double this. Some of this variation could be attributed to study design because some studies may rely on self-disclosure alone.

Apart from exceptionally high rates of childhood abuse and neglect, and with the exception of an ID and convictions of sexual assault, many of the socio-demographic characteristics of the CT sample are also found in general offender populations (Lund 1990; Farrington 1995; Winter et al. 1997; Murphy and Mason 1999; Holland et al. 2002). In relation to the overrepresentation of convictions of sexual assault in the CT sample, one possible explanation is the suitability of the CT treatment and accommodation to manage or reduce this type of offending.

This research described the characteristics and accommodation changes of the only group of individuals to have completed a term of CT under the Disability Act (Victorian Government 2006a). Although the legal framework was likely to have influenced the accommodation pathways of the group, examining other effects, such as the professional judgements of expert decision makers, would probably be fruitful. Despite some limitations to the reliability and comparability of the accommodation variables, mapping these accommodation changes showed a flexible system that is adaptable to the complex circumstances of individuals. Although substantive conclusions cannot be drawn about recipient outcomes, the results revealed that CT was increasingly used to service people with ID who are leaving prison on court orders, rather than on civil orders as a diversion from the CJS. Compiling various findings in relation to the two groups divided by whether or not they had been recently imprisoned raises a new hypothesis.

The first of the two proposed subpopulations is older than the second. Their 'offending cycle' could be described as stable and their problematic behaviours are improving or at least being managed in SSA, where they are likely to be developing supportive relationships and engaging in meaningful daily activity. Although they would probably have a history of imprisonment and convictions, these are historical. They would also be unlikely to experience current substance misuse issues and their mental health is more stable. At the time of their previous imprisonments, alternatives would not have been available and disability support was more limited.

This stands in contrast to a younger group of offenders whose 'offending cycle' could be described as active. This group are more likely to move between unsupported private accommodation and incarceration. Although they may have been diagnosed with a behavioural disorder in childhood, they are unlikely to be known to disability services until they are referred by correctional staff. Their mental health and behaviour are more unstable, as is their compliance with treatment. Therefore, they would be at a higher risk of returning to prison. As the former group age and there is no longer a need for CT, the younger group will continue to dominate referrals for CT.

3.5 A Framework for Protecting the Rights of Persons with Intellectual Disabilities in Correctional Settings

Taking into consideration the imprisonment of recipients of CT, including the greater likelihood of being subject to CT upon release from prison, the final section of this chapter will consider the human rights of recipients of CT who have engaged in offending behaviour and who can be considered both as an offender *and* a person with a disability. This dual role can result in conflicting values between managing the risk of the person as an offender and meeting their needs as a person with a disability (Birgden 2016). In addition, engaging in behaviours that may result in CT requires that treatment providers balance duty of care with dignity of risk. Dignity of risk recognizes that most adults engage in risky behaviour because of some perceived benefit and so a person with a disability ought not to be subject to arbitrary restrictions on their right to choose; they should be able to experience 'bad' decisions and be allowed to take some risks in order to be afforded dignity and autonomy in decision making (Victorian Law Reform Commission 2003). Whilst the Senior Practitioner supports dignity of risk related to life goals, the hazard should not be so great that it will result in harm to self or others (Office of the Senior Practitioner 2012).

Of course, we are talking about prudent risks. People should not be expected to blindly face challenges that without a doubt, will explode in their faces. Knowing which risks are prudent and which are not – this is a new skill that needs to be acquired … a risk is really only when it is not known beforehand whether a person will succeed (Slayter 2007, p. 654, citing disability activist Robert Perske).

3.5.1 CT and Offender Rehabilitation

CT falls under the Disability Act (Victorian Government 2006a) and occurs when a person with an ID is admitted to a secure residential treatment facility under the direction of specific criminal orders or subjected to a civil order under an STO and placed within an SSA service. In this instance, offender rehabilitation is likely to be considered as part of treatment. Birgden (2016) had distinguished between 'habilitation' and 'rehabilitation' – terms applied loosely in the literature and largely undefined in legislation, policy, and practice. Programmes have been described as habilitation (e.g. advocacy, positive role modelling, use of leisure time, academic training and tutoring, obtaining employment, basic hygiene, learning about the law, socialization skills) and rehabilitation (e.g. weekly counselling group, eliminating substance use, and 'rehabilitation') (Petersilia 2000). More recently, in discussing offenders with a hearing disability, habilitation was described as teaching basic skills whilst rehabilitation was described as restoring lost skills, differentiating between learning new skills and re-learning old skills (Glickman et al. 2013). Likewise, Hayes (2007) argued that the critical issues for offenders with ID are to: (i) protect client safety and the safety of the community (duty of care); (ii) reduce re-offending through education, social skills training, welfare services, and offence-specific programmes (i.e. rehabilitation); and (iii) address health through medical, dental, and mental health care (i.e. habilitation). The Convention for the Rights of Persons with Disability (CRPD, United Nations 2006) identifies habilitation and rehabilitation, but simultaneously addressing health, employment, education, and social services without distinguishing between them (Article 26(1)). It seems that treatment can provide formal and informal supports for the person to reconstruct the self (i.e. habilitation) or re-establish a previously adaptive self (i.e. rehabilitation) (Birgden 2016).

3.5.2 Human Rights Framework

Due to the coercive nature of the legislation, a human rights framework is necessary to protect the rights of recipients of CT. The CRPD (United Nations 2006) provides guidelines relevant to CT recipients (Chan et al. 2012). Most importantly, general principles include: respect for inherent dignity, individual autonomy, including the freedom to make one's own choices, and independence of persons (Article 3a); non-discrimination (Article 3b); and accessibility (Article 3c). Equal recognition before the law (Article 12) safeguards the rights, will, and preferences of the person and legal sanctions are proportional and tailored to their circumstances (Article 12(4)).

A human rights framework has been utilized to balance the rights and needs of persons with ID, emphasizing choice and empowerment for individuals and their families rather than being viewed as 'eternal children, unable to speak on their own behalf and therefore not competent to make their own decisions' (Ward and Stewart 2008, p. 305). This consideration is linked to the notion of dignity of risk. The proposed framework was an extension of a human rights model developed by Ward and Birgden (2007) to address the human rights of offenders in general. Ward and Birgden (2007) proposed that all offenders, as humans, hold human rights – they are fellow human beings rather than aliens or 'the other'. Such a human rights framework views the offenders as both a rights-violator (they have violated the rights of others) and a rights-holder (they can claim certain rights regardless). Human rights consist of positive rights and negative rights. The International Covenant on Economic, Social, and Cultural Rights (United Nations 1966a) ensures that the State has obligations to provide access to programmes and services (i.e. positive rights) whilst the International Covenant on Civil and Political Rights (United Nations 1966b) ensures individual freedom from state interference, such as the right to be free from unlawful restrictive practices (i.e. negative rights). Together, these two documents are encapsulated in the Universal Declaration of Human Rights (UDHR, United Nations 1948). Put another way, an example provided for persons with ID is equality of treatment (a negative right) together with equality that requires special treatment (a positive right) (Young and Quibell 2000). Additionally, we are all duty-bearers – those of us who are responsible for ensuring access to required services and supports together with CT recipients who ought not to harm themselves and others.

There are the universal standard human rights objects of personal freedom, social recognition, material subsistence, personal security, elemental equality, and the local policies and procedures to enact them such as the Charter of Human Rights and Responsibilities Act (Victorian Government 2006b). However, Ward and Birgden (2007) argued that such legal and social rights lacked consideration of moral rights required for offenders. Moral rights are the core values of autonomy and well-being in allowing all persons to function with purpose and human dignity. *Autonomy* involves situations in which coercion is absent allowing for the capacity to form and implement personal valued projects. For CT recipients, as rights-violators, the core value of autonomy is absent leading to restriction on personal freedom (e.g. freedom of movement) and social recognition (e.g. directing the course of their own life). Regardless, *well-being* obliges the State to provide the necessary goods and refrain from interfering with individuals' enjoyment of these rights. For CT recipients, this means they still ought to have unrestricted access to the goods of security (e.g. physical safety and welfare), material subsistence (e.g. physical health and education), and equality (e.g. freedom from discrimination on the grounds of disability or for being an offender).

3.5.3 Practice Principles for CT

Birgden (2016) considered the rehabilitation of offenders with ID within the US prison system and proposed a set of practice principles to reduce the likelihood of discrimination against persons with ID. These practise principles are adapted here and outlined in Table 3.2, and have been restricted to human rights concerns regarding values applied within CT.

CT entails mandatory treatment, requiring human rights protections. Whilst Table 3.2 addresses the human rights of persons with ID within the prison setting, the values and treatment practice principles are equally applicable to CT recipients within other settings. Such protections are particularly important when admitted to a secure residential treatment facility, whether as the result of a criminal order or a civil order. Recipients of CT must experience a balance between their position as rights-holder as well as rights violator. This approach can best be reflected in the treatment plan. As duty-bearers, it is incumbent upon the authorized programme officer and the Senior Practitioner to ensure this balance is realized within the delivery of the treatment plan.

Table 3.2 Practice principles to protect human rights of persons with intellectual disability (ID) in correctional settings.

	Person with an intellectual disability (ID) — As rights-holder	Person as an Offender — As rights-violator	
Positive Human Rights	**Values**		**Negative Human Rights**
	Access to programmes, services, and activities.	Freedom from unlawful restrictive practise.	
	The person is a duty-bearer, able to pursue their own goals.	The person is a duty-bearer, but with obligations towards others.	
	Support the person in exercising their rights, will, and preferences.	Support the person in exercising responsibility for themselves and towards others.	
	Provide information about treatment options, risks, and expected outcomes of compulsory treatment (CT) and support participation in treatment planning and decision making.	Acknowledge that free and informed consent is not obtained.	
	Establish practices, policies, and procedures that enhance access to programmes	Preserve and enhance autonomy and well-being, as much as possible.	
	Treatment		
	Provide programmes in the most integrated environment.	Provide programmes in the least restrictive environment.	
	Provide access to habilitation programmes that are equivalent to those available to disability clients in the community.	Provide access to rehabilitation programmes that are equivalent to those available to offenders in prison.	
	Improve quality of life for the person.	Reduce the likelihood of re-offending, for the community.	
	Work with, not on, persons with an ID to reintegrate a non-offending citizen with full rights and responsibilities who contributes to the community.		

3.6 Conclusions

The CT regime in Victoria offers a powerful model for the legal detention of people with ID who present as being at significant risk of causing serious harm to others, ensuring treatment and offering a diversion from the CJS or a step-down from the correctional system. The Victorian legal framework is increasingly populated by offenders with ID who, for much of their life, have fallen through the gaps between service systems and who have found themselves in prison at least once, and probably multiple times.

Overall the CF group demonstrated higher levels of mental distress and behaviour disorder in childhood. Across the sample there were very high rates of conviction for sexual assault and experiences of childhood abuse and neglect. These results indicate that in addition to the disability sector, other sectors can play a significant role in preventing a pathway to the correctional system, which can further compound disadvantage and lead to greater likelihood of recidivism. The sectors highlighted by the findings of the study include: child protection and family services (high rates of child abuse and neglect and family dysfunction), education (high rates of behavioural disorders and undetected ID), mental health and psychiatry (extremely high rates of mental illness), housing (high rates of homelessness/transience), courts and police (low rates of diversion from the CJS) and the employment sector (low rates of employment).

Of concern, CT has increasingly been used in Victoria to ensure ongoing treatment of individuals exiting prison, rather than as a diversion from the mainstream. The practice principles outlined in the last section of this chapter can serve to strengthen the treatment plan development and implementation process for those in correctional settings by ensuring their human rights protections by duty-bearers as both rights-violators and rights-holders. These principles can also be equally applied in other contexts in the community to those subject to CT, whether on criminal or civil orders.

References

Alexander, R.T., Green, F.N., O'Mahony, B. et al. (2010). Personality disorders in offenders with intellectual disability: a comparison of clinical, forensic and outcome variables and implications for service provision. *Journal of Intellectual Disability Research* 54 (7): 650–658.

Alimovic, S. (2013). Emotional and behavioural problems in children with visual impairment, intellectual and multiple disabilities. *Journal of Intellectual Disability Research* 57 (2): 153–160.

Allen, D. (2008). The relationship between challenging behaviour and mental ill-health in people with intellectual disabilities: a review of current theories and evidence. *Journal of Intellectual Disabilities* 12 (4): 267–294.

Baldry, E., Clarence, M., Dowse, L. et al. (2013). Reducing vulnerability to harm in adults with cognitive disabilities in the Australian criminal justice system. *Journal of Policy and Practice in Intellectual Disabilities* 10 (3): 222–229.

Birgden, A. (2016). Enabling the disabled: a proposed framework to reduce discrimination against forensic disability clients requiring access to programs in prison. *Mitchell Hamline Law Review* 42 (2): 638–696.

Borzycki, M. and Baldrey, E. (2003). *Promoting integration: The provision of prisoner post-release services*, Australian Institute of Criminology: Trends and issues in crime and criminal justice: No. 262. Canberra: AIC.

Chan, J., French, P., Hudson, C. et al. (2012). Applying the CRPD to safeguard the rights of people with a disability in contact with the criminal justice system. *Psychiatry, Psychology and Law* 19 (4): 558–565.

Cooper, S.-A., Smiley, E., Morrison, J. et al. (2007). Mental ill-health in adults with intellectual disabilities: prevalence and associated factors. *The British Journal of Psychiatry* 190 (1): 27–35.

Dinani, S., Goodman, W., Swift, C. et al. (2010). Providing forensic community services for people with learning disabilities. *Journal of Learning Disabilities and Offending Behaviour* 1 (1): 58–63.

Einfeld, S., Tonge, B., and Turner, G. (1999). Longitudinal course of behavioral and emotional problems in Fragile X syndrome. *Amercian Journal of Medcial Genetics* 87 (5): 436–439.

Emerson, E., Moss, S., and Kiernan, C. (1999). The relationship between challenging behaviour and psychiatric disorders in people with severe developmental disabilities. In: *Psychiatric and Behavioural Disorders in Developmental Disabilities and Mental Retardation* (ed. N. Bouras), 38–48. Cambridge: Cambridge University Press.

Farrington, D.P. (1995). The development of offending and antisocial behaviour from childhood: key findings from the Cambridge Study in Delinquent Development. *Journal of Child Psychology and Psychiatry* 36 (6): 929–964.

Gardner, W.I. and Moffatt, C.W. (1990). Aggressive behaviour: definition, assessment, treatment. *International Review of Psychiatry* 2 (1): 91–100.

Glaser, W. and Deane, K. (1999). Normalisation in an abnormal world: a study of prisoners with an intellectual disability. *International Journal of Offender Therapy and Comparative Criminology* 43 (3): 338–356.

Glickman, N.S., Smith, C.M., and Lemere, S. (2013). Engaging deaf persons with language and learning challenges and sexual offending behaviours in sex offender-oriented mental health treatment. *Journal of the American Deafness and Rehabilitation Association* 47 (2): 168–203.

Hayes, S. (2004). Pathways for offenders with intellectual disabilities. In: *Offenders with Developmental Disabilities* (eds. W.R. Lindsay, J.L. Taylor and P. Sturmey), 67–89. Chichester: Wiley.

Hayes, S. (2007). Missing out: offenders with learning disabilities and the criminal justice system. *British Journal of Learning Disabilities* 35 (3): 146–153.

Hayes, S. and McIlwain, D. (1988). *The Prevalence of Intellectual Disability in the New South Wales Prison Population: An Empirical Study*. Sydney: Department of Behavioural Sciences in Medicine, Sydney University.

Hogue, T., Steptoe, L., Taylor, J.L. et al. (2006). A comparison of offenders with intellectual disability across three levels of security. *Criminal Behaviour and Mental Health* 16 (1): 13–28.

Holland, S. and Persson, P. (2011). Intellectual disability in the Victorian prison system: characteristics of prisoners with an intellectual disability released from prison in 2003–2006. *Psychology, Crime & Law* 17 (1): 25–41.

Holland, T., Clare, I., and Mukhopadhyay, T. (2002). Prevalence of 'criminal offending' by men and women with intellectual disability and the characteristics of 'offenders': implications for research and service development. *Journal of Intellectual Disability Research* 46 (1): 6–20.

Lindsay, W.R. (2002). Integration of recent reviews on offenders with intellectual disabilities. *Journal of Applied Research in Intellectual Disabilities* 15 (2): 111–119.

Lindsay, W.R., Steele, L., Smith, A.H.W. et al. (2006). A community forensic intellectual disability service: twelve year follow up of referrals, analysis of referral patterns and assessment of harm reduction. *Legal and Criminological Psychology* 11: 113–130.

Lindsay, W.R., O'Brien, G., Carson, D. et al. (2010). Pathways into services for offenders with intellectual disabilities childhood experiences, diagnostic information, and offense variables. *Criminal Justice and Behaviour* 37 (6): 678–694.

Lund, J. (1990). Mentally retarded criminal offenders in Denmark. *The British Journal of Psychiatry* 156 (5): 726–731.

McGillivray, J.A. and Moore, M.R. (2001). Substance use by offenders with mild intellectual disability. *Journal of Intellectual and Developmental Disability* 26 (4): 297–310.

McGrath, R.J., Livingston, J.A., and Falk, G. (2007). Community management of sex offenders with intellectual disabilities: characteristics, services, and outcome of a statewide program. *Intellectual and Developmental Disabilities* 45 (6): 391–398.

Murphy, G. and Mason, J. (1999). People with developmental disabilities who offend. In: *Psychiatric and Behavioural Disorders in Developmental Disabilities and Mental Retardation* (ed. N. Bouras), 226–246. Cambridge: Cambridge University Press.

Nøttestad, J.A. and Linaker, O.M. (2005). People with intellectual disabilities sentenced to preventive supervision–mandatory care outside jails and institutions. *Journal of Policy and Practice in Intellectual Disabilities* 2 (3–4): 221–228.

Office of the Senior Practitioner (2012). *Roadmap Resource for Achieving Dignity without Restraint*. Victoria: Department of Health and Human Services.

Palucka, A.M., Raina, P., Shi-Kai, L. et al. (2012). The clinical profiles of forensic inpatients with intellectual disabilities in a specialised unit. *Journal of Learning Disabilities and Offending Behaviour* 3 (4): 219–227.

Petersilia, J. (2000). *Doing Justice? Criminal Offenders with Developmental Disabilities*. Berkeley: California Policy Research Center.

Plant, A., McDermott, E., Chester, V. et al. (2011). Substance misuse among offenders in a forensic intellectual disability service. *Journal of Learning Disabilities and Offending Behaviour* 2 (3): 127–135.

Raina, P., Arenovich, T., Jones, J. et al. (2013). Pathways into the criminal justice system for individuals with intellectual disability. *Journal of Applied Research in Intellectual Disabilities* 26 (5): 404–409.

Reed, S., Russell, A., Xenitidis, K. et al. (2004). People with learning disabilities in a low secure in-patient unit: comparison of offenders and non-offenders. *The British Journal of Psychiatry* 185 (6): 499–504.

Skrzypiec, G., Wundersitz, J., and McRostie, H. (2004). *Magistrates Court Diversion Program: An Analysis of Post-Program Offending: Evaluation Findings*. Adelaide: Office of Crime Statistics and Research.

Slayter, E.M. (2007). Substance abuse and mental retardation: balancing risk management with the 'dignity of risk'. *Families in Society: The Journal of Contemporary Social Services* 88 (4): 651–659.

Taylor, J. (2002). A review of the assessment and treatment of anger and aggression in offenders with intellectual disability. *Journal of Intellectual Disability Research* 46 (1): 57–73.

Tonge, B.J. and Einfeld, S.L. (2003). Psychopathology and intellectual disability: the Australian child to adult longitudinal study. In: *International Review of Research in Mental Retardation* (ed. L.M. Glidden), 61–91. San Diego, CA: Academic Press.

United Nations (1948). *Universal Declaration of Human Rights*. https://www.un.org/en/universal-declaration-human-rights/index.html (accessed 8 December 2007).

United Nations (1966a). *International Covenant on Economic, Social and Cultural Rights*. https://www.ohchr.org/en/professionalinterest/pages/cescr.aspx (accessed 18 May 2019).

United Nations (1966b). *International Covenant on Civil and Political Rights*. https://www.ohchr.org/en/professionalinterest/pages/ccpr.aspx (accessed 18 May 2019).

United Nations (2006). *Convention on the Rights of Persons with Disabilitie*s. https://www.un.org/development/desa/disabilities/convention-on-the-rights-of-persons-with-disabilities.html (accessed 18 May 2019).

Victorian Government (1986a). *Guardianship and Administration Act 1986, No. 58 (1986)*. Melbourne: Victoria State Government.

Victorian Government (1986b). *Corrections Act 1986, No. 117 (1986)*. Melbourne: Victoria State Government.

Victorian Government (2006a). *Disability Act 2006, No. 23 (2006)*. Melbourne: Victoria State Government.

Victorian Government (2006b). *Charter of Human Rights and Responsibilities Act 2006, No. 43 (2006)*. Melbourne: Victoria State Government.

Victorian Government (2009). *Serious Sex Offenders (Detention and Supervision) Act 2009, No. 91 (2009)*. Melbourne: Victoria State Government.

Victorian Law Reform Commission (2003). *People with Intellectual Disabilities at Risk: A Legal Framework for Compulsory Care*. Melbourne: Victorian Law Reform Commission 166 pp.

Ward, T. and Birgden, A. (2007). Human rights and correctional practice. *Aggression and Violent Behaviour* 12: 628–643.

Ward, T. and Stewart, C. (2008). Putting human rights into practice with people with an intellectual disability. *Journal of Developmental and Physical Disabilities* 20 (3): 297–311.

Webber, L.S., Lambrick, F., Donley, M. et al. (2010). Restraint and seclusion of people on compulsory treatment orders in Victoria, Australia in 2008–2009. *Psychiatry, Psychology and Law* 17 (4): 562–573.

Wheeler, J.R., Holland, A.J., Bambrick, M. et al. (2009). Community services and people with intellectual disabilities who engage in anti-social or offending behaviour: referral rates, characteristics, and care pathways. *Journal of Forensic Psychiatry & Psychology* 20 (5): 717–740.

Winter, N., Holland, A., and Collins, S. (1997). Factors predisposing to suspected offending by adults with self-reported learning disabilities. *Psychological Medicine* 27 (3): 595–607.

Young, D.A. and Quibell, R. (2000). Why rights are never enough: rights, intellectual disability and understanding. *Disability and Society* 15 (5): 747–764.

Part II

Phenotypes and Genotypes and Offending Behaviour

4

Behavioural and Cognitive Phenotypes in Genetic Disorders Associated with Offending

Lauren J. Rice[1], Stewart L. Einfeld[1], and Patricia Howlin[1,2]

[1] *The Brain and Mind Centre, University of Sydney, Camperdown, New South Wales, Australia*
[2] *The Institute of Psychiatry, Psychology and Neuroscience, King's College London, London, UK*

4.1 Introduction

Whilst there is considerable literature on the characteristics of offending in the general and intellectual and developmental disability (IDD) populations, there is very little specific information on offending by individuals with genetic disorders. For this reason, this chapter begins with an overview of the behavioural and cognitive characteristics associated with offenders with IDD more generally. Most of this literature focuses on individuals with borderline or mild IDD (intelligence quotient [IQ] between 55–79) since those with more severe intellectual impairment (i.e. moderate to profound IDD) are usually considered to lack the capacity of intent (*mens rea*) to commit a crime (Holland 2004). We then discuss genetic syndromes associated with these characteristics, with the emphasis being on syndromes associated with mild IDD.

4.2 Types of Offending Behaviours in People with ID

Early studies of offending by people with IDD suffered from significant bias since they tended to recruit participants from services where patients were likely to have more severe behaviour problems than the general IDD population. For example, there were suggestions that people with IDD were more likely to commit arson and sex-related offences than offenders without IDD (Robertson 1981; Walker and McCabe 1973). However, more recent studies have shown that rates of arson and sex-related offences committed by people with IDD vary depending on whether participants are recruited from low, medium, or high-security settings (Lindsay et al. 2010).

To minimise the risk of sampling bias, the Northgate, Cambridge, Abertay Pathways (NCAP) project (O'Brien et al. 2010) recruited participants from a range of IDD service settings in three health areas in the UK. Information about offending behaviours was collected from the case notes of 477 adults with Intellectual Disability (ID). More than

The Wiley Handbook on What Works for Offenders with Intellectual and Developmental Disabilities: An Evidence-Based Approach to Theory, Assessment, and Treatment, First Edition.
Edited by William R. Lindsay, Leam A. Craig, and Dorothy Griffiths.
© 2020 John Wiley & Sons Ltd. Published 2020 by John Wiley & Sons Ltd.

one incident was reported for most participants. Offences against the person were more common than non-person offences. Aggression was the most common offence, with physical aggression reported in 50% of cases and verbal aggression in 33% of cases. Other common behaviours included damage to property (19%), inappropriate sexual contact (15%) and inappropriate sexual non-contact (14%). Substance abuse, theft, cruelty, or neglect of children, fire-setting and stalking were less commonly reported (O'Brien et al. 2010). Other studies report similar patterns of offending behaviour amongst individuals with ID, with aggression being the most common (McBrien et al. 2003; Wheeler et al. 2013). This is not surprising given aggression is also the most common form of challenging behaviour reported in the broader IDD population (Emerson 2001).

4.3 Characteristics of Offending in the ID Population

It is well established that a number of individual and external factors are associated with offending in the general population. These include younger age (typically adolescent) (Farrington 1986; Piquero et al. 2015), male gender (Steffensmeier and Allan 1996), low IQ (Farrington 1986; Lindsay et al. 2004), high impulsivity (Lipsey and Derzon 1998) and presence of a psychiatric illness (Arseneault et al. 2000). External factors include low parental education, poor parental supervision, poor child-rearing skills, parental discord, family size, and socio-economic status (Derzon 2010).

The characteristics of people with IDD who engage in offending-type behaviour are similar to those in the general population. These individuals are also typically young and male; they have high rates of unemployment and frequently have a background of a single-parent household, socio-economic disadvantage and familial offending (Emerson and Halpin 2013; Winter et al. 1997). We now discuss some of the cognitive characteristics associated with offenders in IDD.

4.4 Intelligence

The role of intelligence in criminality is complex. Within the scientific literature, this complexity is at least partly driven by methodological discrepancies and ambiguity in how intellectual ability and offending are defined (Holland 2004; Lindsay et al. 2004). For example, whilst low IQ is known to be a risk factor for offending (Farrington and Welsch 2006), research has found that individuals with an IQ in the intellectual disability range (i.e. below 70) are less likely to offend than those of borderline IQ (i.e. IQ between 70 and 85) (Lindsay et al. 2004). Thus, amongst individuals with IDD referred to the criminal justice system, around 10% have mild IDD (IQ between 55 and 69) whereas 25–30% are of borderline ID (Baldry et al. 2013; Hayes et al. 2007; McLachlan 2016). Mears and Cochran (2013) also found that individuals with the lowest (<88) and highest (>125) IQs were less likely to offend than people with an average IQ. A particular feature of the Mears and Cochran study is that offending was measured by participants' self-reports of whether they had engaged in any of 20 different offending behaviours, regardless of whether they had been charged or convicted. In contrast, other studies have defined offending as coming into contact with the criminal justice system or being formally charged (Lyall et al. 1995; McNulty et al. 1995). The problem with the latter definition is that carers often choose not to report offences committed by people with lower IQs due to the view that they are considered less responsible for their crimes (Holland 2004).

The disproportionate number of people with IDD in the criminal justice system does not, of course, mean that intellectual impairment is a direct cause of offending. Emerson and Halpin (2013) examined parent-reported contact with police and self-reported rates of offending-type behaviours in 13- to 15-year old adolescents with and without mild to moderate IDD. They found that parents of adolescents with IDD were more often contacted by the police on account of their child's behaviours than were parents of typically developing (TD) controls. Adolescents with IDD also self-reported higher rates of offending behaviours than their TD peers. However, the IDD group also experienced higher rates of social deprivation, such as low family income, and living in single-parent households and/or disadvantaged neighbourhoods. After controlling for these external factors, individuals with IDD displayed fewer offending-type behaviours than TD controls. This study suggests that, once social factors are accounted for, rates of offending may, in fact, be lower in people with IDD than the general population and highlights the importance of external risk factors in offending.

4.5 External Factors

People with IDD experience higher rates of early psychosocial adversities relative to their TD peers. These adversities include poorer health, poverty and socio-economic disadvantage, social exclusion from education and community participation as well as higher rates of bullying and abuse (Allerton et al. 2011; Department for Children Schools and Families 2008; Emerson 2013; Emerson et al. 2005; Fisher et al. 2012; Inclusion International 2006; Leonard et al. 2005; McLachlan 2016; Oeseburg et al. 2011; United Nations 2011). Early exposure to psychosocial adversities has been linked to higher rates of psychopathology (Emerson and Hatton 2007) and offending in later life in people with IDD (Put et al. 2014). One study found that as many as 70% of offenders with IDD had been abused and/or neglected compared to only 42% of offenders without IDD. Moreover, the relationship between childhood maltreatment and sexual offending was stronger in offenders with IDD than those without ID (Put et al. 2014). Offenders with IDD are also more likely to have lived in institutions or temporary care and are less likely to have paid employment, educational qualifications, and social support than are offenders without IDD (Ali et al. 2016).

4.6 Moral Reasoning

The moral reasoning abilities of individuals with IDD is developmentally immature compared to that of the general population (Langdon et al. 2011). Two studies in the UK found that, with regard to legal issues, non-offenders with IDD were at the earliest stage of moral development, which was associated with adhering to rules and avoiding punishment. Offenders with IDD were at stage two, which was concerned with personal needs and social exchanges. In contrast, participants without IDD, regardless of whether they did or did not offend, were at stage three, which involves the ability to consider multiple aspects of a situation and to understand others' emotional states (Langdon et al. 2011; McDermott and Langdon 2016). These findings suggest that individuals with IDD who do offend may do so, at least partly, due to a delay in moral development that places them at stage where legal issues are considered in relation to self-interest rather than adherence to rules or consideration for others.

4.7 Impulsivity

Definitions of impulsivity vary according to whether the context is related to biology, personality, or cognition. The lack of an agreed definition has meant that impulsivity is sometimes confused with sensation seeking, extraversion, or risk-taking (Snoyman and Aicken 2011). One of the more generally accepted definitions of impulsiveness is 'a predisposition toward rapid, unplanned reactions to internal or external stimuli without regard to the negative consequences of these reactions to the impulsive individuals or others' (Moeller et al. 2001, p. 1784). Impulsivity is not thought to be directly related to intelligence. It can, however, influence performance on intelligence tests (Vigil-Colet and Morales-Vives 2005). Although several researchers suggest that impulsivity is one of the strongest predictors of offending and antisocial behaviour in the general population (Farrington 2017; Lipsey and Derzon 1998; Pallone and Hennessy 1996), only a few studies have examined the role of impulsivity in offending in IDD. These studies suggest that impulsivity is lowest in sex offenders and highest in people who have committed violent offences (Parry and Lindsay 2003; Snoyman and Aicken 2011). Consistent with this latter finding, impulsivity has been shown to be strongly associated with aggression in both the TD (Barratt 1994) and ID populations (Crocker et al. 2007).

4.8 Co-morbidity

Young people with IDD have rates of psychopathology that are approximately three to four times higher than in the TD population (Dekker et al. 2002; Einfeld and Tonge 1996; Einfeld et al. 2006). In turn, psychopathology can limit the access of individuals with IDD to community residential placement (Bruininks et al. 1988), the workforce (Anderson et al. 1992), and community and recreational placement (Parmenter et al. 1998).

Of the 477 offenders with IDD examined in the NCAP project (O'Brien et al. 2010), 32% had a psychiatric disorder in childhood and 46% had a psychiatric diagnosis in adulthood. The most common childhood disorders were Attention Deficit Hyperactivity Disorder (ADHD) (15%) and Autism Spectrum Disorders (ASDs) (10%) and the most common disorders in adulthood were anxiety and obsessive-compulsive disorder (13%), depression (11%), personality disorder (11%), schizophrenia (9%), and other nonorganic psychotic disorders (9%). A follow-up study found that compared to offenders without ADHD those with ADHD displayed higher rates of physical aggression, damage to property, and substance abuse. ADHD participants also exhibited more persistent offending patterns, had elevated rates of abuse in childhood, and more psychiatric diagnoses. It is important to note that only 15% of participants in the NCAP study had ADHD (Coolidge et al. 2009; O'Brien et al. 2010); thus, the presence of ADHD is only one of many factors that may increase the risk of offending behaviour.

People with IDD are typically less likely to use illicit drugs and alcohol than are the general population (Chapman and Wu 2012). However, the small number of people with IDD who do use illicit drugs and alcohol are at a heightened risk for substance abuse (McGillicuddy 2006) and offending behaviours (Lindsay et al. 2013a; McGillivray and Moore 2001). A recent study found that substance use was similar in offenders with and without IDD one year before their gaol terms as was participation in drug and alcohol treatment programmes. Nevertheless, offenders with IDD were less likely to complete their drug and alcohol treatment programmes. These findings suggest that current drug and alcohol treatment programmes may not be adequately addressing the cognitive or learning needs of individuals with IDD (McGillivray et al. 2016).

4.9 Offending by People with Genetic Disorders

4.9.1 Behavioural Phenotypes

A behavioural phenotype is a specific pattern of behaviours associated with a genetic disorder. A behaviour is considered part of the behavioural phenotype if there is evidence that the behaviour occurs more frequently in a disorder than in an appropriate control group (Einfeld and Hall 1994). However, behaviours are not driven by genes alone. Instead, they are contingent on social and/or environmental circumstances (Griffiths et al. 2010). For example, the genetic abnormality associated with Prader-Willi syndrome (PWS) increases the risk of temper outbursts amongst individuals with this condition; however, such outbursts tend to be associated with excessive distress. Social and environmental factors can also influence the development of behaviours. For example, Hessl et al. (2001) found that educational and therapeutic services, as well as parental psychological problems, predicted internalising and externalising behaviour problems for boys with Fragile X syndrome (FXS) (Hessl et al. 2001). It is therefore essential that the genetic, psychological, social, and environmental contexts be considered together when examining the cause of a behaviour.

Although there are many genetic disorders associated with IDD, there is almost no systematic information on the prevalence of offending behaviours in individuals with these disorders. In the following sections of this chapter, therefore, we focus first on ASDs, as this is the one condition where there has been some systematic research on offending. Following this, we examine certain genetic conditions in which specific aspects of the behavioural phenotype are associated with behaviours that, potentially, are risk factors for offending. However, because of their obvious genetic disorder, and their impaired intellectual ability, such individuals rarely come to the attention of the criminal justice system. In selecting these disorders, we have focused primarily on conditions associated with mild ID, and in which the behavioural phenotype includes two or more characteristics that are potential risk factors for offending. The disorders selected as examples here are FXS, Smith-Magenis Syndrome (SMS) and PWS, and 47,XYY syndrome.

Finally, we examine situations in which, rather than being offenders, individuals with IDD and genetic conditions are more likely to be victims of crime.

4.9.1.1 Offending in Autism

In the Diagnostic and Statistical Manual of Mental Disorders, fifth edition (DSM-V; APA 2013) autistic disorder, Asperger's syndrome disorder, childhood disintegrative disorder, and pervasive developmental disorder not otherwise specified have been amalgamated into one category, ASD. The estimated prevalence of ASD is 1% for both children (Baird et al. 2006) and adults (Brugha et al. 2011), with a ratio of three to one for males and females (Loomes et al. 2017). In 70% of cases, the cause of ASD is unknown. For the remaining 30%, autism is thought to arise from other genetic disorders, such as tuberous sclerosis complex, chromosomal deletions, duplications or copy number variations (Beaudet 2007; Jacquemont et al. 2006).

4.9.1.1.1 Behavioural phenotype of ASD

The core symptoms of ASD are a persistent deficit in social interaction and communication and the presence of restricted interests, and repetitive behaviours (APA 2013). Levels of intellectual ability vary from superior intelligence to severe intellectual impairment (Developmental Disabilities Monitoring Network Surveillance Year 2010 Principal Investigators, Centers for Disease Control and Prevention (CDC) 2014). Females with ASD tend to be more intellectually impaired than males (Tonge and Einfeld 2003) although this may be because diagnostic rates amongst higher functioning females are thought to be unduly low (Loomes et al. 2017). Young people with ASD exhibit higher levels of overall emotional and behavioural problems and are more disruptive, self-absorbed, and anxious than are young people with mixed causes of IDD. They also have higher levels of depressive and attention deficit hyperactivity symptoms (Brereton et al. 2006; Simonoff et al. 2008). The rate of emotional and behavioural problems declines slightly as individuals move into adulthood (Gray et al. 2012).

4.9.1.1.2 Prevalence of offending in ASD and types of offences

Media reports of high-profile cases, such as Gary McKinnon and Adam Lanza, have suggested that people with autism or Asperger syndrome are at an increased risk of committing a crime (Brewer and Young 2015). However, systematic reviews of prevalence studies consistently conclude that individuals with ASD are no more likely to offend than individuals in the general population (Ghaziuddin et al. 1991; King and Murphy 2014; Mouridsen 2012). Several studies have examined whether ASD influences the type of crimes committed. A well-controlled study found that adolescents with ASD were more likely to commit crimes against people, such as assault, robbery, and sex-related offences, and less likely to commit crimes against property, such as trespassing or arson, than were youth without ASD (Cheely et al. 2012). Whilst, some studies support these findings (Helverschou et al. 2015; Kumagami and Matsuura 2009) others do not (Hare et al. 1999; Mouridsen et al. 2008; Woodbury-Smith et al. 2005). These inconstancies are likely attributable to methodological differences. For example, not all studies compared the types of offending in ASD with a control group; others recruited participants through forensic services, which tends to inflate the prevalence of severe crimes and underestimate the rate of minor offences. It may also be that ASD alone does not directly influence the type of offence. Rather, offending in ASD involves a complex interaction between individual and environmental risk factors (Murphy 2017) and thus variability in the nature of offending is to be expected.

4.9.1.1.3 Characteristics of offenders with ASD

There are various anecdotal accounts of people with autism who have come into contact with the criminal justice system. These case studies, as well as reports from clinical experience, highlight several factors that may contribute to offending behaviours in ASD. Amongst the most notable of these are deficits in empathy or theory of mind (Wing 1981), poor emotion regulation (Lerner et al. 2012), social impairments, restricted interests (Howlin 2004), and co-morbidity (Newman and Ghaziuddin 2008). These risk factors are discussed in the following subsections.

Empathy and theory of mind: Theory of mind refers to the ability to understand one's own or others' mental states, including thoughts, intentions, desires, emotions, and goals. Empathy refers to the ability to recognise the mental state of others and respond with appropriate emotion (Rueda et al. 2015). Although individuals with ASD tend to show deficits in both of these areas (Mathersul et al. 2013) only one study has directly investigated the role of theory of mind and empathy in offending in ASD (Woodbury-Smith et al. 2005). The authors found that individuals with ASD who had committed an offence had greater difficulty recognising fear than did non-offenders with ASD. Both groups, however, had similar difficulties with theory of mind, executive functioning, and recognising sadness (Woodbury-Smith et al. 2005). In line with these findings, Rogers et al. (2006) found that adolescents with ASD and callous-unemotional traits were more likely to express antisocial, violent behaviour and had greater difficulty recognising signs of distress in others than did adolescents with ASD without callous-unemotional traits (Rogers et al. 2006). A deficit in recognising signs of distress, particularly fearful expressions, has been robustly linked with antisocial behaviours in the general population (Marsh and Blair 2008). Together these findings suggest that a deficit in recognising fear in others may be a risk factor for assault-like offences both for individuals with ASD and the general population.

Emotion regulation: Individuals with ASD have difficulty both in understanding and controlling emotions, and poor emotion regulation may manifest in the form of temper outbursts and aggression (Mazefsky and White 2014). A recent study conducted with a representative sample of 920 adolescents and young adults with ASD found that high rates of externalising behaviours, such as aggression, were associated with increased contact with police (Rava et al. 2017). Several smaller studies have also found offending to be higher in individuals with a history of aggression or violent behaviour (Tint et al. 2017; Woodbury-Smith et al. 2006). However, other studies have reported no difference in rates of aggression between individuals with ASD who have and have not offended. More research is needed to understand the role of emotion regulation in aggression in ASD.

Social impairment: Autism is associated with particular difficulties in understanding social situations and in interpreting non-verbal social cues. Inability to understand what others are thinking or feeling often gives rise to social misunderstanding and misinterpretation of social situations. For example, someone with ASD who has a crush or intense interest in another person may not recognise when that person wants to be left alone, leading to accusations of stalking (Attwood 2006). Stokes et al. (2007) found that compared to their TD peers, male and female adolescents and adults with ASD were more likely to believe that their feelings towards someone were reciprocated and they would, therefore, continue to pursue the person for longer. The ASD group also showed different patterns of courtship behaviours. Whilst TD participants tended to initiate social contact by approaching, calling or emailing someone to ask them out on a date, individuals with ASD displayed a range of unconventional behaviours. They were more likely to monitor the person's activities, try to persuade them threateningly, or follow or touch them inappropriately (Stokes et al. 2007). The influence of ASD should, therefore, be taken into consideration when individuals are prosecuted for stalking.

A few studies have investigated the motives behind offences committed by people with ASD (Allen et al. 2008; Woodbury-Smith and Dein 2014). One study found that the motives or reasons provided by offenders with ASD often differed from the reasons proposed by the forensic experts. Thus, whilst the individuals with ASD were more likely to report stress, excitement, and social misunderstandings as the reason for their offence, the forensic experts most often reported idiosyncratic beliefs (unusual or irrational ideas or explanations), rigidity, social naivety, and victimisation as common motives. The only motive that both groups seemed to agree on was obsessions or restricted interests. These discrepancies may reflect differences in perspective and experience as well as a potential lack of understanding of people with ASD in forensic settings (Helverschou et al. 2017). Helverschou et al. (2015) also collected information about motives or explanations for offending from forensic reports for all individuals with ASD who had committed a crime in Norway between 2000 and 2010. Again, the most common motives reported were idiosyncratic beliefs, restricted interests, social naivety, revenge, and social misunderstandings (Helverschou et al. 2015) The idiosyncratic or unusual explanations for offending in ASD are also highlighted in case reports (Chesterman and Rutter 1993; Mawson et al. 1985). For example, Howlin (2004) describes the case of a man with ASD who lost his job for attacking a cloakroom attendant. The man believed that his actions were completely justified because she had given him the wrong ticket. Similarly, Chesterman and Rutter (1993) reported the case of a man who struck a police officer for accusing him of burglary after he was found inside a stranger's house. The man took offence to the accusation because in his opinion a burglar is someone who steals valuable items and he merely wanted to use the washing machine and take an item of little value. These unusual thought processes are likely associated with a range of social and cognitive deficits common to ASD, such as difficulty perceiving the view of others, a rigid interpretation of rules, and difficulty generalising information.

Restricted interests: Although restricted interests or obsessions are amongst the core deficits of ASD, only one study has investigated the relationship between restricted interests and offending in this population (Woodbury-Smith et al. 2010). All the participants in this study were convicted of causing harm to someone or threatening to cause harm. The authors found that offenders with ASD were more likely to report violent interests than were non-offenders with ASD. For a third of offenders, the offence seemed to be related to his or her interest. For one of these participants the connection was clear, an interest in fire and a conviction of arson. However, for the other three participants, the link between the interest and the crime was less direct. These findings suggest that restricted interests involving violent content may increase the risk of offending. However, if the interest is limited to reading about a topic then this may simply need to be monitored to ensure that it does not interfere with other aspects of life (Woodbury-Smith et al. 2010). Case studies suggest that non-violent obsessions can also play a role in offending in ASD. For example, Wing (1981) described how a man interested in trains tried to drive off with an unattended railway engine. Similarly, Chesterman and Rutter (1993) described the case of a man obsessed with lingerie who was convicted for breaking in and stealing lingerie from clothes lines or laundry baskets.

External factors: As would be expected, external factors are associated with offending in ASD as much as in the general population and broader ID community. These factors include poor educational levels, low employment status, limited social networks outside the family and a higher rate of adverse childhood abuse and neglect (Helverschou et al. 2015; Kawakami et al. 2012; Kumagami and Matsuura 2009). These findings suggest that individuals with ASD who are highly vulnerable, lonely, and dependent on families or service providers may be at a greater risk of offending (Helverschou et al. 2015). Limited social skills and a lack of social support can also make people with ASD more susceptible to misuse by others, which can lead to offending. For example, Howlin (2004) reported the case of a young man who, as an adolescent, was used by others to carry out petty thefts. This resulted in his being thrown out of home and on one occasion he was hospitalised for being forcibly injected with drugs; on another, he was charged for driving a car with stolen goods, whilst those who stole the goods got away.

Co-morbidity: Several studies report high rates of co-morbidity in offenders with ASD, including higher rates of psychosis and personality disorder (Hare et al. 1999; King and Murphy 2014; Långström et al. 2009; Wahlund and Kristiansson 2006). However, as King and Murphy (2014) highlighted, most of the participants in these studies were recruited through mental health settings, which would very likely provide an overrepresentation of mental health problems. Other studies have found that affective and personality disorders, as well as alcohol and substance abuse, were lower in ASD offenders (Helverschou et al. 2015; Woodbury-Smith et al. 2005). A recent study conducted with a representative population in Sweden found that individuals with ASD, particularly those without ID, appeared to be more likely to be convicted of a violent crime than were individuals without autism. A diagnosis of ADHD, conduct disorder, psychotic disorder, personality disorder, and drug and alcohol misuse were all associated with violent offences. However, when participants were stratified by the presence or absence of ADHD or a conduct disorder, the risk of violence in the ASD group significantly reduced (Heeramun et al. 2017). This suggests that ADHD and conduct disorders, rather than ASD per se may increase the risk of violence. ADHD has been identified as a risk factor for offending in the broader ID community (Lindsay et al. 2013b) and in the general population and is much more common in ASD (28%) than in the general population (5%) (Erskine et al. 2017; Simonoff et al. 2008). However, more recent studies suggest that it is specific symptoms associated with ADHD and conduct disorders, such as impulsivity and emotional problems that are better predictors of offending than the broader diagnosis (Aguilar-Cárceles and Farrington 2017).

4.9.1.1.4 Summary of offending in ASD

Individuals with ASD are no more likely to offend than the general population. Some of the cognitive characteristics and external factors associated with offending in the general population, such as difficulty interpreting emotions, ADHD and childhood adversities, appear to be associated with offending in ASD. However, there are also some characteristics that are more specific to ASD that may influence the context of the offence. For example, limited social skills and restricted interests can lead to social misunderstandings and accusation of offensive behaviour, particularly in relation to stalking and confrontations. Idiosyncratic beliefs or unusual thought processes can also play a role in the justification or reasoning behind offending behaviours. Furthermore, limited social understanding, unusual thought processes, and a lack of social support may place people with ASD at a greater risk of being used for crimes or for being a victim of crimes. The latter is discussed in more detail in the section on victimisation.

4.9.1.2 Characteristics Potentially Associated with Offending in Other Behavioural Phenotypes

4.9.1.2.1 *Prader-Willi Syndrome*

PWS is caused by the lack of paternal expression within the 15q11-q13 region (Smith 1999). PWS occurs in about one in 15 000 live births (Lionti et al. 2015). The most common physical features include hypotonia, hypogonadism, small hands and feet, and characteristic facial features. Individuals with PWS have abnormal growth, an excessive appetite, temperature control dysregulation, somnolence, and emotion dysregulation; all of which are likely to be associated with hypothalamic dysfunction (Swaab et al. 1995).

Behavioural phenotype of PWS: Approximately 70% of people with PWS have a mild to moderate intellectual impairment. The remaining 30% have a borderline or normal IQ (Einfeld et al. 1999). The behavioural phenotype of PWS includes excessive eating, temper outbursts, obsessions, skin-picking, stealing, stubbornness, underactivity, and a tendency to get upset over small changes in their routine or environment (Einfeld et al. 1999; Holland et al. 2003).

Behaviours and cognitive characteristics potentially associated with offending: Temper outbursts are one of the most common forms of maladaptive behaviour exhibited by individuals with PWS (Dykens and Cassidy 1995; Einfeld et al. 1999; Holland et al. 2003). Behaviours that can occur during outbursts include yelling, arguing, cursing, destruction of property, and assault (Stein et al. 1994). Aggressive behaviours usually only occur during an outburst (Holland et al. 2003) but not all outbursts include aggressive behaviour. In fact, rates of verbal and physical aggression are no higher in PWS than in the broader ID population (Einfeld et al. 1999). The frequency and severity of outbursts and physical and verbal aggression are equal for males and females with PWS and persist throughout childhood and adolescence. Physical aggression and tantrums show a small decline in adulthood (Rice et al. 2015).

The causal mechanisms of PWS outbursts are not entirely understood, although it is thought that PWS is associated with an arrest in brain development, which causes a delay in emotional maturity (Holland et al. 2003). Based on clinical observations it has been hypothesised that emotional development in adults with PWS is at a similar level to that of TD two to three-year-olds (Rice and Einfeld 2015). If this is the case, then emotional development is much more delayed in this population than are cognitive abilities. In support of this hypothesis individuals with PWS have been shown to have greater difficulty dealing with emotionally arousing situations, such as frustration and teasing, than people with a non-specified diagnosis of ID (Dykens and Rosner 1999). People with PWS also have deficits in identifying emotions (Whittington and Holland 2011), interpreting social information (Koenig et al. 2004) and in theory of mind

(Lo et al. 2013). As in autism, these emotional and cognitive deficits are highly likely to play a role in antisocial or offending behaviours. Also, many adolescents and adults with PWS have a strong sense of injustice, and they may be over-sensitive to perceived slights. For example, a young man with PWS who was troubled by mosquito bites developed an obsession with spiders after he learnt that spiders eat mosquitos. When a female resident in his group home killed a spider he believed she had done so intentionally to upset him so called the police to report her. He became excessively distressed over the incident which led to him having a temper outburst and hitting the resident. She reported him to the police who treated his behaviours as a domestic violence offence. Although it is uncommon for incidents in residential units to result in court action, residents with PWS and other disabilities can become frustrated with each other and, due to limited coping skills, they may push or hit out at others. In this case, the incident occurred in a jurisdiction where anyone charged with a domestic violence offence must go before the courts. Although the young man was not convicted the process cost the family a great deal of time, money, and stress.

Another characteristic of people with PWS is their tendency to become extremely fixed on an idea and unable to be flexible when the idea is inappropriate (Einfeld et al. 1999). The idea may involve an obsession with an object or person, or it may be a compulsion to hoard, order, rewrite or ask questions. It is thought that these behaviours do not involve the same thought processes as seen in obsessive–compulsive disorders but rather they reflect the restricted interests and repetitive and ritualistic behaviours that are also characteristic of autism (Dykens et al. 2011). They may also be due to delayed development more generally (Clarke et al. 2002). Obsessions and compulsions can also play a role in the increased risk of stealing in PWS, particularly when the person steals non-food items.

Finally, one of the most common characteristics of individuals with PWS is hyperphagia or excessive eating which is thought to be associated with an aberrant satiety response (Holland et al. 2003). The desire for food is so extreme that many families need to lock the fridge and kitchen cupboards to stop their son or daughter from eating themselves to death (Dykens et al. 2007). Hyperphagia can cause people with PWS to eat non-food items and take food from bins (Einfeld et al. 1999). This intense desire for food can lead to stealing.

4.9.1.2.2   Fragile X Syndrome

FXS is caused by a mutation in the FMR1 gene on the long arm of the X chromosome at Xq27.3. Individuals with 55–200 repeats of CGG in this region are classed as having a pre-mutation. These individuals are carriers of FXS and usually show few to no symptoms. People with more than 200 CGG repeats are classed as having the full mutation. The estimated prevalence of the pre-mutation is 1 in 850 males, and 1 in 300 females and the full mutation is 1 in 7000 males and 1 in 11 000 females (Hunter et al. 2014). Females with FXS are usually less affected than males' due to an additional normally functioning X chromosome. Although variable, the physical features of FXS include a characteristic facial appearance, soft skin, flat feet, post-pubertal macroorchidism in males, neuroendocrine problems, and dysplasia of the connective tissue resulting in hyperflexible joints (Hagerman and Hagerman 2002).

Behavioural phenotype in FXS: Intellectual abilities range from above average intelligence to moderate IDD for females and from mild to severe IDD for males (Freund and

Reiss 1991; Turner et al. 1980). The behavioural phenotype of males with FXS includes inattention, hyperactivity, social impairments, social anxiety, hyperarousal, speech and language abnormalities, and unusual responses to sensory stimuli (Baumgardner et al. 1995; Cohen et al. 1988). Speech and language delays are characterised by dysfluent conversation, incomplete sentences, echolalia, and perseveration (Belser and Sudhalter 2001; Martin et al. 2012). The behavioural phenotype of females with FXS includes social avoidance, anxiety, depression, and attention difficulties (Freund et al. 1993; Hagerman et al. 1992).

Characteristics potentially associated with offending in FXS: Although we are unaware of any research directly investigating the prevalence or nature of offending in FXS. FXS is associated with increased risk of impulsivity and ADHD (Grefer et al. 2016; Sullivan et al. 2006). Aggression also occurs in a subgroup of people with FXS and can result in minor injury or property damage (Hall et al. 2016). For males, aggression occurs in approximately 38% with a full mutation and 19% with a pre-mutation. The rate of aggression for females is 14% with a full mutation and 4% with a pre-mutation (Bailey et al. 2008). Reactive aggression (arguing, tantrums) is more common than proactive aggression (bullying, threatening) for both genders (Wheeler et al. 2016). Physical aggression is also common to both genders, and these behaviours typically decline in adolescence (Rice et al. 2015). Sensory issues and escaping a situation are the most common reason for aggression in FXS (Langthorne and McGill 2012; Langthorne et al. 2011; Wheeler et al. 2016). Although the pathophysiological mechanisms for aggression in FXS are not yet understood, one study found that individuals with FXS who had a genetic polymorphism causing hyperactive serotonin reuptake, therefore, reduced serotonin, had higher rates of aggression than those without the polymorphism (Hessl et al. 2001).

Individuals with Fragile X, also show social impairments, language difficulties, and unusual responses to sensory stimuli (Baumgardner et al. 1995; Cohen et al. 1988) and, as with autism, deficits in these areas may also be associated with inappropriate social overtures or response to social situations. Nevertheless, it is important to bear in mind that the genetic defect, itself, is rarely directly connected with the offending behaviour. For example, the girlfriend of a man with FXS took out an apprehended violence order after he assaulted her whilst intoxicated. He then breached the order, again whilst intoxicated, and was sent to gaol. Although it might be argued that the offence was 'due to' his genetic abnormality, in fact, he did not exhibit any behaviour problems when sober and up until this point had managed to maintain a relationship and full-time employment. Since the offender's mother and brother also abused alcohol, but neither had FXS, the violent behaviour and breach were considered most likely to be due to an alcohol addiction that was unrelated to the genetic disorder.

4.9.1.2.3   Smith-Magenis Syndrome

SMS is caused by a chromosomal deletion or heterozygous point mutation at 17p11.2 (Dubourg et al. 2014). SMS occurs in 1 in 25 000 live births (Greenberg et al. 1991). Physical characteristics include infantile hypotonia, short stature, short limbs, small broad hands, and distinct facial features (Poisson et al. 2015).

Behavioural phenotype of SMS: Most individuals with SMS have a mild to moderate ID, speech and language delays (Udwin et al. 2001), and deficits in short-term memory and sequential processing (Dykens et al. 1997; Osório et al. 2012). The behavioural phenotype includes sleep and toileting problems, aggression, social difficulties, mood swings, somatic problems, attention-seeking behaviours, overeating, obsessions, and self-stimulatory or self-injurious behaviours, including, skin-picking, nail-biting, and inserting objects into body orifices are also common (Dykens and Smith 1998). Self-hugging is a common reaction to happiness or positive excitement (Finucane et al. 1994).

Characteristics potentially associated with offending: Obsessions, social difficulties, and aggressive behaviours have all been associated with offending in ASD and hence may also have relevance for unacceptable or inappropriate behaviours in SMS. Attention seeking behaviour, physical discomfort, and sleep disturbance are thought to be the primary causes of aggression (Dykens and Smith 1998; Langthorne and McGill 2012), which typically manifests as hitting, grabbing, kicking, pinching, and biting (Sloneem et al. 2011).

Self-stimulatory activities in SMS can also involve inappropriate sexual behaviours. Griffiths et al. (2010) describe a young man with SMS who was referred to specialist clinical services for rubbing himself against others and inserting objects into his orifices. Staff also noted that he engaged in aggressive hugging and tended to strip off his clothes. There is little evidence that such behaviours are driven by sexual pleasure (Griffiths et al. 2010), and the authors propose that the rubbing and inserting objects may have been due to peripheral neuropathy whilst the stripping was likely associated with a tactile sensitivity (Griffiths et al. 2010). Nevertheless, and this is not unique to SMS, sexual gratification can sometimes arise from sensory-related or self-stimulating behaviours, which may then become the intrinsic reinforcement for the behaviour (Griffiths et al. 2010). These behaviours may be considered an offence if they involve another person or are conducted in the presence of others. Education about the rights of others and when and where it is appropriate to engage in sexual behaviours can help to minimise inappropriate behaviours.

Finally, sleep disturbance is almost universal in SMS (Greenberg et al. 1996) and this, too, may result in daytime behavioural problems. It is thought that sleep problems in SMS may be caused by reduced night-time and increased daytime melatonin release. This can be improved in some individuals by administering a β1-adrenergic antagonist to reduce melatonin release in the day and a low dose of melatonin before bed to increase melatonin at night (De Leersnyder et al. 2001, 2003). The authors of these trials also reported a reduction in problem behaviour, including tantrums, following such treatment.

4.9.1.2.4 Williams Syndrome

Williams syndrome (WS) is caused by a microdeletion on chromosome 7q11.23 and has a prevalence of one in 7500 (Strømme et al. 2002). The physical characteristics include distinct facial features, short stature, connective tissue abnormalities, and cardiovascular disease (Morris et al. 2000). Their chronic physical problems can lead many adults to become very anxious and concerned about their state of health. Hyperacusis or oversensitivity to sound is another, very common and often distressing problem.

Behavioural phenotype of WS: Most individuals with WS have mild to moderate ID. However, ID can range from borderline to severe (Einfeld et al. 1997). Expressive language and facial processing skills are better preserved than general intellectual ability and visuospatial processing skills (Bellugi et al. 2006). One of the primary characteristics of WS is a social and friendly nature. However, this is coupled with social naivety and difficulty interpreting social rules (Davies et al. 1998). People with WS are more anxious, distractible, and hyperactive and have an increased risk of specific phobias than do individuals with ID due to mixed causes (Dykens 2003; Einfeld et al. 1997; Martens et al. 2008). There is also a tendency to develop rather fixed patterns of interests or behaviour.

Behaviours and cognitive characteristics potentially associated with offending: Although there are few reports of serious offending in individuals with WS, their sociable nature, coupled with a tendency to develop very strong interests in certain people can lead to behaviours that are tantamount to stalking. This is because they fail to appreciate the intrusiveness of their behaviours and are thus very resistant to complaints, or to instructions that they should leave the individual who is at the centre of their attention alone. Impaired understanding of social cues can also result in their taking offence for little or no reason. For, example, they may become unduly distressed or angered if someone inadvertently pushes into them, or says something that they do not like. This can give rise to many difficulties for adults living in residential settings as they can become both verbally and physically aggressive towards other residents who they believe have offended them. They may make unwarranted accusations to staff or even call the police to have the offender 'taken away'.

Other problems can result if individuals are not allowed to do something they believe is within their rights. In several instances, this has led to the individual with WS making formal accusations of physical or sexual abuse against family members or staff. Such complaints can be extremely difficult to deal with as it may be very challenging to verify the truth of what is claimed. Sometimes it seems the accusation is made simply to get rid of someone with whom there has been a disagreement; at other times, of course, there may well be a foundation for the complaints.

4.9.1.2.5   Down Syndrome

Down syndrome (DS) is caused by a complete or partial trisomy of chromosome 21. DS occurs in approximately 1 in 732 live births (Canfield et al. 2006), making it the most common cause of ID. The physical characteristics of DS include short stature, hypotonia, dysmorphic facial features, broad hands, motor dysfunction, and associated medical conditions.

Behavioural phenotype of DS: ID is universal in DS and ranges from mild to profound (Rachidi and Lopes 2007). People with DS typically display relative strengths in visuospatial processing (Klein and Mervis 1999) social function and daily living skills (Dykens et al. 2006) and weaknesses in long-term (Jarrold et al. 2007) and verbal short-term memory (Jarrold and Baddeley 2001). Receptive language skills are typically better than expressive skills. Deficits in speech are often associated with hearing impairments or specific facial characteristics, such as a large tongue and narrow palate (Martin et al. 2009). People with DS exhibit fewer behavioural problems than the broader ID population (Dykens et al. 2002; Walz and Benson 2002). However, some individuals do display aggression, stubbornness, hyperactivity, inattention, disobedience, and impulsivity. For these individuals, rates of aggression typically decrease during adolescence (Dykens et al. 2002). Approximately two-thirds of individuals with DS will develop a form of dementia by the age of 60 (McCarron et al. 2014; Zigman et al. 2002). A small number of people with DS also meet the criteria for ASD. These individuals tend to exhibit higher rates of emotional and behavioural problems than individuals with DS without ASD (Warner et al. 2014).

Behaviours and cognitive characteristics potentially associated with offending: There are few reports of a person with DS being charged with a crime and even fewer of a person with DS being convicted. Poor expressive language skills may lead to misunderstandings and in some incidence altercation where a person with DS might push another person. Although not as common as in ASD or PWS, individuals with DS can also have intense interests or obsessions, which in certain circumstances could lead to inappropriate behaviour. For example, one adolescent male with DS was caught breaking into cars. It was later determined that the boy had a strong interest in music and was only breaking into cars to access the radio.

Puberty can sometimes be delayed in adolescents with DS. When it does occur, individuals with DS experience the same physical signs of sexual maturation as the TD population (Arnell et al. 1996). However, they can display inappropriate sexual behaviours such as touching private parts or masturbating in public, speaking about sexual activities inappropriately, staring at, and touching. The higher rate of inappropriate behaviours in DS compared to the general population is not due to an increased sex-drive but rather a limited understanding of social norms and lack of adequate sex education (Ginevra et al. 2016).

4.9.1.2.6   47, XYY Syndrome

Finally, we consider the risk of offending in individuals with chromosomal disorders resulting in a male inheriting an additional Y chromosome (Robinson and Jacobs 1999). The most common cause of XYY syndrome is a non-disjunction event in paternal meiosis, with the estimated prevalence being 1 in 1000 males (Morris et al. 2008). For some decades, it was claimed that the presence of the extra Y chromosome was associated with criminality and aggression (Casey et al. 1966; Hook and Kim 1970; Jacobs et al. 1965). The argument behind this assumption was that, since men with a single Y chromosome are more likely to commit acts of violence than women, then the presence of two Y chromosomes would significantly increase the risk of such behaviour. The extra Y chromosome was even called 'the chromosome of crime'. However, there is no statistical evidence to support the link between 47, XXY and violence or deviant behaviour. A systematic review of studies concerning 47, XXY over the past 50 years concluded that the only characteristics frequently correlated with the 47, XXY genotype are tall stature, intellectual deficit, language delays, and social–emotional problems (Re and Birkhoff 2015). A study of 161 men with 47, XXY syndrome showed that when adjusting for socio-economic status the risk of conviction in 47, XXY men was similar to that of TD controls (Stochholm et al. 2012). Nevertheless, despite the lack of evidence, the stigma associated with this myth persists (Shani and Barilan 2012).

4.10   Victimisation of People with ID

Although there is no evidence that individuals with genetic disorders and IDD have a high risk of offending, the presence of IDD is, in contrast, a significant risk factor for becoming a victim of crime (Fisher et al. 2016; Wilson and Brewer 1992).

The highest risks are for sexual abuse, assault, and robbery (Lin et al. 2009; Wilson and Brewer 1992) but a range of other crimes has also been reported (Lewin 2007; McMahon et al. 2004). A review of 23 studies relating to victimization of adults with IDD found that perpetrators were more likely to be male than female and victims most often knew the perpetrator. The most common relationship perpetrators had to their victim were residential care staff and acquaintances, although this varied widely (Fisher et al. 2016). The characteristics that increased a person's vulnerability to victimization were the presence of ID, higher rate of behaviour problems (Fisher et al. 2012), poor decision-making skills (Hickson et al. 2008), poor interpersonal competence (Wilson et al. 1996) and lack of education on rights and sexuality (McCabe et al. 1994). Specific characteristics of genetic disorders can also increase the risk of victimization. For example, the inherent sociability of individuals with DS or WS may increase their vulnerability to abuse. Thus, a heightened risk of sexual abuse, amongst individuals with WS, is associated with their sociable nature and eagerness to please, coupled with impairments in social understanding (Davies et al. 1998).

Only one study has directly examined whether victimization differs across genetic disorders (Fisher et al. 2013). This study examined the rate and types of victimization as well as social vulnerabilities in individuals with ASD, DS, and WS. Contrary to expectations, the rates and types of victimization were similar across the three groups. There were, however, important differences in the type of social vulnerabilities identified. Individuals with ASD had less social protection from peers, e.g. fewer friends and were less likely to be a part of a peer network. Both individuals with ASD and DS were rated as being less aware of risks than the WS group. This included being less likely to tell people in authority about bullying or abusive behaviour, less likely to know that they have a disability, and less able to describe their disability to others. In contrast, the vulnerability of individuals with WS was associated with having greater independence from parents. Individuals with WS were more likely to be left alone overnight and allowed to be left alone with someone of the opposite sex. Both the DS and WS participants were reported to appear more vulnerable than the ASD group, probably because both conditions are associated with distinct facial features that make the disability more recognizable. Alternatively, individuals with ASD do not typically differ in appearance to the general population. These differences in social vulnerabilities suggest that interventions designed to address potential risk factors should be tailored to the different conditions.

4.11 Conclusion

Few studies have investigated the nature of offending in genetic disorders associated with IDD, presumably because there is little evidence that these disorders increase the risk of offending. Nevertheless, research conducted in the broader ID community and ASD have highlighted several potential behavioural and cognitive characteristics associated with offending. Aggression is one of the most common behaviours associated with offending in IDD, and this is unsurprising given that aggression is the most common form of maladaptive behaviour in the IDD population and some genetic syndromes. For people with IDD, aggression is more often reactive than proactive and is likely associated with impaired emotion regulation. This is particularly evident in PWS where aggression usually occurs only during a temper outburst. In individuals with SMS and FXS, too, aggression tends to be associated with sleep and sensory problems, respectively. When aggression is premeditated, it may be associated with a misunderstanding due to poor social skills, emotional immaturity or unusual beliefs and thought processes. These cognitive deficits are also involved in other forms of offending and can also increase the risk of victimisation. External factors may have a greater impact on offending in IDD and ASD than in the TD population. These factors often include poor social support, childhood adversities, and limited access to employment and services. Educating people with IDD about social norms, sex-related behaviours, their rights and the rights of others can help to minimise the risk of offending and victimisation. It is also important that caregivers are aware of the risk factors of offending or victimisation associated with the individual's disorder, since some behaviours, such as sociability in DS and WS, may only be problematic under certain conditions, such as with increased independence.

References

Aguilar-Cárceles, M.M. and Farrington, D.P. (2017). Attention deficit hyperactivity disorder, impulsivity, and low self-control: which is most useful in understanding and preventing offending. *Crime Psychology Review* 3 (1): 1–22.

Ali, A., Ghosh, S., Strydom, A. et al. (2016). Prisoners with intellectual disabilities and detention status. Findings from a UK cross sectional study of prisons. *Research in Developmental Disabilities* 53: 189–197.

Allen, D., Evans, C., Hider, A. et al. (2008). Offending behaviour in adults with Asperger syndrome. *Journal of Autism and Developmental Disorders* 38: 748–758.

Allerton, L.A., Welch, V., and Emerson, E. (2011). Health inequalities experienced by children and young people with intellectual disabilities: a review of literature from the United Kingdom. *Journal of Intellectual Disabilities* 15 (4): 269–278.

American Psychiatric Association (APA) (2013). *Diagnostic and Statistics Manual of Mental Disorders*, 5e. Arlington, VA: American Psychiatric Publishing.

Anderson, D.J., Lakin, K.C., Hill, B.K. et al. (1992). Social integration of older persons with mental retardation in residential facilities. *American Journal on Mental Retardation* 96 (5): 488–501.

Arnell, H., Gustafsson, J., Ivarsson, S.A. et al. (1996). Growth and pubertal development in Down syndrome. *Acta Paediatrica* 85 (9): 1102–1106.

Arseneault, L., Moffitt, T.E., Caspi, A. et al. (2000). Mental disorders and violence in a total birth cohort: results from the Dunedin Study. *Archives of General Psychiatry* 57 (10): 979–986.

Attwood, T. (2006). *The Complete Guide to Asperger's Syndrome*. Chicago: Jessica Kingsley Publishers.

Bailey, D.B., Raspa, M., Olmsted, M. et al. (2008). Co-occurring conditions associated with FMR1 gene variations: findings from a national parent survey. *American Journal of Medical Genetics Part A* 146 (16): 2060–2069.

Baird, G., Simonoff, E., Pickles, A. et al. (2006). Prevalence of disorders of the autism spectrum in a population cohort of children in South Thames: the Special Needs and Autism Project (SNAP). *The Lancet* 368 (9531): 210–215.

Baldry, E., Clarence, M., Dowse, L. et al. (2013). Reducing vulnerability to harm in adults with cognitive disabilities in the Australian criminal justice system. *Journal of Policy and Practice in Intellectual Disabilities* 10 (3): 222–229.

Barratt, E.S. (1994). Impulsiveness and aggression. *Violence and Mental Disorder: Developments in Risk Assessment* 10: 61–79.

Baumgardner, T.L., Reiss, A.L., Freund, L.S. et al. (1995). Specification of the neurobehavioral phenotype in males with fragile X syndrome. *Pediatrics* 95 (5): 744–751.

Beaudet, A.L. (2007). Autism: highly heritable but not inherited. *Nature Medicine* 13 (5): 534–536.

Bellugi, U., Lichtenberger, L., Jones, W. et al. (2006). I. The neurocognitive profile of Williams Syndrome: a complex pattern of strengths and weaknesses. *Journal of Cognitive Neuroscience* 12: 7–29.

Belser, R.C. and Sudhalter, V. (2001). Conversational characteristics of children with fragile X syndrome: repetitive speech. *American Journal on Mental Retardation* 106 (1): 28–38.

Brereton, A.V., Tonge, B.J., and Einfeld, S.L. (2006). Psychopathology in children and adolescents with autism compared to young people with intellectual disability. *Journal of Autism and Developmental Disorders* 36 (7): 863–870.

Brewer, N. and Young, R.L. (2015). *Crime and Autism Spectrum Disorder: Myths and Mechanisms*. London: Jessica Kingsley.

Brugha, T.S., McManus, S., Bankart, J. et al. (2011). Epidemiology of autism spectrum disorders in adults in the community in England. *Archives of General Psychiatry* 68 (5): 459–465.

Bruininks, R.H., Hill, B.K., and Morreau, L.E. (1988). Prevalence and implications of maladaptive behaviors and dual diagnosis in residential and other service programs. In: *Mental Retardation and Mental Health* (eds. J.A. Stark, F.J. Menolascino, M.H. Albarelli, et al.), 3–29. New York: Springer.

Canfield, M.A., Honein, M.A., Yuskiv, N. et al. (2006). National estimates and race/ethnic-specific variation of selected birth defects in the United States, 1999–2001. *Birth Defects Research Part A: Clinical and Molecular Teratology* 76 (11): 747–756.

Casey, M.D., Segall, L.J., Street, D.R.K. et al. (1966). Sex chromosome abnormalities in two state hospitals for patients requiring special security. *Nature* 209 (5023): 641–642.

Chapman, S.L.C. and Wu, L.-T. (2012). Substance abuse among individuals with intellectual disabilities. *Research in Developmental Disabilities* 33 (4): 1147–1156.

Cheely, C.A., Carpenter, L.A., Letourneau, E.J. et al. (2012). The prevalence of youth with autism spectrum disorders in the criminal justice system. *Journal of Autism and Developmental Disorders* 42 (9): 1856–1862.

Chesterman, P. and Rutter, S.C. (1993). Case report: Asperger's syndrome and sexual offending. *The Journal of Forensic Psychiatry* 4 (3): 555–562.

Clarke, D.J., Boer, H., Whittington, J. et al. (2002). Prader-Willi syndrome, compulsive and ritualistic behaviours: the first population-based survey. *The British Journal of Psychiatry* 180 (4): 358–362.

Cohen, I.L., Fisch, G.S., Sudhalter, V. et al. (1988). Social gaze, social avoidance, and repetitive behavior in fragile X males: a controlled study. *American Journal on Mental Retardation* 92 (5): 436–446.

Coolidge, F.L., Segal, D.L., Klebe, K.J. et al. (2009). Psychometric properties of the Coolidge Correctional Inventory in a sample of 3,962 prison inmates. *Behavioral Sciences & the Law* 27 (5): 713–726.

Crocker, A.G., Mercier, C., Allaire, J. et al. (2007). Profiles and correlates of aggressive behaviour among adults with intellectual disabilities. *Journal of Intellectual Disability Research* 51 (10): 786–801.

Davies, M., Udwin, O., and Howlin, P. (1998). Adults with Williams syndrome. Preliminary study of social, emotional and behavioural difficulties. *The British Journal of Psychiatry* 172 (3): 273–276.

De Leersnyder, H., Bresson, J.L., de Blois, M.C. et al. (2003). β1-adrenergic antagonists and melatonin reset the clock and restore sleep in a circadian disorder, Smith-Magenis syndrome. *Journal of Medical Genetics* 40: 74–78.

De Leersnyder, H., de Blois, M.C., Vekemans, M. et al. (2001). β1-adrenergic antagonists improve sleep and behavioural disturbances in a circadian disorder, Smith-Magenis syndrome. *Journal of Medical Genetics* 38: 586–590.

Dekker, M.C., Koot, H.M., Ende, J.V.D. et al. (2002). Emotional and behavioral problems in children and adolescents with and without intellectual disability. *Journal of Child Psychology and Psychiatry* 43 (8): 1087–1098.

Department for Children, Schools and Families (2008). *Bullying Involving Children with Special Educational Needs and Disabilities*. London: Department for Children, Schools and Families.

Derzon, J.H. (2010). The correspondence of family features with problem, aggressive, criminal, and violent behavior: a meta-analysis. *Journal of Experimental Criminology* 6 (3): 263–292.

Developmental Disabilities Monitoring Network Surveillance Year 2010 Principal Investigators; Centers for Disease Control and Prevention (CDC) (2014). Prevalence of autism spectrum disorder among children aged 8 years-autism and developmental disabilities monitoring network, 11 sites, United States, 2010. *Morbidity and Mortality Weekly Report: Surveillance Summaries* 63 (2): 1.

Dubourg, C., Bonnet-Brilhault, F., Toutain, A. et al. (2014). Identification of nine new RAI1-truncating mutations in Smith-Magenis syndrome patients without 17p11. 2 deletions. *Molecular Syndromology* 5 (2): 57–64.

Dykens, E.M. (2003). Anxiety, fears, and phobias in persons with Williams syndrome. *Developmental Neuropsychology* 23 (1–2): 291–316.

Dykens, E. and Cassidy, S. (1995). Correlates of maladaptive behavior in children and adults with Prader-Willi syndrome. *American Journal of Medical Genetics* 60 (6): 546–549.

Dykens, E.M., Finucane, B.M., and Gayley, C. (1997). Brief report: cognitive and behavioral profiles in persons with Smith-Magenis syndrome. *Journal of Autism and Developmental Disorders* 27 (2): 203–211.

Dykens, E., Hodapp, R., and Evans, D. (2006). Profiles and development of adaptive behavior in children with Down syndrome. *Down Syndrome Research and Practice* 9 (3): 45–50.

Dykens, E., Lee, E., and Roof, E. (2011). Prader-Willi syndrome and autism spectrum disorders: an evolving story. *Journal of Neurodevelopmental Disorders* 3 (3): 225–237.

Dykens, E.M., Maxwell, M.A., Pantino, E. et al. (2007). Assessment of hyperphagia in Prader-Willi syndrome. *Obesity* 15 (7): 1816–1826.

Dykens, E.M. and Rosner, B.A. (1999). Refining behavioral phenotypes: personality, motivation in Williams and Prader-Willi syndromes. *American Journal on Mental Retardation* 104 (2): 158–169.

Dykens, E.M., Shah, B., Sagun, J. et al. (2002). Maladaptive behaviour in children and adolescents with Down's syndrome. *Journal of Intellectual Disability Research* 46 (6): 484–492.

Dykens, E.M. and Smith, A.C.M. (1998). Distinctiveness and correlates of maladaptive behaviour in children and adolescents with Smith-Magenis syndrome. *Journal of Intellectual Disability Research* 42: 481–489.

Einfeld, S.L. and Hall, W. (1994). When is a behavioural phenotype not a phenotype. *Developmental Medicine & Child Neurology* 36 (5): 467–470.

Einfeld, S.L., Piccinin, A.M., Mackinnon, A. et al. (2006). Psychopathology in young people with intellectual disability. *The Journal of the American Medical Association* 296 (16): 1981–1989.

Einfeld, S., Smith, A., Durvasula, S. et al. (1999). Behavior and emotional disturbance in Prader-Willi syndrome. *American Journal of Medical Genetics* 82 (2): 123–127.

Einfeld, S.L. and Tonge, B.J. (1996). Population prevalence of psychopathology in children and adolescents with intellectual disability: II epidemiological findings. *Journal of Intellectual Disability Research* 40 (2): 99–109.

Einfeld, S.L., Tonge, B.J., and Florio, T. (1997). I. The neurocognitive profile of Williams syndrome: a complex pattern of strengths and weaknesses. *Journal of Cognitive Neuroscience* 12: 7–29.

Emerson, E. (2001). *Challenging Behaviour: Analysis and Intervention in People with Severe Intellectual Disabilities*. Cambridge: Cambridge University Press.

Emerson, E. (2013). Commentary: childhood exposure to environmental adversity and the well-being of people with intellectual disabilities. *Journal of Intellectual Disability Research* 57 (7): 589–600.

Emerson, E., Graham, H., and Hatton, C. (2005). Household income and health status in children and adolescents in Britain. *The European Journal of Public Health* 16 (4): 354–360.

Emerson, E. and Halpin, S. (2013). Anti-social behaviour and police contact among 13-to 15-year-old English adolescents with and without mild/moderate intellectual disability. *Journal of Applied Research in Intellectual Disabilities* 26 (5): 362–369.

Emerson, E. and Hatton, C. (2007). Mental health of children and adolescents with intellectual disabilities in Britain. *The British Journal of Psychiatry* 191 (6): 493–499.

Erskine, H.E., Baxter, A.J., Patton, G. et al. (2017). The global coverage of prevalence data for mental disorders in children and adolescents. *Epidemiology and Psychiatric Sciences* 26 (4): 395–402.

Farrington, D.P. (1986). Age and crime. In: *Crime and Justice: An Annual Review of Research*, vol. 7 (eds. M. Tonry and N. Morris), 189–250. Chicago, IL: University of Chicago Press.

Farrington, D.P. (2017). Psychological contributions to the explanation and prevention of offending. *RPsych Rechtspsychologie* 3 (1): 31–47.

Farrington, D.P. and Welsch, B.C. (2006). Individual factors. In: *Saving Children from a Life of Crime: Early Risk Factors and Effective Interventions* (eds. D.P. Farrington and B.C. Welsh), 37–54. Oxford: Oxford University Press.

Finucane, B.M., Konar, D., Givler, B.H. et al. (1994). The spasmodic upper-body squeeze: a characteristic behavior in Smith-Magenis syndrome. *Developmental Medicine & Child Neurology* 36 (1): 78–83.

Fisher, M.H., Baird, J.V., Currey, A.D. et al. (2016). Victimisation and social vulnerability of adults with intellectual disability: a review of research extending beyond Wilson and Brewer. *Australian Psychologist* 51 (2): 114–127.

Fisher, M.H., Moskowitz, A.L., and Hodapp, R.M. (2012). Vulnerability and experiences related to social victimization among individuals with intellectual and developmental disabilities. *Journal of Mental Health Research in Intellectual Disabilities* 5 (1): 32–48.

Fisher, M.H., Moskowitz, A.L., and Hodapp, R.M. (2013). Differences in social vulnerability among individuals with autism spectrum disorder, Williams syndrome, and Down syndrome. *Research in Autism Spectrum Disorders* 7 (8): 931–937.

Freund, L.S. and Reiss, A.L. (1991). Cognitive profiles associated with the fragile X syndrome in males and females. *American Journal of Medical Genetics Part A* 38 (4): 542–547.

Freund, L.S., Reiss, A.L., and Abrams, M.T. (1993). Psychiatric disorders associated with fragile X in the young female. *Pediatrics* 91 (2): 321–329.

Ghaziuddin, M., Tsai, L., and Ghaziuddin, N. (1991). Brief report: violence in Asperger syndrome, a critique. *Journal of Autism and Developmental Disorders* 21 (3): 349–354.

Ginevra, M.C., Nota, L., and Stokes, M.A. (2016). The differential effects of Autism and Down's syndrome on sexual behavior. *Autism Research* 9 (1): 131–140.

Gray, K., Keating, C., Taffe, J. et al. (2012). Trajectory of behavior and emotional problems in autism. *American Journal on Intellectual and Developmental Disabilities* 117 (2): 121–133.

Greenberg, F., Guzzetta, V., de Oca-Luna, R.M. et al. (1991). Molecular analysis of the Smith-Magenis syndrome: a possible contiguous-gene syndrome associated with del (17) (p11. 2). *American Journal of Human Genetics* 49 (6): 1207–1218.

Greenberg, F., Lewis, R.A., Potocki, L. et al. (1996). Multi-disciplinary clinical study of Smith-Magenis syndrome (deletion 17p11. 2). *American Journal of Medical Genetics Part A* 62 (3): 247–254.

Grefer, M., Flory, K., Cornish, K. et al. (2016). The emergence and stability of attention deficit hyperactivity disorder in boys with fragile X syndrome. *Journal of Intellectual Disability Research* 60 (2): 167–178.

Griffiths, D., Fedoroff, P., and Richards, D. (2010). Sexual and gender identity disorders. In: *Assessment and treatment of sexual offenders with intellectual disabilities: a handbook* (eds. L.A. Craig, K.D. Browne and W.R. Lindsay), 111–135. Chicester, UK: Wiley.

Hagerman, R.J. and Hagerman, P.J. (2002). Fragile X syndrome. In: *Outcomes in Neurodevelopmental and Genetic Disorders* (eds. P. Howlin and O. Udwin), 198–219. Cambridge: Cambridge University Press.

Hagerman, R.J., Jackson, C., Amiri, K. et al. (1992). Girls with fragile X syndrome: physical and neurocognitive status and outcome. *Pediatrics* 89 (3): 395–400.

Hall, S.S., Barnett, R.P., and Hustyi, K.M. (2016). Problem behaviour in adolescent boys with fragile X syndrome: relative prevalence, frequency and severity. *Journal of intellectual Disability Research* 60 (12): 1189–1199.

Hare, D.J., Gould, J., Mills, R. et al. (1999). *A preliminary study of individuals with autistic spectrum disorders in three special hospitals in England*. London: National Autistic Society/Department of Health.

Hayes, S., Shackell, P., Mottram, P. et al. (2007). The prevalence of intellectual disability in a major UK prison. *British Journal of Learning Disabilities* 35: 162–167.

Heeramun, R., Magnusson, C., Gumpert, C.H. et al. (2017). Autism and convictions for violent crimes: population-based cohort study in Sweden. *Journal of the American Academy of Child and Adolescent Psychiatry* 56 (6): 491–497.

Helverschou, S.B., Rasmussen, K., Steindal, K. et al. (2015). Offending profiles of individuals with autism spectrum disorder: a study of all individuals with autism spectrum disorder examined by the forensic psychiatric service in Norway between 2000 and 2010. *Autism* 19 (7): 850–858.

Helverschou, S.B., Steindal, K., Nøttestad, J.A. et al. (2017). Personal experiences of the criminal justice system by individuals with autism spectrum disorders. *Autism* https://doi.org/10.1177/1362361316685554.

Hessl, D., Dyer-Friedman, J., Glaser, B. et al. (2001). The influence of environmental and genetic factors on behavior problems and autistic symptoms in boys and girls with fragile X syndrome. *Pediatrics* 108 (5): e88.

Hickson, L., Khemka, I., Golden, H. et al. (2008). Profiles of women who have mental retardation with and without a documented history of abuse. *American Journal on Mental Retardation* 113 (2): 133–142.

Holland, A.J. (2004). Criminal behaviour and developmental disability: an epidemiological perspective. In: *Offenders with Developmental Disabilities* (eds. W.R. Lindsay, J.L. Taylor and P. Sturmey), 23–34. Chichester, UK: Wiley.

Holland, A.J., Whittington, J.E., Butler, J. et al. (2003). Behavioural phenotypes associated with specific genetic disorders: evidence from a population-based study of people with Prader-Willi syndrome. *Psychological Medicine* 33 (01): 141–153.

Hook, E.B. and Kim, D.S. (1970). Prevalence of XYY and XXY karyotypes in 337 non-retarded young offenders. *New England Journal of Medicine* 283 (8): 410–411.

Howlin, P. (2004). *Autism and Asperger Syndrome: Preparing for Adulthood*. London: Routledge.

Hunter, J., Rivero Arias, O., Angelov, A. et al. (2014). Epidemiology of fragile X syndrome: a systematic review and meta analysis. *American Journal of Medical Genetics Part A* 164 (7): 1648–1658.

Inclusion International (2006). *Hear Our Voices: A Global Report – People with an Intellectual Disability and their Families Speak out on Poverty and Exclusion*. London: University of East London, The Rix Centre.

Jacobs, P.A., Brunton, M., Melville, M.M. et al. (1965). Aggressive behaviour, mental sub-normality and the XYY male. *Nature* 208 (5017): 1351–1352.

Jacquemont, M.-L., Sanlaville, D., Redon, R. et al. (2006). Array-based comparative genomic hybridisation identifies high frequency of cryptic chromosomal rearrangements in patients with syndromic autism spectrum disorders. *Journal of Medical Genetics* 43 (11): 843–849.

Jarrold, C. and Baddeley, A. (2001). Short-term memory in Down syndrome: applying the working memory model. *Down Syndrome Research and Practice* 7 (1): 17–23.

Jarrold, C., Baddeley, A.D., and Phillips, C. (2007). Long-term memory for verbal and visual information in Down syndrome and Williams syndrome: performance on the doors and people test. *Cortex* 43 (2): 233–247.

Kawakami, C., Ohnishi, M., Sugiyama, T. et al. (2012). The risk factors for criminal behaviour in high-functioning autism spectrum disorders (HFASDs): a comparison of childhood adversities between individuals with HFASDs who exhibit criminal behaviour and those with HFASD and no criminal histories. *Journal of Interpersonal Violence* 6 (2): 949–957.

King, C. and Murphy, G.H. (2014). A systematic review of people with autism spectrum disorder and the criminal justice system. *Journal of Autism and Developmental Disorders* 44 (11): 2717–2733.

Klein, B.P. and Mervis, C.B. (1999). Contrasting patterns of cognitive abilities of 9-and 10-year-olds with Williams syndrome or Down syndrome. *Developmental Neuropsychology* 16 (2): 177–196.

Koenig, K., Klin, A., and Schultz, R. (2004). Deficits in social attribution ability in Prader Willi syndrome. *Journal of Autism and Developmental Disorders* 34 (5): 573–582.

Kumagami, T. and Matsuura, N. (2009). Prevalence of pervasive developmental disorder in juvenile court cases in Japan. *The Journal of Forensic Psychiatry & Psychology* 20 (6): 974–987.

Langdon, P.E., Murphy, G.H., Clare, I.C.H. et al. (2011). Relationships among moral reasoning, empathy, and distorted cognitions in men with intellectual disabilities and a history of criminal offending. *American Journal of Intellectual and Developmental Disabilities* 116: 438–456.

Långström, N., Grann, M., Ruchkin, V. et al. (2009). Risk factors for violent offending in autism spectrum disorder: a national study of hospitalized individuals. *Journal of Interpersonal Violence* 24 (8): 1358–1370.

Langthorne, P. and McGill, P. (2012). An indirect examination of the function of problem behavior associated with fragile X syndrome and Smith-Magenis syndrome. *Journal of Autism and Developmental Disorders* 42 (2): 201–209.

Langthorne, P., McGill, P., O'Reilly, M.F. et al. (2011). Examining the function of problem behavior in fragile X syndrome: preliminary experimental analysis. *American Journal of Intellectual and Developmental Disabilities* 116 (1): 65–80.

Leonard, H., Petterson, B., De Klerk, N. et al. (2005). Association of sociodemographic characteristics of children with intellectual disability in Western Australia. *Social Science & Medicine* 60 (7): 1499–1513.

Lerner, M.D., Haque, O.S., Northrup, E.C. et al. (2012). Emerging perspectives on adolescents and young adults with high-functioning autism spectrum disorders, violence, and criminal law. *Journal of the American Academy of Psychiatry and the Law Online* 40 (2): 177–190.

Lewin, B. (2007). Who cares about disabled victims of crime? Barriers and facilitators for redress. *Journal of Policy and Practice in Intellectual Disabilities* 4 (3): 170–176.

Lin, L.-P., Yen, C.-F., Kuo, F.-Y. et al. (2009). Sexual assault of people with disabilities: results of a 2002–2007 national report in Taiwan. *Research in Developmental Disabilities* 30 (5): 969–975.

Lindsay, W.R., Carson, D., Holland, A.J. et al. (2013a). Alcohol and its relationship to offence variables in a cohort of offenders with intellectual disability. *Journal of Intellectual and Developmental Disability* 38 (4): 325–331.

Lindsay, W.R., Carson, D., Holland, A.J. et al. (2013b). The impact of known criminogenic factors on offenders with intellectual disability: previous findings and new results on ADHD. *Journal of Applied Research in Developmental Disabilities* 26 (1): 71–80.

Lindsay, W.R., Law, J., and MacLeod, F. (2004). Intellectual disabilities and crime: issues in assessment, intervention and management. In: *Applying Psychology to Forensic Practice* (eds. A. Needs and G. Towl), 97–114. Oxford, UK: Blackwell Publishing Ltd.

Lindsay, W.R., O'Brien, G., Carson, D. et al. (2010). Pathways into services for offenders with intellectual disabilities: childhood experiences, diagnostic information, and offense variables. *Criminal Justice and Behavior* 37 (6): 678–694.

Lionti, T., Reid, S.M., White, S.M. et al. (2015). A population based profile of 160 Australians with Prader Willi syndrome: trends in diagnosis, birth prevalence and birth characteristics. *American Journal of Medical Genetics Part A* 167 (2): 371–378.

Lipsey, M.W. and Derzon, J.H. (1998). Predictors of violent or serious delinquency in adolescence and early adulthood: a synthesis of longitudinal research. In: *Serious and Violent Juvenile Offenders: Risk Factors and Successful Interventions* (ed. D.P. Farrington), 86–105. Thousand Oaks: CA: Sage.

Lo, S.T., Siemensma, E., Collin, P. et al. (2013). Impaired theory of mind and symptoms of Autism Spectrum Disorder in children with Prader-Willi syndrome. *Research in Developmental Disabilities* 34 (9): 2764–2773.

Loomes, R., Hull, L., and Mandy, W.P.L. (2017). What is the male-to-female ratio in autism spectrum disorder? A systematic review and meta-analysis. *Journal of the American Academy of Child & Adolescent Psychiatry* 56 (6): 466–474.

Lyall, I., Holland, A.J., Collins, S. et al. (1995). Incidence of persons with a learning disability detained in police custody. A needs assessment for service development. *Medicine, Science and the Law* 35: 61–71.

Marsh, A.A. and Blair, R.J.R. (2008). Deficits in facial affect recognition among antisocial populations: a meta-analysis. *Neuroscience & Biobehavioral Reviews* 32 (3): 454–465.

Martens, M.A., Wilson, S.J., and Reutens, D.C. (2008). Research review: Williams syndrome: a critical review of the cognitive, behavioral, and neuroanatomical phenotype. *Journal of Child Psychology and Psychiatry* 49 (6): 576–608.

Martin, G.E., Klusek, J., Estigarribia, B. et al. (2009). Language characteristics of individuals with Down syndrome. *Topics in Language Disorders* 29 (2): 112–132.

Martin, G.E., Roberts, J.E., Helm-Estabrooks, N. et al. (2012). Perseveration in the connected speech of boys with fragile X syndrome with and without autism spectrum disorder. *American Journal on Intellectual and Developmental Disabilities* 117 (5): 384–399.

Mathersul, D., McDonald, S., and Rushby, J.A. (2013). Understanding advanced theory of mind and empathy in high-functioning adults with autism spectrum disorder. *Journal of Clinical and Experimental Neuropsychology* 35 (6): 655–668.

Mawson, D.C., Grounds, A., and Tantam, D. (1985). Violence and Asperger's syndrome: a case study. *The British Journal of Psychiatry* 147: 566–569.

Mazefsky, C.A. and White, S.W. (2014). Emotion regulation: concepts & practice in autism spectrum disorder. *Child and Adolescent Psychiatric Clinics of North America* 23 (1): 15–24.

McBrien, J., Hodgetts, A., and Gregory, J. (2003). Offending and risky behaviour in community services for people with intellectual disabilities in one local authority. *Journal of Forensic Psychiatry & Psychology* 14 (2): 280–297.

McCabe, M.P., Cummins, R.A., and Reid, S.B. (1994). An empirical study of the sexual abuse of people with intellectual disability. *Sexuality and Disability* 12 (4): 297–306.

McCarron, M., McCallion, P., Reilly, E. et al. (2014). A prospective 14-year longitudinal follow-up of dementia in persons with Down syndrome. *Journal of Intellectual Disability Research* 58 (1): 61–70.

McDermott, E. and Langdon, P.E. (2016). The moral reasoning abilities of men and women with intellectual disabilities who have a history of criminal offending behaviour. *Legal and Criminological Psychology* 21 (1): 25–40.

McGillicuddy, N.B. (2006). A review of substance use research among those with mental retardation. *Developmental Disabilities Research Reviews* 12 (1): 41–47.

McGillivray, J.A., Gaskin, C.J., Newton, D.C. et al. (2016). Substance use, offending, and participation in alcohol and drug treatment programmes: a comparison of prisoners with and without intellectual disabilities. *Journal of Applied Research in Intellectual Disabilities* 29 (3): 289–294.

McGillivray, J.A. and Moore, M.R. (2001). Substance use by offenders with mild intellectual disability. *Journal of Intellectual and Developmental Disability* 26 (4): 297–310.

McLachlan, K. (2016). Intellectual disability among offenders in correctional forensic settings. In: *Handbook of Forensic Mental Health Services* (eds. R. Roesch and A.N. Cook), 344–368. New York: Taylor & Francis.

McMahon, B.T., West, S.L., Lewis, A.N. et al. (2004). Hate crimes and disability in America. *Rehabilitation Counselling Bulletin* 47 (2): 66–75.

McNulty, C., Kissi-Deborah, R., and Newsome-Davies, I. (1995). Police involvement with clients having intellectual disabilities: a pilot study in South London. *Journal of Applied Research in Intellectual Disabilities* 8 (2): 129–136.

Mears, D.P. and Cochran, J.C. (2013). What is the effect of IQ on offending? *Criminal Justice and Behavior* 40 (11): 1280–1300.

Moeller, F.G., Barratt, E.S., Dougherty, D.M. et al. (2001). Psychiatric aspects of impulsivity. *American Journal of Psychiatry* 158 (11): 1783–1793.

Morris, J.K., Alberman, E., Scott, C. et al. (2008). Is the prevalence of Klinefelter syndrome increasing? *European Journal of Human Genetics* 16: 163–170.

Morris, M.D., Colleen, A., Mervis, P.D. et al. (2000). Williams syndrome and related disorders. *Annual Review of Genomics and Human Genetics* 1: 461–484.

Mouridsen, S.E. (2012). Current status of research on autism spectrum disorders and offending. *Research in Autism Spectrum Disorders* 6 (1): 79–86.

Mouridsen, S.E., Rich, B., Isager, T. et al. (2008). Pervasive developmental disorders and criminal behaviour: a case control study. *International Journal of Offender Therapy and Comparative Criminology* 52 (2): 196–205.

Murphy, D. (2017). Sense and sensibility: forensic issues with Autism Spectrum Disorders. In: *Autism Spectrum Disorders in Adults* (eds. B.B. Corrêa and R.J. van ger Gaag), 247–266. Cham: Springer.

Newman, S.S. and Ghaziuddin, M. (2008). Violent crime in Asperger syndrome: the role of psychiatric comorbidity. *Journal of Autism and Developmental Disorders* 38 (10): 1848.

O'Brien, G., Taylor, J., Lindsay, W. et al. (2010). A multi-centre study of adults with learning disabilities referred to services for antisocial or offending behaviour: demographic, individual, offending and service characteristics. *Journal of Learning Disabilities and Offending Behaviour* 1 (2): 5–15.

Oeseburg, B., Dijkstra, G.J., Groothoff, J.W. et al. (2011). Prevalence of chronic health conditions in children with intellectual disability: a systematic literature review. *Intellectual and Developmental Disabilities* 49 (2): 59–85.

Osório, A., Cruz, R., Sampaio, A. et al. (2012). Cognitive functioning in children and adults with Smith-Magenis syndrome. *European Journal of Medical Genetics* 55 (6): 394–399.

Pallone, N.J. and Hennessy, J.J. (1996). *Tinder-Box Criminal Aggression: Neuropsychology, Demography, Phenomenology*. New Brunswick: Transaction Publishers.

Parmenter, T.R., Einfeld, S.L., Tonge, B.J. et al. (1998). Behavioural and emotional problems in the classroom of children and adolescents with intellectual disability. *Journal of Intellectual and Developmental Disability* 23 (1): 71–77.

Parry, C.J. and Lindsay, W.R. (2003). Impulsiveness as a factor in sexual offending by people with mild intellectual disability. *Journal of Intellectual Disability Research* 47 (6): 483–487.

Piquero, A.R., Jennings, W.G., Diamond, B. et al. (2015). A systematic review of age, sex, ethnicity, and race as predictors of violent recidivism. *International Journal of Offender Therapy and Comparative Criminology* 59 (1): 5–26.

Poisson, A., Nicolas, A., Cochat, P. et al. (2015). Behavioral disturbance and treatment strategies in Smith-Magenis syndrome. *Orphanet Journal of Rare Diseases* 10 (1): 111.

Put, C.E., Asscher, J.J., Wissink, I.B. et al. (2014). The relationship between maltreatment, victimisation and sexual and violent offending: differences between adolescent offenders with and without intellectual disability. *Journal of Intellectual Disability Research* 58 (11): 979–991.

Rachidi, M. and Lopes, C. (2007). Mental retardation in Down syndrome: from gene dosage imbalance to molecular and cellular mechanisms. *Neuroscience Research* 59 (4): 349–369.

Rava, J., Shattuck, P., Rast, J. et al. (2017). The prevalence and correlates of involvement in the criminal justice system among youth on the autism spectrum. *Journal of Autism and Developmental Disorders* 47 (2): 340–346.

Re, L. and Birkhoff, J.M. (2015). The 47, XYY syndrome, 50 years of certainties and doubts: a systematic review. *Aggression and Violent Behavior* 22: 9–17.

Rice, L.J. and Einfeld, S.L. (2015). Cognitive and behavioural aspects of Prader-Willi syndrome. *Current Opinion in Psychiatry* 28 (2): 102–106.

Rice, L.J., Gray, K.M., Howlin, P. et al. (2015). The developmental trajectory of disruptive behavior in Down syndrome, fragile X syndrome, Prader–Willi syndrome and Williams syndrome. *American Journal of Medical Genetics Part C: Seminars in Medical Genetics* 169 (2): 182–187.

Robertson, G. (1981). The extent and pattern of crime amongst mentally handicapped offenders. *British Journal of Learning Disabilities* 9 (3): 100–103.

Robinson, D.O. and Jacobs, P.A. (1999). The origin of the extra Y chromosome in males with a 47, XYY karyotype. *Human Molecular Genetics* 8 (12): 2205–2209.

Rogers, J., Viding, E., Blair, R.J. et al. (2006). Autism spectrum disorder and psychopathy: shared cognitive underpinnings or double hit. *Psychological Medicine* 36: 1789–1798.

Rueda, P., Fernández-Berrocal, P., and Baron-Cohen, S. (2015). Dissociation between cognitive and affective empathy in youth with Asperger syndrome. *European Journal of Developmental Psychology* 12 (1): 85–98.

Shani, R. and Barilan, Y.M. (2012). Excellence, deviance, and gender: lessons from the XYY episode. *The American Journal of Bioethics* 12 (7): 27–30.

Simonoff, E., Pickles, A., Charman, T. et al. (2008). Psychiatric disorders in children with autism spectrum disorders: prevalence, comorbidity, and associated factors in a population-derived sample. *Journal of the American Academy of Child and Adolescent Psychiatry* 47 (8): 921–929.

Sloneem, J., Oliver, C., Udwin, O. et al. (2011). Prevalence, phenomenology, aetiology and predictors of challenging behaviour in Smith-Magenis syndrome. *Journal of Intellectual Disability Research* 55 (2): 138–151.

Smith, A. (1999). The diagnosis of Prader–Willi syndrome. *Journal of Paediatrics and Child Health* 35 (4): 335–337.

Snoyman, P. and Aicken, B. (2011). Self-reported impulsivity in male offenders with low cognitive ability in New South Wales prisons. *Psychology, Crime & Law* 17 (2): 151–164.

Steffensmeier, D. and Allan, E. (1996). Gender and crime: toward a gendered theory of female offending. *Annual Review of Sociology* 22: 459–487.

Stein, D.J., Keating, J., Zar, H.J. et al. (1994). A survey of the phenomenology and pharmacotherapy of compulsive and impulsive-aggressive symptoms in Prader-Willi syndrome. *The Journal of Neuropsychiatry and Clinical Neurosciences* 6: 23–29.

Stochholm, K., Bojesen, A., Jensen, A.S. et al. (2012). Criminality in men with Klinefelter's syndrome and XYY syndrome: a cohort study. *BMJ Open* 2 (1): e000650.

Stokes, M., Newton, N., and Kaur, A. (2007). Stalking, and social and romantic functioning among adolescents and adults with autism spectrum disorder. *Journal of Autism and Developmental Disorders* 37: 1969–1986.

Strømme, P., Bjømstad, P.G., and Ramstad, K. (2002). Prevalence estimation of Williams syndrome. *Journal of Child Neurology* 17 (4): 269–271.

Sullivan, K., Hatton, D., Hammer, J. et al. (2006). ADHD symptoms in children with FXS. *American Journal of Medical Genetics Part A* 140 (21): 2275–2288.

Swaab, D.F., Purba, J.S., and Hofman, M.A. (1995). Alterations in the hypothalamic paraventricular nucleus and its oxytocin neurons (putative satiety cells) in Prader-Willi syndrome: a study of five cases. *Journal of Clinical Endocrinology & Metabolism* 80 (2): 573–579.

Tint, A., Palucka, A.M., Bradley, E. et al. (2017). Correlates of police involvement among adolescents and adults with autism spectrum disorder. *Journal of Autism and Developmental Disorders* 47: 2639–2674.

Tonge, B.J. and Einfeld, S.L. (2003). Psychopathology and intellectual disability: the Australian child to adult longitudinal study. *International Review of Research in Mental Retardation* 26: 61–91.

Turner, G., Daniel, A., and Frost, M. (1980). X-linked mental retardation, macro-orchidism, and the Xq27 fragile site. *The Journal of Pediatrics* 96 (5): 837–841.

Udwin, O., Webber, C., and Horn, I. (2001). Abilities and attainment in Smith-Magenis syndrome. *Developmental Medicine and Child Neurology* 43 (12): 823–828.

United Nations (2011). *Status of the Convention on the Rights of the Child: Report of the Secretary-General*. New York: United Nations.

Vigil-Colet, A. and Morales-Vives, F. (2005). How impulsivity is related to intelligence and academic achievement. *The Spanish Journal of Psychology* 8 (2): 199–204.

Wahlund, K. and Kristiansson, M. (2006). Offender characteristics in lethal violence with special reference to antisocial and autistic personality traits. *Journal of Interpersonal Violence* 21 (8): 1081–1091.

Walker, N. and McCabe, S. (1973). *Crime and Insanity in England*, vol. 2. Edinburgh: Edinburgh University Press.

Walz, N.C. and Benson, B.A. (2002). Behavioral phenotypes in children with Down syndrome, Prader-Willi syndrome, or Angelman syndrome. *Journal of Developmental and Physical Disabilities* 14 (4): 307–321.

Warner, G., Moss, J., Smith, P. et al. (2014). Autism characteristics and behavioural disturbances in ~500 children with Down's syndrome in England and Wales. *Autism Research* 7 (4): 433–441.

Wheeler, J.R., Clare, I.C.H., and Holland, A.J. (2013). Offending by people with intellectual disabilities in community settings: a preliminary examination of contextual factors. *Journal of Applied Research in Intellectual Disabilities* 26: 370–383.

Wheeler, A.C., Raspa, M., Bishop, E. et al. (2016). Aggression in fragile X syndrome. *Journal of Intellectual Disability Research* 60 (2): 113–125.

Whittington, J. and Holland, T. (2011). Recognition of emotion in facial expression by people with Prader Willi syndrome. *Journal of Intellectual Disability Research* 55 (1): 75–84.

Wilson, C. and Brewer, N. (1992). The incidence of criminal victimisation of individuals with an intellectual disability. *Australian Psychologist* 27 (2): 114–117.

Wilson, C., Seaman, L., and Nettelbeck, T. (1996). Vulnerability to criminal exploitation: influence of interpersonal competence differences among people with mental retardation. *Journal of Intellectual Disability Research* 40 (1): 8–16.

Wing, L. (1981). Asperger's syndrome: a clinical account. *Psychological Medicine* 11 (1): 115–129.

Winter, N., Holland, A.J., and Collins, S. (1997). Factors predisposing to suspected offending by adults with self-reported learning disabilities. *Psychological Medicine* 27 (3): 595–607.

Woodbury-Smith, M.R., Clare, I.C.H., Holland, A.J. et al. (2006). High functioning autistic spectrum disorders, offending and other law-breaking: findings from a community sample. *The Journal of Forensic Psychiatry and Psychology* 17 (1): 108–120.

Woodbury-Smith, M.R., Clare, I.C.H., Holland, A.J. et al. (2005). A case-control study of offenders with high functioning autistic spectrum disorders. *Journal of Forensic Psychiatry & Psychology* 16 (4): 747–763.

Woodbury-Smith, M., Clare, I., Holland, A.J. et al. (2010). Circumscribed interests and 'offenders' with autism spectrum disorders: a case-control study. *The Journal of Forensic Psychiatry & Psychology* 21 (3): 366–377.

Woodbury-Smith, M. and Dein, K. (2014). Autism spectrum disorder (ASD) and unlawful behaviour: where do we go from here. *Journal of Autism and Developmental Disorders* 44 (11): 2734–2741.

Zigman, W.B., Schupf, N., Urv, T. et al. (2002). Incidence and temporal patterns of adaptive behavior change in adults with mental retardation. *American Journal on Mental Retardation* 107 (3): 161–174.

Part III

Validated Assessments

5

Diagnosis of Personality Disorder in Offenders with Intellectual and Developmental Disabilities

Nigel Beail

South West Yorkshire Partnership NHS Foundation Trust and the University of Sheffield, Sheffield, UK

5.1   Introduction

Personality is a term that has become embedded in popular culture; we have television personalities, sport personalities, and so on. In general conversation people use adjectives to describe others and their own personality. So how do we evaluate others and our own personally. Livesley (2001) noted that the term personality has had many definitions but found that there is a consensus concerning the fundamental elements and concepts which comprise it. First it is reflected in the way a person behaves and how they interact with others. Second it comprises the persons experience in the world; how they think, perceive the world, and how they feel. All these occur regularly and consistently across a range of situations and across the life span. So over time the person develops individual traits and attributes that form a coherent integrated system. The person then is perceived by others as having a set of characteristics and qualities that are used to define them.

Personality as a subject has been considered from many theoretical perspective from the more qualitative descriptive psychoanalytic model (Freud 1923) to the more quantitative trait approach (Cattell 1946). Quantitative research on personality has resulted in two structural models to have become established – the Five Factor Model (Cattell 1946) (extraversion-introversion, agreeableness, conscientiousness, neuroticism, and openness to experience) and the Circumplex Model (Wiggins 1982) where individual responses to questionnaires will place them on an octant of a circle with the dimensions dominance/submissiveness and hostility/nurturance. These models have been found to be robust and to complement each other. Unfortunately for some people the process of personality formation does not go so well and they are experienced and experience themselves as not so coherent or integrated. Their personality traits are inflexible and maladaptive and cause significant functional impairment or subjective distress (American Psychiatric Association 2013). These individuals have come to be described

The Wiley Handbook on What Works for Offenders with Intellectual and Developmental Disabilities:
An Evidence-Based Approach to Theory, Assessment, and Treatment, First Edition.
Edited by William R. Lindsay, Leam A. Craig, and Dorothy Griffiths.
© 2020 John Wiley & Sons Ltd. Published 2020 by John Wiley & Sons Ltd.

in clinical service systems as having a personality disorder (PD). In the chapter the focus is on PD and its relationship with offending behaviour in adults who have intellectual disabilities.

5.2   Definitions

There are two standard classificatory systems for mental disorders; the Diagnostic and Statistical Manual of Mental Disorders-V (DSM-V) (American Psychiatric Association 2013) and the International Classification of Diseases-10 (World Health Organisation 1992). Both describe and classify a range of PDs. Both have a categorical structure to classification and both have supplementary manuals for their use with people who have intellectual and developmental disabilities (IDD) (DMID-2, Fletcher et al. 2016) and DC-LD, Royal College of Psychiatrists 2001). DSM-V with DMID-2 has been the most recently revised and published; ICD-11 is under development. In view of this, and the fact that the 2016 DMID-2 has been so recently produced by a team of experts on IDD and PD from around the world, it seems more relevant to use DSM-V and DMID-2 in this chapter. PD has been described by the American Psychiatric Association (2013) as 'an enduring pattern of inner experience and behaviour that deviates markedly from the expectations of the individual's culture and is manifested in at least two of the following areas: cognition, affectivity, interpersonal functioning or impulse control' (APA 2013, p. 647). The definition goes on the state that this enduring pattern is inflexible and pervasive across a broad range of personal and social situations and leads to clinically significant distress or impairments in social, occupational, and other areas of functioning. Thus the DSM-V definition (APA 2013) emphasizes the impact that PD has on the person's life: 'personality disorders are associated with ways of thinking and feeling about oneself and others that significantly and adversely affect how an individual functions in many aspects of life'. These inner experiences and patterns of behaviour can lead to difficulties in living with oneself and other people. These 'failures to achieve adaptive solutions to life tasks' (Livesley 2001, p. 13) can include problems in relationships and relating to others, struggles with emotion control and regulation, and can be associated with, or result in, offending behaviour.

It should be noted that the definition and classification of PD in DSM-V has changed very little from DSM-IV (APA 1994). However, in their deliberations the experts working on the PD chapter in DSM-V did consider dimensional models as opposed to the categorical approach. The same deliberations are being made in the development of ICD-11. The categorical model retained in DSM-V contains 10 specific PDs and one nonspecific PD. The 11 PDs are grouped into three clusters based on their descriptive similarities. It needs to be made clear that these categories have no empirical basis; they were largely developed through the basis of clinical consensus. It is also important to note that there is considerable overlap between the categories especially within each cluster.

Cluster A contains paranoid, schizoid, and schizotypal PDs and individuals in this cluster are described as appearing odd and eccentric:

- Paranoid PD involves the person presenting with pervasive distrust and suspiciousness of others that is without sufficient evidence. The person believes that others are exploiting, deceiving, demeaning, or harming them in some way. They feel others are a threat and may also hold grudges against others.

- Schizoid PD presents as a pattern of detachment from social relationships, accompanied by a restricted range of emotional expression. The person does not enjoy close relationships, appears detached, and chooses solitary activities.
- Schizotypal PD also shows discomfort and capacity for close relationships, but also a range of cognitive distortions including magical thinking, suspiciousness, and unusual perceptual experiences.

Cluster B is defined as containing people who are dramatic, emotional, and erratic and includes antisocial, borderline, histrionic, and narcissistic PD:

- Antisocial PD is the type most frequently associated with offending behaviour. It presents as a pervasive pattern of disregard for and violation of the rights of others. This may include a failure to conform to societal norms, as disrespect of the law, and engaging in criminal acts. Other features may be deceitfulness, impulsiveness, irritability, aggression, reckless behaviour, and a lack of remorse.
- Borderline Personality Disorder (BPD) presents as a pervasive pattern of instability in the persons relationships. This can present in extreme feelings of idealization and devaluation towards others. Offending may be associated with BPD as they can present with intense feelings of anger which can result in physical aggression. However, this can also be turned towards the self in the form of suicidal and self-harming behaviour.
- Histrionic PD features excessive emotional feelings and behaviour and attention seeking. They like to be the centre of attention. Those with this disorder may come into contact with the criminal justice system due to inappropriate and provocative sexual behaviour.
- Narcissistic PD is characterized by grandiosity, lack of empathy, and a need for admiration. The person is preoccupied with power and success and believes they are special. They may come into contact with the criminal justice system through their engagement in exploitative behaviours.

Cluster C is defined as containing people who often appear anxious or fearful and includes Avoidant, Dependent, and Obsessive–Compulsive PDs.

- Avoidant PD presents as social inhibition, a preoccupation with rejection, feelings of being inadequate, and over sensitivity to criticism.
- Dependent PD is characterized by a preoccupation with needing to be taken care of and fear of separation or loss.
- Obsessive–compulsive PD presents as a preoccupation with orderliness and perfectionism. The person can be stubborn, likes to be in control and lacks flexibility.

5.3 Issues Related to Diagnosis in People with IDD

In DM-ID 2 (Fletcher et al. 2016), Lindsay et al. (2016) considered a number of issues in relation to people with IDD when considering diagnoses of PDs. They pointed out that people with IDD are likely to experience developmental delay that may result in immature and or a less completely developed personality which may cause them to have traits or features of PD. They suggested that we need to keep in mind more general work on personality structure that employs developmental models. However, they were also cognizant of the fact that this could lead to simple conclusions that people with IDD are immune from PD. The alternative DSM-V model for PD states consideration should be given to whether the person's individual personality trait expression is not better understood as typical for the individual's developmental stage. The DC-ID (Royal College of Psychiatrists 2001) stated that a diagnosis of PD should take account of the person's developmental delay and personality formation. The personality of people with IDD continues to develop through adolescence and the RCP argue that a diagnosis of PD in people with IDD should not be made until the person is 21 years old. Lindsay et al. (2016) endorse this recommendation in DMID-2.

One particular feature of many PDs is the concept of empathy. Researchers on empathy with offenders who have IDD (Procter and Beail 2007; Ralfs and Beail 2012) have employed Marshall et al.'s (1995) four stage process model of empathy. The stages are Emotion Recognition (the ability to recognize another person's emotions), Perspective Taking (the ability to see another person's point of view), Emotion Replication (the ability to feel the same emotion as another person), and Response Decision (the ability to make a decision about how to act based on the other stages). Marshall et al. (1995) propose that individuals can have deficits at different stages, such that one person can be deficient in 'perspective taking' and another deficient in 'emotion replication'. Each would lead to a deficit in the overall ability to empathize with another person. Lindsay et al. (2016) argue that these are developmental skills and so for individuals with IDD it is likely that their empathy skills will be impaired.

A further issue that Lindsay et al. (2016) draw attention to is that some people with IDD could have experienced institutional life, which may contribute to behavioural patterns that are consistent with some features of PD. However, for a diagnosis of PD the presentation must be consistent across environments. It may be that with environmental change or psychological intervention such behaviours may change and more adaptive behaviour develops.

Several items across the 11 PD diagnoses include issues relating to intimate and sexual relationships. Consideration needs to be given to the personal history of people with IDD as they may have been protected from gaining knowledge and experience in this area. Another feature of some PDs is dependency and fear of failure. People who have IDD are most likely dependent on others for some support in their lives and this may be minimal or extensive. In view of this Lindsay et al. (2016) are clear that dependent PD cannot be diagnosed in people with IDD.

An issue in the consideration of avoidant PD is the ability to make decisions. People with IDD may have compromised capacity and ability in this area due to their IDD and cultural experience (i.e. protection from carers).

Expressions of anger and aggression are considered across a range of PDs and antisocial PD in particular. Anger is a common presentation in people who have IDD and has been the most researched area of psychological intervention (Nicoll et al. 2013). Thus Lindsay et al. (2016) stated that anger and aggression should not be considered the defining characteristic in the absence of other diagnostic features.

The last issue Lindsay et al. (2016) considered is suggestibility. This is because people with IDD can be easily led and suggestible in some contexts (Beail 2002). They argued this is a cultural factor that should be taken into account. In summary Lindsay et al. (2016) found that nine of the ten PDs could apply to people who have IDD if consideration of specific factors characteristic of people with IDD are considered in the assessment and diagnostic process. Offending and PD are two constructs that have developed quite a significant association. This relationship has also become of interest in services for offenders who have IDD.

5.4   Epidemiology

The bulk of the literature on PD to date has concerned people who access mainstream mental health and forensic services. The issue of co-morbidity of IDD and PD is starting to attract research interest, and there is now an emerging literature on PD in people with IDD and a small literature on forensic IDD populations.

Diagnostic rates for PD in the general population have been reported to be around 4.4% in the UK (Coid et al. 2006) and 9% in the USA (Lewin et al. 2005). However, in forensic settings the prevalence rates have been found to be much higher. Moran (1999) reported a rate of 60% in male prisoners, and Fazel and Danesh (2002) report a rate of 42% for male and female offenders. In high secure settings rates have been around 50% (Hogue et al. 2006, Lindsay et al. 2017).

Alexander and Cooray (2003) noted a high range in variation in the diagnosis of PD in populations of people with IDD. The range they found was huge from 1% to 91% in community settings and 2% to 92% in hospital settings. They concluded that such ranges are too large to be explained by real differences. They suggested that the high rates of co-morbidity raise questions about the validity and reliability of diagnosis. They noticed a lack of diagnostic tools, use of different diagnostic systems and difficulties in distinguishing between PDs from other problems associated with IDD. In a more recent study of patients seen in two clinical services in the Netherlands, Wieland et al. (2015) found that 33.6% of 152 people who had mild IDD (IQ 50–70) were given a diagnosis of PD using DSM-IV and DM-ID. The majority of these (64%) were given a diagnosis of PD Not Otherwise Specified. There were no Cluster A diagnoses; and none with anti-social PD and nearly a quarter received a diagnosis of borderline PD. The focus of this study was people with borderline intellectual functioning and so the distribution of PDs in the mild ID clinical group was not commented upon. It is not clear over what time span the 152 people came into services. Such data inform on the frequency of PD in clinical services but does not help with understanding the prevalence in the population.

A study frequently referred to for prevalence rates of mental health difficulties in people who have ID living in the community is that of Cooper et al. (2007). They completed an administrative population study of all service users (N = 1025) with ID over the age of 16 years living in the Glasgow area of Scotland. They found a prevalence rate of 1% presenting with a PD. They do not report the breakdown of PDs found. However, such a low prevalence rate is difficult to reconcile with the rates reported by Wieland et al. (2015) in their clinical population. In their review of studies of the prevalence of PD in people with IDD who offend, Rayner et al. (2015) found five reports representing three studies which sampled from forensic ID populations across the spectrum of community services to high secure hospitals. These studies, like Wieland et al.'s were retrospective and based on file information (Devapriam et al. 2007; Hogue et al. 2006; Lindsay et al. 2006, 2007; Mannysalo et al. 2009). Lindsay et al. (2006, 2007), and Hogue et al. (2007) studied 164 men from three forensic ID services, with a comparison of the prevalence of PD between forensic community, medium/low, and high secure settings. Of the sample, 39.3% met the diagnostic criteria for at least one PD. Lindsay et al. (2017) carried out a study across the same three forensic settings and found a prevalence rate of 41.9% using a structured diagnostic approach, but a rate of only 25% using a file review approach. These figures are within the same ball park as those of Wieland et al. (2015). What is different about the findings in forensic settings is that, as would be expected, antisocial PD is the largest category followed by borderline PD (Devapriam et al. 2007; Hogue et al. 2007; Mannysalo et al. 2009). High secure settings were found to present at least one PD in half of its cases, with fewer cases in medium/low secure and community settings (Hogue et al. 2006; Lindsay et al. 2017). However, Lindsay et al.'s (2017) study found the prevalence rate in community IDD forensic services was significantly different depending on the assessment process. File data found prevalence rate of only 1.5%, but a structured assessment process based on DSM-IV found a rate of 40.6%. They speculated that community-based clinicians may not consider PD as a diagnosis and focus more on other mental health presentations, or are reluctant to use this due to the negative images which such diagnoses make. Indeed having a PD has been found to be one of three variables that predict placement in secure settings (Hogue et al. 2006).

5.5 Co-morbidity

In their general clinical population study, Wieland et al. (2015) found that 80.4% of people with mild IDD who have a PD had a co-morbid mental health difficulty. Mannysalo et al. (2009) found that a third of their sample of 44 people who had ID and a forensic history in Finland had a 'triple diagnosis' of ID, mental disorder (including mental illness or PD), and substance misuse. Alexander et al. (2012) found that 33% of the ID-PD co-morbid group had two to five previous convictions, the highest in comparison to the ID and PD alone groups.

5.6 Assessment

Lindsay et al. (2017) stated that in clinical practice most cases of PD diagnosis are established on the basis of an interview only. However, this approach is believed to be associated with significant underestimates (Taylor and Novaco 2013). Lindsay et al. (2017) compared diagnoses recorded in clinical files of offenders who have IDD with a structured system of diagnosis using DSM-IV (APA 1994) and the Structured Assessment of Personality (SAP, Pilgrim and Mann 1990). This process involves an assessment based on a file review, an assessment with a clinician familiar with the patient, an assessment with nursing or care staff who know the patient, and then a structured interview with the SAP with direct care staff. The final diagnosis is made on the presence or absence of the 93 individual traits in DSM against the 11 subtypes of PD. Using this approach they found that in high secure settings the diagnosis rates were roughly the same for both approaches, however, in medium/low and community settings the prevalence rates were much higher using a structured diagnostic approach. In considering which is the best approach, they examined the two approaches predictive validity. They point out that PD diagnosis is associated with violence in men. They found that only the structured diagnostic system could predict violence. The diagnoses extracted from case files did not predict incidents of violence at a rate better than chance.

The structured diagnostic approach may be preferable but many services lack the resources to assess everyone this way. Recognizing this, Taylor and Novaco (2013) developed the Personality Disorder Characteristics Checklist (PDCC). This is a brief screening instrument for the two most prevalent PDs in IDD forensic services – emotionally unstable (borderline) and dissocial (antisocial) PD. The population on which this study was carried out were 159 inpatients in medium- and low-secure services for offenders who have IDD. This is an 18-item staff-rated measure based on IDC-10 diagnostic criteria. They found 48% of the patients had at least three traits which are required for diagnosis. Internal reliability was good being above 0.8. The scale also correlated well with the PD and Adjustment Disorder subscales of the Psychiatric Inventory for Mentally Retarded Adults (PIMRA) (Matson et al. 1984). The scale also correlated with violent offences and assaultive behaviour in hospital. They suggested this brief screen serves to identify high-risk clients who are referred to forensic services who require particular attention to their clinical and management needs. However, they recommend that those clients identified through the PDCC should then undergo a full diagnostic assessment. Since Lindsay et al. (2017) completed their research DSM-V has been published and also DMID-2 (Fletcher et al. 2016). It is this system that is described and discussed in the definitions section of this chapter and the approach that should be used in any structured multidisciplinary assessment.

In view of the high rates of co-morbidity with other mental health problems the assessors also need to consider for the presence of these. This may be facilitated by the use of the Psychiatric Assessment Schedule for Adults who have Developmental Disabilities (Moss 2016) and other single trait and multi-trait tools that have appropriate psychometric properties (see Vlissides et al. 2016, for a review).

5.7 Interventions

The UK National Institute for Health and Care Excellence (NICE) website (nice.org.uk) is a valuable resource for clinicians seeking to provide the most evidenced-based treatments for their clients. The dilemma in services for people who have IDD is that specific advice is very limited. So there is no specific advice on the best treatment options for offenders who have PD who have IDD. There is guidance on mental health problems for people who have IDD, but PD is not covered because there is no evidence base on which to draw. However, in the absence of any evidence base for people with IDD, NICE (2016) refers you to the guidance for the general population. With regard to PD there is guidance, and some of this refers to offenders who have PD (NICE 2009a, 2009b). The two main PD's in the offender population are Borderline and Antisocial. Most NICE (2009a, 2009b) guidance and other offender literature (e.g. Davies and Nagi 2017) focus on these two presentations of PD. NICE (2009a) recommends that practitioners should ensure interventions for people with a diagnosis of PD or associated problems are supportive, facilitate learning, and develop new behaviours and coping strategies. The guidance recommends attention needs to be paid to problem-solving abilities, emotion regulation and impulse control, managing interpersonal relationships, managing self-harm and the use of medicine (including reducing polypharmacy). NICE further states that practitioners should be aware people with mental health problems and PD may reduce the effectiveness of interventions. They suggest that people may need extra support, longer-term or more frequent therapy. For people with borderline PD comprehensive multidisciplinary care plans are recommended. These should identify clear roles and responsibilities for those involved and contain short-term treatment plans and longer-term goals. It is also recommended that a crisis plan should be in place.

5.8 Psychologically Based Interventions for PD

NICE (2009a) does not explicitly recommend a particular treatment approach, but recommends an integrated theoretical approach should be used by both the treatment team and the therapist, which is shared with the service user. An example is Livesley's (2007) integrated stage model of treating PD. This approach focuses on safety and containment in the first stage. The therapist and the team provide support, validation, empathy, and emotional regulation. When the patient has developed a feeling of safety and containment they can start to develop self-regulation skills before developing more adaptive ways of thinking, behaving, and relating to others. NICE recommends that the frequency of therapy sessions should be adapted to the person's needs and context of living and that twice-weekly sessions may be considered. Brief psychological interventions are not recommended.

Early works on the use of psychological therapies with people who have borderline PD suggest that several approaches may be helpful. As evidence is emerging for the use of psychodynamic (Town et al. 2011), and Cognitive Analytic Therapy (CAT) with adolescents (Chanen et al. 2008) and adults (Clarke et al. 2013), they are being recommended. A recent theoretical model to emerge from psychodynamic psychotherapy is mentalization-based treatment (McGauley 2017). This was originally developed for the treatment of people who have borderline PD. The original study of its efficacy was embedded in an 18-month hospital programme. However, recipients showed significant improvements in their mood and interpersonal functioning (Bateman and Fonagy 2001). Its efficacy has resulted in this approach being used in forensic settings, but so far this has not been evaluated. As mentalization-based therapy brings about improvements in interpersonal functioning it seems worthwhile to explore this. Psychodynamic psychotherapy has a small evidence base with people who have IDD (Shepherd and Beail 2017) and mentalization therapy is also now being used with people who have IDD (Dekker-van der Sande and Sterkenburg 2016). In view of this there seems no reason why this should not be explored with offenders who have Borderline PD and IDD.

Shannon and Pollock (2017) suggest CAT should be explored with offenders who have PD. CAT has also been adapted for people who have IDD (Beard et al. 2016; Lloyd and Clayton 2014), and Clayton and Crowther (2014) describe how this model can be used in an integrated therapeutic community approach.

Schema therapy has been explored mainly with women who have borderline PD. This approach is now being explored with offenders who have PD (Keulen-de Vos and Bernstein 2017) and a large study of its effectiveness is taking place in the Netherlands.

For women with borderline PD for whom reducing self-harming behaviour is a priority, NICE (2009a) suggest a dialectical behaviour therapy programme. This approach has also been adapted for people who have IDD (Lippold 2016).

The evidence base for the treatment of antisocial PD is quite weak. NICE (2009b) suggest offering group-based cognitive and behavioural interventions, in order to address problems such as impulsivity, interpersonal difficulties, and antisocial behaviour. For offenders with antisocial PD they also suggest group-based cognitive and behavioural interventions focused on reducing offending and other antisocial behaviour. Of the psychological therapies Cognitive Behaviour Therapy (CBT; i.e. Nicoll et al. 2013) has the largest evidence base with people who have IDD, but this is largely for the treatment of anger problems. However, anger is a significant feature of antisocial PD. McGauley (2017) points out that the mental states associated with antisocial PD are underpinned by deficits in mentalization.

Willmot and McMurran (2016) explored the process of change amongst high secure male offenders with a primary diagnosis of PD. They tested out an attachment-based model of change and found support for a limited reparenting attachment-based model of therapeutic change. They reported that the behaviour of therapists was particularly important throughout treatment, and in the later stages of therapy this extended to the wider staff team. They argued that a secure attachment between client and therapist can be seen as enabling the development of self-regulation and mentalization and a widening range of relationships. They argued that treatment can be understood as a process of enhancing attachment security. Of relevance to here are British Psychological Society's (2017) Faculty for People who have Intellectual Disabilities' guidance on incorporating attachment theory into clinical work. In summary research on using psychological approaches to support people with PDs is still in its infancy.

5.9   Pharmacological Interventions for PD

NICE (2009a) are clear that drug treatment should not be used specifically for BPD or for the individual symptoms or behaviour associated with the disorder including self-harm, marked emotional instability, risk-taking behaviour, and transient psychotic symptoms. However, they state that sedative medication may be considered cautiously as part of the overall treatment plan for people with BPD in a crisis.

5.10   Treatment of Co-morbid Conditions

People who have PDs frequently present with co-morbid mental health difficulties such as anxiety, depression, or post-traumatic stress disorder, to name a few. NICE (2009a) recommend that these problems should be treated within a well-structured treatment programme for BPD. For some conditions such as psychosis or severe eating disorders they recommend referral to an appropriate service. For people with antisocial PD NICE (2009a) suggested treatment for any co-morbid disorders should be in line with recommendations in the relevant NICE clinical guideline. For people who have IDD, NICE (2016) recommends that the same treatments should be provided as for the general population. For a review of the wide range of psychological therapies available to people who have IDD, see Beail (2016), Fletcher (2011) and Taylor et al. (2013). Pharmacological interventions for co-morbid mental disorders, in particular depression and anxiety, should be in line with recommendations in the relevant NICE clinical guideline. For guidance on the use of psychotropic medication with people who have IDD and mental health problems see Royal College of Psychiatrists (2016).

5.11 Conclusions

This chapter suggests that we have a long way to go in developing an understanding of the presentation of PDs in people who have IDD and even more so in offenders who have IDD. Extensive work has examined the diagnostic criteria for PDs in people who have IDD and for the most part little modification in criteria are recommended especially for the two most frequent PD's found in offenders who have IDD, borderline, and antisocial PD. The literature suggests that diagnosis should be structured and made within a multidisciplinary context informed by DSM-V and DM-ID. For all people who have IDD a specialist in IDD and mental health should always be involved (NICE 2009a). Treatment options for people with IDD and PD who offend can only be based on the developing research on interventions with people who have PD in the general population, offenders with PD in the general population, and the emerging research on the effectiveness of psychological interventions for people who have IDD. Being able to say what works for whom is an aspiration, but an enterprise with significant research potential.

References

Alexander, R.T., Chester, V., Gray, N.S. et al. (2012). Patients with personality disorders and intellectual disability – closer to personality disorders or intellectual disability? A three-way comparison. *Journal of Forensic Psychiatry and Psychology* 23: 435–451.

Alexander, R. and Cooray, S. (2003). Diagnosis of personality disorders in learning disability. *The British Journal of Psychiatry* 182: 28–31.

American Psychiatric Association (1994). *Diagnostic and Statistical Manual for Mental Disorders – fourth edition*. Washington DC: American Psychiatric Association.

American Psychiatric Association (2013). *Diagnostic and Statistical Manual for Mental Disorders – fifth edition*. Arlington, VA: American Psychiatric Association.

Bateman, A.W. and Fonagy, P. (2001). Treatment of borderline personality disorder with psychoanalytically orientated partial hospitalisation: an 18 month follow-up. *The American Journal of Psychiatry* 158: 36–42.

Beail, N. (2002). Interrogative suggestibility, memory and intellectual disability. *Journal of Applied Research in Intellectual Disabilities* 15: 129–137.

Beail, N. (2016). *Psychological Therapies and People Who Have Intellectual Disabilities*. Leicester: British Psychological Society.

Beard, K., Greenhill, B., and Lloyd, J. (2016). Cognitive analytic therapy. In: *Psychological Therapies and People Who Have Intellectual Disabilities* (ed. N. Beail), 35–43. Leicester: British Psychological Society.

British Psychological Society (2017). *Incorporating Attachment Theory into Clinical Practice with People Who Have Intellectual Disabilities*. Division of Clinical Psychology Faculty for People Who Have Intellectual Disabilities. Leicester: British Psychological Society.

Cattell, R.B. (1946). Confirmation and clarification of primary personality factors. *Psychometrika* 12: 197–220.

Chanen, A.M., Jackson, H.J., McCutcheon, L.K. et al. (2008). Early intervention for adolescents with borderline personality disorder using cognitive analytic therapy: randomised controlled trial. *The British Journal of Psychiatry* 193: 477–484.

Clarke, S., Thomas, P., and James, K. (2013). Cognitive analytic therapy for personality disorder: a randomised controlled trial. *The British Journal of Psychiatry* 202: 129–134.

Clayton, P. and Crowther, S. (2014). Cognitive analytic therapy integrated into a therapeutic community. In: *Cognitive Analytic Therapy for People with Learning Disabilities and Their Carers* (eds. J. Lloyd and P. Clayton), 191–202. London: Jessica Kingsley.

Coid, J., Yang, M., Tyrer, P. et al. (2006). Prevalence and correlates of personality disorder in Great Britain. *British Journal of Psychiatry* 188: 423–431.

Cooper, S.A., Smiley, E., Morrison, J. et al. (2007). Mental ill-health in adults with intellectual disability; prevalence and associated factors. *British Journal of Psychiatry* 190: 27–35.

Davies, J. and Nagi, C. (eds.) (2017). *Individual Psychological Therapies in Forensic Settings*. London: Routledge.

Dekker-van der Sande, F. and Sterkenburg, P. (2016). *Mentalization Can Be Learned*. Doorn, NL: Bartimeus.

Devapriam, J., Raju, L.B., Singh, N. et al. (2007). Arson: characteristics and predisposing factors in offenders with intellectual disabilities. *The British Journal of Forensic Practice* 9: 23–27.

Fazel, S. and Danesh, J. (2002). Serious mental disorder in 23 000 prisoners: a systematic review of 62 surveys. *The Lancet* 359: 545–550.

Fletcher, R.J. (ed.) (2011). *Psychotherapy for Individuals with Intellectual Disability*. New York: NADD Press.

Fletcher, R.J., Barnhill, J., and Cooper, S.A. (eds.) (2016). *Diagnostic Manual – Intellectual Disabilities-2*. New York: NADD Press.

Freud, S. (1923). The ego and the id. In: *The Standard Edition of the Complete Psychological Works of Sigmund Freud*, vol. 19 (ed. J. Strachey), 1–59. Oxford: Macmillan.

Hogue, T.E., Mooney, P., Morrissey, C. et al. (2007). Emotional and behavioural problems in offenders with intellectual disabilities: comparative data from three forensic services. *Journal of Intellectual Disability Research* 51: 778–785.

Hogue, T.E., Steptoe, L., Taylor, J.L. et al. (2006). A comparison of offenders with intellectual disabilities across three levels of security. *Criminal Behaviour and Mental Health* 16: 13–28.

Keulen-de Vos, M. and Bernstein, D.P. (2017). Schema therapy. In: *Individual Psychological Therapies in Forensic Settings* (eds. J. Davies and C. Nagi), 157–179. London: Routledge.

Lewin, T.J., Slade, T., Andrews, G. et al. (2005). Assessing personality disorders in a national mental health survey. *Social Psychiatry and Psychiatric Epidemiology* 40: 87–98.

Lindsay, W.R., Hogue, T., Taylor, J.L. et al. (2006). Two studies on the prevalence and validity of personality disorder in three forensic intellectual disability samples. *The Journal of Forensic Psychiatry and Psychology* 17: 485–506.

Lindsay, W.R., Lawrence, D.A., Alexander, R.T. et al. (2016). Personality disorders. In: *Diagnostic Manual- Intellectual Disabilities-2* (eds. R.J. Fletcher, J. Barnshill and S.-A. Cooper), 599–636. New York: NADD Press.

Lindsay, W.R., Steptoe, L., Hogue, T.E. et al. (2007). Internal consistency and factor structure of personality disorders in a forensic intellectual disability sample. *Journal of Intellectual and Developmental Disability* 32: 134–142.

Lindsay, W.R., van Logten, A., Didden, R. et al. (2017). The validity of two diagnostic systems for personality disorder in people with intellectual disabilities: a short report. *Journal of Intellectual Disabilities and Offending Behaviour* 8: 104–110.

Lippold, T. (2016). Dialectical behaviour therapy. In: *Psychological Therapies and People Who Have Intellectual Disabilities* (ed. N. Beail), 55–60. Leicester: British Psychological Society.

Livesley, W.L. (2001). Conceptual and taxonomic issues. In: *Handbook of Personality Disorders: Theory, Research and Treatment* (ed. W.L. Livesley), 3–38. London: Guildford Press.

Livesley, W.J. (2007). An integrated approach to the treatment of personality disorder. *Journal of Mental Health* 16: 131–148.

Lloyd, J. and Clayton, P. (eds.) (2014). *Cognitive Analytic Therapy for People with Learning Disabilities and their Carers*. London: Jessica Kingsley.

Mannysalo, L., Putkonen, H., Lindberg, N. et al. (2009). Forensic psychiatric perspective on criminality associated with intellectual disability: a nationwide register-based study. *Journal of Intellectual Disability Research* 53: 278–288.

Marshall, W.L., Hudson, S.M., Jones, R. et al. (1995). Empathy in sex offenders. *Clinical Psychology Review* 15: 99–113.

Matson, J.L., Kazdin, A.E., and Senatore, V. (1984). Psychometric properties of the psychopathology instrument for mentally retarded adults. *Applied Research in Mental Retardation* 5: 881–889.

McGauley, G. (2017). Mentalisation based treatments. In: *Individual Psychological Therapies in Forensic Settings* (eds. J. Davies and C. Nagi), 100–120. London: Routledge.

Moran, P. (1999). The epidemiology of antisocial personality disorder. *Social Psychiatry and Psychiatric Epidemiology* 34: 231–242.

Moss, S. (2016). *The Mini PAS-ADD Interview*. Hove: Pavilion.

NICE (2009a). Bordeline personality disorder: recognition and management. https://www.nice.org.uk/guidance/cg78 (accessed 22 May 2019).

NICE (2009b). Anti-social personality disorder: prevention and management. https://www.nice.org.uk/guidance/cg77 (accessed 22 May 2019).

NICE (2016). Learning disabilities: identifying and managing mental health problems. https://www.nice.org.uk/guidance/qs142 (accessed 22 May 2019).

Nicoll, M., Beail, N., and Saxon, D. (2013). Cognitive behavioural treatment for anger in adults with intellectual disabilities: a systematic review and meta-analysis. *Journal of Applied Research in Intellectual Disabilities* 26: 47–62.

Pilgrim, J. and Mann, A. (1990). The use of IDC-10 version of standardised assessment of personality to determine the prevalence of personality disorder in psychiatric in-patients. *Psychological Medicine* 20: 985–992.

Proctor, T. and Beail, N. (2007). Theory of mind and empathy in offenders with intellectual disabilities. *Journal of Intellectual and Developmental Disabilities* 32: 82–93.

Ralfs, S. and Beail, N. (2012). Assessing components of empathy in sex-offenders with intellectual disabilities. *Journal of Applied Research in Intellectual Disabilities* 25: 50–59.

Rayner, K., Wood, H., Beail, N. et al. (2015). Intellectual disability, personality disorder and offending: a systematic review. *Advances in Mental Health and Intellectual Disability* 9: 50–61.

Royal College of Psychiatrists (2001). *DC-LD*. London: Gaskell.

Royal College of Psychiatrists (2016). Psychotropic drug treatment for people with intellectual disability, mental health problems and/or behaviours that challenge: practice guidelines. Faculty Report FR/ID/09. London: Royal College of Psychiatrists.

Shannon, K. and Pollock, P. (2017). Cognitive analytic therapy. In: *Individual Psychological Therapies in Forensic Settings* (eds. J. Davies and C. Nagi), 41–58. London: Routledge.

Shepherd, C. and Beail, N. (2017). A systematic review of the effectiveness of psychoanalysis, psychoanalytic and psychodynamic psychotherapy with adults with intellectual and developmental disabilities: progress and challenges. *Psychoanalytic Psychotherapy* 31: 94–117.

Taylor, J.L., Lindsay, W.R., Hastings, R. et al. (2013). *Psychological Therapies for Adults with Intellectual Disabilites*. Chichester: Wiley-Blackwell.

Taylor, J.L. and Novaco, R. (2013). A brief screening instrument for emotionally unstable and dissocial personality disorder in male offenders with intellectual disabilities. *Research in Developmental Disabilities* 34: 546–553.

Town, J.M., Abbas, A., and Hardy, G. (2011). Short-term psychodynamic psychotherapy for personality disorders: a critical review of randomised controlled trails. *Journal of Personality Disorders* 23: 723–740.

Vlissides, N., Golding, L., and Beail, N. (2016). A systematic review of the outcome measures used in psychological therapies with adults with ID. In: *Psychological Therapies and People Who Have Intellectual Disabilities* (ed. N. Beail), 115–139. Leicester: British Psychological Society.

Wieland, J., van den Brinke, A., and Zitman, F.G. (2015). The prevalence of personality disorders in psychiatric outpatients with borderline intellectual functioning. *Nordic Journal of Psychiatry* 69: 599–604.

Wiggins, J.S. (1982). Circumplex models of interpersonal behaviour in clinical psychology. In: *Handbook of Research Methods in Clinical Psychology* (eds. P.S. Kendall and J.N. Butcher), 183–221. New York: Wiley.

Willmot, P. and McMurran, M. (2016). An attachment-based model of therapeutic change process in the treatment of personality disorder among male forensic patients. *Legal and Criminological Psychology* 21: 390–406.

World Health Organisation (1992). *International Classification of Diseases- Tenth Edition*. Geneva: World Health Organisation.

6

Assessment of Anger and Aggression

Paul Willner[1], Andrew Jahoda[2], and Ken MacMahon[3]

[1] Department of Psychology, Swansea University, Swansea, UK
[2] Institute of Health and Wellbeing, University of Glasgow, Glasgow, UK
[3] Department of Clinical and Health Psychology, University of Edinburgh, Edinburgh, UK

6.1   Introduction

Aggression is essentially an interpersonal act, relating to harm to others or the intent to cause or threaten harm to others (Nelson and Traynor 2007). Aggression is therefore subject to social norms and the criminal code. Understanding the psychological processes that drive aggression within an individual may, depending on offence-type, be a keystone of risk assessment and management.

When referring to offenders with an intellectual disability who are acting with intent, we are referring to individuals whose intellectual disabilities (ID) would be considered to be milder. Those with more significant impairments would, in general, not be considered to have responsibility for their actions under the law – essentially, they may lack *mens rea* ('to have criminal intent') and their aggressive behaviour might be described as behaviours that challenge; albeit that this distinction is not always clear (Steans and Duff 2018). Hence, this chapter focuses upon assessments developed or adapted for people with more mild to moderate ID.

When defining aggression, a distinction is often made between instrumental and reactive types. Reactive aggression describes a tendency to respond in an angry way to perceived threats, slights, or problems. In contrast, instrumental aggression is when someone behaves aggressively to achieve their goals. There is a notion that these more calculated forms of aggression are less driven by emotion and that perpetrators feel less guilt for their actions and less emotional empathy with victims (Orobio de Castro et al. 2005). In practice, however, it can be difficult to distinguish between these different types of behaviour because individuals who engage in premeditated aggressive acts may have on-going conflict with others, whilst those who have significant problems with reactive anger may ruminate about anger provoking events, leading to aggressive acts that are distant from the original perceived slight or provocation.

The Wiley Handbook on What Works for Offenders with Intellectual and Developmental Disabilities: An Evidence-Based Approach to Theory, Assessment, and Treatment, First Edition.
Edited by William R. Lindsay, Leam A. Craig, and Dorothy Griffiths.

Problems of aggression are presented by a significant minority of people with mild ID and are a major source of referrals to psychological services working with offenders with ID (e.g. Taylor 2002; Cooper et al. 2009). When reflecting on the causes of aggression presented by people with ID, there has been a tendency to assume that episodes of aggression are linked to cognitive deficits that are inherent to the person's ID (Jahoda et al. 2001). This rather circular argument is undermined by the fact that only a minority of people with ID present problems of aggression. However, it is still worth considering whether there are specific cognitive deficits or ways of processing the world that are likely to increase the likelihood of behaving aggressively and should be considered as part of any assessment.

The Social Information Processing (SIP) model described by Crick and Dodge (1996), teases out the following six different cognitive processes involved in interpersonal encounters that might result in aggressive behaviour: (i) encoding of cues, which involves socio-emotional understanding and focus and attention, (ii) interpreting the cues based on past experience and knowledge, (iii) response clarification stage, considering the social goals for the interaction, (iv) response access/construction, including generation of possible responses and problem solving, (v) response decision process involving evaluation of the possible outcomes and selection of the response, and finally (vi) the enactment of the response.

Although there is an absence of research concerning the SIP of violent offenders with an ID, Larkin et al. (2013) reviewed the broader literature concerning the SIP steps and people with ID who are frequently aggressive. When compared with those without aggression, it was interesting the studies largely showed no difference between the ability of aggressive and non-aggressive individuals' socio-emotional understanding (Jahoda et al. 2006a). However, there was a suggestion that there might be a tendency to interpret social situations differently, with a bias towards an attribution of hostile intent (Pert et al. 1999; Jahoda et al. 2006b). The clearest evidence was in terms of a response decision phase and a greater tendency for aggressive individuals to endorse the choice of aggressive responses. However, the participants in those studies did not lack the ability to produce nonaggressive response options, rather they appeared to prefer the aggressive option as a way of dealing with perceive threat (Kirk et al. 2008). Thus, the available evidence does not support the view that particular socio-cognitive deficits increase the likelihood of people with ID behaving aggressively. Instead, it appears to be their interpretation of events and their choice of aggression as a strategy for dealing with situations of perceived threat that largely differentiates the aggressive participants from their nonaggressive peers.

Whilst the SIP model presents a series of consecutive steps involved in generating a social response, the process involved in a real-life dynamic social situations is more complex. There will be an interplay between the different steps, depending on the unfolding situation and the person's emotional state and ability to regulate their emotions (Larkin et al. 2013). Emotion plays a central role in theories of aggression, with Dollard et al.'s (1939) original proposition that frustration leads to aggression, either directed towards those blocking goal directed behaviour or elsewhere. However, Berkowitz (1978) argued that frustration leads to aggression only when the person becomes angry. Taylor (2002), has pointed out that feelings of anger are neither sufficient nor necessary for aggressive acts to occur. However, anger is closely linked to aggression (Novaco 1994), and self-reports of anger by people with ID have been found to be strongly associated with aggressiveness.

6.2   Interventions for Aggression

Anger management interventions are one of the primary forms of psychological intervention used with offenders who have an ID, and are National Institute for Health and Care Excellence (NICE)-recommended interventions for aggression by people with mild ID (National Collaborating Centre for Mental Health, 2015). Anger management interventions adopt a cognitive behavioural approach, and are based on Meichenbaum's (1985) stress inoculation model. The three main elements of the approach consist of (i) cognitive work concerning perceived provocation and beliefs about aggression, (ii) learning to control one's level of arousal, and (iii) skills training in relation to problem solving and more appropriate ways of dealing with anger-provoking situations. In some cases, group-based anger management packages may differ from individual anger management treatment, with the latter more based on an individual formulation.

As noted above, understanding the processes that underlie aggressive behaviour are key, and hence assessments of anger may offer helpful – and necessary – insights into people's difficulties. This will support the development of psychological formulations that can inform risk management, through direct interventions, as well as wider social and contextual changes that may support individuals to reduce their offending behaviour. For example, a provocation inventory (PI) might help the therapist to identify the kind of situations the person finds anger provoking. Equally, it is self-evident that aggression usually occurs in particular contexts and in relation to particular types of social interactions. The behaviour of offenders living in secure settings is often carefully managed through the procedural, physical, and relational security of that institution, resulting in a reduction in acts of aggression, even though the individuals continue to have anger management problems that make them more likely to behave aggressively. The use of anger assessments can help to identify whether psychological interventions have been successful in reducing anger management problems in the absence of behavioural evidence.

This chapter consists of two main sections. The first section will review current anger management assessments, with the second detailing the underpinning evidence for their use, and then measures of aggression will then be outlined. The relevance of assessments of aggression to risk assessment and management for offenders with ID is discussed.

6.3   Questionnaire Measures of Anger

6.3.1   The State-Trait Anger Expression Inventory (STAXI)

The STAXI (Spielberger 1999) is a self-report instrument that provides a profile of an individual's experience, expression, and control of anger. It was originally designed to assess the components of anger associated with different personality variables and to measure the impact of anger on various medical conditions, but not specifically for individuals with ID. The STAXI is not underpinned by a model of anger: hence, this measure has limited utility in the clinical formulation of treatment needs.

The current version, the STAXI-II, has 57 items and includes measures of State Anger, Trait Anger, and Anger Expression. Each has several subscales: for example, the Anger Expression Index is calculated from the four self-explanatory sub-scales of

Anger Expression-Out, Anger Expression-In, Anger Control-Out and Anger Control-In (Spielberger 1999). State Anger reflects momentary 'subjective feelings that can vary in intensity from mild irritation to intense fury and rage'; trait anger describes 'individual differences in the disposition to perceive a wide range of situations as annoying or frustrating and by the tendency to respond to such situations with elevations in state anger' (Spielberger 1999). The STAXI-II has good psychometric properties, established in large samples of participants, and has been used in hundreds of research studies and translated into many languages: it is the most widely used anger assessment in clinical settings (Novaco and Taylor 2004; Culhane and Morera 2010). Psychiatric patients score higher than the general population on all STAXI-II scales and sub-scales. The only gender differences found in the general population were that men have higher scores on State Anger and Anger Expression-Out, whereas women have higher Anger Control-In scores (Spielberger 1999).

A recent review of the use of the STAXI-II in forensic populations (Schamborg et al. 2016) concluded that whilst the instrument has satisfactory psychometric properties in this context it does not capture all aspects of the construct of anger. Specifically, the STAXI-II does not capture the notion of angry mood, which is neither fixed in the present nor considered as a lasting predisposition (Fernandez 2013), and it does not assess the full range of ways that anger may be expressed (Martin and Dahlen 2007). The STAXI-II (in common with other self-report measures) is also subject to a social desirability bias that should be, but is not always, assessed (McEwan et al. 2009). Nevertheless, STAXI-II scores are reliably higher in offenders than in non-offenders. For example, men convicted of domestic violence were more predisposed to outwardly express their anger than non-violent men, and reported considerably lower anger control (Barbour et al. 1998). Prisoners had higher STAXI scores than a community sample (Spielberger 1991); violent female prisoners on parole had higher Trait anger and Anger Expression-Out scores than a non-violent group (Cherek et al. 2000); and forensic out-patients had higher STAXI-II scores than general psychiatric out-patients (Lievaart et al. 2016). One study has reported higher scores on most STAXI scales in female, relative to male prisoners (Suter et al. 2002), but this was hypothesized to reflect greater psychopathology in the female group. No gender difference was observed in another study with youth offenders (Swaffer and Epps 1999). STAXI-II scores decreased following a course of anger management training in Trinidadian prisons (Hutchinson et al. 2017).

An important issue for present purposes is whether high scores on the STAXI predict aggressive behaviour. Whilst the STAXI was not designed for this purpose, there is a theoretical expectation that aggression might be predicted by scores on Trait Anger and Anger Expression-Out (Cornell et al. 1999). And indeed, several studies have reported that Trait Angers scores do predict aggressive behaviour (Deffenbacher et al. 1996; Cornell et al. 1999; Parrott and Zeichner 2001; Giancola 2002), though some studies did not observe this relationship (Loza and Loza-Fanous 1999; Mills and Kroner 2003).

6.3.2 The Northgate Modification of the STAXI

The original 44-item STAXI has been adapted for people with ID, using the same questions, but simpler language and verbal prompts (Novaco and Taylor 2004). For example, each of the 10 State Anger items were prefixed with the temporal anchor

'Right now', and six were modified by a brief elaboration of the key word – for example, 'furious' was elaborated by 'really angry; or in a rage'; 'irritated' was elaborated by 'bad tempered, annoyed, or cross'; 'breaking things' was elaborated by 'smashing stuff up'. Similarly, key words were elaborated for each of the 10 Trait Anger items (for example, 'quick tempered' was elaborated by 'short-tempered, have a short fuse, touchy'). Each of the 24 *Anger Expression* items were prefixed with 'When I'm angry' as a contextual cue, and nine of them were altered to make the meaning more explicit (For example, 'I strike out at whatever infuriates me' became 'When I'm angry – I hit out at whatever is making me furious').

In a sample of >100 male forensic patients with mild or borderline ID, the modified instrument had excellent internal consistency (alpha >0.86 for State and Trait Anger) and good test–retest reliability (r > 0.5) over several months for Trait Anger and Anger Expression. Trait Anger and Anger Expression scores were significantly correlated with the number of physical assaults on staff or other patients; however, the significance was lost in a multiple regression analysis that included a range of control variables, with much of the variance accounted for by Full-Scale IQ and Extraversion scores (Novaco and Taylor 2004). Anger Expression scores were also significantly correlated with reports of parental aggression and a history of physical abuse (Novaco and Taylor 2008). Forensic patients with ID and those with IQs in the 'borderline' range showed a decrease in Anger Expression (Trait Anger was not tested in this study), in a small controlled trial of individual cognitive-behavioural anger treatment (Taylor et al. 2005). A later, some-what larger, uncontrolled study in the same population reported significant decreases in Trait Anger as well as Anger Expression and Anger Control, maintained at 12-month follow-up (Taylor et al. 2009). In another uncontrolled study of 50 patients, reductions in assaults following anger treatment were associated with reductions on the Anger-Out measure, but not with other STAXI measures (Novaco and Taylor 2015).

6.3.3 The Novaco Anger Scale (NAS)

The NAS is a 60-item self-report instrument that measures an individual's experience of anger in the Behavioural, Arousal, and Cognitive domains, as well as Anger Regulation (Novaco 2003). Whilst differing from the STAXI in being grounded in a theoretical model of anger, the NAS covers some of the same ground as the STAXI: the Behavioural and Arousal domains loosely correspond to STAXI Trait Anxiety, and Anger Regulation loosely corresponds to STAXI Anger Expression. There are numerous significant inter-correlations when the two instruments are used together. The main differences are that the NAS does not have the immediacy of the State Anxiety measure, whilst the STAXI does not address the cognitive dimension of anger, which includes constructs of justifi-cation, suspiciousness, rumination, and hostile attitude (Novaco 2003).

The NAS was designed to be readable by persons with elementary reading ability. It was standardized on a large non-clinical sample (>1500) spanning an age range from 8 to 84, and two sets of norms were produced, for ages 9–18 and 19+. Scores are similar in male and female samples; there are some significant differences between racial groups, but the effects sizes are small. The NAS has shown to be highly reliable in many different samples. For example, the overall internal consistency of the standardization sample was 0.94, with r = 0.76–0.89 for the sub-scales, and similar levels of test–retest reliability (Novaco 2003). A factor analytic study of the normative sample identified three factors, 'aggressively striking out', 'hot reaction high intensity arousal', and 'cognitive disturbance' (Novaco 2003), though this factor structure has not generally been confirmed (e.g. Novaco 2003; Hornsveld et al. 2011; Moeller et al. 2016). There are Danish (Moeller et al. 2016), Dutch (Nederlof et al. 2009), Swedish (Lindqvist et al. 2005), and Urdu (Naz and Khalily 2016) translations.

Unlike the STAXI, the NAS was explicitly developed and validated for use in forensic populations: specifically, the MacArthur Violence Risk Assessment Study (MVRAS) (Monahan et al. 2001). Consequently, the NAS has been extensively used and validated in this context (Mills et al. 1998; Novaco 2003; Doyle and Dolan 2006a, 2006b; Baker et al. 2008; Hornsveld et al. 2011; Swogger et al. 2012; Moeller et al. 2016). Like the STAXI, the NAS is subject to a social desirability bias that can influence the results (Baker et al. 2008). In general, NAS total and sub-scale scores do not discriminate between offenders and non-offender control groups (Novaco 2003). Nevertheless, there is a strong relationship between scores on the NAS (high behaviour, arousal, and cognitive scores; low anger control) and past or future acts of physical violence (Mills et al. 1998; Doyle and Dolan, 2006a,b; Swogger et al. 2012; Ullrich et al. 2014; Moeller et al. 2016).

6.3.4 The Northgate Modification of the NAS

Like the Northgate STAXI, the Northgate modification of the NAS includes the same questions as the parent instrument, adapted for ease of completion by people with ID, with changes of wording and some items rewritten (e.g. 'People act like they are being honest when they really have something to hide' was changed to 'People pretend they are telling the truth, when they are really telling lies') (Novaco and Taylor 2004). In the same sample of male forensic patients with ID tested with the modified STAXI, the modified NAS had excellent internal consistency (alpha = 0.92) and good test–retest reliability over a period of months (r = 0.52). The NAS score was predictive of physical violence, and this relationship survived in a multiple regression analysis alongside a raft of control variables (Novaco and Taylor 2004). The Northgate NAS may not suffer from the social desirability bias reported for the parent instrument (Baker et al. 2008). Novaco and Taylor (2004) reported that their participants did not appear guarded in disclosing their anger and staff ratings, based on ward observations, correlated significantly with patient self-reports, albeit that the correlations were relatively low.

In a small controlled trial in forensic patients with IDD, individual cognitive-behavioural anger treatment resulted in a decrease in NAS total and Arousal scores; results for the Behavioural and Cognitive scales were in the predicted direction but not significant, perhaps reflecting the small sample size (Taylor et al. 2005). A later, somewhat larger, uncontrolled study in the same population reported significant decreases in all four measures, maintained at 12-month follow-up (Taylor et al. 2009). In another uncontrolled study of 50 patients with mild or borderline ID, a reduction in violence following cognitive-behavioural anger treatment was predicted by the gain in NAS Total and Behavioural scores, but not by changes in the Arousal and Cognitive scores (Novaco and Taylor 2015). In addition to these forensic studies by the Novaco-Taylor group, the NAS total score was decreased in a small controlled-trial of a group-based anger management intervention in a community ID sample (Hagiliassis et al. 2009).

6.3.5 The Novaco PI

The PI is a 25-item instrument that was developed as an add-on to the NAS (it is sometimes referred to as the NAS part B) but is now a separate instrument. The PI measures the propensity to respond in an angry manner to hypothetical provocative situations. Each item is a potential provocation (e.g. 'Someone makes fun of the clothes you are wearing', which is rated on a five-point scale for the degree of anger it would evoke. The PI is sometimes administered alongside the NAS and sometimes used independently. It contains five groups of five items, but factor analyses do not support a corresponding five-factor structure, and indeed, do not encourage the use of sub-scales, so the PI is always reported as a single score. It has excellent internal consistency (typically >0.9) and test–retest reliability (typically >0.8) in non-clinical, clinical and forensic samples. Across several studies, PI scores were found to correlate strongly with other anger measures (including STAXI Trait Anxiety and Anger Expression, and other NAS scales) (Novaco 2003).

There is somewhat less literature on the relationship of the PI to violence, relative to the NAS, and the results are equivocal. PI scores did not discriminate a variety of groups of offenders from their respective control groups (Novaco 2003). Higher PI scores were reported in hospital patients with violent thoughts relative to those without (Grisso et al. 2000), but in the large MacArthur study, the correlation between PI scores and violent acts was very small ($r = 0.15$), albeit significant because the sample was very large (Monahan et al. 2001).

6.3.6 The Northgate Modification of the PI

Like the STAXI and the NAS, the PI has been modified by the Northgate group to improve acceptability to people with ID, involving some changes of wording and explanatory expansion of some items (Novaco and Taylor 2004). In some studies of people with ID, the PI was used as a third-party instrument, with ratings by a carer of their perceptions of the participant's disposition to anger. This version of the PI has good reliability (alpha >0.89) when rated either by people with ID themselves (Novaco and Taylor 2004; Willner et al. 2013), or by their key-workers or home carers (Willner et al. 2013). However, first-person and third-party ratings are not equivalent: the first-person ratings correlated significantly with subjective measures of mental health, whereas the third-party ratings correlated significantly with measures of challenging behaviour (Rose et al. 2013).

The modified PI has been used with people with ID in a number of treatment studies. In two controlled trials in community samples, decreases in PI scores were reported both by participants and their carers following a group-based cognitive-behavioural anger management intervention (Willner et al. 2002, 2005). However, this finding was not replicated in a large randomized controlled trial, possibly because the focus of that intervention was on anger control, which increased substantially, rather than feelings of anger per se (Willner et al. 2013). Individual cognitive-behavioural anger treatment did not significantly improve PI scores in a small controlled trial in a forensic ID setting (Taylor et al. 2005). In a larger uncontrolled study, the PI score did decrease significantly following treatment, but to a much lesser extent than the NAS or the STAXI (Taylor et al. 2009). And in a later study, the change in PI score following treatment did not predict subsequent acts of violence (Novaco and Taylor. 2015). Overall, the value of the PI for predictive studies in people with ID is questionable.

6.3.7 The Anger Inventory (AI)

The AI (Benson et al. 1986) is a 34-item self-report questionnaire that was developed by adaptation of an unpublished instrument developed to measure anger in children; to our knowledge, it has only been used with adults with ID. The AI closely resembles the PI insofar as the items measure the propensity to respond in an angry manner to hypothetical provocative situations (Benson and Ivens 1992). The AI has been used in several evaluations of interventions for anger in people with ID. The first was a study of four active interventions that found a decrease in AI scores in all groups (Benson et al. 1986). Subsequently, it was used alongside the PI in four studies of group-based cognitive-behavioural interventions, with very similar outcomes on both measures (Willner et al. 2002, 2005), and in a further series of studies of cognitive-behavioural interventions using both group and individual formats (Rose et al. 2000, 2005, 2008, 2009; Rose 2010). Like the PI, the AI has also been administered as a third-party instrument with ratings of participants' anger as perceived by their carers (Willner et al. 2002; Rose and Gerson 2009; Rose 2010). The AI does not have any obvious advantage over the PI when used with people with ID, and lacks the PI's large hinterland of studies in the general population.

6.3.8 Dundee Provocation Inventory (DPI)

Like the AI, the DPI (Alder and Lindsay 2007) is another instrument for reporting the propensity to respond to hypothetical provocations that was developed specifically for use with people with ID, with explicit reference to the Novaco model of anger (Novaco 1994). The parallel development of the PI and DPI is explained by the fact that the Dundee studies commenced in 1991 (Lindsay et al. 2003, 2004) when the NAS-PI was also in its infancy. The DPI is somewhat shorter than the AI and PI, with 20 items; the current version has good reliability (alpha >0.9) and scores correlate significantly with the NAS ($r = 0.57$) and PI ($r = 0.77$) (Alder and Lindsay 2007). A factor analytic study produced a five-factor solution (Alder and Lindsey 2007), but given the instability of factor structures seen with other instruments, this requires replication. The DPI has been used in a controlled trial of a cognitive-behavioural anger intervention with forensic patients (Lindsay et al. 2004) and in long-term (12- and 20-year) post-treatment follow-ups of violent offenders with ID (Lindsay et al. 2006, 2013). Like the AI, the DPI has no obvious advantage over the PI, other than its genesis within ID services.

6.3.9 The Ward Anger Rating Scale (WARS)

Unlike the self-report instruments described so far, the WARS was developed by Novaco (1994) alongside the NAS as an instrument on which ward staff rate their perceptions of the levels of anger and aggression of hospitalized patients. It was designed for ease of recording in busy clinical settings. Part A consists of 18 yes-no ratings of whether verbal and physical behaviours associated with anger and aggression occurred in the past week. Five of these items are summed for a measure, the Antagonistic Behaviour Index, of overt verbal and physical aggression directed at another person. Part B consists of seven items regarding anger attributes rated on a 5-point scale, which are summed to produce a staff-rated Anger Index. Good inter-rater reliability was found for both indices (r = 0.79 and 0.82, respectively), as well as significant associations with other staff-rated and self-report measures of anger/aggression and with reports of violent incidents in an unpublished study by Novaco and Renwick (2002; reported by Novaco and Taylor 2004). Other studies have confirmed that the WARS Anger Index predicts aggressive behaviour amongst hospitalized patients (Taylor et al. 2004b; Doyle and Dolan 2006a; Vitacco et al. 2009).

The WARS was used in the Northgate studies of anger and aggression in people with ID in a forensic hospital. Staff-rated anger correlated significantly with patients' NAS total and Anger Expression scores, and also with the number of physical assaults recorded (Novaco and Taylor 2004). In common with the other anger measures (see above), the decrease in WARS anger scores was not significant in a small controlled study (Taylor et al. 2005) but was significant in a larger uncontrolled study (Taylor et al. 2009), and the change in the WARS anger score during treatment was predictive of subsequent physical assaults (Novaco and Taylor 2015).

6.4 Scenario-based Measures of Anger, Coping, and Cognitions

6.4.1 The Imaginal Provocation Test (IPT)

The PI, AI, and DPI all ask participants to respond to hypothetical situations, which may or may not command attention and may or may not be meaningful to the participant. The IPT (Taylor et al. 2004a) is a more ecologically valid method, in which participants are asked to imagine themselves in each of four situations that are presented as scenarios, with greater contextual detail and temporal development. After experiencing each scenario, participants are asked to rate their level of anger, and the likelihood of various behavioural reactions (e.g. 'You would want to hit the person'). Finally, they are asked to rate the ease of imagining the situation and its clarity, and to recall the scenario. The IPT has been used in a single published study of patients with mild or borderline ID (Taylor et al. 2004a). The scenarios reliably elicited anger, which was correlated with IPT measures of behavioural reactions and anger regulation, and with the NAS Total, Arousal, and PI scores; and the behavioural reactions measure correlated with almost all NAS and STAXI scores. A small controlled trial confirmed that the IPT is sensitive to change: anger and behavioural reaction measures were decreased by cognitive-behavioural anger treatment. Potential confounds (scene clarity and memory) were unaffected by treatment (Taylor et al. 2004a).

6.4.2 The Profile of Anger Coping Skills (PACS)

The IPT is a standardized test that does not address individual concerns, which could vary greatly between different participants. An alternative is to take an ideographic approach in which anger experiences recalled by individual participants are used as the basis for anger ratings (Tafrate et al. 2002). This approach is used in the PACS, which was developed to measure coping skills in people with mild to moderate ID undertaking anger management training (Willner et al. 2005). The PACS is based around three anger-provoking scenarios that are personalized individually for each participant, followed by questions about the usage of a specified set of coping skills in each situation. The PACS was originally developed as a third-party instrument for carers to report on the coping skills of those they were supporting (Willner et al. 2005; Willner and Tomlinson 2007). This version of the PACS has good test–retest reliability (r = 0.78) and acceptable inter-rater reliability (r = 0.57) and provided evidence of significant and sustained increases in use of anger-coping skills following a group-based cognitive-behavioural intervention (Willner et al. 2005; Willner and Tomlinson 2007).

Subsequently, a self-report version of the PACS was developed (Willner et al. 2013). This version incorporates a rating of the anger evoked by each scenario, which corresponds to the IPT, except that it is based on actual rather than hypothetical scenarios. In a large randomized controlled trial of anger management, the PACS was completed by both participants with mild ID and their carers (Willner et al. 2013). Prior to treatment, service users rated themselves as coping better than did their carers, and PACS ratings correlated significantly with PI scores for service-users but not for carers, again suggesting a difference between carer perceptions of services users and service-user self-perceptions (cf. Rose et al. 2013). In this study, treatment did not decrease PI scores (as noted above), but PACS-IPT anger scores did show a decrease, which was maintained at a 4-month post-treatment follow-up. PACS coping-skills scores increased substantially, as reported by service users, with an even larger increase reported by their key-workers (Willner et al. 2013).

A recent study reported that both people with ID and university students were able reliably to generate two anger-provoking scenarios, but the reliability of a third scenario was much lower. Therefore, it is now recommended that administration of the PACS should be based on two scenarios rather than the original three (Richardson et al. 2015).

6.4.3 The Profile of Anger Cognitions (PAC)

The PAC was designed as an add-on the PACS, with the two instruments presented together as the Profile of Anger Coping Skills and Cognitions (PACSAC) (Richardson et al. 2015), though the PAC could also be presented separately. Drawing on SIP theory (Crick and Dodge 1996; Larkin et al. 2013), the PAC focuses on the interpersonal domain in which most incidents of anger arise and addresses four cognitive determinants that are prominent in the anger literature: attribution of hostile intent, perceptions of injustice, perceptions of self as victim, and inability to cope with social demands. Each dimension is assessed by asking the participant to talk about the general issue (e.g. 'Does X treat you differently from some other people'), followed if necessary by a request to focus on the specific issue (e.g. 'Do you think X was picking on you'), and finally, a request for a rating (e.g. 'How much did X pick on you') using a four-point scale. This procedure is applied to each of the scenarios generated for the PACS. The PAC thus comprises two elements: a set of individualized anger-provoking interpersonal scenarios, provided by the participant as reports of recent incidents, followed by ratings of the intensity of anger elicited by each event and the four anger-related cognitions. It differs from the IPT in being based on actual rather than hypothetical events, and focusing on cognitions rather than behaviour (Richardson et al. 2015).

The PAC was administered to small samples of university students and people with ID who were identified as having difficulties with anger control (Richardson et al. 2015).

As noted above, test–retest reliability was good (r > 0.8) for two scenarios, but poor for a third scenario in both groups. The ID group also showed good internal consistency (alpha = 0.75), though the student group did not (alpha = 0.12). In both groups, PAC cognitions scores were correlated with ratings of anger intensity, and with NAS Anger Regulation but not with other NAS or STAXI scores. The predominant cognitions reported were perceptions of unfairness and helplessness. People with ID and university students were in most respects very similar in both the psychometric analyses and the content analyses of their verbal responses. The PAC had high acceptability both to people with ID and to clinicians. Its sensitivity to change following anger treatment, or relationship to incidents of violence, have not yet been determined.

6.5 Measures of Aggression

6.5.1 The Buss-Perry Aggression Questionnaire (BPAQ)

Several questionnaire measures of aggression have been developed, of which the BPAQ (often known simply as the Aggression Questionnaire) is the gold standard. The BPAQ is a 28-item self-report questionnaire that provides, four measures, derived by factor analysis: Physical Aggression, Verbal Aggression, Hostility, and Anger (Buss and Perry 1992). The reliability and validity of the BPAQ are well established in numerous studies: it is widely used and has been extensively translated. However, to our knowledge it has never been used with people with ID. This is, presumably, because many of the questions are somewhat complex and would not be accessible to people with ID. However, they are not obviously more complex than the items included in the original versions of other questionnaires that have been modified for use by people with ID. It seems likely that modification of the BPAQ for people with ID would be a straightforward project to accomplish.

6.5.2 The Modified Overt Aggression Scale (MOAS)

Aggression by people with ID is typically assessed by observer (typically, staff) ratings rather than self-ratings. The Overt Aggression Scale (OAS) (Silver and Yudovsky 1991) was developed to record characteristics of aggressive episodes during the past week, with a view to assessing the effectiveness of treatment interventions for violent patients. It comprises a checklist of four instances of each of four types of aggression: verbal, and physical aggression against objects, self, and other people. The severity of each incident is scored and the four categories are weighted differently (verbal lowest, interpersonal highest) when deriving a total aggression score (Silver and Yudovsky 1991). The MOAS (Alderman et al. 1997) retained the same structure as the OAS but expanded the section of the OAS that describes interventions in use, introduced a crude frequency measure (< 10 or > 10 observations) in the previous seven days, and modified the language to increase its suitability in a UK context. Another version, the Institute of Basic Research MOAS (IBR-MOAS) added a further category of Verbal aggression towards self (Cohen et al. 2010). The IBR-MOAS, originally used with adults on the autism spectrum (Cohen, et al. 2010), was also subsequently used to examine the association of aggressive behaviour with psychiatric disorders in people with ID (Tsiouris et al. 2011).

The first use of the MOAS with people with ID was by Oliver and colleagues in 2007, in the context of a randomized controlled trial of neuroleptic medication for aggressive challenging behaviour. In a small sample (23 carers of 14 patients) they reported high (r = 0.9) inter-rater reliability for verbal aggression and physical aggression against others, with lower levels of agreement for aggression against self and property (Oliver et al. 2007). The MOAS has subsequently been used as standard in studies needing to measure aggressive behaviour in people with ID (e.g. Bhaumik et al. 2009; Drieschner et al. 2013; Willner et al. 2013; Unwin and Deb 2014; Tyrer et al. 2017).

6.5.3 The WARS

As described earlier, the WARS includes staff-rated measures of both anger and aggression. Although the WARS was used in all of the Northgate studies on people with ID in forensic settings, only one study reported data for the aggression measure, the Antagonistic Behaviour Index, scores on which were higher for patients with a history of violence (Novaco and Taylor 2004). Only the anger measure was used in subsequent studies (e.g. Taylor et al. 2004a, 2005), perhaps because the studies also drew on incident reports of aggressive behaviour in hospital records.

6.5.4 The How I Think Questionnaire (HIT-Q)

The HIT-Q is a 54-item self-report instrument, originally developed for use with adolescents, which measures four types of self-serving cognitive distortions, Self-Centred cognitions, Minimizing/Mislabelling cognitions, Blaming Others cognitions and Assuming the Worst cognitions (Barriga and Gibbs 1996). It is not aggression specific, but the cognitions measured are relevant to interpersonal aggression (as well as to other forms of offending) and the instrument includes a number of sub-scales assessing behavioural variables, one of which is physical aggression. The overall reliability and validity of the HIT-Q are good (Barriga et al. 2001) and it has been translated into several languages. A meta-analysis of studies using the HIT-Q reported that it had excellent internal consistency and discriminated well between offenders and non-offenders (Gini and Pozzoli 2013).

Langdon et al. (2011) used the HIT-Q in a study of men with ID and confirmed the discrimination between offenders and non-offenders. The same authors subsequently developed an ID version of the HIT-Q, the HIT-ID, to increase its accessibility to people with ID. This involved replacing some American words with British words, increasing readability, and simplifying the response scale. The modified instrument again had good internal consistency and discriminated well between offenders and non-offenders: the relevance for present purposes is that this was also true of the physical violence sub-scale (Daniel et al. 2017).

6.6 Assessment and Management of Risk of Violence

Within forensic settings, risk assessment and management typically form the cornerstone of work with offenders. Risk assessments are typically used to inform decisions regarding necessary interventions, both in terms of the restrictions that may be placed upon an individual (including detention within hospital or prison) as well as psychological or pharmacological interventions. Actuarial assessments provide a rough estimate of the likelihood of offending or re-offending, based on a combination of static factors which cannot change (e.g. IQ, offending history) and dynamic factors that could change in either direction (e.g. social circumstances, attitudes to offending). One of the most commonly used is the Violence Risk Appraisal Guide (VRAG) (Quinsey et al. 1998). The VRAG is a static tool (i.e. it does not consider dynamic factors). It is considered to be 70–75% accurate in predicting long-term risk amongst male offenders, but does not accurately predict short-term risk (SBU 2005). Some problems in replicating findings with the VRAG have been noted (Rossegger et al. 2013).

Lofthouse et al. (2013) completed the VRAG, alongside two actuarial assessments of the risk of sexual offending, for men with ID. They found that dynamic factors were the most useful predictors of sexual re-offending, and the VRAG, which only includes static factors, performed less well as a predictor of violent re-offending. Nevertheless, other studies have reported that the VRAG accurately predicted institutional violence (Fitzgerald et al. 2013) and reconviction (Gray et al. 2007) amongst offenders with ID. Similarly, a study in sex offenders with ID reported that the VRAG was predictive of both sexual and violent offending (Federoff et al. 2016). However, a recent study reported that the VRAG did not predict aggressive behaviour amongst institutionalized offenders with ID, and the authors questioned its usefulness in this context (Pouls and Jeandarme 2018).

Although there continues to be a focus upon estimating the risk of re-offending, using actuarial measures of risk, in both mainstream and ID fields, there has been a move towards the use of structured professional judgement assessments (SPJ).

With SPJ assessments, the user is required to identify key factors that are implicated in offending behaviour, but, crucially, offending behaviour is formulated from a psychological perspective, with effective risk management processes arising from this. In the field of ID, recent years have seen greater research focus upon validation tools within this population (e.g. Hounsome et al. 2018). There is now good evidence that such assessments have validity in estimating risk and, more importantly, identifying management strategies to reduce the risk of re-offending. Judicious use of measures of anger and aggression can help to identify underlying cognitions and contextual factors that are implicated in offending behaviour and thereby direct towards risk management. Anger frequently holds the key to a range of offences, therefore detailed assessment is a necessary part of forensic work and existing measures, as outlined above, can provide a wealth of relevant clinical information.

6.7 Discussion

This review highlights an array of measures and assessments that clinicians may choose to use in their assessment of anger and aggression with offenders with ID. Crucially, authors of measures have made attempts to adapt a number of these assessments specifically to make them more accessible to individuals with ID. Duration and ease of delivery are factors when determining whether clinicians can make use of them in routine practice. However, the degree to which an individual can comprehend the questions used and scenarios posed, is perhaps of more central importance.

There is a growing interest in implementation research, regarding the delivery of evidence-based interventions (Powell et al. 2015). However, it is interesting that little attention is paid to encouraging the collection and use of assessment data in routine clinical practice. There is no information about the use of these measures in practice or which of the measures and assessments are used by whom in their work with offenders. It would be particularly interesting to know what assessments have particular value in terms of their contribution to risk assessment and risk management.

Clearly, assessments need to serve a purpose for the clinicians and all of the anger assessments provide information that could be used to help with the formulation of an individual's problems with anger and aggression. A particular strength of the adapted Northgate Anger Scale is that it is based upon the theory that underpins current anger management interventions. However, there can be problems with using questionnaires with people who have ID. First, as noted earlier, the respondents might have difficulty understanding the questions, even if they are adapted. Second, because offenders with ID will be acutely aware that their responses are likely to have an impact on how they are perceived by professionals working in the forensic health or criminal justice system, as with any individual in such circumstances, there may be a tendency to provide socially desirable responses (McEwan et al. 2009). Interestingly, anger management work (as with any other psychological intervention) encourages people to talk more openly about their difficulties, as part of the process of learning to recognize and gain control over their arousal and behaviour. Thus, paradoxically, it is conceivable that individuals' scores on anger management assessments increase over the course of an anger management intervention. This was a problem highlighted by Willner et al. (2013).

Although measures and assessments that are currently available are valuable to the clinician, there is a clear opportunity to further develop this field. As we noted at the start of this chapter, aggression is typically an interpersonal act, with anger often (although not always) implicated within it. However, aggressive acts (and underlying anger) can have complex contextual factors that may be idiosyncratic to the individual, that existing measures may not be sufficient to tease-out. If episodes of aggressive behaviour are viewed in the context of the SIP Model, there are clearly elements of this which are not covered by current instruments. Some of the assessments, such as the IPT and PAC, do have the advantage of, respectively, trying to engage individuals emotionally by asking the respondents to imagine themselves facing different types of provocation, asking respondents to imagine themselves facing provocation that they find personally salient. However, areas such as attention to and encoding of cues within 'real-life' situations, and structured assessments of social goals, are absent. These are factors that are relevant to whether anger develops and whether an aggressive act is 'chosen' in response to this.

References

Alder, L. and Lindsay, W.R. (2007). Exploratory factor analysis and convergent validity of the Dundee Provocation Inventory. *Journal of Intellectual and Developmental Disabilities* 32: 190–199.

Alderman, N., Knight, C., and Morgan, C. (1997). Use of a modified version of the Overt Aggression Scale in the measurement and assessment of aggressive behaviours following brain injury. *Brain Injury* 11: 503–523.

Baker, M.T., Van Hasselt, V.B., and Sellers, A.H. (2008). Validation of the Novaco Anger Scale in an incarcerated offender population. *Criminal Justice and Behavior* 35: 741–754.

Barbour, K.A., Eckhardt, C.I., Davidson, G.C. et al. (1998). The experience and expression of anger in maritally violent and maritally discordant-nonviolent men. *Behavior Therapy* 29: 173–191.

Barriga, A.Q. and Gibbs, J.C. (1996). Measuring cognitive distortion in antisocial youth: development and preliminary validation of the "How I Think" questionnaire. *Aggressive Behavior* 22: 333–343.

Barriga, A.Q., Gibbs, J.C., Potter, G.B. et al. (2001). *Test Manual for the How I Think Questionnaire*. Champaign, IL: Research Press.

Benson, B. and Ivins, J. (1992). Anger, depression and self-concept in adults with mental retardation. *Journal of Intellectual Disability Research* 36: 169–175.

Benson, B., Johnson-Rice, C., and Miranti, S.V. (1986). Effects of anger management training with mentally retarded adults in group treatment. *Journal of Consulting and Clinical Psychology* 54: 728–729.

Berkowitz, L. (1978). Whatever happened to the frustration-aggression hypothesis? *American Behavioral Scientist* 21: 691–708.

Bhaumik, S., Watson, J.M., Devapriam, J. et al. (2009). Brief report: aggressive challenging behaviour in adults with intellectual disability following community resettlement. *Journal of Intellectual Disability Research* 53: 298–302.

Buss, A.H. and Perry, M. (1992). The aggression questionnaire. *Journal of Personality and Social Psychology* 63: 452–459.

Cherek, D.R., Lane, S.D., Dougherty, D.M. et al. (2000). Laboratory and questionnaire measures of aggression among female parolees with violent or nonviolent histories. *Aggressive Behavior* 26: 291–307.

Cohen, I.L., Tsiouris, J.A., Flory, M.J. et al. (2010). A large scale study of the psychometric characteristics of the IBR Modified Overt Aggression Scale: findings and evidence for increased self-destructive behaviors in adult females with autism spectrum disorder. *Journal of Autism and Developmental Disorders* 40: 599–609.

Cooper, S.A., Smiley, E., Jackson, A. et al. (2009). Adults with intellectual disabilities: prevalence, incidence and remission of aggressive behaviour and related factors. *Journal of Intellectual Disability Research* 53: 217–232.

Cornell, D.G., Peterson, C.S., and Richards, H. (1999). Anger as a predictor of aggression among incarcerated adolescents. *Journal of Consulting and Clinical Psychology* 67: 108–115.

Crick, N.I. and Dodge, K.A. (1996). Social information-processing mechanisms in reactive and proactive aggression. *Child Development* 67: 993–1002.

Culhane, S.E. and Morera, O.F. (2010). Reliability and validity of the Novaco Anger Scale and Provocation Inventory (NAS-PI) and State-Trait Anger Expression Inventory–2 (STAXI2) in Hispanic and non-Hispanic White student samples. *Hispanic Journal of Behavioral Sciences* 32: 586–606.

Daniel, M.R., Sadek, S.A., and Langdon, P.E. (2017). The reliability and validity of a revised version of the How I Think Questionnaire for people who have intellectual disabilities. *Psychology, Crime & Law* 24: 379–390.

Deffenbacher, J.L., Oetting, E.R., Thwaites, G.A. et al. (1996). State-Trait Anger Theory and the utility of the Trait Anger Scale. *Journal of Counseling Psychology* 43: 131–148.

Dollard, J., Miller, N., Mowrer, O. et al. (1939). *Frustration and Aggression*. New Haven, CT: University Press.

Doyle, M. and Dolan, M. (2006a). Evaluating the validity of anger regulation problems, interpersonal style, and disturbed mental state for predicting inpatient violence. *Behavioral Sciences & the Law* 24: 783–798.

Doyle, M. and Dolan, M. (2006b). Predicting community violence from patients discharged from mental health services. *British Journal of Psychiatry* 189: 520–526.

Drieschner, K.H., Marrozos, I., and Regenboog, M. (2013). Prevalence and risk factors of inpatient aggression by adults with intellectual disabilities and severe challenging behaviour: a long-term prospective study in two Dutch treatment facilities. *Research in Developmental Disabilities* 34: 2407–2418.

Fedoroff, J.P., Richards, D., Ranger, R. et al. (2016). The predictive validity of common risk assessment tools in men with intellectual disabilities and problematic sexual behaviors. *Research in Developmental Disabilities* 57: 29–38.

Fernandez, E. (2013). Anger dysfunction and its treatment. In: *Treatments for Anger in Specific Populations: Theory, Application, and Outcome* (ed. E. Fernandez), 1–14. New York: Oxford University Press.

Fitzgerald, S., Gray, N.S., Alexander, R.T. et al. (2013). Predicting institutional violence in offenders with intellectual disabilities: the predictive efficacy of the VRAG and the HCR-20. *Journal of Applied Research in Intellectual Disabilities* 26: 384–393.

Giancola, P.R. (2002). The influence of trait anger on the alcohol-aggression relation in men and women. *Alcoholism: Clinical & Experimental Research* 26: 1350–1358.

Gini, G. and Pozzoli, T. (2013). Measuring self-serving cognitive distortions: a meta-analysis of the psychometric properties of the How I Think Questionnaire (HIT). *European Journal of Developmental Psychology* 10: 510–517.

Gray, N.S., Fitzgerald, S., Taylor, J. et al. (2007). Predicting future reconviction in offenders with intellectual disabilities: the predictive efficacy of VRAG, PCL-SV, and the HCR-20. *Psychological Assessment* 19: 474–479.

Grisso, T., Davis, J., Vesselinov, R. et al. (2000). Violent thoughts and violent behavior following hospitalization for mental disorder. *Journal of Consulting and Clinical Psychology* 68: 388–398.

Hagiliassis, N., Gulbenkoglu, H., Di Marco, M. et al. (2009). The Anger Management Project: a group intervention for anger in people with physical and multiple disabilities. *Journal of Intellectual and Developmental Disability* 30: 86–96.

Hornsveld, R.H., Muris, P., and Kraaimaat, F.W. (2011). The Novaco Anger Scale-Provocation Inventory (1994 version) in Dutch forensic psychiatric patients. *Psychological Assessment* 23: 937–944.

Hounsome, J., Whittington, R., Brown, A. et al. (2018). The structured assessment of violence risk in adults with intellectual disability: a systematic review. *Journal of Applied Research in Intellectual Disabilities* 31 (1): e1–e17.

Hutchinson, G., Willner, P., Rose, J. et al. (2017). CBT in a Caribbean context: a controlled trial of anger management in Trinidadian prisons. *Behavioural and Cognitive Psychotherapy* 45: 1–15.

Jahoda, A., Pert, C., and Trower, P. (2006a). Socioemotional understanding and frequent aggression in people with mild to moderate intellectual disabilities. *American Journal on Mental Retardation* 111: 77–89.

Jahoda, A., Pert, C., and Trower, P. (2006b). Frequent aggression and attribution of hostile intent in people with mild to moderate intellectual disabilities: an empirical investigation. *American Journal on Mental Retardation* 111: 90–99.

Jahoda, A., Trower, P., Pert, C. et al. (2001). Contingent reinforcement or defending the self? A review of evolving models of aggression in people with mild learning disabilities. *British Journal of Medical Psychology* 74: 305–321.

Kirk, J.D., Jahoda, A., and Pert, C. (2008). Beliefs about aggression and submissiveness: a comparison of aggressive and nonaggressive individuals with mild intellectual disability. *Journal of Mental Health Research in Intellectual Disabilities* 1: 191–204.

Langdon, P.E., Murphy, G.H., Clare, I.C.H. et al. (2011). Relationships among moral reasoning, empathy and distorted cognitions amongst men with intellectual disabilities and a history of criminal offending. *American Journal on Intellectual and Developmental Disabilities* 116: 438–456.

Larkin, P., Jahoda, A., and MacMahon, K. (2013). The Social Information Processing model as a framework for explaining frequent aggression in adults with mild to moderate intellectual disabilities: a systematic review of the evidence. *Journal of Applied Research in Intellectual Disabilities* 26: 447–465.

Lievaart, M., Franken, I.H., and Hovens, J.E. (2016). Anger assessment in clinical and nonclinical populations: further validation of the State-Trait Anger Expression Inventory-2. *Journal of Clinical Psychology* 72: 263–278.

Lindqvist, J.K., Dåderman, A.M., and Hellström, Å. (2005). Internal reliability and construct validity of the Novaco Anger Scale-1998-S in a sample of violent prison inmates in Sweden. *Psychology, Crime & Law* 11: 223–237.

Lindsay, W.R., Allan, R., Macleod, F. et al. (2003). Long term treatment and management of violent tendencies of men with intellectual disabilities convicted of assault. *Mental Retardation* 41: 47–56.

Lindsay, W.R., Allan, R., Parry, C. et al. (2004). Anger and aggression in people with intellectual disabilities: treatment and follow-up of consecutive referrals and a waiting list comparison. *Clinical Psychology and Psychotherapy* 11: 255–264.

Lindsay, W.R., Steele, L., Smith, A.H.W. et al. (2006). A community forensic intellectual disability service: twelve year follow-up of referrals, analysis of referral patterns and assessment of harm reduction. *Legal & Criminological Psychology* 11: 113–130.

Lindsay, W.R., Steptoe, L., Wallace, L. et al. (2013). An evaluation and 20-year follow-up of a community forensic intellectual disability service. *Criminal Behaviour and Mental Health* 23: 138–149.

Lofthouse, R.E., Lindsay, W.R., Totsika, V. et al. (2013). Prospective dynamic assessment of risk of sexual reoffending in individuals with an intellectual disability and a history of sexual offending behaviour. *Journal of Applied Research in Intellectual Disabilities* 26: 394–403.

Loza, W. and Loza-Fanous, A. (1999). Anger and prediction of violent and nonviolent offenders' recidivism. *Journal of Interpersonal Violence* 14: 1014–1029.

Martin, R.C. and Dahlen, E.R. (2007). Anger response styles and reaction to provocation. *Personality and Individual Differences* 43: 2083–2094.

McEwan, T.E., Davis, M., MacKenzie, R. et al. (2009). The effects of social desirability response bias on STAXI-2 profiles in a clinical forensic sample. *British Journal of Clinical Psychology* 48: 431–436.

Meichenbaum, D. (1985). *Stress Inoculation Training*. Oxford: Pergamon Press.

Mills, J.F. and Kroner, D.G. (2003). Anger as a predictor of institutional misconduct and recidivism in a sample of violent offenders. *Journal of Interpersonal Violence* 18: 282–294.

Mills, J.F., Kroner, D.G., and Forth, A.E. (1998). Novaco Anger Scale: reliability and validity within an adult criminal sample. *Assessment* 5: 237–248.

Moeller, S.B., Novaco, R.W., Heinola-Nielsen, V. et al. (2016). Validation of the Novaco Anger Scale-Provocation Inventory (Danish) with nonclinical, clinical, and offender samples. *Assessment* 23: 624–636.

Monahan, J., Steadman, H.J., Silver, E. et al. (2001). *Rethinking Risk Assessment: The MacArthur Study of Mental Disorder and Violence*. New York: Oxford University Press.

National Collaborating Centre for Mental Health (UK) (2015). *Challenging Behaviour and Learning Disabilities: Prevention and Interventions for People with Learning Disabilities Whose Behaviour Challenges*. London: National Institute for Health and Care Excellence.

Naz, S. and Khalily, M.T. (2016). Indigenous adoption of Novaco's model of anger management among individuals with psychiatric problems in Pakistan. *Journal of Religion Health* 55: 439–447.

Nederlof, A.F., Hovens, J.E., Muris, P. et al. (2009). Psychometric evaluation of a Dutch version of the dimensions of anger reactions. *Psychological Reports* 105: 585–592.

Nelson, R.J. and Traynor, B.C. (2007). Neural mechanisms of aggression. *Nature Reviews in Neuroscience* 8: 536–546.

Novaco, R.W. (1994). Anger as a risk factor for violence among the mentally disordered. In: *Violence and Mental Disorder: Developments in Risk Assessment* (eds. J. Monahan and H.J. Steadman), 21–59. Chicago: University of Chicago Press.

Novaco, R.W. (2003). *The Novaco Anger Scale and Provocation Inventory*. Los Angeles: Stern Psychological Services.

Novaco, R.W. and Taylor, J.L. (2004). Assessment of anger and aggression in male offenders with developmental disabilities. *Psychological Assessment* 16: 42–50.

Novaco, R.W. and Taylor, J.L. (2008). Anger and assaultiveness of male forensic patients with developmental disabilities: links to volatile parents. *Aggressive Behaviour* 34: 380–393.

Novaco, R.W. and Taylor, J.L. (2015). Reduction of assaultive behavior following anger treatment of forensic hospital patients with intellectual disabilities. *Behaviour Research and Therapy* 65: 52–59.

Oliver, P.C., Crawford, M.J., Rao, B. et al. (2007). Modified Overt Aggression Scale (MOAS) for people with intellectual disability and aggressive challenging behaviour: a reliability study. *Journal of Applied Research in Intellectual Disabilities* 20: 368–372.

Orobio de Castro, B., Merk, W., Koops, W. et al. (2005). Emotions in social information processing and their relations with reactive and proactive aggression in referred aggressive boys. *Journal of Clinical Child and Adolescent Psychology* 34: 105–116.

Parrott, D.J. and Zeichner, A. (2001). Effects of alcohol and trait anger on physical aggression in men. *Psychology of Men & Masculinity* 6: 3–17.

Pert, C., Jahoda, A., and Squire, J. (1999). Attribution of intent and role-taking: cognitive factors as mediators of aggression with people who have mental retardation. *American Journal on Mental Retardation* 104 (5): 399–409.

Pouls, C. and Jeandarme, I. (2018). Predicting institutional aggression in offenders with intellectual disabilities using the Violence Risk Appraisal Guide. *Journal of Applied Research in Intellectual Disabilities* 31: e265–e271.

Powell, B.J., Waltz, T.J., Chinman, M.J. et al. (2015). A refined compilation of implementation strategies: results for Expert Recommendations for Implementing Change (ERIC) project. *Implementation Science* 10: 21.

Quinsey, V.L., Rice, M.E., Harris, G.T. et al. (1998). *Violent Offenders: Appraising and Managing Risk*. Washington, DC: American Psychological Association.

Richardson, C., Killeen, S., Jahoda, A. et al. (2015). Assessment of anger-related cognitions of people with intellectual disabilities. *Behavioural and Cognitive Psychopharmacology* 44: 580–600.

Rose, J. (2010). Carer reports of the efficacy of cognitive behavioral interventions for anger. *Research in Developmental Disability* 31: 1502–1508.

Rose, J.L., Dodd, L., and Rose, N. (2008). Individual cognitive behavioral intervention for anger. *Journal of Mental Health Research in Intellectual Disabilities* 1: 97–108.

Rose, J.L. and Gerson, D.F. (2009). Assessing anger in people with intellectual disability. *Journal of Intellectual and Developmental Disability* 34: 116–122.

Rose, J., Loftus, M., Flint, B. et al. (2005). Factors associated with the efficacy of a group intervention for anger in people with intellectual disabilities. *British Journal of Clinical Psychology* 44: 305–317.

Rose, J., O'Brien, A., and Rose, D. (2009). Group and individual cognitive behavioural interventions for anger. *Advances in Mental Health and Learning Disabilities* 3: 45–50.

Rose, J., West, C., and Clifford, D. (2000). Group interventions for anger in people with intellectual disabilities. *Research in Developmental Disability* 21: 171–118.

Rose, J., Willner, P., Shead, J. et al. (2013). Different factors influence self-reports and third-party reports of anger by adults with intellectual disabilities. *Journal of Applied Research in Intellectual Disabilities* 26: 410–419.

Rossegger, A., Gerth, J., Seewald, K. et al. (2013). Current obstacles in replicating risk assessment findings: a systematic review of commonly used actuarial instruments. *Behavioral Science and Law* 31: 154–164.

SBU (2005). *Psychiatric risk assessment methods: Are violent acts predictable?: A systematic review*. Stockholm: Swedish Council on Health Technology Assessment in Healthcare (SBU). SBU Report no. 175.

Schamborg, S., Tully, R.J., and Browne, K.D. (2016). The use of the State-Trait Anger Expression Inventory-II with forensic populations: a psychometric critique. *International Journal of Offender Therapy and Comparative Criminology* 60: 1239–1256.

Silver, J.M. and Yudofsky, S.C. (1991). The Overt Aggression Scale: overview and guiding principles. *Journal of Neuropsychiatry and Clinical Neuroscience* 3: S22–S29.

Spielberger, C.D. (1991). *State-Trait Anger Expression Inventory: STAXI Professional Manual*. Lutz, FL: Psychological Assessment Resources.

Spielberger, C.D. (1999). *State-Trait Anger Expression Inventory-2: Revised Research Edition: Professional Manual*. Odessa, FL: Psychological Assessment Resources.

Steans, J. and Duff, S. (2018). Perceptions of sex offenders with intellectual disability: a comparison of forensic staff and the general public. *Journal of Applied Research in Intellectual Disabilities* https://doi.org/10.1111/jar.12467.

Suter, J.M., Byrne, M.K., Byrne, S. et al. (2002). Anger in prisoners: women are different from men. *Personality and Individual Differences* 32: 1087–1100.

Swaffer, T. and Epps, K. (1999). The psychometric assessment of anger in male and female adolescents resident at a secure youth treatment centre. *Journal of Adolescence* 22: 419–422.

Swogger, M.T., Walsh, Z., Homaifar, B.Y. et al. (2012). Predicting self- and other-directed violence among discharged psychiatric patients: the roles of anger and psychopathic traits. *Psychological Medicine* 42: 371–379.

Tafrate, R.C., Kassinove, H., and Dundin, L. (2002). Anger episodes in high- and low-trait-anger community adults. *Journal of Clinical Psychology* 58: 1575–1590.

Taylor, J.L. (2002). A review of the assessment and treatment of anger and aggression in offenders with intellectual disability. *Journal of Intellectual Disability Research* 46 (s1): 57–73.

Taylor, J.L., DuQueno, L., and Novaco, R.W. (2004b). Piloting a ward anger rating scale for older adults with mental health problems. *Behavioural and Cognitive Psychotherapy* 32: 467–479.

Taylor, J.L., Novaco, R.W., Gillmer, B.T. et al. (2005). Individual cognitive-behavioural anger treatment for people with mild-borderline intellectual disabilities and histories of aggression: a controlled trial. *British Journal of Clinical Psychology* 44: 367–382.

Taylor, J.L., Novaco, R.W., Guinan, C. et al. (2004a). Development of an imaginal provocation test to evaluate treatment for anger problems in people with intellectual disabilities. *Clinical Psychology and Psychotherapy* 11: 233–246.

Taylor, J.L., Novaco, R.W., and Johnson, L. (2009). Effects of intellectual functioning on cognitive behavioural anger treatment for adults with learning disabilities in secure settings. *Advances in Mental Health and Intellectual Disabilities* 3: 51–56.

Tsiouris, J.A., Kim, S.Y., Brown, W.T. et al. (2011). Association of aggressive behaviours with psychiatric disorders, age, sex and degree of intellectual disability: a large-scale survey. *Journal of Intellectual Disability Research* 55: 636–649.

Tyrer, P., Tarabi, S.A., Bassett, P. et al. (2017). Nidotherapy compared with enhanced care programme approach training for adults with aggressive challenging behaviour and intellectual disability (NIDABID): cluster-randomised controlled trial. *Journal of Intellectual Disability Research* 61: 521–531.

Ullrich, S., Keers, R., and Coid, J.W. (2014). Delusions, anger, and serious violence: new findings from the MacArthur Violence Risk Assessment Study. *Schizophrenia Bulletin* 40: 1174–1181.

Unwin, G. and Deb, S. (2014). Caregiver's concerns-quality of life scale (CC-QoLS): development and evaluation of psychometric properties. *Research in Developmental Disabilities* 35: 2329–2340.

Vitacco, M.J., Van Rybroek, G.J., Rogstad, J.E. et al. (2009). Predicting short-term institutional aggression in forensic patients: a multi-trait method for understanding subtypes of aggression. *Law and Human Behavior* 33: 308–319.

Willner, P., Brace, N., and Phillips, J. (2005). Assessment of anger coping skills in individuals with intellectual disabilities. *Journal of Intellectual Disability Research* 49: 329–339.

Willner, P., Jones, J., Tams, R. et al. (2002). A randomised controlled trial of the efficacy of a cognitive-behavioural anger management group for adults with learning disabilities. *Journal of Applied Research in Intellectual Disabilities* 15: 224–235.

Willner, P., Rose, J., Jahoda, A. et al. (2013). A cluster randomised controlled trial of a manualised cognitive behavioural anger management intervention delivered by supervised lay therapists to people with intellectual disabilities. *Health Technology Assessment* 17: 21.

Willner, P. and Tomlinson, S. (2007). Generalization of anger-coping skills from day-service to residential settings. *Journal of Applied Research in Intellectual Disabilities* 20: 553–562.

7

Psychological Assessment Procedures for Sex Offenders with Intellectual and Developmental Disabilities

Lesley R. Steptoe[1,2] and Amanda M. Michie[3]

[1] *NHS Tayside, Dundee, UK*
[2] *Abertay University, Dundee, UK*
[3] *NHS Lothian, Edinburgh, UK*

7.1 Introduction

In this chapter, we consider the important variables in the assessment of sexual offenders with intellectual developmental disabilities (IDD: APA 2013). We aim to outline and evaluate the available psychometric assessments commonly used when assessing psychological constructs with sexual offenders with IDD. We have provided a brief overview of some psychometric principles. We also review the area of risk assessment and its growing development in relation to sexual offenders with IDD.

There are noted similarities between sex offenders with IDD and their mainstream counterparts (Craig and Hutchinson 2005), therefore it would be easy to assume, in relation to assessment and intervention, what is applicable to one group should be pertinent to all. However, methodological differences between studies of these two groups and the difficulties of standardization of normative data within assessment measures for sexual offenders with IDD provides challenge to this assumption.

7.1.1 Psychometrics

The importance of having normative data on assessments used to measure constructs of attitudes, emotional stability, values, and beliefs of sexual offenders with IDD is crucial to the assessment of risk. Goals of treatment also require careful consideration, and any assessment process should include a wide range of psychological constructs to inform subsequent formulation. Psychometric assessment is an objective measurement of a particular psychological construct with accuracy and reliability. For a valid assessment result, it is essential that the outcome data from the assessment scale is first, truly representative of the construct being assessed (construct validity), and second provides an indication of the individual's performance in comparison to others, within a representative standardized normative sample. To achieve this aim, the standardized normative data used as a comparison for the individuals responses on the assessment scale must have been standardized on the population it is to be used with (Craig et al. 2010). If these criteria are met, the evaluation of the response sets in comparison to normative data, allows a judgement to be made as to how closely the participants score is to the mean of the normal distribution.

There are a variety of psychological constructs relative to sexual offending behaviour and a number of varied assessments that facilitate their measurement. A significant challenge for those working with sex offenders with IDD, is that many of these assessments lack standardized normative data for that population. This throws doubt onto the reliability of outcomes when such assessments are used with this cohort, as it makes any comparison to normative data questionable. Given this deficit, it is not possible to ascertain whether the assessment has construct validity for use with that client group and whether it can differentiate between groups (e.g. sex offenders and non-sex offenders). Part of the problem with standardization of assessments is the question of how valid the sample used for obtaining standardized normative data is (Fisher et al. 1999). For example, a number of assessments used to measure psychological constructs in sexual offenders have produced standardized normative data from college students or other non-sexually offending group populations (Craig et al. 2010). These groups from which this normative data has been obtained may differ significantly from sexual offenders in many aspects such as social class, life experience, and so on.

7.1.2 Determining Intellectual Disability

Three criteria are required to meet the diagnosis of intellectual disability as set out in Diagnostic and Statistical Manual 5th Edition (DSM-V):

- the individual should have a full-scale Intelligence Quotient (IQ) of less than 70 as measured by a reliable and valid test of intellectual functioning;
- there should be at least two deficits of adaptive behaviour; and
- onset should be pre-18 years.

Authors such as Lezak et al. (2004) or Kaufman and Lichtenberger (1999) provide an in-depth review of the cognitive assessment. The detail these authors provide is extensive and more comprehensive than can be discussed within the limits of this chapter. However, there are two fundamental aspects of cognitive assessment that should guide assessment with all clients with ID. Primarily it is important to assess the basic level of intellectual ability for the individual client, in order to be able to structure the assessment process. There is a clear relationship between an individual's level of intellectual functioning and the level of difficulty within the understanding of the assessment process (Lindsay 2009). The assessor needs to be sensitive to the need to utilize adaptation in all aspects of client assessment, from the interview process, through psychometric assessment and resultant formulation from the assessment process (Table 7.1). The Wechsler Adult Intelligence Scale – Fourth Edition UK (WAIS-IV-UK) (Wechsler 2008) is produced to the highest psychometric standards and is internationally recognized regarding its psychometric properties relative to the evaluation of intellectual functioning. The scale provides a full scale intelligent quotient (FSIQ) and allows a determination of four index scores relative to verbal comprehension, perceptual reasoning, working memory and the speed of processing of information presented to them. If indicated, an evaluation of differences in index ratings for statistical significance should be carried out and in certain cases, the

Table 7.1 Initial assessments of intellectual disability and adaptive functioning.

Domain	Assessment
Assessment of Intellectual Functioning	Wechsler Adult Intelligence Scale IV edition (WAIS IV)
Assessment of Adaptive Behaviour	Vineland Scales of Adaptive Behaviour (Sparrow et al. 1984). Adaptive Behaviour Scale: Residential and Community (Nihira et al. 1993)

determination of optional index ratings such as the General Ability Index (GAI) and/or the Cognitive Proficiency Index (CPI) can be additionally informative. Where statistically significant differences exist between index ratings the GAI provides an estimate of general intellectual ability, with less emphasis being placed on working memory and processing speed components of cognitive functioning, and is determined through the addition of the standardized rating for solely the Verbal Comprehension Index and the Perceptual Reasoning Index. The CPI is derived from the core Working Memory and Processing Speed indices and represents the individual's proficiency with cognitive processing. The cognitive assessment is an extremely important part of the initial evaluation; however, a full-scale IQ of less than 70 IQ points should not be considered as definitive of intellectual disability on its own as all three criteria should be met.

7.1.2.1 Adaptive Functioning

Adaptive functioning can be understood as, the ability to blend into society un-noticed. Deficits that result in failure to meet the sociocultural standards for personal independence and social responsibility may be described as deficits in adaptive behaviour. Constructs such as communication, social participation, and independent living are evaluated within the assessment process.

To be considered as relevant, deficits identified must be pervasive across settings such as home, school, work, and leisure. Adaptive functioning is generally assessed through clinical observation and standardized assessment carried out with a knowledgeable informant, for example, a family member or support worker and also the individual to the extent that this may be possible. Assessments such as the Adaptive Behaviour Scale – Residential and Community (ABS-RC2) or the Vineland's Adaptive Behaviour Scale (VABS) are well recognized assessments in the field and provide appropriately standardized normative comparisons for interpretation of results. It is worth noting that adaptive functioning may be more difficult to assess in a controlled setting, such as a prison or hospital setting, due to the institutional nature of such settings. If feasible, information regarding the individual's adaptive functioning outside those setting should be obtained.

7.1.2.2 Onset pre-18

The third criterion to be met is onset of developmental disability pre-18 years. Background information is the source of information to determine whether this criterion is met. Interview with the individual, file review of any available child and adolescent mental health or social work information can also be invaluable. Exploration of educational support, special needs schooling, record of needs as a child in education may all assist in the determination of a psychological profile relative to intellectual ability at an early age. It is also worth noting any suspension or exclusion from school as a measure of behavioural issues and also potential interruption to educational progress.

7.2 Characteristics of Sex Offenders with IDD

Empirical studies have identified certain characteristics that are likely to present within sex offenders with IDD. These studies have suggested that this client group in particular, has a higher incidence of family psychopathology, psycho-social deprivation, behavioural disturbances at school, higher prevalence of psychiatric illness, social and sexual naivety, poor ability to form normal sexual and personal relationships, poor impulse control, and lower levels of conceptual/abstract reasoning (Allam et al. 1997; Awad et al. 1984; Caparulo 1991; Day 1994; Lambrick and Glaser 2004; Winter et al. 1997). From these identified characteristics, researchers have put forward several potential hypotheses regarding factors that may underpin sexually deviant behaviour in men with IDD. Some of the evaluations have been made within the context of forensic intellectual disability services that apply a holistic approach to individuals including psychiatric review, occupational placement, nursing interventions, community support and management, criminal justice involvement, and in some cases, 24-hour supervision.

Carrying out a holistic multidisciplinary assessment is clearly a helpful process and facilitates the assessment of a number of factors simultaneously by professionals. Factors such as mental illness, lack of skills and difficulties in adaptive functioning, and, not least, aspects pertinent to sexual deviancy, will give way to a formulation-based approach which may either include, or indeed exclude, factors that may assist in identifying risk and needs analysis for future intervention and provision. If this amalgamation of assessment leads to a more holistic multifactorial approach to intervention, one would anticipate that as a result, as there is an increased response to intervention and support needs, over the longer term this would lead to an increased ability in the offender's desistance from offending. If this can be achieved from a dispositional and/or situational pathway, then it can be viewed as a positive outcome from the identified needs from the assessment process. Unfortunately, even when such services are recognized as effective (Lindsay and Michie 2013), there is the possibility of risk of retraction under the current auspices of National Health Service (NHS) redevelopment and funding issues.

Lanyon (2001) highlights the need for a structured assessment format that delineates the relevant issues. To aid the understanding of the relevant issues we first need to understand the aetiology of sexual offending behaviour in men with IDD. A number of aetiological factors have been identified as relevant to sexual offending behaviour. Those that may be considered relevant to sexual offenders with IDD are worthy of consideration at this point.

7.2.1 Counterfeit Deviance Theory

The theory of Counterfeit Deviance was first mentioned by Hingsburger et al. (1991) and was noted as the most influential basis for the development of treatment services for this client group (Luiselli 2000). Counterfeit Deviance refers to behaviour, which is without doubt deviant but which may be precipitated by a lack of sexual knowledge, poor social skills, limited opportunities to establish sexual relationships, and sexual naivety rather than a deviant sexual interest. Therefore, assessment should also consider these issues in addition to sexuality.

Murphy et al. (1983) noted that sex offenders with IDD display deviant sexual arousal and cognitive distortions rather than sexual naivety. In comparison to controls, sexual offenders with IDD, had higher levels of sexual knowledge, Michie et al. (2006). To test this theory Lunsky et al. (2007) compared the sexual knowledge of two samples of individuals with IDD who had a history of sexual offending and two matched samples of individuals with IDD with no sexual offences. These authors found that offenders with IDD who had previously engaged in inappropriate sexual behaviour such as masturbation in public or touching someone inappropriately showed no difference relative to level of sexual knowledge from their matched sample of individuals with IDD with no sexual offence history. Those offenders who had committed more serious offences were found to have greater sexual knowledge than matched non-offenders. When only those individuals who had received prior sex education were compared in terms of sexual knowledge, there were no differences between groups. However, sex offenders who had perpetrated serious offences, expressed more liberal attitudes than sex offenders who were considered to have perpetrated inappropriate behaviour and non-offenders towards same-sex activities. However, Lindsay (2009) suggests that sex offenders with IDD may not have full comprehension of the social sexual rules and norms of society, which, if coupled with deviant sexual interests, may lead to sexually offending behaviour. This is supported by Griffiths et al. (2013) who suggest that inappropriate sexual behaviour may be precipitated by: lack of sexual knowledge, poor social and interpersonal skills, limited opportunities to establish appropriate sexual relationships, and sexual naiveté rather than deviant sexual interest.

7.2.2 Sexual Abuse

In some cases, there would be an element of face validity in the suggestion that there may be an association between the experience of sexual abuse in childhood and sexual offending in adolescence or adulthood. Briggs and Hawkins (1996) noted that not all individuals who have been a victim of sexual abuse will go on to abuse. There are few existing studies on sexual abuse in people with IDD that suggest behaviour problems such as sexual disinhibition, are as a consequence of past sexual abuse (Sequeira and Hollins 2003). Lindsay et al. (2000) reported a significantly higher rate of sexual abuse 38% vs 12.7% when comparing 48 sex offenders with 50 non-sex offenders. However, Lindsay and MacLeod (2001) highlighted, that in a population of offenders with IDD, not all sex offenders have been sexually abused. Lindsay et al. (2001) compared the physical and sexual abuse histories of 46 sexual and 48 non-sexual offenders with learning disabilities and found 38% of the sexual offenders and 12.7% of the non-sexual offenders had experienced sexual abuse, while 13% of the sexual offenders and 33% of the nonsexual offenders had experienced physical abuse.

7.2.3 Mental Illness

Within a retrospective review of psychiatric case notes for 47 male patients with IDD having been referred for antisocial sexual behaviour, Day (1994) found 32% of the men had a psychiatric diagnosis. This prevalence rate was also supported by Lindsay (2002).

However, Lund (1990) utilized the Danish Central Criminal register to extract data on 274 learning disabled offenders serving statutory care orders on two census days, the first in 1973 and the second in 1984. Of the offences registered 20.9% were sexual and in 12.9% a sexual offence was the only offence with which the individual had been charged. Results indicated that 91.7% (87.5% categorized as behaviour disorders) had a diagnosis of mental illness. Variations in definitions of mental illness may account for this discrepancy as behaviour disorders were reported separately in both the Day and Lindsay studies (Lindsay 2004).

7.2.4 Impulsivity

The term Impulsivity connotes a, 'react first think later' presentation and is suggested as relevant to the presentation of sex offenders with IDD. This factor therefore assumes that sexual offenders with IDD will be more impulsive than their non-disabled counterparts. Empirical testing of this hypothesis by Parry and Lindsay (2003) found that levels of impulsivity in sexual offenders with IDD compared with those of non-IDD sexual offenders revealed no significant differences. Lindsay (2004) suggested that there is little evidence that sexual offenders with IDD are more impulsive with regard to their offending. They have been shown to demonstrate delayed gratification through the display of simple grooming behaviours. Similarly, to non-IDD sex offenders, they may delay gratification until an opportunity presents itself. This data suggests that impulsivity requires careful assessment.

7.2.5 Lack of Discrimination

It is suggested that sex offenders with IDD are less discriminating in their victim choice. Studies suggest that 68% had previous offending (Scorzelli and Reinke-Scorzelli 1979) with 62% having previous sexual offending (Lindsay et al. 2002). The findings of Scorzelli and Reinke-Scorzelli (1979) reported that 68% of a mixed group of offenders with IDD had committed previous sexual offences. Of the sample, 33% of the offences were against adults, 28% were against children and 18% consisted of indecent exposure. Although sex offenders with intellectual disabilities tend to have low specificity for age and sex of their victims (Craig and Hutchinson 2005; Gilby et al. 1989; Griffiths et al. 1985), they have a greater tendency to offend against male children and younger children (Blanchard et al. 1999; Brown and Stein 1997; Rice et al. 2008).

7.2.6 Empathy Deficits

A national study of sexual offender treatment providers noted that 93% recognized that developing offender empathy for victims is an important treatment component (Knopp and Stevenson 1989). Empathy has been noted to be positively related to prosocial behaviour and an inhibitor of aggression (Miller and Eisenberg 1988).

Ward et al. (1998) noted that the literature on sexual offending shows many offenders demonstrate problems in perspective taking and empathy. For example, many offenders have difficulty in understanding their victim's distress and appreciating the subsequent consequences to victims and the victim's wider circle of support, such as family and friends (Hanson and Scott 1995; Keeling et al. 2007a; Malmuth and Brown 1994; Williams et al. 2007).

Some research has directly related empathy to offenders with IDD, Jolliffe and Farrington (2004) studied 349 offenders and found that ability to demonstrate empathy was directly related to IQ. Those with lower intellectual ability showed greater deficits in empathy. Proctor and Beail (2007) compared 25 offenders with 35 non-offenders on the Davis Interpersonal Reactivity Index (IRI) (Davis 1980) and found that the offender group showed greater levels of empathic response than the non-offender group suggesting that empathy training may not be necessary for this group. Consistent with Marshall et al. (1995), this may suggest that offenders may have specific deficits in relation to their own offence.

Keenan and Ward (2000) suggest that the 'theory of mind' literature provides a conceptual framework that may serve to explain some aspects that are identified as underpinning this aspect of sexual offending behaviour. 'Theory of mind' is a descriptive term that refers to the ability of the individual to attribute mental states to others. Deficits in theory of mind may take the form of a pervasive and profound deficit in perspective taking (Keenan and Ward 2000). These authors suggested that deficits in theory of mind could result from genetic or organic factors, but might also result from the individual's developmental experience within the family and within their social environment. For example, a background of abuse or neglect may act as a risk factor for entry to a deviant developmental pathway, leading eventually to sexual offending. Such experiences exist in the backgrounds of many sexual offenders (Prentky et al. 1989). Researchers have attributed a relationship between the development of theory of mind and the communicative relationship between child and parent critical for the development of attachment bonds (Fonagy et al. 1997). Similarly, research on individual differences in the development of theory of mind have shown early factors such as security of attachment between infant and caregiver, are associated with the rate of theory of mind acquisition (Fonagy et al. 1997). Many sex offenders have disturbed family backgrounds and are known to show high rates of insecure attachment (Ward et al. 1996). Whilst the hypothesis that sexual offenders' difficulties of theory of mind, with delayed acquisition of theory of mind due to attachment difficulties may be plausible, Proctor and Beail (2007), within their comparison of 25 offenders with IDD and 25 non-offenders with IDD on two empathy and three theory of mind tasks, found offenders with IDD had better, rather than poorer empathy and theory of mind abilities than non-offenders. Equally there is support for a 'delay hypothesis' in the development of theory of mind relative to verbal cognition and the understanding of causes and consequences of emotions in children and adolescents (Thirion-Marissiaux and Nader-Grosbois 2008). These latter authors suggested that if delayed development continues into adulthood, it may result in difficulties of perspective taking and the understanding of others mental representations for offenders with IDD.

While some research suggests that sexual offenders with IDD may be no worse than other men with IDD in their empathic responses (Proctor and Beail 2007), there may still be some benefit in developing better empathic responses, which may increase self-regulation skills and as such promote restraint in personal relapse prevention.

7.3 Assessment of Sexual Offence Related Issues

A growing body of empirical studies have identified several factors that appear to be crucial ingredients in the underpinnings of sexual abuse (Keenan and Ward 2000). This has led to a variety of empirical measures for the assessment of sexual offenders (non-IDD) with psychometric assessments being plentiful to assess a number of constructs (see Beech et al. 2003; Craig and Beech 2010). Constructs include assessment of sexual interests, distorted sexual attitude, affectivity, impulsivity, and self-management/ self-regulation. Until the 1990s there has been a dearth of empirically tested psychometric measures for sexual offenders with IDD with appropriate normative samples for comparison, however, the 1990s provided a change with some development of empirically validated psychometric measures specifically standardized for use with this cohort of individuals. Craig and Rettenberger (2016) conducted a comprehensive review of risk assessment in sex offenders and considered the developments in this area. They highlighted the importance of protective factors and the consideration of issues such as responsivity.

To set out the needs within the assessment process we have used the conceptual framework of the Structured Risk Assessment (SRA) model (Craig and Rettenberger 2016, 2017; Thornton 2002). Within the SRA model Thornton (2002) suggest that the main dynamic risk factors fall into four domains of interest: Sexual Interests, Distorted Attitudes, Social and Emotional Functioning, and Self-Management. In Table 7.2 we have utilised these four domains to conceptualize the psychometric assessment process for sex offenders with IDD (Craig et al. 2010).

Table 7.2 Psychometric assessments of sexual deviancy in sex offenders with intellectual developmental disabilities (IDD).

Domain	Assessment
Sexual Interests	Multiphasic Sex Inventory (MSI) (Nichols and Molinder 1984)
	Sexual Attitudes and Knowledge Assessment (SAK) (Heighway and Webster, 2007).
Distorted Attitudes	Adapted Victim Empathy (Beckett and Fisher 1994)
	The Adapted Victim Consequences Task – adapted from the Victim Empathy Questionnaire (Bowers et al. 1995)
	Questionnaire on Attitudes Consistent with Sexual Offenders (QACSO) (Broxholme and Lindsay 2003; Lindsay et al. 2000)
	Abel and Becker Cognition Scale (Abel et al. 1984)
	Sex Offences Self-Opinion Scale (SOSAS: Bray and Forshaw 1996)
Social and Emotional Functioning	Adapted Self-Esteem Questionnaire – adapted version of Thornton's Brief Self-Esteem Scale (Thornton et al. 2004)
	Adapted Emotional Loneliness Scale – adapted from Russell et al.'s (1980) UCLA Emotional Loneliness scale
	Adapted Relationship Questionnaire (ARQ) – adapted version of the Relationship Questionnaire (RQ) – Bartholomew and Horowitz (1991) adapted by (Steptoe 2011)
	The Norwicki-Strickland Internal-External Locus of Control Scale (Nowicki 1976)
	Adapted Relapse Prevention Interview (Beckett et al. 1997)
Self-Management	The Psychopathy Checklist – Revised (PCL-R; Hare 1991) (adapted by Morrissey 2003)

7.3.1 Sexual Interests

There is a considerable range of assessments for the purpose of assessing deviant sexual interest including phallometric technology (Marshall and Fernandez 2003; Reyes et al. 2017), attention-based measures (Mokros et al. 2013), self-report measures of sexual interest (Laws et al. 2000) and psychometric measures (Craig and Beech 2010). Evidence suggests that both sexual interests and sexual drive are considered as primary motivators by several authors (Blanchard et al. 1999; Harris et al. 2003). In particular, the assessment of deviant sexual preferences in sexual offenders has been shown to determine those sexual offenders who show continuity of offence pathways (Craig et al. 2010; Hanson and Bussière 1998; Hanson and Morton-Bourgon 2005). Thornton (2002) suggests that within this domain, the level of intensity of both sexual preoccupation and offence related sexual preferences are a consideration.

7.3.1.1 Multiphasic Sex Inventory (MSI) (Nichols and Molinder 1984)

The MSI is designed to assess psychosocial aspects of the sex offender's presentation (rapists, child molesters, exhibitionists) and shows good psychometric and risk assessment properties (Craig et al. 2006a, 2007). The MSI provides data that corroborates with physiological indices of arousal (Barnard et al. 1989). Although this scale was developed for use with non-IDD sex offenders, it has been used to evaluate cognitive shift in sexual offenders with lower levels of cognitive functioning (mean IQ = 70) who were treatment completers (Craig et al. 2006b). Good predictive utility was found relative to risk probability with the sexual obsession scale (area under the curve [AUC] = 0.85), child molester scale, Rape scale, and the Paraphilia scale each reaching an AUC of 0.74. There is some caution however, as this scale was developed and standardized for non-IDD offenders and it remains unclear to what extent the standardized sample can translate as normative data for offenders with IDD. Craig et al. (2006b) suggest the application of some caution in utilizing this measure and to what extent the MSI items and language may be suitable for people with IDD. It may not be sensitive to the more subtle changes of cognitions for people with IDD.

7.3.1.2 Sexual Attitudes and Knowledge Assessment (SAK) (Heighway and Webster 2007)

This assessment is designed to assess sexual knowledge across four domains such as sexual awareness, assertiveness, understanding relationships, and social interaction. The scale consists of a series of questions that are supported with pictorial information. The SAK may be used to identify knowledge gaps and learning needs, to complete evaluations to design an individual programme of intervention according to need and for post-evaluations of treatment effectiveness.

7.3.2 Distorted Sexual Attitudes

It is reasonable to suggest that sexual offenders may have distorted beliefs about their victims or potential victims (Keenan and Ward 2000) and that these beliefs functionally facilitate and maintain their offending behaviour (Abel et al. 1984; Burt 1980; Ward et al. 1997). Distorted cognitions in sexual offenders have a considerable evidence base within research literature (Abel et al. 1984; Beech et al. 1999; Burt 1980; Hanson and

Harris 2000; Lindsay et al. 2007; Marolla and Scully 1986; Pithers et al. 1988; Stermac and Segal 1989; Ward et al. 1995, 1997). These distorted cognitions refer to faulty thought processes about victims, sexuality, or the offences themselves, that serve to justify sexual offending behaviour. The meta-analysis carried out by Hanson and Morton-Bourgon (2005) found denial and minimization unrelated to sexual recidivism while more general attitudes showing a tolerance for sexual offending behaviour being associated with sexual recidivism.

7.3.2.1 Adapted Victim Empathy (Beckett and Fisher 1994)

This scale is designed to evaluate a sex offender's expression of empathy towards a victim. Scores are expressed as percentages with a higher percentile score delineating a lower level of empathy expressed toward the victim. Adaptation of the scale was carried out by Keeling et al. (2007b). These authors report the adapted scale shows psychometric equivalence, when compared to the original with good internal consistency and a significant correlation with large effect size between the adapted and original scale. There was also good test–retest reliability and a high correlation with other adapted empathy scales, suggesting good convergent validity (Craig et al. 2010).

7.3.2.2 Adapted Victim Consequences Task: (Bowers et al. 1995)

The adapted Victim Empathy Consequences task is a nine-item interview requiring participants to list the good and bad things that happened to their victim as a result of the offence. It is an adaptation from the Victim Empathy Questionnaire.

7.3.2.3 Questionnaire on Attitudes Consistent with Sexual Offenders (QACSO) (Lindsay et al. 2000)

The QACSO is a 63-item questionnaire specifically designed for use with sex offenders with IDD. The scale is designed to measure cognitive distortions over several domains such as: rape and attitudes to women, voyeurism, exhibitionism, dating abuse, homosexual assault, offences against children, stalking and sexual harassment, and also has a domain measuring social desirability. The QACSO has been standardized on sex offenders with IDD, non-sexual offenders with IDD, non-offenders with IDD, and mainstream males. The scale has been found to discriminate sexual offenders with IDD from non-sexual offenders, indicating particular cognitive distortions which may serve to underpin offending behaviour in sex offenders and which may be a focus of intervention. Internal consistency of each domain on the scale revealed alphas of around 0.8. The QACSO has adequate test–retest reliability for all groups with the exception of the 'Rape and Attitudes towards Women' domain for non-sexual offenders without intellectual disability.

7.3.2.4 Sex Offenders Opinion Test (SOOT) (Bray 1997)

The original SOOT is a 28-item scale measuring attitudes regarding victims of sexual offences in general. Of the 28 items, 7 items measure lying, with the remaining 21 items being rated on a five-point Likert scale. Total scores relate to levels of distortions: the higher the score the greater the pattern of distorted thought processes relative to victims of sexual offences. The scale has been shown to have good internal consistency and is sensitive to treatment effects (Williams et al. 2007).

7.3.2.5   Sex Offences Self-Appraisal Scale (SOSAS) (Bray and Forshaw 1996):
This 20-item scale uses a five-point Likert scale, which presents statements that form attractive excuses likely to elicit agreement from sexual offenders. Alongside a total score, this scale also provides information on six domains: social desirability, victim blaming, denial, blame, minimization, and realism. The measures assess openness and objectivity identifying levels of denial, blame, and minimization in relation to offending behaviour. The item responses on the Likert scale are summed to give a total score, with higher scores relating to greater denial/distortions (range 0–95). The scale has been shown to have good internal consistency and a factor analysis revealed two distinct factors, denial of responsibility and denial of future risk (Williams et al. 2007). This scale has also been shown to measure cognitive shift following intervention and distinguishes between high- and low-risk groups. It has been used with sex offenders with IDD (Murphy et al. 2010).

7.3.3   Social and Emotional Functioning

The development of healthy attachment bonds to a primary caregiver in childhood emanates in social competence and a self-assured individual, whilst insecure attachment orientations clearly lead to maladaptive emotional regulation strategies, and poor coping methods based on less than optimal expectations of responsivity and supportiveness from primary attachment figures (Steptoe 2011). Attachment formation is a complex association of cognitive, affective, and behavioural mechanisms within the attachment system.

Difficulties in social and/or emotional functioning of sex offenders have been investigated relative to the formation of secure/insecure attachment bonds formed in childhood. Consistent with the attachment literature, Marshall and colleagues suggested that poor quality of parent–child attachments may lead to low self-confidence, poor social skills, little understanding of relationship issues and a lack of empathy (Garlick et al. 1996). Poor childhood attachment has been noted widely in sexual offenders' histories (Becker 1998; Browne and Herbert 1997; Marshall et al. 2000; Steptoe 2011). Hirschi (1969) identifies attachment as a critical factor to an individual's ability to identify positively with the expectations and values of others within society. Attachment style refers to the way individuals relate to other people and the emotions underpinning these social interactions. When writing regarding juvenile sex offenders, Ryan (1999) reports that when physical violence, sexual abuse, and parental neglect are included as maltreatment factors 'almost the whole population of juvenile sex offenders can be seen to have experienced some form of maltreatment' (p. 134). An important link to the development of adolescent offending in general may in part be due to the insecure and damaged attachment that develops between children and parents as a result of neglect and maltreatment Pithers et al. (1998). In a review of the literature Craissati et al. (2002) found that family backgrounds of sex offenders are typified by neglect, violence, and disruption, with parents of adolescent sex offenders found to be rejecting, abusive, or emotionally detached towards their children (Awad et al. 1984). Support for these findings was provided by Craissati et al. (2002) who concluded that an affectionless control style of parenting was reported as being highly prevalent in the parents of sex offenders. Whilst insecure attachment style could not be considered as the only contributory factor to sexual offending behaviour it can be considered as a developmental risk factor, whilst secure attachment could be considered as a protective factor (Rich 2006).

Insecure attachment is generally associated with negative affect (Consedine and Magai, 2003). Negative emotional states such as anxiety, depression, and low levels of self-esteem and also anger (Hanson and Harris 2000; Pithers et al. 1998; Proulx et al. 1999) have been identified in the literature as precursors to offences. Additionally, factors such as low self-esteem, loneliness, and external locus of control seem to distinguish child abusers from comparison groups (Beech et al. 1999). The meta-analysis carried out by Hanson and Morton-Bourgon (2005) lends support to the relevance of emotional congruence and emotional over identification with children and to a lesser extent hostility, as important factors relative to recidivism. Lindsay (2009) suggests the innate drive for sexual contact alongside emotional closeness may continue resulting in them seeking these basic human needs through forced sex or sexual deviancy. Theories of intimacy deficits have been muted as a contributory factor to sexual offending behaviour in adult males (Marshall 1989).

7.3.3.1 Adapted Relationship Questionnaire (ARQ) (Steptoe 2011)

Adapted from the Relationship Questionnaire (RQ) (Bartholomew and Horrowitz 1991), the ARQ is a 15-item scale that delineates three attachment styles, Secure, Anxious Avoidant, and Dismissing Avoidant. The scale accounts for attachment within two continuums of attachment anxiety and behavioural avoidance and shows a good level of internal consistency. The client is asked to rate their concordance with the statements in the scale over a four-part Likert scale of 'Not like me; A bit like me; Quite like me; and Very like me'. A pictorial representation in the form of a bar chart is provided as representative of each category on the Likert scale to aid decision making. The scale has been developed with offenders with IDD inclusive of sex offenders with IDD and has been tested on comparative controls. This is a preliminary screening measure; empirical evaluation found the scale to have good internal consistency and construct validity. Whilst this scale is one of the first to find good internal consistency and construct validity when attempting to measure the construct of attachment with this client group, one difficulty with the scale is the retrospective self-report response system within the scoring and evaluation, which may be subject to issues of participant memory or bias. Additional perceived parenting measures were also conducted at the same time and provided adequate correlation to the attachment measure, however further development of additional qualitative measures such as an attachment interview are required for the assessment of attachment in offenders with IDD to provide a holistic assessment.

7.3.3.2 Adapted Self Esteem Questionnaire

The Adapted Self Esteem Questionnaire is an adapted version of the Brief Self Esteem Scale (Thornton et al. 2004). The scale consists of eight items used to evaluate self-esteem. The items have been reworded using simpler phrasing and respondents rate items on a dichotomous yes/no scale. High scores relate to high self-esteem (range 0–8). The measure has been shown to have good internal consistency and is sensitive to treatment effect with participants scoring higher post treatment indicating increased self-esteem.

7.3.3.3 Adapted Emotional Loneliness Scale

This scale is utilized in Her Majesty's Prison (HMP) Service assessment battery and is adapted from the Russell et al.'s (1980) UCLA Emotional Loneliness scale. The scale consists of 18 items measuring the individual's own feelings of emotional loneliness. Responses are given through a three-point Likert scale of 'yes', 'no', and 'don't know'. The range of scores is 0–18, the higher the score the more emotional loneliness. This scale was noted as having good internal consistency, it was found to be insensitive to treatment effects (Williams et al. 2007). The scale is thought to be most useful in its application as a pre-treatment measure of emotional loneliness to inform clinical assessment rather than as a measure of sexual deviancy or cognitive shift in perception of emotional loneliness.

7.3.3.4 The Nowicki-Strickland Internal-External Locus of Control Scale (Nowicki 1976)

This scale consists of 40 items with response set of the simple 'yes' or 'no'. The scale evaluates the extent to which an individual believes that events have occurred as a result of their own behaviour (internal locus of control) or as a result of events outside their control such as luck or fate (external locus of control). Test re-test results evaluating reliability has been reported to be $r = 0.83$ (Nowicki and Duke 1974). This scale has been used with adults with IDD (Wehmeyer 1994; Wehmeyer and Palmer 1997), including sex offenders with IDD (Langdon and Talbot 2006; Rose et al. 2002) as well as non-IDD sex offenders (Fisher et al. 1998). Scores of 11 or less represent the endorsement of an internal locus of control whereas scores of 12 or more endorse an external locus of control (Fisher and Beech 1998).

7.3.4 Self-Management

This domain refers to the individual's ability to plan, problem solve, and regulate dysfunctional impulses that might lead down a pathway of sexual offending behaviour (Pithers et al. 1988; Ward et al. 1998). Patterns of antisocial behaviour and impulsivity have been identified as precursors of sexual recidivism (Prentky and Knight 1991). Thornton (2002) draws similarities between this concept and Factor 2 in the Psychopathy Checklist – Revised (PCL-R) (Hare 1991) which has been found to predict sexual recidivism (Firestone et al. 1999; Rice and Harris 1997).

Lindsay (2009) provides an evaluation of the literature regarding the Ward and Hudson (1998) Self-Regulation Pathways Model which he notes has been particularly fruitful with regards to studies on offenders with IDD. For example, Keeling and Rose (2005) note that this population is characterized by low self-esteem, low self-worth, poor assertiveness and problem-solving skills. They conclude that sex offenders with IDD would be more likely to be aligned with passive, automatic styles of self-regulation and less likely to engage in explicit planning. These authors hypothesized that sex offenders with IDD would tend to use avoidant/passive or approach/automatic pathways. However, sex offenders with IDD tended to use approach pathways with equal numbers distributed between active and passive self-regulation strategies (Keeling et al. 2006; Langdon et al. 2007; Lindsay et al. 2008). As the majority of the men in the three studies identified are assessed as using approach goals, this suggests that there are very few who actively attempt to inhibit their sexual desires. Secondly Ward and Hudson

(2000) hypothesized that approach/explicit offenders would have a higher rate of recidivism. However, in their study, Lindsay et al. (2008) found the opposite, with approach/explicit offenders having a significantly lower rate of recidivism following treatment. Lindsay (2009) suggests this reinforces the conclusion that these men may not have internalized the extent to which their behaviour contravenes conventions of society and suggests a revision to the Counterfeit Deviance hypothesis is warranted.

7.3.4.1 Adapted Relapse Prevention Interview (Beckett et al. 1997)

This interview schedule is designed for use with people with IDD and can be utilized either at time of assessment for potential attendance at group therapy or within the first week of attendance at therapeutic intervention. The scale is divided into questions that focus on awareness of risk factors and questions that focus on the use of appropriate strategies to avoid, escape, or cope safely with risky scenarios. The scale has the ability to differentiate between different areas of relapse knowledge and can inform on the effectiveness of a relapse prevention intervention. The scale has been adapted for use with sex offenders with ID and is noted to have a good measure of internal consistency with sensitivity to treatment effects (Williams et al. 2007). It should be administered and scored by the responsible clinician for the treatment programme.

7.3.4.2 Psychopathy Checklist – Revised (PCL-R) (Hare 1991, 2003) (adapted by Morrissey 2003)

The PCL-R is a 20-item semi-structured interview schedule of psychopathic personality traits. Each of the items is scored on a three-point scale, 0; 1; 2, from file review and semi-structured interview. Maximum score attained is 40, with categorical cut off scores and more dynamic scoring also being used to allocate levels of psychopathy in an individual case. Of the 20 items, 18 are categorized into two factors: Interpersonal/Affective (Factor 1) and Social Deviance (Factor 2), each factor having two facets. The outcome of this assessment may have a significant effect on the individual's future, and because the potential for harm if the test is used or administered incorrectly is considerable, Hare argues that the test should be considered valid only if administered by a suitably qualified and experienced clinician.

An ongoing criticism of the PCL-R is that interrater reliability is noted as much lower in the real world than stated in the manual (Hare 2003; Hare and Neumann 2006). In relation to the issue of interrater reliability, Daderman and Hellstrom (2018) noted the importance of knowledge about factors that can affect scoring of forensic assessment such as education, training, experience, motivation, rater's personality, and quality of file data. With regards to the assessment of offenders with IDD, Morrisey (2003) developed clinical guidelines for the use of the PCL-R with offenders with IDD in order to facilitate research in the field. On the basis of these guidelines Morrisey et al. (2005) reported findings on the applicability, reliability, and validity of the PCL-R in 203 offenders with IDD. These authors reported acceptable internal consistency for the measure with reasonable ($\alpha = 0.82$) and interrater reliability for the total score was also good (ICC = 0.89). Reliability for affective and interpersonal facets was also reasonable ($\alpha = 0.74$–0.79) and somewhat poorer reliability for lifestyle and antisocial facets was noted ($\alpha = 0.62$–0.64) convergent and discriminant validity being similar to those observed in other populations. FSIQ was not found to be correlated with the PCL-R total score on either Factor 1 (affective and interpersonal style) of Factor 2 (antisocial lifestyle). Morrisey et al. (2007) further reviewed the use of the PCL-R in 73 participants in a high secure intellectual disability setting by investigating the relationship between PCL-R score with treatment progress over a two-year period. They found that PCL-R total score and Factor 1 scores (interpersonal and affective aspects) were significantly and inversely associated with moves from high to medium secure settings within the follow up period. The PCL-R scores were also significantly associated with negative treatment progress with personality aspects, specifically, deficient affective experiences being stronger predictors of progress than the behavioural or antisocial aspects. Lindsay (2009) noted that studies have reported equivalent numbers of sex offenders with IDD across levels of security. From this he suggests that a relatively significant number of individuals are likely to be appropriate for sex offender treatment in the community as well as other secure settings. If personality features are related to treatment engagement and progress, then it is important for therapists to consider these features relative to motivational procedures to ensure progress.

Further exploratory studies using the PCL – Youth version (PCL-YV) (Forth et al. 2003) and PCL-Screening version (PCL-SV) (Hart et al. 1995) resulted in better content validity and improved psychometric properties for these scales as compared to the PCL-R (C. Morrisey, personal commuication). These findings provide preliminary evidence that the PCL-YV and PCL-SV may have promise as more IDD appropriate measures of psychopathy. At present therefore, some caution is advised in the use of the PCL-R in offenders with IDD, particularly where clinical decision making may be influenced as a result of the outcome.

7.4 Sexual Recidivism

There are various rates of prevalence reported for sex offending in offenders with IDD. Lund (1990) found a doubling of the incidence of sex offending when comparing sentencing in 1973 with 1983 however this was a short time after the deinstitutionalization of individuals with intellectual disabilities and may be a reflection of individuals now being opened to opportunity that had previously been managed in the institutional setting. Gross (1985) found that between 21 and 50% of offenders with intellectual disabilities had committed a sexual crime. Walker and McCabe (1973) in their study of patients committed under a hospital order, found that of 331 men with an intellectual disability, 28% had committed a sexual offence. A high rate of serious crimes including sexual offences was found in a study by Sundram (1990) with 38% of inmates with an IQ below 70 in New York State prisons committing or attempting to commit murder, manslaughter, assault, and sexual offences. In relation to rates of recidivism, within a two year follow up study, an overall rate of recidivism of 41.3% in previous prison inmates with IDD and 34% recidivism in sexual offenders with IDD (Klimecki et al. 1994). Gibbens and Robertson (1983) reported a reconviction rate of 68% in 250 male patients with IDD detained under hospital orders. Craig and Hutchinson (2005) estimated sex offenders with IDD reoffend at a rate of six times that of non-IDD sexual offenders at two-years and three times that of non-IDD sexual offenders at four-years. Recidivism is more likely to occur in the first year following discharge (Day 1993, 1994; Klimecki et al. 1994). The assessment of risk probability is an important factor within the formulation of risk, need, and responsivity for the sex offender with IDD.

7.5 Risk Assessment

Risk assessment is related to the future likelihood of whether the offender may commit a further sexual offence. Risk assessment methods have developed over time to reach the holistic methods used today. The previously used, unstructured professional judgement approach, led to the development of the second-generation actuarial approach (See Bonta and Andrews 2017) for an extensive overview. However, limitations identified with using solely actuarial risk assessment, led to the further development of Structured Professional Judgement (SPJ) approaches. We will provide an overview of the development of the risk assessment process over time prior to providing information on specific risk assessments which may be used with offenders with IDD (Table 7.3).

7.5.1 Unstructured Professional Judgement of Risk

Looking back to the 1950s and 1960s, unstructured clinical judgement was the most common approach used to determine an individual's risk for violence or sexual violence. By definition, it is based primarily on professional opinion, intuition, and clinical experience. The assessors have absolute discretion in terms of selecting risk factors to consider, how to conceptualize them for relevance and prioritization, and how to interpret this information to provide an ultimate prediction of risk probability. As such, this method is essentially informal and subjective and not without the possibility of human bias in the risk-judgement process. Although clinical judgement is a routine and necessary component within many clinical decision-making contexts, the defining feature of clinical judgement in terms of prediction is the lack of rules to integrate case information. Although this permits flexibility, ostensible widespread applicability, and relevance to the individual patient, there are several difficulties with this approach.

Table 7.3 Risk assessment measures for use with sex offenders with intellectual developmental disabilities (IDD).

Domain	Assessment
Actuarial Risk Assessment Instruments (ARAIs)	Rapid Risk Assessment for Sexual Offence Recidivism (RRASOR)
	Static-99 (Hanson and Thornton 1999, 2000)
	Minnesota Sex Offender Screening Tool–Revised (MnSOST-R) (Epperson et al. 1998)
	Sex Offender Risk Appraisal Guide (SORAG) (Quinsey et al. 2006)
Structured Professional Judgement (SPJ) measures	Sexual Violence Risk-20 (SVR-20) (Boer et al. 1997) adaptation guidelines (Boer et al. 2010).
	Historical Clinical Risk-20 (HCR-20) (Webster et al. 1997, Douglas et al. 2013)
	Risk of Sexual Violence Protocol (RSVP) (Hart et al. 2003)
Dynamic risk assessment	Assessment of Risk and Manageability of Individuals with Developmental and Intellectual Limitations Who Offend – Sexually (ARMIDILO-S) Boer et al. (2012)

First, because of the lack of rules there is low interrater reliability. Critics contend that the technique generally lacks consistency because independent clinicians may focus on dissimilar sources of information and subsequently form disparate conclusions. Second, there is low content validity in this method, as clinicians may or may not attend to variables that actually relate to violent or sexually violent behaviour. Third, there is low predictive validity as either failing to attend to important risk factors, attending to irrelevant variables, or giving improper weight to risk factors, will inevitably decrease the accuracy of decisions and may lead to false negative or false positive decisions being made relative to risk probability. Research bears these weaknesses out (see Goldberg 1968; Quinsey et al. 2001). As a response to the difficulties identified, researchers attempted to provide a more structured approach to the assessment of risk probability for offending behaviour in both violent and sexual offenders. This research led to the development of statistically driven actuarial risk assessments which are continuing to be used within a holistic risk assessment framework present day.

7.5.2   Actuarial Risk Assessment Instruments (ARAIs)

There are a number of shared characteristics within ARAIs, for example they represent highly SRA scales using combinations of empirically determined and thoroughly operationalized predictor variables which correlate with sexual recidivism. The scores derived on each of the scales correspond to risk categories (low, medium, high), which indicate a prediction of future risk probability. This may be explained in term of percentage risk of recidivism over a specific time frame, for example 45% for an individual of risk over a 10-year period. In their validation study of risk assessment tools for offenders with IDD Lindsay et al. (2008) tested the predictive validity of a number of risk assessment scales inclusive of the Static-99 (Hanson and Thornton 1999) and the Violence Risk Appraisal Guide (VRAG: Quinsey et al. 1998) with significant positive results. However, adaptations to scoring these tools were required in two areas. First, within the Static-99, in relation to the number of charges and convictions attained, it was consistently noted in file review that, despite behaviours being acknowledged that could be considered as sexual offending behaviour, no charge was brought. This was particularly evident in the hospital setting. Equally where a charge was brought, it was apparent that offenders with IDD are more likely to be diverted from the criminal justice system and therefore convictions may not ensue. Second, with regard to the evaluation of the ability to form meaningful relationships, offenders with IDD have less opportunity to establish such relationships. Each of these factors underpinned the need for some adaptation in scoring on actuarial measures (Lindsay et al. 2008). Several empirically derived actuarial risk measures have been developed. The most widely used of these in relation to risk of sexual offending behaviour are the Rapid Risk Assessment of Sexual Offence Recidivism (RRASOR; Hanson 1997), Static-99 (Hanson and Thornton 1999), Minnesota Sex Offender Screening Tool–Revised (MnSOST-R) (Epperson et al. 1998), the Sex Offender Risk Appraisal Guide (SORAG) (Quinsey et al. 1998). We provide an overview of these assessment scales.

7.5.2.1 Rapid Risk Assessment for Sexual Offence Recidivism (RRASOR: Hanson 1997)

Hanson commenced the development of the RRASOR in 1997 using seven empirically derived variables that correlated to sexual recidivism. Initial regression analysis identified four variables that could account for almost all of the variance across six aggregated samples. These four variables were: prior sex offences, offender under 25 years of age, ever having a male victim, and ever having an extra familial victim. These variables were then combined to form the RRASOR. Dichotomous scoring is used for three items and scoring the item on 'prior sex offences' involves a four-tiered structure, with scores in the higher elevations relating to higher risk probability. The scores for each item are totalled and the scale offers recidivism rates for each of six ranked score levels (0 through to 5) for 5 and 10 year follow up periods. Predictive accuracy was tested within developmental studies through the use of Receiver Operating Characteristic (ROC) Curves and was found to range between 0.62 and 0.77 across the seven samples used for development of the scale. Interrater reliability tests have typically found the scales reliability to fall in the 0.90 to 0.94 range, however this is not unexpected given the few items involved in the scale. Wilcox et al. (2009) compared the RRASOR with the Static-99 and Risk Matrix (RM2000) in predicting sexual recidivism in offenders with IDD. They found that the Static-99 predicted as well as guided clinical judgements (AUC = 0.64) performing better than RM2000 (AUC = 0.58) and the RRASOR (AUC = 0.42).

7.5.2.2 Static-99 (Hanson and Thornton 1999, 2000)

The Static-99 is a development of a second-generation scale and combined items from both the RRASOR and the Structured Anchored Clinical Judgement (SAC-J-MIN) (Grubin 1998) and could be considered the most widely used actuarial risk assessment for sexual recidivism. Developed from three Canadian samples of sexual offenders from mental health and correctional facilities it was subsequently cross validated on 563 sexual offenders released from HMP settings in England and Wales in 1979, with follow up over a period of 16 years and has been validated for predictive accuracy when used with sex offenders with IDD (Lindsay et al. 2008). The items in the scale are: young age, single (ever lived with a lover for at least two years), index non-sexual violence (conviction), prior non-sexual violence (conviction), prior sex offences, prior sentencing dates, any convictions for non-contact sex offences, unrelated victims, stranger victims, and male victims. Each item is scored and the item scores are added together to attain a total score for the scale. Scores may range from 0 to 12. The Static-99 provides four potential risk probability levels, which correlate with the total score attained. The levels are described as low, medium-low, medium-high, and high risk. The Static-99 showed moderate predictive accuracy for both sexual recidivism (r = 0.33, AUC 0.71) and violent recidivism (r = 0.32, AUC 0.69).

7.5.2.3 Minnesota Sex Offender Screening Tool–Revised (MnSOST-R: Epperson et al. 1998)

This is a 16-item actuarial risk assessment developed in 1991 on 256 incarcerated non-IDD sex offenders in Minnesota who were released primarily in 1988 or 1990. The 16 items include 12 historical/static items and 4 institutional/dynamic variables. The 12 historical variables include the number of convictions for sex offences, length of sex offending history, commission of a sex offence while under court supervision, commission of a sex offence in a public place, use or threat of force in any sex offence, perpetration of multiple sex acts in a single event contact, offending against victims from multiple age groups, offending against a 13–15-year-old victim with more than a 5-year age difference between the offender and the victim, victimization of a stranger, persistent pattern of adolescent antisocial behaviour, recent pattern of substantial substance abuse, and recent employment history. The four institutional variables included discipline history, chemical dependency treatment recommendations and outcomes, sex offender treatment recommendations and outcomes, and age of the offender at the time of release. The AUC of the Receiver Operating Characteristic (ROC) is the preferred analysis used to measure the predictive accuracy of a scale. A perfectly accurate prediction would yield a ROC hit rate or AUC of 1.0 with a hit rate (AUC) of 0.5 indicating a result no better than chance. The predictive utility of the total MnSOST-R score in relation to sexual recidivism showed a ROC AUC of 0.77 (95% confidence interval [CI] of 0.71–0.83). Total MnSOST-R scores were equally predictive of sexual recidivism in the development sample for rapists (AUC = 0.79) and molesters (AUC = 0.75) and for minorities (AUC = 0.75) and non-minorities (AUC = 0.77). This scale has not been evaluated for offenders with IDD.

7.5.2.4   Sex Offender Risk Appraisal Guide (SORAG: Quinsey et al. 2006)

The SORAG is a 14-item actuarial scale designed to predict violence, including 'hands on' sexual recidivism among men who have committed a 'hands on' sexual offence on at least one previous occasion. The 14 items consist of: lived with both biological parents until age 16, elementary school maladjustment, history of alcohol problems, never been married at time of index offence, criminal history score for nonviolent offences, criminal history score for violent offences, number of convictions for previous sexual offences, history of sexual offences only against girls below 14 years of age (negatively scored), failure on prior conditional release, age at index offence (negatively scored), diagnosis of any personality disorder, diagnosis of schizophrenia (negatively scored), phallometric test results indicating deviant sexual interests, and psychopathy (PCL-R score). The Child and Adolescent Taxon (CAT) scale can be used as a substitute in the absence of a PCL-R rating. The SORAG has been tested across various settings, countries, and follow up time. The predictive utility has been found to lie about 0.75, meaning that 75% of randomly selected violent recidivists have higher SORAG scores than randomly chosen men who are not violent recidivists.

Whilst the empirical development of actuarial risk assessments facilitated predictive accuracy, one critique of these measures is the lack of ability to evaluate more dynamic factors that may be relative to risk. The concentration on historical factors does not facilitate an evaluation relative to protective factors that may have developed in the individuals' life.

To address the identified difficulties empirical studies derived a more SPJ approach. Similar to actuarial approaches, the SPJ approach specifies a fixed set of operationally defined risk factors with explicit, manual based, coding procedures. The purpose of this structure is to facilitate both inter-rater reliability and content validity. SPJ approaches attempt to optimize the relevance of specifically derived risk factors, which, whether for legal, clinical, or risk management purposes, inform the decision-making process relative to risk probability of recidivism. Consideration is given to the number, priority, and relevance of risk factors present in the case and the needs, relative to any identified intervention or management strategies to mitigate risk, lead to final decisions of low, moderate, or high-risk probability by decision makers. The SPJ model does not provide estimated numerical probability levels of future violence for the individual case but rather concentrates on the process of risk formulation.

7.5.3 SPJ of Risk

7.5.3.1 Sexual Violence Risk–20 (SVR-20: Boer et al. 1997)

The SVR-20 consists of 20 items formulated from a systematic review of the scientific and professional literature in the areas of sexual violence, sexual offender recidivism, and sexual offender treatment. The 20 factors selected for inclusion are divided into three domains: psychosocial adjustment, sexual offences, and future plans.

Psychosocial Adjustment: Factors include: sexual deviation, victim of childhood abuse, psychopathy, major mental illness, substance use problems, suicidal/homicidal ideation, relationship problems, employment problems, past nonsexual violent offences, past nonviolent offences, and past supervision failures.

Sexual Offences: Factors include: high-density sex offences, multiple types of sex offences, physical harm to victim(s) (in sex offences), use of weapons or threats of death (in sex offences), escalation in frequency or severity (of sex offences), extreme minimization or denial of sex offences, and attitudes that support or condone sex offences.

Future Plans: This comprises two items: lacks realistic plans, and negative attitude toward intervention.

The assessor may also include 'other considerations' unique to the individual case that are considered to be important to the determination of risk. Boer et al. (2010) developed guidelines for the use of the SVR-20 with IDD violent and sex offenders.

7.5.3.2 Historical Clinical Risk-20-3rd Edition (HCR-20-III: Douglas et al. 2013)

The HCR-20 version 3 assesses clinical evaluations of sexual risk across a broad range of populations and settings in the three domains of historical, clinical, and risk management items.

There are 10 *historical* items consisting of: violence, other antisocial behaviour, relationships, employment; substance use, major mental disorder, personality disorder, traumatic experiences, violent attitudes, and treatment or supervision response.

Clinical scales consist of: recent problems with insight, violent ideation or intent, symptoms of major mental disorder, instability, and treatment or supervision response.

Risk management items consist of: professional services and plans, living situation, personal support, treatment or supervision response, stress or coping.

The scale is rated with reference to the user's manual which provides extensive guidance on the indicators relevant within each item. It is intended to structure clinical decisions about the risk for violence posed by adult forensic psychiatric patients, civil psychiatric patients, and criminal offenders (whether mentally disordered or not). The main aim of the HCR-20-III is to structure the assessor within a risk formulation approach. Decision making regarding importance and relevance of items to risk is made alongside the development of three scenarios appertaining to risk. In constructing scenarios, it is important to consider: nature, severity, imminence, frequency, or duration and likelihood of an offence occurring in a given potential situation. Formulation of risk-management strategies and review timeframes are included. Lindsay et al. (2008) found good predictive validity of the HCR-20 Version 2, the predictive utility of the HCR-20-III for use with offenders with IDD has still to be ascertained in its entirety. Boer et al. (2010) suggested a revised scoring/coding system for offenders with IDD which is yet to be tested.

7.5.3.3   Risk of Sexual Violence Protocol (RSVP: Hart et al. 2003)

The RSVP is an SPJ scale whose target population consisting of 22 items divided into five sections:

1) Sexual violence historical – chronicity of sexual violence, diversity of sexual violence, escalation of sexual violence, physical coercion in sexual violence, psychological coercion in sexual violence.
2) Psychological adjustment – extreme minimization or denial, attitudes that support or condone sexual violence, problems with self-awareness, problems with stress and coping, problems resulting from child abuse.
3) Mental disorder – sexual deviance, psychopathic personality disorder, major mental illness, problems with substance abuse, and violent or suicidal ideation
4) Social adjustment – problems with intimate relationships, problems with non-intimate relationships, problems with employment, and non-sexual criminality
5) Manageability – problems with planning, problems with treatment, problems with supervision.

Each item is coded three times: for presence in the past, recent presence, and future relevance. Each of these ratings is on a three-point scale: no evidence, partial evidence, or definite evidence. The assessor must determine the relevance of the individual risk factors with respect to potential future sexual violence, the development of risk-management plans, describe the most plausible scenarios of future sexual violence, and recommend strategies for managing sexual violence risk in light of the relevant factors and scenarios. The scale aims to identify potential risk factors (presence) and facilitate decision makers to make a determination of their importance to future offending (relevance). The RSVP emphasizes the complexity of sex offender risk assessment, prediction, and management and underlines the importance of avoiding reductionist approaches.

Consideration of risk management strategies includes monitoring, treatment, supervision, victim safety planning, with one item facilitating any 'other considerations' deemed relevant to the case being assessed. Finally, the formulation of summary judgements includes case prioritization – low (routine), moderate (elevated), high (urgent) – and risk of serious harm – low (routine), moderate (elevated), high (urgent) – alongside the 'need for immediate action'? (yes/no). The next step is to consider any 'other risks indicated'. These may be relative to – non-sexual violence or non-sexual criminality. The final aspect of the RSVP assessment is to indicate the time frame required for case review, e.g. every 6–12 months routinely, or, more frequently for moderate-high risk. To date there is no published empirical data to support the predictive accuracy of the RSVP assessment with sex offenders with and without IDD.

7.6 Dynamic Risk Management

A further innovative approach to SPJ of risk probability is the development of the Assessment of Risk and Manageability of Individuals with Developmental and Intellectual Limitations who Offend – Sexually (ARMIDILO-S) (Boer et al. 2012).

7.6.1 Assessment of Risk and Manageability of Individuals with Developmental and Intellectual Limitations Who Offend – Sexually (ARMIDILO-S) (Boer et al. 2012)

The ARMIDILO-S is a scale designed specifically for use with individuals with borderline intelligence, or a mild intellectual impairment, with or without learning disabilities, who have offended sexually or have displayed sexually inappropriate behaviour. The ARMIDILO-S has been shown to have good predictive validity with different samples of sex offenders and has been positively evaluated in qualitative studies as a case management instrument. The authors advise that the ARMIDILO-S, is used with an actuarial test and an appropriate structured clinical guideline (SVR-20 or RSVP), and is part of an assessment procedure that combines the assessment of risk and risk manageability in one assessment. The items in the scale are distributed amongst: staff/environment and client dynamic factors, both of which are further differentiated into stable and acute dynamic groups.

Item classification:

1) Stable Dynamic Items (staff and environment).
2) Acute Dynamic Items (staff and environment).
3) Stable Dynamic Items (client).
4) Acute Dynamic Items (client).

All items are as related to risk as they are to manageability in institutional or community settings. Each assessment requires the assessor to determine which variables are of most relevance to their client and determine which items are or are not indicative of elevated risk for the client.

7.6.2 Evaluation of Risk Assessment Scales

Several studies have evaluated the various risk assessment scales and it is not within the scope of this chapter to provide an extensive evaluation. We have provided limited evaluations and would advise the reader to look to further comparative studies to form a full evaluation of risk assessment tools. There is a large body of evidence evaluating the reliability and validity of various risk assessment tools for use with violent and sex offenders. However there continues to remain a shortage of research regarding their reliability and predictive validity specifically with the IDD offender population. This raises some contentious issues around the use of current risk assessment measures in the development of risk management plans for this offender group (McMillan et al. 2004).

With regard to actuarial risk assessments, Barbaree et al. (2001) compared the VRAG, SORAG, RRASOR, and Static-99 for 215 non-IDD sex offenders in Canada who had been released from prison for an average of 4.5 years. This study found that the VRAG, SORAG, RRASOR, and Static-99 successfully predicted general recidivism and sexual recidivism. The RRASOR, which includes only four easily scored items, was superior to the other instruments in predicting sexual recidivism. Lindsay et al. (2008) compared the Static-99 and RM2000-S relative to sexual incidents in a sample of 212 offenders in each setting with IDD. Participants within this cohort were selected from high secure, medium/low secure, and community settings, with over 50% of the cohort in each setting having at least one sexual offending conviction. The Static-99 achieved significant predictive value (AUC = 0.71, p = 0.000), and the RM2000-S fell just short of significance (AUC = 0.61, p = 0.08). The HCR–20 (Version 2) also showed significant values of predictive accuracy with this cohort HCR-20-H (AUC = 0.68, p = 0.000), HCR-20-C (AUC = 0.67, p = 0.000), and HCR-20-R (AUC = 0.62, p = 0.02).

Comparison of the Static-99, RRASOR, MnSOST-R, and SORAG in predicting recidivism in 251 non-IDD sexual offenders in the USA found that none of the four tests had consistent predictive validity across categories. However, the Static-99 and SORAG emerged as the most consistent instruments in terms of predictive accuracy (Bartosh et al. 2003).

The evaluation of the VRAG, SORAG, Static-99 and HCR-20 version 2 in the study conducted by Cooke et al. (2002) with 250 violent offenders in Scotland found that each instrument predicted recidivism with similar accuracy to that of other studies.

With regard to the SVR-20 (Boer et al. 1997) the predictive accuracy of the SVR-20, the RRASOR, the PCL-R, and the VRAG on prediction of recidivism among 51 men convicted of rape and followed for 92 months in Sweden was evaluated. Only the RRASOR showed predictive accuracy for sexual recidivism, whereas the other assessments showed some predictive accuracy with violent non-sexual recidivism (Sjostedt and Langstrom 2002). Blacker et al. (2011) reported the predictive validity of the SVR-20 in a study of 44 participants with special needs, 10 of whom had IDD. The SVR-20 had poor predictive validity for the special needs group relative to sexual incidents (AUC 0.45) but for the small group of sex offenders with IDD it had a large effect size (AUC 0.75).

In relation to sex offence recidivism, Hanson and Harris (2000) reviewed the comprehensive range of stable and acute dynamic risk factors in 208 sex offence recidivists and 201 non-recidivists. They found that the most predictive variables associated with recidivism were poor social supports, antisocial lifestyle, poor self-management strategies, difficulties cooperating with supervision, anger, and subjective distress just before the offence, and attitudes tolerant of sexual assault. In their study of 52 sex offenders and abusers with IDD, Lindsay et al. (2004) found several dynamic variables in line with those found in mainstream empirical studies of sex offenders without IDD, for example; poor response to treatment (r = 0.45**); poor compliance with management/treatment routine (r = 415*); allowances made by staff (r = 0.409**), low self-esteem (r = 0.374**); poor relationship with mother (r = 0.346*); denial of crime (r = 0.335*), sexual abuse (r = 0.327*); antisocial attitude (r = 0.309*), and low treatment motivation (r = 0.303*), offence involving violence (r = 0.295*), juvenile crime (r = 0.284*). Several other variables were found not to be predictive such as employment history, diverse sexual crimes, deviant victim choice, prior non-sexual offences, criminal lifestyle, criminal companions, social and emotional isolation, and mental illness, and showed no relationship to the dependant variables of reoffending or suspicion of reoffending.

Within the realms of dynamic risk of sexual offending Lofthouse et al. (2013) evaluated the ARMIDILO-S alongside a static risk assessment for sexual offending (Static-99), and a static risk assessment for violence (VRAG) within a sample of 64 adult males with IDD who had a history of sexual offending behaviour. The use of a dynamic risk tool for sexual offenders with IDD resulted in the best prediction of sexual reoffending (ARMIDILO-S total score AUC = 0.92) which was an improvement on the established sexual offending static risk tool (Static-99 AUC = 0.75). As would be expected the more general static risk assessment for violent reoffending, did not perform as well in predicting sexual reoffending in this group (VRAG: AUC = 0.58). These authors suggest that in line with the findings of Lindsay et al. (2007) dynamic variables are useful in predicting sexual reoffending with individuals with IDD. Overall the ARMIDILO-S was found to be a promising dynamic risk-assessment tool for individuals with an IDD. To further assess the utility of the ARMIDILO-S Blacker et al. (2011) examined the predictive validity of four risk assessment instruments: the RRASOR, SVR-20, RM2000-V, and the ARMIDILO-Stable, and -Acute dynamic client subscales within a sample of 88 offenders, which consisted of 44 mainstream sex offenders and 44 sexual offenders with special needs, who had been matched on risk items within the RRASOR tool. Instruments were coded retrospectively from file information. Sexual reconviction data was used, in conjunction with sexual recidivism data based on unofficial data sources, over a mean follow-up period of 8.8 years. The results of this study found that the ARMIDILO-S instrument was the best predictor for sexual reconviction among offenders with special needs (ARMIDILO-Stable, AUC = 0.60; ARMIDILO-Acute, AUC = 0.73). While, the predictive validities of the RRASOR (AUC = 0.53) and the RM2000-V (AUC = 0.50) were little better than chance. In contrast, the SVR-20 yielded a higher score (AUC =0.73) for the non-IDD sample, than for the intellectually disabled sample (AUC =0.45). Within the special needs group, the ARMIDILO-S Acute, SVR-20 Psychosocial Affect, and Overall scales were better predictors of sexual recidivism for the cohort of offenders with intellectual and developmental disability (AUCs ranging from 0.75 to 0.88).

7.7 Conclusion

Assessment measures for use with sex offenders with IDD have been growing in breadth due to adaptations and empirical testing of validity in addition to the provision of appropriate normative samples for this client group. This is an area of specific research growth, which is not without its challenges due to the smaller sized cohorts within studies. There have been successful adaptations to existing measures for a variety of constructs, which increases validity and the predictive utility of measures in many respects. Assessment is the critical factor to inform risk, needs, and responsivity in respect of treatment. Those individuals scoring on higher levels of deviancy should be prioritized for treatment and appropriate risk management whether within an institutional setting or community. The development of risk-assessment measures through actuarial and SPJ scales has also led to evaluation of these measures, which highlight some differences in predictive utility between actuarial measures in evaluation of risk for mainstream sex offenders and sex offenders with IDD. Scales for SPJ risk assessment are encouraging with their focus on risk formulation with the more dynamic risk scales such as the

ARMIDILO- S. Subject to ongoing validation, these scales will provide a welcome added next generation of risk assessments to the existing stock. The essential quality of all assessment processes is to ensure the use of a number of complementary assessment measures to provide a holistic formulation from the assessment process. This is an important factor of all assessment processes for sex offenders with IDD.

References

Abel, G.G., Becker, J.V., and Cunningham-Rathner, J. (1984). Complications, consent and cognitions in sex between children and adults. *International Journal of Law and Psychiatry* 7: 89–103.

Allam, J.A., Browne, K.D., and Middleton, D. (1997). Different clients, different needs? Practice issues in community-based treatment for sex offenders. *Criminal Behaviour and Mental Health* 7: 69–84.

American Psychiatric Association (2013). *Diagnostic and Statistical Manual of Mental Disorders: DSM-5*. Washington, DC: APA.

Awad, G., Saunders, E., and Levene, J. (1984). A clinical study of male adolescent sexual offenders. *International Journal of Offender Therapy and Comparative Criminology* 28: 105–116.

Barbaree, H.E., Seto, M.C., Langton, C.M. et al. (2001). Evaluating the predictive accuracy of six risk assessment instruments for adult sex offenders. *Criminal Justice and Behavior* 28: 490–521.

Barnard, G.W., Fuller, A.K., Robbins, L. et al. (1989). *The Child Molester: An Integrated Approach to Evaluation and Treatment*, Brunner/Mazel clinical psychiatry series, No. 1. Philadelphia, PA: Brunner/Mazel.

Bartholomew, K. and Horowitz, L.M. (1991). Attachment styles among young adults: a test of a four-category model. *Journal of Personality and Social Psychology* 61: 226–244.

Bartosh, D.L., Garby, T., Lewis, L. et al. (2003). Differences in the predictive validity of actuarial risk assessments in relation to sex offender type. *International Journal of Offender Therapy and Comparative Criminology* 47 (4): 422–438.

Becker, J.V. (1998). What we know about the characteristics and treatment of adolescents who have committed sexual offenses. *Child Maltreatment: Journal of the American Professional Society on the Abuse of Children* 3: 317–329.

Beckett, R.C. and Fisher, D. (1994). *Assessing victim empathy: A new measure*. Paper presented at the 13th Annual Conference of ATSA (the Association for the Treatment of Sexual Abusers), San Francisco, CA.

Beckett, R.C., Fisher, D., Mann, R. et al. (1997). The relapse prevention questionnaire and interview. In: *Therapists Guide for Maintaining Change: Relapse Prevention Manual for Adult Male Perpetrators of Child Sexual Abuse* (ed. H. Eldridge), 124–128. Thousand Oaks, CA: SAGE.

Beech, A.R., Fisher, D., and Beckett, R.C. (1999). *Step 3: An evaluation of the Prison Sex Offender Treatment Programme, report for the Home Office*. Available from the Information and Publication Group, Room 201, Home Office, 50 Queen Anne's Gate. London, SW1H 9AT.

Beech, A.R., Fisher, D., and Thornton, D. (2003). Risk assessment of sex offenders. *Professional Psychology: Research and Practice* 34 (4): 339–352.

Blacker, J., Beech, A.R., Wilcox, D.T. et al. (2011). The assessment of dynamic risk and recidivism in a sample of special needs sex offenders. *Psychology, Crime and Law* 17 (1): 75–92.

Blanchard, R., Watson, M.S., Choy, A. et al. (1999). Paedophiles: mental retardation, maternal age, and sexual orientation. *Archives of Sexual Behavior* 28: 111–127.

Boer, D., Haaven, J., Lambrick, F. et al. (2012). http://www.armidilo.net/files/Web-Version-1-1-2013-Intro-Manual.pdf (accessed 30 May 2019).

Boer, D.P., Frize, M., Pappas, R. et al. (2010). Suggested adaptations to the SVR-20 for offenders with intellectual disabilities. In: *Assessment and Treatment of Sexual Offenders with Intellectual Disabilities: A Handbook* (eds. L.A. Craig, W.R. Lindsay and K.D. Browne), 193–209. Chichester, UK: Wiley.

Boer, D.P., Hart, S.D., Kropp, P.R. et al. (1997). *Manual for the Sexual Violence Risk-20: Professional Guidelines for Assessing Risk of Sexual Violence.* Vancouver, Canada: The Mental Health, Law, and Policy Institute, Simon Fraser University.

Bonta, J. and Andrews, D.A. (2017). *The Psychology of Criminal Conduct*, 6e. New York: Routledge.

Bowers, L.E., Mann, R.E., and Thornton, D. (1995). *The Consequences Task.* Unpublished manuscript.

Bray, D. (1997). The sex offender's opinion test (SOOT). Preston, UK: Lancashire Care NHS Trust.

Bray, D., and Forshaw, N. (1996). *Sex Offender's Self-Appraisal Scale. Version 1.1.* Preston. UK: Lancashire Care NHS Trust; North Warwickshire NHS Trust.

Briggs, F. and Hawkins, R.M.F. (1996). A comparison of the childhood experiences of convicted male child molesters and men who were sexually abused in childhood and claimed to be nonoffenders. *Child Abuse & Neglect* 20 (3): 221–233.

Brown, H. and Stein, J. (1997). Sexual abuse perpetrated by men with intellectual disabilities: a comparative study. *Journal of Intellectual Disability Research* 41: 215–224.

Browne, K.D. and Herbert, M. (1997). *Preventing Family Violence.* Chichester, UK: Wiley.

Broxholme, S.L. and Lindsay, W.R. (2003). Development and preliminary evaluation of a questionnaire on cognitions related to sex offending for use with individuals who have mild intellectual disabilities. *Journal of Intellectual Disability Research* 47 (6): 472–482.

Burt, M. (1980). Cultural myths and support for rape. *Journal of Personality and Social Psychology* 38 (2): 217–230.

Caparulo, F. (1991). Identifying the developmentally disabled sex offenders. *Sexuality and Disability* 2: 253–268.

Consedine, N.S. and Magai, C. (2003). Attachment and emotion experience in later life: the view from emotions theory. *Attachment & Human Development* 5 (2): 165–187.

Cooke, D.J., Michie, S., and Ryan, J. (2002). *Evaluating Risk for Violence: A Preliminary Study of the HCR-20, PCL-R and VRAG on a Scottish Prison Population.* Edinburgh, UK: Scottish Prison Service.

Craig, L. and Hutchinson, R.B. (2005). Sexual offenders with learning disabilities: risk, recidivism and treatment. *Journal of Sexual Aggression* 11: 289–304.

Craig, L., Lindsay, W.R., and Browne, K.D. (2010). *Assessment and Treatment of Sexual Offenders with Intellectual Disabilities, a Handbook.* Chichester, UK: Wiley.

Craig, L.A. and Beech, A.R. (2010). Towards a guide to best practice in conducting actuarial risk assessments with sex offenders. *Aggression and Violent Behavior* 15 (4): 278–293.

Craig, L.A., Browne, K.D., Beech, A. et al. (2006a). Differences in personality and risk characteristics in sex, violent and general offenders. *Criminal Behaviour and Mental Health* 16 (3): 183–194.

Craig, L.A. and Rettenberger, M. (2016). A brief history of sexual offender risk assessment. In: *Treatment of Sexual Offenders: Strengths and Weaknesses in Assessment and Intervention* (eds. D.R. Laws and W. O'Donohue), 19–44. New York: Springer.

Craig, L.A. and Rettenberger, M. (2017). Risk assessment for sexual offenders: where to from here? In: *The Wiley Handbook on the Theories, Assessment and Treatment of Sexual Offending, Vol. 2: Assessment* (eds. L. Craig and M. Rettenberger), 1–12. Chichester: Wiley.

Craig, L.A., Stringer, I., and Moss, T. (2006b). Treating sexual offenders with learning disabilities in the community. *International Journal of Offender Therapy and Comparative Criminology* 50: 369–390.

Craig, L.A., Thornton, D., Beech, A. et al. (2007). The relationship of statistical and psychological risk markers to sexual reconviction in child molesters. *Criminal Justice and Behavior* 34: 314–329.

Craissati, J., McClurg, G., and Browne, K. (2002). The parental bonding experiences of sex offenders: a comparison between child molesters and rapists. *Child Abuse & Neglect* 26: 909–921.

Daderman, A.M. and Hellstrom, A. (2018). Inter-rater reliability of psychopathy checklist-revised, results on multiple analysis levels for a sample of patients undergoing forensic psychiatric evaluation. *Criminal Justice and Behavior* 45 (2): 234–263.

Davis, M.H. (1980). A multidimensional approach to individual differences in empathy. *JSAS Catalog of Selected Documents in Psychology* 10: 85.

Day, K. (1993). Crime and mental retardation: a review. In: *Clinical Approaches to the Mentally Disordered Offender* (eds. K. Howells and C.R. Hollin), 111–144. Cambridge: Wiley.

Day, K. (1994). Male mentally handicapped sex offenders. *British Journal of Psychiatry* 165: 630–639.

Douglas, K.S., Hart, S.D., Webster, C.D. et al. (2013). *HCR-20: Assessing Risk for Violence*, 3e. Vancouver, Canada: Mental Health, Law and Policy Institute, Simon Fraser University.

Douglas, K.S., Hart, S.D., Webster, C.D. et al. (2013). *HCR-20V3: Assessing Risk of Violence – User Guide*. Burnaby, Canada: Mental Health, Law, and Policy Institute, Simon Fraser University.

Epperson, D.L., Kaul, J.D., and Hesselton, D. (1998). Final report of the development of the Minnesota Sex Offender Screening Tool-Revised (MnSOST-R). Presentation at the 17th Annual Research and Treatment Conference of the Association for the Treatment of Sexual Abusers, Vancouver, British Columbia, Canada.

Firestone, P., Bradford, J.M., McCoy, M. et al. (1999). Prediction of recidivism in incest offenders. *Journal of Interpersonal Violence* 14: 511–531.

Fisher, D., Beech, A., and Browne, K. (1999). Comparison of sex offenders to nonoffenders on selected psychological measures. *International Journal of Offender Therapy and Comparative Criminology* 43 (4): 473–491.

Fisher, K. and Beech, A. (1998). Reconstituting families after sexual abuse: the offender's perspective. *Child Abuse Review* 7: 420–434.

Fonagy, P., Redfern, S., and Charman, T. (1997). The relationship between belief-desire reasoning and a projective measure of attachment security. *British Journal of Developmental Psychology* 15: 51–61.

160

Forth, A.E., Kosson, D., and Hare, R. (2003). *The Hare Psychopathy Checklist: Youth Version*. New York: Multi-Health Systems.

Garlick, Y., Marshall, W.L., and Thornton, D. (1996). Intimacy deficits and attribution of blame among sexual offenders. *Legal and Criminological Psychology* 1: 251–258.

Gibbens, T.C. and Robertson, G. (1983). A survey of the criminal careers of restriction order patients. *British Journal of Psychiatry* 143: 370–375.

Gilby, R., Wolf, L., and Goldberg, B. (1989). Mentally retarded adolescent sex offenders. A survey and pilot study. *Canadian Journal of Psychiatry* 34 (6): 542–548.

Goldberg, L.R. (1968). Simple models or simple processes? Some research on clinical judgements. *American Psychologist* 23: 483–496.

Griffiths, D., Hingsburger, D., Hoath, J. et al. (2013). 'Counterfeit deviance' revisited. *Journal of Applied Research in Intellectual Disabilities* 26 (5): 471–480.

Griffiths, D.M., Hingsburger, D., and Christain, R. (1985). Treating developmentally handicapped sexual offenders: the York management services treatment program. *Psychiatric Aspects of Mental Retardation Reviews* 4: 49–52.

Gross, G. (1985). *Activities of a Development Disabilities Adult Offender Project*. Olympia, WA: Washington State Developmental Disabilities Planning Council.

Grubin, D. (1998). *Sex Offending Against Children: Understanding the Risk*. Police Research Series Paper 99. London: Home Office.

Hanson, R.K. (1997). *The development of a brief actuarial risk scale for sexual offense recidivism (User Report 97–04)*. Ottawa, Canada: Department of the Solicitor General of Canada.

Hanson, R.K. and Bussière, M.T. (1998). Predicting relapse: a meta-analysis of sexual offender recidivism studies. *Journal of Consulting and Clinical Psychology* 66: 348–362.

Hanson, R.K. and Harris, A. (2000). *The Sex Offender Need Assessment Rating (SONAR): A method for measuring change in risk levels (User Report 2000–01)*. Ottawa, Canada: Department of the Solicitor General of Canada.

Hanson, R.K. and Morton-Bourgon, K.E. (2005). The characteristics of persistent sexual offenders: a meta-analysis of recidivism studies. *Journal of Consulting and Clinical Psychology* 73: 1154–1163.

Hanson, R.K. and Scott, H. (1995). Assessing perspective taking among sexual offenders, non-sexual criminal and non-offenders. *Sexual Abuse: A Journal of Research and Treatment* 7: 259–277.

Hanson, R.K. and Thornton, D. (1999). *Static-99: Improving Actuarial Risk Assessments For Sex Offenders. User Report 99-02*. Ottawa: Department of the Solicitor General of Canada.

Hanson, R.K. and Thornton, D. (2000). Improving risk assessments for sex offenders: a comparison of three actuarial scales. *Law and Human Behavior* 24: 119–136.

Hare, R.D. (1991). *Manual for the Revised Psychopathy Checklist*. Toronto, ON: Multi-Health Systems.

Hare, R.D. (2003). *Manual for the Revised Psychopathy Checklist*, 2e. Toronto, ON: Multi-Health Systems.

Hare, R.D. and Neumann, C.N. (2006). The PCL-R assessment of psychopathy: development, structural properties, and new directions. In: *Handbook of Psychopathy* (ed. C. Patrick), 58–88. New York: Guilford.

Harris, G.T., Rice, M.E., Quinsey, V.L. et al. (2003). A multi-site comparison of actuarial risk instruments for sex offenders. *Psychological Assessment* 15: 413–425.

Hart, S.D., Cox, D.N., and Hare, R.D. (1995). *The Hare PCL:SV*. Toronto, ON: Multi-health Systems.

Hart, S.D., Kropp, P.R., Laws, D.R. et al. (2003). *The Risk for Sexual Violence Protocol (RSVP): Structured Professional Guidelines for Assessing Risk of Sexual Violence*. Vancouver: Simon Fraser University.

Heighway, S.M. and Webster, S.K. (2007). *STARS: Skills Training for Assertiveness, Relationships Building and Sexual Awareness*. Arlington, TX: Future Horizons.

Hingsburger, D., Griffiths, D., and Quinsey, V. (1991). Detecting counterfeit deviance: differentiating sexual deviance from sexual inappropriateness. *The Habilitative Mental Healthcare Newsletter* 10 (9): 514.

Hirschi, T. (1969). *Causes of Delinquency*. Berkeley, CA: University of California Press.

Jolliffe, D. and Farrington, D.P. (2004). Empathy and offending: a systematic review and meta-analysis. *Aggression and Violent Behavior* 9 (5): 441–476.

Kaufman, A.S. and Lichtenberger, E.O. (1999). *Essentials of WAIS-3 Assessment*. New York: John Wiley & Sons.

Keeling, J.A., Beech, A.R., and Rose, J.L. (2007a). Assessment of intellectually disabled sexual offenders: the current position. *Aggression and Violent Behavior* 12: 229–241.

Keeling, J.A. and Rose, J.L. (2005). Relapse prevention with intellectually disabled sexual offenders. *Sexual Abuse: A Journal of Research and Treatment* 17: 407–423.

Keeling, J.A., Rose, J.L., and Beech, A.R. (2006). A comparison of the application of the self-regulation model of the relapse process for mainstream and special needs sexual offenders. *Sexual Abuse* 18 (4): 373–382.

Keeling, J.A., Rose, J.L., and Beech, A.R. (2007b). Comparing sexual offender treatment efficacy: mainstream sexual offenders and sexual offenders with special needs. *Journal of Intellectual & Developmental Disability* 32 (2): 117–124.

Keenan, T. and Ward, T. (2000). A theory of mind perspective on cognitive, affective, and intimacy deficits in child sexual offenders. *Sexual Abuse: A Journal of Research and Treatment* 12: 49–58.

Klimecki, M., Jenkinson, J., and Wilson, L. (1994). A study of recidivism amongst offenders with an intellectual disability. *Australia and New Zealand Journal of Developmental Disabilities* 19: 209–219.

Knopp, F.H. and Stevenson, W.L. (1989). *National Survey of Juvenile and Adult Sex Offender Treatment Programs and Models:1988*. Orwell, VT: Safer Society Press.

Lambrick, F. and Glaser, W. (2004). Sex offenders with an intellectual disability. *Sexual Abuse: A Journal of Research and Treatment* 16 (4): 381–392.

Langdon, P.E., Maxted, H., and Murphy, G.H. (2007). An exploratory evaluation of the Ward and Hudson offending pathways model with sex offenders who have intellectual disabilities. *Journal of Intellectual and Developmental Disabilities* 32: 94–105.

Langdon, P.E. and Talbot, T.J. (2006). Locus of control and sex offenders with an intellectual disability. *International Journal of Offender Therapy and Comparative Criminology* 50 (4): 391–401.

Lanyon, R.I. (2001). Psychological assessment procedures in sex offending. *Professional Psychology: Research and Practice* 32 (3): 253–260.

Laws, D.R., Hanson, R.K., Osborn, C.A. et al. (2000). Classification of child molesters by plethysmographic assessment of sexual arousal and a self-report measure of sexual preference. *Journal of Interpersonal Violence* 15 (12): 1297–1312.

Lezak, M.D., Howieson, D.B., and Loring, D.W. (2004). *Neuropsychological Assessment.* Oxford: Oxford University Press.

Lindsay, W.R. (2002). Research and literature on sex offenders with intellectual and developmental disabilities. *Journal of Intellectual Disability Research* 46: 74–85.

Lindsay, W.R. (2004). Sex offenders: conceptualisation of the issues, services, treatment and management. In: *Offenders with Developmental Disabilities* (eds. W.R. Lindsay, J.L. Taylor and P. Sturmey), 163–186. Chichester, UK: Wiley.

Lindsay, W.R. (2009). *The Treatment of Sex Offenders with Developmental Disabilities: A Practice Workbook.* Chichester, UK: Wiley.

Lindsay, W.R., Carson, D., and Whitefield, E. (2000). Development of a questionnaire on attitudes consistent with sex offending for men with intellectual disabilities. *Journal of Intellectual Disability Research* 44: 368–374.

Lindsay, W.R., Elliot, S.F., and Astell, A. (2004). Predictors of sexual offence recidivism in offenders with intellectual disabilities. *Journal of Applied Research in Intellectual Disabilities* 17 (4): 299–305.

Lindsay, W.R., Law, J., Quinn, K. et al. (2001). A comparison of physical and sexual abuse: histories of sexual and non-sexual offenders with learning disabilities. *Child Abuse and Neglect* 25: 989–995.

Lindsay, W.R. and MacLeod, F. (2001). A review of forensic learning disability research. *The British Journal of Forensic Practice* 3: 4–10.

Lindsay, W.R. and Michie, A.M. (2013). Individuals with developmental delay and problematic sexual behaviors. *Current Psychiatry Reports* 15 (4): 1–6.

Lindsay, W.R., Smith, A.H.W., Law, J. et al. (2002). A treatment service for sex offenders and abusers with intellectual disability: characteristics or referrals and evaluation. *Journal of Applied Research in Intellectual Disabilities* 15: 166–174.

Lindsay, W.R., Steptoe, L.R., and Beech, A.T. (2008). The Ward and Hudson pathways model of the sexual offence process applied to offenders with intellectual disability. *Sexual Abuse* 20 (4): 379–392.

Lindsay, W.R., Whitefield, E., and Carson, D. (2007). An assessment for follow-up: sex offenders with intellectual disabilities 31 attitudes consistent with sex offending for use with offenders with intellectual disabilities. *Legal and Criminological Psychology* 12: 55–68.

Lofthouse, R.E., Lindsay, W.R., Totsika, V. et al. (2013). Prospective dynamic assessment of risk of sexual reoffending in individuals with an intellectual disability and a history of sexual offending behaviour. *Journal of Applied Research in Intellectual Disabilities* 26: 394–403.

Luiselli, J.K. (2000). Presentation of paraphilias and paraphilia-related disorders in young adults with mental retardation: two case profiles. *Mental Health Aspects of Developmental Disabilities* 3: 42–46.

Lund, J. (1990). Mentally retarded criminal offenders in Denmark. *British Journal of Psychiatry* 156: 726–731.

Lunsky, Y., Frijters, J., Watson, S. et al. (2007). Sexual knowledge and attitudes of men with intellectual disabilities who sexually offend. Special issue on offenders with ID/IDD. *Journal of Intellectual and Developmental Disabilities* 32 (2): 74–81.

Malmuth, N.M. and Brown, L.M. (1994). Sexually aggressive men's perceptions of women's communications: testing three explanations. *Journal of Personality and Social Psychology* 67 (4): 699–712.

Marolla, J. and Scully, D. (1986). Attitudes toward women, violence, and rape: a comparison of convicted rapists and other felons. *Deviant Behavior* 7 (4): 337–355.

Marshall, W.L. (1989). Invited essay: intimacy, loneliness and sexual offenders. *Behaviour Research and Therapy* 27: 491–503.

Marshall, W.L. and Fernandez, Y.M. (2003). *Phallometric Testing with Sexual Offenders: Theory, Research, and Practice*. Brandon, VT: Safer Society Press.

Marshall, W.L., Hudson, S.M., Jones, R. et al. (1995). Empathy in sex offenders. *Clinical Psychology Review* 15: 99–113.

Marshall, W.L., Serran, G.A., and Cortoni, F.A. (2000). Childhood attachments and sexual abuse and the effect on adult coping in child molesters. *Sexual Abuse: A Journal of Research and Treatment* 12: 17–26.

McMillan, D., Hastings, R.P., and Coldwell, J. (2004). Clinical and actuarial prediction of physical violence in a forensic intellectual disability hospital: a longitudinal study. *Journal of Applied Research in Intellectual Disability* 17 (4): 255–265.

Michie, A.M., Lindsay, W.R., Martin, V. et al. (2006). A test of counterfeit deviance: a comparison of sexual knowledge in groups of sex offenders with intellectual disability and controls. *Sexual Abuse: A Journal of Research and Treatment* 18 (3): 271–278.

Miller, P.A. and Eisenberg, N. (1988). The relation of empathy to aggressive and externalising/antisocial behaviour. *Psychological Bulletin* 103: 324–344.

Mokros, A., Hollerbach, P., Vohs, K. et al. (2013). Normative data for the psychopathy checklist–revised in German-speaking countries: a meta-analysis. *Criminal Justice and Behaviour* 40 (12): 1397–1412.

Morrisey, C., Hogue, T., Mooney, P. et al. (2005). Applicability, reliability and validity of the Psychopathy Checklist – Revised in offenders with intellectual disabilities: some initial findings. *International Journal of Forensic Mental Health* 4: 207–220.

Morrisey, C., Mooney, P., Hogue, T. et al. (2007). Predictive validity of psychopathy in offenders with intellectual disabilities in a high security hospital: treatment progress. *Journal of Intellectual and Developmental Disabilities* 32: 125–133.

Morrissey, C. (2003). The use of the PCL-R in forensic populations with learning disability. *The British Journal of Forensic Practice* 5: 20–24.

Murphy, G.H., Sinclair, N., Hays, S. et al. (2010). Effectiveness of group cognitive behavioural treatment for men with intellectual disabilities at risk of sexual offending. *Journal of Applied Research in Intellectual Disabilities* 23 (6): 537–551.

Murphy, W.D., Coleman, E.M., and Abel, G.G. (1983). Human sexuality in the mentally retarded. In: *Clinical Approaches to Sex Offenders and their Victims* (eds. J.L. Matson and F. Andrasik), 77–92. Chichester: John Wiley.

Nichols, H.R. and Molinder, I. (1984). *Manual for the Multiphasic Sex Inventory*. Tacoma, WA: Crime and Victim Psychology Specialists.

Nihira, K., Leland, H., and Lambert, N. (1993). *Adaptive Behaviour Scale-Residential and Community (Second Edition): Examination Booklet*. Austin, TX: PRO-ED.

Nowicki, S. Jr. and Duke, M.P. (1974). A locus of control scale for noncollege as well as college adults. *Journal of Personality Assessment* 38: 136–137.

Nowicki, S. (1976). Factor structure of locus of control in children. *Journal of Genetic Psychology* 129: 13–17.

Parry, C.J. and Lindsay, W.R. (2003). Impulsiveness as a factor in sexual offending in people with mild intellectual disability. *Journal of Intellectual Disability Research* 47 (6): 483–487.

Pithers, W.D., Gray, A.S., Busconi, A. et al. (1998). Caregivers of children with sexual behavior problems: psychological and familial functioning. *Child Abuse and Neglect* 22: 43–55.

Pithers, W.D., Kashima, K.M., Cumming, G.F. et al. (1988). Relapse prevention. A method of enhancing maintenance of change in sex offenders. In: *Treating Child Sex Offenders and Victims: A Practical Guide* (ed. A.C. Salter), 131–170. Newbury Park, CA: Sage.

Prentky, R., Burgess, A., Rokous, F. et al. (1989). The presumed role of fantasy in serial sexual homicide. *American Journal of Psychiatry* 146: 887–891.

Prentky, R.A. and Knight, R.A. (1991). Identifying critical dimensions for discriminating among rapists. *Journal of Consulting and Clinical Psychology* 59 (5): 643–661.

Proctor, T. and Beail, N. (2007). Empathy and theory of mind in offenders with intellectual disability. *Journal of Intellectual & Developmental Disability* 32 (2): 82–93.

Proulx, J., Ouimet, M., Pellerin, B. et al. (1999). Posttreatment recidivism rates in sexual aggressors: a comparison between dropouts and non-dropout subjects. In: *The Sex Offender* (ed. B.K. Schwartz), 15(1)–15(13). Kingston, NJ: Civic Research Institute.

Quinsey, V.L., Harris, G.T., Rice, M.E. et al. (1998). *Violent Offenders: Appraising and Managing Risk*. Washington, DC: American Psychological Association.

Quinsey, V.L., Harris, G.T., Rice, M.E. et al. (2001). Violent offenders. *Psychology, Public Policy, and Law* 7 (2): 409–443.

Quinsey, V.L., Harris, G.T., Rice, M.E. et al. (2006). *Violent Offenders: Appraising and Managing Risk*, 2e. Washington, DC: American Psychological Association.

Reyes, J.R., Vollmer, T.R., and Hall, A. (2017). Comparison of arousal and preference assessment outcomes for sex offenders with intellectual disabilities. *Journal of Applied Behaviour Analysis* 50 (1): 27–37.

Rice, M.E. and Harris, G.T. (1997). Cross-validation and extension of the violence risk appraisal guide for child molesters and rapists. *Law and Human Behavior* 21: 231–241.

Rice, M.E., Harris, G.T., Lang, C. et al. (2008). Sexual preference and recidivism of sex offenders with mental retardation. *Sexual Abuse: A Journal of Research and Treatment* 20: 409–425.

Rich, P. (2006). *Attachment and Sexual Offending*. Chichester: Wiley.

Rose, J., Jenkins, R., O'Connor, C. et al. (2002). A group treatment for men with intellectual disabilities who sexually offend or abuse. *Journal of Applied Research in Intellectual Disabilities* 15: 138–150.

Russell, D., Peplau, L.A., and Cutrona, C.E. (1980). The revised UCLA loneliness scale: concurrent and discriminate validity evidence. *Journal of Personality and Social Psychology* 39: 472–480.

Ryan, G. (1999). Treatment of sexually abusive youth. The evolving consensus. *Journal of Interpersonal Violence* 14: 422–436.

Scorzelli, J.F. and Reinke-Scorzelli, M. (1979). Mentally retarded offenders: a follow-up study. *Rehabilitation Counselling Bulletin* 23: 70–73.

Sequeira, H. and Hollins, S. (2003). Clinical effects of sexual abuse on people with learning disability: critical literature review. *British Journal of Psychiatry* 182: 13–19.

Sequeira, H., Howlin, P., and Hollins, S. (2003). Psychological disturbance associated with sexual abuse in people with learning disabilities. Case-control study. *British Journal of Psychiatry* 183: 451–456.

Sjostedt, G. and Langstrom, N. (2002). Assesment of risk for criminal recidivism among rapists: a comparison of four different measures. *Psychology, Crime & Law* 8: 25–40.

Sparrow, S.S., Balla, D.A., and Cicchetti, D.V. (1984). *A Revision of the Vineland Social Maturity Scale by E.A. Doll*. MN: American Guidance Service, Inc.

Steptoe, L. R. (2011). *Attachment,* Childhood *Adversity, emotional problems and personality disorder in offenders with mild intellectual disability*. Doctoral Thesis, Abertay University, Dundee, Scotland https://rke.abertay.ac.uk/en/studentTheses/ attachment-childhood-adversity-emotional-problems-and-personality (accessed 30 May 2019).

Stermac, L.E. and Segal, Z.V. (1989). Adult sexual contact with children: an examination of cognitive factors. *Behavior Therapy* 20: 573–584.

Sundram, C. (1990). *Inmates with developmental disabilities in New York Correctional Facilities*. Albany, NY: New York State Commission on Quality of Care for the Mentally Disabled.

Thirion-Marissiaux, A.F. and Nader-Grosbois, N. (2008). Theory of mind 'emotion', developmental characteristics and social understanding in children and adolescents with intellectual disabilities. *Research in Developmental Disabilities* 29: 414–430.

Thornton, D. (2002). *Scoring Guide for Risk Matrix 2000*. Madison, WI: Thornton.

Thornton, D., Beech, A., and Marshall, W.L. (2004). Pre-treatment self-esteem and post-treatment sexual recidivism. *International Journal of Offender Therapy and Comparative Criminology* 48: 587–599.

Walker, N. and McCabe, S. (1973). *Crime and Insanity in England*, vol. 2. Edinburgh: University Press.

Ward, T., Hudson, S., Johnston, L. et al. (1997). Cognitive distortions in sexual offenders: an integrative review. *Clinical Psychology Review* 17: 479–507.

Ward, T., Hudson, S., and Marshall, W.L. (1996). Attachment style in sex offenders: a preliminary study. *Journal of Sex Research* 33: 17–26.

Ward, T. and Hudson, S.M. (1998). A model of the relapse process in sexual offenders. *Journal of Interpersonal Violence* 13: 700–725.

Ward, T. and Hudson, S.M. (2000). A self-regulation model of relapse prevention. In: *Remaking Relapse Prevention with Sex Offenders: A Sourcebook* (eds. D.R. Laws, S.M. Hudson and T. Ward), 79–101. Thousand Oaks: Sage.

Ward, T., Hudson, S.M., and Keenan, T. (1998). A self-regulation model of the sexual offence process. *Sexual Abuse: A Journal of Research and Treatment* 10: 141–157.

Ward, T., Louden, K., Hudson, S.M. et al. (1995). A descriptive model of the offense chain for child molesters. *Journal of Interpersonal Violence* 10: 452–472.

Webster, C.D., Douglas, K.S., Eaves, D. et al. (1997). *HCR-20: Assessing Risk for Violence Version 2*. Mental Health, Law and Policy Institute, Simon Fraser University.

Wechsler, D. (2008). *Manual for the Wechsler Adult Intelligence Scale*, 4e. San Antonio, TX: Pearson.

Wehmeyer, M.L. (1994). Perceptions of self-determination and psychological empowerment of adolescents with mental retardation. *Education and Training in Mental Retardation and Developmental Disability* 29: 9–21.

Wehmeyer, M.L. and Palmer, S.B. (1997). Perceptions of control of students with and without cognitive disabilities. *Psychological Reports* 81: 195–206.

Wilcox, D., Beech, A., Markhall, H.F. et al. (2009). Actuarial risk assessment and recidivism in a sample of UK intellectually disabled sexual offenders. *Journal of Sexual Aggression* 15 ((1): 97–106.

Williams, F., Wakeling, H., and Webster, S. (2007). A psychometric study of six self-report measures for use with sexual offenders with cognitive and social functioning deficits. *Psychology, Crime & Law* 13 (5): 505–522.

Winter, N., Holland, A.J., and Collins, S. (1997). Factors predisposing to suspected offending by adults with self-reported learning disabilities. *Psychological Medicine* 27: 595–607.

8

Assessment for Social Problem-Solving, Social Information Processing, and Criminal Thinking

Peter E. Langdon

Centre for Educational Development, Appraisal and Research, University of Warwick

8.1 Introduction

Problem-solving, or in other words, 'the self-directed cognitive-behavioural process by which a person attempts to identify or discover effective or adaptive solutions for specific problems encountered in everyday living' (D'Zurilla and Nezu 2001, p. 212) is an area of marked interest to those who work with people who have intellectual disabilities, especially problem-solving within the social domain. Social problem-solving, or the, 'the process of problem solving as it occurs in the natural environment, or "real world"' (D'Zurilla et al. 2004, p. 11), has been an area of focus for many researchers and clinicians working with people who have intellectual disabilities as attempts to improve it have been associated with increasing integration into community settings (Loumidis 1992; Loumidis and Hill 1997), with more recent authors using social problem-solving interventions with offenders with intellectual disabilities (Lindsay et al. 2010).

The development of social behaviour and the associated processes have been subject to many empirical investigations, especially behaviour and decision making that violate social norms, including behaviour that would be considered criminal. Some early theorists attempted to describe the steps involved when making social decisions and enacting behaviour, often in an attempt to outline the biopsychosocial variables that are thought to be involved when engaging in social problem-solving. For example, D'Zurilla and Goldfried (1971) theorized that problem-solving comprised five stages or steps – (i) general-orientation, (ii) problem definition and formulation, (iii) generation of solutions or alternatives, (iv) decision-making, and (v) solution implementation or verification – and went on to develop a model of *social* problem-solving (D'Zurilla et al. 2004). This model of social problem-solving was simplified, and comprised only two steps: (i) problem orientation, which were meta-cognitive skills, and (ii) problem-solving skills, which comprised four skills referred to as problem definition and formulation, the generation of alternative solutions, decision-making, and solution implementation and verification (D'Zurilla et al. 2004).

The Wiley Handbook on What Works for Offenders with Intellectual and Developmental Disabilities: An Evidence-Based Approach to Theory, Assessment, and Treatment, First Edition.
Edited by William R. Lindsay, Leam A. Craig, and Dorothy Griffiths.

Other theorists focused more heavily upon 'online' social information processing, which cannot be ignored when discussing social problem-solving, as social information processing is inherently necessary for social problem-solving; models of social information processing share similarities with the earlier work of D'Zurilla and Goldfried (1971). The most well-known theory is the model of social information processing developed by Crick and Dodge (1994, 1996, Dodge 1986, Dodge and Price 1994) to help understand behavioural disorders in children and adolescents. Crick and Dodge (1994, 1996) theorized that behaviour is determined by the processing of contextual cues, and ability, which is biologically determined, as well as our stored knowledge that has been generated as a consequence of experience. Social information processing involved six steps: (i) encoding of cues, (ii) interpretation of cues, (iii) clarification of goals, (iv) response access or construction, (v) response decision, and (vi) behavioural enactment. The steps occur rapidly and in parallel, are affected by our knowledge store, which can be modified with experience, and developmental maturation occurs over time.

These aforementioned theories are cognitive in theoretical orientation, and whilst they incorporate developmental perspectives, others have nested developmental psychology more centrally, helping to further explain how social problem-solving and information processing develops or changes with age, and how such may lead to the occurrence of problematic social behaviour. For example, almost 20 years ago, Lemerise and Arsenio (2000) incorporated emotion recognition and regulation, along with temperament into social information processing theory and went on to integrate moral or social domain theory (Smetana 1999; Turiel 1983, 2002) in order to further define latent mental structures and online information processing together, expanding social information processing theory (Arsenio and Lemerise 2004). However, theories from developmental moral psychology are varied, and whilst there are differences, there are many similarities, with all attempting to explain decision making within the moral domain and how decision making changes over time as a consequence of increasing maturity and experience (Gibbs 2003, 2010, 2013; Haidt 2008; Hoffman 2000; Rest et al. 1999). This is of course relevant to our understanding of criminal offending behaviour as there is evidence of a relationship between moral development and criminal behaviour, where developmental lags are associated with conduct (Stams et al. 2006).

8.2 The Social Information Processing – Moral Decision-Making Framework

More recently, Garrigan et al. (2016, 2017) completed a meta-analytic study of the neural correlates of moral decision making, and went on to develop the Social Information Processing-Moral Decision-Making (SIP-MDM) framework, integrating social information processing and moral development in order to help further our understanding of social decision making (Garrigan et al. 2018). As part of this, they outlined the psychological processes and constructs relevant to decision making within this domain which included: (i) cognitive components, such as working memory, cognitive perspective taking, attention, abstract thought and reasoning, logical reasoning, self-control, attributions, and the development of schemas and scripts, (ii) affective components, including affective empathy, emotion recognition and regulation, somatic markers and intuition, (iii) social components, including social functioning and competence or skills, peer socialization and interaction, socio-economic factors, culture, and parenting or family functioning, and (iv) other factors such as brain development and integrity, temperament and personality, as well as online processing such as social information processing which is affected by all of the above mentioned components, growing increasingly mature with age (Garrigan et al. 2018).

Garrigan et al. (2018) integrated social information processing and moral development, outlining the developmental psychological constructs which change over time and have an impact upon the process of decision-making and behavioural enactment. For example, within the SIP-MDM framework the initial step within the process of behavioural enactment is: (i) the encoding of cues, which requires the processing of situation cues, emotion recognition, empathic responsiveness, and attentional resources, followed by (ii) the interpretation of these cues, drawing on skills such as perspective taking and theory of mind, causal and intent attributions, working memory, and moral judgements, which leads to (iii) a clarification of the goals, where situational factors, arousal regulation, and abstract thought are needed, and then, (iv) response access of construction occurs, where situation factors, somatic markers, and abstract thought is further required, leading to a (v) moral response decision, further relying on an evaluation of the likely outcome, empathy, situation factors, self-control and response inhibition, working memory, and moral reasoning skills, before (vi) the behaviour occurs. Throughout the process of online reasoning, where the relationships between steps are multidirectional, developmental factors, including the development of the brain, emotional processes, social factors, and the sum total knowledge stored within the database are required and influence the process of decision making. These factors develop over time as a consequence of maturation and developmental influences such as peer socialization, parenting, culture, and social and domain knowledge. The framework is meant to be dynamic, and development is gradual, where components develop with age and experience, directly and indirectly as a consequence of brain maturation. However, whilst atypical development may occur as a consequence of socialization which will impact upon brain maturation, atypical development may also occur as a consequence of physical brain damage or pre-existing developmental conditions such as intellectual disabilities where cognitive development, and, for example, some of the associated constructs such as logical and abstract reasoning, perspective-taking, speed of processing, attentional resources, and working memory may have an atypical developmental trajectory, which will affect decision making and behaviour.

8.3 People with Intellectual Disabilities

There are implications for our understanding of social decision making by people with intellectual disabilities who have a differing developmental trajectory that is rather heterogeneous, varying from person to person. However, this does not mean that people with intellectual disabilities are somehow destined to engage in social decision making and social problem solving that is associated with problematic behaviour. In fact, there is some evidence to the contrary; that is, people with intellectual disabilities may be less likely to engage in problematic behaviour that may be considered illegal. Langdon et al.

(2011a), having previously reviewed the literature in this area (Langdon et al. 2010a), argued that some people with intellectual disabilities are likely to engage in moral reasoning at an earlier developmental stage, and as such, they may be less likely to engage in illegal behaviour. They suggested that the relationship between moral development and illegal behaviour should be curvilinear, rather than linear, and those reasoning at earlier and later moral developmental stages should present with a reduced propensity to engage in illegal behaviour. The crux of this argument is that reasoning at earlier developmental stages is associated with an avoidance of punishment and adherence to rules, whilst later developmental stages, which are associated with prioritizing one's own needs, are hypothesized to be more prevalent amongst those with a history of engaging in illegal behaviour; this has been reported in several studies (Daniel et al. 2018; Langdon et al. 2010b, 2010c, 2011b; McDermott and Langdon 2016). This reasoning remains 'developmentally delayed' and Gibbs (2003, 2010, 2013) has argued that this is associated with cognitive distortions, or offence-supportive beliefs, and social skills deficits that increase the probability of illegal behaviours, commonly seen amongst offenders, including young-offenders.

8.4 Social Problem-Solving and Information Processing

There is evidence that groups of people with intellectual disabilities have difficulties with social problem-solving and social information processing. Children with intellectual disabilities have been shown to encode more negative cues within social vignettes (van Nieuwenhuijzen et al. 2004a), and that they may respond more submissively to social problems, and consider aggressive and submissive responses as more favourable (van Nieuwenhuijzen et al. 2004a, 2004b). Further, there is evidence that the working memory, perspective-taking, and emotional recognition skills predict emotional cue encoding in children with intellectual disabilities (van Nieuwenhuijzen and Vriens 2012). These authors also reported that the ability to recognize emotions and interpret problems predicted the ability to generate and select responses.

Considering adults with intellectual disabilities, there is evidence that those with problems with aggression have a hostile attributional bias, but those with and without a history of aggression were able to generate assertive and passive solutions to problems (Pert et al. 1999). Jahoda et al. (2006a) demonstrated that those with a history of aggressive behaviour did attribute more hostility to characters in stories when hostility was directed at participants, but not when it was directed at someone else. However, this was not the case within ambiguous stories, but those who had been aggressive gave more aggressive responses. Jahoda et al. (2006b) reported that there was no differences between aggressive and non-aggressive adults with intellectual disabilities on an emotional-recognition task, which is inconsistent with theory. Others have reported that adults with intellectual disabilities who have a history of engaging in illegal behaviour have a hostile attributional bias and social problem-solving difficulties, as would be predicted by our theory (Basquill et al. 2004), but this has not always consistent (Fuchs and Benson 1995), and may be associated with the type of assessments used, for example, vignettes and stories, as opposed to situations where relevant emotions and schemas are likely to be elicited.

There is evidence that adults with intellectual disabilities who have a history of engaging in illegal behaviour tend to endorse distorted, or offence-supportive beliefs, consistent with biased social information processing (Broxholme and Lindsay 2003; Langdon and Talbot 2006; Langdon et al. 2011b; Lindsay and Michie 2004; Lindsay et al. 2006), whilst others have also reported difficulties with empathy, and again, those with a history of illegal behaviour tend to present with reduced empathy (Hockley and Langdon 2015; Langdon and Hockley 2012). This difference has not been consistently reported, and there is some evidence that offenders with intellectual disabilities do not have difficulties with empathy (Beail and Proctor 2004; Langdon et al. 2011b; Proctor and Beail 2007; Ralfs and Beail 2012). This could be related to increasing developmental maturity, or possibly difficulties with how empathy is measured within this population.

8.5 Assessment of Social Problem-Solving and Criminal Thinking

There are substantial challenges when undertaking formalized psychological assessments of constructs related to social problem-solving, social information processing, and criminal thinking with people who have intellectual disabilities. Psychological measurement has been a longstanding and challenging problem with this population because of the potential difficulties with understanding assessment materials and providing responses, much of which requires cognitive and other related skills. Hartley and MacLean (2006) reviewed studies making use of assessment tools with Likert scales and found that response rates were low, and response bias was evident when tools were used with people with moderate to profound intellectual disabilities, whilst increased reliability and validity were noted when these assessments were used with people who have mild to borderline general intellectual functioning. The inclusion of pictures, clarifying questions, and fewer and simpler response choices were recommended. The majority of methods available to assess social problem-solving and related constructs tend to be questionnaires or semi-structured interviews, whilst within research, there are newer emerging methods that have promise and future clinical utility.

8.5.1 Social Problem-Solving Inventory – Revised

Bearing these issues in mind, one of the most commonly used measures of social problem-solving was developed by D'Zurilla et al. (2002) and based upon their social problem-solving theory (D'Zurilla et al. 2004). The Social Problem-Solving Inventory – Revised (SPSI-R) has been used widely, and was adapted by Lindsay et al. (2010) for use with people who have intellectual disabilities. Lindsay et al. (2010) administered the SPSI-R to 132 adults with intellectual disabilities who had committed a criminal offence, or had engaged in aggressive behaviour. The SPSI-R is a short 25-item questionnaire which aims to measure (i) problem orientation, either positive or negative, and (ii) problem-solving style, defined as rational, impulsive, or avoidant. Lindsay et al. (2010) simplified the questions and confirmed the modified items were consistent with the original meaning of the items, and made use of a diagram displaying increasing filled rectangles to represent the Likert response scale. They also read all the items to respondents.

Lindsay et al. (2010) reported good internal consistency for the modified SPSI-R, and completed a factor analysis indicating a four-factor solution, which was consistent with the previous findings of D'Zurilla et al. (2002), and concluded that the modified SPSI-R was a robust tool for use with people who have mild intellectual disabilities. They went on to make use of this modified measure to evaluate outcomes from the Social Problem-Solving and Offence Related Thinking (SPORT) programme (Lindsay et al. 2010). This is a 12 to 15-week programme which aims to improve the social problem-solving abilities of people with intellectual disabilities who had a history of engaging in illegal behaviour. Making use of a single-group design in order to model the effects of the intervention, the authors reported a significant reduction in impulsive and avoidant social problem-solving, and a significant increase in positive problem orientation, following treatment, bearing in mind that there were no methods used to guard against bias (e.g. masked assessors, randomization, control group, allocation concealment).

8.5.2 'How I Think' Questionnaire

Theories of social problem-solving and social information processing all consider the importance of causal or intent attributions with respect to determining behaviour. Cognition, and in particular, offence-supportive cognitions, have been shown to be related to illegal behaviour, and many psychological intervention programmes aim to reduce offence-supportive cognitions and attitudes (Banse et al. 2013; Bowes and McMurran 2013; Helmond et al. 2015). Measuring these distorted cognitions with offenders with intellectual disabilities is relevant to our understanding or both dynamic risk and treatment outcomes.

The How I Think Questionnaire (HIT; Barriga and Gibbs 1996; Barriga et al. 2001) was developed for use with adolescents and was shown to correlate with self-report and informant-reported antisocial behaviour. A meta-analysis showed that the HIT has excellent internal consistency and discriminated well between those with and without a history of engaging in crime (Gini and Pozzoli 2013).

Langdon et al. (2011b) first used an unmodified version of the HIT with a sample of men with and without intellectual disabilities who had, or did not have, a history of criminal offending behaviour. They reported that offenders with intellectual disabilities scored significantly higher than non-offenders with intellectual disabilities. They went on to demonstrate that a significant relationship between empathy and distorted cognitions was mediated by moral development. Following this study, they adapted the HIT by changing some of the words to reflect British culture, made some of the items easier to read, and reduced the Likert-scale from six responses to four. They administered the revised HIT to a sample of men with intellectual disabilities with and without a history of criminal offending behaviour and demonstrated improved internal consistency, and good test–retest reliability, and reported that those with a history of criminal offending scored higher than those without such a history. There was also a significant relationship between the HIT, moral development, and empathy (Daniel et al. 2018).

8.5.3 Sociomoral Reflective Measure – Short Form

Moral development, and the process of engaging in reasoning within the moral domain, are relevant to social decision-making, as many of these decisions fall within the moral domain, especially where behaviour may be considered illegal. The moral 'domain' by-and-large covers situations where principles related to justice, harm, fairness, and care are activated, but these may differ between cultures and religions, and measures tend to try to capture or characterize moral schema. Previously, Langdon et al. (2010a) reviewed the literature within this area and concluded that development for people with intellectual disabilities tends to occur at a slower rate than chronologically age-matched peers, and this difference tends to disappear when comparisons are made between groups which general intellectual functioning is controlled.

Langdon et al. (2010b, 2011b) went on to test out the Sociomoral Reflective Measure – Short Form (SRM-SF; Gibbs et al. 1992) with men with intellectual disabilities, including those with a history of criminal offending behaviour, and latterly, women (McDermott and Langdon 2016). The SRM-SF is a short semi-structured interview which has 11 questions, and takes about 20 minutes to complete The questions relate to the following seven constructs, (i) Contract (questions 1–3), (ii) Truth (question 4), (iii) Affiliation (questions 5 and 6), (iv) Life (questions 7 and 8), (v) Property (question 9), (vi) Law (question 10), and (vii) Legal Justice (question 11). Verbatim answers to the questions are scored according to a set of complex rules and heuristics, and the development of proficient and reliable scoring occurs through the use of practice scoring material. Responses to each question are assigned a developmental rating which corresponds to a moral stage associated with Gibb's Socio-Moral Reasoning Theory. Generally, across studies, men and women with intellectual disabilities who have a history of criminal offending tend to present with immature moral reasoning, but this is developmental mature in comparison their peers without a history of criminal offending. As previously discussed, the argument is that reasoning at earlier developmental stages is associated with an avoidance of punishment and adherence to rules, whilst later developmental stages are associated with prioritizing one's own needs and more prevalent amongst those with a history of engaging in illegal behaviour (Daniel et al. 2018; Langdon et al. 2010b, 2010c, 2011b; McDermott and Langdon 2016).

8.5.4 Questionnaire on Attitudes Consistent with Sexual Offending

Another well-known assessment tool for distorted cognitions is the Questionnaire on Attitudes Consistent with Sexual Offending (QACSO; Lindsay and Michie 2004; Lindsay et al. 2006, 2007) which was developed for use with sexual offenders. The QACSO has been shown to be a reliable and valid assessment tool (Broxholme and Lindsay 2003), and requires respondents to answer 'yes' or 'no' in response to a series of statements which are normally read aloud by the examiner. There is evidence that scores decrease on this questionnaire following psychological treatment for sexual offending (SOTSEC-ID 2010).

8.5.5 Sexual Offenders Self-Appraisal Scale

The Sexual Offenders Self-Appraisal Scale (SOSAS; Bray and Forshaw 1996) is another measure of distorted cognitions which was developed for use with people with intellectual disabilities. Statements are presented to respondents who are asked to indicate their level of agreement by posting a statement into one of five small boxes which represent a five-point Likert scale. Both Langdon et al. (2007) and Williams et al. (2007)

demonstrated that the SOSAS had substantial internal consistency, but there appear to be problems with the use of double-negatives for some of the items which have been seen to confuse some respondents, whilst Williams et al. (2007) suggested that there may be some associated issues with the underlying factor structure.

8.5.6 Sex Offenders Opinion Test

The Sex Offenders Opinion Test (SOOT; Bray 1997) is another assessment tool meant for use with sexual offenders who have intellectual disabilities and aims to examine attitudes towards victims of sexual offenders. The SOOT has been reported to have good internal consistency and a two-factor structure (Williams et al. 2007).

8.5.7 Other Methods

Within research studies, a variety of other methods have been used to assess social problem-solving and social information processing. Some of these studies had attempted to assess aspects of the process of social problem-solving, or information processing, whilst others have attempted to assess the various steps or associated processes in some manner using a method that involves the manipulation of variables.

One of the more common methods used for assessing social problem-solving and information processing has been the use of vignettes, or problem-based stories, which are presented to a respondent who is invited to tell the researcher their reasoning or decision. For example, van Nieuwenhuijzen et al. (2011) developed a series of hypothetical scenarios comprised of cartoons, pictures, and videos which were presented to children with intellectual disabilities. The behaviour of the antagonist within each scenario was ambiguous, intentional, or accidental. The scenarios were used to measure social information processing steps, including the encoding of information, attributions, goals, response generation, evaluation, self-efficacy, and response selection by asking a series of questions in response to various stimuli that were presented to children.

Similarly with adults with intellectual disabilities, Jahoda et al. (2006a) presented vignettes to those with and without a history of aggressive behaviour. They demonstrated that those with a history of aggression attributed more hostility to characters within the vignettes when hostility was directed at the respondent compared to when it was directed at another character in the vignettes. Those with a history of aggression tended to respond with more frequent aggressive responses, but a hostile attributional response was not present when the situation was ambiguous. Related methods making use of vignettes have been used by other groups (Basquill et al. 2004).

More recently, and considering that the initial step within any social decision is the encoding of information, Langdon et al. (2016) examined attentional bias towards positive and negative images amongst men with intellectual disabilities, some of whom had a history of criminal offending. They made use of a dot-probe paradigm to present the images to respondents. The dot-probe paradigm involved the presentation of an initial central cross on a computer screen, followed by the sequential presentation of pairs of images for a short period, usually a few hundred milliseconds, which is then followed by the presentation of a dot within the location of one of the images. The respondent must then make a response using a key press to indicate the location of the dot. Attentional resources may be allocated towards the images as they are presented, and assuming that one of the images may have drawn a respondent's attention, and this is congruent with the location of the subsequent appearance of the dot, they may respond with a key press slightly faster than when their attention is allocated differently. The results indicated that those without a history of engaging in criminal offending had an attention bias away from negative images, whilst offenders had a slight bias towards negative images. There was a noted significant positive correlation between pro-offence distorted cognitions and attentional bias towards negative images, and a negative correlation between empathy and an attentional bias towards negative images.

Further, increasing reliance on computerized methods for the assessment and treatment of social problem-solving and social skills are emerging within the literature, including with offenders who have intellectual disabilities. Langdon and Archibald (2016) tested virtual immersion therapy (VIT) with 12 offenders with intellectual and/ or autism as a method for both assessing and teaching social problem-solving and social skills. The system allows for someone to be 'immersed' in a social problem situation which is displayed on a television (Figure 8.1). The person taking part in the scenario is captured live by a video camera and immersed into the social problem situation which they view on the television. They are required to interact with actors within the problem situation and observe themselves responding, as they respond. The initial findings indicated that emotion recognition, quality of verbal responses, and social problem-solving skills improved following the intervention, but this was not consistent for everyone.

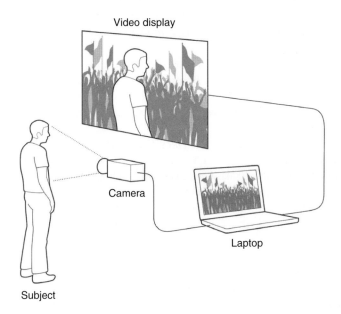

Figure 8.1 Representation of Virtual Immersion Therapy (VIT).

8.6 Conclusions

Models of social problem-solving and related theoretical perspectives, such as social information processing have been augmented to incorporate developmental perspectives, mainly drawn from moral psychology (Garrigan ct al. 2018). The SIP-MDM framework integrated several previous theoretical perspectives into a single framework that attempts to capture variables and constructs that develop over time, whilst also attempting to consider how real time decision making and social problem-solving occurs.

There are a variety of component processes and steps in the model that lead to the occurrence of behaviour, drawing upon affective, cognitive, and developmental constructs as processing occurs. Whilst some of these processes and steps have been investigated with people who have intellectual disabilities, there has been very little research within this area. There have been some attempts to examine social information processing within children, adolescents, and adults with intellectual disabilities, but there are by-and-large only a few studies. Methods of assessing social problem-solving and pro-offence distorted cognitions are limited to questionnaire-based or semi-structured interviews, and there are very few well developed and validated tools for use with this population. Looking forward, we need to focus on the development of modern and robust methods of assessment, and where possible, consider using technology which may help to enable more effective communication and participation, not only within assessment procedures, but eventually within interventions.

References

Arsenio, W.F. and Lemerise, E.A. (2004). Aggression and moral development: integrating social information processing and moral domain models. *Child Development* 75 (4): 987–1002.

Banse, R., Koppehele-Gossel, J., Kistemaker, L.M. et al. (2013). Pro-criminal attitudes, intervention, and recidivism. *Aggression and Violent Behavior* 18 (6): 673–685.

Barriga, A.Q. and Gibbs, J.C. (1996). Measuring cognitive distortion in antisocial youth: development and preliminary validation of the 'how I think' questionnaire. *Aggressive Behavior* 22 (5): 333–343.

Barriga, A.Q., Gibbs, J.C., Potter, G.B. et al. (2001). *How I Think (HIT) Questionnaire Manual*. Champaign, IL: Research Press.

Basquill, M.F., Nezu, C.M., Nezu, A.M. et al. (2004). Aggression-related hostility bias and social-problem solving deficits in adult males with mental retardation. *American Journal on Mental Retardation* 109: 255–263.

Beail, N. and Proctor, T. (2004). Empathy and theory of mind: a study of offenders and non-offenders with intellectual disabilities (ID). *Journal of Intellectual Disability Research* 48: 466–466.

Bowes, N. and McMurran, M. (2013). Cognitions supportive of violence and violent behavior. *Aggression and Violent Behavior* 18 (6): 660–665.

Bray, D. (1997). *The Sex Offenders Opinion Test (SOOT)*. Preston, UK: Lancashire Care NHS Trust.

Bray, D. and Forshaw, N. (1996). *Sex Offenders Self Appraisal Scale (Version 1.1.)*. Preston, UK: Lancashire Care NHS Trust.

Broxholme, S.L. and Lindsay, W.R. (2003). Development and preliminary evaluation of a questionnaire on cognitions related to sex offending for use with individuals who have mild intellectual disabilities. *Journal of Intellectual Disability Research* 47: 472–482.

Crick, N.R. and Dodge, K.A. (1994). A review and reformation of social information-processing mechanisms in children's social adjustment. *Psychological Bulletin* 115: 74–99.

Crick, N.R. and Dodge, K.A. (1996). Social information-processing mechanisms in reactive and proactive aggression. *Child Development* 67: 993–1002.

Daniel, M.R., Sadek, S.A., and Langdon, P.E. (2018). The reliabilty and validity of a revised version of the How I Think Questionnaire for men who have intellectual disabilities. *Psychology, Crime & Law* 24 (4): 379–390.

Dodge, K.A. (1986). A social information processing model of social competence in children. In: *The Minnesota Symposium on Child Psychology*, vol. 18 (ed. M. Perlmutter), 37–51. Hillsdale, NJ: Erlbaum.

Dodge, K.A. and Price, J.M. (1994). On the relation between social information-processing and socially competent behavior in early school-aged children. *Child Development* 65: 1385–1397.

D'Zurilla, T.J. and Goldfried, M.R. (1971). Problem solving and behavior modification. *Journal of Abnormal Psychology* 78 (1): 107.

D'Zurilla, T.J. and Nezu, A.M. (2001). *Problem-Solving Therapies*, 2e. New York: Guildford Press.

D'Zurilla, T.J., Nezu, A.M., and Maydeu-Olivares, A. (2002). *Social Problem Solving Inventory Revised (SPSI-R): Technical Manual*. New York: Multihealth Systems, Inc.

D'Zurilla, T.J., Nezu, A.M., and Maydeu-Olivares, A. (2004). Social problem solving: theory and assessment. In: *Social Problem Solving: Theory, Research and Training* (eds. E.C. Chang, T.J. D'Zurilla and L.J. Sanna), 11–27. Washington, DC: American Psychological Association.

Fuchs, C. and Benson, B.A. (1995). Social information processing by aggressive and nonaggressive men with mental retardation. *American Journal on Mental Retardation* 100: 244–252.

Garrigan, B., Adlam, A.L.R., and Langdon, P.E. (2016). The neural correlates of moral decision-making: a systematic review and meta-analysis of moral evaluations and response decision judgements. *Brain and Cognition* 108: 88–97. https://doi.org/10.1016/j.bandc.2016.07.007.

Garrigan, B., Adlam, A.L.R., and Langdon, P.E. (2017). Corrigendum to 'the neural correlates of moral decision-making: a systematic review and meta-analysis of moral evaluations and response decision judgements' [Brain Cogn. 108 (2016) 88–97]. *Brain and Cognition* 111: 104–106. https://doi.org/10.1016/j.bandc.2016.10.002.

Garrigan, B., Adlam, A.L., and Langdon, P.E. (2018). Moral decision-making and moral development: toward an integrative framework. *Developmental Review* 49: 80–100.

Gibbs, J.C. (2003). *Moral Development and Reality: Beyond the Theories of Kohlberg and Hoffman*. London: Sage Publications.

Gibbs, J.C. (2010). *Moral Development and Reality: Beyond the Theories of Kohlberg and Hoffman*, 2e. Boston: Pearson, Allyn & Bacon.

Gibbs, J.C. (2013). *Moral Development and Reality: Beyond the Theories of Kohlberg, Hoffman, and Haidt*. Oxford: Oxford University Press.

Gibbs, J.C., Basinger, K.S., and Fuller, D. (1992). *Moral Maturity: Measuring the Development of Sociomoral Reflection*. Hillsdale, NJ: Erlbaum.

Gini, G. and Pozzoli, T. (2013). Measuring self-serving cognitive distortions: a meta-analysis of the psychometric properties of the How I Think Questionnaire (HIT). *European Journal of Developmental Psychology* 10 (4): 510–517.

Haidt, J. (2008). Morality. *Perspectives on Psychological Science* 3 (1): 65–72.

Hartley, S.L. and MacLean, W.E. (2006). A review of the reliability and validity of Likert-type scales for people with intellectual disability. *Journal of Intellectual Disability Research* 50: 813–827.

Helmond, P., Overbeek, G., Brugman, D. et al. (2015). A meta-analysis on cognitive distortions and externalizing problem behavior: associations, moderators, and treatment effectiveness. *Criminal Justice and Behavior* 42 (3): 245–262.

Hockley, O. and Langdon, P.E. (2015). Men with intellectual disabilities with a history of sexual offending: empathy for victims of sexual and non-sexual crimes. *Journal of Intellectual Disability Research* 59 (4): 332–341.

Hoffman, M.L. (2000). *Empathy and Moral Development: Implications for Caring and Justice*. Cambridge, UK: Cambridge University Press.

Jahoda, A., Pert, C., and Trower, P. (2006a). Frequent aggression and attribution of hostile intent in people with mild to moderate intellectual disabilities: an empirical investigation. *American Journal of Mental Retardation* 111: 90–99.

Jahoda, A., Pert, C., and Trower, P. (2006b). Socioemotional understanding and frequent aggression in people with mild to moderate intellectual disabilities. *American Journal on Mental Retardation* 111: 77–89.

Langdon, P.E. and Archibald, S. (2016). Using virtual immersion therapy to teach offenders with intellectual and developmental disabilities social skills: a modelling study. *Journal of Intellectual Disability Research* 60: 693.

Langdon, P.E. and Hockley, O. (2012). Empathy towards victims of sexual and non-sexual crimes amongst men with intellectual disabilities who are convicted sexual offenders. *Journal of Intellectual Disability Research* 56: 688.

Langdon, P.E. and Talbot, T.J. (2006). Locus of control and sex offenders with an intellectual disability. *International Journal of Offender Therapy and Comparative Criminology* 50: 391–401.

Langdon, P.E., Maxted, H., Murphy, G.H. et al. (2007). An exploratory evaluation of the Ward and Hudson offending pathways model with sex offenders who have intellectual disability. *Journal of Intellectual and Developmental Disability* 32: 94–105.

Langdon, P., Clare, I., and Murphy, G. (2010a). Developing an understanding of the literature relating to the moral development of people with intellectual disabilities. *Developmental Review* 30 (3): 273–293. https://doi.org/10.1016/j.dr.2010.01.001.

Langdon, P., Murphy, G., Clare, I. et al. (2010b). The psychometric properties of the Socio-Moral Reflection Measure - Short Form and the moral theme inventory for men with and without intellectual disabilities. *Research in Developmental Disabilities* 31 (6): 1204–1215. https://doi.org/10.1016/j.ridd.2010.07.025.

Langdon, P.E., Clare, I.C.H., and Murphy, G.H. (2010c). Illegal behaviour and moral reasoning amongst men with and without ID. *Journal of Applied Research in Intellectual Disabilities* 23 (5): 428–428.

Langdon, P.E., Clare, I.C.H., and Murphy, G.H. (2011a). Moral reasoning theory and illegal behaviour by adults with intellectual disabilities. *Psychology, Crime & Law* 17 (2): 101–115.

Langdon, P.E., Murphy, G.H., Clare, I.C.H. et al. (2011b). Relationships among moral reasoning, empathy and distorted cognitions amongst men with intellectual disabilities and a history of criminal offending. *American Journal on Intellectual and Developmental Disabilities* 116: 438–456.

Langdon, P.E., Sadek, S., and Daniel, M.R. (2016). Attentional bias towards positive and negative images amongst offenders and non-offenders with intellectual disabilities. *Journal of Intellectual Disability Research* 60: 794.

Lemerise, E.A. and Arsenio, W.F. (2000). An integrated model of emotion processes and cognition in social information processing. *Child Development* 71 (1): 107–118.

Lindsay, W.R. and Michie, A.M. (2004). Two studies using the questionnaire on attitudes consistent with sexual offending (QACSO) to discriminate between categories of sex offenders. *Journal of Intellectual Disability Research* 48: 464–464.

Lindsay, W.R., Michie, A.M., Whitefield, E. et al. (2006). Response patterns on the questionnaire on attitudes consistent with sexual offending in groups of sex offenders with intellectual disabilities. *Journal of Applied Research in Intellectual Disabilities* 19 (1): 47–53.

Lindsay, W.R., Whitefield, E., and Carson, D. (2007). An assessment for attitudes consistent with sexual offending for use with offenders with intellectual disabilities. *Legal and Criminological Psychology* 12: 55–68.

Lindsay, W.R., Hamilton, C., Moulton, S. et al. (2010). Assessment and treatment of social problem solving in offenders with intellectual disability. *Psychology, Crime & Law* 17: 181–197.

Loumidis, K. (1992). Can social problem-solving training help people with learning difficulties? In: *The Promotion of Mental Health* (ed. D.R. Trent). Aldershot: Avebury Press.

Loumidis, K. and Hill, A. (1997). Social problem-solving groups for adults with learning disabilities. In: *Cognitive-Behavioural Therapy for People with Learning Disabilities* (eds. B. Stenfert Kroese, D. Dagnan and K. Loumidis), 86. London: Routledge.

McDermott, E. and Langdon, P.E. (2016). The moral reasoning abilities of men and women with intellectual disabilities who have a history of criminal offending behaviour. *Legal and Criminological Psychology* 21: 25–40. https://doi.org/10.1111/lcrp.12051.

van Nieuwenhuijzen, M. and Vriens, A. (2012). (Social) cognitive skills and social information processing in children with mild to borderline intellectual disablities. *Research in Developmental Disabilities* 33: 426–434.

van Nieuwenhuijzen, M., Orobio de Castro, B., Wijnroks, L. et al. (2004a). The relations between intellectual disabilities, social information processing and behaviour problems. *European Journal of Developmental Psychology* 1: 215–229.

van Nieuwenhuijzen, M., Orobio de Castro, B.O., Wijnroks, L. et al. (2004b). The relation between social information processing and behaviour problems in children with mild intellectual disabilities (MID). *Journal of Intellectual Disability Research* 48: 291–291.

Pert, C., Jahoda, A., and Squire, J. (1999). Attribution of intent and role-taking: cognitive factors as mediator of aggression with people who have mental retardation. *American Journal on Mental Retardation* 104: 399–409.

Proctor, T. and Beail, N. (2007). Empathy and theory of mind in offenders with intellectual disability. *Journal of Intellectual and Developmental Disability* 32: 82–93.

Ralfs, S. and Beail, N. (2012). Assessing components of empathy in sex-offenders with intellectual disabilties. *Journal of Applied Research in Intellectual Disabilities* 25: 50–59.

Rest, J., Narvaez, D., Bebeau, M. et al. (1999). A neo-Kohlbergian approach: the DIT and schema theory. *Educational Psychology Review* 11: 291–324.

Smetana, J.G. (1999). The role of parents in moral development: a social domain analysis. *Journal of Moral Education* 28 (3): 311–322.

SOTSEC-ID (2010). Effectiveness of group cognitive behavioural treatment for men with intellectual disabilities at risk of sexual offending. *Journal of Applied Research in Intellectual Disabilities* 23: 537–551.

Stams, G.J., Brugman, D., Deković, M. et al. (2006). The moral judgement of juvenile delinquents: a meta-analysis. *Journal of Abnormal Child Psychology* 34: 697–713.

Turiel, E. (1983). *The Development of Social Knowledge: Morality and Convention.* Cambridge, UK: Cambridge University Press.

Turiel, E. (2002). *The Culture of Morality: Social Development, Context and Conflict.* Cambridge, UK: Cambridge University Press.

Van Nieuwenhuijzen, M., Vriens, A., Scheepmaker, M. et al. (2011). The development of a diagnostic instrument to measure social information processing in children with mild to borderline intellectual disabilities. *Research in Developmental Disabilities* 32 (1): 358–370.

Williams, F., Wakeling, H., and Webster, S. (2007). A psychometric study of six self-report measure for use with sexual offenders with cognitive and social functioning deficits. *Psychology Crime and Law* 13: 505–522.

9

Assessment of Alcohol Use Disorder and Alcohol-Related Offending Behaviour

Joanne E.L. VanDerNagel[1,2,3]*, Neomi van Duijvenbode*[1,2,4]*, and Robert Didden*[4,5]

[1] *Tactus, Deventer, the Netherlands*
[2] *Radboud University Nijmegen, Nijmegen Institute for Scientist-Practitioners in Addiction, Nijmegen, the Netherlands*
[3] *Aveleijn, Borne, the Netherlands*
[4] *Radboud University Nijmegen, Behavioural Science Institute, Nijmegen, the Netherlands*
[5] *Trajectum, Zwolle, the Netherlands*

9.1 Introduction

Individuals with intellectual and developmental disabilities (IDD) are known to use and misuse a range of substances including tobacco, alcohol, cannabis, and other drugs. Alcohol is the main substance used and misused in individuals with IDD, followed by cannabis and stimulants (e.g. Carroll Chapman and Wu 2012; Van Duijvenbode et al. 2015; VanDerNagel et al. 2017a). These substances are used for similar reasons as those found in persons in the general population. That is, individuals with IDD might engage in substance use because of its psychoactive effects (for example to feel 'high' after smoking cannabis or 'tipsy' after drinking alcohol), to conform to social norms or for social enhancement, and/or to self-medicate against negative experiences in life (Taggart et al. 2006).

The prevalence of substance use amongst individuals with IDD seems to be lower than in the general population. They are – however – considered a risk group for developing substance use-related problems and substance use disorders (SUD) (Carroll Chapman and Wu 2012). Several studies underscore that substance use amongst this population may adversely interact with some of the characteristics associated with IDD (e.g. cognitive limitations, overly compliant dispositions) (McGillivray and Moore 2001). In addition, substance use and SUDs are highly prevalent in some subgroups of individuals with IDD, for example in those with mental health and/or forensic issues (Carroll Chapman and Wu 2012; Van Duijvenbode et al. 2015).

Unfortunately, individuals with IDD and SUD seem to be less likely to receive treatment or to remain in addiction treatment (Hassiotis et al. 2011; Carroll Chapman and Wu 2012). First, SUDs in individuals with IDD are probably underdiagnosed (e.g. VanDerNagel 2016). Second, they experience more difficulties in accessing addiction

The Wiley Handbook on What Works for Offenders with Intellectual and Developmental Disabilities: An Evidence-Based Approach to Theory, Assessment, and Treatment, First Edition.
Edited by William R. Lindsay, Leam A. Craig, and Dorothy Griffiths.
© 2020 John Wiley & Sons Ltd. Published 2020 by John Wiley & Sons Ltd.

treatment due to for instance poverty, lack of transportation to treatment facilities, or simply not knowing they might need help or how to get a referral for addiction treatment. In addition, traditional treatment programmes generally are not adapted to the needs and characteristics of those with IDD, making it less likely for them to benefit from treatment and more likely to drop out prematurely. This treatment gap may increase the likelihood of substance use-related problems. This gap may be a risk factor for offending behaviour (Kiewik et al. 2017). Recent studies have found substance use and SUDs to be highly prevalent amongst individuals with IDD in forensic settings (e.g. Bhandari et al. 2015; Luteijn et al. 2017).

In this chapter, we summarize research on the prevalence of SUD – particularly alcohol use disorder (AUD) – amongst individuals with IDD in a forensic context and its relationship to offending behaviour. We then provide suggestions for the assessment of substance use in individuals with IDD in a forensic context. Treatment of AUD in the forensic context will be discussed in Chapter 18 (Newton and McGillivary, this volume).

9.2   AUD in Individuals with IDD

AUD is one of the diagnoses in the DSM-V chapter *Substance-related and addictive disorders* (American Psychiatric Association [APA] 2013). The chapter encompasses diagnoses related to (excessive) use of 10 classes of psychoactive substances as well as gambling disorders. Although several classes of drugs are distinguished, all types of substances activate the brain reward system in such an intense way that normal activities may be neglected. In the DSM-V, SUD is defined by 11 criteria related to: (i) impaired control over quantity and duration of substance use; (ii) social impairment due to substance use; (iii) risky use; and (iv) tolerance and withdrawal. Specifiers for each of the SUDs indicate the severity of the disorder: mild (two to three symptoms), moderate (four to five symptoms), or severe (six or more symptoms). According to the Diagnostic Manual – Intellectual Disability 2[1] the DSM-V diagnostic criteria can be applied to individuals with mild to moderate ID 'assuming that one has access to accurate information concerning the four groups of criteria [...]. However, it may be difficult to obtain reliable information about several criteria that include difficult to observe or interpret behaviour' (p. 564) (Mikkelsen et al. 2016). These validity issues regarding the assessment of substance use and substance use in individuals with IDD are discussed later.

9.2.1   Prevalence of AUD in Individuals with IDD

It is not possible to present conclusive data on prevalence rates of AUD amongst individuals with IDD. In part this is because there is lack of systematic assessment of alcohol and other drug use amongst this group of individuals as well as a relative lack of empirical research on this topic. Another part of the problem is that, amongst the group of individuals with IDD, there are subgroups with an increased risk for SUDs (e.g. Carroll Chapman and Wu 2012). The reported prevalence rates in studies thus varies greatly.

---

1 The DM-ID-2 (Fletcher et al. 2016) is an adaptation of the DSM-IV-TR for use with individuals with IDD.

Indeed, studies report prevalence rates of AUD ranging from 0.5 to 1% in the wider ID population or amongst community based samples (Sturmey et al. 2003; Cooper et al. 2007) to over 60% in individuals with IDD in forensic settings (e.g. Männynsolo et al. 2009; Hassiotis et al. 2011). The wide range reflects differences between studies regarding sample characteristics and assessment methods. A number of things stand out in the prevalence studies. First, regarding substance use amongst individuals with IDD, an 'all-or-nothing' principle seems to be at play: large proportions of those with IDD are reported not using substances at all. But those who do generally are seen to be at increased risk for developing problematic substance use, including SUD (Taggart et al. 2006). Second, individuals with IDD seem to be more susceptible to negative psychosocial consequences of substance use. That is, relatively little substance use can cause rather serious problems, including work-related problems and social problems (Taggart et al. 2006). The relatively high prevalence of co-occurring use of prescribed psychotropic medication and mental disorders further increases the chance of experiencing negative consequences of substance use (Slayter 2010). Third, the wide range reflects that subgroups of those with IDD – especially those with mild to borderline IDD (IQ range 50–85) and those with IDD and forensic or mental health issues – are at an even higher risk for developing SUD, compared to, for example, individuals with IDD in the lower IQ range or those without co-occurring mental health or forensic issues (Carroll Chapman and Wu 2012).

9.2.2 Prevalence of AUD in Individuals with IDD in Forensic Settings

Similar to prevalence rates in the wider IDD population, the prevalence rates of SUD amongst individuals with IDD in forensic settings differ across studies. Lindsay et al. (2013) suggest that there are discrepancies between studies from different parts of the world, with for example, higher rates of SUDs amongst offenders in Australia, than in studies from for instance Canada (rates between 11 and 38%), and the United Kingdom (rates between 4 and 50%). Indeed, an Australian study found that 81% of the soon-to-be-released prisoners with IDD used alcohol in the 12 months prior to incarceration (Bhandari et al. 2015). In a large-scale prison survey in the UK 28% of the IDD population (defined as an estimated IQ < 65) was found to have scores indicative of alcohol related problems on the Alcohol Use Disorder Identity Test (AUDIT; Babor et al. 2001), and an additional 33% to have scores indicative for an AUD (Hassiotis et al. 2011). Also, a Finnish study reported that 68% of the offenders with IDD had a SUD (Männynsolo et al. 2009). Rates of SUDs may also vary across security levels in forensic settings. Several authors report about a history of alcohol related problems in approximately 10% of the individuals with IDD and forensic issues in community settings (e.g. Hogue et al. 2006; Lindsay et al. 2013), and in medium or maximum secure settings rates of 27% (Hogue et al. 2006) to 50% (Lindsay et al. 2013) are reported. These studies show that – despite a wide range of prevalence rates – substance use and SUD are highly prevalent amongst individuals with IDD in forensic settings.

Even though individuals with IDD and forensic issues do have higher prevalence rates of SUDs, rates are still low compared to the non-IDD forensic population (e.g. Lindsay et al. 2013). For instance, though Lunsky et al. (2011) reported 11% of a sample of individuals with IDD and forensic issues to have SUDs (compared to 5% in a sample of individuals with IDD without forensic issues), this rate is substantially lower than the reported 28% in the non-IDD forensic population. Also, in a Dutch pretrial report Vinkers (2013) found lower rates of alcohol misuse in individuals with an IQ below 70 (11% alcohol misuse), than in those with an IQ above 85 (15% alcohol misuse). However, Crocker et al. (2007) found in pre-trial reports that individuals with IDD were as likely as those with borderline intellectual functioning or average intellectual disabilities to have a SUD (60.4, 61.9, and 61.1%, respectively).

9.3   AUD in Relation to Offending Behaviour

Substance use and offending behaviour are closely related (Lindsay et al. 2013) and this relationship can be explained in several ways (European Monitoring Centre for Drugs and Drug Addiction [EMCDDA] 2007). First, substance use can lead to offending behaviour. For example, crimes committed under the influence or during withdrawal of substances (pharmacological crimes) or crimes committed to purchase substances (acquisitive crimes). Substance use can also lead to offending behaviour if the crimes are connected to the illegal drug market (systemic crimes) or if the person violates the drug laws (consensual crimes). Though in use of illicit substances acquisitive crimes are common, pharmacological effects may better explain the relationship between alcohol use and offending behaviour, especially for violent crimes as alcohol intoxication is related to aggression (Giancola et al. 2001). Second, the criminal context can also lead to (increased) substance use itself (Maruna 2001). This can be the case if a criminal subculture provides the context for drug use or social situations in which substance use is condoned or encouraged. Third and last, substance use and offending behaviour can be indirectly related, with general psychosocial risk factors, genetic traits, and subcultural norms increasing the risk for both SUD and offending behaviour (Gorman and White 1995).

9.3.1   Relations Between Alcohol Use and Offending in Individuals with IDD

Despite the (potential) relationship between alcohol use (disorder) and offending behaviour, several studies report low levels of substance use involvement in index offences. For instance, McGillivray et al. (2016) found similar rates of substance use in prisoners with and without IDD in the year prior to their imprisonment, but a much lower rate (32% versus 64% in the non-IDD population) of substance use as an antecedent for the index offence. In addition, when reviewing the files of 477 patients of forensic IDD services, Lindsay et al. (2013) found only 6% of index offences that had alcohol use as part of the description or charges. Nevertheless, in the same study it was mentioned that more than 20% had a history of AUD, and such a history was associated with a history of problems including physical aggression, contact sexual offences, theft, property damage, fire setting, and road traffic offences, and having previous charges (Lindsay et al. 2013). Thus, as Lindsay et al. (2013) remarked regarding the reported lower percentages of involvement of alcohol use (disorder) in offending behaviour in individuals with IDD: 'A study such as this is dependent on the quality of the information in the case notes, and it may have been that the presence of alcohol as a contributing factor has not been documented'. In another series of case studies in 14 individuals with mild ID to borderline intellectual functioning (IQ 50–85) in the Netherlands, SUD was linked to offending behaviour. This link was mostly a pharmacological relationship (n = 10, 71%), but also indirect relationships, for instance when substance used increased pre-existing symptoms of mental disorders (n = 6, 42%) (VanDerNagel et al. 2014).

9.4 Assessment of AUD in Individuals with IDD

The diagnosis of AUD is primarily related to impaired control over quantity and duration of substance use, social impairment due to substance use, risky use, and tolerance and withdrawal. When this information is available, the diagnosis of AUD is relatively straightforward in individuals with IDD (Mikkelsen et al. 2016). However, AUD is probably under-diagnosed in the IDD population, as individuals tend to underreport their substance use, and signs and symptoms of SUD may remain undetected, or are wrongfully misattributed to behavioural problems, other mental disorders or the IDD itself (e.g. Van Duijvenbode et al. 2015; VanDerNagel 2016). The lack of procedures and methods of systematic screening and assessment of alcohol use and AUD adapted to and validated for use in individuals with IDD also contribute to the under-diagnosis (VanDerNagel 2016).

9.4.1 Assessment of Alcohol Use (Disorder)

There are several ways to assess alcohol use (disorder), relying on self-report (e.g. using structured questionnaires or clinical interviews), collateral-report (including reports from next of kin, or professional caregivers), case files (including police and forensic reports), and biomarker analysis (such as breath, blood, or urine analysis). These methods have been compared in a range of studies (see e.g. Connors and Maisto 2003; de Beaurepaire et al. 2007; Stasiewicz et al. 2008). Outcomes of these studies show that all methods have their pros and cons. For example, there are several self-report instruments available for screening for AUD, such as the CAGE questionnaire (Mayfield et al. 1974), Michigan Alcoholism Screening Test (MAST; Selzer 1971) and Alcohol Use Disorder Identification Test (AUDIT; Babor et al. 2001). In addition, diagnostic assessment instruments such as the Composite International Diagnostic Interview-Substance Abuse (CIDI-SAM; Cottler 2000) or the Structured Clinical Interview for DSM-V disorders (SCID-5-CV; First et al. 2015) are available. Whilst self-report is the easiest way of assessing alcohol and other substance use, relatively high rates of under-reported use (i.e. no self-reported use whilst biomarker analysis was positive) have been found for this method. In addition, whilst biomarker analysis may quantify and objectively detect substance use, it also has its limitations. First, false positive or negative testing can occur due to due to tampering with the sample ('cheating the drug test') or dilution of the substance in incidental use (Fendrich et al. 2004; Hoiseth et al. 2008). Also, both the window of detection of substance use and the threshold of detectable use vary across different types of biomarker analysis (e.g. Wojcik and Hawthorne 2007; Hoiseth et al. 2008). Further, biomarker testing generally depends on subject cooperation as well as availability of test kits and laboratory facilities that may not be available (Fendrich et al. 2004). Another major limitation of biomarker testing is that it cannot be used to assess the AUD criteria (see Section 9.2). Thus, information on impaired control over alcohol use, social impairment due to this use, risky use, and tolerance and withdrawal needs to be assembled using both self-report and collateral report.

When assessing alcohol use (disorder), it is important to bear in mind that co-morbidity of alcohol related problems with other substance use disorders and/or other mental health conditions is common (e.g. Petrakis et al. 2002). Thus, special attention should be given to the possibility of polysubstance use and co-occurring symptoms of a mental disorder. The latter can be both be the result of, and a risk factor for AUD, and generally warrants a comprehensive multicomponent assessment.

9.4.2   Assessment of Alcohol Use (Disorders) in Individuals with IDD

Widely used screening and assessment instruments for AUD are less suitable for individuals with IDD. They are often too complex (e.g. use of difficult wording and lengthy phrases) and do not take into account the tendency of individuals with IDD to acquiescence (i.e. to agree with whatever statement has been given) as well as to 'say nay' regarding questions relating to social taboos such as illicit substance use (Van Duijvenbode et al. 2015; VanDerNagel 2016). For instance, for an individual with IDD it may not be evident that the term 'alcohol' not only refers to strong spirits but also to beer. To add to this: the straightforward focus and style of mainstream questionnaires on the topic of an individual's substance use may evoke evasive responses, especially when the individual fears negative consequences of admitting to using substances, such as may be the case in forensic settings.

For the above reasons, VanDerNagel et al. (2011) developed the Substance Use and Misuse in Individuals with Intellectual Disability-Questionnaire (SumID-Q, VanDerNagel et al. 2011). As far as we know, this instrument (and its translations into Flemish and Danish) is the only screening instrument as of yet available which is designed for individuals with IDD. The SumID-Q uses pictures of both legal substances (tobacco and alcohol) and pictures of illicit drugs (cannabis, cocaine, and so on) to evaluate the respondent's familiarity with substances in general and to assess the terminology the client uses for each substance (e.g. 'booze' for strong liquor). Then the respondent is interviewed on his or her knowledge of and attitude towards substance use. After this, substances in the individual's social environment (e.g. family, professional caregivers, peers) are inventoried. Only after this initial phase, in which the clients experience that they can talk freely about substances, is their own substance use addressed. This strategy – though time-consuming – elicits valuable information and is well-appreciated by both clients and professionals (VanDerNagel et al. 2013, 2017b). Further studies into the validity and feasibility of the SumID-Q and its translation into other languages are underway.

Another line of research that has addressed the assessment of alcohol use (disorder) amongst individuals with IDD has focused on the use of implicit or indirect measures (see Van Duijvenbode 2016). Research has shown that problematic alcohol use is associated with disruptions in the motivational, reward, and inhibitory control processes of the brain (Nestler 2005; Hyman et al. 2006; Koob 2013). For example, as a result of adaptations in the motivational and reward systems, alcohol-related stimuli acquire 'incentive salience' and therefore seem attractive, 'grab attention' and elicit approach behaviour (Robinson and Berridge 2008). In addition, problematic alcohol use has been associated with executive dysfunction as a result of disruptions in the inhibitory control system. These disruptions can be measured with implicit or indirect measures. Such measures provide indirect measures of automatic cognitive processes (such as attention allocation, interpretation, and approach tendencies) derived from reaction times (Wilson et al. 2000) and are thought to reduce social desirability (Stacy and Wiers 2010). Despite these promising qualities, however, Van Duijvenbode (2017, Van Duijvenbode et al. 2017) conclude that the current evidence of their usefulness and effectiveness to screen, assess, and treat alcohol use (disorder) is scarce yet. They therefore discourage using these measures for clinical purposes.

9.4.3 Assessment of Alcohol Use in IDD in Forensic Settings

Assessment of AUD amongst individuals with IDD may be especially problematic in forensic settings. Often, there are reasons for the respondent to deny alcohol use or to downplay their problems with (former) substance use. For instance, offenders may be reluctant to admit to AUD, fearing that this may influence sentencing or may lead to court mandated treatment. Also, individuals with IDD in forensic settings may have a number of other issues, including psychiatric co-morbidity (Hassiotis et al. 2011) and social issues (e.g. Bhandari et al. 2015). These issues may overshadow alcohol use related signs and symptoms, and thus may contribute to AUD remaining undetected, especially in the absence of systematic screening. Giving the relationship of AUD to offending and reoffending, systematic screening and assessment (preferably with instruments adapted for individuals with IDD) for alcohol and other SUDs should be in place for individuals with IDD and offending behaviour.

In the assessment of AUD in forensic contexts special attention is warranted for possible relationships between alcohol use and the index offence and alcohol use as a predictor for reoffending. For example, forensic risk assessment instruments such as the Historical Clinical Risk Management-20 scale (HCR20, Douglas et al. 2013) and the Dynamic Risk Outcome Scales (DROS, Delforterie et al. 2018) include substance use both as a historic and a clinical item. As a historic item, the history of substance use prior to the current treatment or detention is scored, whilst as a clinical item substance use during current treatment or detention period is scored. These instruments thus only report *if* substance use occurred – now or in the past – but provide little information on motives, frequency, quantity, and consequences of substance use, nor do they provide information about the relationship between substance use and offending behaviour. In that light, another instrument worth mentioning is the MATE-Crimi (Schippers and Broekman 2012), a Dutch instrument that focuses on assessing the severity of substance use related problems and its relationship with offending behaviour. Based on case files, the caregiver or therapist reports if there is a pattern of substance use in relation to offending behaviour, and – if so – how the two factors are related to each other. This information can then be used in risk assessment for reoffending and treatment interventions aimed at preventing reoffending. However, this instrument has not been validated in the IDD population.

9.5 Conclusions

Individuals with IDD in forensic contexts are a risk group for alcohol use related problems and AUD. The topics of alcohol use and AUD amongst individuals with IDD have gained much attention during the last decade, with a growing number of studies on prevalence, assessment, prevention, and treatment of alcohol misuse and AUD. That said, there is still a lack of understanding of its risk factors, and how it relates to offending behaviour in this target group, especially given the conflicting reports of involvement of AUD in the index offences.

Systematic screening and assessment of alcohol use and AUD in individuals with IDD in forensic contexts is relevant for both the offender (given the importance of timely case identification) and society in general (given de socio-economic consequences of AUD, as well as the risk of reoffending). Special attention should be paid to the possibility that alcohol use continues in prison and forensic treatment settings (Bhandari et al. 2015), the influence that intoxication can have on other assessments (including IQ testing), and the reduced understanding of the factors (including AUD) in their offending behaviour many offenders with IDD have (McGillivray et al. 2016). In addition, the recognition that individuals with IDD in (forensic) settings are at risk for AUD does not imply that appropriate interventions are available. In fact, several authors report that individuals with IDD and substance use related problems in forensic settings are less likely to receive treatment or substance use education compared to individuals without ID (Hassiotis et al. 2011; Kiewik et al. 2017). Treatment of AUD in the forensic context will be further discussed in Chapter 18.

References

American Psychiatric Association (2013). *Diagnostic and Statistical Manual of Mental Disorders: DSM-5*. Washington DC: American Psychiatric Association.

Babor, T.F., Higgins-Biddle, J.C., Saunders, J.B. et al. (2001). *AUDIT. The Alcohol Use Disorders Identification Test: Guidelines for Use in Primary Care*, 2e. Geneva: World Health Organisation.

Bhandari, A., Van Dooren, K., Eastgate, G. et al. (2015). Comparison of social circumstances, substance use and substance-related harm in soon-to-be-released prisoners with and without intellectual disability. *Journal of Intellectual Disability Research* 59: 571–579.

Carroll Chapman, S.L. and Wu, L.-T. (2012). Substance abuse among individuals with intellectual disability. *Research in Developmental Disabilities* 33: 1147–1156.

Connors, G.J. and Maisto, S.A. (2003). Drinking reports from collateral individuals. *Addiction* 98 (Suppl 2): 21–29.

Cooper, S.A., Smiley, E., Morrison, J. et al. (2007). Mental ill-health in adults with intellectual disabilities: prevalence and associated factors. *British Journal of Psychiatry* 190: 27–35.

Cottler, L.B. (2000). *Composite International Diagnostic Interview—Substance Abuse Module (SAM)*. St. Louis, MO: Department of Psychiatry, Washington University School of Medicine.

Crocker, A.G., Côte, G., Toupin, J. et al. (2007). Rate and characteristics of men with an intellectual disability in pre-trial detention. *Journal of Intellectual & Developmental Disability* 2: 143–152.

de Beaurepaire, R., Lukasiewicz, M., Beauverie, P. et al. (2007). Comparison of self-reports and biological measures for alcohol, tobacco, and illicit drugs consumption in psychiatric inpatients. *European Psychiatry* 22: 540–548.

Delforterie, M., Hesper, B., and Didden, R. (2018). Psychometric properties of the Dynamic Risk Outcome Scales (DROS) for use in individuals with mild intellectual disability or borderline intellectual functioning and externalizing behaviour problems. *Journal of Applied Research in Intellect Disabilities*: 1–11. https://doi.org/10.1111/jar.12546.

Douglas, K.S., Hart, S.D., Webster, C.D. et al. (2013). *HCR-20: Assessing Risk of Violence – User Guide*. Burnaby, Canada: Mental Health, Law, and Policy Institute, Simon Fraser University.

European Monitoring Centre for Drugs and Drug Addiction (2007). Drugs and crime, a complex relationship. Towards a definition of drug-related crime. *Drugs in Focus* 16: 1–4.

Fendrich, M., Johnson, T.P., Wislar, J.S. et al. (2004). The utility of drug testing in epidemiological research: results from a general population survey. *Addiction* 99: 197–208.

First, M.B., Williams, J.B.W., Karg, R.S. et al. (2015). *Structured Clinical Interview for DSM-5 Disorders, Clinical Version*. Washington, DC: American Psychiatric Publishing.

Fletcher, R., Barnhill, J., and Cooper, S.-A. (2016). *Diagnostic Manual – Intellectual Disability. DM-ID-II. A Textbook of Diagnosis of Mental Disorders in Persons with Intellectual Disability*. Washington, DC: NADD Press.

Giancola, P.R., Helton, E.L., Osborne, A.B. et al. (2001). The effects of alcohol and provocation on aggressive behavior in men and women. *Journal of Studies on Alcohol* 63: 64–73.

Gorman, D.M. and White, H.R. (1995). You can choose your friends, but do they choose your crime? Implications of differential association theories for crime prevention policy. In: *Criminology and Public Policy: Putting Theory to Work* (ed. H. Barlow), 131–155. Boulder, CO: Westview Press.

Hassiotis, A., Gazizova, D., Akinlonu, L. et al. (2011). Psychiatric morbidity in prisoners with intellectual disabilities: analysis of prison survey data for England and Wales. *The British Journal of Psychiatry: The Journal of Mental Science* 199: 156–157.

Hogue, T., Steptoe, L., Taylor, J.L. et al. (2006). A comparison of offenders with intellectual disability across three levels of security. *Criminal Behaviour and Mental Health* 16: 13–28.

Hoiseth, G., Bernard, J.P., Stephanson, N. et al. (2008). Comparison between the urinary alcohol markers EtG, EtS, and GTOL/5-HIAA in a controlled drinking experiment. *Alcohol and Alcoholism* 43: 187–191.

Hyman, S.E., Malenka, R.C., and Nestler, E.J. (2006). Neural mechanisms of addiction: the role of reward-related learning and memory. *Annual Review of Neuroscience* 29: 565–598.

Kiewik, M., VanDerNagel, J.E.L., Engels, R.C.M.E. et al. (2017). Intellectually disabled and addicted: a call for evidence based tailor-made interventions. *Addiction* 112: 2067–2068.

Koob, G.F. (2013). Addiction is a reward deficit and stress surfeit disorder. *Frontiers in Psychiatry* 4: 1–18.

Lindsay, W.R., Carson, D., Holland, A.J. et al. (2013). Alcohol and its relationship to offence variables in a cohort of offenders with intellectual disability. *Journal of Intellectual and Developmental Disability* 38: 325–331.

Lunsky, Y., Gracey, C., Koegl, C. et al. (2011). The clinical profile and service needs of psychiatric inpatients with intellectual disabilities and forensic involvement. *Psychology, Crime & Law* 17: 9–23.

Luteijn, I., Didden, R., and VanDerNagel, J.E.L. (2017). Individuals with mild intellectual disability or borderline intellectual functioning in a forensic addiction treatment Centre: prevalence and clinical characteristics. *Advances in Neurodevelopmental Disorders* 1: 240–251.

Männynsolo, L., Putkonen, H., Lindberg, N. et al. (2009). Forensic psychiatric perspective on criminality associated with intellectual disability: a nationwide register-based study. *Journal of Intellectual Disability Research* 53: 279–288.

Maruna, S. (2001). *Making Good: How Ex-Convicts Reform and Rebuild their Lives.* Washington, DC: American Psychological Association.

Mayfield, D., McLeod, G., and Hall, P. (1974). The CAGE questionnaire: validation of a new alcoholism screening instrument. *American Journal of Psychiatry* 131: 1121–1123.

McGillivray, J.A., Gaskin, C.J., Newton, D.C. et al. (2016). Substance use, offending, and participation in alcohol and drug treatment programmes: a comparison of prisoners with and without intellectual disabilities. *Journal of Applied Research in Intellectual Disabilities* 29: 289–294.

McGillivray, J.A. and Moore, M.R. (2001). Substance use by offenders with mild intellectual disability. *Journal of Intellectual & Developmental Disability* 26: 297–310.

Mikkelsen, E.J., VanDerNagel, J.E.L., and Lindsay, W.R. (2016). Substance related and addictive disorders. In: *Diagnostic Manual – Intellectual Disability. DM-ID-II. A Textbook of Diagnosis of Mental Disorders in Persons with Intellectual Disability* (eds. R. Fletcher, J. Barnhill and S.-A. Cooper), 561–572. Washington, DC: NADD Press.

Nestler, E.J. (2005). Is there a common molecular pathway for addiction? *Nature Neuroscience* 8: 1445–1449.

Petrakis, I.L., Gonzalez, G., Rosenheck, R. et al. (2002). Comorbidity of alcoholism and psychiatric disorders: an overview. *Alcohol Research* 26: 81–89.

Robinson, T.E. and Berridge, K.C. (2008). The incentive sensitization theory of addiction: some current issues. *Philosophical Transaction of the Royal Society of London: Series B, Biological Sciences* 363: 3137–3146.

Schippers, G. M. and Broekman, T. G. (2012). *MATE-Crimi 2.1 Handleiding en protocol.* [MATE-Crimi 2.1. Manual and protocol]. Nijmegen, the Netherlands: Bêta Boeken.

Selzer, M.L. (1971). The Michigan alcoholism screening test: the quest for a new diagnostic instrument. *American Journal of Psychiatry* 127: 1653–1658.

Slayter, E.M. (2010). Demographic and clinical characteristics of people with intellectual disabilities with and without substance abuse disorders in a Medicaid population. *Intellectual and Developmental Disabilities* 48: 417–431.

Stacy, A.W. and Wiers, R.W. (2010). Implicit cognition and addiction: a tool for explaining paradoxical behavior. *Annual Review of Clinical Psychology* 6: 551–575.

Stasiewicz, P.R., Vincent, P.C., Bradizza, C.M. et al. (2008). Factors affecting agreement between severely mentally ill alcohol abusers' and collaterals' reports of alcohol and other substance abuse. *Psychology of Addictive Behaviors* 22: 78–87.

Sturmey, P., Reyer, H., Lee, R. et al. (2003). *Substance-Related Disorders in Persons with Mental Retardation.* Kingston: NADD.

Taggart, L., McLaughlin, D., Quinn, B. et al. (2006). An exploration of substance misuse in people with intellectual disabilities. *Journal of Intellectual Disability Research* 50: 588–597.

Van Duijvenbode, N. (2016). *"It's all between my ears!" Deficiencies in information processing in problematic drinkers with mild to borderline intellectual disability.* Doctoral thesis, Radboud University Nijmegen, the Netherlands.

Van Duijvenbode, N. (2017). The potential usefulness of implicit measures to assess and treat problematic substance use in individuals with mild to borderline intellectual disability: setting a research agenda. *Advances in Neurodevelopmental Disorders* 1: 107–109.

Van Duijvenbode, N., Didden, R., Korzilius, H. et al. (2017). The usefulness of implicit measures for the screening, assessment and treatment of problematic alcohol use in individuals with mild to borderline intellectual disability. *Advances in Neurodevelopmental Disorders* 1: 42–51.

Van Duijvenbode, N., VanDerNagel, J.E.L., Didden, R. et al. (2015). Substance use disorders in individuals with mild to borderline intellectual disability: current status and future directions. *Research in Developmental Disabilities* 38: 319–328.

VanDerNagel, J., Kiewik, M., Van Dijk, M. et al. (2011). *Handleiding SumID-Q, Meetinstrument voor het in kaart brengen van Middelengebruik bij mensen met een lichte verstandelijke beperking* [Manual of Substance use and misuse in Intellectual Disability Questionnaire]. Deventer: Tactus.

VanDerNagel, J., Duijvenbode, N. van, Trentelman, M., and Didden, R. (2014). Middelengebruik en delictgedrag bij forensische cliënten met een licht verstandelijke beperking. [Substance use and offending behaviour in forensic clients with mild intellectual disability or borderline intellectual functioning]. *Nederlands Tijdschrift voor de Zorg aan mensen met een verstandelijke beperking,* 4, 288–304.

VanDerNagel, J. E. L. (2016). *Is it just the tip of the Iceberg? Substance use and misuse in Intellectual Disability (SumID).* Doctoral thesis, Radboud University Nijmegen, the Netherlands.

VanDerNagel, J.E.L., Kemna, L., and Didden, R. (2013). Substance use among persons with mild intellectual disability: approaches to screening and interviewing. *NADD Bulletin* 16: 87–92.

VanDerNagel, J.E.L., Kiewik, M., Didden, R. et al. (2017a). Substance use in individuals with mild to borderline intellectual disability in the Netherlands: an exploration of risks and rates. *Advances in Neurodevelopmental Disorders* 1: 283–293.

VanDerNagel, J.E.L., Kiewik, M., van Dijk, M. et al. (2017b). Substance use in individuals with mild to borderline intellectual disability: a comparison between self-report, collateral-report and biomarker analysis. *Research in Developmental Disabilities* 63: 151–159.

Vinkers, D.J. (2013). Pre-trial reported defendants in the Netherlands with intellectual disability, borderline and normal intellectual functioning. *Journal of Applied Research in Intellectual Disabilities* 26: 357–361.

Wilson, T.D., Lindsey, S., and Schooler, T.Y. (2000). A model of dual attitudes. *Psychological Review* 107: 101–126.

Wojcik, M.H. and Hawthorne, J.S. (2007). Sensitivity of commercial ethyl glucuronide (ETG) testing in screening for alcohol abstinence. *Alcohol and Alcoholism* 42: 317–320.

10

Assessing People with Intellectual Disabilities Who Have Engaged in Fire Setting

Samuel J. Tromans[1], Verity Chester[2], and Regi T. Alexander[3]

[1] *Department of Health Sciences, University of Leicester and Leicestershire Partnership NHS Trust, Leicester, UK*
[2] *Norwich Medical School, St Johns House, Norfolk, UK*
[3] *Leicestershire Partnership NHS Trust & Hertfordshire Partnership University NHS Foundation Trust, Norwich, UK*

10.1 Introduction

Fires represent a major societal issue, producing considerable devastation to both property and human life. There were 376 000 fire-related incidents attended by fire and rescue services in England between April 2015 to March 2016, with an associated 303 fatalities and 7661 casualties (Smalldridge 2017). Large-scale epidemiological surveys estimate a lifetime prevalence of fire-setting of around 1.0% (Vaughn et al. 2010). A variety of terms are used to refer to fire setting within the literature, often interchangeably. However, there are important distinctions between key terms, largely in regards to the individual's intent regarding the fire set, and legal factors, which are summarized in Box 10.1. The term 'fire-setting' is used throughout this chapter, and where other terms are used, this is to refer to terminology used by cited authors.

Fire setting behaviours amongst individuals with Intellectual Developmental Disorder (IDD) present numerous challenges for assessment and management by healthcare professionals, requiring coordinated multidisciplinary team input, and treatment programmes adapted for their level of intellectual functioning. IDD is defined as a disorder with onset during the developmental period (first 18 years of life), which includes deficits in both intellectual and adaptive functioning in conceptual, social, and practical domains (American Psychiatric Association 2013). The degree can be mild, moderate, severe, or profound, with over 90% of those with IDD falling within the mild range (Department of Health 2001).

10.2 Epidemiology

It is frequently suggested that fire setting is more prevalent amongst individuals with IDD, and that individuals with IDD are overrepresented in arson relative to other types of offences (Enayati et al. 2008). Prins et al. (1985) suggested that IDD in themselves

The Wiley Handbook on What Works for Offenders with Intellectual and Developmental Disabilities: An Evidence-Based Approach to Theory, Assessment, and Treatment, First Edition.
Edited by William R. Lindsay, Leam A. Craig, and Dorothy Griffiths.

Box 10.1 Fire Setting Terms and Definitions	
Fire setting	Refers to a behaviour encompassing both accidental and intentional setting of fires (Burton et al. 2012). This can be for a multitude of reasons, including the perpetrator having not been identified or being below the age of criminal conviction, uncertainty pertaining to whether the fire was deliberate and instances where any property damage was negligible (Alexander et al. 2015).
Arson	A subcategory of fire setting, describes a criminal offence whereby the fire is set deliberately and with malicious intent. This may be with the direct intent of harming another person, or rather a reckless disregard as to whether others are harmed from the act (Alexander et al. 2015; Burton et al. 2012).
Pyromania	Also known as pathological fire setting, pyromania is a psychiatric disorder described by ICD-10 as being 'characterized by multiple acts of, or attempts at, setting fire to property or other objects, without apparent motive, and by a persistent preoccupations with subjects related to fire and burning' (World Health Organization 1993). In clinical practice, pyromania is a rare diagnosis (Geller et al. 1997).

have been thought to directly predispose to fire-setting. This idea has been challenged (Holland et al. 2002), and others have suggested that it cannot be reliably evidenced by the current available literature (Alexander et al. 2015). It is possible that this perception developed partly because people with IDD were less capable of concealing their fire setting behaviours, and thus were more likely to get caught (Alexander et al. 2015). People with IDD are often being processed differently by the legal system compared to their non-IDD peers (Tranah and Nicholas 2013), and authors have suggested carers may be reluctant to report fire-setting behaviours in people with IDD to the police (Alexander et al. 2006).

Reliable prevalence estimates are lacking, and rates vary widely between published studies, as shown in Table 10.1, largely due to methodological variations. Whether studies focus on strict legal definitions of arson, rather than the wider definition of fire setting, and the inclusion of participants with borderline intellectual functioning within the study population, can markedly impact prevalence estimates (Taylor et al. 2002). Reporting of highly selected populations, such as specialist forensic services and prisons can also skew estimates (Alexander et al. 2015). In a retrospective study of the records of 90 fire-setting recidivists across a 21-year period, Lindberg et al. (2005) found 16 to have IDD, a disproportionately high percentage when taking into account a prevalence of around 2–3% of IDD within the general population (Daily et al. 2000). A recent large-scale comparison of long-stay forensic psychiatric inpatients with and without IDD within medium-high secure settings reported an increased rate of arson in those with IDD (25.8 vs. 18.6%), though the difference between the two groups was not statistically significant (Chester et al. 2018).

10.3 Characteristics and Risk Factors

The risk factors for fire-setting in persons with IDD are complex and often interwoven, much like in the non-IDD population.

Table 10.1 Reported prevalence of arson and fire setting in populations of people with ID.

Study	Sample/population	Total n	Country	Definition	Reported prevalence (%)
Taylor et al. (2002)	Men with ID admitted to an inpatient forensic service.	129	England	Arson	25
Alexander et al. (2002)	Referrals to a forensic ID service.	79	England	Arson	10.4
Alexander et al. (2006)	Inpatients discharged from a medium-secure ID service.	64	England	Arson	15
Hogue et al. (2006)	Offenders with ID from three levels of security: medium (M), low (L), community (Com).	212	UK – 3 regions	Arson	M/L– 21.4 Com – 2.9
Devapriam et al. (2007)	Adults (19+) with ID who had been in contact with community psychiatric services during a 20-year period.	1100	England	Arson	1.36
Enayati et al. (2008)	Arsonists referred for inpatient forensic psychiatric examination over a 5-year period (1997–2001).	214	Sweden	Arson	9.8
Wheeler et al. (2009)	Referrals to community ID team.	237	UK – 3 regions	Fire starting	1
Alexander et al. (2010, 2011, 2015)	Secure/ forensic inpatient ID service.	138	England	Arson / Fire setting	10 / 22
Lindsay et al. (2010)	Offenders with ID accepted into forensic services	477	20	Fire starting	4.2
Chester et al. (2018)	All long-stay medium- and high-secure forensic psychiatric inpatients with ID in England.	66	England	Arson	25.8

10.3.1 Sociodemographic

As in the general population, where approximately 40% of fire setting is carried out by young people, most fire setting appears to be undertaken by younger patients with IDD (Rice and Harris 1991; Tranah and Nicholas 2013). Additionally, a younger age of first fire-setting episode is, along with a past history of fire-setting, one of the strongest factors predictive of future fire-setting (Repo et al. 1997a; Rice and Harris 1996).

A systematic review of 12 papers on fire setting in IDD by Lees-Warley and Rose (2015) provided collated data on the demographic characteristics of fire setters with IDD. Across the 12 studies involving a total of 200 participants, they found a preponderance of males relative to females (126 males, 37 females, 37 gender not reported), as well as the vast majority of having either borderline intellectual functioning (n = 36) or mild

IDD (n = 59), rather than moderate IDD (n = 2). It is unlikely that individuals with severe or profound IDD would possess the functional capacity to enable the execution of fire setting. A Finish-based study of 98 fire-setters (a combination of IDD and non-IDD) similarly found that the vast majority were male, with poor educational attainment, unemployment, and having lived in rural areas (Räsänen et al. 1995). Additionally, most fire setters are single in terms of relationship status (O'Sullivan and Kelleher 1987) and have higher rates of homelessness (Leong 1992). Puri et al. (1995) reviewed the characteristics of 36 fire setters (both with IDD and without IDD) referred to a forensic psychiatry service between the years of 1987–1991. In terms of gender, 22 (72%) of the patients were male, similar to the male to female ratio of 9 : 1 observed in the non-IDD population (Devapriam et al. 2007), and 85% lived alone.

10.3.2 Background/Developmental

Childhood maltreatment appears to play an aetiological role in later fire-setting in the general population (Saunders and Awad 1991), and it is conceivable that such an association may follow for those with IDD. Additionally, Root et al. (2008) demonstrated that amongst a population of fire-setting juveniles, those whom had experienced childhood maltreatment demonstrated a more severe course of fire-setting behaviour, with a greater likelihood of recidivism. Paternal alcoholism (Repo et al. 1997a) and social isolation in adulthood appear to be associated with fire-setting (Rice and Harris 1991). Alexander et al. (2015) found significantly higher levels of physical abuse amongst forensic inpatients with IDD and histories of fire setting, compared to those without fire-setting histories, and higher levels of sexual abuse, although this was non-significant.

10.3.3 Personality and Other Associated Traits

Certain personality traits appear to be more prevalent amongst fire setters. Räsänen et al. (1996) evaluated texts written by 15 patients whom had committed fire-setting offences and subsequently been asked to write their life stories leading up to the offence. They found that the patients viewed themselves as inconsistent, unbalanced, and emotionally unstable, with episodes of loss of self-control, often precipitated by alcohol intoxication. They had low self-worth and a high dependency on others, though struggled greatly to maintain close, lasting, and satisfying relationships. In a study within a specialist inpatient IDD forensic service, it was reported that 24 of 30 (80%) with histories of fire setting had diagnoses of personality disorder, a finding which was significantly higher than patients without a history of fire setting (Alexander et al. 2015). The high rates of emotional instability amongst this patient group are further supported by the relatively high frequency of suicide attempts (McKerracher and Dacre 1966).

10.3.4 Neuropsychological and Biological

Dolan et al. (2002) investigated neuropsychological test performance between violence, sex, and arson offenders. They found no significant group differences in age, IQ, or educational attainment, and neuropsychological test performances did not differ significantly. The reasons for such a difference are unclear, as they could not be explained by differences in anxiety or depression scores within the arsonist group. Though there has been limited research into the relationship between specific genetic syndromes and fire-setting, there is some limited evidence supportive of associations with both Klinefelter's syndrome (Miller and Sulkes 1988; Nielsen 1970) and possibly XYY syndrome (Nielsen 1970).

Describing two patient case reports, (Meinhard et al. 1988) suggested that flames may represent a self-induced stimulus in patients with photosensitive epilepsy, though larger scale studies are required to establish whether this phenomenon is more widely observed. Whilst the evidence is also limited to case reports, authors have suggested that brain injury, particularly affecting the frontal regions, could lead to fire setting behaviours, as a manifestation of the irritability and impairment of behavioural regulation associated with such damage (Carpenter and King 1989; Friedman and Clayton 1996). Equally, damage to other brain regions can have an indirect effect, via disconnection of neural pathways to the frontal lobe, as explained by Bosshart and Capek (2011) in a case report of fire setting in a patient following a lacunar infarction. Labree et al. (2010) explored the characteristics of 25 arsonists within a maximum-security hospital, comparing them with 50 inpatient controls, without a history of arson. Differences were observed with arsonists scoring comparatively higher on impulsivity, but lower on superficial charm and juvenile delinquency items of the Psychopathy Checklist (PCL–R) (Hare 1991).

10.3.5 Psychiatric

In a recent literature review, Tyler and Gannon (2012) advised that despite a developing body of research into fire setting involving psychiatric populations, there remains a limited understanding of the this group, as well as how they compare with fire-setters without mental disorder.

Puri et al. (1995) reported high rates of alcohol abuse (42%), other psychoactive substance misuse (33%) and sexual abuse (18% of men and 44% of women) in their sample. Männynsalo et al. (2009) suggested that offenders with the 'triple diagnosis' – that is, substance abuse, mental illness, and IDD – represent a small but particularly high-risk group with complex needs, requiring cross-specialty input from IDD, mental health, and substance abuse services. Indeed, alcoholism has been found to be significantly associated with arson, when compared with other offences, such as homicide (Räsänen et al. 1995). However, the role of other illicit substances is also important; a case series of 34 arsonists found that nearly half had cannabis abuse, with opioids and polysubstance abuse in a third of cases (Jayaraman and Frazer 2006). Those with a clinical diagnosis of pyromania have high rates of psychiatric co-morbidity, including disorders of mood and impulse control (Grant and Won Kim 2007).

In a large scale North American epidemiological survey, involving structured interviews of 43 093 persons, several factors were found to be strongly associated with fire setting following multiple logistic regression analysis, including antisocial and obsessive–compulsive personality disorders, as well as a family history of antisocial behaviour (Vaughn et al. 2010). A Swedish-based case–control study (Anwar et al. 2009) found that both schizophrenia and other psychoses were significantly associated with an increased risk of arson, even more so than for other violent crimes in psychotic patients. Reviewing 30 patients with a history of fire setting in a forensic IDD psychiatry service, Alexander et al. (2015) found that fire setting was associated with significant psychiatric morbidity (including personality disorder, severe mental illness, autism spectrum disorder, alcohol abuse, and illicit substance misuse), in keeping with the findings of other researchers (Devapriam et al. 2007; Enayati et al. 2008).

Findings from a Finnish study of 90 arson recidivists suggest that people with IDD who commit arson are usually 'pure arsonists' – in that arson is the only form of crime they have committed – a pattern also observed amongst those with psychotic disorders. In contrast, those with a diagnosis of personality disorder (Lindberg et al. 2005), particularly antisocial personality disorder (Repo et al. 1997a) typically committed a range of crimes in addition to arson. Repo and Virkkunen (1997) report that fire setters with schizophrenia and alcoholism have a higher rate of offending when compared to their peers without alcoholism.

10.3.6   Forensic

Research has suggested that offenders with IDD and histories of fire setting are more likely to be subject to a criminal section, or restriction order when compared to those without fire setting histories (Alexander et al. 2015). This suggests this behaviour receives harsher sentencing options, and as such the assessment of people who have set fires or committed arson is often a priority of courts (Dickens et al. 2009) and a prerequisite for determining treatment and intervention need within forensic settings, as well as assessing response to treatment and risk of future recidivism.

10.4   Assessing the Needs and Recidivism Risks of Fire Setters with IDD

Assessing fire setters with IDD should follow the same approach as those without an IDD, but with a number of additional considerations. The first stage of this process is to determine the need for assessment of fire-setting behaviour. Whilst this need may be very clear for those referred to forensic psychiatric services or sent to prison following a conviction of arson, it can be less clear for others admitted to criminal justice services. Histories of fire-setting behaviour often become evident when reviewing the case histories of people with IDD within criminal justice settings, even if this is not the index offence, and numerous studies have identified significant discrepancies in the number of people with convictions for arson, versus those with fire-setting behaviours documented within their case files (Devapriam and Bhaumik 2012).

Alexander et al. (2015) examined the prevalence and correlates of fire-setting histories in a cohort of 138 offenders with IDD within a specialist forensic service in the UK. Whilst 14 of the participants had a conviction for arson, this figure increased to 30 when detailed file reviews of case histories were undertaken. This is due to the phenomena of people with IDD being less likely to be processed through the criminal justice system, the blurred dividing line between criminal and challenging behaviour in people with IDD, and the reluctance of carers and family members to report such behaviours to authorities (Lyall and Kelly 2007; Wheeler et al. 2009). Such findings underscore the importance of systematic history taking when undertaking risk assessment for individuals with IDD, as solely relying on convictions in this population risks overlooking an important need.

10.5 Assessing Fire Setting in the General Offending Population

Once fire setting has been established as a treatment need, a useful starting point is to consider how fire setting risks and needs are assessed in the general offending population, and to ascertain the utility of these processes and measures to people with IDD. All of the aspects highlighted in the risk factors section (e.g. treatment of underlying mental disorder, impulse control, and so on) should be considered when assessing an individual with a fire setting history, alongside factors specific to fire setting. Fire setting specific factors include the extent to which individuals may identify with fire, fire interest, attitudes supporting fire setting, fire safety knowledge lacking or minimized, and the perception that setting fires is normal or common (Ó Ciardha et al. 2015).

Further to this, theoretical developments provide useful considerations for assessment. Reviewing 175 cases of arson, Canter and Fritzon (1998) suggested four themes of arson according to motivation, including two expressive subtypes (related to the arsonist's feelings, equivalent to suicide/those that are acted on objects), and two instrumental subtypes (related to personal indulgence, including revenge, or related to objects, such as destroying evidence pertaining to a crime). These themes may form a basis for informing the subsequent treatment approach. In the multi-trajectory theory of adult fire setting (M-TTAF), Gannon et al. (2012) organized research into hypothesized dynamic risk factors or vulnerabilities associated with the facilitation and maintenance of fire-setting behaviour. This theory incorporated background characteristics and proximal factors that represent an immediate vulnerability as contributors to fire setting; identified key factors associated with repeated fire setting and fire setting desistence; and described five key fire-setting trajectories (patterns of characteristics leading to fire setting). These are antisocial cognition, grievance, fire interest, emotionally expressive/need for recognition, and multifaceted.

A fire-setting offence chain model for mentally disordered offenders was subsequently developed (Tyler et al. 2014). Offence chain models have shed light on the offence processes of different types of offenders and highlighted focus points for treatment that had previously been overlooked. The model outlined the sequence of thoughts, feelings, behaviours, and events that precede and surround a single incidence of fire setting in mentally disordered offenders, and is divided into four main phases: (i) background Factors, which accounts for historical factors in the offender's childhood and adolescence; (ii) early adulthood; (iii) pre-offence period, factors that occur in the offender's early adulthood and in the period up until immediately prior to the fire; and (iv) offence and post offence period.

10.6 Fire Setting Assessments

A number of specific fire setting assessments exist, and are described in Table 10.2, alongside details of their use in persons with IDD, and psychometric properties. Some of the measures are designed in order to guide and support functional analysis and clinical interview, such as The Tranah Firesetting Inventory (TFI) (Tranah and Nicholas 2013) and the Pathological Fire Setters Interview (PFSI) (Taylor et al. 2004) and the

Table 10.2 Fire setting assessments / measures.

Measure	Authors	Description	Clinical Use in ID populations	Research in ID populations	Psychometric Properties
Fire Interest Rating Scale (FIRS)[a]	Murphy and Clare (1996)	This scale examines self-reported affect when imagining various fire-related situations (e.g. 'Watching a person with his clothes on fire') on a Likert scale from (1) most upsetting or absolutely horrible to (7) very exciting. Higher scores on this measure indicate increased levels of fire interest.	Developed specifically for people with ID. Regularly used in clinical practice (Curtis et al. 2012).	Used as an outcome measure in Taylor et al. (2002, 2006).	Limited psychometric examination (Curtis et al. 2012). Incorporated into a factor analysis by Ó Ciardha et al. (2015) who recommended combining these scales using a scoring template that will generate an overall combined score of five core fire setting factors.
Fire Attitude Scale (FAS)[a]	Muckley (1997)	A self-report scale examining fire-supportive attitudes (e.g. 'if you've got problems, a small fire can help you sort them out') rated on a 5-point scale (1 = strongly disagree, 5 = strongly agree).	Regularly used in clinical practice (Curtis et al. 2012).	Used as an outcome measure Taylor et al. (2002, 2006).	Limited psychometric examination (Curtis et al. 2012). Acceptable internal consistency (Barrowcliffe and Gannon 2015). Incorporated into a factor analysis by Ó Ciardha et al. (2015) who recommended combining these scales using a scoring template that will generate an overall combined score of five core fire-setting factors.

Pathological Fire Setters Interview (PFSI)	Taylor et al. (2004)	A structured interview which is supplemented with (i) demographics, personal, family, and past history of offending, (ii) personal circumstance conditions, (iii) situational setting conditions, (iv) antecedents to fire setting, (v) motives for fire settings (vi) consequences (thoughts, feelings, and actual fire setting) information from patient records, staff observations, and patient / informant completed clinical assessments, which contribute to a formulation of risk, need, and intervention plans.	Developed specifically for people with ID.	Used within case study methodologies (Davies and Beech 2012).	Yet to be evaluated (Davies and Beech 2012)
Northgate Firesetter Risk Assessment (NFRA)	Taylor and Thorne (2005)	This measure captures information on risk factors for fire setting. The items include five historical items (e.g. a previous history of fire setting) which can guide formulation, and six clinical items (such as stress, depression, and anger) which can monitor fluctuation of risk through treatment.	This measure was designed for and with adults with ID.	None published.	The NFRA has not been subjected to rigorous evaluation for reliability and validity (Watt and Ong 2016).
Identification with Fire Questionnaire (IFQ)[a]	Gannon et al. (2011)	A self-report measure of identification and affinity with fire (e.g. 'fire is almost part of my personality') rated on a 5-point scale (1 = strongly disagree, 5 = strongly agree).	Regularly used in clinical practice (Curtis et al. 2012).	None published.	Acceptable internal consistency has been reported (Barrowcliffe and Gannon 2015). Incorporated into a factor analysis by Ó Ciardha et al. (2015) who recommended combining these scales using a scoring template that will generate an overall combined score of five core fire setting factors.

(Continued)

Table 10.2 (Continued)

Measure	Authors	Description	Clinical Use in ID populations	Research in ID populations	Psychometric Properties
Fire Proclivity Scale (FPS)	Gannon and Barrowcliffe (2012)	The FPS provides an indication of an individual's propensity to engage in fire setting. Participants read six hypothetical vignettes describing fire setting situations of varying degrees of severity, are asked to imagine themselves as the fire-setting protagonist, and then are requested to respond to four questions using a 5-point Likert scale assessing: (i) fascination with the fire described in the scenario, (ii) behavioural propensity to act similarly (iii) general arousal to the fire described in the scenario, and (iv) general antisocialism.	No reports of clinical use with the ID population. Respondents with ID are likely to have difficulties in reading or understanding information from the vignettes, and may need it reading to them.	None published.	Subscales and overall total score reported to have acceptable to good internal consistency (Barrowcliffe and Gannon 2015; Gannon and Barrowcliffe 2012)
The Fire Setting Scale (FSS).	Gannon and Barrowcliffe (2012)	The FSS is a 20 item scale measuring antisocial behaviour (e.g. I am a rule breaker) and Fire Interest (e.g. I get excited thinking about fire). The items are rated using a 7-point Likert scale (1 = not at all like me, 7 = very strongly like me).	No reports of clinical use with the ID population. People with ID may struggle with the number of Likert scale response options (Chester et al. 2015).	None published.	Studies have reported internal consistency ranging from acceptable to excellent (Barrowcliffe and Gannon 2015; Gannon and Barrowcliffe 2012).

Instrument	Reference	Description			
St Andrew's Fire and Arson Risk Instrument (SAFARI)	Long et al. (2014)	A semi structured interview developed for use with forensic psychiatric settings examining the antecedents, behaviour, and consequences associated with fire setting, readiness to change, fire setting self-efficacy, the future probability of fire setting, barriers to change, and understanding of fire-setting behaviours.	None published.	No reports of clinical use with the ID population.	Psychometric evaluation carried out on 15 female fire setters detained in a mental health service, which reported good interrater reliability, internal consistency, and convergent validity with a risk management tool (Long et al. 2014).
The Tranah Firesetting inventory (TFI)	Tranah and Nicholas (2013)	The TFI was developed for young people with ID (no definition of 'young' is provided). The TFI gathers information from reports / records, from informants and the respondent, to establish the history of fire setting, completes a functional analysis of their fire-setting behaviour, examines fire knowledge and fire-safety skills, explores fire interest, assesses the risk of future fires and evaluates treatment needs.	Not yet used within published research.	Developed specifically for people with ID.	Yet to be evaluated.

[a] Practitioners can combine and collate the scores on the FIRS, FAS, and IFQ using a scoring template that will generate an overall combined score of five core fire setting factors as detailed in Ó Ciardha et al. (2015).

St Andrew's Fire and Arson Risk Instrument (SAFARI) (Long et al. 2014). These assessments are suited to serve as a basis for clinical assessments of fire setters with ID. The Northgate Firesetter Risk Assessment (NFRA) (Taylor and Thorne 2005) was the first attempt to develop a structured clinical judgement tool for fire setters. Further measures aim to capture constructs specific to fire setting and are regularly used in research evaluating the outcomes of fire-setting treatment programmes, pre and post-treatment. These include the Fire Interest Rating Scale (FIRS) (Murphy and Clare 1996), the Fire Attitude Scale (FAS) (Muckley 1997), the Identification with Fire Questionnaire (IFQ) (Gannon et al. 2011), and the Fire Proclivity Scale (FPS) and Fire Setting Scale (FSS) (Gannon and Barrowcliffe 2012).

As evident within Table 10.2, there are a number of issues that should be considered when using these instruments, particularly when working with individuals with IDD. Minimal research has examined the validity, reliability, and psychometric properties of available measures. Furthermore, authors have noted that development of the FIRS and FAS predated more recent progression in the theoretical literature, and do not appear to capture all the information relevant to fire-setting behaviour, such as how fire might be seen as soothing, as a way to communicate emotions, or as a powerful tool with which to send a message (Ó Ciardha et al. 2015).

A further drawback is that only some of the tools have been designed for the IDD population. Many of the core deficits associated with IDD can challenge reliable and valid self-reporting, and the linguistic content of self-report questions and response format used can present cognitive demands (Chester et al. 2015). Some people with IDD have difficulties with receptive language and limitations in understanding (determining the meaning of questions), cognitive processing (recalling information, ordering information, or making comparisons), and expression (articulating a response) (Chester et al. 2015). Difficulty also arises when using subjective, or abstract concepts, and negative or passive phrases (Emerson et al. 2013). Short-term memory difficulties may prevent the person from holding questions in their memory whilst they decide upon an appropriate response (Kells 2011), particularly when interpreting sentences which use complex or unusual structures. In addition, various response biases are common amongst people with IDD; acquiescence (the tendency to say yes to questions regardless of content) and recency bias (the tendency to select the last option mentioned in multiple-choice questions, irrespective of one's true opinion) (Emerson et al. 2013), nay-saying (saying no to every question), and suggestibility (Kells 2011). Some response formats are more susceptible to such biases (Kells 2011), such as complex Likert rating scales (Emerson et al. 2013), with simpler response scales (e.g. yes, sometimes, no) being a better option. Indeed, many self-report scales were designed, or adapted specifically for people with IDD, using simplified question wording and response formats, minimizing the afore-described cognitive and linguistic difficulties (Emerson et al. 2013).

10.7 Assessing Fire Setting Amongst People with IDD

Fire setters with IDD have a set of distinctive needs that will require specialist treatment responses (Curtis et al. 2012). For example, their understanding of the extent and severity of the consequences of their actions is limited (Curtis et al. 2012). Moral reasoning delays may affect the extent to which they take into account (or are concerned with) the needs of others (Kohlberg and Candee 1984). Comprehension of the circumstances, and their ability to identify and moderate emotional impulses that might be the precursor to offending might also be impaired (Curtis et al. 2012).

When assessing those with IDD who have engaged in fire-setting behaviours, Tranah and Nicholas (2013) recommended considering the person's level of IDD, whether there are any associations between their IDD and the fire setting, any previous fire setting, current fire setting risk, the underlying purpose of the fire setting, and treatment needs. Assessing the function of fire-setting behaviour is essential, as it can highlight treatment needs and inform the subsequent management approach. However, this can be challenging, and in some instances it is not possible to establish the underlying motivation for fire-setting, described by Barnett and Spitzer (1994) as 'arson without motive', though this is perhaps something of a misnomer, as a motive may still be present, just not established by healthcare professionals. A study focusing on arson perpetrators without IDD reported that motivation could not be established in 40% of cases (Hill et al. 1982). It is possible that this may appear to be the case in a greater proportion of people with IDD relative to the non-IDD population, due to the associated communication issues and difficulties with emotional introspection. However, in interviews with adult fire setters with IDD, Murphy and Clare (1996) found that most individuals were able to identify the emotional states that had been present at the time they started the fire, and these included anger, sadness, excitement, and depression.

A further issue regarding the intention, or underlying function of fire setting behaviour, is regarding fire fascination and fire play. Whilst fire fascination is a normal phenomenon experienced by most children between the ages of 3 and 5 years, the majority of children have learnt the rules of fire safety and prevention by the age of 10 years (Tranah and Nicholas 2013). Whether the pathway from fire fascination and fire play to intentional fire setting is the same for both populations is not clear (Tranah and Nicholas 2013). However, it is likely that learning the dangers of fire may be delayed amongst those with IDD. As such, it must be considered whether the fire setting behaviour being assessed truly reflects intentional fire setting, or whether it appears more attributable to fire play, particularly amongst adolescents and young adults with IDD. Establishing the underlying purpose, or function of the fire setting can direct the most appropriate intervention, e.g. for fire 'play', education and monitoring may be more appropriate. A number of authors endorse Jackson et al's (1987) method of functional analysis for the conceptual basis for fire-setting assessment. The model promotes the development of a hypothetical working model of the problem behaviour, to include: (i) information on the situations in which fire-setting occurs; (ii) which responses (emotional, physiological, cognitive, overt) behaviours occur; and (iii) the consequences of fire-setting that might reinforce future fire-setting.

Rose et al. (2016) conducted a series of semi-structured interviews of inpatients within a forensic IDD hospital, and found that their first fires often occurred in childhood, often in response to some form of abuse. Reasons for subsequent fires varied, but emergent themes included escaping distress, to enable positive emotional experiences (including a feeling of control and the sensory experiences associated with a fire) and as a means of communicating with services (either a desire for containment or discontent with their current care).

Devapriam et al. (2007) reviewed 15 patients with IDD who had committed arson, finding that revenge was the underlying motivation in nine (60%) of the patients, followed by suggestibility in three, pyromania in two, and other mental illness in one patient. From this patient group, 11 were living in the community at the time of the offence, demonstrating the risks that such behaviour presents to the general public. Puri et al. (1995) found revenge to be the underlying reason for fire setting in only two (6%) of the 36 patients reviewed, with schizophrenia or psychosis (10 patients, 28% of study population), psychoactive substance misuse (6, 17%), pleasure from fires (6, 17%), depression (5, 14%), and burglary (4, 11%) all being found to be more commonly cited reasons. This finding appears to contradict previous research, which reported that revenge was the main motive in their respective studies of fire-setting adults (Bradford 1982; O'Sullivan and Kelleher 1987; Rix 1994).

10.8 Gender Considerations

Gender considerations apply when assessing the function of fire setting. The general recognition that fire-setting is more prevalent in males has led to female fire setters being an under-researched population, with significantly less known about the specific characteristics and treatment needs of this patient group (Gannon 2010). Whilst literature focusing on female-perpetrated fire setting is scarce (Gannon et al. 2012), a number of gender differences have been highlighted (Dickens et al. 2007). For example, women have been highlighted as being more likely than men to set fires as a 'cry for help' (Dickens et al. 2007), to report fire setting in the context of distressing life experiences (Cunningham et al. 2011), to commit their offences in or close to their place of residence (Wachi et al. 2007), to be older in age, and more likely to have psychiatric co-morbidity and a history of sexual abuse (Dickens et al. 2007). Earlier studies reported common motivators for women to be: revenge, attention seeking, conflict with authority (hospital, prison, work), and self-harm (Stewart 1993; Tennent et al. 1971). Stewart (1993) found that approximately one-third of the population had multiple motives for fire setting (e.g. revenge and mental illness), and that for 20%, fire setting was instrumental.

A particular subtype of fire setting appears more prevalent in females; that of self-immolation. Though such occurrences are relatively rare, a case series of 12 patients (O'Donoghue et al. 1998) demonstrated that 10 had a history of psychiatric illness, and 8 were psychiatric inpatients when they committed the act. The mortality rate within this group was 33%, underlining the seriousness of this specific manifestation of fire-setting behaviour. However, the reason for self-immolation appears to be somewhat variable based on culture; in Indian and Sri-Lankan populations, where this behaviour is more prevalent, motives including interpersonal problems and political protest are more commonly observed (Laloë 2004).

10.9 Future Recidivism Risk

Assessing the future recidivism risk of those with histories of fire setting is challenging. Conviction rates for arson have a very low base rate, with only 9% of arson fires in England and Wales resulting in a suspect being charged or cautioned (Department for

Communities and Local Government 2006). Much of the research on recidivism amongst fire setters has been carried out on child and adolescent populations, which may be difficult to generalize to adults. Sakheim et al. (1991) highlighted a number of psychological characteristics that consistently identified children who are most seriously at risk for future fire-setting. These included; intense feelings of anger and resentment at maternal neglect, rejection, deprivation, or abandonment; feelings of impotent rage at insults or humiliations inflicted by peers or adults, resulting in a narcissistic injury and aggressive retaliatory wishes; excitement, pleasure, or sexual arousal stimulated by lighting or watching fires; fire preoccupation as revealed on projective tests, in an interview, or in therapy; poor judgement in social situations; weak social anticipation, poor planning, and competence; impulsivity and poor self-control; a tendency to experience little guilt or remorse about previous acts of fire-setting; cruelty to children or animals, and finally, a psychiatric diagnosis of aggressive conduct disorder.

Similarly, Kennedy et al. (2006) conducted a systematic review to identify potential predictors of recidivism in children and adolescents who set fires. The authors reported that previous involvement in fire-setting behaviour was found to be the best single predictor of recidivistic fire-setting. Recidivists had greater levels of interest in fire and fire-related activities, displayed more covert antisocial behaviours, and were more likely to be male and older than non-recidivists. Recidivists also reported poorer social skills and higher levels of family dysfunction than other fire-setters.

In terms of historical factors in fire-setters, those associated most strongly with perceived dangerousness by psychiatrists are setting fire to an occupied building and an apparent intention to endanger life (Sugarman and Dickens 2009). Dickens et al. (2009) compared the characteristics of one-time only and multiple fire setters, and analysed the characteristics of those who had set serious fires causing serious injury, loss of life, or extensive damage. The authors reported that repeat arsonists were younger, single, and more likely to have experienced childhood disturbance. Personality disorder and previous time in prison were also associated with repeat fire setting. Recidivism was not associated with the setting of serious fires. Very few variables were able to predict whether subjects had set a serious fire although intentional behaviours such as multiple-point fire setting and the use of fuel and accelerants appear to indicate highly dangerous fire setting behaviour.

Whilst many of the tools in Table 10.2 refer to considerations for assessing risk of future recidivism amongst fire setters, the predictive validity of these assessments have not been assessed, and there are currently no specific fire risk assessments available. As such, Gannon and Pina (2010) have recommended use of existing violence risk tools, such as the HCR–20 (Webster and Eaves 1995), in instances where the fire setting is viewed as violent in its intent, due to significant overlaps between predictors for fire setting recidivism and both violent and non-violent recidivism.

10.10 Clinical Interview

In interviewing a person with IDD who has been engaging in fire setting, many of the usual principles for clinical interview in this patient group apply, including ensuring that the setting is relaxed and using language appropriate to the person's level of communication skills. The breadth of information to be covered may mean that multiple

---

Box 10.2 Areas of Specific Focus for a Clinical Interview in a Patient with IDD Who Has Engaged in Fire-Setting Behaviours

---

Risk factors – Both pertaining to index/most recent fire-setting event and recidivism
Motivation for fire setting
Psychiatric co-morbidity
Substance abuse
Personality features
Measured IQ and adaptive functioning
Treatability, including willingness to engage

---

interviews are required before having a thorough understanding of the patient and their fire setting; this will also likely help in fostering rapport (Hall 2000). Areas of specific focus for a clinical interview of a patient whom has engaged in fire setting are outlined in Box 10.2.

One should be aware that people with IDD are considered more suggestible in interview settings, and there is a risk of obtaining inaccurate details of the fire-setting event, or potentially, the patient confessing to a crime they did not commit. Suggestibility assessment tools, such as the Gudjonsson Suggestibility Scale (Gudjonsson 1984) can be useful in assessing this, though as it was developed for use in the general population, its clinical utility in those with IDD is questionable, and as such it should be used with caution (Beail 2002).

Collateral history is invaluable, as carers, friends, or family members, who know the patient well will likely have extensive knowledge of the patient's baseline mental state and functioning, as well as potentially having information specific to the fire-setting incident, such as the preceding circumstances and possible underlying motives (Hall 2000).

It is essential to get a thorough history of any previous offending behaviours, particularly previous instances of fire setting, as well as details pertaining to the severity of such offences and the circumstances of their occurrence. In terms of historical factors in fire-setters, those associated most strongly with perceived dangerousness by psychiatrists are setting fire to an occupied building and an apparent intention to endanger life (Sugarman and Dickens 2009). Of course, risk assessment should not be solely focussed on future fire setting, as self-injurious and suicidal behaviours are common amongst this patient group. Factors associated with suicide attempts in fire-setters include mood disorder, paternal alcoholism, self-injurious behaviour, and a suicidal motive of fire setting (Repo et al. 1997b).

It is also important to consider the risk of diagnostic overshadowing, whereby signs of mental illness are instead attributed to the person's IDD (Mason and Scior 2004). Mental illness often manifests differently in individuals with IDD, particularly those with moderate–severe IDD, so one should consider use of diagnostic classification tools appropriate to their developmental level, such as the Diagnostic Criteria for Psychiatric Disorders for Use with Adults with Learning Disabilities (DC–-LD) (Royal College of Psychiatrists 2001).

Establishing the treatability of the patient is also a key component of the clinical interview. For example, factors such as substance abuse may be remediable provided the patient can comply with the related treatment plan, whereas facets of the individual's core personality, such as impulsivity, may be associated with a poorer treatment response and greater likelihood of recidivism (Mikkelsen 2004). Other factors that appear to be associated with recidivism include being younger, single, having features suggestive of childhood trauma, personality disorder, and having spent more time in prison (Dickens et al. 2009). Additionally, a German-based population study (Barnett et al. 1997) found that arsonists with psychiatric co-morbidity had significantly higher recidivism rates than those with no mental health problems (11 vs. 4%). However, data on recidivism rates amongst populations of fire setters varies greatly amongst studies (from 4 to 60%), challenging the traditionally held belief these individuals were inherently dangerous (Brett 2004).

10.11 Treating Fire Setters with IDD

Fire setters share many of the same characteristics as those who commit other types of crime (Gannon and Pina 2010). As such, their treatment needs may align with those of other offender groups (e.g. offence supportive beliefs, social problem-solving deficits). In this sense, the 10-point treatment programme for offenders with IDD becomes relevant (Alexander et al. 2011), as it identifies the importance of a comprehensive assessment process which focuses on a multi-axial diagnosis, psychological formulation, and risk factors, which will in turn inform the specific programme of treatment and therapy that is followed. The treatment programme consists of a combination of 'foundation treatments' which may consist of motivational work, emotional regulation, and so on prior to or as part of offence-specific treatments, alongside occupational and pharmacotherapy, as directed by the assessment.

A number of offence-specific treatments for fire-setting behaviour in IDD populations exist. Clare et al. (1992) described the application of a cognitive behavioural model with a 23-year-old man with mild IDD, using a case-study methodology. The initial assessment found that the participant set fires in order to reduce negative emotions and gain attention. His treatment plan incorporated assertiveness, social skills, coping strategies, graded exposure, and relaxation techniques. Furthermore, covert sensitization was implemented, where imagined fire-setting activities became associated with punishment and seclusion. After a 30 month follow up, no further fire-setting offences were reported.

Taylor and colleagues developed the Northgate treatment programme and its outcomes within a number of patient cohorts (2002). The treatment is a 40-session group-based intervention which targets criminogenic factors associated with fire setting, e.g. fire interest and attitudes towards fire and fire setting. Utilizing a cognitive behavioural framework, each participant's offence cycle is analysed in turn in the group sessions with regard to: (i) antecedent factors and triggers; (ii) the cognitions, emotions, and behaviour they experienced at the time fires were started; and (iii) the positive and negative consequences of their fire-setting behaviour. Participants also received education (provided by the local Fire and Rescue Service) concerning the dangers and costs associated with setting fires. The group focuses on skill development, in order to enhance future coping with emotional and interpersonal problems associated with previous fire-setting behaviour, and personalized relapse prevention plans are integral to the treatment.

The first cohort of study participants, 14 inpatients with IDD and arson convictions detained in a low-secure unit were assessed pre- and post-treatment on a range of fire-specific and clinical self- and staff-rated measures, and followed up for a period of two years (Taylor et al. 2002). Participants displayed significant improvements, with reduced fire interest and anger, as well as improved self-esteem. Subsequently, Taylor et al. (2006) described the outcomes of a group psychological intervention using a case series methodology, for six female fire setters with mild and borderline IDD. Participants indicated improved levels of anger, self-esteem, and depression on the post-group assessments, and demonstrated improved attitudes towards fire, with no offending behaviour reported at follow-up, although there was some within group variability in treatment response.

Taylor (2014) reported on a follow-up of 24 fire setters (16 men and 8 women) with ID who had completed treatment. The follow-up period ranged between 4 and 13 years post-treatment. Seventeen participants were living in the community, four remained in hospital placements and two women were deceased. At follow-up there had been no further arrests or convictions for arson in this cohort. File data available for 17 study participants showed that prior to treatment that sub-group had been responsible for setting a total of 425 fires. This suggests that the intervention was associated with a significant harm-reduction effect. The authors concluded that the results suggest that female fire setters with IDD can successfully engage in and benefit from the therapeutic approach described in this study and that these gains appear to be reflected in an absence of fire-setting behaviour in the short to medium term.

These studies, excepting Taylor (2014), were the subject of a systematic review (Curtis et al. 2012). Curtis et al. (2012) noted that whilst all of the studies demonstrated reduced fire setting following programme completion, their research designs were far from robust. Thus, they concluded there is a lack of truly evidence-based IDD-specific treatment programmes, though the option of adapting programmes used in the non-IDD population (such as fire safety education and cognitive behavioural therapy-based approaches) merited further exploration.

Whilst this may be the case, the literature thus far highlights a number of factors which should be taken into account when facilitating therapy and treatments for this population. First, the need for therapies to have their foundation in a comprehensive functional analysis. Second, it clarifies the need for fire-setting treatments to address a broad range of identified psychological difficulties, and to be delivered by experienced clinicians (Tranah and Nicholas 2013). Furthermore, a number of factors can preclude meaningful participation in both individual and group-based interventions for people with IDD, and thus treatment responsivity (Curtis et al. 2012). Reading and other receptive communication deficits should be considered in the provision of verbal and written information. This population can find generalizing learning acquired in one setting (e.g. group work in a custodial facility) to another (e.g. a community setting when released) particularly challenging (Curtis et al. 2012). As such, 'one-off' educational interventions are likely to be insufficient for many patients, and a combined approach involving education and cognitive behavioural therapy is recommended (Tranah and Nicholas 2013).

Finally, it has been noted that despite the long-term nature of the deficits intrinsic to IDD, there has been very little discussion in the literature regarding the importance of long-term support and supervision of offenders with IDD in the community (Chaplin and Henry 2016). The authors note that these issues often necessitate lifelong involvement from multiple agencies, in order to carry out supervision, as well as to support transition back into the community after prolonged durations.

10.12 Conclusions

The fire-setting behaviours amongst individuals with IDD presents numerous challenges for assessment and management by healthcare professionals. Establishing the need for fire-setting behaviour is less straightforward amongst this population, as behaviours may not have come to the attention of authorities, for a variety of reasons. As such, a thorough review of file note information and clinical interview of each case is required to establish need. The clinician should then consider the use of specific psychometric measures to further assess factors that influence or maintain fire-setting behaviour. However, attention should be paid to the accessibility of measures which will be administered directly to the client, and many measures have not been validated for use with people with IDD. However, this lack of research should not preclude assessment of this issue, and many available measures have been used routinely within clinical practice and research. It is recommended that further research should focus on establishing the accessibility and validity of psychometric measures that assess domains of relevance to fire-setting behaviour in people with IDD.

A number of treatments have been described that target fire-setting behaviour and aim to reduce the risk of future re-offending. Many of these are grounded in psychological theory and have demonstrated positive results in a variety of clinical settings, although a number of methodological difficulties are evident. Nonetheless, the interventions described share a number of components which appear to contribute to their efficacy. One is that treatments should be grounded in a thorough functional analysis, aiming to ascertain the function of fire-setting behaviour to the individual. Furthermore, treatments should be carried out over a period of time, giving participants opportunity to practise and apply their learning in settings outside the therapy space. Finally, treatments should take into account a number of factors which can affect accessibility for people with IDD, such as language and reading deficits.

References

Alexander, R.T., Chester, V., Green, F.N. et al. (2015). Arson or fire setting in offenders with intellectual disability: clinical characteristics, forensic histories, and treatment outcomes. *Journal of Intellectual and Developmental Disability* 40 (2): 189–197.

Alexander, R., Crouch, K., Halstead, S. et al. (2006). Long-term outcome from a medium secure service for people with intellectual disability. *Journal of Intellectual Disability Research* 50 (4): 305–315.

Alexander, R.T., Green, F., O'mahony, B. et al. (2010). Personality disorders in offenders with intellectual disability: a comparison of clinical, forensic and outcome variables and implications for service provision. *Journal of Intellectual Disability Research* 54 (7): 650–658.

Alexander, R., Hiremath, A., Chester, V. et al. (2011). Evaluation of treatment outcomes from a medium secure unit for people with intellectual disability. *Advances in Mental Health and Intellectual Disabilities* 5 (1): 22–32.

Alexander, R., Piachaud, J., Odebiyi, L. et al. (2002). Referrals to a forensic service in the psychiatry of learning disability. *The British Journal of Forensic Practice* 4 (2): 29–33.

American Psychiatric Association (2013). *Diagnostic and Statistical Manual of Mental Disorders (DSM-5)*. Washington, DC: American Psychiatric Publishing.

Anwar, S., Långström, N., Grann, M. et al. (2009). Is arson the crime most strongly associated with psychosis? A national case-control study of arson risk in schizophrenia and other psychoses. *Schizophrenia Bulletin* 37 (3): 580–586.

Barnett, W., Richter, P., Sigmund, D. et al. (1997). Recidivism and concomitant criminality in pathological firesetters. *Journal of Forensic Science* 42 (5): 879–883.

Barnett, W. and Spitzer, M. (1994). Pathological fire-setting 1951–1991: a review. *Medicine, Science and the Law* 34 (1): 4–20.

Barrowcliffe, E.R. and Gannon, T.A. (2015). The characteristics of un-apprehended firesetters living in the UK community. *Psychology, Crime & Law* 21 (9): 836–853.

Beail, N. (2002). Interrogative suggestibility, memory and intellectual disability. *Journal of Applied Research in Intellectual Disabilities* 15 (2): 129–137.

Bosshart, H. and Capek, S. (2011). An unusual case of random fire-setting behavior associated with lacunar stroke. *Forensic Science International* 209 (1): e8–e10.

Bradford, J.M. (1982). Arson: a clinical study. *The Canadian Journal of Psychiatry* 27 (3): 188–193.

Brett, A. (2004). 'Kindling theory' in arson: how dangerous are firesetters? *Australian and New Zealand Journal of Psychiatry* 38 (6): 419–425.

Burton, P.R., McNiel, D.E., and Binder, R.L. (2012). Firesetting, arson, pyromania, and the forensic mental health expert. *The Journal of the American Academy of Psychiatry and the Law* 40 (3): 355–365.

Canter, D. and Fritzon, K. (1998). Differentiating arsonists: a model of firesetting actions and characteristics. *Legal and Criminological Psychology* 3 (1): 73–96.

Carpenter, P.K. and King, A.L. (1989). Epilepsy and arson. *The British Journal of Psychiatry: The Journal of Mental Science* 154: 554–556.

Chaplin, E. and Henry, J. (2016). Assessment and treatment of deliberate firesetters with intellectual disability. In: *The Psychology of Arson* (eds. R. Doley, G.L. Dickens and T.A. Gannon), 55–67. Abingdon, UK: Routledge.

Chester, V., McCathie, J., Quinn, M. et al. (2015). Clinician experiences of administering the Essen climate evaluation schema (EssenCES) in a forensic intellectual disability service. *Advances in Mental Health and Intellectual Disabilities* 9 (2): 70–78.

Chester, V., Völlm, B., Tromans, S. et al. (2018). Long-stay forensic psychiatric patients with and without intellectual disability: a comparison of characteristics and needs. *British Journal of Psychiatry Open* 4 (4): 226–234.

Clare, I.C., Murphy, G.H., Cox, D. et al. (1992). Assessment and treatment of fire-setting: a single-case investigation using a cognitive-behavioural model. *Criminal Behaviour and Mental Health* 2 (3): 253–268.

Cunningham, E.M., Timms, J., Holloway, G. et al. (2011). Women and firesetting: a qualitative analysis of context, meaning, and development. *Psychology and Psychotherapy: Theory, Research and Practice* 84 (2): 128–140.

Curtis, A., McVilly, K., and Day, A. (2012). Arson treatment programmes for offenders with disability: a systematic review of the literature. *Journal of Learning Disabilities and Offending Behaviour* 3 (4): 186–205.

Daily, D.K., Ardinger, H.H., and Holmes, G.E. (2000). Identification and evaluation of mental retardation. *American Family Physician* 61 (4): 1059–1067.

Davies, G.M. and Beech, A.R. (2012). *Forensic Psychology: Crime, Justice, Law, Interventions*. Hoboken, NJ: Wiley.

Department for Communities and Local Government (2006). *Annual report 2006.* Wetherby: DCLG publications http://Webarchive.nationalarchives.gov. uk/20120919224253/www.communities.gov.uk/documents/fire/pdf/154145.pdf (accessed 28 May 2019.

Department of Health (2001). *Valuing People: A New Strategy for Learning Disability for the 21st Century*. London, UK: Departmnet of Health.

Devapriam, J. and Bhaumik, S. (2012). Intellectual disability and arson. In: *Firesetting and Mental Health* (eds. G.L. Dickens, P.A. Sugarman and T.A. Gannon), 107–125. London, England: RCPsych Publications.

Devapriam, J., Raju, L., Singh, N. et al. (2007). Arson: characteristics and predisposing factors in offenders with intellectual disabilities. *The British Journal of Forensic Practice* 9 (4): 23–27.

Dickens, G., Sugarman, P., Ahmad, F. et al. (2007). Gender differences amongst adult arsonists at psychiatric assessment. *Medicine, Science and the Law* 47 (3): 233–238.

Dickens, G., Sugarman, P., Edgar, S. et al. (2009). Recidivism and dangerousness in arsonists. *The Journal of Forensic Psychiatry & Psychology* 20 (5): 621–639.

Dolan, M., Millington, J., and Park, I. (2002). Personality and neuropsychological function in violent, sexual and arson offenders. *Medicine, Science and the Law* 42 (1): 34–43.

Emerson, E., Felce, D., and Stancliffe, R.J. (2013). Issues concerning self-report data and population-based data sets involving people with intellectual disabilities. *Intellectual and Developmental Disabilities* 51 (5): 333–348.

Enayati, J., Grann, M., Lubbe, S. et al. (2008). Psychiatric morbidity in arsonists referred for forensic psychiatric assessment in Sweden. *The Journal of Forensic Psychiatry & Psychology* 19 (2): 139–147.

Friedman, C. and Clayton, R. (1996). Juvenile fire setting after bilateral frontal lobe damage. *Archives of Clinical Neuropsychology* 11 (5): 392.

Gannon, T.A. (2010). Female arsonists: key features, psychopathologies, and treatment needs. *Psychiatry: Interpersonal and Biological Processes* 73 (2): 173–189.

Gannon, T.A. and Barrowcliffe, E. (2012). Firesetting in the general population: the development and validation of the fire setting and fire proclivity scales. *Legal and Criminological Psychology* 17 (1): 105–122.

Gannon, T., Ciardha, C., and Barnoux, M. (2011). The identification with fire questionnaire. Unpublished manuscript, School of Psychology, University of Kent, UK.

Gannon, T.A., Ciardha, C.Ó., Doley, R.M. et al. (2012). The multi-trajectory theory of adult firesetting (M-TTAF). *Aggression and Violent Behavior* 17 (2): 107–121.

Gannon, T.A. and Pina, A. (2010). Firesetting: psychopathology, theory and treatment. *Aggression and Violent Behavior* 15 (3): 224–238.

Geller, J.L., McDermeit, M., and Brown, J. (1997). Pyromania? What does it mean? *Journal of Forensic Science* 42 (6): 1052–1057.

Grant, J.E. and Won Kim, S. (2007). Clinical characteristics and psychiatric comorbidity of pyromania. *The Journal of Clinical Psychiatry* 68 (11): 1717–1722.

Gudjonsson, G.H. (1984). A new scale of interrogative suggestibility. *Personality and Individual Differences* 5 (3): 303–314.

Hall, I. (2000). Young offenders with a learning disability. *Advances in Psychiatric Treatment* 6 (4): 278–285.

Hare, R.D. (1991). *The Hare Psychopathy Checklist-Revised*. Toronto, Ontario, Canada: Multi-health systems.

Hill, R., Langevin, R., Paitich, D. et al. (1982). Is arson an aggressive act or a property offence? A controlled study of psychiatric referrals. *The Canadian Journal of Psychiatry* 27 (8): 648–654.

Hogue, T., Steptoe, L., Taylor, J.L. et al. (2006). A comparison of offenders with intellectual disability across three levels of security. *Criminal Behaviour and Mental Health* 16 (1): 13–28.

Holland, T., Clare, I., and Mukhopadhyay, T. (2002). Prevalence of 'criminal offending' by men and women with intellectual disability and the characteristics of 'offenders': implications for research and service development. *Journal of Intellectual Disability Research* 46 (s1): 6–20.

Jackson, H.F., Glass, C., and Hope, S. (1987). A functional analysis of recidivistic arson. *British Journal of Clinical Psychology* 26 (3): 175–185.

Jayaraman, A. and Frazer, J. (2006). Arson: a growing inferno. *Medicine, Science and the Law* 46 (4): 295–300.

Kells, M. (2011). The psychometric assessment of offenders with an intellectual disability PhD dissertation, University of Birmingham.

Kennedy, P.J., Vale, E.L., Khan, S.J. et al. (2006). Factors predicting recidivism in child and adolescent fire-setters: a systematic review of the literature. *The Journal of Forensic Psychiatry & Psychology* 17 (1): 151–164.

Kohlberg, L. and Candee, D. (1984). The relationship of moral judgment to moral action. *Morality, Moral Behavior, and Moral Development* 52: 73.

Labree, W., Nijman, H., Van Marle, H. et al. (2010). Backgrounds and characteristics of arsonists. *International Journal of Law and Psychiatry* 33 (3): 149–153.

Laloë, V. (2004). Patterns of deliberate self-burning in various parts of the world: a review. *Burns* 30 (3): 207–215.

Lees-Warley, G. and Rose, J. (2015). What does the evidence tell us about adults with low intellectual functioning who deliberately set fires? A systematic review. *International Journal of Developmental Disabilities* 61 (4): 242–256.

Leong, G.B. (1992). A psychiatric study of persons charged with arson. *Journal of Forensic Science* 37 (5): 1319–1326.

Lindberg, N., Holi, M.M., Tani, P. et al. (2005). Looking for pyromania: characteristics of a consecutive sample of Finnish male criminals with histories of recidivist fire-setting between 1973 and 1993. *BMC Psychiatry* 5 (1): 47.

Lindsay, W.R., O'Brien, G., Carson, D. et al. (2010). Pathways into services for offenders with intellectual disabilities: childhood experiences, diagnostic information, and offense variables. *Criminal Justice and Behavior* 37 (6): 678–694.

Long, C.G., Banyard, E., Fulton, B. et al. (2014). Developing an assessment of fire-setting to guide treatment in secure settings: the st Andrew's fire and arson risk instrument (SAFARI). *Behavioural and Cognitive Psychotherapy* 42 (5): 617–628.

Lyall, R. and Kelly, M. (2007). Specialist psychiatric beds for people with learning disability. *The Psychiatrist* 31 (8): 297–300.

Männynsalo, L., Putkonen, H., Lindberg, N. et al. (2009). Forensic psychiatric perspective on criminality associated with intellectual disability: a nationwide register-based study. *Journal of Intellectual Disability Research* 53 (3): 279–288.

Mason, J. and Scior, K. (2004). 'Diagnostic overshadowing' amongst clinicians working with people with intellectual disabilities in the UK. *Journal of Applied Research in Intellectual Disabilities* 17 (2): 85–90.

McKerracher, D.W. and Dacre, A.J. (1966). A study of arsonists in a special security hospital. *The British Journal of Psychiatry: The Journal of Mental Science* 112 (492): 1151–1154.

Meinhard, E.A., Oozeer, R., and Cameron, D. (1988). Photosensitive epilepsy in children who set fires. *British Medical Journal (Clinical Research Ed.)* 296 (6639): 1773.

Mikkelsen, E.J. (2004). The assessment of individuals with developmental disabilities who commit criminal offenses. *Offenders with Developmental Disabilities* 3: 111.

Miller, M.E. and Sulkes, S. (1988). Fire-setting behavior in individuals with klinefelter syndrome. *Pediatrics* 82 (1): 115–117.

Muckley, A. (1997). Firesetting: Addressing offending behaviour, A resource and training manual. Middlesbrough: Redcar and Cleveland Psychological Service.

Murphy, G.H. and Clare, I.C. (1996). Analysis of motivation in people with mild learning disabilities (mental handicap) who set fires. *Psychology, Crime and Law* 2 (3): 153–164.

Nielsen, J. (1970). Criminality among patients with klinefelter's syndrome and the XYY syndrome. *The British Journal of Psychiatry: The Journal of Mental Science* 117 (539): 365–369.

Ó Ciardha, C., Tyler, N., and Gannon, T.A. (2015). A practical guide to assessing adult firesetters' fire-specific treatment needs using the four factor fire scales. *Psychiatry* 78 (4): 293–304.

O'Donoghue, J., Panchal, J., O'sullivan, S. et al. (1998). A study of suicide and attempted suicide by self-immolation in an Irish psychiatric population: an increasing problem. *Burns* 24 (2): 144–146.

O'Sullivan, G.H. and Kelleher, M.J. (1987). A study of firesetters in the south-west of Ireland. *The British Journal of Psychiatry: The Journal of Mental Science* 151: 818–823.

Prins, H., Tennent, G., and Trick, K. (1985). Motives for arson (fire raising). *Medicine, Science and the Law* 25 (4): 275–278.

Puri, B.K., Baxter, R., and Cordess, C.C. (1995). Characteristics of fire-setters. A study and proposed multiaxial psychiatric classification. *The British Journal of Psychiatry: The Journal of Mental Science* 166 (3): 393–396.

Räsänen, P., Hakko, H., and Väisänen, E. (1995). The mental state of arsonists as determined by forensic psychiatric examinations. *Journal of the American Academy of Psychiatry and the Law Online* 23 (4): 547–553.

Räsänen, P., Puumalainen, T., Janhonen, S. et al. (1996). Fire-setting from the viewpoint of an arsonist. *Journal of Psychosocial Nursing and Mental Health Services* 34 (3): 16–21.

Repo, E. and Virkkunen, M. (1997). Criminal recidivism and family histories of schizophrenic and nonschizophrenic fire setters: comorbid alcohol dependence in schizophrenic fire setters. *The Journal of the American Academy of Psychiatry and the Law* 25 (2): 207–215.

Repo, E., Virkkunen, M., Rawlings, R. et al. (1997a). Criminal and psychiatric histories of Finnish arsonists. *Acta Psychiatrica Scandinavica* 95 (4): 318–323.

Repo, E., Virkkunen, M., Rawlings, R. et al. (1997b). Suicidal behavior among Finnish fire setters. *European Archives of Psychiatry and Clinical Neuroscience* 247 (6): 303–307.

Rice, M.E. and Harris, G.T. (1991). Firesetters admitted to a maximum security psychiatric institution: offenders and offenses. *Journal of Interpersonal Violence* 6 (4): 461–475.

Rice, M.E. and Harris, G.T. (1996). Predicting the recidivism of mentally disordered firesetters. *Journal of Interpersonal Violence* 11 (3): 364–375.

Rix, K.J. (1994). A psychiatric study of adult arsonists. *Medicine, Science and the Law* 34 (1): 21–34.

Root, C., Mackay, S., Henderson, J. et al. (2008). The link between maltreatment and juvenile firesetting: correlates and underlying mechanisms. *Child Abuse & Neglect* 32 (2): 161–176.

Rose, J., Lees-Warley, G., and Thrift, S. (2016). The subjective experiences of firesetting by men with mild intellectual disabilities detained in a secure hospital. *International Journal of Offender Therapy and Comparative Criminology* 60 (11): 1278–1297.

Royal College of Psychiatrists (2001). *DC-LD: Diagnostic Criteria for Psychiatric Disorders for Use with Adults with Learning Disabilities/Mental Retardation (Occasional Paper OP 48)*. Exeter, UK: Edward Gaskell Publishers.

Sakheim, G.A., Osborn, E., and Abrams, D. (1991). Toward a clearer differentiation of high-risk from low-risk fire-setters. *Child Welfare: Journal of Policy, Practice, and Program* 70 (4): 489–503.

Saunders, E.B. and Awad, G.A. (1991). Adolescent female firesetters. *The Canadian Journal of Psychiatry* 36 (6): 401–404.

Smalldridge, G. (2017). *Fire Statistics: England April 2015 to March 2016*. London, UK: Home Office.

Stewart, L.A. (1993). Profile of female firesetters. Implications for treatment. *The British Journal of Psychiatry: The Journal of Mental Science* 163: 248–256.

Sugarman, P. and Dickens, G. (2009). Dangerousness in firesetters: a survey of psychiatrists' views. *The Psychiatrist* 33 (3): 99–101.

Taylor, J. L. (2014). Roots, referrals, risks and remedies for offenders with intellectual disabilities. Paper presented to 'A risky business' BPS conference, October 2014, University of Manchester, UK.

Taylor, J.L., Robertson, A., Thorne, I. et al. (2006). Responses of female fire-setters with mild and borderline intellectual disabilities to a group intervention. *Journal of Applied Research in Intellectual Disabilities* 19 (2): 179–190.

Taylor, J. and Thorne, I. (2005). Northgate firesetter risk assessment. Unpublished Manual, Gosforth: Northgate and Prudhoe NHS Trust.

Taylor, J.L., Thorne, I., Robertson, A. et al. (2002). Evaluation of a group intervention for convicted arsonists with mild and borderline intellectual disabilities. *Criminal Behaviour and Mental Health* 12 (4): 282–293.

Taylor, J.L., Thorne, I., and Slavkin, M.L. (2004). Treatment of fire-setting behaviour. *Offenders with Developmental Disabilities* 3: 221.

Tennent, T.G., McQuaid, A., Loughnane, T. et al. (1971). Female arsonists. *The Journal of Mental Science* 119 (552): 497–502.

Tranah, T. and Nicholas, J. (2013). Interventions for young people with intellectual disabilities who commit arson. *Advances in Mental Health and Intellectual Disabilities* 7 (2): 72–81.

Tyler, N. and Gannon, T.A. (2012). Explanations of firesetting in mentally disordered offenders: a review of the literature. *Psychiatry: Interpersonal & Biological Processes* 75 (2): 150–166.

Tyler, N., Gannon, T.A., Lockerbie, L. et al. (2014). A firesetting offense chain for mentally disordered offenders. *Criminal Justice and Behavior* 41 (4): 512–530.

Vaughn, M.G., Fu, Q., DeLisi, M. et al. (2010). Prevalence and correlates of fire-setting in the United States: results from the national epidemiological survey on alcohol and related conditions. *Comprehensive Psychiatry* 51 (3): 217–223.

Wachi, T., Watanabe, K., Yokota, K. et al. (2007). Offender and crime characteristics of female serial arsonists in Japan. *Journal of Investigative Psychology and Offender Profiling* 4 (1): 29–52.

Watt, B. and Ong, S. (2016). Current directions of risk assessment in deliberate firesetters. In: *The Psychology of Arson* (eds. R. Doley, G.L. Dickens and T.A. Gannon), 167–183. Abingdon, UK: Routledge.

Webster, C. D. and Eaves, D. (1995). *The HCR-20 scheme: The assessment of dangerousness and risk*. Burnaby: Mental Health, Law and Policy Institute, Department of Psychology, Simon Fraser University and Forensic Psychiatric Services Commission of British Columbia.

Wheeler, J.R., Holland, A.J., Bambrick, M. et al. (2009). Community services and people with intellectual disabilities who engage in anti-social or offending behaviour: referral rates, characteristics, and care pathways. *The Journal of Forensic Psychiatry & Psychology* 20 (5): 717–740.

World Health Organization (1993). *The ICD-10 Classification of Mental and Behavioural Disorders: Diagnostic Criteria for Research*. Geneva: World Health Organization.

11

Biopsychosocial Assessment Approach for Offenders with Intellectual Disabilities

Deborah Richards[1], Tyler Oswald[2], and J. Paul Fedoroff[3]

[1] *Pelham Psychotherapy & Consulting Services, Fonthill, Ontario, Canada*
[2] *Hamilton Health Sciences, McMaster University, Hamilton, Ontario, Canada*
[3] *The Royal Hospital, University of Ottawa, Ottawa, Ontario, Canada*

11.1   Introduction

> Jeremy is a 20-year old male with a history of abuse and neglect and a suspected diagnosis of Fetal Alcohol Spectrum Disorder (FASD). At 18 years of age he was charged and convicted with physical assault with a weapon. While on probation he was charged with two counts of sexual interference involving a 9-year-old male child. While he was facing the sexual assault charges, Jeremy's lawyer requested the court to order a neuropsychological assessment to confirm his suspicion of FASD as well as to confirm the presence of intellectual disability and mental health issues. This request was granted by the court as well as a request from the crown to provide a sexual risk assessment.

Evolving research has demonstrated that people with intellectual and developmental disabilities (IDD) have an increased vulnerability towards mental and emotional disorders. Four out of 10 people with IDD are estimated to have both mental health problems and behavioural disorders (Riches et al. 2006). It is also well documented that people with IDD experience a higher rate of abuse, neglect, and adverse environmental conditions that contribute to the quality of their emotional well-being (Bradley and Burke 2002; Putnam 2009; Sobsey 1994). These vulnerabilities require careful assessment to determine their aetiologies and contributory factors. Individuals with IDD who present with extreme and challenging behaviours are often not easily understood (Gardner 1998).

Reflecting on the disadvantages and vulnerabilities that people with IDD experience throughout their formative years, it is not surprising that they have an increased likelihood of becoming involved in the criminal justice system (CJS). It is also not surprising that these disadvantages play a role on an individual's mental well-being and emotional state (Putnam 2009). When a person with IDD intersects with the CJS there is an even

The Wiley Handbook on What Works for Offenders with Intellectual and Developmental Disabilities:
An Evidence-Based Approach to Theory, Assessment, and Treatment, First Edition.
Edited by William R. Lindsay, Leam A. Craig, and Dorothy Griffiths.
© 2020 John Wiley & Sons Ltd. Published 2020 by John Wiley & Sons Ltd.

greater responsibility for clinicians to gain an understanding of these vulnerabilities through comprehensive assessments. The main goal is to ensure that the best possible treatment strategies and outcomes are in place to avoid future offences.

In particular, it is important to have early detection to determine the presence of both an intellectual disability and mental health diagnoses (Beail 2002). Hobson and Rose (2008) found that mental health diagnoses of individuals with ID may not be discovered until after they have entered the criminal system. This makes the issue of appropriate assessment especially important given the overrepresentation of this group within the CJS (Richards et al. accepted for publication). There is now a universal concern about the treatment of offenders with ID due to the historic lack of understanding about the individual complexities of their involvement in the CJS (Richards et al. accepted for publication).

These challenging behaviours may be influenced by medical, psychiatric, psychological, and social or environmental factors and may present in multiple forms. For example, the presentation of some behaviours can have the appearance of psychopathy when in fact it may well be the appearance of psychopathology triggered by a phenotype secondary to a genetic disorder (Levitas et al. 2007; Watson et al. 2012). Another consideration can present itself when an individual with ID has been sexually or physical abused and they in turn learn maladaptive behaviours as a way to cope within their environments. Family separation is a common occurrence with people who have ID, and especially frequent for children who have a diagnosis of FASD, as they are often removed early on from their homes because of neglect and abuse. Thereby, family separation is a loss that can often affect an individual's abilities to emotionally connect and relate to those around them (Bradley and Burke 2002). These three examples represent only a small portion of the vast range of presenting problems clinicians are faced with trying to determine the instigating and precipitating factors that influence these vulnerabilities. This process is at the core of the assessment process.

Over the past two decades, examination of the biomedical, emotional or psychological, and socio-environmental factors through integrating information from a multidisciplinary perspective has become the practice of choice in the development of assessment and treatment for individuals who have been dually diagnosed (Ingham et al. 2008). This chapter explores various assessment strategies via a biopsychosocial approach (BPS) for individuals with ID who have also been labelled as offenders. In order to understand the intricacies of establishing a diagnosis through careful assessment, this case study will be threaded through the chapter to illustrate a recommended diagnostic approach.

11.2 Biological-Medical Assessment

Jeremy has been described as having complex mental health problems and been given a number of diagnoses by numerous psychiatrists throughout his life. Reports describe a wide range of diagnoses including Attention Deficit Hyperactivity Disorder (ADHD); Foetal Alcohol Spectrum Disorder (FASD); Obsessive Compulsive Disorder (OCD); Oppositional Defiant Disorder (ODD); Conduct Disorder (CD); Reactive Attachment Disorder (RAD); Generalized

Anxiety Disorder (GAD); Depression; Suicidal Behaviour Disorder; and Attachment-based Anxiety. From age 5, Jeremy has been prescribed various medications for depressed mood and impulsivity. By age 12, several medications had also been prescribed to treat anger and aggressiveness. There did not appear to be follow-up records indicating the efficacy of any of these medications or the length of time he was on them.

As one element of a complete bio-psycho-social assessment, the biomedical lens offers psychiatric diagnoses and can identify targets for pharmacological intervention. Offenders with ID often present significant diagnostic challenges.

The psychiatric assessment of a person with ID proceeds as in persons without ID, but with special attention being paid to the potential challenges of developing a clear understanding of a person's internal world. These can include barriers to receptive and expressive communication, efforts by a patient to hide their disabilities via a 'cloak of competence' (Edgerton 1967), and a potential tendency to try to please the examiner via 'acquiescence bias'. These can result in 'diagnostic overshadowing'. This later term refers to the phenomenon that odd or abnormal behaviours displayed by patients with ID are often assumed to be related to developmental delay or other impairments. In this way, symptoms of mental illness can be lost or misinterpreted in the shadow of a patient's larger clinical picture (Reiss et al. 1982). The diagnostician's task is to apply standard diagnostic criteria in the highly unique situations of each individual patient.

The Diagnostic Manual – Intellectual Disability 2 (DM-ID2; Fletcher et al. 2016) is a tool that was designed to take into consideration these notable problems whilst acting as a complementary manual to the DSM-5 (American Psychiatric Association [APA], 2013). The DM-ID-2, like the DSM-5, is evidence-based and places a focus on the assessment and diagnostic process in terms of adaptations and special considerations for individuals with ID. The availability of such tools is an important step towards recognizing mental health disorders in individuals who have an ID (Lunsky and Bradley 2001).

The psychiatric assessment begins with history taking and includes a thorough canvassing of a patient's current and past presentations. Various approaches exist, but areas of interest include details about the current problem bringing the patient to clinical attention; past psychiatric history including previous diagnoses, admissions, and treatments; family psychiatric history; birth and developmental history including pre-natal and post-natal exposure to teratogens (including alcohol), developmental milestones, and any other identified delays; social history including relationship, educational, work, and legal history; substance use both past and present; sexual history; and medical history including conditions and treatments. A detailed exploration of current and past psychiatric symptoms is necessary, with particular focus on relevant conditions. Depending on the case, other areas may also be important. For example, a detailed sleep history may be important in patients presenting with anger or irritability (Booth et al. 2006). Collateral information from caregivers is essential when assessing a person with ID, as is a review of medical and legal records.

Persons with ID and significant behavioural disturbance may have had numerous contacts with mental health systems especially if aggression and violence are factors. Due to the complexity of their presentations, past clinicians may have offered a variety of diagnoses in an effort to categorize a patient and offer help as is seen in the case of Jeremy.

It is important to appreciate that this list may represent the efforts of many clinicians over many years and circumstances, and that some of these diagnoses may not accurately reflect the patient's current difficulties. It is of paramount importance that clinicians take a fresh look at each newly referred offender with ID and consider a range of possible alternative causes and explanations for a patient's presentation.

Given that a person with ID symptoms may be presenting in attenuated form, it is necessary to begin with a wide-ranging list of possible causes to develop a differential diagnosis that can be explored to prove or disprove each possibility. The first assessment encounter(s) are often the beginning of the therapeutic relationship. The most effective therapeutic relationships empower the patient to make decisions about their care. When first establishing this relationship, it is essential to positively reinforce the patient's decision to seek help, and explicitly support this throughout the assessment and treatment (Richards and Fedoroff 2016). The following sections will touch on common psychiatric diagnoses, and offer suggestions for assessment of these conditions in offenders with ID.

11.2.1 Genetic or Neurodevelopmental Disorders

A wide range of genetic or neurodevelopmental disorders can include behavioural disturbance as part of their constellation of symptoms, and it is important to consider this when assessing offenders with ID. Common disorders that include behavioural components include FASDs, autism spectrum disorders (ASD), and others. These disorders can have genetic or environmental causes; some disorders are considered to arise from a combination of the two. When assessing an offender with ID, a clinician should be sensitive to features suggestive of neurodevelopmental disorders: dysmorphic features, a history of teratogen exposure, or a behavioural syndrome compatible with a known neurodevelopmental disorder. Impairments will be traceable to childhood.

Alcohol is a known teratogen, and in-utero exposure in some cases is known to cause deleterious effects on the foetus. Degree of exposure is thought to correlate to degree of effect on foetus, but the relationship is not known precisely. In-utero exposure to alcohol can have physical, cognitive, neurologic, or behavioural effects. Various diagnostic labels exist to capture different combinations of these effects; the broadest term describing these conditions is FASD.

According to Vidovic (2012) FASD can include characteristic dysmorphic features. Known nervous system effects of alcohol exposure include structural brain abnormalities, neurologic impairments (e.g. seizure disorders, hearing loss, poor fine motor skills), and functional impairments (behavioural or cognitive abnormalities, including intellectual impairment, problems with learning, impulse control, memory, and other domains). It is of importance to note, people can be affected by FASD and experience neurologic and functional impairments, without exhibiting physical dysmorphic features. The presence of a reported history of pre-natal alcohol exposure, characteristic dysmorphic features, characteristic behavioural features should prompt consideration of FASD as a diagnostic possibility. Correctly identifying offenders with FASD can direct treatment towards interventions that are known to be more effective and avoid erroneous diagnoses and ineffective treatments. To date, validated FASD assessments are infrequently conducted due to high cost and it is therefore difficult to locate clinical services for identification (Vidovic 2012). However, there are an increasing number of resource groups, researchers, and clinicians who have expertise in FASD that can be utilized.

11.2.2 Attention Deficit Hyperactivity Disorder (ADHD)

ADHD is a condition characterized by symptoms of inattention and/or hyperactivity, with symptoms manifesting prior to the age of 12 years and lasting 6 months or more and causing the patient impairment or distress. Symptoms must be present in two or more settings (e.g. at home and at school) (DSM-5; American Psychiatric Association 2013).

Humphries (2007) states that the prevalence of ADHD amongst typically developing children ranges from 3 to 7%, as compared to children with ID where rates are 10–20%. Although prevalence has proven to be much higher, the diagnosis can be complicated by the likelihood of co-morbidity (Xenitidis et al. 2010). For example, a person with the diagnosis of FASD will be more likely to have an additional diagnosis of ADHD.

ADHD is based on the severity of one's behaviour rather than a reliance on the frequency or presence of symptoms (Haut and Brewster 2010). Characteristically, inattention, impulsivity, and hyperactivity are key features of ADHD. However, these very characteristics have long been noted in individuals who have an intellectual disability (Haut and Brewster 2010; Lindsay et al. 2009; Xenitidis et al. 2010). This is an example of how diagnostic overshadowing may lead to difficulty in identifying ADHD (Xenitidis et al. 2010).

Despite the challenges to diagnosing ADHD in individuals with ID, it has been found that noncompliance and aggression are the most frequent characteristics in identifying ADHD in both children and adults with ID, unrelated to the aetiology of the ID (Haut and Brewster 2010; Humphries 2007). Xenitidis et al. (2010) stated that the onset of significant behavioural problems increases through childhood into adolescent years for individuals with ID who had a previous diagnosis of ADHD. This does not suggest that the primary DSM-5 (American Psychiatric Association 2013) criteria of inattention, hyperactivity-impulsivity, or a combination of both are not relevant, it simply means that there may also be aggression and non-compliance. These were in fact the very factors that contributed to Jeremy's initial intersections with the legal system.

ADHD has been known to be a childhood risk factor for future offending behaviour. In a study of 477 individuals with ID who also had a history of criminal offences, Lindsay et al. (2009) found ADHD and CD to have the most common association with offending behaviour. Understanding this risk, Lindsay et al. (2009) recommended that any referrals into developmental services following a diagnosis of ADHD as a co-morbid condition should be considered high on the priority list for relevant services, both pharmacological and psychological.

There is some overlap between the presentation of patients with ASD and those with ADHD; it has been suggested that if patients present with symptoms consistent with ADHD, this should be seen as a concurrent diagnosis (Hellings et al. 2016). The same can be said about FASD and ADHD.

A number of rating scales exist to screen for ADHD; these are helpful for collecting standardized measures of symptoms. The diagnostic criteria for ADHD are anchored in behaviours, making application to persons with ID relatively straightforward.

Youth scales include the Connors Comprehensive Behaviour Rating Scale, and the SNAP-IV. Adult scales include the Adult ADHD Self-Report Scale, and the ADHD Rating Scale-IV. Scales exist that can assist in the collection of information about hyperactive or disruptive behaviours in persons with ID; these include the Aberrant Behaviours Checklist (ABC). Whilst this scale may assist in the collection of information related to a diagnosis of ADHD, it is not specific for this purpose.

11.2.3 Depression

Whilst mood problems present in persons with ID at increased rates relative to the general population (Kiddle and Dagnan (2011), identification can be challenging. Key aspects of biomedical assessment include careful history taking to detect changes in baseline function, thorough application of standard diagnostic symptoms, and a proper medical workup to identify underlying medical issues that may be exacerbating mood problems or masquerading as them. Identification of genetic syndromes is also important as some conditions leave people more prone to depression (Dykens and Hodapp 2001).

The classic depressive illness is Major Depressive Disorder. This condition is characterized by discrete episodes of depressed mood or anhedonia lasting two weeks or longer, along with a number of other symptoms including sleep problems, loss of interest in activities, feelings of guilt, low energy, concentration problems, appetite changes, increases, or decreases in psychomotor behaviours (agitation or lassitude), and suicidal thoughts. Whilst changes from baseline functioning and an episodic course are key features of a history, persons with ID can exhibit what appear to be episodic changes that are in fact the result of environmental factors such as changes in staffing or allergies (Charlot et al. 2016)

These symptoms appear to rely heavily on a patient's ability to express their inner experience. As noted earlier, assessing the internal world of persons with communication deficits can be challenging. Persons with ID can also exhibit impairments in developmental level. It is necessary to consider the developmental level of a patient and understand the ways in which the well-validated symptoms of depression would be expressed. People with mild to moderate ID can express the full range of depressive symptoms, and core symptoms appear to be expressed in the same ways as in the non-ID population (Charlot et al. 2016). Some symptoms relying on cognitive capacity may not be present in persons with profound ID and persons with profound ID may not meet full criteria for a Major Depressive Episode and may be diagnosed with Other Specific Depressive Disorder.

Depending on degree of ID, patients with depressed mood can exhibit dramatic externalizing behaviours. Whilst this may be a change in baseline function and in fact may be related to an active mood disorder, aggression is not specific to mood problems and is a part of many other psychiatric syndromes in the context of ID. Given that disruptive behaviours can overshadow more subtle symptoms of depression (sleep and appetite changes), a careful assessment including collateral information from caregivers who would have detailed knowledge of a patient's daily functioning, is critical. Expressions of aggression can include self-injurious behaviour; this is also not a specific symptom of depressive illnesses. Identification of any genetic syndromes is also essential, as some conditions can include self-harm behaviour (e.g. Lesch–Nyhan syndrome).

11.2.4 Anger and Aggression

Anger and aggression is a common presenting problem in the context of persons with ID who are also labelled offenders, and more than any other requires a comprehensive assessment approach. As noted earlier, this symptom is not specific to a single psychiatric diagnosis. Anger and aggression are best understood as a symptom resulting from the dynamic interaction of biological, social, and psychological factors (Gardner 2002).

Anger and aggression are described as a final common pathway for a number of interacting problems. When considering the biomedical aspects of assessment, various biological and psychiatric causes need to be considered, appreciating that elements of a patient's social and psychological context can attenuate or adjust expressions of anger. As per Fletcher et al. (2007), 'the tendency to focus on just the aggression may be the most critical contributing factor in the variability and inaccuracy of psychiatric diagnoses for people with ID' (p. 267).

When beginning an assessment in which aggression is the focus, a complete history of the aggressive behaviour is necessary. Information about environment and patient are important. This includes time of day, relation to mealtimes or activities, specific staff present and other environmental data. Information about onset, frequency, intensity, provoking, and palliating factors are all relevant (Gardner 2002). Course is important, as new or rapid-onset of aggressive behaviours suggests some aetiologies over others and should emphasize the need for a thorough medical assessment.

Given the barriers to communication in some cases of aggression, a thorough medical evaluation is necessary. This would include physical exam and lab work. Specific laboratory tests will be guided by the patient's presentation. If there are concerns about sexual aggression, testing of hormone levels is indicated; see the later section on assessment of sexual behaviour disorders. Common medical conditions that can precipitate aggressive behaviour include faecal impaction, pain (e.g. secondary to infection or other cause), seizure disorders and post-ictal confusion, delirium, headaches, menstrual discomfort, sleep difficulties, allergic reactions, skin disorders, gastrointestinal problems (Barnhill et al. 2016). Identification of genetic syndromes is also valuable, as some phenotypes more often include aggressive behaviour (Levitas et al. 2007)

A comprehensive psychiatric assessment is required, as many psychiatric illnesses can predispose a patient to anger and aggressive behaviours. A non-exhaustive list of possible psychiatric causes includes mood disorders (depression, mania), schizophrenia and other psychotic illnesses, ADHD, anxiety disorders, OCD, and Post-traumatic stress disorder (PTSD). Each of these illnesses would have its own characteristic age of onset, presentation(s), and course.

A review of all current and past medications is required as some prescription and over-the-counter medications have the potential to precipitate aggressive behaviour. Benzodiazepine medications are associated with disinhibition in some cases, and antipsychotic medications can cause restlessness (akathisia) as a side effect. Consideration should be given to substance use, and a review of the patient's current pattern of use should be undertaken. If appropriate, urine or serum testing could be undertaken to identify substance use. Intoxication, withdrawal, and chronic use can all precipitate aggressive behaviour.

The goal of a biomedical assessment is to identify diagnoses predisposing to aggression; these diagnoses can then become targets for treatment. Once identified through biomedical assessment, the expression of these factors must then be placed in the unique social and psychological context of the patient.

11.2.5 Personality Disorders

A personality disorder is defined by the DSM-5 as 'an enduring pattern of inner experience and behaviour that deviates markedly from the expectations of the individual's culture, is pervasive and inflexible, has an onset in adolescence or early adulthood, is stable over time, and leads to distress or impairment'. Personality disorders are grouped into three 'clusters': A (odd, eccentric), B (dramatic-emotional), and C (anxious-fearful).

Diagnosing personality pathology requires a detailed knowledge of a patient's presentation over time. As noted earlier, barriers to communication can make accessing information about a patient's inner experience challenging. For this reason, the diagnosis of personality disorders is confined to adult patients with mild or moderate ID; the inner experience of patients with severe or profound ID is generally seen as too remote to permit accurate diagnosis of a personality disorder. Additionally, patients with ID generally have delays in development and these include delays in personality development; patients with severe or profound ID have delays in personality development such that diagnoses of personality disorder cannot be reliably made.

No effective structured diagnostic inventory tools exist for the identification of personality disorders in patients with ID. Use of questionnaires in the ID population can be problematic. People with ID may not be able to read or write. They may not be able to comprehend or focus sufficiently to accurately respond to a long questionnaire. As a necessary part of history taking involves the collection of patient symptoms over time, collateral information from informants is essential to the assessment of personality pathology in this population.

Whilst diagnosis of personality disorders in this population ultimately rely on the application of standard criteria, it is important to recognize the unique context of patient with ID. The nature of their care needs may have necessitated long relationships of dependence and they may be inexperienced in navigating relationships (sexual or otherwise). Many criteria for diagnosis of personality disorder rely on the detection of sophisticated and abstract concepts like a sense of internal 'emptiness' – communication barriers may make such symptoms impossible to reliably elicit. Some concepts like empathy involve abstract reasoning that is beyond the capacity of some patients with ID. Key to the application of standard diagnostic criteria is an appreciation of a patient's neurodevelopmental and environmental context. It is also important to remember that an inability to appreciate or describe a symptom (e.g. anhedonia) does not mean the person is not experiencing the symptom and suffering from its effects.

11.2.6 Post-Traumatic Stress Disorder (PTSD)

PTSD describes a condition in which, following exposure to a traumatic experience, a patient develops a constellation of symptoms involving intrusive memories or dreams, avoidance of certain stimuli, negative changes in mood or cognition, and increase in arousal or reactivity. It is known that patients with ID experience abuse and neglect at greater frequencies than the general population (Ammerman et al. 1989; Sobsey 1994). According to Razzo and Tomasulo (2005), the sexual trauma experienced by an individual with ID places them in a particularly exaggerated state of vulnerability. In fact, a study conducted by Sequeira et al. (2003) found a higher incidence of depression, anxiety, and sexual maladjustment, with a higher proportion meeting criteria overall for a psychiatric diagnosis. Specifically, a higher incidence of DSM-IV-TR (APA 2000) diagnostic criteria for the clustering of symptoms consistent with PTSD was found in the group who had ID. Importantly, Sequeira et al. (2003) discovered that there was a significant and higher incidence of inappropriate sexual behaviour within the group who had ID. Lindsay et al. (2009) found that men with ID who had been involved in the legal system had a higher rate of sexual abuse than men without ID.

Central challenges in the assessment of PTSD in patients with ID involve the effects of a patient's developmental level on the experience of trauma and the expression of its symptoms. Given the developmental level of patients with ID, it is an open question as to what degree of stressor can constitute a traumatic experience. There is some suggestion that 'lesser' degrees of trauma are required to produce PTSD in persons with ID (McCarthy et al. 2016). Significant stressors could include the departure of a beloved staff member, a move, or another highly significant subjective loss. A careful assessment of a patient's history and records is necessary in order to identify past traumatic experiences. In the case of Jeremy, there was a significant trauma history from early childhood that evolved over several years in multiple forms of abuse and neglect.

11.2.7 Sexual Behaviour Disorder

In terms of biomedical diagnosis, problematic sexual behaviour can fall within the definition of paraphilic disorders. The DSM-5, defines a paraphilia as 'any intense and persistent sexual interest other than sexual interest in genital stimulation or preparatory fondling with phenotypically normal, physically mature, consenting human partners' (American Psychiatric Association 2013, p. 685). A paraphilia becomes a disorder when it causes distress or impairment to the patient, or harm (or risk of harm) to the patient or another person.

A variety of behaviours and sexual interests can form the basis for a paraphilic disorder. These include voyeurism, exhibitionism, frotteurism, sadism, masochism, fetishism, transvestitism, and paedophilia. It should be noted that hypersexuality is not a DSM-5 diagnosis. Whilst all these diagnoses can lead a person to criminal charges, common diagnoses presenting for psychiatric assessment in offenders with ID are paedophilia and exhibitionism (Day 1994).

In order to determine whether or not a patient meets the DSM-5 diagnostic criteria for paedophilia, there has to be a period of 6 months of recurrent, intense, sexually arousing fantasies, with action taken upon these feelings with a child or children who is generally aged 13 years or younger, whilst the person with the disorder being 16 years of age and older. Research over the past decade has been unravelling the contributing factors that are early onset predictors of sexual offending behaviours for individuals with ID. In order to establish a psychiatric diagnosis that meets the criteria for paedophilia, a comprehensive evaluation is needed to determine the biomedical, psychological, and socio-environmental influences (Fedoroff and Richards 2010). Both psychological and socio-environmental factors will be discussed later in their respective sections.

Psychiatric assessment in cases of sexual behaviour disorders proceeds as it would for other presenting problems and includes gathering information from the patient and collateral sources (medical and legal records, caregivers, and family members). In advance of the first appointment, questionnaires can be completed by the patient (with assistance, as required) and caregivers to collect relevant information. Areas to explore include demographic and social history information, developmental and behavioural history, relationship history, legal history including details about past offences and victims, the patient's own history of sexual or physical abuse, detailed sexual history, substance use history, medical and current medications, and information about any past assessments and treatments.

The sexual history should include information about the patient's sexual development, sexual interests and fantasies, and sexual activities including frequency (sex with a partner, masturbation, pornography use). Details are required, including specifics about sexual behaviours and interests.

As part of the medical assessment, lab work could include luteinizing hormone (LH), follicular stimulation hormone (FSH), and free testosterone. Assessment of sexual interests in males can be most objectively done via phallometric testing. Whilst this testing is fraught with challenges for people with ID, it can provide objective information about sexual arousal patterns (Fedoroff and Richards 2010, 2013). The use of this tool for people who sexually offend and have ID should be used with caution and only used as one of the tools in an overall assessment as there is limited research for this population. This assessment is able to identify penile tumescence in response to images or audiotaped scenarios involving males and/or females, to children and/or adults, and to coercive stimuli. The patient should understand the nature of the testing and be able to provide informed consent.

11.3 Psychological and Emotional Assessment

> Jeremy was taken from his biological mother at the age of 4 years due to severe neglect, physical abuse, and suspected sexual abuse. His mother was reported to be a sex trade worker with a drug and alcohol problem. He was placed in approximately 5 foster homes by the age of 12. He was described by teachers and foster parents as angry, aggressive with severe behavioural problems, and impulsive in his actions. He received a number of suspensions throughout his school years due to aggressive behaviour. At age 8 he reported being sexually abused by 2 foster brothers who were 14 and 15 years of age. Because of ongoing behavioural problems, he was placed in several behavioural group homes from ages 12 to 18 years. His first arrest was at 13 years of age for physical assault and stealing from the group home. At 15 years of age he was charged with sexual interference involving a 9-year-old male. And then at 18 years of age, Jeremy was charged with assault with a weapon to a peace officer upon his arrest where he was then formally charged as an adult with 2 counts of sexual interference of a 9-year old male.

In order to understand what shapes a person's life it is important to gather information from early childhood to current age by way of doing a psychosocial history. Taking a thorough history is a way to evaluate and understand the circumstances that prompt emotional reactions, social interactions as well as medical occurrences. Summers et al. (2002) explained that an evaluation should include history of abuse or neglect, significant medical procedures that may have been perceived as invasive or long-term hospital stays, violence in the family home, educational experiences, environmental factors related to significant changes, employment history, or socio-economic status, grief, and loss that can also involve perceived abandonment. Taking this into account, in Jeremy's childhood history of abuse and neglect there are possible indicators to assist the clinician in understanding what prompted the challenging behaviours. From early on he experienced violence. When he should have been safe from abuse after being apprehended from his biological mother, he was placed into foster care where he was once again subjected to sexual abuse and violence. As demonstrated by this hypothetical but typical case, by obtaining a history even though this is a quick overview, a clinician is able to ascertain that Jeremy has had a significant history of victimization that has caused emotional reactions throughout his life. These life circumstances are likely to have contributed to his offending behaviour and must be taken into account.

Of particular importance during this process is knowing the person's intellectual functioning and their ability to reason and solve problems. Associated with intellectual functioning is adaptive functioning. In identifying these deficits and strengths it is easier to understand how the person handles the demands of life. Functional assessments are also an essential component in understanding that a combination of the numerous influences can often result in challenging behaviours (Gardner 1998). In the case of Jeremy, these multiple influences from early childhood to adulthood, had a negative impact on his day-to-day functioning eventually leading to his arrest. This section will demonstrate how psychological and emotional factors can be assessed as a means to formulate a treatment plan.

If the offender has problematic sexual behaviours it is important to assess risk of committing a sex offence or of re-offending. There are a number of sexual risk assessments that estimate the level of risk the offender poses regarding future recidivism, whilst also providing a direction for management and prevention (Fedoroff et al. 2016). There are two types of risk assessments, actuarial and dynamic risk assessments. According to Langdon and Murphy (2010) sexual risk assessments are multidimensional and are related to the biopsychosocial functioning of an individual. It is suggested that sexual risk identifiers are no different than it is for people without ID, but it is recommended that assessments need to also incorporate a clinical interview and mental status examination, functional analysis, assessment of the dynamic risk factors, and actuarial risk assessment tools keeping in mind that this particular assessment may have potential problems for people with ID (Langdon and Murphy 2010).

Whilst there are a number of assessment tools, The Risk and Manageability of Individuals with Developmental and Intellectual Limitations who Offend – Sexually (ARMIDILO-S; Blacker et al. 2011) is considered one of the more applicable tools because of its dynamic factors and specificity for people with ID who sexually offend (Fedoroff et al. 2016). In the case of Jeremy, the Judge has ordered a sexual risk assessment and with the employment of this tool, although risk cannot be certain with any assessment tool, this one is believed to outline the most applicable factors. It is comprised of static and dynamic variables that include environment and societal factors that are often related to individuals with ID and recidivism (Blacker et al. 2011; Boer et al. 2004). Because of the predictive value of this assessment, the CJS order can be fulfilled. Additionally, this assessment provides a range of areas identified as risk factors that have a practical implication for recommendations and future treatment.

Understanding a person's history, a clear understanding of the environment, and the circumstances surrounding the sexual offence is needed (Griffiths et al. 1989). It is important to determine whether or not a person with ID has a paraphilic disorder or alternatively, Griffiths et al. (1989) has suggested that an individual's sexual knowledge base, interpersonal relationship skills, coping skills, along with sexual interests and arousal patterns should also be assessed. The clinician may be able to determine if the sexually offensive behaviours of the offender could be the result of experiential, environmental and/or medical factors. People can display behaviours encompassed within the coined term 'counterfeit deviance'. These include, for example, impairments in sexual problem solving, problems in impulse control, lack of skills in respecting appropriate boundaries. In the case of Jeremy, it could be suggested that his past childhood experiences of being sexually abused may have contributed to his actions of sexually assaulting others. Using Griffiths et al.'s (1989) counterfeit deviance theory, Jeremy's sexually offensive behaviour could be the result of modelling or faulty education. Understanding the personal history and the offence history is an important aspect of determining whether or not a person could meet the criteria for a sexual disorder or is better understood as the result of counterfeit deviance, or possibly a combination of the two.

An additional approach to consider in the assessment of problematic sexual behaviours is to gather information on what the person has come to know and believe in regard to sexual knowledge, personal boundaries, and intimate relationships. This can be done with the Social Sexual Knowledge and Attitudes Tool - Revised (SSKAAT-R) (Griffiths and Lunsky 2003; Lunsky et al. 2007). This is a criterion-based assessment tool that evaluates specific areas of socio-sexual functioning and attitudes. For example, if the offender has been a victim of abuse as an adolescent and has never received abuse prevention training or sex education, he may not understand the legal implications of touching a child. It is important to remember that the 'determination of paraphilia or counterfeit deviance can only be accomplished by a comprehensive evaluation for the individual in relation to the behaviour in question' (Griffiths et al. accepted for publication).

Assessing aggression and violence from a psychological perspective is important as these may or may not be related to a psychiatric condition. Children and adolescents with ID who have lived in abusive and neglectful environments have an increased prevalence of aggression and anger (Fudge-Schormans and Sobsey 2007). In fact, the presence of a childhood history of sexual abuse accompanied by a lack of attachment with primary caregivers can profoundly impact the ability to express appropriate emotions and establish meaningful relationships later on in life. Clinically significant problems of aggression and other related disruptive actions may represent a number of defined psychiatric disorders or may also be greatly influenced by psychological conditions that were present during the developmental years and continued over the person's life span. Gardner (2002) suggests that the functionality of these impulse-driven aggressive acts become habitually relevant as a coping option. Until new replacement strategies are formulated and learned the negative responses will continue.

In response to these acts of anger and aggression, it is recommended that a comprehensive functional assessment and analysis be done as a means to understand the function of the negatively impacting behaviours. Recommended by Gardner (2002) is a case formulation including a multimodal assessment that takes into account biomedical and psychosocial elements to account for the reinforcing influences of aggressive and disruptive behaviours. There are six domains that need to be considered in this analysis; physical environment, social situations, programme situations, psychological situations, medical conditions, and psychiatric-neuropsychiatric interventions. Functional assessments are meant to gather information about the events before the disruptive behaviour takes place or antecedents and the function of the behaviour (Summers et al. 2002). Once this assessment is completed it requires behavioural analysis. An action plan can then be put into place to teach alternative positive replacement behaviours.

Trauma-based histories are increased for people with ID and can come in many forms. Martorell et al. (2009) found that 75% of individuals with mild to moderate ID had at least one clinically significant traumatic event during their lifespan. Individuals with ID may experience abuse and neglect, witnessed violence, or have experienced abandonment. In fact, people with ID are at an increased risk of abuse and neglect and because of this have increased risk of adverse psychological effects (Sobsey 1994). These traumatic experiences can cause difficulty in regulating emotions as well as disclosing feelings. It has been found that more frequently *only* maladaptive behaviours are typically addressed and the root cause of the behaviour is largely *ignored* (Martorell et al. 2009). Trauma assessments need to include the history of trauma, mental health symptoms, maladaptive behaviour and its presentation, and the current safety and support within the individuals' current environment so that further trauma does not continue. The DSM-5 (APA 2013) outlines trauma-based diagnoses and the use of comprehensive and integrated approaches, which take into account the mental health diagnosis and the role that the instigating factors contribute to the behaviours as related to the trauma. By identifying the trauma and not just the resulting behaviour, the identification of trauma-informed care can be implemented (Cox-Lindenbaum and Watson 2002). Assessing offenders with ID who have experienced trauma is not something that has been a priority for offenders as the aggression and violence typically is at the forefront. However, in order to get to the root cause of these challenging behaviours a clinician needs to be open to the possibility that there is a direct link to early childhood trauma.

11.4 Socio-environmental Assessment

Currently, Jeremy is 20 years old and residing in a for-profit boarding home with 20 other individuals who experience mental health and/or developmental disorders. This is not an ideal situation for Jeremy as the crowded environment creates problems around aggression for him. However, prior to this arrangement he was homeless for approximately a year. He receives monthly disability funds. Referrals have been placed in developmental disability service agencies and mental health but has been waitlisted. He is on probation for the next three years. He is on the Sex Offender Registry. Jeremy has difficulty developing and maintaining healthy relationship. He is a pleasant and engaging young man but also presents as someone that can become easily agitated and angers quickly. Upon the first psychiatric visit, Jeremy stated that he needs help with his decision making and has made bad choices throughout his life. He also states that he wants to get a job and wants to live in his own flat, as he doesn't like living with so many people who have the same problems as he does. There have been reports from his probation officer that he has been using marijuana and alcohol. His probation officer states that he attends appointments with her weekly and she has set up a system to ensure he makes the visits and she has had no problems with his compliance at this point.

Within a socio-environmental framework there are three areas that require planning in order to promote success for an offender that include (i) adequate housing and residential placements; (ii) supports and services, and (iii) healthy relationships. It is suggested to consider the analysis from the three sources that was gathered from the sexual risk assessment, psychological assessment including the adaptive functioning testing, and the functional analysis. The ARMIDILO-S identifies risk of recidivism. Information from this assessment can identify the stable and acute dynamic factors associated with supervision and treatment compliance, sexual pre-occupation and deviance, emotional coping, offence management, relationship, impulsivity, mental health, and lifestyle Understanding the needs and protective factors of the offender with ID can aid in the assessment process leading to an effective support plan. Psychological and adaptive functioning testing is the second source that is critical in planning. Consideration of cognitive limitations and strengths can promote appropriate delivery of service, and guide support staff in communicating and training strategies that will benefit the person best. Adaptive functioning is based on the conceptual, social, and practical abilities. Lastly, the analysis of the functional assessment can assist in understanding the instigating behaviours within the environment and how it directly impacts individual behaviour. Assessing the current physical environment and social situation and their positive or negative impact on the offender with ID is of importance. The integration of the results of these assessments can provide a framework that is person centred.

Understanding the biomedical and psychological needs of the offender allows for a comprehensive examination of the socio-environmental factors and what is necessary to promote appropriate services and supports. According to Brown and Percy (2007) there are five basic assessment considerations that can be used across all significant domains of support interventions. These include an examination of the following;

1) Attend to the current problem or situation that is occurring in the persons' life (In Jeremy's situation it is his legal problems);
2) Gather as much information as possible about the situation;
3) Determine what has been working and what has not worked in regards to the problem;
4) Understand what factors improve the situations and those that hinder the process; and lastly,
5) Determine an intervention plan that will improve or enhance the person's life.

Additionally, Griffiths et al. (1998) looked at the features that promote a habilitative environment and found that gathering information of five key elements needs to be considered. These elements include examination of whether or not the environment is as typical as possible, there is promotion of learning a prosocial alternative to challenging behaviours, there is an enriched lifestyle incorporating quality of life factors, and the individual is seen as a unique person with goals and dreams. Griffiths et al. (1998) point out that the environmental quality can either add to or interfere with the person's ability to benefit from the key factors of an engaging life. Individuals with ID who are also labelled offenders are often living in sub-standard conditions that can greatly impact on their emotional state and well-being.

With a comprehensive screening of these areas that also includes analysis of the assessments suggested from the psychological assessment domain, offenders with ID along with their support team can begin the person-centred planning process. This identifies specific goals, expected outcomes and recognition of specialized support services (Brown and Percy 2007). These specialized support services in Jeremy's case should consider skill building based upon the findings of the assessments in terms of mental health and well-being, learning style and cognitive limitations, along with functional analysis results with an emphasis on risk management. Lastly, it is critical to evaluate the support system in place regarding care providers to determine the level of knowledge and attitudes towards offenders, problematic sexual behaviours, FASD, or other genetic syndromes and dual diagnosis.

11.5 Conclusions

Employing a systematic and comprehensive assessment approach to address the maladaptive problems experienced by offenders who have ID is necessary in developing the effective treatment strategies (Jones 2007). Determining the function and purpose of the challenging problems of each unique individual needs to go beyond the label of offender. Integrating clinical information from a multidisciplinary perspective with the common goal leading to effective care and support is encouraged (Ingham et al. 2008). Utilizing a BPS approach to minimize the maladaptive behaviours and increase prosocial skills is essential. Ingham et al. (2008) state that the apparent overlap in mental health concerns and challenging behaviour is cause to integrate the BPS assessment when formulating a plan. Fedoroff and Richards (2010) suggest that understanding there is an overarching need to gather information from all aspects of a person's life is essential in determining diagnoses in order to move forward into developing a treatment plan. This is especially true when there is evidence to show that over 30% of individuals with ID who also have a label of offender have mental health issues (Haut and Brewster 2010).

As a demonstration of how a BPS approach can successfully be integrated in supporting an offender with ID, Jeremy's case will be used in regards to two of his problems (sexual offending and aggression). Biomedically Jeremy will undergo a number of assessments including laboratory testing to determine his sexual arousal patterns, which may include testosterone levels, and penile plethysmograph (PPG) testing. In addition, Jeremy's mental health is carefully assessed, and a framework of care can be determined based on the diagnoses. Psychological and emotional factors are also closely examined to first determine his sexual knowledge or lack thereof, in addition to considering other factors through a counterfeit deviance theory in identifying possible alternative reasons he may have committed a sexual crime. Because aggression has played a major role in his criminal behaviour, an integration of the biomedical finding and the results from the functional analysis along with an evaluation of the environmental factors is required. Understanding that there is a link within each of these components will enrich the clinician's ability to build comprehensive and inclusive assessments. One is not any more important than the other in determining what is instigating the criminal behaviour but rather an integration of the BPS needs enhances the final results.

Working within an integrated framework of a BPS can better support the whole person. The case of Jeremy was a demonstration of how each separate area has a method of seeking out the instigating causes and more often than not, those causes are interrelated. The judge's order to undergo assessment was the most critical factor towards ensuring that a solid understanding of Jeremy's needs and complexities were being met within the CJS. It is not until this integration of a biomedical, psychological, and socio-environmental conditions are met that offenders with ID are able to live a life that has personal gain and autonomy.

References

American Psychiatric Association (APA) (2000). *Diagnostic and Statistical Manual of Mental Disorders: DSM-IV-TR*, 4e. Washington, DC: American Psychiatric Association.

American Psychiatric Association (2013). *Diagnostic and Statistical Manual of Mental Disorders*, 5e. Washington, DC: American Psychiatric Association.

Ammerman, R.T., VanHasselt, V.B., Herson, M. et al. (1989). Abuse and neglect in psychiatrically hospitalized multi-handicapped children. *Child Abuse and Neglect* 13: 335–343.

Barnhill, J., McLean, L.K., Ogletree, B.T. et al. (2016). Communication disorders. In: *Diagnostic Manual – Intellectual Disability – 2: A Textbook of Diagnosis of Mental Disorders in Persons with Intellectual Disability* (eds. R.J. Fletcher, J. Barnhill and S. Cooper), 91–114. Kingston, NY: NADD Press.

Beail, N. (2002). Constructive approaches to the assessment, treatment and management of offenders with intellectual disabilities. *Journal of Applied Research in Intellectual Disabilities* 15: 179–182.

Blacker, J., Beech, A.R., Wilcox, D.T. et al. (2011). The assessment of dynamic risk and recidivism in a sample of special needs sexual offenders. *Psychology, Crime & Law* 17 (1): 75–92.

Boer, D.P., Tough, S., and Haaven, J. (2004). Assessment of risk manageability of intellectually disabled sex offenders. *Journal of Applied Research in Intellectual Disabilities* 17: 275–283.

Booth, B., Fedoroff, J.P., Curry, S. et al. (2006). Sleep apnea as a possible factor contributing to aggression in sex offenders. *The Journal of Forensic Sciences* 51: 1178–1181.

Bradley, E. and Burke, L. (2002). Offenders who have a developmental disability. In: *Dual Diagnosis: An Introduction to the Mental Health Needs of Persons with Developmental Disabilities* (eds. D. Griffiths, C. Stavrakaki and J. Summers), 45–79. Sudbury, ON: Habilitative Mental Health Resource Network.

Brown, I. and Percy, M. (2007). An introduction to assessment, diagnosis, intervention, and services. In: *A Comprehensive Guide to Intellectual & Developmental Disabilities* (eds. I. Brown and M. Percy), 335–350. Baltimore, MD: Paul, H. Brookes Publishing Co.

Charlot, L.R., Benson, B.A., Fox, M. et al. (2016). Depressive Disorders. In: *Diagnostic Manual – Intellectual Disability – 2: A Textbook of Diagnosis of Mental Disorders in Persons with Intellectual Disability* (eds. R.J. Fletcher, J. Barnhill and S. Cooper), 265–302. Kingston, NY: NADD Press.

Cox-Lindenbaum, D. and Watson, S. (2002). Sexual assault against persons with developmental disabilities. In: *Sexuality: Ethical Dilemmas* (eds. D. Griffiths, D. Richards, P. Fedoroff, et al.), 293–330. Kingston, NY: NADD Press.

Day, K. (1994). Male mentally handicapped sex offenders. *British Journal of Psychiatry* 165: 630–639.

Dykens, E.M. and Hodapp, R.M. (2001). Research in mental retardation: toward an etiologic approach. *Journal of Child Psychology and Psychiatry* 42 (1): 49–71.

Edgerton, R.B. (1967). *The Coak of Competence: Stigma in the Lives of the Mentally Retarded*. San Francisco: University of California Press.

Fedoroff, J.P. and Richards, D. (2010). Sexual disorders and intellectual disabilities. In: *Handbook of Clinical Sexuality for Mental Health Professionals*, 2e (ed. S. Levine), 451–468. New York, NY: Brunner/Routledge.

Fedoroff, J.P. and Richards, D. (2013). An experiment concerning ethical issues in the care of people with intellectual disailities and potentially problematic sexual behaviours. *Journal of Ethics in Mental Health* 7: 1–9.

Fedoroff, J.P., Richards, D., Ranger, R. et al. (2016). Factors related to sexual re-offense in men with intellectual disabilities and problematic sexual behaviour. *Research in Developmental Disabilities* 57: 29–38.

Fletcher, R.J., Loschen, E., Stavrakaki, C. et al. (2007). *Diagnostic Manual-Intellectual Disability: A Clinical Guide for Diagnosis of Mental Disorders in Persons with Intellectual Disability*. Kingston, NY: NADD Press.

Fletcher, R.J., Barnhill, J., and Cooper, S. (2016). *Diagnostic Manual – Intellectual Disability – 2: A Textbook of Diagnosis of Mental Disorders in Persons with Intellectual Disability*, 33–62. Kingston, NY: NADD Press.

Fudge-Schormans, A. and Sobsey, D. (2007). Maltreatment of children with developmental disabilities. In: *A Comprehensive Guide to Intellectual & Developmental Disabilities* (eds. I. Brown and M. Percy), 467–488. Baltimore, MD: Paul, H. Brookes Publishing Co.

Gardner, W.I. (1998). Understanding challenging behaviours. In: *Behavioural Supports: Individual Centred Interventions, a Multimodal Functional Approach* (eds. D.M. Griffiths, W.I. Gardner and J. Nugent), 7–16. Kingston, NY: NADD Press.

Gardner, W.I. (2002). Origins of aggression and related disruptive behaviours. In: *Aggression and Other Disruptive Behavioural Challenges: Biomedical and Psychosocial Assessment and Treatment* (ed. W.I. Gardner), 43–68. Kingston, NY: NADD Press.

Griffiths, D.M., Gardner, W.I., and Nugent, J.A. (eds.) (1998). Introduction. In: *Behavioural Supports: Individual Centred Interventions, a Multimodal Functional Approach*, 1–6. Kingston, NY: NADD Press.

Griffiths, D. and Lunsky, Y. (2003). *Sociosexual Knowledge and Attitudes Assessment Tool (SSKAAT-R)*. Wood Dale, IL: Stoelting Company.

Griffiths, D.M., Quinsey, V.L., and Hingsburger, D. (1989). *Changing Inappropriate Sexual Behavior: A Community Based Approach for Persons with Intellectual Disabilities*. Baltimore, MD: Paul H. Brookes Publishing.

Griffiths, D.M., Hoath, J., Ioannou, S. et al. (accepted for publication). *Sex Offending Behaviour of Persons with an Intellectual Disability: A Multi-Component Applied Behaviour Analytic Approach*. Kingston, NY: NADD Press.

Haut, F. and Brewster, E. (2010). Psychiatric illness, pervasive developmental disorders and risk. In: *Assessment and Treatment of Sexual Offenders with Intellectual Disabilities: A Handbook* (eds. L.A. Craig, W.R. Lindsay and K.D. Browne), 89–110. Chichester, UK: Wiley.

Hellings, J.A. et al. (2016). Attention-deficit/hyperactivity disorder. In: *Diagnostic Manual-Intellectual Disability textbook of Mental Disorders in Persons with Intellectual disability (DM-ID 2)* (eds. R.J. Fletcher, J. Barnhill and S.-A. Cooper). New York: NADD Press.

Hobson, B. and Rose, J.L. (2008). The mental health of people with intellectual disabilities who offend. *The Open Criminology Journal* 1: 12–18.

Humphries, T. (2007). Attention-deficit/hyperactivity disorder. In: *A Comprehensive Guide to Intellectual & Developmental Disabilities* (eds. I. Brown and M. Percy), 295–308. Baltimore, MD: Paul H. Brookes Publishing.

Ingham, B., Clarke, L., and James, I.A. (2008). Biospsychosocial case formulation for people with intellectual disabilities and mental health problems: a pilot study of a training workshop for direct care staff. *The British Journal of Developmental Disabilities* 54 (106): 41–54.

Jones, J. (2007). Persons with intellectual disabilities in the criminal justice system. *International Journal of Offender Therapy and Comparative Criminology* 651 (6): 723–733.

Kiddle, H. and Dagnan, D. (2011). Vulnerability to depression in adolescents with intellectual disabilities. *Advances in Mental Health and Intellectual Disabilities* 5 (1): 3–8.

Langdon, P.E. and Murphy, G.H. (2010). Assessing treatment need in sexual offenders with intellectual disabilities. In: *Assessment and Treatment of Sexual Offenders with Intellectual Disabilities: A Handbook* (eds. L.A. Craig, W.R. Lindsay and K.D. Browne), 233–251. Chichester, UK: Wiley.

Levitas, A., Dykens, E., Finucane, B. et al. (2007). Behavioral phenotypes of genetic disorders. In: *Diagnostic Manual – Intellectual Disability: A Textbook of Diagnosis of Mental Disorders in Persons with Intellectual Disability* (eds. R. Fletcher, E. Loschen, C. Stavrakaki, et al.), 33–62. Kingston, NY: NADD Press.

Lindsay, W.R., Holland, A.J., Taylor, J.L. et al. (2009). Diagnostic information and adversity in childhood for offenders with learning disabilities referred to and accepted into forensic services. *Advances in Mental Health and Learning Disabilities* 3 (4): 19–24.

Lunsky, Y. and Bradley, E. (2001). Developmental disability training in Canadian psychiatry residency program. *Canadian Journal of Psychiatry* 46: 138–143.

Lunsky, Y., Frijters, J., Griffiths, D.M. et al. (2007). Sexual knowledge and attitudes of men with intellectual disability who sexually offend. *Journal of Intellectual & Developmental Disability* 32 (2): 74–81.

Martorell, A., Tsakanikos, E., Pereda, A. et al. (2009). Mental health in adults with mild and moderate intellectual disabilities: the role of recent life events and traumatic experiences across the life span. *The Journal of Nervous and Mental Disease* 197 (3): 182–186.

McCarthy, J., Blanca, R.A., Gaus, V.L. et al. (2016). Trauma and stressor related disorders. In: *Diagnostic Manual – Intellectual Disability – 2: A Textbook of Diagnosis of Mental Disorders in Persons with Intellectual Disability* (eds. R.J. Fletcher, J. Barnhill and S. Cooper), 353–400. Kingston, NY: NADD Press.

Putnam, C., (2009). Guidelines for understanding and serving people with ID and mental, emotional and behavioural disorders. Tallahassee: Florida Developmental Disabilities Council. http://www.nasddds.org/uploads/documents/Florida_DD_Council_Guidelines_for_Dual_Diagnosis.pdf (accessed 5 March 2018).

Razzo, N.J. and Tomasulo, D.J. (2005). *Healing Trauma: The Power of Group Treatment for People with Intellectual Disabilities*. Washington, DC: American Psychological Association.

Reiss, S., Levitan, G., and Szyszko, J. (1982). Emotional disturbance and mental retardation: diagnostic overshadowing. *American Journal of Mental Deficiency* 86: 567–574.

Richards, D. and Fedoroff, J.P. (2016). Helping those with intellectual disabilities. In: *Handbook of Clinical Sexuality for Mental Health Professionals*, 2e (eds. S.B. Levine, C.B. Risen and S.E. Althof), 250–262. New York: Brunner/Routledge.

Richards, D., Stromski, S., and Griffiths, D. (accepted for publication). Challenges in community supports for offenders who have intellectual disabilities. In V. Marinos, S. Stromski, L. Whittingham et al. (ed.), Navigating the Justice System: Offenders Who Have an Intellectual Disability.

Riches, V.C., Parmenter, T.R., Wiese, M. et al. (2006). Intellectual disability and mental illness in the NSW criminal justice system. *International Journal of Law and Psychiatry* 29: 386–396.

Sequeira, H., Howlin, P., and Hollins, S. (2003). Psychological disturbance associated with sexual abuse in people with learning disabilities. *British Journal of Psychiatry* 183: 451–456.

Sobsey, D. (1994). Sexual abuse of individuals with intellectual disability. In: *Practice Issues in Sexuality and Learning Disabilities* (ed. A. Craft), 91–111. London: Routledge.

Summers, J., Stavrakaki, C., Griffithe, D.M. et al. (2002). Comprehensive screening and assessment. In: *Dual Diagnosis: An Introduction to the Mental Health Needs of Persons with Developmental Disabilities* (eds. D.M. Griffiths, C. Stavrakaki and J. Summers), 151–191. Sudbury, ON: Habilitative Mental Health Resource Network.

Vidovic, P.J. (2012). Neuro-cognitive impairments and the criminal justice system: A case analysis of the impact of diagnoses of FASD and ADHD on the sentencing of offenders in the courts of three Canadian provinces. Dissertation, Simon Fraser University, British Columbia, Canada. http://summit.sfu.ca/system/files/iritems1/12312/etd7253_PJonasVidovic.pdf (accessed 5 November 2017).

Watson, S., Richards, D., Miodrag, N. et al. (2012). Sex and genes part I: sexuality and Down, Prader Willi, and Williams syndromes. *American Association for Intellectual and Developmental Disabilities, (AAIDD)* 50 (2): 155–168.

Xenitidis, K., Paliokosta, E., Rose, E. et al. (2010). ADHD symptom presentation and trajectory in adults with borderline and mild intellectual disability. *Journal of Intellectual Disability Research* 54 (7): 668–677.

12

Using a Multicomponent Model in the Assessment of Persons with Intellectual Disabilities and Problems in Sexual Behaviour

Robin J. Wilson[1,2]*, Stephanie Ioannou*[3]*, and Kendra Thomson*[4]

[1] *McMaster University, Hamilton, Canada*
[2] *Wilson Psychology Services LLC, Sarasota, FL, USA*
[3] *Kerry's Place Autism Services, Aurora, Canada*
[4] *Brock University, St. Catharines, Canada*

12.1 Introduction

Whether or not treatment reduces recidivism in persons who have sexually offended is still something of an unanswered question, in that reviews typically point to less than advantageous research methods as hindering full demonstration of efficacy (e.g. Långström et al. 2013). As a subpopulation, the treatment experiences and successes or failures of individuals with Intellectual and Developmental Disorders (IDD – American Psychiatric Association [APA] 2013) who have sexually offended are also a matter of debate. Although current discussions have focused on the relative benefits or inadequacies of the research methods used to demonstrate efficacy, there has been a tendency to see the glass as half-empty when considering the treatment and risk management of those who engage in sexual violence.

The 'nothing works' perspective that grew out of ultimately incorrect findings about the relative benefit of rehabilitative programming over sanction-alone has been one of the most enduring myths in correctional practice (Martinson 1974). Although Martinson sought to clarify his original proclamation (1979), there is still a nagging belief amongst many corrections administrators that 'treatment doesn't work' and that it is therefore not worth paying for. A case in point is the USA where criminal sanction has generally taken precedence over options for rehabilitative interventions. Sentences in the USA are typically significantly longer than most other countries and the per capita rate of incarceration remains the highest in the world. Often, the US approach has been to 'lock' em up and throw away the keys'. Alarmingly, aspects of this approach to crime reduction have taken hold in other international jurisdictions, in the form of mandatory minimum sentences and highly restrictive post-release conditions that ultimately promote return to custody for violations more often than for commission of new crimes. This is particularly true of persons convicted of sexual offences. Because

The Wiley Handbook on What Works for Offenders with Intellectual and Developmental Disabilities: An Evidence-Based Approach to Theory, Assessment, and Treatment, First Edition.
Edited by William R. Lindsay, Leam A. Craig, and Dorothy Griffiths.
© 2020 John Wiley & Sons Ltd. Published 2020 by John Wiley & Sons Ltd.

they represent an often misunderstood group, individuals with IDD may actually receive more restrictive care than their neuro-typical peers. Further, because of their some-times complex presentations, clients with IDD are also more likely to already have been subject to placement in a care facility (e.g. hospital, group home, etc.) where their freedoms have already been curtailed.

Individuals who commit sexual offences are amongst the most reviled persons in the world, and contemporary criminal justice approaches to sexual violence prevention have tended to emphasize containment over rehabilitation. Examples include enhanced sentencing guidelines, public registries and notification, residency restrictions, and other measures intended to contain risk for reoffending, but that might actually pro-duce iatrogenic results through social isolation and inability to develop stability in the community (Levenson and Hern 2007). Further, opportunities for rehabilitative pro-gramming are often few and far between. In the USA, nearly half of the country utilizes sex offender civil commitment (SOCC) – essentially, post-sentence involuntary and indeterminate detention in a 'state hospital' for 'care, control, and treatment' (see Brandt et al. 2015). Although SOCC has traditionally been a US-only approach, other jurisdic-tions (e.g. Australia) have been experimenting with similar approaches. In many instances – at least in the USA – persons who had committed sexual offences were not afforded an opportunity to complete sexual behaviour process treatment whilst in prison prior to being considered for SOCC. In some cases, this process may delay reha-bilitative attention to the problem leading to criminal sanction until literally decades after the offence(s) occurred. The personal experiences of author Robin J. Wilson with SOCC would suggest that the patient censuses of such centres typically include 10–20% persons with IDD who have sexually offended.

Although the literature regarding the relative benefits of treatment for persons who have sexually offended is by no means clear, every meta-analysis completed to date – whether with neuro-typical clients (e.g. Hanson et al. 2002; Schmucker and Lösel 2015) or clients with IDD (e.g. Cohen and Harvey 2016; Marotta 2017) – has shown a small but significant decrease in rates of reoffending for those who complete treatment. Theoretically, that would mean that waiting until sentence completion to offer treat-ment and then using SOCC on the back end may not be a reasonable expenditure of public funds. It stands to reason that a system that 'believed' in rehabilitative efforts would not want to wait until after someone has served a lengthy period of incarceration before offering programming aimed at rehabilitation. A cynical person might opine that SOCC merely represents a way to keep those 'reviled' individuals out of the public eye for as long as possible, and that rehabilitation may not be the major goal of SOCC – in spite of the fact that US Supreme Court findings have traditionally focused more on treatment than incapacitation (see Brandt et al. 2015).

Given the findings of several meta-analyses (e.g. Smith et al. 2002; Aos et al. 2006; Lipsey and Cullen 2007), there can be little doubt that using incarceration and other containment-style approaches without significant focus on rehabilitation will ultimately not substantively contribute to public safety. The findings of these large-scale studies-of-studies show clearly that punishment alone will not reduce bad behaviour and that it is only through the application of human service programming that individuals who have offended will be able to make significant strides towards leading lives marked by prosociality, lifestyle balance, and effective self-determination. In our work with persons with IDD who have sexually offended, we are continually reminded that *disabled* does not mean *disinclined* and that different levels of *capability* can be accommodated through individualized programming emphasizing attention to the responsivity principle (see next section; also Peel Behavioural Services and Wilson 2017).

12.2 Effective Interventions

In answer to Martinson's nothing works proclamation, criminology researchers sought to gain a better understanding of the relationship between interventions and outcomes. The most prominent of these researchers were Andrews and Bonta from Canada. Their seminal text – *The Psychology of Criminal Conduct* – is now in its sixth edition (Bonta and Andrews 2017) and the risk-need-responsivity (RNR) model included in that work now underpins the majority of Western correctional services. Although often misunderstood as a model of treatment, RNR is more properly described as an overarching framework in which interventions are more likely to succeed.

Simply put, the RNR model posits that effective interventions will appropriately match intensity of intervention to assessed level of risk whilst attending to criminogenic needs in a manner that promotes motivation to change and accommodates client learning styles and other idiosyncratic elements. Problems arise when intensity and risk are mismatched, and this is not only true when high-risk individuals are under-serviced, it also applies when low-risk individuals are over-serviced. Similarly, problems also arise when focus in interventions is on issues unrelated to propensity for re-engagement in criminal conduct – for example, focus on self-esteem when such focus is unrelated to risk for reoffence. Bonta and Andrews (2017) show clearly that the focus should be on dynamic risk variables on which the individual has demonstrated difficulty (e.g. substance abuse, lack of social skills, antisocial orientation). However, notwithstanding potential issues with implementation along the risk and need dimensions, it appears that problems are most likely to arise in regard to responsivity.

12.2.1 Responsivity

Ensuring that clients who have offended are able to better understand their problematic attitudes and behaviours and to make realistic prosocial changes in their lives can be a tall order. This is likely to be complicated from the beginning by the prevalence of Antisocial Personality Disorder, which ranges from 35% to nearly 50% amongst male prison inmates depending on which study you endorse (see Black et al. 2010 or Busari 2015, respectively). So, encouraging persons who have offended to abandon their natural tendency to eschew correctional interventions will present difficulties as many clients referred to programming will initially present as precontemplative and unwilling to consider that their current predicament is related to things that they did (see DiClemente and Prochaska 1998); with respect to sexual offenders, see also Stirpe et al. 2001; Barrett et al. 2003). This can be particularly true for persons convicted of sexual offences who are keenly aware of what life in the community will look like for them as members of that aforementioned highly reviled group. All of this presents potent barriers to change and ultimate success in the community.

A major component to ensuring that interventions are responsive to the clients they seek to assist is consideration of client learning styles and intellectual abilities. By way of a simple example, it stands to reason that persons who are illiterate or who demonstrate cognitive limitations (e.g. clients with intellectual disability, brain injuries, or severe mental illness) will likely do poorly in manualized programmes with significant cognitive load. Indeed, in such situations, many such clients will withdraw, become apathetic, or drop out of interventions. And, whilst these outcomes may be reasonable given client inabilities to appropriately respond to programming, those outcomes are also often interpreted as lack of motivation for change, resistance, or antisocial obstinance. Accordingly, providing interventions that adhere to the responsivity principle is of paramount importance and, actually, we would suggest that responsivity has to pervade all aspects of our work with clients who have engaged in problematic behaviours. Craig and Hutchinson (2005) argued that persons with IDD who have sexually offended are unlikely to complete programmes that are not adapted to meet their needs. Barron et al. (2004) found little evidence for the efficacy of therapeutic interventions that were non-specific to people with learning disabilities. As such, attention to responsivity concerns for clients with IDD is of the utmost importance.

12.2.2 Attending to Responsivity When Applying the Risk and Need Principles

The last 30 years have been witness to considerable advances in risk assessment methods for persons who have sexually offended, with some of those advancements having been specific to persons with IDD. Advancements and refinements have been made to testing procedures designed to highlight inappropriate/paraphilic sexual interests or preferences (Wilson and Miner 2016; Thornton et al. 2018). Further, the late 1990s saw the introduction of actuarial risk assessment instruments (ARAI; e.g. Static-99-R – see Hanson et al. 2017) which, in many ways, revolutionized the risk-assessment process by injecting a much-needed element of science and objectivity. Although controversy remains as to the true predictive value of such measures (Campbell and DeClue 2010; Wilson and Looman 2010), we also now have several options for structured and empirically informed consideration of dynamic factors (i.e. lifestyle management and personality variables also sometimes referred to as criminogenic needs – see Hanson et al. 2007; McGrath et al. 2012; Brankley et al. 2017). One such dynamic risk tool created specifically for use with persons with IDD who have sexually offended is the Assessment of Risk and Manageability for Individuals with Developmental and Intellectual Limitations who Offend-Sexually (ARMIDILO-S; Boer et al. 2013), which we will discuss in greater detail below.

A major difficulty in the development of methods to assess risk and need has been that the majority of those methods have focused on clients without IDD. Although it may be true that many instruments include some number of individuals with disabilities or severe mental illness, there are very few mainstream tools that focus precisely on these clients. Although research on the utility of ARAIs has been conducted on persons with IDD and sexual offence histories (Lindsay et al. 2008), it seems that the field continually tries to make the clients conform to the tools rather than the tools to the clients. It is reasonable to conclude that the inappropriate behaviours of many clients with IDD may not always have the same aetiology, life course, or treatment prognosis as their neuro-typical peers (Blasingame et al. 2014).

Many practitioners working with persons with IDD who have sexually offended approach treatment from an applied behaviour analytic framework (ABA; see Griffiths et al. 2019, described later) in their attempts to better understand why their clients did what they did and how best to help them avoid such actions in the future. In this vein, considering who the client is and understanding his life circumstances, prior to engaging in assessment or treatment construction, will likely lead to better outcomes. We are also aware that punitive measures involving aversive consequences have often been used under the guise of behavioural approaches – especially with disabled persons – and we wish to draw a clear distinction between those methods and the ABA processes we are advocating here. As noted elsewhere in this chapter, punishment alone has a particularly poor history in regard to efficacy, whereas the ABA framework holds greater promise for long-term effects (see Griffiths et al. 2019).

Current research supports a holistic, strength-based, multifactorial approach to working with persons with IDD and sexual offending behaviour. In practice however, consensus is lacking as to which assessment methods are most effective for determining appropriate interventions. In 1996, Wulfert and colleagues proposed a logical functional analysis that suggested if functional clusters of behaviour could be identified for sexually offensive behaviour (specifically, paedophilia), then a stronger link could be formed between assessment and treatment (Wulfert et al. 1996). This approach has been validated for treating other challenging behaviours such as aggression and self-injury in persons with IDD for many years in the field of ABA.

Griffiths et al. (2019) proposed a multicomponent, function-based decision model based on Wulfert et al. (1996) and many years of well-established behavioural analytic methodologies (see Figure 12.1). The model is not new conceptually, but rather a refinement of strategies that have empirical support with the neuro-typical population,

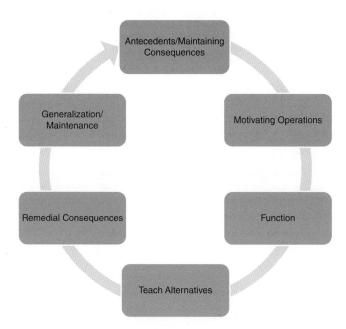

Figure 12.1 Components of the decision model for assessment and intervention for sexualized offending behaviour. *Source:* Reprinted with permission from Griffiths et al. (2019).

applied to people with IDD and sexualized offending behaviour. Written for individuals with backgrounds in behaviour analytic principles, Griffiths et al. (2019) present a comprehensive and function-based behavioural assessment model including nuances that are vital for guiding effective intervention for persons with IDD and sexualized offending behaviour. The six components of the model assemble into three categories: (i) *Assessment,* which includes determining the variables that contribute to the function (cause) of the behaviour; (ii) *Treatment* based on the assessment results, which includes teaching alternative or coping skills, and providing remedial consequences; and (iii) *Generalization and Maintenance*, which aims to ensure that positive outcomes maintain over time and occur across various conditions, people, settings, and situations.

12.3   Assessment of Sexual Offending Behaviour within a Multicomponent ABA Treatment Program

Assessment of sexual offending behaviour utilizing the principles of ABA should follow the same process as behavioural assessment for other problematic behaviours, within a holistic comprehensive approach. Although some theoretical explanations for sexual offending behaviours exist, they often do not take into consideration contextual variables and, therefore, do not directly determine function.

12.3.1   Functional Behaviour Assessment

Determining the cause(s) of a behaviour through a comprehensive functional behaviour assessment (FBA) that evaluates variables associated with challenging behaviours and designs treatment based on results, is considered best practice for persons with IDD (Dixon et al. 2012). This assessment approach as traditionally applied has not typically been employed to assess and treat sexualized offending behaviour although these behaviours also serve functions that need to be considered in treatment. The FBA process gathers information about the variables that are functionally related to the behaviour, which then helps practitioners to identify an effective treatment for the problem behaviour (Miltenberger 1997). That is, comprehensive interventions that include functional replacement training require a complete understanding of which variables motivate and maintain the behaviour in order to identify more appropriate replacement behaviours that serve the same function. This process needs careful consideration when behaviours are sexual in nature, as the functional categories are complex due to people with IDD having drastically different life experiences, cultural mores, learning styles, and personal histories. These influencing factors are a critical aspect of a comprehensive behavioural assessment.

The FBA process includes a combination of indirect measures (interviews, questionnaires, and so on), descriptive/direct measures (direct observation without manipulation, antecedent, behaviour, consequence data, and so on), and experimental functional analysis (EFA) (direct observation with systematic manipulation of environmental events) (Iwata et al. 1982, 1990, 1994; Hanley 2012). The key features to be assessed in this process are described in Table 12.1.

Table 12.1 Key features of functional behaviour assessment (FBA).

Motivating Operations	Include both: 1) Value-altering effects (increases or decreases the value of a stimulus as a reinforcer or punisher) 2) Behaviour-altering effects (increases or decreases behaviours associated with obtaining or avoiding the stimulus).
Setting Event	Increases the likelihood that an antecedent will trigger behaviour and vary in their temporal extent from the behaviour occurring (e.g. emotional states may increase the likelihood of certain behaviours occurring).
Antecedent	Any environmental condition or stimulus change that precedes a behaviour and exerts control over the behaviour. Identifiable antecedents can be modified to impact behaviour.
Behaviour	Anything an individual says or does that has an impact on the environment (can include private events such as verbal behaviour)
Consequence	Any environmental condition or stimulus change that follows a behaviour and has varying effects on the probability of the behaviour occurring in the future. Determines what variables maintain the behaviour through positive or negative reinforcement, or positive or negative punishment). Identifiable consequences can be modified to impact behaviour.
Reinforcement	*Positive reinforcement* – a desirable consequence follows a behaviour (e.g. attention or sexual gratification). *Negative reinforcement* – an aversive consequence is removed or avoided as a result of a behaviour (e.g. termination of an aversive emotional state, such as anger). Both reinforcement processes lead to an increase in the likelihood that the behaviour will occur in the future.
Punishment	*Positive punishment* – an aversive stimulus follows a behaviour (e.g. legal sanctions). *Negative punishment* – a desirable stimulus is removed following a behaviour (e.g. loss of privileges). Both punishment processes lead to a decrease in the probability of the behaviour occurring in the future.

12.3.1.1 Direct Observation Methods

Directly observing the antecedents and consequences to behaviour without manipulating variables in the environment provides structural information about *what* is happening and can provide valuable information in predicting *why* it is occurring. Therefore, direct observations provide useful predictive information, but do not provide definitive information about causal factors, or *why* a behaviour is occurring (Wacker et al. 2011). Direct observation of sexualized offending behaviour is challenging due to practical and ethical considerations. These behaviours are difficult to predict and typically occur at low frequency, with significant and immediate consequences. Further, it is far too dangerous to evoke these behaviours for the purposes of direct assessment especially given that other vulnerable persons may be in the environment (Vollmer et al. 2012). When the behaviours do occur, they often occur in private, and individuals typically go to great extremes to conceal the behaviour due to the reinforcing and potentially punishing consequences. Given the challenges with direct observation of sexual offending behaviours clinicians may need to be creative in the assessment process, by directly observing the precursor behaviours with careful clinical and ethical review to ensure they are justifiable and properly conducted (Griffiths et al. 2019), as well as relying more on indirect functional assessment methodology.

12.3.1.2 Indirect Functional Assessment

Indirect assessment methods can include gathering information from past incidences, reviewing evaluation reports, and conducting behavioural interviews/questionnaires with the individual and others familiar with the individual. The Functional Assessment Interview (FAI; O'Neill et al. 1997) is often used to assess persons with challenging behaviours and can also be used to gather information on inappropriate sexual behaviour. Fredericks and Nishioka-Evans (1999) suggested that a comprehensive assessment of sexual violence potential includes a social and family history and a review of medical, clinical, and psychiatric reports, as well as a behavioural history. The individual themselves can also provide important data for the functional assessment (Fredericks and Nishioka-Evans 1999), which may be potentially biased by both the secretive nature of the behaviours and the threat of punishment. The individual may also face challenges due to communication skills, expression of feelings, and in providing pertinent details such as a timeframe. The therapist can seek information from the person about the offences, the onset of offending, sexual preferences, and specific circumstances surrounding the offence. Lindsay et al. (2007) suggested that another key factor to examine is the individual's knowledge of the mores and laws of society, and understanding regarding which are applicable to the individual and have real consequences. The intended outcome of indirect functional assessments is to generate objective information. However, the process contains inherent limitations such as biases and/or inaccurate information. Therefore, these methods must be combined using direct methods or experimental analyses of directly observable precursor behaviours.

Table 12.2 includes an example of a man who touched a young boy's genitals in the washroom stall of a department store and demonstrates how the key components of FBA of behaviour relate to the behaviour. We recognize that the example in Table 12.2 is a very simplistic example of a behaviour that is much more complex and multifaceted. However, all behaviour occurs in a context, and it is important to assess and analyse sexual behaviour both in the context of the contingencies that have impacted the individual throughout their life as well as at the time of the offence. This is a defining feature of the multicomponent model.

Table 12.2 Example of sexual offending behaviour within the context of the key features of the functional behaviour assessment FBA process.

Motivating Operations	Setting Events	Antecedents	Behaviour	Consequences
In a state of sexual arousal but deprived of appropriate sexual gratification	Feeling angry about a change in routine Lack of self-regulation or/coping skills	Alone in the washroom Saw a young boy who was also alone	Touched the young boy's genitals	Sexual gratification (automatic reinforcement) No negative repercussions

12.3.1.3 EFA Methods

The aim of an EFA is to determine the cause of behaviour, or *why it* is occurring. The process involves manipulating motivating operations/setting events/antecedent stimuli and consequent events/stimuli to evoke the target behaviour in order to determine which variables are maintaining the behaviour.

Classic research studies involving persons with IDD have provided empirical support for functional categories for behaviour including: (i) socially mediated positive reinforcement (e.g. behaviour that is maintained by access to desired stimuli such as attention or preferred items – see Lovaas et al. 1965; Carr 1977); (ii) socially and non-socially mediated negative reinforcement (e.g. behaviour that is maintained by escape or avoidance of aversive stimuli/situations, such as pain reduction or demands – see Carr et al. 1980); and (iii) automatic reinforcement (e.g. behaviour that is maintained by the reinforcement that is produced automatically when the behaviour occurs – see Skinner 1957; Rincover et al. 1979). It is also possible, and common, for behaviour to be maintained by a combination of functions or be under the control of idiosyncratic variables such as the presence of certain stimuli in the environment (e.g. attention from a specific individual vs. attention in general). More recent research in ABA has shown that these contingencies can operate on their own or simultaneously and can be assessed as such, described further later (Hanley et al. 2014).

Although the EFA methodology has been empirically validated for determining the function of various challenging behaviours and in turn, prioritizing areas for individualized treatment (Iwata et al. 1982, 1994; McGuire 2001), EFAs for sexual behaviour are rife with ethical and practical challenges. Similar to assessing other severe behaviours such as self-injurious behaviour, it is difficult, and potentially unethical, to set up conditions to evoke the behaviour. Some exceptions in the literature exist (e.g. Smith and Churchill 2002) which have evaluated the value of examining the function of precursor behaviours that are associated with a specific dangerous behaviour. Also, Najdowski et al. (2008) identified that there was functional similarity between the strength of precursor behaviours and severity of problem behaviours, such as those that are sexually inappropriate. In these cases, conducting a functional analysis may be unethical, and therefore the identification of the function of precursor behaviours may serve as a basis for development of functional-based treatment (see also Wright et al. 1992; Fyffe et al. 2004). To address the ethical and practical challenges of using EFA with sexual offending behaviour, it is applicable to use this methodology on precursor sexual offending behaviours that are non-contact offences. For example, an EFA could be utilized with precursor behaviours for public masturbation, public exposure, stalking, or accessing child pornography.

12.3.1.4 Other Components of the FBA Process

A comprehensive FBA for sexualized behaviour should include other types of assessments such as: biomedical, risk, deviance/paraphilia (see American Psychiatric Association 2013), cognitive distortion/attitudes, and sexual knowledge/skill deficits.

12.3.1.4.1 Biomedical

A physical examination by a qualified medical professional should precede behavioural interventions to explore and rule out biomedical influences such as pain, discomfort, psychiatric conditions, and medication side effects (Axelrod 1987). Baker et al. (2002)

suggested that current behavioural assessments should be adapted to also evaluate the role that biomedical issues may play in presenting a behavioural symptom. They suggested, for example, that physiological arousal might be seen as an antecedent event for many problem behaviours. Gardner (2002) cautioned, however, that physical, psychiatric, or physiological challenges do not trigger the occurrence of a challenging behaviour; rather, they represent a vulnerability that may contribute to the behaviour in the presence of other environmental stimuli (such as specific social triggers). However, as Baker et al. (2002) suggested, adaptations to the traditional behavioural assessment could be made to expand the observations to include these factors.

12.3.1.4.2 Risk Assessment

Specialized methods to assess clients with IDD and sexual behaviour problems have included questionnaires tailored to the population, as well as measures of dynamic risk potential (and, more recently, preventive factors). Regarding the former, Broxholme and Lindsay (2003) developed the Questionnaire on Attitudes Consistent with Sexual Offending (QACSO), which has been validated for assessment of individuals with IDD and has good psychometric support. With respect to dynamic risk potential, the (ARMIDILO-S; Boer et al. 2013) is a measure of structured professional judgement specifically aimed at identifying dynamic risk and preventive factors. Modelled after the Stable-2007 (Hanson et al. 2007; Brankley et al. 2017), the ARMIDILO-S has the benefit of not only considering client-driven sources of risk or protection, but also sources of strength or difficulty that emanate from the environment in which clients live. Given that a large number of persons with IDD reside in care facilities (e.g. hospitals, group homes) or work in sheltered workshops (e.g. ARC Industries), it is of critical importance that issues of environment or external influence (staff, peers, and so on) be considered.

The Static-99R (Hanson et al. 2017) is a commonly used risk assessment that assesses static (unchanging) risk factors amongst the typically developing population. Some of the items on the Static-99R have the capacity to inflate the risk score for people with IDD, due to the nature of the lives people with IDD live (i.e. many people with IDD have not lived with a partner for more than two years). In one study, the Rapid Risk Assessment of Sexual Offence Recidivism (RRASOR; Hanson 1997) was suggested to be a better predictor of risk for people with IDD, potentially due to greater focus on variables relevant to this population (Tough 2001). However, more recent cross-validation studies have shown that the Static-99R is the best predictor for sexual reoffence for people with IDD (Lindsay et al. 2008; Hanson et al. 2013).

Sexual Deviance vs. Counterfeit Deviance: An important aspect of assessment is to determine if the individual's behaviour is sexually deviant (or paraphilic, such as sexual interest in children or forced sexual activity) or counterfeit deviant. Counterfeit deviance refers to behaviours that are topographically similar to sexual offences but are not motivated by deviant or sensory functions and may be due to various antecedent conditions or consequences that could be modified. Counterfeit deviance can be the product of experiential, environmental, or medical factors including lack of privacy in the environment, modelling by others, inappropriate partner selection or courtship, lack of sexual knowledge or moral training, a maladaptive learning history, medical disorders, or medication effects (Hingsburger et al. 1991; Griffiths et al. 2013). Assessing for sexual deviance has traditionally been done using penile plethysmography (phallometric testing), however using this method with people with IDD is questionable since it was validated on the neuro-typical population (Wilson and Burns 2011). Many methods for assessing sexual interests in people with IDD are not standardized but are 'the best we have', such as a card sort test. Typical cart sort test includes a series of pictures of men, women, adolescents, and children, and the individual is asked a series of questions such as, 'Pick who you would like to date', 'Pick who you would like to kiss', and 'Pick who you would like to have sex with'. To account for the individual answering in ways they know is the socially acceptable answer, an additional question can be included: 'If there were no rules, no laws, and nobody would ever find out, who would you pick to have sex with?' The card sort also includes an age discrimination portion, where the individual is asked to differentiate between age groups (e.g. 'show me all the children').

Arousal graphs (Worling 2006) are a self-report method used to assess for sexual interest in typically developing adolescents, and have been successfully used in practice with people with IDD. The individual is presented with a simple line graph, where the x-axis represents different age groups, and the y axis represents level of sexual arousal (1 = low arousal, 10 = high arousal; with force or without force). The clinician identifies the age group being assessed, and then asks the individual to rate their level of arousal by drawing a mark on the graph.

Cognitive Distortions/Attitudes Consistent with Offending: Cognitive distortions, or the individual's attitudes that facilitate and support offending, serve as rule-governed behaviour and increase the likelihood of a sexual offence (Wulfert et al. 1996; Lindsay et al. 2007). An offender's faulty rule statements may allow them to deny, minimize, rationalize, and justify their behaviour (Maruna and Mann 2006). Cognitive distortions are assessed using the QASCO (described earlier in this chapter), as well as the Bumby RAPE and MOLEST scales (Bumby 1996).

Sexual Knowledge and Skill Deficits: People with IDD do not receive the same sexual education as neuro-typical people (are often shielded from any sexual education), and live in environments where they do not have the same opportunities to learn or engage in healthy relationships. The Socio-Sexual Knowledge and Attitudes Assessment Tool Revised (SSKAAT-R; Griffiths and Lunsky 2003) is a validated tool that evaluates anatomy, women's, and men's bodies, intimacy, pregnancy, childbirth, birth control/STDs, and healthy boundaries. A lack of sexual knowledge can be a factor in offending within the Counterfeit Deviant group, as people with IDD and sexual deviance have been found to have high sexual knowledge (Michie et al. 2006).

Other skill deficits that should be assessed under a multicomponent behavioural model are understanding of consent (including who can and cannot consent), coping/self-regulation skills such as impulsivity (Barratt Impulsiveness Scale – Patton et al. 1995), as well as looking at skill deficits that were identified from assessing the function of behaviour (e.g. communication skills, anger management, and so forth).

12.3.2 Treatment Based on FBA

Once the function of behaviour has been determined in the assessment phase, intervention strategies must be implemented to address whatever is causing and maintaining the problem behaviour. Next, preventative coping skills and replacement behaviours should be taught. In the case of sexual offending behaviour, treatment may include teaching individuals how to get their sexual needs met in a non-offending way (McGuire 2001) – the most common treatment programmes today are strength-based and focus on self-regulation and the securing of life goals that are common to most people (Yates et al. 2010; Marshall et al. 2011). Achievement of lifestyle balance and self-determinism are central to effective interventions in an RNR framework wherein the responsivity principle requires keen attention (Wilson and Yates 2009). In keeping with the ABA focus of this chapter, consequences for behaviour can be reinforcement or punishment based, natural or contrived. Treatment should consider all environmental variables to which the individual is exposed and attempt to begin with the least intrusive and/or reinforcement-based intervention strategies. It is important to note, however that for very severe problem behaviour, a punishment procedure such as response cost (e.g. loss of privileges) may be a more ethical treatment option than a reinforcement procedure since punishment strategies (which do not necessarily mean aversive) tend to lead to more immediate decreases in behaviour. Other ethical considerations in treatment include the use of psychotropic intervention, isolation, and so forth (Ioannou 2013).

It is most effective to teach alternative functional replacement behaviour in any behaviour-reduction programme (Evans and Meyer 1985). That is, simply reducing the problem behaviour is not sufficient and any treatment gains will likely not maintain or generalize. Clinicians need to ensure that any punishment procedures are supplemented with other reinforcement-based strategies as non-contingent reinforcement, differential reinforcement, and extinction in addition to teaching alternative and more appropriate functionally equivalent behaviour. Also important to consider, is that individuals do not all commit sexualized acts for the same reasons, nor are they reinforced in similar manners (McGuire 2001). Therefore, strategies that may be effective in reducing offences for one individual may have the opposite effects on another and may actually lead to strengthening of their motivation to offend (Hazelwood and Harpold 1986).

12.3.3 Generalization and Maintenance of Treatment Effects

When developing and implementing intervention programmes, it is imperative to consider how to maintain and generalize reductions in inappropriate behaviours and increases in alternative behaviours. Behaviour change is considered generalized if it occurs at other times, with other people and in other places than the intervention setting, without being re-trained, or if a behaviour that is functionally equivalent to the target behaviour emerges untrained (Cooper et al. 2007). A challenging goal of any behavioural treatment programme is to produce desirable outcomes that generalize across people, environments, and behaviours (Stokes and Baer 1977). This is a particularly difficult outcome to achieve in persons with IDD and sexually offending behaviour since the risks for recidivism must be minimized whilst the treatment gains are maximized. Although it is important for any generalized behaviour change to maintain after an intervention is terminated or faded out, it is especially important for any reduction/elimination of sexual offending behaviour as it is vital to the person's future and the safety of others.

Lindsay argued that extended community supervision was more effective than long-term institutionally based programming when considering persons with IDD who have sexually offended (personal communication). This is generally in keeping with the prescriptions of the RNR model regarding a preference for treatment in the community, when safe and feasible (Bonta and Andrews 2017). General strategies to promote generalization and maintenance of treatment gains in any behaviour-reduction programme include selecting target behaviours that will meet naturally occurring contingencies of reinforcement in the individual's environment, specifying all desired variations of the behaviour and the settings and situations where it should and should not occur, teaching the full range of relevant stimulus conditions and response requirements, making the instructional setting similar to the generalization setting, and maximizing the person's contact with reinforcement in the generalization setting, amongst others. We will explore the components of the model in two composites.

12.3.3.1 Composite 1: Tim

Tim is a 25-year-old man with IDD and autism spectrum disorder and was living at home with his mother, father, and younger brother at the time of the index offence. Tim's primary method of communication is gesturing and showing people what he wants; he sometimes verbally says 'yes' and 'no'. He had attended a day programme in his town but was told he could no longer attend due to his offending behaviour against the other clients, and the staff were unable to manage it. Every day at the day programme, he would either pull his trousers down to his ankles and touch his genitals over his underwear, or expose himself to other staff and clients. At home, he would often not go out for weeks at a time because he would do the same in the community. On one occasion when he was grocery shopping with his mother, he dropped his pants and began touching himself in the aisle. Tim was admitted to a mental health unit in a hospital for over a year. The clinicians at the hospital completed assessments and wrote in his file that he was 'sexually deviant'.

An external behavioural consultant then took on Tim's case. The goal was to get him out of the mental health unit, living back at home, and attending his day programme. Both direct and indirect assessments were completed. Tim was observed on multiple occasions on the mental health unit, in which the consultant did observe him pull his pants down and touch himself in common areas of the unit. Indirect assessments (FAI, sexual interest assessments) were completed with his former day programme staff, his mother, and his primary workers on the mental health unit. A complete review of his files was also conducted, including incident reports from the day programme and assessment reports from the mental health unit. The consultant noted that Tim was not taking any medication (thus to rule out potential medication side effects). The consultant administered Sections 3 and 7 (Men's Bodies, Healthy Boundaries) of the SSKAAT-R to determine any possible deficits in sexual knowledge related to this behaviour.

Results from the indirect assessments showed that this was a relatively new behaviour; he had no other history of 'sexual deviance' or inappropriate sexual behaviour. All of Tim's likes and dislikes were noted in the assessments. A review of the incident reports and information gathered from interviews clearly outlined what happened before (antecedents), during (behaviour), and after (consequences) he pulled his trousers down. The exact topography of the behaviour was also noted, and importantly, it was reported that Tim never had an erection during these incidences. The results of the SSKAAT-R showed that Tim had high levels of sexual knowledge in the two areas that were assessed, ruling out a sexual knowledge deficit.

The direct observations on the mental health unit were most telling. The following is a summary of what the consultant observed, on multiple occasions (with some variations). Tim was watching TV (an activity he disliked). He would get up several times and bang on the nursing station window. They repeatedly redirected him back to the TV as they were busy with paperwork. This would occur several times over approximately 30 minutes. Tim would then stand up, pull his trousers down and start touching himself in the common area. Three nurses would come running out to pull his trousers up, and then redirect him to another, more enjoyable activity with 1:1 support to ensure he kept his pants on.

The four-term contingencies in this case were clearly evident across all environments (community, day programme, hospital unit). When Tim was bored, deprived of attention, and/or doing an activity he didn't like (*MO, setting event, antecedent*), he would pull down his trousers, expose, and touch himself (*behaviour*). As a result, he would get out of the activity he disliked, be part of a spectacle of attention and engagement, and be able to do an activity he likes (*maintaining consequences in form of positive reinforcement*).

Tim was not 'sexually deviant' as indicated in reports from the hospital unit. Tim was engaging in a very effective form of escape and attention maintained behaviour, under clear setting events and antecedent conditions.

His parents and day programme staff were trained on the four-term contingency with practical examples related to Tim. Antecedents were modified to ensure he has opportunities to participate in activities he enjoys with other people he could engage with. Tim was taught to functionally communicate when he doesn't like something and socially acceptable ways to get other's attention. At the same time, his caregivers were taught how and when to respond to his communication, including ways to provide high quality attention such that he was not deprived of attention and would seek it inappropriate ways. During the teaching phases, if the behaviour occurred, it could not be completely ignored. However, the amount and quality of attention given to it was significantly reduced, by caregivers/staff responding as minimally and neutral as possible.

The case of Tim highlights an example of counterfeit deviance and the improper application of the risk and responsivity principles. Improper assessments led to the damning label of 'sexual deviance' which resulted in Tim being removed from his home and community and placed in a highly restrictive environment. Through a comprehensive, multicomponent assessment of Tim's life across multiple environments and multiple people, an accurate, individualized intervention could be created that led to functional skill development and active participation in his community.

12.3.3.2 Composite 2: Mark

Mark is a 35-year-old man who was adopted as a baby and lives at home in a small town with his mother and maternal aunt. He is described as a very happy and social man; he is diagnosed with mild intellectual disability and suspected foetal alcohol syndrome disorder (FASD). Mark was very involved in his small town and was well liked by his neighbours. He had seasonal summer jobs for which he was paid to cut all the lawns and shovel the snow in his neighbourhood. Mark has a long history of sexually offensive behaviour with children, which started when he was around 15-years-old and escalated to a contact offence at the age of 35.

As part of a typical assessment, a review of historical factors was completed, through interviews with his mother and aunt, Mark's self-reports, reviewing a psychoeducational report from years prior when Mark was still in school, victim statements, and police reports.

Mark had a history of frequently visiting McDonalds, beaches, parks, and other places that children were likely to be, bringing with him different toys to encourage children to approach and interact with him. His family saw this as innocent, since he is 'like a kid himself'. Mark was active on social media, where he would engage in long chats with the neighbourhood kids. Right after these online chats, he would, on numerous occasions, leave his house and ask the children in the neighbourhood to pull their pants down, at which time the police were called. The police had a firm discussion with Mark and told his mother to keep an eye on him, but determined that there were no major concerns, as Mark did not understand what he was doing.

One day Mark saw one of the neighbourhood children playing outside whilst he was cutting their lawn. He invited the child over to his house to play video games, and whilst they were alone together in the basement, he sexually assaulted the child. The child told his own parents who called the police. Mark was charged with Sexual Assault and Sexual Interference, but the charges were dropped down to Assault conditional on attending a treatment centre.

At the treatment centre, sessions were adapted to encompass lots of concrete examples with visuals, repetition, and role-play due to Mark's intellectual disability and FASD (*responsivity principle*). The behaviour consultant worked directly with Mark on his self-reporting and a comprehensive assessment measuring risk factors (ARMIDILO-S), cognitive distortions and attitudes supportive of offending (QACSO, Bumby MOLEST scale), sexual knowledge (SSKAAT-R), age discrimination and sexual interest/preferences (card sort, arousal graphs), and problem-solving skills and impulsivity (Barratt Impulsiveness Scale).

Due to the seriousness of Mark's offences involving children, the behaviour consultant relied on indirect and descriptive behaviour analysis for the assessment. The behaviour consultant worked with Mark on creating timelines of events for his past offending behaviour, including the most recent offence, attempting to specify components of the four-term contingency. Included in the timelines were his grooming behaviours of going to places with children and chatting with neighbourhood children on social media. Mark would be feeling aroused and be deprived of sexual attention or gratification, so he would actively engage in behaviours to attract or gain access to children such as chatting on social media or going near their houses in the neighbourhood (*motivating operation*). Once he was alone with the child in his basement (*antecedent*), he sexually assaulted him, which provided immediate gratification (*consequence which resulted in the behaviour being maintained by positive reinforcement*).

Mark had a long reinforcement history for this behaviour, with repeated access to children with no aversive or punishing consequences, which served to strengthen his offending behaviour pathway repeatedly over time (*positive reinforcement*).

Mark reported on all of the sexual preference assessments that he has sexual interest in boys with blonde hair, aged 7–10, but also young men (in their 20s). This was consistent with his victim's age groups and appearance descriptions. His risk factors noted in the ARMIDILO-S were high (sexual deviance, sexual preoccupation, coping ability, impulsivity, supervision, victim access, attitudes towards him) with some notable protective factors (relationships, compliance with treatment, lack of substance abuse).

Mark reported attitudes consistent with offending, in that children who are nice to him want to have sex with him, children like sexual activity, sexual activity with men is a good way for children to learn about sex, and so forth. Mark had high levels of sexual knowledge according to the SSKAAT-R, except for major deficits in Section 7, Healthy Boundaries.

Due to Mark's level of risk to offend against children, he required supervision and restrictive environmental modifications to prevent another offence whilst he was in treatment (*risk principle*).

All of the aforementioned assessment findings were found to be directly related to his offending behaviour (*need principle*). Therefore, a comprehensive multicomponent treatment plan focused on shaping his sexual preferences more towards men in their 20s (increasing opportunities and teaching relationship/dating skills, including healthy boundaries), teaching emotional regulation and self-management skills, and working extensively on his cognitive distortions and attitudes supportive of offending. Treatment also focused on building on his protective factors and strengths, to practise skills and create prosocial opportunities that provide a dense schedule of reinforcement.

After two years in intensive treatment, Mark was able to learn the self-management skills to have reduced supervision and eliminating restrictive environmental modifications. Part of his ongoing generalization and maintenance plan is to avoid children or be closely supervised if he needs to attend an event where children are present. Mark is living semi-independently in an adult-oriented neighbourhood, with regular check ins from a staff member who is aware of his history, to ensure he is continuing to use his skills learned in treatment.

12.4   ABA Is Not Just for People with IDD

Throughout this chapter, we have advocated for the use of behaviour analysis as a means to better assess sexually inappropriate conduct engaged in by persons with IDD and other conditions that could serve to limit their understanding of their actions. As we have argued, it is not always the goal that the client is trying to meet that is the problem – it is often the means by which the goal is achieved that leads to difficulties. This includes situations that we have suggested lead to a misappraisal of 'counterfeit deviance' – behaviour that looks deviant on the surface, but that may not actually be when we consider what the client was attempting to achieve. For instance, some of our clients with IDD have a hard time distinguishing general kindness from romantic overtures. In such a scenario, our client misinterprets a warm hello and a pat on the back from an attractive person as 'we should be in an intimate relationship.' If our client then touches the attractive person inappropriately, it may very well be because he misinterpreted the social cues. He did not necessarily intend to offend the other person, he simply did not have the intellectual wherewithal to negotiate the scenario safely.

In considering the inappropriate sexual behaviours engaged in by persons without IDD, how often is it possible that the goal (intimacy) was intact whilst the means of achieving the goal was actually the problem? It is a well-known fact that not all persons who engage in sexually offensive conduct do so because they had strong sexual interest in or a sexual preference for the persons or activities involved in their offending. Not all people who sexually offend are necessarily paraphilic; they often engage in offending behaviour for reasons other than sexual deviance (although the behaviours themselves may be 'deviant' in and of themselves). For example, a man who is at odds with his partner, is experiencing high levels of stress, is self-medicating with alcohol, and who ultimately seeks comfort and intimacy from his 12-year-old daughter has clearly engaged in inappropriate behaviour, but the need for comfort and intimacy is understandable given the other circumstances. In such a situation, some degree of FBA and replacement skills teaching would be helpful in understanding the man's actions and in devising appropriate interventions to help prevent him from employing similarly damaging means in the future.

Although ABA has been extensively supported for people with IDD, there are reasons why we might employ such approaches with clients who might not traditionally be viewed as having special needs. First, it is important to acknowledge the emerging literature regarding adverse childhood experiences (ACE) in the life trajectories of persons who later become involved in criminal conduct, including sexual misconduct (see Reavis et al. 2013; Levenson et al. 2016). People who have experienced significant childhood trauma often engage in highly damaging behaviours (directed both internally and externally) that – like the counterfeit deviance example explained in this chapter – are often poorly contrived means by which to achieve what were likely otherwise intact social and personal goals. For example, some children sexually abused as prepubescents misunderstand sexuality as a means to exhibit love and closeness; that is, they demonstrate sexual reactivity in their attempts to establish important social and comfort relationships with peers and others.

Another observation we have made through our clinical work with persons who have been incarcerated for extended periods of time, is that some of those individuals appear to demonstrate a sort of *acquired* intellectual disability. Given the general lack of opportunities to express true agency or to exert any degree of self-determination whilst incarcerated/hospitalized, combined with few options for intellectual growth, it is not surprising that some individuals display psychological laziness and a generalized helplessness. In attempting to devise effective interventions for individuals in these situations, employment of ABA principles and practices would no doubt be helpful.

12.5 Conclusions

In this chapter, we have written about assessment processes for persons with IDD who have engaged in sexually offensive conduct, focusing largely on principles and practices associated with Applied Behaviour Analysis (ABA). We believe that in order to truly understand what someone did, you also need to have a good sense of why they did it. Is it the goal that was the problem, or the means by which the goal was achieved? Distinguishing between these two options can have a dramatic effect on what topics you might approach in treatment and by what methods. It is no doubt true that you cannot engage in effective treatment without first completing a comprehensive assessment. In this chapter, we have made several suggestions about how best to complete an evaluation incorporating ABA techniques.

We began this chapter by outlining the principles of effective interventions – relying mostly on the Andrews and Bonta RNR model. It is important to reiterate that the RNR model is not a treatment model in and of itself; rather, it is an overarching framework in which good treatment is more likely to occur. There has been some debate in the literature regarding the relative areas of focus between RNR and the currently-popular

Good Lives Model (Yates et al. 2010; Peel Behavioural Services and Wilson 2017); however, this is likely something of a red herring as long as you remember the distinction between *framework* and *programme* (Wilson and Yates 2009). And, to be sure, we always need to remember that not all interventions will work equally well with all potential clients. The responsivity principle is of utmost importance when working with clients with IDD. If we are to assist our clients in achieving the balanced, self-determined lifestyles they so dearly desire, remembering that they are individuals with unique personality traits will be crucial.

References

American Psychiatric Association (2013). *Diagnostic and Statistical Manual of Mental Disorders*, 5e. Washington, DC: APA.

Aos, S., Miller, M., and Drake, E. (2006). *Evidence-based adult corrections programs: what works and what does not*. Olympia, WA: Washington State Institute for Public Policy.

Axelrod, S. (1987). Functional and structural analyses of behavior: approaches leading to reduced use of punishment procedures? *Research in Developmental Disabilities* 8: 165–178.

Baker, D.J., Blumberg, R., and Freeman, R. (2002). Considerations for functional assessment of problem behavior among persons with developmental disabilities and mental illness. In: *Programs and Services for People with Dual Developmental and Psychiatric Disabilities* (eds. J. Jacobson, J. Mulick and S. Holburn), 51–66. Kingston, NY: National Association for Dual Diagnosis.

Barrett, M., Wilson, R.J., and Long, C. (2003). Measuring motivation to change in sexual offenders from institutional intake to community treatment. *Sexual Abuse* 15: 269–283.

Barron, P., Hassiotis, A., and Banes, J. (2004). Offenders with intellectual disability: a prospective comparative study. *Journal of Intellectual Disability Research* 48: 66–76.

Black, D.W., Gunter, T., Loveless, P. et al. (2010). Antisocial personality disorder in incarcerated offenders psychiatric comorbidity and quality of life. *Annals of Clinical Psychiatry* 22: 113–120.

Blasingame, G.D., Boer, D.P., Guidry, L. et al. (2014). *Assessment, Treatment, and Supervision of Individuals with Intellectual Disabilities and Problematic Sexual Behaviors*. Beaverton, OR: Association for the Treatment of Sexual Abusers. Available from www.atsa.com.

Boer, D.P., Haaven, J.L., Lambrick, F. et al., (2013). *The Assessment of Risk and Manageability of Individuals with Developmental and Intellectual Limitations Who Offend – Sexually (ARMIDILO-S)*. www.armidilo.net (accessed 30 May 2019).

Bonta, J. and Andrews, D.A. (2017). *The Psychology of Criminal Conduct*, 6e. Cincinnati, OH: Anderson.

Brandt, J., Wilson, R.J., and Prescott, D.S. (2015). Doubts about SVP programs: a critical review of sexual offender civil commitment in the US. In: *The Sex Offender*, vol. 8 (ed. B. Schwartz), 5-1–5-29. Kingston, NJ: Civic Research Institute.

Brankley, A., Helmus, L.M., and Hanson, R.K. (2017). *Stable-2007 Evaluator Workbook: Revised 2017*. Ottawa, ON: Public Safety Canada.

Broxholme, S.L. and Lindsay, W.R. (2003). Development and preliminary evaluation of a questionnaire on cognitions related to sex offending for use with individuals who have mild intellectual disabilities. *Journal of Intellectual Disability Research* 47: 472–482.

Bumby, K.M. (1996). Assessing the cognitive distortions of child molesters and rapists: development and validation of the MOLEST and RAPE scales. *Sexual Abuse* 8: 37–54.

Busari, A.O. (2015). Antisocial personality disorder among prison inmates: the mediating role of schema-focused therapy. *International Journal of Emergency Mental Health and Human Resiliency* 17: 327–332.

Campbell, T.W. and DeClue, G. (2010). Maximizing predictive accuracy in sexually violent predator evaluations. *Open Access Journal of Forensic Psychology* 2: 148–232.

Carr, E.G. (1977). The motivation of self-injurious behavior: a review of some hypotheses. *Psychological Bulletin* 84: 800–816.

Carr, E.G., Newsom, C.D., and Binkoff, J.A. (1980). Escape as a factor in the aggressive behavior of two retarded children. *Journal of Applied Behaviour Analysis* 13: 101–117.

Cohen, G. and Harvey, J. (2016). The use of psychological interventions for adult male sex offenders with a learning disability: a systematic review. *Journal of Sexual Aggression* 22: 206–233.

Cooper, J.O., Heron, T.E., and Heward, W.L. (2007). *Applied Behavior Analysis*, 2e. Upper Saddle River, NJ: Pearson Education Inc.

Craig, L. and Hutchinson, R.B. (2005). Sexual offenders with learning disabilities: risk, recidivism and treatment. *Journal of Sexual Aggression* 11: 289–304.

DiClemente, C.C. and Prochaska, J.O. (1998). Toward a comprehensive, transtheoretical model of change: stages of change and addictive behaviors. In: *Treating Addictive Behaviors: Applied Clinical Psychology*, 2e (eds. W.R. Miller and N. Heather), 3–27. New York: Springer.

Dixon, D.R., Vogel, T., and Tarbox, J. (2012). A brief history of functional analysis and applied behavior analysis. In: *Functional Assessment for Challenging Behaviors* (ed. J.L. Matson), 3–24. New York: Springer Science and Business Media.

Evans, I.M. and Meyer, L.H. (1985). *An Educative Approach to Behavior Problems: A Practical Decision Model for Interventions with Severely Handicapped Learners.* Baltimore, MD: Paul H. Brookes.

Fredericks, B. and Nishioka-Evans, V. (1999). Functional assessment for a sex offender population. In: *Functional Analysis of Problem Behavior: From Effective Assessment to Effective Intervention* (eds. A.C. Repp and R.H. Horner), 279–303. Belmont, CA: Wadsworth.

Fyffe, C.E., Kahng, S., Fittro, E. et al. (2004). Functional analysis and treatment of inappropriate sexual behavior. *Journal of Applied Behavior Analysis* 37: 401–404.

Gardner, W.I. (2002). *Aggression and Other Disruptive Behavioral Challenges: Biomedical and Psychosocial Assessment and Treatment*, 325–398. New York: National Association for Dual Diagnosis.

Griffiths, D., Hingsburger, D., Hoath, J. et al. (2013). 'Counterfeit deviance' revisited. *Journal of Applied Research in Intellectual Disabilities* 26: 471–480.

Griffiths, D. and Lunsky, Y. (2003). *Socio-Sexual Knowledge and Attitudes Assessment Tool (SSKAAT-R).* Wood Dale, IL: Stoelting.

Griffiths, D.M., Thomson, K., Ioannou, S. et al. (2019). *Sex Offending Behaviour of Persons with an Intellectual Disability: A Multi-Component Applied Behaviour Analytic Approach.* Kingston, NY: National Association for Dual Diagnosis (NADD).

Hanley, G.P. (2012). Functional assessment of problem behavior: dispelling myths, overcoming implementation obstacles, and developing new lore. *Behavior Analysis in Practice* 5: 54–72.

Hanley, G.P., Jin, C.S., Vanselow, N.R. et al. (2014). Producing meaningful improvements in problem behavior of children with autism via synthesized analyses and treatments. *Journal of Applied Behavior Analysis* 47: 16–36.

Hanson, R.K. (1997). *The Development of a Brief Actuarial Risk Scale for Sexual Offense Recidivism*. (User report 1997-04). Ottawa, ON: Department of the Solicitor General of Canada.

Hanson, R.K., Babchishin, K.M., Helmus, L.M. et al. (2017). Communicating the results of criterion-referenced prediction measures: risk categories for the Static-99R and Static-2002R sexual offender risk assessment tools. *Psychological Assessment* 29: 582–597.

Hanson, R.K., Gordon, A., Harris, A.J.R. et al. (2002). First report of the collaborative outcome data project on the effectiveness of treatment for sex offenders. *Sexual Abuse* 14: 169–194.

Hanson, R.K., Harris, A.J.R., Scott, T.L. et al. (2007). *Assessing the Risk of Sexoffenders on Community Supervision: The Dynamic Supervision Project*. (User Report 2007–05). Ottawa, ON: Public Safety Canada.

Hanson, R.K., Sheahan, C.L., and VanZuylen, H. (2013). Static-99 and RRASOR predict recidivism among developmentally delayed sexual offenders: a cumulative meta-analysis. *Sexual Offender Treatment* 8: 1862–2941.

Hazelwood, R.R. and Harpold, J.A. (1986). Rape: the dangers of providing confrontational advice. *FBI Law Enforcement Bulletin* 55 (6): 1–5.

Hingsburger, D., Griffiths, D., and Quinsey, V. (1991). Detecting counterfeit deviance: differentiating sexual deviance from sexual inappropriateness. *Habilitation Mental Health Care Newsletter* 10: 51–54.

Ioannou, S. (2013). *Managing risk in a culture of rights: Providing support and treatment for sex offenders with intellectual disability in community-based settings*. Unpublished Master's Thesis. Brock University, St. Catharines, Ontario, Canada.

Iwata, B.A., Dorsey, M.F., Slifer, K.J. et al. (1982). Toward a functional analysis of self-injury. *Analysis and Intervention in Developmental Disabilities* 2: 3–20.

Iwata, B.A., Dorsey, M.F., Slifer, K.J. et al. (1994). Toward a functional analysis of self-injury. *Journal of Applied Behavior Analysis* 27: 197–209.

Iwata, B.A., Vollmer, T.R., and Zarcone, J.R. (1990). The experimental (functional) analysis of behavior disorders: methodology, applications, and limitations. In: *Perspectives on the Use of Nonaversive and Aversive Interventions for Persons with Developmental Disabilities* (eds. A.C. Repp and N.N. Singh), 301–330. Sycamore, IL: Sycamore.

Långström, N., Enebrink, P., Laurén, E.-M. et al. (2013). Preventing sexual abusers of children from reoffending: systematic review of medical and psychological interventions. *BMJ: British Medical Journal*: 347–358.

Levenson, J.S. and Hern, A.L. (2007). Sex offender residence restrictions: unintended consequences and community reentry. *Justice Research and Policy* 9: 59–73.

Levenson, J.S., Willis, G.M., and Prescott, D. (2016). Adverse childhood experiences in the lives of male sex offenders and implications for trauma-informed care. *Sexual Abuse* 28: 340–359.

Lindsay, W.R., Hogue, T.E., Taylor, J.L. et al. (2008). Risk assessment in offenders with intellectual disability: a comparison across three levels of security. *International Journal of Offender Therapy and Comparative Criminology* 52: 90–111.

Lindsay, W.R., Whitefield, E., and Carson, D. (2007). An assessment for attitudes consistent with sexual offending for use with offenders with intellectual disabilities. *Legal and Criminological Psychology* 12: 55–68.

Lipsey, M.W. and Cullen, F.T. (2007). The effectiveness of correctional rehabilitation: a review of systematic reviews. *Annual Review of Law and Social Science* 3: 297–320.

Lovaas, O.I., Frietag, G., Gold, V.J. et al. (1965). Experimental studies in childhood schizophrenia. *Journal of Experimental Child Psychology* 2: 67–84.

Marotta, P.L. (2017). A systematic review of behavioral health interventions for sex offenders with intellectual disabilities. *Sexual Abuse* 29: 148–185.

Marshall, W.L., Marshall, L.E., Serran, G.A. et al. (2011). *Rehabilitating Sexual Offenders: A Strength-Based Approach*. Washington, DC: American Psychological Association.

Martinson, R. (1974). Nothing works: questions and answers about prison reform. *The Public Interest* 35: 22–54.

Martinson, R. (1979). New findings, new views: a note of caution regarding sentencing reform. *Hofstra Law Review* 7: 242–258.

Maruna, S. and Mann, R.E. (2006). A fundamental attribution error? Rethinking cognitive distortions. *Legal and Criminological Psychology* 11: 155–177.

McGrath, R.J., Lasher, M.P., and Cumming, G.F. (2012). The Sex Offender Treatment Intervention and progress cale (SOTIPS): psychometric properties and incremental predictive validity with Static-99R. *Sexual Abuse* 24: 431–458.

McGuire, T. (2001). Sex offending: behavioral analysis perspective. *Advances in Psychology Research* 6: 129–155.

Michie, A.M., Lindsay, W.R., Martin, V. et al. (2006). A test of counterfeit deviance: a comparison of sexual knowledge in groups of sex offenders with intellectual disabilities and controls. *Sexual Abuse* 18: 271–278.

Miltenberger, R. (1997). *Behavior Modification: Principles and Practice*. Pacific Grove, CA: Brooks/Cole.

Najdowski, A., Wallace, M., Ellsworth, C. et al. (2008). Functional analyses and treatment of precursor behavior. *Journal of Applied Behavior Analysis* 41: 97–105.

O'Neill, R.E., Horner, R.H., Albin, R.W. et al. (1997). *Functional Assessment and Program Development for Problem Behavior: A Practical Handbook*. Pacific Grove, CA: Brooks/Cole.

Patton, J.H., Stanford, M.S., and Barratt, E.S. (1995). Factor structure of the Barratt impulsiveness scale. *Journal of Clinical Psychology* 51: 768–774.

Peel Behavioural Service and Wilson, R.J. (2017). *Passport to Independence*. Holyoke, MA: NEARI Press.

Reavis, J., Looman, J., Franco, K. et al. (2013). Adverse childhood experiences and adult criminality: how long must we live before we possess our own lives? *The Permanente Journal* 17: 44–48.

Rincover, A., Cook, R., Peoples, A. et al. (1979). Sensory extinction and sensory reinforcement principles for programming multiple adaptive behavior change. *Journal of Applied Behavior Analysis* 12: 221–233.

Schmucker, M. and Lösel, F. (2015). The effects of sexual offender treatment on recidivism: an international meta-analysis of sound quality evaluations. *Journal of Experimental Criminology* 11: 597–630.

Skinner, B.F. (1957). *Verbal Behavior*. New York: Appleton-Century-Crofts.

Smith, R.G. and Churchill, R.M. (2002). Identification of environmental determinants of behavior disorders through functional analysis of precursor behaviors. *Journal of Applied Behavior Analysis* 35: 125–136.

Smith, P., Goggin, C., and Gendreau, P. (2002). *The Effects of Prison Sentences and Intermediate Sanctions on Recidivism: General Effects and Individual Differences*. (User Report 2002-01). Ottawa, ON: Solicitor General Canada.

Stirpe, T., Wilson, R.J., and Long, C. (2001). Goal attainment scaling with sexual offenders: a measure of clinical impact at post treatment and at community follow-up. *Sexual Abuse* 13: 65–77.

Stokes, T.F. and Baer, D.M. (1977). An implicit technology of generalization. *Journal of Applied Behavior Analysis* 10: 349–367.

Thornton, D., Ambroziak, G., Kahn, R.E. et al. (2018). Advances in the assessment of sexual deviance. *Current Psychiatry Reports* 20 (8): 55.

Tough, S.E. (2001). Validation of two standardized risk assessments (RRASOR, 1997; Static-99, 1999) on a sample of adult males who are developmentally disabled with significant cognitive deficits. *Masters Abstracts International* 39: 1626B.

Vollmer, T.R., Reyes, J.R., and Walker, S.F. (2012). Behavioral assessment and intervention for sex offenders with intellectual and developmental disabilities. In: *A Handbook of High-Risk Challenging Behaviors in People with Intellectual and Developmental Disabilities* (ed. J.K. Luiselli), 121–144. Baltimore, MD: Paul H. Brookes.

Wacker, D.P., Berg, W.K., Harding, J.W. et al. (2011). Functional and structural approaches to behavioral assessment of problem behavior. In: *Handbook of Applied Behavior Analysis* (eds. W.W. Fisher, C.C. Piazza and H.S. Roane), 165–181. New York: Guildford Press.

Wilson, R.J. and Burns, M. (2011). *Intellectual Disability and Problems in Sexual Behaviour: Assessment, Treatment, and Promotion of Healthy Sexuality*. Holyoke, MA: NEARI Press.

Wilson, R.J. and Looman, J. (2010). What can we reasonably expect to accomplish in conducting actuarial risk assessments with sexual offenders in civil commitment settings? A response to Campbell and DeClue: 'maximizing predictive accuracy in sexually violent predator evaluations'. *Open Access Journal of Forensic Psychology* 2: 306–321.

Wilson, R.J. and Miner, M.H. (2016). Measurement of male sexual arousal and interest using penile plethysmography and viewing time. In: *Treatment of Sex Offenders: Strengths and Weaknesses in Assessment and Intervention* (eds. D.R. Laws and W.T. O'Donohue), 107–131. New York: Springer.

Wilson, R.J. and Yates, P.M. (2009). Effective interventions and the Good Lives Model: maximizing treatment gains for sexual offenders. *Aggression and Violent Behavior* 14: 157–161.

Worling, J.R. (2006). Assessing sexual arousal with adolescent males who have offended sexually: self-report and unobtrusively measured viewing time. *Sexual Abuse* 18: 383–400.

Wright, D., Herzog, G., and Seymour, J. (1992). Treatment of a constellation of inappropriate sexual and social behaviors in a 20-year old man with Down syndrome. *Sexuality and Disability* 10: 57–61.

Wulfert, E., Greenway, D., and Dougher, M.J. (1996). A logical functional analysis of reinforcement-based disorders: alcoholism and pedophilia. *Journal of Consulting and Clinical Psychology* 64: 1140–1151.

Yates, P.M., Prescott, D.S., and Ward, T. (2010). *Applying the Good Lives and Self-Regulation Models to Sex Offender Treatment: A Practical Guide for Clinicians*. Brandon, VT: Safer Society Press.

Part IV

Treatment

13

Supporting People with Intellectual and Developmental Disabilities Leaving Prison

Kathy Ellem[1], Michelle Denton[1], and Danielle Davidson[2]

[1] School of Nursing, Midwifery and Social Work, University of Queensland, Brisbane, Queensland, Australia
[2] School of Public Health and Social Work, Queensland University of Technology, Brisbane, Queensland, Australia

13.1 Introduction

Whilst there is a growing body of research about individual and group psychological treatments particularly focused on criminogenic risk for people with intellectual and developmental disabilities (IDD) leaving prison (Lindsay and Michie 2013), there are very few studies that focus on transition support for this population that fit the 'what works' criteria as outlined in Chapter 1, or rise above the lowest levels of evidence within this system. Notwithstanding the difficulties in precise definitions of intellectual disability and diagnosis of co-occurring problems, identification can be difficult and unreliable in the criminal justice system and the prevalence of people with IDD in prisons varies markedly between studies and jurisdictions (Hayes 2012). Overall however, the research suggests that this population is overrepresented in prisons and probation and parole services (Hayes 2012); they are a profoundly disadvantaged and vulnerable group within the criminal justice system (Jones and Talbot 2010); and they have high recidivism rates (see for example, Holland and Persson 2011).

Prison-to-community transition is a complex psychosocial phenomenon that requires a broad interdisciplinary perspective beyond the important contribution of psychological treatment, the impact of which is often measured by the single indicator of recidivism (McNeill 2012). Failure to shift beyond this lens when considering the transition support needs of people with IDD has the potential to undermine and limit the effectiveness of evidence-based treatment and approaches (Barrenger and Draine 2013). For many offenders with IDD there are many individual and systemic factors that play a part in their experience of transition. Hence, we propose in this chapter that a wide range of evidence, not normally considered within the 'what works' framework, is drawn from criminology, sociology, and public health to understand what may work in transition support for people with intellectual disability. This approach provides a multidimensional understanding of evidence that includes

The Wiley Handbook on What Works for Offenders with Intellectual and Developmental Disabilities: An Evidence-Based Approach to Theory, Assessment, and Treatment, First Edition.
Edited by William R. Lindsay, Leam A. Craig, and Dorothy Griffiths.

consumer wisdom, professional experience, and findings from qualitative research that can stand as equal partners with more traditional forms of evidence that has been developed from experimental research (Petr and Walter 2009).

Drawing on the literature and our own research, we understand post-prison support needs using a number of theoretical frames. We describe the experience and support needs of people with IDD leaving prison using an adapted version of Graffam and Shinkfield's reintegration theory (2012). This ecological framework consists of the following domains: intrapersonal conditions; subsistence conditions; and support conditions. These domains are considered separately and in combination to gain a more holistic perspective on prison-to-community transition.

Many of the findings in this chapter align with the values espoused by both desistance and complexity theorists, where successful reintegration and abstinence from criminal activity is regarded as a process that is influenced by a myriad of psychological, developmental, and sociological factors (Maruna 2001; Pycroft 2014). It is argued that successful reintegration is best supported by the cumulative effect of a wide spectrum of interventions with attention given to a prosocial identity in ex-prisoners with IDD (Lewis 2014; Ward and Gannon 2006).

It is this multiplicity and interconnectivity of factors at play that underpins our analysis of 'what works' in supporting ex-prisoners with IDD to transition and reintegrate into the community. The next two sections discuss the intrapersonal and subsistence conditions of people with IDD leaving prison, identifying specific individual issues related to cognition and behaviour, as well as social influences regarding housing, income, and employment conditions. Section 13.3 then reviews recent research in formal and informal supports for ex-prisoners with IDD and provides some insight into 'what works' in prison-to-community transition.

13.2 Intrapersonal Conditions of People with IDD Who Leave Prison

Intrapersonal conditions refer to the individual factors which have influence on ex-prisoners when they return to their local community (Graffam and Shinkfield 2012). For ex-prisoners with IDD, the interplay of cognitive and behavioural challenges with physical and mental health conditions are important considerations in community reintegration. This section provides a brief summary of these issues and includes recent research on problematic substance use and gambling addiction in this population: the impact of impairment, physical and mental health, substance abuse, and gambling.

13.2.1 The Impact of Impairment

When the term 'intellectual disability' is applied to alleged offenders entering the criminal justice system, it often refers to people with 'borderline' (IQ range of 70–80) or 'mild' (IQ 50–69) intellectual impairment and in some cases, people with 'moderate' intellectual impairment (IQ 35–49) (World Health Organisation 2007). People with intellectual disability often experience challenges in learning, reasoning, and problem solving, as well as language and literacy, self-direction, social skills, and activities of daily living (Schalock et al. 2010). For many offenders within this group the causal nature of their impairment is not always clear, and some of the challenges they may experience could also be attributed to other disabilities such as acquired brain injury and other co-morbid conditions (Baldry et al. 2013).

Given the multiple combinations of disorders and disadvantages experienced by this group (Baldry et al. 2013), it can be difficult to determine the degree of influence these disorders have on a person's behaviour and their success in achieving community reintegration. The literature refers to characteristics of intellectual impairment which can pose challenges, such as communication and social skill difficulties; poor judgement or impulse control; suggestibility and exploitability; and delays in moral development (Clare and Gudjonsson 1993; Lindsay et al. 2004). All of these factors can contribute to offending behaviour and can also impact on a person's quality of life upon release from prison. For example, challenges in cognition and social skills can create difficulties accessing appropriate rehabilitation programmes within prison that can assist early release (Ellem 2013). It can also affect a person's understanding and ability to adhere to requirements of parole (Hayes 2012), and to understand the implications of association with others engaged in criminal acts (Kaal et al. 2012). Diminished cognitive capacity, lack of confidence, poor literacy and numeracy skills can also prove problematic when accessing mainstream services and supports in the community (Abbott and McConkey 2006).

An understanding of a person's disability and its effects is important in the context of community reintegration, and lack of understanding by mainstream service providers and the broader community can lead to poor outcomes. The experience of cognitive impairment requires service and community responses to better cater for heterogeneity. In addition, there is a need to recognize the added complexity of a heightened risk of physical and mental health conditions in offenders with IDD.

13.2.2 Physical and Mental Health

Research investigating the physical and mental health status and needs of people with intellectual disability consistently find that this group experience elevated rates of unrecognized health problems, chronic and infectious disease, inadequate health screening, higher rates of hearing, visual, and speech impairment, higher rates of mental illness, premature death, and disparity in health care service delivery (Fisher 2004; Krahn and Fox 2014). Adults with intellectual disability have also been found to have high rates of co-existing psychiatric disorders with estimates that depression, schizophrenia, and bipolar in this population is twice that identified in the general population (Cooper and van der Speck 2009).

Within the Australian context, prisoners with IDD have been found to be at high risk of a number of physical and mental health concerns. In a study in Queensland, Australia of a large sample of 1279 prisoners within six weeks from release of custody, those who were identified with intellectual disability (115, 9%), were more likely than their peers to be diagnosed with medical conditions such as heart disease and hearing problems and to be obese, and were less likely to have received screening and preventive care interventions (Dias et al. 2013a). This study also identified that half of the prisoners with intellectual disability experienced a lifetime and current prevalence of co-occurring mental disorder and 13.5% reported very high levels of psychological distress (Dias et al. 2013b).

Whilst chronic, complex physical health conditions and mental health disorders are shared with peers in prison and post release, this group may have difficulty accessing health services in prison and post release, communicating their health needs to medical staff, and disclosing their disability. Psychiatric disorders are not always detected in this group or presented to healthcare professionals due to misdiagnosis, diagnostic overshadowing, and service-access difficulties (Cooper and van der Speck 2009). Young et al. (2016) advocate for individualized support to navigate complex health systems; maintain healthy lifestyles; understand and adhere to medical advice; actively participate in healthcare decisions; and enhance capacity for self-management and health-related autonomy. Such recommendations would require whole systems case management and mutual cooperation between relevant agencies post release (Pycroft 2014).

13.2.3 Substance Use

In addition to issues related to cognition, behaviour, and physical and mental health, ex-prisoners with IDD may also experience challenges with problematic alcohol and substance use. Available data suggest that although people with intellectual disability overall may use less alcohol and other substances than people in the general population, those who do use substances are at greater risk of developing substance-related problems (Didden et al. 2009). Substance-related problems for people with an intellectual disability can lead to significant health issues including an increase in cognitive decline, poor impulse control, physical impairment, loss of self-care skills, and heightened irritability (Slayter 2008). When a person also has co-occurring mental illness and uses psychotropic medications, there may be further negative effects from substance use such as suicidal thoughts and ideation (Taggart et al. 2006). People with intellectual disability who have alcohol and drug use problems may also experience physical, psychological, financial, and sexual exploitation by peers (Taggart et al. 2006).

In Lindsay and others' (2013a) recent study of the alcohol-related crime history of 477 people with intellectual disability who were referred to forensic intellectual disability services, a relationship was found between a person's alcohol abuse history and a number of offences, including contact sexual offences, property damage, physical aggression, fire setting, road traffic offences, and theft. Alcohol abuse was considered a risk factor for offending, particularly when there was also a history of childhood adversity and psychiatric problems (Lindsay et al. 2013a). Despite these findings, McGillivray et al. (2016) have speculated that prisoners with an intellectual disability may not always associate their offending with substance abuse because they may have a reduced understanding of the contributing factors that influence their offending.

Whilst there appears to be an association between alcohol/substance abuse and offending for people with an IDD, the literature indicates that rehabilitation programme responses in prison are generally ineffective in addressing the issue (Hassiotis et al. 2011; McGillivray and Moore 2001). A study by Hassiotis and others (2011) on the psychiatric morbidity of prisoners with IDD found that those with drug use and alcohol dependence received less treatment for drug addiction in prison than prisoners in the general population with substance problems. There were also a smaller number of prisoners with IDD who had received any drug education when compared to the general population. McGilllivray et al. (2016) speculated that high dropout rates in these programmes may be an indicator of failing to adapt the content to people's learning styles and a lack of strategies to ensure successful access and participation.

Treating a person with an IDD for substance issues can present certain challenges. A person with an intellectual disability may present with behaviours that appear to be associated with their disability but may actually mask substance use problems (Slayter and Steenrod 2009). There may be communication and comprehension challenges in relation to treatment. For example, the person may have difficulties recalling their history of substance use (Miller and Whicher 2009); have limited vocabularies; and difficulty understanding and retaining information relevant to treatment (Burgard et al. 2000).

A person with an IDD is likely to need concurrent support in addressing issues of substance use, managing symptoms of mental illness, and negotiating fundamental resources to live in their local community. The skill set to address all of these issues is seldom present in the one service and there is a need for cross-systems collaboration. People with an IDD may be in a constant cycle of re-referral to various generic service providers, who are not trained in appropriate therapeutic approaches, as is evident in the mental health sector (Slayter 2008).

13.2.4 Gambling

Another significant challenge for ex-prisoners with IDD can be problem gambling. Gambling disorder has been defined in the Diagnostic and Statistical Manual of Mental Disorders V as gambling behaviour which is 'persistent and recurrent', 'leading to clinically significant impairment or distress' (American Psychiatric Association 2013, section 312.13). Problem gambling is associated with mental health concerns, such as depression, anxiety, and personality disorders and can co-occur with problematic substance and alcohol use (Shaffer et al. 2004).

Several studies of the general offender population have found a significant proportion of offenders have difficulties associated with problem gambling and associated debt (for example, Kuoppamaki et al. 2014; Riley and Oakes 2015). Whilst the extent of gambling-related crime in the community has not been adequately measured, there is some evidence that gambling behaviours are associated with theft, fraud, family violence, sexual assault, child neglect, drug and alcohol related offences, drink driving, and weapons offences (Griffiths et al. 2005; May-Chahal et al. 2012). In their study of 140 incarcerated offenders in Canada, Lloyd et al. (2014) found that offenders with problem-gambling histories were a particularly at-risk group for future crime, and that this warranted intervention programmes within prison to address these issues.

Very little research has been conducted on offenders with IDD who have problem-gambling behaviours, both in terms of prevalence and intervention approaches, yet this may be an important avenue to pursue. An internal report on compulsory treatment orders for people with IDD commissioned by the Department of Human Services in Victoria, Australia touches briefly on this issue (McLeod 2014). There was mention of gambling habits in all of the files on participants with IDD who had entered correctional facilities at the time of the study, but the severity of gambling and its implications were not explored. A US study by Morasco and Petry (2006) compared the gambling habits of people receiving disability benefits for medical or psychiatric conditions to a general population and found that the former group showed higher rates of problem gambling. Problem gambling may therefore be an important aspect in a person's life which may be overlooked in specialized interventions for offenders with IDD.

13.3 Subsistence Conditions

The previous section provided a brief summary of the literature relating to individual conditions that have an impact on the reintegration of offenders with IDD. The complex interaction between cognitive impairment, challenging behaviour, mental health, problematic substance use, and gambling disorder can all influence a person's ability to secure housing, employment, and maintain an income. These subsistence conditions, including income and employment, and housing, are explored in the following subsections.

13.3.1 Income and Employment

Most prisoners have little in the way of financial resources when they re-enter the community and often need to rely on the assistance of others, including support from community agencies and informal supports from any social connections they have (Draine et al. 2005). Lack of income and an inability to acquire it is likely to influence a person's reintegration success, leading to significant stressors in acquiring fundamental needs such as food and housing and exacerbating the associated risk of reoffending (Harley et al. 2014). Social security measures are often considered inadequate in alleviating poverty (Australian Council of Social Service 2016; Feist-Price et al. 2014). Nevertheless, additional support may be needed to help people to apply for and access such resources (Ellem 2013).

The ability to generate income through paid employment is a challenge for any ex-prisoner. The stigma associated with having a criminal history and difficulties keeping up with changing technologies on the outside can reduce opportunities to obtain work (Harley et al. 2014; Lepage et al. 2011). Ex-prisoners with IDD are likely to flounder in the job market independent of their criminal record (World Health Organisation 2011). Rates of competitive employment for adults with IDD are estimated at only 25% in Canada (Domin and Butterworth 2013) and 6% in England (Hatton et al. 2016).

There are mixed results in relation to the impact of employment on reducing recidivism for ex-offenders in the general population, which calls for further research in this area (Harley et al. 2014). There are some studies that indicate that employment can lead to a lower rate of reoffending (Graffam et al. 2014) and a longer time to reincarceration (Tripodi et al. 2010). Certainly, for ex-offenders with IDD this may be an area that warrants further exploration in improving the outcomes of their reintegration, although it is unlikely that employment opportunities on their own would be sufficient to prevent further offending in this group (Tripodi et al. 2010).

13.3.2 Housing

A strong association has been found between homelessness and incarceration and that these factors increase the risk of each other in the general offender population (Brackertz et al. 2016). In the first major study on the housing status of released prisoners in Australia, Baldry et al. (2006) found that 50% of participants in the study (n = 238) who moved accommodation more than twice in the first nine months post-release were up to eight times more likely to be re-incarcerated during that time. Moving often, lack of family and professional support, lack of employment, and worsening drug use were all associated with poor housing and return to prison.

Less definitive data has been specifically gathered regarding ex-prisoners with IDD. A recent paper by Young et al. (2017) found that ex-prisoners who had been screened as potentially having an intellectual disability were more likely to be living alone, in unstable accommodation, or back in prison six months after release. Murphy et al.'s (2017a) study in the UK found that whilst healthcare staff were seeking to establish a logical care pathway for people with IDD leaving prison towards the least possible restrictive setting, the data regarding where people with IDD went to live did not marry with this intention. People with IDD appeared to transition into living arrangements based on factors of convenience, such as the availability of family members to take them in, rather than by any standardized risk assessments.

Obtaining and maintaining stable housing requires a degree of financial literacy and ability to keep the home environment in liveable order (Backer and Howard 2007). This may be difficult for someone with IDD who may not always comply with rules in a supported housing arrangement leading to impairment-related disruptive behaviour (HCH Clinicians' Network 2003). Quirouette (2016) found in her study of homeless shelters in Toronto, Canada, that people with complex needs such as ex-prisoners with IDD were often 'remarginalized' by practices that assumed clients had a high level of motivation and ability to access resources, could cooperate with case management goals, and quickly reintegrate into the community.

Programmes such as the Housing First Model (HFM) which provides permanent supportive housing for chronically homeless individuals with serious mental illness and substance use disorder may be equally beneficial for ex-prisoners with IDD (Brackertz et al. 2016). Guided by a human rights perspective, HFM was first developed in the 1990s as an alternative to 'Treatment First' approaches, which demand abstinence/sobriety, medication compliance, and responsivity to therapeutic interventions (Watson et al. 2013).

To date, there is robust evidence to suggest that the HFM is successful in ensuring sustained tenancies for people with mental illness and substance use disorder, but it is unclear how well the model addresses issues of social inclusion, mental health issues, and problematic substance use (Brackertz et al. 2016). The intent behind the HFM aligns with strengths-based values inherent in desistance promotion strategies (McNeill et al. 2012), but further research is needed regarding its application with ex-prisoners with IDD.

13.4 Support Conditions

Support conditions and the ways in which they are implemented are critical in determining positive outcomes for ex-prisoners with IDD returning to community. The following subsections review current research on social support, disability service support, and criminal justice intervention for ex-prisoners with IDD.

13.4.1 Social Support

Studies on offender reintegration in the general population have increasingly high-lighted the need for positive and supportive relationships for ex-prisoners to aid in desistance from crime (Chui and Cheng 2014). Social support can be defined as 'the perceived and actual amount of instrumental and expressive/emotional supports that one receives from primary relationships, social networks, and communities' (Hochstetler et al. 2010, p. 590). Positive social support, such as a supportive family network may reinforce prosocial norms, values, and expectations as well as assist a person to find employment and accommodation (Markson et al. 2015).

Given the myriad of concerns facing ex-prisoners with IDD as outlined in this chapter, their need for social support may be even more salient than other ex-prisoners. Numerous studies have reported the difficulties people with IDD have in overcoming loneliness and stigma and developing social connections (for example, Ali et al. 2015; Duggan and Linehan 2013), yet there is very little research evidence regarding the social networks of ex-prisoners with IDD. Murphy et al. (2017a) found that in the small sample of ex-prisoners with IDD, the average social network size (M = 29) was low. Men who lived with families or alone with some support had a lower number of social networks, compared to those living in large restrictive units. Some men living with families reported times where local communities ostracized them, indicating that experiences of stigmatization may be common upon re-entry.

A number of evaluative studies have reported the success of Circles of Support and Accountability (CoSAs) in mitigating the risk of 'high risk' sex offenders in the general prison population when they re-enter the community (Fox 2014; Wilson et al. 2009). Whilst little research has explored the efficacy of such models with ex-prisoners with IDD (regardless of offence type), the principles of engaging community volunteers to offer assistance to the released ex-prisoner may have some merit. Community engagement has long been considered an important component in supporting people with a disability, and disability service provision has adopted similar models of practice in the area of person-centred planning which could be adapted for this purpose (Sanderson et al. 2006).

13.4.2 Disability Support

Both generic IDD services and specialized forensic services within the community, play an important part in the reintegration of ex-prisoners with IDD. Community disability support is cost-effective and provides an opportunity for ex-prisoners with IDD to engage in situation specific learning (Taylor 2002), and to generalize any prosocial skills learned within correctional settings (McDermott 2010). An individual's human rights for freedom of movement need to be considered alongside the need for community protection. A supervised residential placement that involves individualized planning may often be necessary for ex-prisoners with IDD (Hayes 2007). This response involves a gradual reduction in restrictive practices, and legal checks and balances (McLeod 2014). Managing risk to individuals and the broader community are important considerations in such arrangements. A review of qualitative studies on the perspectives of people with IDD in restrictive settings found that many people reported feelings of helplessness, frustration, and anger living in institutional residential placements (Griffith et al. 2013). A person's sense of autonomy is likely to be restored when they no longer reside in a secure unit, but the onus on community services is to ensure intervention continues (Lindsay et al. 2013b).

Entry into disability-specific services in many contexts can be problematic for ex-prisoners with mild or borderline IDD (Ellem et al. 2013). The eligibility for service ideally should be based on the support needs of the individual rather than just the assessed IQ score (Nouwens et al. 2017), but many generic intellectual disability services rely on psychometric measures that exclude people with IDD with higher IQ scores. Referral pathways to particular services are also complicated by whether a person's behaviour is defined as 'offending' or 'challenging' (Reed et al. 2004). The former descriptor is likely to lead to referrals to forensic disability services where such services are available, and may result in exclusion from generic community disability services. A person defined as having 'challenging' behaviour may be someone who has a severe or profound IDD and referred to supervisory practices within generic disability services (Wheeler et al. 2009). Agencies need to take into account their own capacity to provide support and any issues that could potentially arise when the person with IDD interacts with other clients in a service. Further research is needed regarding how particular behaviours are interpreted by the sector and the implications this presents for service responses (Wheeler et al. 2009).

Generic intellectual disability services in the community often have a wide-ranging purview of practice, which may include supporting people with IDD who present with many complex issues, such as managing a mental illness, dealing with family breakdown, and struggling to maintain current living arrangements (Lindsay et al. 2013b). The focus on valued social roles of people with a disability and the drive to establish a strong community presence for individuals are the hallmarks of contemporary disability service provision in Western countries (Wolfensberger and Race 2003). These approaches adopt an individualized and holistic approach to support and may be considered a more empowering model for ex-prisoners with IDD than the focus given in corrective services on deterrence, incapacitation, and rehabilitation (Coyle 2005). If the agency and its workers are able to maintain a broad focus on all life domains, they can play a crucial role in facilitating the interaction between ex-prisoners with IDD and specialist services, by assisting in locating resources, making referrals, providing important contextual information, and acting as a mediator when disputes and conflicts arise (Raeymaeckers 2016).

Such a broad focus on the part of generic disability services may also present with significant challenges. The diversity of issues these services seek to address may mean they do not have the staffing or resources to address criminogenic issues adequately (Lindsay et al. 2013b). The services may therefore assume a degree of competency on the part of ex-prisoners with IDD to make prosocial choices that may not exist. These services typically do not have the high level of expertise needed to address the ideological tension which can occur around 'care and control' when working with offenders with IDD (Williams 2009).

The services provided under forensic intellectual disability community agencies is a large focus of this current book. Treatment that is specifically designed to address emotional difficulties, fire raising, anger and violence, and inappropriate sexual behaviour in offenders with IDD are all services provided by such agencies. Much of the focus of these interventions is to define clearly the behaviours associated with index offences, specify skills and competencies required to address these behaviours, and provide empirical evidence of the efficacy of interventions in reducing recidivism (Blom 2004). Forensic intellectual disability services can delineate a clear role and level of expertise in the 'what works' paradigm through targeted goals and discrete measures of success. The availability of such services is predicated on the priorities of government spending however, with governments often not recognizing the unmet individual and community needs of supporting offenders with IDD. These programmes may also have difficulties addressing concerns for ex-prisoners with IDD outside their areas of specialization (Ellem et al. 2012). Clearly, there is a need for flow of information and skills between both generic and forensic disability service systems to account for the wide range of biopsychosocial factors that lead to reoffending in this population (Pycroft 2014).

13.4.3   Criminal Justice Responses

For some ex-prisoners with IDD there may have been no contact with any kind of disability service due to a failure of systems to identify the nature of their impairment. Therefore, ex-prisoners with IDD may be very reliant on appropriate responses from the criminal justice system during reintegration.

Ongoing throughcare and aftercare for offenders with IDD are certainly warranted but rarely implemented. There are often inadequate mechanisms in place to identify prisoners with IDD, as full assessments for IQ and adaptive behaviour are both costly and time consuming within the correctional context (Murphy et al. 2017b). Failure to identify a prisoner's disability can lead to many difficulties, including vulnerability to physical, emotional, and sexual assault from other prisoners (Boodle et al. 2014). People with IDD may become entrenched in a culture of criminality and be easily influenced by other prisoners to engage in illegal activities such as drug dealing (New South Wales Sentencing Council 2004).

If a person is identified as having an IDD in prison, they are likely to be housed in a high-security setting for the duration of their sentence. Whilst such arrangements may afford the person some protection in a custodial setting, it can also act as a barrier to learning skills of independent living and undermine any rehabilitative efforts (Holland and Persson 2011). Mainstream rehabilitative and work programmes may also be denied to prisoners with IDD, as they are not suitably adapted to the person's learning needs. The lack of opportunity to participate in such programmes has negative implications for parole applications and a graduated release into the community becomes less likely (Murphy and Mason 2014). Many prisoners with IDD serve short sentences or on remand (Hassiotis et al. 2011). The short duration of their stay does not allow time for correctional staff to coordinate supports or for the person to access any rehabilitative programmes and a person can continually cycle in and out of prison as a result (Baldry 2011).

For those prisoners with IDD who are able to achieve parole, there may be inherent difficulties complying with the conditions of the post-release order. This can include challenges in remembering and keeping appointments with a parole officer and understanding the specific conditions of the parole order (Mason and Morris 2000; Mason and Murphy 2002). Some authors such as Mason and Morris (2000) and Parsons and Sherwood (2016) have trialled plain English versions of information relating to community corrections orders and police custody. Whilst such initiatives improve the readability of vital documents, Parsons and Sherwood (2016) note that the success of such initiatives is dependent on the ability of the system to account for any significant stressors a person may be under at the time, and the level of understanding criminal justice professionals have about the particular characteristics of a person with IDD.

Ex-prisoners with IDD can experience significant challenges in their contact with police and in court. In Murphy et al.'s (2017a) study of ex-prisoners with IDD, over half of the men in her sample ($n = 21$) had been in contact with police. Police not only can act in a law-enforcement role, but may also have to decide if a person needs referral to a mental-health facility (Spivak and Thomas 2013). There may be problems in appropriately identifying the person as having an IDD, and adapting communication styles (Henshaw and Thomas 2012). Initiatives such as the use of an independent third person (Spivak and Thomas 2013), police contact and collaboration with relevant disability service agencies (Henshaw and Thomas 2012), and the involvement of family members and advocates (Eadens et al. 2016), have all been regarded as helpful safeguards, provided these are appropriately resourced.

The involvement of an appropriate adult is also an important consideration when supporting someone with IDD to appear in court (Todd 2015). A person's competence needs to be assessed in such contexts (Cederborg et al. 2009). An ex-prisoner with IDD may have difficulties remembering court-appearance dates, fail to understand the gravity of offending behaviour and its legal consequences, and experience anxiety issues related to court attendance (Mercier and Crocker 2011). Suggestions made in the literature to overcome some of these challenges include the use of court accompaniment services; video links for interviewing; adapted written information for ease of understanding; judicial processes occurring within the person's regular environment; and shortening the time between the offence and court procedures so that the person is able to fully understand the consequences of their behaviour (Mercier and Crocker 2011). Specialist mental health courts that apply the principles of therapeutic jurisprudence to criminal behaviour can also be effective if they can refer a person to effective rehabilitative programmes in lieu of incarceration (Lim and Day 2016).

13.5 Conclusions

This chapter reviewed the current literature on supports and intervention for people with IDD leaving prison. Although there is a need for further research in this area, the existing evidence suggests there are many variables that impact on successful reintegration for this group. Given this, we have gone beyond a purely psychological and clinical focus that is often found in the 'what works' literature, to a non-linear and non-reductionist way of understanding multiplicity of need (Pycroft 2014). Using the organizing concepts found in Graffam and Shinkfield's (2012) reintegration model, we have outlined the necessity of holistic interventions that target a broad spectrum of intrapersonal, subsistence, and support dimensions in the process of reintegration.

Our analysis of the support needs of people with IDD leaving prison resonates with contemporary thought on complexity theory. Within this frame, it is recognized that specific interventions that target certain domains of a person's life are affected by the mediating impact of social context (Fish and Hardy 2015). Complexity theory, therefore, argues for a localized response to social problems that takes into account specific contexts and local populations (Pycroft 2014; Whitehead 2010). This chapter has attempted to describe a number of influences on transition support for ex-prisoners with IDD, but these are not exhaustive. A localized response would also need to consider all individual factors, such as a person's culture, gender, and offence type, as well as important macro considerations, such as government policy and practice.

The literature on desistance processes in the general offender population describes the journey away from crime as a challenging process, often involving a 'zig-zag' pattern, where a person moves in and out of criminal activity before achieving sustained desistance (Maruna 2001). There is some evidence in the research on ex-prisoners with IDD to suggest similar processes (Holland and Persson 2011). It would, therefore, be unreasonable to assume that any of the interventions discussed in this chapter on their own would produce an immediate, positive outcome for offenders with IDD. Instead, what is called for is an appreciation of the layers of interaction that exist between systems. Coordinated intervention targeting multiple issues is likely to have a cumulative effect on reintegration processes (Lewis 2014). Support must therefore be of a long-term nature and be open to positive future possibilities for individuals, in the face of likely moments of relapse into offending (Fish and Hardy 2015; McNeill et al. 2012).

The research reviewed in this chapter highlights the potential usefulness of a whole-systems case-management model that is both relational and flexible in its approach when working with ex-prisoners with IDD. This is not a simple task. As Pycroft (2014) attests, case management in the field of probation and parole grapples with many dilemmas. These can include addressing diversity of need; adopting appropriate assessment tools; determining if generic or specialist agency intervention is warranted; acquiring the necessary resources and funding; and determining what constitutes a good outcome from the intervention. These tasks become all the more challenging in systems where supports and services are fragmented and can espouse contradictory aims and philosophies. Case management for ex-prisoners with IDD must traverse all these issues, and embrace the complexity of practice. There needs to be an active process of information sharing between systems and between practitioners and people with IDD (Snowden 2002); and an active engagement of families, communities, civil society and state (McNeill et al. 2012).

References

Abbott, S. and McConkey, R. (2006). The barriers to social inclusion as perceived by people with intellectual disabilities. *Journal of Intellectual Disabilities* 10 (3): 275–287. https://doi.org/10.1177/1744629506067618.

Ali, A., King, M., Strydom, A. et al. (2015). Self-reported stigma and symptoms of anxiety and depression in people with intellectual disabilities: findings from a cross sectional study in England. *Journal of Affective Disorders* 187: 224–231. https://doi.org/10.1016/j.jad.2015.07.046.

American Psychiatric Association (2013). *Diagnostic and Statistical Manual of Mental Disorders: DSM-5*. Arlington, VA: American Psychiatric Association.

Australian Council of Social Service (2016). *Poverty in Australia 2016*. http://www.acoss.org.au/wp-content/uploads/2016/10/Poverty-in-Australia-2016.pdf (accessed 30 May 2019).

Backer, T.E. and Howard, E.A. (2007). Cognitive impairments and the prevention of homelessness: research and practice review. *The Journal of Primary Prevention* 28 (3): 375–388. https://doi.org/10.1007/s10935-007-0100-1.

Baldry, E. (2011). Women in transition: from prison to…. *Current Issues in Criminal Justice* 22 (3): 267.

Baldry, E., Clarence, M., Dowse, L. et al. (2013). Reducing vulnerability to harm in adults with cognitive disabilities in the Australian criminal justice system: reducing vulnerability to harm. *Journal of Policy and Practice in Intellectual Disabilities* 10 (3): 222–229. https://doi.org/10.1111/jppi.12039.

Baldry, E., McDonnell, D., Maplestone, P. et al. (2006). Ex-prisoners, homelessness and the state in Australia. *The Australian and New Zealand Journal of Criminology* 39 (1): 20–33.

Barrenger, S.L. and Draine, J. (2013). 'You don't get no help': the role of community context in effectiveness of evidence-based treatments for people with mental illness leaving prison for high risk environments. *American Journal of Psychiatric Rehabilitation* 16 (2): 154–178. https://doi.org/10.1080/15487768.2013.789709.

Blom, B. (2004). Specialization in social work practice: effects on interventions in the personal social services. *Journal of Social Work* 4 (1): 25–46. https://doi.org/10.1177/1468017304042419.

Boodle, A., Ellem, K., and Chenoweth, L. (2014). Anna's story of life in prison. *British Journal of Learning Disabilities* 42 (2): 117–124.

Brackertz, N., Fotheringham, M., and Winter, I. (2016). *Effectiveness of the homelessness service system*. https://www.ahuri.edu.au/research/research-papers/effectiveness-of-the-homelessness-service-system (accessed 30 May 2019).

Burgard, J.F., Donohue, B., Azrin, N.H. et al. (2000). Prevalence and treatment of substance abuse in the mentally retarded population: an empirical review. *Journal of Psychoactive Drugs* 32 (3): 293–298. https://doi.org/10.1080/02791072.2000.10400452.

Cederborg, A., Danielsson, H., La Rooy, D. et al. (2009). Repetition of contaminating question types when children and youths with intellectual disabilities are interviewed. *Journal of Intellectual Disability Research* 53: 440–449.

Chui, W.H. and Cheng, K.K.-Y. (2014). Challenges facing young men returning from incarceration in Hong Kong. *The Howard Journal of Criminal Justice* 53 (4): 411–427. http://dx.doi.org/10.1111/hojo.12088.

Clare, I. and Gudjonsson, G. (1993). Interrogative suggestibility, confabulation, and acquiescence in people with mild learning-disabilities (mental handicap) – implications for reliability during police interrogations. *British Journal of Clinical Psychology* 32: 295–301.

Cooper, S.A. and van der Speck, R. (2009). Epidemiology of mental ill health in adults with intellectual disabilities. *Current Opinion in Psychiatry* 22 (5): 431–436. https://doi.org/10.1097/YCO.0b013e32832e2a1e.

Coyle, A. (2005). *Understanding Prisons*, vol. 1. Milton Keynes: Open University Press.

Dias, S., Ware, R.S., Kinner, S.A. et al. (2013a). Physical health outcomes in prisoners with intellectual disability: a cross-sectional study. *Journal of Intellectual Disability Research* 57 (12): 1191–1196. https://doi.org/10.1111/j.1365-2788.2012.01621.x.

Dias, S., Ware, R.S., Kinner, S.A. et al. (2013b). Co-occurring mental disorder and intellectual disability in a large sample of Australian prisoners. *Australian and New Zealand Journal of Psychiatry* 47 (10): 938–944. https://doi.org/10.1177/0004867413492220.

Didden, R., Embregts, P., van der Toorn, M. et al. (2009). Substance abuse, coping strategies, adaptive skills and behavioral and emotional problems in clients with mild to borderline intellectual disability admitted to a treatment facility: a pilot study. *Research in Developmental Disabilities* 30 (5): 927–932. https://doi.org/10.1016/j.ridd.2009.01.002.

Domin, D. and Butterworth, J. (2013). The role of community rehabilitation providers in employment for persons with intellectual and developmental disabilities: results of the 2010–2011 national survey. *Intellectual and Developmental Disabilities* 51 (4): 215–225. https://doi.org/10.1352/1934-9556-51.4.215.

Draine, J., Wolff, N., Jacoby, J.E. et al. (2005). Understanding community re-entry of former prisoners with mental illness: a conceptual model to guide new research. *Behavioral Sciences & The Law* 23 (5): 689–707. https://doi.org/10.1002/bsl.642.

Duggan, C. and Linehan, C. (2013). The role of 'natural supports' in promoting independent living for people with disabilities; a review of existing literature. *British Journal of Learning Disabilities* 41 (3): 199–207. https://doi.org/10.1111/bld.12040.

Eadens, D.M., Cranston-Gingras, A., Dupoux, E. et al. (2016). Police officer perspectives on intellectual disability. *Policing-an International Journal of Police Strategies & Management* 39 (1): 222–235. https://doi.org/10.1108/pijpsm-03-2015-0039.

Ellem, K. (2013). Experiences of leaving prison for people with intellectual disability. *Journal of Learning Disabilities and Offending Behaviour* 3 (3): 127–138.

Ellem, K., O'Connor, M., Wilson, J. et al. (2013). Social work with marginalised people who have a mild or borderline intellectual disability: practicing gentleness and encouraging hope. *Australian Social Work* 66 (1): 56–71. https://doi.org/10.1080/0312407X.2012.710244.

Ellem, K., Wilson, J., and Chui, W.H. (2012). Effective responses to offenders with intellectual disabilities: generalist and specialist services working together. *Australian Social Work* 65 (3): 398–412. https://doi.org/10.1080/0312407x.2011.625433.

Feist-Price, S., Lavergne, L., and Davis, M. (2014). Disability, race and ex-offender status: the tri-vector challenge to employment. *Journal of Applied Rehabilitation Counseling* 45 (4): 25–34.

Fish, S. and Hardy, M. (2015). Complex issues, complex solutions: applying complexity theory in social work practice. *Nordic Social Work Research* 5 (sup1): 98–114. https://doi.org/10.1080/2156857X.2015.1065902.

Fisher, K. (2004). Health disparities and mental retardation. *Journal of Nursing Scholarship* 36 (1): 48–53. https://doi.org/10.1111/j.1547-5069.2004.04010.x.

Fox, K.J. (2014). Restoring the social: offender reintegration in a risky world. *International Journal of Comparative and Applied Criminal Justice* 38 (3): 235–256. https://doi.org/10.1080/01924036.2013.848221.

Graffam, J. and Shinkfield, A.J. (2012). The life conditions of Australian ex-prisoners: an analysis of intrapersonal, subsistence, and support conditions. *International Journal of Offender Therapy and Comparative Criminology* 56 (6): 897–916. https://doi.org/10.1177/0306624X11415510.

Graffam, J., Shinkfield, A.J., and Lavelle, B. (2014). Recidivism among participants of an employment assistance program for prisoners and offenders. *International Journal of Offender Therapy and Comparative Criminology* 58 (3): 348–363. https://doi.org/10. 1177/0306624X12470526.

Griffith, G.M., Hutchinson, L., and Hastings, R.P. (2013). 'I'm not a patient, I'm a person': the experiences of individuals with intellectual disabilities and challenging behavior—a thematic synthesis of qualitative studies. *Clinical Psychology: Science and Practice* 20 (4): 469–488. https://doi.org/10.1111/cpsp.12053.

Griffiths, M., Parke, A., and Parke, J. (2005). Gambling-related violence: an issue for the police? *The Police Journal: Theory, Practice and Principles* 78 (3): 223–227. https://doi. org/10.1350/pojo.2005.78.3.223.

Harley, D.A., Cabe, B., Woolums, R. et al. (2014). Vulnerability and marginalization of adult ex-offenders with disabilities in community and employment reintegration. *Journal of Applied Rehabilitation Counseling* 45 (4): 4–14.

Hassiotis, A., Gazizova, D., Akinlonu, L. et al. (2011). Psychiatric morbidity in prisoners with intellectual disabilities: analysis of prison survey data for England and Wales. *British Journal of Psychiatry* 199 (2): 156–157. https://doi.org/10.1192/bjp. bp.110.088039.

Hatton, C., Glover, G., Emerson, E. et al. (2016). *People with learning disabilities in England 2015: main report*. London: Public Health England. https://assets.publishing.service.gov. uk/government/uploads/system/uploads/attachment_data/file/613182/PWLDIE_2015_ main_report_NB090517.pdf (accessed 30 May 2019).

Hayes, S. (2007). Missing out: offenders with learning disabilities and the criminal justice system. *British Journal of Learning Disabilities* 35: 146–153.

Hayes, S. (2012). People with intellectual and developmental disabilities in the criminal justice system. In: *High Risk Challenging Behaviors in People with Intellectual and Developmental Disabilities* (ed. J. Luiselli), 211–228. Baltimore, MD: Paul H. Brookes.

HCH Clinicians' Network (2003). Dealing with disability: cognitive impairments and homelessness. *Healing Hands* 7 (1): 1–6.

Henshaw, M. and Thomas, S. (2012). Police encounters with people with intellectual disability: prevalence, characteristics and challenges. *Journal of Intellectual Disability Research* 56 (6): 620–631. https://doi.org/10.1111/j.1365-2788.2011.01502.x.

Hochstetler, A., DeLisi, M., and Pratt, T.C. (2010). Social support and feelings of hostility among released inmates. *Crime & Delinquency* 56 (4): 588–607. https://doi.org/10. 1177/0011128708319926.

Holland, S. and Persson, P. (2011). Intellectual disability in the Victorian prison system: characteristics of prisoners with an intellectual disability released from prison in 2003–2006. *Psychology, Crime & Law* 17 (1): 25–41. https://doi.org/10.1080/ 10683160903392285.

Jones, G. and Talbot, J. (2010). No one knows: the bewildering passage of offenders with learning disability and learning difficulty through the criminal justice system. *Criminal Behaviour and Mental Health* 20 (1): 1–7. https://doi.org/10.1002/ cbm.746.

Kaal, H., Brand, E., and van Nieuwenhuijzen, M. (2012). Serious juvenile offenders with and without intellectual disabilities. *Journal of Learning Disabilities and Offending Behaviour* 3 (2): 77–84.

Krahn, G.L. and Fox, M.H. (2014). Health disparities of adults with intellectual disabilities: what do we know? What do we do? *Journal of Applied Research in Intellectual Disabilities* 27 (5): 431–446. https://doi.org/10.1111/jar.12067.

Kuoppamaki, S.M., Kaariainen, J., and Lind, K. (2014). Examining gambling-related crime reports in the National Finnish Police Register. *Journal of Gambling Studies* 30 (4): 967–983. https://doi.org/10.1007/s10899-013-9393-6.

Lepage, J.P., Washington, E.L., Lewis, A.A. et al. (2011). Effects of structured vocational services on job-search success in ex-offender veterans with mental illness: 3-month follow-up. *Journal of Rehabilitation Research and Development* 48 (3): 277–286. https://doi.org/10.1682/JRRD.2010.03.0032.

Lewis, S. (2014). Responding to domestic abuse: multi-agented systems, probation programmes and emergent outcomes. In: *Applying Complexity Theory: Whole Systems Approaches to Criminal Justice and Social Work*, vol. 47181 (eds. A. Pycroft and C. Bartollas), 220–245. Bristol: The Policy Press.

Lim, L. and Day, A. (2016). Mental health diversion courts: a prospective study of reoffending and clinical outcomes of an Australian mental health court program. *Journal of Offender Rehabilitation* 55 (4): 254–270. https://doi.org/10.1080/10509674. 2016.1159639.

Lindsay, W.R., Carson, D., Holland, A.J. et al. (2013a). Alcohol and its relationship to offence variables in a cohort of offenders with intellectual disability. *Journal of Intellectual and Developmental Disability* 38 (4): 325–331. https://doi.org/10.3109/ 13668250.2013.837154.

Lindsay, W.R., Holland, A.J., Carson, D. et al. (2013b). Responsivity to criminogenic need in forensic intellectual disability services. *Journal of Intellectual Disability Research* 57 (2): 172–181. https://doi.org/10.1111/j.1365-2788.2012.01600.x.

Lindsay, W. and Michie, A. (2013). What works for offenders with intellectual disabilities. In: *What Works in Offender Rehabilitation: An Evidence-Based Approach to Assessment and Treatment* (eds. L.A. Craig, L. Dixon and T. Gannon), 285–304. Chichester, UK: Wiley-Blackwell.

Lindsay, W.R., Sturmey, P., and Taylor, J.L. (2004). Natural history and theories of offending in people with developmental disabilities. In: *Offenders with Developmental Disabilities* (eds. W.R. Lindsay, J.L. Taylor and P. Sturmey), 3–22. Chichester: Wiley.

Lloyd, C.D., Chadwick, N., and Serin, R.C. (2014). Associations between gambling, substance misuse and recidivism among Canadian offenders: a multifaceted exploration of poor impulse control traits and behaviours. *International Gambling Studies* 14 (2): 279–300. https://doi.org/10.1080/14459795.2014.913301.

Markson, L., Lösel, F., Souza, K. et al. (2015). Male prisoners' family relationships and resilience in resettlement. *Criminology & Criminal Justice* 15 (4): 423–441. https://doi. org/10.1177/1748895814566287.

Maruna, S. (2001). *Making Good: How Ex-Convicts Reform and Rebuild Their Lives.* Washington, DC: American Psychological Association.

Mason, J. and Morris, L. (2000). Improving understanding and recall of the probation service contract. *Journal of Community and Applied Social Psychology* 10 (3): 199–210. https://doi.org/10.1002/1099-1298(200005/06)10:3<199::AID-CASP565>3.0.CO;2-9.

Mason, J. and Murphy, G. (2002). Intellectual disability amongst people on probation: prevalence and outcome. *Journal of Intellectual Disability Research* 46: 230–238. https://doi.org/10.1046/j.1365-2788.2002.00399.x.

May-Chahal, C., Wilson, A., Humphreys, L. et al. (2012). Promoting an evidence-informed approach to addressing problem gambling in UK prison populations. *The Howard Journal of Criminal Justice* 51 (4): 372–386. https://doi.org/10.1111/j.1468-2311.2012.00723.x.

McDermott, B. (2010). Individuals with developmental disabilities in correctional settings. In: *Handbook of Correctional Mental Health*, 2e (ed. C. Scott), 515–541. Washington, DC: American Psychiatric Publishing.

McGillivray, J. and Moore, M. (2001). Substance use by offenders with mild intellectual disability. *Journal of Intellectual and Developmental Disability* 26 (4): 297–310. https://doi.org/10.1080/13668250120087317.

McGillivray, J.A., Gaskin, C.J., Newton, D.C. et al. (2016). Substance use, offending, and participation in alcohol and drug treatment programmes: a comparison of prisoners with and without intellectual disabilities. *Journal of Applied Research in Intellectual Disabilities* 29 (3): 289–294. https://doi.org/10.1111/jar.12175.

McLeod, D. (2014). *Accommodation Changes and Characteristics of People with an Intellectual Disability Under Compulsory Treatment in Victoria (2007–2014)*. Melbourne: Department of Human Services.

McNeill, F. (2012). Four forms of 'offender' rehabilitation: towards an interdisciplinary perspective. *Legal and Criminological Psychology* 17 (1): 18–36. https://doi.org/10.1111/j.2044-8333.2011.02039.x.

McNeill, F., Farrall, S., Lightfowler, C. et al. (2012). *How and why people stop offending: discovering desistance*. https://www.iriss.org.uk/resources/insights/how-why-people-stop-offending-discovering-desistance (accessed 30 May 2019).

Mercier, C. and Crocker, A.G. (2011). The first critical steps through the criminal justice system for persons with intellectual disabilities. *British Journal of Learning Disabilities* 39 (2): 130–138. https://doi.org/10.1111/j.1468-3156.2010.00639.x.

Miller, H. and Whicher, E. (2009). Substance misuse. In: *Intellectual Disability Psychiatry: A Practical Handbook* (eds. A. Hassiotis, D. Barron and I. Hall), 101–114. London: Wiley.

Morasco, B.J. and Petry, N.M. (2006). Gambling problems and health functioning in individuals receiving disability. *Disability & Rehabilitation* 28 (10): 619–623. https://doi.org/10.1080/09638280500242507.

Murphy, G., Chiu, P., Triantafyllopoulou, P. et al. (2017a). Offenders with intellectual disabilities in prison: what happens when they leave? *Journal of Intellectual Disability Research* 61 (10): 957–968.

Murphy, G. and Mason, J. (2014). Forensic and offending behaviours. In: *Handbook of Psychopathology in Intellectual Disability: Research, Practice, and Policy* (eds. E. Tsakanikos and J. McCarthy), 281–303. London: Springer.

Murphy, G.H., Gardner, J., and Freeman, M.J. (2017b). Screening prisoners for intellectual disabilities in three English prisons. *Journal of Applied Research in Intellectual Disabilities* 30 (1): 198–204. https://doi.org/10.1111/jar.12224.

New South Wales Sentencing Council (2004). *Abolishing prison sentences of six months or less: final report*. http://www.sentencingcouncil.justice.nsw.gov.au/Documents/Projects_Complete/Short_Sentences/abolish_report_final.pdf (accessed 30 May 2019).

Nouwens, P.J.G., Lucas, R., Embregts, P.J.C.M. et al. (2017). In plain sight but still invisible: a structured case analysis of people with mild intellectual disability or borderline intellectual functioning. *Journal of Intellectual and Developmental Disability* 42 (1): 36–44. https://doi.org/10.3109/13668250.2016.1178220.

Parsons, S. and Sherwood, G. (2016). Vulnerability in custody: perceptions and practices of police officers and criminal justice professionals in meeting the communication needs of offenders with learning disabilities and learning difficulties. *Disability & Society* 31 (4): 553–572. https://doi.org/10.1080/09687599.2016.1181538.

Petr, C.G. and Walter, U.M. (2009). Evidence-based practice: a critical reflection. *European Journal of Social Work* 12 (2): 221–232. https://doi.org/10.1080/13691450802567523.

Pycroft, A. (2014). Probation practice and creativity in England and Wales: a complex system analysis. In: *Applying Complexity Theory: Whole Systems Approaches to Criminal Justice and Social Work* (eds. A. Pycroft and C. Bartollas), 199–220. Bristol: The Policy Press.

Quirouette, M. (2016). Managing multiple disadvantages: the regulation of complex needs in emergency shelters for the homeless. *Journal of Poverty* 20 (3): 316–339. https://doi.org/10.1080/10875549.2015.1094774.

Raeymaeckers, P. (2016). A specialist's perspective on the value of generalist practice: a qualitative network analysis. *Journal of Social Work* 16 (5): 610–626. https://doi.org/10.1177/1468017316644693.

Reed, S., Russell, A., Xenitidis, K. et al. (2004). People with learning disabilities in a low secure in-patient unit: comparison of offenders and non-offenders. *The British Journal of Psychiatry* 185 (6): 499–504. https://doi.org/10.1192/bjp.185.6.499.

Riley, B. and Oakes, J. (2015). Problem gambling among a group of male prisoners: lifetime prevalence and association with incarceration. *Australian and New Zealand Journal of Criminology* 48 (1): 73–81. https://doi.org/10.1177/0004865814538037.

Sanderson, H., Thomspon, J., and Kilbane, J. (2006). The emergence of person-centred planning as evidence-based practice. *Journal of Integrated Care* 14 (2): 18–25.

Schalock, R., Borthwick-Duffy, S., Bradley, V. et al. (2010). *Intellectual Disability: Definition, Classification, and Systems of Support*, 11e. Washington, DC: American Association on Intellectual and Developmental Disabilities.

Shaffer, H.J., LaPlante, D.A., LaBrie, R.A. et al. (2004). Toward a syndrome model of addiction: multiple expressions, common etiology. *Harvard Review of Psychiatry* 12 (6): 367–374. https://doi.org/10.1080/10673220490905705.

Slayter, E. and Steenrod, S.A. (2009). Addressing alcohol and drug addiction among people with mental retardation in non-addiction settings: a need for cross-system collaboration. *Journal of Social Work Practice in the Addictions* 9 (1): 71–90. https://doi.org/10.1080/15332560802646547.

Slayter, E.M. (2008). Understanding and overcoming barriers to substance abuse treatment access for people with mental retardation. *Journal of Social Work in Disability & Rehabilitation* 7 (2): 63–80. https://doi.org/10.1080/15367100802009780.

Snowden, D. (2002). Complex acts of knowing: paradox and descriptive self-awareness. *Journal of Knowledge Management* 6 (2): 100–111. https://doi.org/10.1108/13673270210424639.

Spivak, B.L. and Thomas, S.D.M. (2013). Police contact with people with an intellectual disability: the independent third person perspective. *Journal of Intellectual Disability Research* 57 (7): 635–646. https://doi.org/10.1111/j.1365-2788.2012.01571.x.

Taggart, L., McLaughlin, D., Quinn, B. et al. (2006). An exploration of substance misuse in people with intellectual disabilities. *Journal of Intellectual Disability Research* 50 (8): 588–597. https://doi.org/10.1111/j.1365-2788.2006.00820.x.

Taylor, J.L. (2002). A review of the assessment and treatment of anger and aggression in offenders with intellectual disability. *Journal of Intellectual Disability Research* 46 (s1): 57–73. https://doi.org/10.1046/j.1365-2788.2002.00005.x.

Todd, A. (2015). Addressing the needs of people with learning disabilities who have offended. In: *Intellectual Disability in Health and Social Care* (eds. S. Atkinson, J. Lay, S. McAnelly, et al.), 410–437. London: Routledge.

Tripodi, S.J., Kim, J.S., and Bender, K. (2010). Is employment associated with reduced recidivism? The complex relationship between employment and crime. *International Journal of Offender Therapy and Comparative Criminology* 54 (5): 706–720. https://doi.org/10.1177/0306624X09342980.

Ward, T. and Gannon, T.A. (2006). Rehabilitation, etiology, and self-regulation: the comprehensive good lives model of treatment for sexual offenders. *Aggression and Violent Behavior* 11 (1): 77–94. https://doi.org/10.1016/j.avb.2005.06.001.

Watson, D.P., Wagner, D.E., and Rivers, M. (2013). Understanding the critical ingredients for facilitating consumer change in housing first programming: a case study approach. *The Journal of Behavioral Health Services & Research* 40 (2): 169–179. https://doi.org/10.1007/s11414-012-9312-0.

Wheeler, J.R., Holland, A.J., Bambrick, M. et al. (2009). Community services and people with intellectual disabilities who engage in anti-social or offending behaviour: referral rates, characteristics, and care pathways. *Journal of Forensic Psychiatry & Psychology* 20 (5): 717–740. https://doi.org/10.1080/14789940903174048.

Whitehead, P. (2010). *Exploring Modern Probation: Social Theory and Organisational Complexity*. Bristol: Policy Press.

Williams, I. (2009). Offender health and social care: a review of the evidence on inter-agency collaboration. *Health and Social Care in the Community* 17 (6): 573–580. https://doi.org/10.1111/j.1365-2524.2009.00857.x.

Wilson, R.J., Cortoni, F., and McWhinnie, A.J. (2009). Circles of support & accountability: a Canadian national replication of outcome findings. *Sexual Abuse: A Journal of Research and Treatment* 21 (4): 412–430. https://doi.org/10.1177/1079063209347724.

Wolfensberger, W. and Race, D.G. (2003). *Leadership and Change in Human Services: Selected Readings from Wolf Wolfensberger*; compiled and edited by (ed. D.G. Race). New York and London: Routledge.

World Health Organisation (2007). *The ICD-10 Classification of Mental and Behavioural Disorders: Clinical Descriptions and Diagnostic Guidelines*. Geneva: World Health Organisation.

World Health Organisation. (2011) *World Report on Disability*. http://www.who.int/disabilities/world_report/2011/report/en (accessed 30 May 2019).

Young, J.T., Cumming, C., van Dooren, K. et al. (2017). Intellectual disability and patient activation after release from prison: a prospective cohort study. *Journal of Intellectual Disability Research* 61 (10): 939–956. https://doi.org/10.1111/jir.12349.

Young, J., van Dooren, K., Fernando, C. et al. (2016). Transition from prison for people with intellectual disability: a qualitative study of service professionals. *Trends & Issues in Crime and Criminal Justice* 528: 1–12.

14

Prison-based Programmes for People with Intellectual and Developmental Disabilities

Phillip Snoyman, Berindah Aicken, and Jayson Ware

Corrective Services New South Wales, Department of Justice, Sydney, Australia

14.1   Introduction

The prevalence of people with intellectual and developmental disabilities (IDD) in the community is just over 1% according to a meta-analysis of 52 studies (Maulik et al. 2011). Unfortunately, a significant number of these individuals will have some contact with the criminal justice system and a disproportionate percentage of inmates in prisons may have IDD (Dowse et al. 2009; Hayes 2007). Despite a general consensus that people with IDD are over-represented in prisons, relatively little research has been published relating to the assessment, risk, and treatment of these individuals. The existing research has also been naturally hampered by definitional and identification issues, methodological inconsistencies, small sample sizes, and specific to treatment, a lack of high quality rigorous approaches such as the use of controlled randomized studies.

Within this chapter, we explore these definitional and identification issues specific to prisons, consider what treatment for people with IDD in prison seeks to achieve, and carefully review the existing research specific to prison-based programmes for people with IDD. We conclude with our considerations for future treatment programmes and research.

14.2   Definitional and Identification Issues for People with IDD in Prison

There is a lack of consensus as to who has IDD and who should be involved in treatment programmes for people with IDD. The lack of strict *definitions* which include Intelligence Quotient (IQ, generally a full scale IQ score) range, levels of adaptive functioning, and age of onset has resulted in publication of data that includes a heterogeneous group of people including those with IDD, autism spectrum disorder (ASD), borderline cognitive functioning, low literacy, acquired brain injury, or other cognitive impairment.

*The Wiley Handbook on What Works for Offenders with Intellectual and Developmental Disabilities:
An Evidence-Based Approach to Theory, Assessment, and Treatment*, First Edition.
Edited by William R. Lindsay, Leam A. Craig, and Dorothy Griffiths.

A view commonly held is that if a person is not suitable for a mainstream programme, that person should be placed in an 'adapted' programme which may be more accessible (Keeling et al. 2006). Alternatively, adapted treatments may be indicated for people who score low on a cognitive assessment yet high on some psychometric instruments indicating specific deficits or treatment needs (Newberry and Shuker 2011). It is now accepted that people with intellectual disability may also have co-morbid disorders such as personality disorder (Alexander et al. 2010; Rayner et al. 2015; Taylor 2014; Taylor and Morrissey 2012) or substance abuse (Day et al. 2016; van Dooren et al. 2015). The focus of treatment may then vary according to the complex interaction between the IDD and the co-morbidity.

Identification of people with IDD within the criminal justice system (Snoyman 2010) is a difficult process. This said, the police often have brief interventions for offenders identified as having IDD that are directed at crime prevention or reduction (Eadens et al. 2016; Henshaw and Thomas 2012). The judicial courts tend not to focus on disability aside from some considerations around mitigation or diversion (Astor et al. 2012; Shaw 2016). Whilst gaols and other correctional facilities have more time to work with prisoners, the main focus is on safe and humane treatment or treatment of high-risk inmates rather than identification of a disability that is often not readily evident (Board et al. 2015). People with mild IDD frequently do not appear different from their peers, and by the time they reach adulthood, have either become 'street-smart' or have learned to mask their limited abilities. There are small numbers of people with severe IDD, with most falling into the so called 'mild' range of intellectual disability (Bogart and Bruce 2009).

Florio and Trollor (2015) note that in a community sample of people with intellectual disability, only 18–22% were diagnosed because of the presence of a co-morbid mental illness. In prisons there is an overrepresentation of people with mental illness, particularly in females (Dean 2016; Fazel et al. 2016). Indigenous people have been assessed as being over-represented in prisons and are greatly over-represented within cohorts of inmates with intellectual disability (McCausland et al. 2015; McEntyre 2015). It is therefore likely that some people with IDD in custody are never identified particularly when they choose not to identify as having a disability.

14.3 What Constitutes Treatment for People with IDD?

More recent thinking, which moves from offence-specific interventions to an analysis of pathways through the criminal justice system (Baldry 2010; Lindsay et al. 2010a), indicates that there are both: (i) a large group who commit less serious offences but are frequently incarcerated and (ii) a smaller group of high-risk high-need offenders who commit serious violent or sexual offences. These two groups may require different treatment programmes.

In prisons, it appears that the prevailing focus (for both of these groups) is on providing treatment specific to identified criminogenic needs rather than disability needs. Mainstream treatment programmes tend to be 'adapted' or 'modified' so that people with IDD can not only attend but also benefit from the programmes (Craig and Hutchinson 2005; Eccleston et al. 2010; Keeling et al. 2007b; Lindsay et al. 2013; Oakes et al. 2016; Sakdalan and Collier 2012; Taylor 2013; Taylor et al. 2012; West 2007;

Williams and Mann 2010). People with IDD who offend have the same criminogenic needs as people without IDD who offend. However, the former also have a number of compounding and intersecting disability-related issues that cannot be separated from the individual in their treatment. There is a requirement for treatment programmes designed to meet the unique needs of people with IDD who offend rather than adapting pre-existing programmes.

14.4 Adapted Programmes or Additional Supports?

Treatment programmes for people with IDD have been slower to develop than mainstream programmes. Most of these have been adapted from adult mainstream programmes (Wilcox 2004) and modified for use with offenders with intellectual disabilities by simplifying the concepts and using visual imagery and other tools and interventions from the disability field to complement the offence-specific models (Lambrick and Glaser 2004). However, there is a need to provide specific services for this client group as opposed to simply modifying a mainstream treatment programme which is unlikely to take into consideration the complexity and compounding nature of the needs of people who have both IDD and who offend.

Lambrick and Glaser (2004) suggest that the specific needs of people with IDD be taken into account. They advocate for the simplification of concepts, use of visual imagery, emphasis on the generalization of skills developed in treatment to the day-to-day and the use of assessments and intervention methods historically used in the field of intellectual disability. Thus, the literature in the field of the assessment and treatment of offenders with IDD demonstrates that this client group can be effectively treated if programmes are specifically designed and delivered in a manner consistent with their level of functioning (Haaven and Coleman 2000; Lambrick and Glaser 2004; Lindsay 2002; Lindsay et al. 2006). The key differences in such programmes compared with mainstream programmes are the duration, level of external support, focus on behavioural application of treatment principles across contexts, and level of post-treatment follow-up or maintenance.

Within the prison setting in New South Wales, Australia, the need for additional programmes to meet the specific needs of people with IDD was identified in response to offenders with IDD being excluded from mainstream programmes, and high attrition rates of people with IDD in adapted programmes. These additional programmes should include interventions that are responsive to the cognitive, psychosocial capacities and learning style of the client group. The Self-Regulation Program (SRP) suite of programmes, including programmes for people with IDD who sexually offend (SRP-SO), who violently offend (SRP-VO) and those with general offending (SRP-GO) were developed in 2011 (Aicken et al. 2011). The programmes sit beside mainstream programmes and differ in terms of length of programme, number of participants (8–10), utilizing multiple modalities for learning, focus on experiential learning and generalizability, and maintaining structure yet providing a great deal of opportunity for process work.

People with IDD require additional supports when transitioning to, and residing within, the community. Bhandari et al. (2015) note that there is a lack of an evidence base to inform transitional interventions for people with IDD. Bhandari et al. note the complex presentation of many offenders with IDD including health- and disability-related

Table 14.1 Overlap of criminogenic and disability needs.

Criminogenic Needs	Disability Needs
• Poor educational attainment • Pre-incarceration unemployment • Increased likelihood of an institutional misconduct or charges laid while on probation • Reliance on social assistance • Poor attitudes towards sentence and supervision • History of mental health treatment • For those who offend, few anti-criminal acquaintances or friends and increased likelihood of drug or substance problems	• Poor educational attainment • Unemployment • Reliance on social assistance • History of mental health treatment • Few peers

needs, substance use, and poor social circumstances including lack of educational attainment, unemployment, and an offence history. The complexity around people with IDD is in stark contrast to the straightforwardness of risk and criminogenic need programmes provided to mainstream offenders. Mainstream offender programmes are more likely to be comprehensively evaluated.

There is currently a greater awareness of disability as a social construct (Snoyman and Aicken 2011), but many factors associated with risk of crime, those so called criminogenic needs (Andrews 1995; Andrews and Bonta 2010), are also prevalent in people with IDD not in contact with the criminal justice system. The overlap between criminogenic and disability needs also complicates decisions around treatment or support needs. This overlap includes factors on the Level of Service Inventory (Revised) (LSI-R – a measure of risk of recidivism and criminogenic need – Andrews and Bonta 1995; Hsu et al. 2011) shown in Table 14.1 People with IDD receive a range of treatments in the community and secure hospital settings (Cohen and Harvey 2016; Lindsay et al. 2011; Marotta 2015). Most studies reporting treatment for people with IDD are located in the community (Lindsay et al. 2010b) or high- or medium-security wards associated with mental health treatment (Alexander et al. 2011). Many of these studies report good outcomes along a range of dimensions including recidivism, or improved knowledge, attitudes, and skills.

14.5 Range of Treatment Modalities Used with People with IDD in Prison

The range of treatment has also been reviewed in relation to people with IDD. A very early review examined the use of antilibidinal drug treatment (Clarke 1989) for people with IDD and aberrant sexual behaviour. More recently Marotta (2015) reviewed programmes in the USA, UK, Australia, and New Zealand for people with IDD who offended sexually. Marotta reported most of the programmes used cognitive behavioural therapy (CBT), but a few used dialectical behaviour therapy (DBT), mindfulness, problem-solving therapy, and relapse prevention, but as there were no randomized control trials and generally small samples, it is difficult to synthesize the qualitative data.

Authors have also presented a range of criminogenic treatment models developed from those established for people with IDD. These include the Good Lives Model (GLM) (Ward and Brown 2004; Ward et al. 2007, 2012); self-regulation model (Keeling and Rose 2012; Lindsay et al. 2007), and various forms of psychotherapy (Cohen and Harvey 2016). The reviews have consistently reported finding a lack of randomized control studies; a wide range of methods; a lack of consistently applied criteria for participation; an assortment of outcomes; a lack of control group or adequate control group; or a combination of these factors.

Finally, there has been a review of outcomes of individual versus group offence-focused therapy (O'Brien et al. 2016) which found only 13 evidence-based studies of individual treatment. None of the studies included people with IDD, three were prison-based and, only two compared group and individual therapy for high-risk and need offenders. Whilst there are comparable outcomes in treatment, the authors discuss when individual therapy may be beneficial and assist in reducing treatment drop-out.

14.6 Evidence for Effectiveness of Prison-based Programmes for People with IDD

There have been a number of reviews, including two Cochrane reviews, around various aspects of treatment programmes for people who offend (Dennis et al. 2012) and people with IDD who offend (Ashman and Duggan 2009). Whilst much has therefore been written about people with IDD who offend (Courtney and Rose 2004; Endicott 1991; Lindsay 2002; Loucks 2007; Marotta 2015), there has not been a comprehensive review of their treatment in a prison setting.

Only five articles appear to provide adequate, albeit limited, evidence regarding the effectiveness of programmes for people with IDD in prison. The programme type, sample size, theoretical model of treatment, evaluation method, and outcome are presented in Table 14.2. The majority of the programmes were for sex offenders, although a substance abuse and a thinking skills programme were noted. No randomized controlled studies were found. The criteria applied for participation in the IDD groups in all but the McGillivray et al. (2016) study, varied, and commonly included people in the range of borderline to low average intellectual functioning (above 70 IQ points), or no adaptive functioning assessment was conducted to meet the criteria for a diagnosis of Intellectual Disability. All, except for the substance abuse programme, were noted to be 'adapted' from mainstream programmes. Although there was a theme across the studies suggesting that responsivity issues should be addressed for people with IDD as mainstream, programmes are not entirely suitable and may lead to higher drop out rates.

The capacity to compare the five studies and draw conclusions from them is limited. Within the studies, the matching of participants was inexact; not all studies assessed the intervention itself but rather focused on changes in participants psychometric scores across time, or on participation rates. For this reason, identification of trends or consistent approaches with which to build an evidence base in the treatment of offenders with IDD is currently lacking.

Table 14.2 Prison studies reporting treatment of people with IDD.

Authors	Purpose	Sample size	Theoretical model / intervention	Evaluation method	Outcome
Keeling et al. (2006)	Evaluating a programme developed for offenders with specific need	18 men; Mean age 35.2; Mean IQ (WAIS-III)[a] 71.78 (range – mild to low average); 18 Australian including 5 ATSI;[b] 5 married, 13 single; 16 left school prior to age 15. Av. Sentence length 7.24 years; Moderate to high risk (Static-99)	CBT group for 12 months, 4 times per week. Adapted for IDD – session duration 2.5 hours from 3; only 4 days per week from 5; programme length 12 months (from 8 to 10); used Old Me / New Me model; fewer written tasks and materials	Pre-post evaluation – no comparison group or follow-up	Programme was successful in reducing supportive attitudes towards sexual offending; increasing victim empathy and self-control
Keeling et al. (2007a)	Comparing self-regulation model for mainstream and 'special needs' sexual offenders	22 men in 2 groups – 11 mainstream and 11 'special needs'. Mainstream X age – 45.73 10 Australian Inc. 1 ATSI IQ – not assessed 73% high risk 0 married 6 divorced 5 single 'Special needs' 37.82 11 Australian Incl. 4 ATSI 71 (63–83) 7 above IQ 70 73% high risk 2 married 4 divorced 5 single	CBT group for 12 months, 4 times per week. Adapted for IDD – session duration 2.5 hours from 3; only 4 days per week from 5; programme length 12 months (from 8 to 10); used Old Me / New Me model; fewer written tasks and materials	Participants matched: risk; victim sex; offence type; age)	Both groups showed lack of significant pre-post-test change. No 'special need' participant convicted for sexual offence after 16 months follow-up. No 'mainstream' data available
Williams et al. (2007)	Evaluating modified instruments for Adapted sex offender programme	211 men; Sample from 8 prisons in England and Wales. Mean age 40.3; Mean IQ (WAIS-R)[c] 71.9 (range 56–80); 191 born in UK; 156 no educational qualification; 123 single; 21 married; 41 divorced; 5 separated	CBT group treatment using Old Me / New Me model; Manualized standardized treatment delivery; multimodal delivery strategies; link emotion and learning; longer time period for treatment. 89 treatment sessions – 200 hours	Pre-treatment and 6 weeks-post- treatment assessment on 6 self-report instruments across 8 prisons. No comparison group; self-report measures; missing data	Significant change found on 5 self-report measures with medium to large effect sizes for most. Higher risk offenders scored lower on risk following treatment

McGillivray et al. (2016)

Evaluated substance use and participation in AOD treatment

449 prisoners in Victoria, Australia

	With ID	Non ID
	180 offenders	269 matched
	93% male	90% male
	Mean age 27 years	Mean age 28 years
	ATSI 17%	ATSI 13%
	Higher proportion used ethanol	
	Offence antecedent was drug 32%	Offence antecedent was drug 64%

With ID treatment	Non ID treatment
Participate alcohol – 0.5	Participate alcohol – 0.55
Complete alcohol – 0.59	Complete alcohol – 0.89
Participate drug – 0.61	Participate drug – 0.71
Complete drug – 0.57	Complete drug – 0.92
Current methadone – 0	Current methadone – 0.01
Current buprenorphine – 0.47	Current buprenorphine – 0.73

Prisoners with and without intellectual disabilities have many similarities relating to substance use

Completion rate of AOD treatment programme by ID participants was substantially lower as was buprenorphine use. Treatment may not be addressing responsivity

Oakes et al. (2016)

Evaluation of an adapted thinking skills programme

Across 3 prisons in England 8 male inmates

Prison number	# 1	# 2	# 3
Prison type	C – closed	C – closed	A – max
Prison size	800–900	700–800	1100–1200
No. participants	8	8	8
Average age	43.7	42.5	43.7
Age range	30–63	30–65	28–73
Average IQ	68.6	73.6	70.7
IQ range	63–73	60–95	64–76

Realistic evaluation model used for the pilot of the Adapted Thinking Skills Program (ATSP) across 3 prisons with different security levels

Evaluation differences not described. Programme consistent across sites. A more robust evaluation is required

Statistically significant improvements for locus of control as well as ability to create assertive social solutions.

---

[a] Wechsler Adult Intelligence Scale – Third Edition (an IQ test)
[b] Aboriginal or Torres Strait Islander
[c] Wechsler Adult Intelligence Scale – Revised Edition (an IQ test)

14.7   Conclusions

So, what are the difficulties that people in prisons experience that impact on the creation of an evidence base? We would argue that some of the issues include identification and the consequential small numbers of people considered suitable for treatment programmes; those small numbers impacting on the ability to randomly allocate to different treatment groups and being further reduced by individual choice around participating in various types of treatment; diagnostic overshadowing; the nature of prisons including the historical reluctance of governments to shine a spotlight on processes and programmes that may impact negatively on public perceptions; and the focus on adapted treatments that are offence specific rather than dealing with the whole person across the span of the sentence including reintegration into the community.

With reasonably small numbers of identified inmates for any treatment group, let alone one specifically for offenders with IDD, there is reduced opportunity for randomization around interventions. The small numbers also impact on available locations for treatment with generally only a single location being available for a treatment group. Treatment suitability, readiness, and even sequencing of programmes (i.e. generally sex offender treatment occurs towards the end of a custodial sentence whilst violent offender treatment can occur at any point of incarceration) further limits research design. There are also limitations around long-term research design in that the prison environment is not static across time, but is governed by changes in policies that impact staffing levels, inmate flows, and inmate motivation to attend treatment. A further restriction is the inmate classification that limits in which prison an inmate may be held and may impact on treatment availability.

Each of the above factors affecting the development of an evidence base for mainstream programmes in prison is true for programmes for offenders with IDD. It is further impacted by the challenges of identification of the client group; the complexity and heterogeneity of people with IDD needing an individualized, flexible approach to group treatment, as well as the significant number of intersectional factors that further burden the person in their capacity to participate in a programme and maintain attendance.

14.8   Future Research

Despite all the limitations and restrictions described in this chapter, treatment in custody does occur and programmes across Australia, including those targeting people with IDD, are detailed (Heseltine et al. 2011). There are programmes that meet criminogenic need and / or disability need. Evaluation questions that still need to be addressed include the role of the therapeutic alliance in relation to the treatment approach i.e. do the results that are being obtained relate to the nature of the treatment (e.g. group based CBT or DBT) or to the therapeutic relationship developed between group members and therapists, or a combination of these factors? What is the impact of different models e.g. Risk/Needs/ Responsivity and Good Lives (Netto et al. 2014) and how does the context of a prison impact on delivery of those models? Do other models such as mindfulness (Singh et al. 2011) and DBT (Frazier and Vela 2014) work differently across various offence types (e.g. anger and violence; sex offending; or arson)? Is it good enough to demonstrate change on psychometric instruments e.g. better attitudes and knowledge, or must treatment extend to a reduction of harm in the community (e.g. future offending has less impact or recidivism is reduced)?

We are not sure whether it is possible to answer some, or any, of these questions when considering treatment in custody because of the many limitations discussed earlier. So, how do we know whether treatment is effective and how can we build an evidence base in a prison context? We believe that for this to occur:

- There must be an overarching policy and strategic imperative to evaluate treatment for people with IDD in prison. This agenda comes with risk, but it is better than the current situation where we are unable to show the public there is an evidence base showing that treatment not only works, but that the public is safer when a person with IDD is released following treatment.
- For treatment to be effective there is also a requirement to identify people with IDD in custody. The identification process may be costly in terms of both financial and human resources, but at present the risk of not identifying this population includes providing treatment that does not meet responsivity principles. The risk of reoffending increases when offenders fail to complete treatment (McMurran and Theodosi 2007; Olver et al. 2011). If that drop-out is due to lack of identification, then the correctional system is inadvertently contributing to an increased risk of reoffending.
- People with IDD must be considered from a holistic perspective. It is not sufficient to conduct a well-constructed programme that has been shown to work for people with IDD in the community or even in prison. The programme that addresses criminogenic needs must be supplemented by one that addresses disability needs. A structure of disability- and offence-related supports in the community is likely to have a greater impact than a treatment programme alone. However, this hypothesis needs to be tested and an evidence base provided.
- There are many papers indicating that serious offenders can be treated in the community. For diversion from a custodial option to occur there needs to be a degree of public support (or even public apathy) as to not incarcerating people with IDD who offend. Diversionary options offer another way to build an evidence base and even the possibility of comparing treatment effectiveness with a community / prison sample using the same programme.
- Finally, we need to address our current reality. As the population increases, so too do the numbers of people with IDD in custody. With better identification, the number of people with IDD becomes even larger. With more people in prison suitable for treatment programmes, the opportunities for evidence-based research become greater. Inmates can be randomly assigned to attend different programmes in different locations providing there is consensus as to the scope of research and methodology prior to treatment. It may even be possible to do research across prison and community settings (notwithstanding individual differences allowing treatment in these various settings; or across states (even with varying legislative requirements) or internationally (despite different treatment settings). Without a coordinated effort to obtain an evidence base, we are likely to be reporting in reviews during the next decade the same words that have been reported in previous reviews i.e. there are promising trends in treatment approaches but no reported evidence-based controlled studies around treatment of people with IDD in prison.

References

Aicken, B., Snoyman, P., and Langton, C. (2011, October). *The self regulation program for sexual offending (SRP-SO)*. Paper presented at the New Paradigms Old Challenges. 6th Forensic Disabilities Conference, Rendezvous Hotel, Melbourne.

Alexander, R.T., Green, F.N., O'Mahony, B. et al. (2010). Personality disorders in offenders with intellectual disability: a comparison of clinical, forensic and outcome variables and implications for service provision. *Journal of Intellectual Disability Research* 54 (7): 650–658. https://doi.org/10.1111/j.1365-2788.2010.01248.x.

Alexander, R., Hiremath, A., Chester, V. et al. (2011). Evaluation of treatment outcomes from a medium secure unit for people with intellectual disability. *Advances in Mental Health and Intellectual Disabilities* 5 (1): 22–32. https://doi.org/10.5042/amhid.2011.0013.

Andrews, D.A. (1995). The psychology of criminal conduct and effective treatment. In: *What Works: Reducing Re-Offending. Guidelines from Research and Practice* (ed. J. Mcguire), 35–62. Chichester, UK: Wiley.

Andrews, D.A. and Bonta, J.L. (1995). *LSI-R, Level of Service Inventory-Revised user's Manual*. Toronto: Multi-health Systems.

Andrews, D.A. and Bonta, J. (2010). Rehabilitating criminal justice policy and practice. *Psychology, Public Policy, and Law* 16 (1): 39.

Ashman, L.L.M. and Duggan, L. (2009). Interventions for learning disabled sex offenders. *Cochrane Database of Systematic Reviews* 1 https://doi.org/10.1002/14651858. CD003682.pub2.

Astor, H., James, G., Sperling, H. et al. (2012). People with cognitive and mental health impairments in the criminal justice system: Diversion - Report 135. Sydney: NSW Law Reform Commission.

Baldry, E. (2010, February). *Pathways to prison: intellectual disability*. Paper presented at the Coalition on ID in the CJS Seminar, UNSW, Sydney, Australia.

Bhandari, A., van Dooren, K., Eastgate, G. et al. (2015). Comparison of social circumstances, substance use and substance-related harm in soon-to-be-released prisoners with and without intellectual disability. *Journal Of Intellectual Disability Research* 59 (6): 571–579. https://doi.org/10.1111/jir.12162.

Board, T., Ali, S., and Bartlett, A. (2015). Intellectual disability screening in women prisoners: preliminary evaluation. *International Journal of Prisoner Health* 11 (4): 243–254. https://doi.org/10.1108/IJPH-09-2014-0027.

Bogart, S. and Bruce, J. (2009). *People with Mental Health Disorders & Cognitive Disabilities in the Criminal Justice System in NSW: Policy & Legislative Impacts*. Sydney: University of New South Wales.

Clarke, D.J. (1989). Antilibidinal drugs and mental retardation: a review. *Medicine, Science and the Law* 29 (2): 136–146. https://doi.org/10.1177/002580248902900209.

Cohen, G. and Harvey, J. (2016). The use of psychological interventions for adult male sex offenders with a learning disability: a systematic review. *Journal of Sexual aggression* 22 (2): 206–223. https://doi.org/10.1080/13552600.2015.1077279.

Courtney, J. and Rose, J. (2004). The effectiveness of treatment for male sex offenders with learning disabilities: a review of the literature. *Journal of Sexual aggression* 10 (2): 215–236. https://doi.org/10.1080/13552600412331286558.

Craig, L.A. and Hutchinson, R.B. (2005). Sexual offenders with learning disabilities: risk, recidivism and treatment. *Journal of Sexual aggression* 11 (3): 289–304.

Day, C., Lampraki, A., Ridings, D. et al. (2016). Intellectual disability and substance use/ misuse: a narrative review. *Journal of Intellectual Disabilities and Offending Behaviour* 7 (1): 25–34. https://doi.org/10.1108/JIDOB-10-2015-0041.

Dean, K. (2016). *Prison Models of Mental Health Care: A Review of the Literature and Relevant Key Principles/Concepts*. Sydney: Justice Health and Forensic Mental Health Network, NSW.

Dennis, J.A., Khan, O., Ferriter, M. et al. (2012). Psychological interventions for adults who have sexually offended or are at risk of offending. *Cochrane Database of Systematic Reviews* (12): CD007507. https://doi.org/10.1002/14651858.CD007507.pub2.

van Dooren, K., Young, J., Blackburn, C. et al. (2015). Substance use interventions for people with intellectual disability transitioning out of prison. *Australian and New Zealand Journal of Public Health* 39 (4): 397–397. https://doi.org/10.1111/1753-6405.12377.

Dowse, L., Baldry, E., and Snoyman, P. (2009). Disabling criminology: conceptualizing the intersection of critical disability studies and critical criminology for people with mental health and cognitive disabilities in the criminal justice system. Relationship to UN convention of the rights of persons with disabilities. *Australian Journal of Human Rights – Disability Studies Special Edition* 15 (1): 29–46.

Eadens, D.M., Cranston-Gingras, A., Dupoux, E. et al. (2016). Police officer perspectives on intellectual disability. *Policing: An International Journal of Police Strategies & Management* 39 (1): 222–235. https://doi.org/10.1108/PIJPSM-03-2015-0039.

Eccleston, L., Ward, T., and Waterman, B. (2010). Applying the self-regulation model to sexual offenders with intellectual disabilities. In: *Assessment and Treatment of Sexual Offenders with Intellectual Disabilities: A Handbook* (eds. L.A. Craig, W.R. Lindsay and K.D. Browne), 69–86. Chichester, UK: Wiley-Blackwell.

Endicott, O.R. (1991). *Persons with intellectual disability who are incarcerated for criminal offences: a literature review*. Research report No. R-14: Research Branch, Corporate Development. Ottawa, ON: Correctional Services Canada.

Fazel, S., Hayes, A.J., Bartellas, K. et al. (2016). Mental health of prisoners: prevalence, adverse outcomes, and interventions. *The Lancet Psychiatry* 3 (9): 871–881. https://doi.org/10.1016/S2215-0366(16)30142-0.

Florio, T. and Trollor, J. (2015, May). *Poor diagnostic recognition of intellectual disability among mental health clinicians*. Paper presented at the IASSID Americas Regional Congress, Honolulu, Hawaii.

Frazier, S.N. and Vela, J. (2014). Dialectical behavior therapy for the treatment of anger and aggressive behavior: a review. *Aggression and Violent Behavior* 19 (2): 156–163. https://doi.org/10.1016/j.avb.2014.02.001.

Haaven, J.L. and Coleman, E.M. (2000). Treatment of the developmentally disabled sex offender. In: *Remaking Relapse Prevention with Sex Offenders: A Sourcebook* (eds. D.R. Laws, S.M. Hudson and T. Ward), 273–285. Thousand Oaks, CA: Sage Publications.

Hayes, S. (2007). Missing out: offenders with learning disabilities and the criminal justice system. *British Journal of Learning Disabilities* 35 (3): 146–153. https://doi.org/10.1111/j.1468-3156.2007.00465.x.

Henshaw, M. and Thomas, S. (2012). Police encounters with people with intellectual disability: prevalence, characteristics and challenges. *Journal of Intellectual Disability Research* 56 (6): 620–631.

Heseltine, K., Sarre, R., and Day, A. (2011). Prison-based correctional rehabilitation: an overview of intensive interventions for moderate to high-risk offenders. *Trends and Issues in Crime and Criminal Justice* 412: 1–6.

Hsu, C.-I., Caputi, P., and Byrne, M.K. (2011). The level of service inventory-revised (LSI-R) and Australian offenders factor structure, sensitivity, and specificity. *Criminal Justice and Behavior* 38 (6): 600–618.

Keeling, J.A. and Rose, J.L. (2012). Implications of the self-regulation model for treatment with sexual offenders with intellectual disabilities. *The British Journal of Forensic Practice* 14 (1): 29–39.

Keeling, J., Rose, J., and Beech, A. (2006). An investigation into the effectiveness of a custody-based cognitive-behavioural treatment for special needs sexual offenders. *Journal of Forensic Psychiatry and Psychology* 17 (3): 372–392.

Keeling, J.A., Rose, J.L., and Beech, A.R. (2007a). Comparing sexual offender treatment efficacy: mainstream sexual offenders and sexual offenders with special needs. *Journal of Intellectual & Developmental Disability* 32 (2): 117–124.

Keeling, J.A., Rose, J.L., and Beech, A.R. (2007b). A preliminary evaluation of the adaptation of four assessments for offenders with special needs. *Journal of Intellectual & Developmental Disability* 32 (2): 62–73.

Lambrick, F. and Glaser, W. (2004). Sex offenders with an intellectual disability. *Sexual Abuse: A Journal of Research and Treatment* 16 (4): 381–392.

Lindsay, W.R. (2002). Research and literature on sex offenders with intellectual and developmental disabilities. *Journal of Intellectual Disability Research* 46: 74–85. https://doi.org/10.1046/j.1365-2788.2002.00006.x.

Lindsay, W.R., Steele, L., Smith, A.H.W. et al. (2006). A community forensic intellectual disability service: twelve year follow up of referrals, analysis of referral patterns and assessment of harm reduction. *Legal & Criminological Psychology* 11 (1): 113–130.

Lindsay, W.R., Ward, T., Morgan, T. et al. (2007). Self-regulation of sex offending, future pathways and the good lives model: applications and problems. *Journal of Sexual Aggression* 13 (1): 37–50.

Lindsay, W.R., Holland, T., Wheeler, J.R. et al. (2010a). Pathways through services for offenders with intellectual disability: a one- and two-year follow-up study. *Suivi de un à deux ans sur les trajectoires de services des contrevenants présentant une déficience intellectuelle* 115 (3): 250–262. https://doi.org/10.1352/1944-7558-115.3-250.

Lindsay, W.R., Michie, A.M., and Lambrick, F. (2010b). Community-based treatment programmes for sex offenders with intellectual disabilities. In: *Assessment and Treatment of Sexual Offenders with Intellectual Disabilities: A Handbook* (eds. L.A. Craig, W.R. Lindsay and K.D. Browne), 271–292. Chichester, UK: Wiley-Blackwell.

Lindsay, W.R., Hastings, R.P., and Beech, A.R. (2011). Forensic research in offenders with intellectual & developmental disabilities 1: prevalence and risk assessment. *Psychology, Crime & Law* 17 (1): 3–7.

Lindsay, W.R., Holland, A.J., Carson, D. et al. (2013). Responsivity to criminogenic need in forensic intellectual disability services. *Journal Of Intellectual Disability Research* 57 (2): 172–181. https://doi.org/10.1111/j.1365-2788.2012.01600.x.

Loucks, N. (2007). *Prisoners with Learning Difficulties and Learning Disabilities – Review of Prevalence and Associated Needs*. London: Prison Reform Trust.

Marotta, P.L. (2015). A systematic review of behavioral health interventions for sex offenders with intellectual disabilities. *Sexual Abuse: A Journal of Research and Treatment*: 1–38. https://doi.org/10.1177/1079063215569546.

Maulik, P.K., Mascarenhas, M.N., Mathers, C.D. et al. (2011). Prevalence of intellectual disability: a meta-analysis of population-based studies. *Research in Developmental Disabilities* 32 (2): 419–436. http://dx.doi.org/10.1016/j.ridd.2010.12.018.

McCausland, R., Baldry, E., and McEntyre, E. (2015, 4 November 2015). Aboriginal people with disabilities get caught in a spiral of over-policing. *The Conversation*. https://theconversation.com/aboriginal-people-with-disabilities-get-caught-in-a-spiral-of-over-policing-49294 (accessed 30 May 2019).

McEntyre, E. (2015, 3 November 2015). How Aboriginal women with disabilities are set on a path into the criminal justice system. *The Conversation*. https://theconversation.com/how-aboriginal-women-with-disabilities-are-set-on-a-path-into-the-criminal-justice-system-48167 (accessed 30 May 2019).

McGillivray, J.A., Gaskin, C.J., Newton, D.C. et al. (2016). Substance use, offending, and participation in alcohol and drug treatment programmes: a comparison of prisoners with and without intellectual disabilities. *Journal of Applied Research in Intellectual Disabilities* 29 (3): 289–294.

McMurran, M. and Theodosi, E. (2007). Is treatment non-completion associated with increased reconviction over no treatment? *Psychology, Crime & Law* 13 (4): 333–343. https://doi.org/10.1080/10683160601060374.

Netto, N.R., Carter, J.M., and Bonell, C. (2014). A systematic review of interventions that adopt the 'good lives' approach to offender rehabilitation. *Journal of Offender Rehabilitation* 53 (6): 403–432. https://doi.org/10.1080/10509674.2014.931746.

Newberry, M. and Shuker, R. (2011). The relationship between intellectual ability and the treatment needs of offenders in a therapeutic community prison. *The Journal of Forensic Psychiatry & Psychology* 22 (3): 455–471. https://doi.org/10.1080/14789949.2011.586715.

Oakes, P., Murphy, G., Giraud-Saunders, A. et al. (2016). The realistic evaluation of an adapted thinking skills programme. *Journal of Intellectual Disabilities and Offending Behaviour* 7 (1): 14–24. https://doi.org/10.1108/JIDOB-05-2014-0006.

O'Brien, K., Sullivan, D., and Daffern, M. (2016). Integrating individual and group-based offence-focussed psychological treatments: towards a model for best practice. *Psychiatry, Psychology & Law* 23 (5): 746–764. https://doi.org/10.1080/13218719.2016.1150143.

Olver, M.E., Stockdale, K.C., and Wormith, J.S. (2011). A meta-analysis of predictors of offender treatment attrition and its relationship to recidivism. *Journal of Consulting and Clinical Psychology* 79 (1): 6–21. https://doi.org/10.1037/a0022200.

Rayner, K., Wood, H., Beail, N. et al. (2015). Intellectual disability, personality disorder and offending: a systematic review. *Advances in Mental Health and Intellectual Disabilities* 9 (2): 50–61. https://doi.org/10.1108/AMHID-04-2014-0007.

Sakdalan, J.A. and Collier, V. (2012). Piloting an evidence-based group treatment programme for high risk sex ofenders with intellectual disability in the New Zealand setting. *New Zealand Journal of Psychology* 41 (3): 6–12.

Shaw, V.L. (2016). Liaison and diversion services: embedding the role of learning disability nurses. *Journal of Intellectual Disabilities and Offending Behaviour* 7 (2): 56–65. https://doi.org/10.1108/JIDOB-09-2015-0039.

Singh, N.N., Lancioni, G.E., Winton, A.S.W. et al. (2011). Can adult offenders with intellectual disabilities use mindfulness-based procedures to control their deviant sexual arousal? *Psychology, Crime & Law* 17 (2): 165–179. https://doi.org/10.1080/10683160903392731.

Snoyman, P. (2010). *Staff in the NSW criminal justice system understanding of people with and without disability who offend*. Unpublished Doctoral discertation, University of New South Wales, Sydney.

Snoyman, P. and Aicken, B. (2011). The concept of intellectual disability, and people with intellectual disability in corrective services NSW. *Australasian Journal of Correctional Staff Development* 6 (2): 1–12.

Taylor, J. (2013). The evolution of a therapeutic community for offenders with a learning disability and personality disorder: part two – increasing responsivity. *Therapeutic Communities: The International Journal of Therapeutic Communities* 34 (1): 29–40. https://doi.org/10.1108/09641861311330482.

Taylor, J. (2014). *The criminogenic needs of offenders with intellectual disability and personality disorder*. Unpublished doctoral discertation in Forensic Psychology Practice, University of Birmingham, United Kingdom.

Taylor, J. and Morrissey, C. (2012). Integrating treatment for offenders with an intellectual disability and personality disorder. *The British Journal of Forensic Practice* 14 (2): 302–315. https://doi.org/10.1108/14636641211283101.

Taylor, J., MacKenzie, J., Bowen, J. et al. (2012). The development and accreditation of a treatment model for prisoners with a learning disability and personality disorder. *Journal of Learning Disabilities & Offending Behaviour* 3 (1): 44–51. https://doi.org/10.1108/20420921211236898.

Ward, T. and Brown, M. (2004). The good lives model and conceptual issues in offender rehabilitation. *Psychology, Crime & Law* 10 (3): 223–227.

Ward, T., Mann, R.E., and Gannon, T.A. (2007). The good lives model of offender rehabilitation: clinical implications. *Aggression and Violent Behavior* 12 (1): 87–107.

Ward, T., Yates, P., and Willis, G. (2012). The good lives model and the risk need responsivity model. *Criminal Justice and Behavior* 39 (1): 94–110.

West, B. (2007). Using the good way model to work positively with adults and youth with intellectual difficulties and sexually abusive behaviour. *Journal of Sexual Aggression* 13 (3): 253–266.

Wilcox, D.T. (2004). Treatment of intellectually disabled individuals who have committed sexual offences: a review of the literature. *Journal of Sexual Aggression* 10 (1): 85–100.

Williams, F. and Mann, R.E. (2010). The treatment of intellectually disabled sexual offenders in the National Offender Management Service: the adapted sex offender treatment programmes. In: *Assessment and Treatment of Sexual Offenders with Intellectual Disabilities: A Handbook* (eds. L.A. Craig, W.R. Lindsay and K.D. Browne), 293–315. Chichester, UK: Wiley-Blackwell.

Williams, F., Wakeling, H., and Webster, S. (2007). A psychometric study of six self-report measures for use with sexual offenders with cognitive and social functioning deficits. *Psychology, Crime & Law* 13 (5): 505–522. https://doi.org/10.1080/10683160601060739.

15

Treatment of Anger and Violence in Individuals with Intellectual Disability

Robert Didden[1,2], Henk Nijman[1,3], Monique Delforterie[2], and Marije Keulen-De Vos[4]

[1] *Radboud University, Nijmegen, The Netherlands*
[2] *Trajectum, Zwolle, The Netherlands*
[3] *Fivoor, Den Dolder, The Netherlands*
[4] *De Rooyse Wissel, Oostrum, The Netherlands*

15.1   Introduction

Problems with anger and violence are the most common reasons for referral to specialized treatment services for individuals with mild intellectual disability or borderline intellectual functioning (MID-BIF; IQ 50–85). Several studies have shown that the most prevalent index behaviour and most common problems in the lives of offenders are aggression and violence (see e.g. Lunsky et al. 2011). In many cases, such problems have high co-morbidity with problems related to mental health (e.g. substance abuse, trauma, personality issues) and social conditions (e.g. financial and interpersonal problems) (see Taylor and Novaco 2013).

Aggressive behaviour has a number of adverse consequences. It may result in re-offending and crisis intervention re-referrals. Many individuals reside in inpatient (forensic) mental health services that often involve high levels of security and/or intrusive pharmacological interventions, seclusion, or sedation. Aggressive behaviour can make it difficult to form and maintain relationships and lead to exclusion from educational, work, and social settings. Furthermore, it may generate stress for family members, is correlated with staff burnout and stress, and may create negative attitudes and interactions with clients (see Jahoda et al. 2013). Without treatment of tendencies to become aggressive, the risk of re-offending is high (Lindsay 2009).

Within a forensic framework, it is generally agreed that treatments that are based on 'What Works' principles are more effective than those that are not based on these principles (see e.g. Andrews and Bonta 2010). The core 'What Works' principles of risk, responsivity, and criminogenic needs are important in the treatment of offenders in general. In the treatment of individuals with MID-BIF, responsivity in particular requires much attention, as this principle means that the treatment should be adapted to the characteristics and learning style of the recipient of the treatment. Besides this,

The Wiley Handbook on What Works for Offenders with Intellectual and Developmental Disabilities: An Evidence-Based Approach to Theory, Assessment, and Treatment, First Edition.
Edited by William R. Lindsay, Leam A. Craig, and Dorothy Griffiths.
© 2020 John Wiley & Sons Ltd. Published 2020 by John Wiley & Sons Ltd.

treatment should be directed at dynamic (i.e. potentially changeable) risk factors of aggression such as anger, substance abuse, impulsivity, hostile attitude, and deficiencies in coping skills, amongst others.

In this chapter, we provide a selective overview of studies published between 2000 and 2018 that assessed effectiveness of cognitive behaviour therapy (CBT) and mindfulness for anger and violence (aggression) in individuals with MID-BIF. Next to this, we give suggestions for adapting CBT for this target group. Also, we review studies that have evaluated programmes for training staff members who are involved in the treatment of clients with ID who present with anger problems and violence.

15.2 Treatments for Anger and Violence

Anger is strongly associated and may even be predictive of (physical) aggression in individuals with ID and histories of violence and offending (Taylor and Novaco 2013). It is therefore often a therapeutic target for individuals with aggressive behaviour. Didden et al. (2016) and Taylor and Novaco (2013) suggested that there are several treatment approaches for anger and aggression in ID: cognitive behavioural therapy, behavioural interventions, mindfulness, and psychotropic medication. In this chapter, the focus will be on CBT and mindfulness for adults with ID. The main reasons for this choice are that both treatments actively promote self-regulation, that they can be implemented both in settings with high or low staff ratios (e.g. inpatient versus community treatment), that they may be used in clients showing low-frequency yet severe aggression and violence, and that they are commonly implemented in forensic services for individuals with ID.

15.2.1 Cognitive Behaviour Therapy

Cognitive behaviour therapy or anger management training (CBT/AMT) is a composite treatment with a number of components designed to address anger in several ways. A basic assumption is that anger is a normal emotion and that it can be dealt with in ways that will not place the individual in difficult situations (Taylor and Novaco 2013). The following are considered essential components of CBT/AMT (also see Didden et al. 2016):

- relaxation: teach skills with which the individual can control their anger or increased arousal. This is often done through the use of relaxation exercises of which the main one is abbreviated progressive relaxation in which the participant tenses and relaxes major muscle groups including arms, torso, head, neck and shoulders, buttocks and thighs, and legs and feet;
- understanding of the person's own and others' emotions;
- keeping a diary of situations that may have caused anger;
- establishing an anger hierarchy: this is made up of a series of situations that make the individual angry;
- cognitive restructuring. This is based on the relationship between arousal and cognitions. Individuals may have a tendency to perceive threat in situations where they feel aroused. This perception of threat may lead to an interpretation of the arousal as one of anger with corresponding behavioural consequences to deal with the perceived

threat (i.e. aggression). Aim is to help the person make realistic appraisals of the situation;

- problem solving. Exercises are likely to involve accurate self-perception, arousal reduction, effective communication, and action alternative to aggression through role-play and discussion;
- stress inoculation. Involves gradually introducing stress-inducing stimuli to the individual under conditions where they are supported to control their arousal and stress reactions. It can be done in imagination, through role-play, and in actual situations whilst supporting the client to use coping skills they have learned during anger management training (AMT).

15.2.2 Research on CBT

15.2.2.1 Single Case or Case Series Studies

Howells et al. (2000) used group-wise CBT in three men and two women with mild ID. CBT consisted of several of the above techniques during 2-hour sessions that were held during 12 weeks. CBT resulted in improvements in anger control in all participants.

Allan et al. (2001) and Lindsay et al. (2003) published a series of case studies on violent offenders with ID. Allan et al. treated five women with mild ID who had convictions for violence. They used group CBT including psycho-education, arousal reduction, role-play of anger provocation incidents, problem-solving exercises, exercises on emotional recognition, and stress inoculation through imagination of anger-provoking situations. Treatment lasted 40 sessions and was assessed using self-report measures, reports of aggressive incidents, and an anger diary. Participants were also assessed using videotaped role-plays in anger-provoking situations. Improvements were reported on all measures for all the women and these improvements maintained to 15-month follow-up. Only one of the women had another incident of violence. In a follow-up study, Lindsay et al. (2003) reported on six men with mild ID who had been involved with the criminal justice system for reasons of aggression and violence. Treatment was similar to that described by Allan et al. and there were improvements on all measures, which were maintained at 15-month follow-up. None of the men had been violent at four-year follow-up. Whilst these case evaluations have all suggested positive outcomes, effectiveness of these methods has not been verified either by staggering the baseline for each of the participants or by a return to baseline conditions.

Burns et al. (2003) presented a case series of three forensic males with MID-BIF on the effects of a group CBT that lasted 12 weeks and consisted of 2.5 hour sessions. Data that were collected in an ABA (baseline – intervention – return to baseline) design showed that CBT resulted in improvements in anger levels. However, Burns et al. (2003) noted that maintenance treatment is required to prevent anger levels increasing to pre-test levels following treatment.

15.2.2.2 Group Studies

Rose et al. (2000) used a group CBT in 23 men and 2 women with mild to moderate ID. CBT consisted of relaxation training, coping skills training, role-play with video feedback, and emotion recognition. The intervention lasted 16 weeks and weekly sessions lasted 2 hours. The intervention resulted in a reduction in expressed anger which was maintained at 6- and 12-months follow-up.

Willner et al. (2002) conducted a randomized control study with 14 participants with mild ID who were randomly allocated to a 9-session treatment group (AMT) and a waiting list control condition. Data were collected through an anger questionnaire and a provocation index completed by both participants and their careers. Participants in the treated group showed substantial improvements in anger ratings that further improved relative to their own pre-treatment scores at a three-month follow-up. There were no improvements in the control group. The degree of improvement during AMT was strongly and positively correlated with IQ, but the group of treated participants in this study was very small. The intervention was shorter than that reported in previous studies (e.g. Allan et al. 2001) with no apparent loss of efficacy. Taylor et al. (2009) addressed the question if verbal IQ influenced the outcomes of AMT in a larger sample of 83 inpatients with MID-BIF who were inpatients of a forensic facility. The verbal IQ of the 83 participants in the study ranged from 54 to 81 and was found to be statistically unrelated to positive changes in self-reported and staff-reported anger scores. This suggests that a therapy like AMT may indeed be effective also for individuals with rather pronounced intellectual deficiencies.

Taylor and his colleagues have conducted a series of waiting list control studies on the effectiveness of AMT. All participants had been detained for reasons of cognitive impairment and severe aggressive and/or irresponsible and dangerous behaviour. Taylor et al. (2002) compared 10 men with MID-BIF who received AMT with 10 on the waiting list. Treatment was manualized and delivered individually to participants over 18 60-minute sessions. Participants in the treatment group reported significantly lower anger intensity and staff member ratings supported these improvements showing modest gains for the treatment group. Taylor et al. (2005) used the same protocol with 20 participants (some of whom had also been enrolled in their 2002 study) allocated to the AMT condition and 20 to the waiting list control. Scores on self-reported anger disposition and reactivity indices were significantly reduced following intervention in the treatment group compared with scores for the control group and these differences were maintained to a four-month follow-up. Staff ratings of study participants' anger disposition converged with self-report ratings but did not reach statistical significance. Although this study did not randomize participants, it did have the strength of using a treatment manual with a waiting list control condition and a four-month follow-up.

Lindsay et al. (2004) included participants referred from the courts and criminal justice agencies to a community forensic ID service. This was a waiting list control study with several outcome measures, provocation role-plays and self-report diaries that were repeated before treatment and at several points in a follow-up period of 15 months. They compared 33 participants who received 40 sessions of AMT with 14 who made up a waiting list control condition for six months. Control participants were seen by community nursing staff but did not receive any form of anger treatment until after the cessation of the study period. For the AMT group, there were significant within-group improvements on all measures. In post-treatment comparisons between the two groups, there were no differences on the Dundee Provocation Inventory whilst the self-report diaries and the anger provocation role-plays showed significant differences between groups. These improvements were maintained at follow-up. The study also reported on the number of aggressive incidents and re-offences recorded for both groups. At the post-waiting-list assessment point (six months follow-up), 45% of the control group had committed another assault whilst at the post-treatment assessment point (nine months),

14% at the treatment group had committed a further incident of assault. Analysis on this data revealed a significant difference between groups. Therefore, although the follow-up period was relatively short, there was some evidence that AMT had a significant impact on the number of aggressive incidents recorded in these participants.

Rose et al. (2005) compared 50 participants with ID who received AMT with 36 controls. Outcome was measured using a provocation inventory administered at pre-treatment, post-treatment, and three to six months follow-up. Between-group comparisons showed a statistically significant treatment effect but examination of clinical significance was more equivocal with only 11 of the 50 participants in the intervention group showing reliable clinical change. A reduction in provocation inventory scores was more likely to occur if a participant was accompanied by a member of staff who knew them. The results on reliable clinical change suggested that although improvement was statistically significant, the approach may not be as effective as seems apparent from the initial statistical analysis.

Willner et al. (2013) conducted a randomized controlled trial of AMT with 179 people with ID having problems with anger. Treatment lasted 12 weeks, was delivered by care staff who were guided by a treatment manual, and assessments were conducted at pre-treatment, post-treatment, and 10-month follow-up. There were no significant improvements on the primary provocation self-report measure and any treatment gains were modest. However, keyworkers reported that treated individuals had significantly lower provocation scores and treated individuals reported significantly greater use of coping skills following treatment.

It is assumed that anger is associated with aggressive behaviour, but few studies have empirically addressed the question whether reduced levels of anger are associated with reduced levels of aggressive behaviour. Novaco and Taylor (2015) addressed this question in their study in which 50 forensic hospital patients (44 males) with MID-BIF were given individual AMT which was delivered twice weekly for 18 sessions. Data were collected on participants' self-reported anger, staff ratings of anger and aggression, and case records of aggressive incidents before and after the treatment. Results showed that the treatment yielded significant reductions in physical aggression. This reduction was associated with reductions in anger levels of participants.

15.2.2.3 Evidence-Base of CBT/AMT

From the above studies it may be concluded that CBT/AMT may be effective in reducing anger control problems and aggressive behaviour in individuals with ID in community settings and inpatient settings with offender clients (also see Didden et al. 2016; Taylor and Novaco 2013; Vereenooghe and Langdon 2013). These outcomes are in agreement with those of AMT/CBT studies conducted in samples of individuals without MID-BIF (see Lee and DiGuiseppe 2018). CBT is a treatment package and it remains unclear which elements contribute to its effectiveness. An important element in this regard is relaxation. Relaxation treatment has been assessed separately in relation to both the reduction of anxiety and the reduction of aggression in individuals with ID. In their systematic review, Bellemans et al. (2019) concluded that progressive muscle relaxation – as a stand-alone intervention – is effective in reducing anger problems and aggression in individuals with MID-BIF.

Another important and effective element of CBT packages is stress inoculation and teaching coping skills. A well-controlled study on three cases has been conducted by

Travis and Sturmey (2013). Three participants with high frequencies of aggressive behaviour were taught to identify anger-provoking situations and 'socially acceptable replacement responses' rather than aggression. The study focused on stress inoculation, using situations that emerged from an anger hierarchy. They used a multiple baseline across-participants design, and results showed a large reduction in aggressive responses with a corresponding increase in replacement responses. There was also a significant increase in escorted community access. However, there was no follow-up in this study and in many services for violent individuals (e.g. offender services) follow-up periods over months and years is an essential aspect of effectiveness.

Results of a study by Rose (2013) amongst 37 participants with ID who lived in the community showed that therapist experience may also play a role in the effectiveness of CBT for anger problems. He found that individuals who were treated by more-experienced therapists reported more clinically significant reliable change than individuals who were treated by less-experienced therapists.

15.2.3   Adapting CBT/AMT to Individuals with ID

Cognitive and adaptive skill deficits have long been regarded as precluding the use of CBT/AMT in individuals with ID due to their limited verbal communication skills, recognizing emotions, executive functioning deficits, and limited working memory, amongst others. Lindsay (2009) noted that psychological therapies require adaptations to be accessible for individuals with ID especially with regard to communication. Adaptation requires for example adjustments of vocabulary and syntax in addition to continuing self-monitoring. He provides the following basic recommendations:

- use short sentences that contain a single concept;
- use words of fewer than three syllables;
- ask clients to summarize the session in order to assess their understanding and retention;
- use inductive methods (e.g. Socratic dialogue);
- use role-play;
- increase motivation to change;
- work with significant others and relatives.

Cooney et al. (2018) conducted a systematic review on skills assisting adults with ID to participate in CBT programmes such as those mentioned in the previous section. The following skills and prompts were identified:

- recognizing emotions by using photographs of people's faces;
- discriminating between thoughts, emotions, and behaviour by using personally relevant scenario's and pictorial stimuli;
- making a connection between events and emotions, and recognizing the mediating role of thoughts in the relationship between thoughts, emotions, and behaviour by using examples of situations and emotions and behaviours that are congruent.

Hronis et al. (2017) provided suggestions for adapting CBT to children with ID who present with cognitive skill deficits. Below are some examples:

- attention: use shorter, more frequent sessions, reduce task length (smaller units), prevent distractions;

- working memory: use memory aids (e.g. visual prompts), present one task at a time, use short, simple, subject-verb-object sentences;
- executive functions: use structured sessions (e.g. visual schedule), minimize switching between tasks, redirect uninhibited responses.

Many of the recommendations mentioned above are aimed at increasing the 'What Works' responsivity principle for individuals with ID. Using more frequent, but shorter, sessions, a lot of repetition, shorter sentences, a lot of visual materials and incorporating a lot of practical exercises and role plays is likely to have a better match with the learning style of individuals with ID.

In clinical practice, however, individuals with ID may lack the prerequisite skills for participating in CBT programmes. They have difficulties understanding the cognitive components of CBT even if the programme is adapted to their learning style and characteristics. It has been suggested that those who lack the prerequisite skills may benefit from pre-therapy in which they are taught CBT basic concepts such as identifying, differentiating, and linking emotions, thoughts, and events (see Tsimopoulou et al. 2018). Tsimoupoulou et al. used a video to teach six adults with mild ID cognitive skills necessary to engage in CBT. The video consisted of simple digital stories (scenario's) that were created using an online comic-making tool and in which examples of emotions, thoughts, and behaviours were presented to the participants. Participants were taught to discriminate between these categories, to link events to emotions, and make associations between mediating cognitions and emotions. Results of this study showed that most participants increased their cognitive mediation skills and that this improvement was maintained at follow-up. These results suggest that individuals with mild ID can learn the prerequisite skills necessary to participate in CBT programmes.

15.3 Mindfulness

A procedure that has received increased attention in the literature on anger and aggression in individuals with intellectual disability is mindfulness. Singh et al. (2008) have developed the meditation procedure 'Soles of the feet' (SoF) with which individuals are taught to recognize the precursors of aggression, to disengage their attention to the precursor(s), and to focus their attention to a neutral point of the body. Precursors of aggression may be behaviours and/or emotions such as anger that increases the likelihood of aggression. Through this procedure the individual is able to focus his mind on the body and calm down and think about alternative ways to react to an event that triggered anger. The individual is guided through the steps of the procedure, which include finding a natural posture, breathing naturally whilst allowing the emotions and thoughts to flow without trying to stop or respond to them, then shifting the attention to the SoF. This is continued until calmness and clarity of mind is established. The final step includes walking away from the situation or a nonaggressive response to the situation. Training is provided during supervised role-play and practice sessions, supplemented with homework practice assignments whereby the client is encouraged to practise in multiple contexts.

Singh et al. have conducted studies on the effectiveness of mindfulness in a variety of target groups and settings (i.e. forensic and community settings). Most studies have employed single subject designs. But, Singh et al. (2013) also performed a randomized controlled trial in which they assessed the effectiveness of the SoF-procedure for the treatment of aggressive behaviour in a sample of 34 individuals (between 17 and 34 years of age) with mild ID who lived in the community. They were assigned to either the SoF group or a waiting list control group. A 12-week baseline phase was followed by a 12-week intervention phase and follow-up. During the SoF training parents and staff taught (through instructions and modelling) the use of various techniques to the individuals and each weekday they practised with the individuals during daily 15–30 minutes sessions. Staff and parents followed the steps outlined in the manualized treatment protocol and reliability measurements yielded high treatment fidelity. Results revealed that the number of both verbal and physical aggression acts was much lower in the SoF condition compared to the control condition. Further significant reductions to (near) zero levels of aggression were seen during the follow-up phases.

The results of the studies by Singh and his colleagues suggest that a mindful-based procedure may be effective in reducing aggressive behaviour of individuals with ID. These results, however, need to be replicated by other independent researchers before conclusions may be drawn on whether mindfulness is an evidence-based practice for aggression in individuals with ID.

15.4 Social Climate and Staff Training

The social environment plays a crucial part in the treatment of anger and violence in clients with MID-BIF. Jahoda et al. (2013) stated that aggression is usually a social act and concerns the dynamic (transactional) relationship between the person and his or her social environment. This may especially hold true for (secure forensic) inpatient settings. Langdon et al. (2006) point to the fact that the social climate in such settings is an important contributor to treatment outcome. Stams and Van der Helm (2017) defined living-group climate as 'the quality of the social and physical environment in terms of the provision of sufficient and necessary conditions for physical and mental health, well-being and personal growth of the residents, with respect for their human dignity and human rights as well as (if not restricted by judicial measures) their personal autonomy, aimed at successful participation in society' (p. 4). A positive living-group climate has been shown to be associated with active coping, improved social information processing, empathy, prosocial behaviour, motivation for treatment, a longer period of treatment (no drop out), and higher levels of internal locus of control in participants. It is also associated with lower levels of aggressive and destructive behaviour of clients in secure care (see Stams and Van der Helm 2017). To create a therapeutic living-group climate staff should be responsive to fulfil the basic psychological needs of the clients, such as the need for autonomy, competence, and relatedness. Surprisingly little research has been done in such settings for people with ID. Langdon et al. (2006) conducted a study on social climate in 18 clients and 37 staff members within a secure setting and found that on average clients and staff differed in their perceptions of the social climate on the wards. Future studies should be conducted on evaluating and improving social climate on wards of treatment facilities for people with ID. To this purpose, the Group Climate Instrument (GCI) – a self-report questionnaire administered to clients through an interview – may be used to explore clients' perceptions of the living-group climate. Neimeijer et al. (2019) examined the psychometric properties of the GCI in a sample of 189 adults (79% male) with MID-BIF who were residents of a (secure) treatment facility in the Netherlands. Analysis showed that the GCI has four factors (i.e. support, growth, group atmosphere, and repression) and a second-order factor overall climate, providing preliminary support for construct validity of the GCI. Reliability coefficients were good for all factors. Preliminary evidence for convergent validity was found in significant moderate associations between subscales and single-item ratings for the factors of group climate.

One way to improve the social climate on wards is through training of staff members responsible for the treatment and care of clients with ID. Relatively many studies have been conducted on staff training in services for individuals with ID. For example, Willner and his colleagues (2013) have adapted the CBT approach to the needs and skill deficits shown by individuals with ID by training staff to deliver the CBT. In this multicentre study, a manualized anger-management group intervention was compared to a waiting-list control condition. Staff or home carers participated as lay therapists and were trained by a clinical psychologist explaining the principles of anger management and the use of the CBT manual. The outcomes showed that anger management resulted in improved anger control by participants with ID and an overall reduction in challenging behaviours. Analyses also showed that staff members delivered the CBT intervention with reasonable fidelity.

During the past decade, positive behaviour support (PBS) has received increased attention in the ID-literature. A PBS programme for staff working in a forensic mental health service may be effective in changing staff's confidence and attributions towards clients with problem behaviours. PBS is a values-led behavioural management framework aimed at preventing and managing problem behaviours such as aggression. Important elements are, amongst others:

- functional analysis of the problem behaviour (understanding the causes of the behaviour)
- service user involvement, increasing quality of life
- feedback, skills training, altering triggers, or reinforcement
- no punitive approaches
- de-escalation and distraction techniques prior to crisis management
- post incident support.

The aim of PBS is that staff members respond to problem behaviours such as aggression in line with therapeutic considerations as opposed to reacting out of anger or fear. PBS is directed at changing the attributions held by staff concerning the degree of control and causality of the problem behaviour displayed by a client. Several studies in forensic settings have shown that if staff believe that problem behaviours are internal and controllable by clients they have more perceptions of 'untreatability', implementation of aversive approaches, and negative attributions (see Davies et al. 2015). Davies et al. assessed the effectiveness of a PBS training package to staff working in a medium-secure forensic mental health service where some clients have borderline intellectual functioning (IQ 70–85) or limited functional skills. Following training staff showed significant increases in attributing the causes of problem behaviour to emotions, reinforcement history, biomedical causes, physical environment, and levels of stimulation. This study showed that training staff in the PBS model is effective in increasing their confidence in working with clients with problem behaviours although results were not maintained at a six-months follow-up. The latter result indicates a need for ongoing training in supporting staff working with these clients.

A recent meta-analysis by Knotter et al. (2018) shows that whilst staff training was moderately effective in changing staff behaviour, no convincing evidence was found for an effect on the reduction of challenging behaviour (e.g. aggression) of persons with ID. These results suggest that training staff members does not result in a reduction of clients' aggressive behaviour. The authors provide several explanations for this negative finding. It may be explained by insufficient power of the meta-analysis due to the small number of studies included, it may be difficult for staff to transfer learned skills or knowledge from a training setting to daily practice in which they care for clients with ID who also show behaviour that challenges, or that training programmes did not aim to reduce the challenging (aggressive) behaviour in the first place.

15.5 Conclusion

During the past decades, significant improvements have been made regarding the treatment of anger and violence in individuals with ID. CBT/AMT is the most often used treatment which – if adapted – may be effective in reducing problems related to anger and aggression (also see Didden et al. 2016; Lindsay 2009; Vereenooghe and Langdon 2013). The specific adaptations that are needed to CBT to increase its responsivity for individuals with ID warrant further study. At present, protocolled treatment programmes are available that have been evaluated in case and group studies (see Taylor and Novaco 2013). The positive results imply that such programmes should be incorporated in a broader treatment approach for individuals with ID who present with anger and aggression problems in institutional and community settings (see Didden et al. 2016; Lindsay 2009). CBT programmes should thus be combined with approaches addressing the social context (through staff training) (see e.g. Jahoda et al. 2013), co-occurring mental health problems (such as trauma and substance abuse), and risk assessment and management of aggressive behaviour (see e.g. Lofthouse et al. 2017) (also see Morrissey et al. 2017). Dagnan et al. (2013) point to the fact that establishing a therapeutic relationship between client and therapist during CBT is of particular importance as this has been viewed by clients as one of the most positive aspects of therapy. A positive relationship improves client's motivation to attend the sessions and his or her confidence in learning skills. Qualitative studies have shown that CBT is experienced by participants with ID as effective and enjoyable (see e.g. MacMahon et al. 2015).

Finally, we would like to point out that gender effects were not reported in the studies that were reviewed in this chapter. Hellenbach et al. (2015) have noted that female offenders differ from male counterparts in relation to index offence, type of mental disorder, sexual abuse (trauma) and anger, and life history, and that forensic mental health services hardly address such differences. It is for example estimated that women constitute 25% of the population of forensic mental health services. Hellenbach et al. conducted a systematic review on evidence-based treatments for women with ID and mental disorder and concluded that the distinct forensic care needs by these women are overlooked in the literature and in clinical practice, and that future research should address gender differences in offenders with ID.

References

Allan, R., Lindsay, W., Macleod, F. et al. (2001). Treatment of women with intellectual disabilities who have been involved with the criminal justice system for reasons of aggression. *Journal of Applied Research in Intellectual Disabilities* 14: 340–347.

Andrews, D. and Bonta, J. (2010). *The Psychology of Criminal Conduct*, 5e. London: Routledge.

Bellemans, T., Didden, R., Van Busschbach, J. et al. (2019). Psychomotor therapy targeting anger and aggressive behavior in individuals with mild or borderline intellectual disabilities: a systematic review. *Journal of Intellectual and Developmental Disabilities* 44: 121–130.

Burns, M., Bird, D., Leach, C. et al. (2003). Anger management training: the effects of a structured programme on the self-reported anger experience of forensic inpatients with learning disability. *Journal of Psychiatric Mental Health Nursing* 10: 569–577.

Cooney, P., Tunney, C., and O'Reilly, G. (2018). A systematic review of the evidence regarding cognitive skills that assist cognitive behavioural therapy in adults who have an intellectual disability. *Journal of Applied Research in Intellectual Disability* 31: 23–42.

Dagnan, D., Jahoda, A., and Kilbane, A. (2013). Preparing people with intellectual disabilities for psychological treatment. In: *Psychological Therapies for Adults with Intellectual Disabilities* (eds. J. Taylor, W. Lindsay, R. Hastings, et al.), 55–68. Chichester: Wiley Blackwell.

Davies, B., Griffiths, J., Liddiard, K. et al. (2015). Changes in staff confidence and attributions for challenging behaviors after training in positive behavioural support within a forensic medium secure service. *The Journal of Forensic Psychiatry & Psychology* 26: 847–861.

Didden, R., Lindsay, W., Lang, R. et al. (2016). Aggression. In: *Clinical Handbook of Evidence-Based Practices for Individuals with Intellectual Disabilities* (ed. N. Singh), 727–750. New York: Springer.

Hellenbach, M., Brown, M., Karatzias, T. et al. (2015). Psychological interventions for women with intellectual disabilities and forensic care needs: a systematic review of the literature. *Journal of Intellectual Disability Research* 59: 319–331.

Howells, P., Rogers, C., and Wilcock, S. (2000). Evaluating a cognitive/behavioural approach to anger management skills in adults with learning disabilities. *British Journal of Learning Disabilities* 28: 137–142.

Hronis, A., Roberts, A., and Kneebone, I. (2017). A review of cognitive impairments with children with intellectual disabilities: implications for cognitive behaviour therapy. *British Journal of Clinical Psychology* 56: 189–207.

Jahoda, A., Willner, P., Pert, C. et al. (2013). From causes of aggression to interventions: the importance of context. *International Review of Research in Developmental Disabilities* 44: 69–104.

Knotter, M., Spruit, A., De Swart, J. et al. (2018). Training direct care staff working with persons with intellectual disabilities and challenging behaviour: a meta-analytic review study. *Aggression and Violent Behaviour* 40: 60–72.

Langdon, P., Swift, A., and Budd, R. (2006). Social climate within secure inpatient services for people with intellectual disabilities. *Journal of Intellectual Disability Research* 50: 828–836.

Lee, A. and DiGuiseppe, R. (2018). Anger and aggression treatments: a review of meta-analyses. *Current Opinion in Psychiatry* 19: 65–74.

Lindsay, W. (2009). Adaptations and developments in treatment programmes for offenders with developmental disabilities. *Psychiatry, Psychology and Law* 16: S18–S35.

Lindsay, W., Allan, R., Macleod, F. et al. (2003). Long term treatment and management of violent tendencies of men with intellectual disabilities convicted of assault. *Mental Retardation* 41: 47–56.

Lindsay, W., Allan, R., Parry, C. et al. (2004). Anger and aggression in people with intellectual disabilities: treatment and follow-up of consecutive referrals and a waiting list comparison. *Clinical Psychology & Psychotherapy* 11: 255–264.

Lofthouse, R., Golding, L., Totsika, V. et al. (2017). How effective are risk assessments/measures for predicting future aggressive behaviour in adults with intellectual disabilities: a systematic review and meta-analysis. *Clinical Psychology Review* 58: 76–85.

Lunsky, Y., Gracey, C., Koegl, C. et al. (2011). The clinical profile and service needs of psychiatric inpatients with intellectual disabilities and forensic involvement. *Psychology, Crime and Law* 17: 9–25.

MacMahon, P., Stenfert Kroese, B., Jahoda, A. et al. (2015). 'It's made all of us bond since that course…': a qualitative study of service users' experiences of a CBT anger management group intervention. *Journal of Intellectual Disability Research* 59: 342–352.

Morrissey, C., Langdon, P., Geach, N. et al. (2017). A systematic review and synthesis of outcome domains for use within forensic services for people with intellectual disabilities. *British Journal of Psychiatry Open* 3: 41–56.

Neimeijer, E., Roest, J., Van der Helm, P. et al. (2019). Psychometric properties of the Group Climate Instrument (GCI) in individuals with mild intellectual disability or borderline intellectual functioning. *Journal of Intellectual Disability Research* 63: 215–224.

Novaco, R. and Taylor, J. (2015). Reduction in assaultive behavior following anger treatment in forensic hospital patients with intellectual disabilities. *Behaviour Research and Therapy* 65: 52–59.

Rose, J. (2013). A preliminary investigation into the influence of therapist experience on the outcome of individual anger interventions for people with intellectual disabilities. *Behavioural and Cognitive Psychotherapy* 41: 470–478.

Rose, J., Loftus, M., Flint, B. et al. (2005). Factors associated with the efficacy of a group intervention for anger in people with intellectual disabilities. *British Journal of Clinical Psychology* 44: 305–317.

Rose, J., West, C., and Clifford, D. (2000). Group interventions for anger in people with intellectual disabilities. *Research in Developmental Disabilities* 21: 171–181.

Singh, N., Lancioni, G., Karazsia, B. et al. (2013). Mindfulness-based treatment of aggression in individuals with mild intellectual disabilities: a waiting list control study. *Mindfulness* 4: 158–167.

Singh, N., Lancioni, G., Winton, A. et al. (2008). Clinical and benefit-cost outcomes of teaching a mindfulness-based procedure to adult offenders with intellectual disabilities. *Behavior Modification* 32: 622–637.

Stams, G.J.J.M. and Van der Helm, G.H.P. (2017). What works in residential programs for aggressive and violent youth? Treating youth at risk for aggressive and violent behavior in (secure) residential care. In: *The Wiley Handbook of Violence and Aggression* (ed. P. Sturmey), 1–12. Chichester: Wiley.

Taylor, J. and Novaco, R. (2013). Anger control problems. In: *Psychological Therapies for Adults with Intellectual Disabilities* (eds. J. Taylor, W. Lindsay, R. Hastings, et al.), 133–155. Chichester: Wiley.

Taylor, J., Novaco, R., Gillmer, B. et al. (2002). Cognitive-behavioural treatment of anger intensity among offenders with intellectual disabilities. *Journal of Applied Research in Intellectual Disabilities* 15: 151–165.

Taylor, J., Novaco, R., Gillmer, B. et al. (2005). Individual cognitive-behavioural anger treatment for people with mild-borderline intellectual disabilities and histories of aggression: a controlled trial. *British Journal of Clinical Psychology* 44: 367–382.

Taylor, J., Novaco, R., and Johnson, L. (2009). Effects of intellectual functioning on cognitive behavioural anger treatment for adults with learning disabilities in secure settings. *Advances in Mental Health and Learning Disabilities* 3: 51–56.

Travis, R. and Sturmey, P. (2013). Using behavioral skills training to teach anger management skills to adults with mild intellectual disability. *Journal of Applied Research in Intellectual Disabilities* 26: 481–488.

Tsimopoulou, I., Stenfert Kroese, B., Unwin, G. et al. (2018). A case series to examine whether people with learning disabilities can learn prerequisite skills for cognitive behaviour therapy. *The Cognitive Behaviour Therapist* 11: e1.

Vereenooghe, L. and Langdon, P. (2013). Psychological therapies for people with intellectual disabilities: a systematic review and meta-analysis. *Research in Developmental Disabilities* 34: 4085–4102.

Willner, P., Jones, J., Tams, R. et al. (2002). A randomised controlled trial of the efficacy of a cognitive-behavioural anger management group for clients with learning disabilities. *Journal of Applied Research in Intellectual Disabilities* 15: 224–235.

Willner, P., Rose, J., Jahoda, A. et al. (2013). Group-based cognitive-behavioural anger management for people with mild to moderate intellectual disabilities: cluster randomised controlled trial. *The British Journal of Psychiatry* 203: 288–296.

16

Treatment of Inappropriate Sexual Behaviour by People with Intellectual Developmental Disabilities

Leam A. Craig[1,2,3]

[1] *Forensic Psychology Practice Ltd., Sutton Coldfield, UK*
[2] *Centre for Applied Psychology, University of Birmingham, Birmingham, UK*
[3] *School of Social Sciences, Birmingham City University, Birmingham, UK*

16.1   Introduction

Since the late 1990s, a number of systems have been introduced that are designed to evaluate the quality of studies on the treatment of offending behaviour; Chambless and colleagues' system (Chambless et al. 1998; Chambless and Hollon 1998; Chambless and Ollendick 2001); Sherman et al.'s (1998) 'levels' system for reviewing the quality of evidence and intervention; and the Cochrane System (Higgins and Green 2011). These systems of evaluation have been subsumed under the category of 'What Works' in offender rehabilitation (see Craig et al. 2013) and share an emphasis on the quality of evidence from research studies and the effectiveness of interventions in the field of criminal behaviour. As an often-neglected group of people, nowhere are the principles of What Works more relevant than for people with intellectual developmental disorder (IDD; APA 2013) who engage in inappropriate sexual behaviour (ISB). The highest quality of evidence of any intervention programme is that of the randomized controlled trial (RCT) followed by highly structured meta-analyses which include RCTs (Higgins et al. 2011, 2016).

However, often in the field of interventions for people with IDD who commit ISB, studies are usually small in scale, single-subject research designs or bespoke case studies that do not lend themselves easily to empirical rigour (Chapman et al. 2013; Cohen and Harvey 2016). The most common designs of intervention studies are multiple case studies, pre-and post-treatment assessments, often in the absence of any control sample or repeated measures follow-up or using RCTs and very few treatment studies have been evaluated (Marotta 2017; Singh et al. 2011; Thom et al. 2017). Based on the 'What Work' principles this limits the extent to which researchers can be confident of demonstrating repeatable treatment effects in this client group. However, treatment efficacy and therapeutic outcomes can also be demonstrated in other ways such as behavioural change, changes in attitudes towards offending, improvements in sexual knowledge and

The Wiley Handbook on What Works for Offenders with Intellectual and Developmental Disabilities: An Evidence-Based Approach to Theory, Assessment, and Treatment, First Edition.
Edited by William R. Lindsay, Leam A. Craig, and Dorothy Griffiths.
© 2020 John Wiley & Sons Ltd. Published 2020 by John Wiley & Sons Ltd.

victim empathy, a reduction in cognitive distortions, and problem sexual behaviours. With this in mind, and as a starting point towards the holy grail of RCTs, clinicians and researchers have developed a number of empirically validated psychometric measures with good psychometric principles for this client group upon which comparisons can be drawn between intervention studies (see Craig and Lindsay 2010b). It is on this basis that the aim of this chapter is to review the treatment of ISB by people with IDD who have completed intervention programmes utilizing psychometric data to demonstrate therapeutic outcome. Before reviewing these intervention programmes, I will first briefly comment on the prevalence of this client group and discuss some of the more robust etiological explanations of sexual offending for people with IDD who commit ISB.

16.2   Prevalence

With the introduction of the Transforming Care Programme (DoH 2015) in the UK, and wider community care policies throughout the Western world, there has been a de-emphasis on institutional care in favour of community care programmes for people with IDD who have forensic histories, including ISB. This has resulted in a 'perceived' increase in the numbers of people with IDD passing through criminal justice settings who would have otherwise been diverted into mental health systems (Keller 2016; Lindsay 2002; Lindsay et al. 2013). Some have estimated the incidence of ISB among people with IDD to be between 15 and 33% (Thom et al. 2017) while others have estimated it to be closer to 6% (Swanson and Garwick 1990; Thompson and Brown 1997) although the nature of any ISB tends to be more socially inappropriate than violative intent.

Within correctional services, there is no accurate recording of the number of people held in prisons or serving probation orders who have an IDD. A recent report by Her Majesty's Inspectorate for Prison and Probation (2015) found that the criminal justice system in England and Wales is currently failing to identify people with 'learning disabilities' and 'learning difficulties' adequately. Independent inspectors found that little thought was given to the need to adapt regimes to meet the needs of prisoners with IDD, that prisoners with IDD or learning difficulties are more likely than other prisoners to have broken a prison rule, five times as likely to have been subject to control and restraint, and over three times as likely to report having spent time in segregation (Talbot 2008). Due to a number of filters that place the person with IDD at a disadvantage within the criminal justice system, there is a perception that there is a higher prevalence of people with IDD within criminal justice although there is no evidence of an over or under-estimation of people with IDD in criminal justice settings (Lindsay 2002; Murphy 2007).

Estimates of people with IDD range from 20% of the prison population (Rack 2005), to 21% of remand prisoners (Murphy et al. 1995), to 22% having self-reported difficulties in reading (Winter et al. 1997), to 30% having an Intelligence Quotient (IQ) less than 80 (Mottram 2007), which is the UK cut off for attending mainstream treatment programmes in prison and probation services in England and Wales. The difficulty in estimating the prevalence of people with IDD who engage in ISB is greater still and both Lindsay (2002) and Craig et al. (2012) have argued there is no conclusive evidence that there is a higher prevalence of sexual offending in men with IDD. While the literature on people with IDD who commit ISB has witnessed a surge in research in the last 10 years (Craig et al. 2010; Keeling et al. 2006; Lindsay 2009; Singh et al. 2011), and despite this 'apparent' over-representation of IDD among sexual offenders (Griffiths and Fedoroff 2014; Hayes et al. 2007; Walker and McCabe 1973), empirical progress continues at a much slower rate than that of non-IDD counterparts.

On 30 September 2017 the male prison population in England and Wales was at 82 040 (Ministry of Justice, 30 September 2017), of which, 13 456 were prisoners serving a sentence for a sex offence (Ministry of Justice, 2017 quarterly report), which represents approximately 17% of the sentenced prison population. The true estimate of the number of people with IDD in prison remains unknown. Based on Racks (2005) estimate of 20%, Mottram's (2007) estimate of 30%, there could be between 2691 and 4036 sexual offenders with IDD currently in prisons in England and Wales.

16.3   Aetiological Explanations of Sexual Offending Behaviour

Of the various theoretical hypotheses that have been generated in attempting to explain ISB in men with IDD (for more detail see Craig and Lindsay 2010a), the Counterfeit Deviance Hypothesis is the most influential (Hingsburger et al. 1991), updated by Griffiths et al. (2013). It attempts to explain ISB in some men with IDD as precipitated by factors such as a lack of sexual knowledge, poor social and interpersonal skills, limited opportunities to establish appropriate sexual relationships, and sexual naivety rather than deviant sexual interests. The hypothesis aims at understanding both the individual and the system in which they live. It suggested some individuals with IDD, as with the typical population, develop sexualized interests that meet the diagnostic criteria of paraphilia. Although counterfeit deviance was posed as an explanation for some ISB, the authors of the concept did not rule out the existence of paraphilia in some individuals with IDD. They described paraphilia as three types: benign – situations where diagnostically significant fetishes or images, although unusual, posed no danger; offensive – involving individuals showing arousal to children or situations involving violence; and hypersexualised – where some individuals were obsessed or controlled by sexual thoughts. Hingsburger et al. (1991) observed that in many cases where persons with IDD were clustered together in shared living environments some benign behaviours were observed by care providers who deemed them problematic, something Coleman and Haaven (2001) also commented on.

The hypothesis attempts to explain that people with IDD often lived in atypical situations that could lead to atypical behaviour and that individual's behaviour should be understood within the context of the environments in which they live, for example, care homes. The theory is made up of 11 hypotheses (see Griffiths et al. 2013) and Griffiths et al. (2013) pointed out, counterfeit deviance did not suggest that any one of the hypotheses was predictive of individual behaviour or was characteristic of sex offenders with IDD. For example, the sexual knowledge hypothesis did not state that someone with an IDD with poor sexual knowledge will sexually offend. Griffiths et al. (2013) posited that the question is not 'Do persons with intellectual disabilities offend sexually because of a lack of sexual knowledge?' but 'Has a lack of sexual knowledge resulted in or contributed to this particular individual acting in a sexually inappropriate way?' (p. 476).

A number of research groups have now tested aspects of the counterfeit deviance hypothesis, much of the research focusing on cognitive processes and knowledge, modelling, and learning theory, with relatively few studies (case studies) examining the structural (living environments) and behavioural hypotheses (see Griffiths et al. 2013). Research has found no significant differences in sexual knowledge between the untreated sex offenders with IDD and the non-offenders with IDD and therefore concluded that limited sexual knowledge was unlikely to be a factor placing men with IDD at risk of committing sexual offences (Talbot and Langdon 2006). Some studies have found that people with IDD who commit ISB have higher levels of sexual knowledge compared to non-offending counterparts (Lunsky et al. 2007; Michie et al. 2006).

Lunsky et al. (2007) however found that among the sample there were two distinctive groups. The first group demonstrated behaviours that were repeated and more predatory, whereas the second group displayed behaviours that were more consistent with counterfeit deviance. When comparing these two groups of offenders sexual knowledge was higher for the first group but diminished in the second group.

This has led some to revise the sexual knowledge hypothesis suggesting that people with IDD who engage in ISB may have higher levels of sexual knowledge than their non-offending counterparts, but their sexual knowledge remains at a stage where it is considerably poorer than that required by non-handicapped men and may not fully understand the illegality of ISB (Lindsay 2009). This relative lack of understanding may interact with a wish or need for sexual contact, or indeed a deviant sexual interest, resulting in episodes of ISB. It has been argued that limited sociosexual education is a large contributor to ISB in people with IDD and intervention is better addressing this area as a target for prevention and treatment (Thom et al. 2017).

More support has been found for the modelling and learning theory aspects of the Counterfeit Deviancy theory which posits that history of abuse may serve as a model to later offending (modelling), which is compounded by the lack of normative sexual experiences (learning history) (Lindsay et al. 2001).

The theory of counterfeit deviance continues to have relevance as a consideration for clinicians when assessing the nature of a sexual offence committed by a person with IDD (Griffiths et al. 2013). Application of the theory can assist clinicians in determining an underlying motivation behind the behaviour, which will in turn direct treatment need by focusing on areas such as, understanding the law, pro-social behaviours, understanding of what is and is not appropriate sexual behaviour, typical components of a treatment programmes for people with IDD who commit ISB (Craig and Hutchinson 2005).

16.4 Treatment

There are very few published empirically validated treatment programmes available and those which are available tend to be 'adapted' from mainstream interventions or based on case studies, small groups and with little or no control group and which have been hampered by poor methodology and non-standardized psychometric measures (Craig and Hutchinson 2005; Craig et al. 2006; Marotta 2017). There are have been several meta-analytical studies examining the effects of treatment for people with IDD who commit ISB, however, due to methodological variations between studies it is often difficult to reach firm empirical conclusions on What Works. In a systematic review of the effectiveness of psychological approaches in the treatment of sex offenders with IDD, Jones and Chaplin (2017) found that although a number of studies appeared to establish positive treatment outcomes (improvements in offence-related attitudes, victim empathy, and sexual knowledge) these results were not consistent across studies with a lack of adequate control comparisons.

Cohen and Harvey (2016) systematically reviewed the evidence base for adapted CBT-based sex offender treatment programmes (10 studies, n = 358) and found that within-treatment findings generally indicated positive cognitive shift, improvements in victim empathy, and increased sexual knowledge on psychometric measures. However, they noted a number of methodological issues with the various studies. Marotta (2017) completed a review of all published peer review treatment studies between 1994 and 2014 for people with IDD who had committed ISB (18 studies). Therapeutic outcomes included changes in attitudes consistent with sexual offending, victim empathy, sexual knowledge, cognitive distortions, and problem sexual behaviours with CBT principles being the most commonly delivered treatment modality. A review of other treatment modalities such as mindfulness techniques have been used with sexual offenders with IDD and demonstrated improvements in aggression and sexual arousal after mindfulness training, although this was only based on seven studies (Chapman et al. 2013). Results in smaller samples using mindfulness techniques have been mixed (Singh et al. 2011).

In making recommendations for treatment design Craig and Lindsay (2010b) highlighted a number of advances that have been made in the development and standardization of psychometric measures specifically designed for people with IDD, many of which overlap with the various theories of the Counterfeit Deviance Hypothesis such as, sexual knowledge and distorted attitudes through social learning.

Craig and Lindsay (2010b) organized a range of psychometric measures for people with IDD who commit ISB into one of four domains consistent with assessments of dynamic risk and treatment need frameworks used with non-IDD sexual offenders. Collectively referred to as Third Generation Risk Assessment frameworks (Bonta and Andrews 2017) the main treatment need assessment frameworks include: the Structured Risk Assessment (Thornton 2002), recently revised to Structured Assessment of Risk and Need-Responsivity (SARN-R: see Craig and Rettenberger 2017); and the STABLE-2007 and ACUTE-2007 (Hanson et al. 2007). Common across these criminogenic frameworks for the assessment of treatment need are four deviancy domains:

- *Sexual Interests*: This domain refers to both the direction and strength of sexual interests and considers offence-related sexual preferences and sexual preoccupation both factors identified as predictive of sexual recidivism.
- *Attitudes Supportive of Sexual Offences*: This domain refers to sets of beliefs about offences, sexuality, or victims that can be used to justify sexual offending behaviour. Denial or minimization of a particular offence is not considered relevant unless it can be linked to more general attitudes.
- *Relationships/Socio-Affective Functioning*: This refers to the ways of relating to other people and to motivating emotions felt in the context of these interactions. Negative

emotional states such as anxiety, depression and low self-esteem, and especially anger have been found to be offence-precursors.

- *Self-Management/Problem Solving*: This refers to an individual's ability to plan, problem solve, and regulate dysfunctional impulses that might otherwise lead to relapse.

(for more information on how deviancy domains map onto psychological risk factors see Craig and Rettenberger 2016, 2017).

Craig and Lindsay (2010b) identified a list of psychometric measures used with sexual offenders with IDD and theoretically mapped these measures onto one of the four deviancy domains. Of these measures, arguably the most researched and empirically validated measures for sexual offenders with IDD include: measures of change in adapted treatment programmes include measures of distorted attitudes, using the Questionnaire on Attitudes Consistent with Sexual Offenders (QACSO: Broxholme and Lindsay 2003; Lindsay et al. 2007); measures of offence-related attitudes, using the Sex Offences Self-Appraisal Scale (SOSAS; Bray and Forshaw 1996); measures of victim empathy, using the Adapted Victim Empathy scale (Beckett and Fisher 1994); and measures of sexual knowledge and attitudes, using the Sexual Attitudes and Knowledge Assessment (SAK, Heighway and Webster 2007). These measures have been specifically designed and empirically validated for sexual offenders with IDD and map onto two of the four deviancy domains, 'Sexual Interests' and 'Attitudes Supportive of Sexual Offences'. Each of these measures has been used across different studies and found to be good indicators of attitudinal change in sexual offenders with IDD following intervention.

As already noted, there are methodological variations between studies that make direct comparison difficult, although a consistent trend in treatment efficacy does emerge.

An early study by Rose et al. (2002) delivered a 16-week group treatment for five men with IDD who had engaged in ISB. The treatment focused on self-control, victim empathy, sex education, assertiveness, and risk avoidance. Although no significant difference in attitudes to offending were found (see Table 16.1), they did report a significant difference on the Nowicki–Strickland (Nowicki 1976) locus of control scale, indicating a more external locus of control after intervention. Ten years later, Rose et al. (2012) did report significant improvements in attitudes related to sexual offending in a community sample of 12 men (mean IQ 58, range 49–70) who had a history of ISB. This time the intervention lasted for more than double the length of time, 40 weeks, and was based on CBT principles. They reported significant changes in attitudes (Table 16.2) and a significant increase in sexual knowledge (Table 16.1) and a small, but non-significant improvement in victim empathy (Table 16.3). It was reported that only one person reoffended during the 18-month follow-up.

Lindsay and colleagues (1998a, b, c, 1999) undertook a series of studies examining treatment styles and approaches for people with IDD who commit ISB, looking at offenders against children, exhibitionists, and stalkers. The primary treatment approach adopted CBT principles in challenging cognitions, denial, and mitigation of the offence. Early studies revealed the importance of the length of intervention on attitude change. Lindsay and Smith (1998) compared the responses to treatment of sex offenders with IDD receiving one- and two-year probationary sentences. Both groups underwent the same form of treatment in small groups of four consisting of weekly sessions lasting around 2.5 hours in which denial, minimization of responsibility, and victim empathy

Table 16.1 Treatment effects on the sexual assault attitudes in sexual offenders with intellectual developmental disorder (IDD).

					Attitudes Supportive of Sexual Offences Domain					
Questionnaire on Attitudes Consistent with Sexual Offenders (QACSO) (Total)	Craig et al. (2012) n = 12	Heaton and Murphy (2013) n = 30	Langdon and Talbot (2006) n = 12	Lindsay and Smith (1998)[a] G1 n = 7 G2 n = 7	Lindsay et al. (2011)[b] G1 n = 15 G2 n = 15	Murphy et al. 2007 n = 10	Murphy et al. (2010) n = 42	Rose et al. (2002) n = 4	Rose et al. (2012) n = 12
Pre-group M (s.d)	45.21 (21.1)	56.6 (24.8)	54.72 (19.8)	G1 93% (7.2) G2 93% (5.5)	G1 33.3(6.5) G2 34.8 (8.2)	40.3	51.4 (20.7)	73	37.33 (10.7)
Post-group M (s.d)	19.25 (11.5)*	35.9 (27.4)*	27.08 (16.6) *c	G1 35% (18.6)* G2 11% (12.6)*	G1 12.5 (4.2)* G2 14.1 (6.3)*	31.0**	28.0 (20.6)*	55	23.45 (7.9)*

Source: Adapted from Craig (2017).

*P < 0.01, **P < 0.05.

[a] Lindsay and Smith (1998) reported QACSO total scores as a percentage of the total scores on measures of exhibitionism and paedophilia for two groups: Group 1 (G1) who were given one year probation order, and Group 2 (G2) who were given a two year probation order.

[b] Lindsay et al. (2011) reported treatment effects on two groups, one group who had committed offence against women and a second group who had committed offences against children.

[c] Non-treatment comparison group (n = 11).

Table 16.2 Treatment effects on sexual attitudes and knowledge (SAK) in sexual offenders with intellectual developmental disorder (IDD).

	Sexual Interests Domain				
SAK (Total)	Craig et al. (2012) n = 12	Heaton and Murphy (2013) n = 30	Murphy et al. (2007) n = 10	Murphy et al. (2010) n = 42	Rose et al. (2012) n = 9
Pre-group M (s.d)	46.25 (1.74)	40.3 (8.1)	39.5	42.0 (6.8)	135.44 (25.7)
Post-group M (s.d)	45.45 (2.63)	44.9 (6.5)*	44.7**	45.1 (7.1)*	159.33 (24.4)* [a]

Source: Adapted from Craig (2017).
*P < 0.01, **P < 0.05.
[a] Rose et al. (2012) used the Socio-Sexual Knowledge and Attitudes Assessment-Revised (SSKAAT-R; Griffiths and Lunsky 2003) which is a measure of sexual knowledge and attitudes similar to the Sexual Attitudes and Knowledge (SAK: Heighway and Webster 2007) assessment.

Table 16.3 Treatment effects on victim empathy in sexual offenders with intellectual developmental disorder (IDD).

	Attitudes Supportive of Sexual Offences Domain				
VES-A[a] (Total)	Craig et al. (2012) n = 12	Heaton and Murphy (2013) n = 30	Murphy et al. (2007) n = 10	Murphy et al. (2010) n = 42	Rose et al. (2002) n = 4
Pre-group M (s.d)	32.21 (21.9)	33.2 (16.7)	35.7	34.5 (18.4)	35.35
Post-group M (s.d)	21.83 (17.0)*	24.6 (17.7)	26.6**	27.1 (17.9)*	33.95

Source: Adapted from Craig (2017).
*P < 0.01, **P < 0.05.
[a] The VES-A is reversed scored where the lower the score (as a percentage) indicates better victim empathy.

were repeatedly dealt with. They found that while both groups showed improvements on attitudes to offending, the group that received two-years' probation were improved more significantly than the group that received one-years' probation.

Lindsay et al. (2011) compared 15 men with IDD who had committed offences against adults with another 15 who had offended against children. All participants attended a 36-month manualized treatment programme and demonstrated a significant reduction in the level of cognitive distortions (Table 16.1). Reoffending at six years follow up was between 20 and 25% for both groups with no significant differences.

In a 20-year follow-up of assessment and treatment services for 309 offenders with IDD (156 sex offenders), Lindsay et al. (2013) reported that 24 men (16%) in the sex offender group reoffended. In the sex offender group, 257 sexual offences were committed before referral to specialist services and 66 were committed after referral. Taking into account the majority of individuals who did not re-offend, the reduction was over 95%.

Like Lindsay and colleagues, Murphy and colleagues embarked on a series of studies validating a manualized treatment for people with IDD who commit ISB. An early pilot study focused on delivering a CBT-based intervention to 15 men with IDD who had committed ISB, evaluated by collecting data on measures of change in sexual knowledge, victim empathy, and cognitive distortions, together with a log of further sexually abusive behaviour. Of the eight men who completed the intervention, significant positive changes in victim empathy (Table 16.3) and attitudes to offending (Table 16.1) were reported (Murphy et al. 2007). Murphy and colleagues extended the pilot study and developed a national research group named, Sex Offender Treatment Services Collaborative – Intellectual Disabilities (SOTSEC-ID). In the first published SOTSEC-ID study, 46 men living in the community participated in treatment that lasted 12-months across multiple sites around the UK. Following treatment, Murphy et al. (2010) found significant reductions in cognitive distortions (Table 16.1) and significant improvements in offence-related appraisal (Table 16.5), victim empathy (Table 16.3) and sexual knowledge (Table 16.3). Few men showed further sexually abusive behaviour during the one-year period when they were attending treatment (three men) or during the six-month follow-up period (four men). Only the presence of autistic spectrum disorders appeared to be related to re-offending.

More recently, Heaton and Murphy (2013) reported on the treatment effects on 34 men who had attended the SOTSEC-ID intervention but who were followed up for 44 months. The group demonstrated that statistically significant improvements in sexual knowledge, victim empathy, and cognitive distortions that occurred during treatment were maintained at follow-up. Eleven men showed further sexually abusive behaviour, but only two of these men received convictions. Consistent with earlier findings, a diagnosis of autism was associated with a higher likelihood of further sexually abusive behaviour.

In an earlier study, Craig et al. (2006) delivered a CBT-based intervention to six men who had been referred to a National Health Service (NHS) intensive support service for people with IDD who had committed ISB. The intervention lasted seven months, two-hour group sessions once a week. Using the Multiphasic Sex Inventory (MSI: Nichols

Table 16.4 Treatment effects on sexual offence appraisal in sexual offenders with intellectual developmental disorder (IDD).

	Attitudes Supportive of Sexual Offences Domain			
SOSAS (Total)	Craig et al. (2012) n = 12	Heaton and Murphy (2013) n = 30	Murphy et al. (2007) n = 10	Murphy et al. (2010) n = 42
Pre-group M (s.d)	50.64 (13.58)	53.8 (8.3)	51.2	55.2 (9.1)
Post-group M (s.d)	46.00 (11.69)	47.0 (12.3)	49.4	51.2 (10.8)*

Source: Adapted from Craig (2017).
*P < 0.05.

Table 16.5 Questionnaire on Attitudes Consistent with Sexual Offenders (QACSO) scores pre- and post-group.

	Pre-Group		Post-Group		
Scale	*M*	*SD*	*M*	*SD*	*t*
QACSO Total	45.21	21.21	19.25	11.56	4.11**
Rape and Attitudes to Women	7.28	4.56	3.75	4.20	2.17*
Voyeurism	7.78	5.13	2.33	2.01	3.59**
Exhibitionism	8.28	3.81	5.33	2.83	2.72**
Dating Abuse	4.14	2.90	1.66	1.96	2.75**
Homosexual Assault	5.21	3.59	2.58	2.71	2.36*
Offences Against Children	5.85	4.11	1.41	1.44	4.18**
Stalking and Sexual Harassment	7.71	6.19	3.41	2.90	2.51*

Source: Reprinted with permission, Craig et al. (2012).
Note: Means and standard deviations ($n = 12$).
*p < 0.05, **p < 0.01.

and Molinder 1984), the Coping Response Inventory (CRI: Moos 1993), the Psychiatric Assessment for Adults With a Developmental Disability (mini-PAS-ADD; Prosser et al. 1997), and the Vineland Adaptive Behavior Scale (VABS: Sparrow et al. 1984) they reported significant improvements on measures of Socialization Domain and Play and Leisure and a non-significant trend in admitting sexual interests and improvements in sexual knowledge, although these were non-significant. A criticism of the study was the use of the non-IDD specialist measures, which it was argued, may not have been sensitive enough to detect subtle changes in cognitive shift in clients with IDD.

In a later study, Craig et al. (2012) delivered a programme of intervention, based on the SOTSEC-ID model, to 12 men with intellectual limitations (mean IQ = 73, range 69–79) using standardized psychometric measures. After a 14-month intervention, they reported significant improvements in victim empathy (Table 16.3) and significant reductions across all QACSO scales (rape and attitudes to women, voyeurism, exhibitionism, dating abuse, homosexual assault, offences against children, and stalking / sexual harassment) (Table 16.5). However, no significant differences were found pre- and post-treatment on the SAK subscales (understanding relationships, social interaction, sexual awareness, and assertiveness: Table 16.2) or on the SOSAS subscales (denial, blame, minimization and real: Table 16.3). Consistent with the SOTSEC-ID findings, the only significant improvements were in attitudes to offending and victim empathy. Due to funding limitations, only six men were followed up for 12 months while the rest were followed up to six months. None of the men were charged or reconvicted for a new sexual offence although one was recalled back to prison for breaching prison licence conditions. A limitation of this study, as is common across similar studies, was small sample sizes, a lack of adequate comparisons and short follow-up period.

Despite the obvious criticism of such studies, the strength in these results lay in the use of manualized programmes with standardized and empirically validated psychometric measures and that the treatment programmes were able to demonstrate cognitive change beyond the end of the intervention. However, as Lindsay and Michie (2013), and Marotta (2017) have argued, a general critique of the research in this area is that all studies lack a no-treatment control comparison, any reported comparisons are comparisons of convenience, there is no random allocation to treatment conditions, the follow up period is typically contaminated by 24 hour supervision, sample sizes are typically small, there are variations in length of treatment and follow-up, and short follow-up times, all of which make it difficult generalize findings on the efficacy of treatment in the longer term. For example, in the Craig et al. (2006) study, all participants were under the care of the NHS Learning Disability Services and subject to 24-hour supervision. Similarly, McGrath et al. (2007) reviewed the treatment and management of 103 adult sex offenders with IDD who had moved from institutions to staffed private houses with 24-hour support.

Emerging research highlights the role of self-regulation in the treatment of sexual offenders, particularly for offenders with serious mental illness and IDD. Stinson et al. (2017) reported the results of an intervention for 156 male psychiatric inpatients who had a history of ISB and who received Safe Offender Strategies (SOS), a manualized sex-offender treatment programme that emphasized the role of self-regulation and self-regulatory skills development particularly for offenders with mental illness and IDD. Of the sample, the most frequently diagnosed symptom category was cognitive disorder (IDD and Autism Spectrum Disorders, 63.5%). At the end of the 24-month intervention results indicated significant decreases in sexual and other aggression and improvements in treatment engagement and compliance with supervision and improvements in self-regulatory abilities and prosocial views. This approach may prove a promising way forward as part of a wider package of intervention and support for people with IDD who commit ISB.

16.5 Conclusions

One of the greatest advances in the theoretical field is the development of hypotheses to explain behaviour and the counterfeit deviance hypothesis in particular has resulted in a great deal of research which has furthered our understanding of the personal histories and experiences of people with IDD who have displayed ISB. This has helped shape and direct treatment interventions and it is encouraging to see the development of specifically designed and validated assessment protocols for people with IDD which can act as an objective indicator of change.

A common criticism of this field is that treatment studies are often based on small samples or case studies, poor or inconsistent methodology between studies, and a lack of adequate control groups. However, although the findings from treatment studies may not necessarily meet the empirical rigour of the core What Works principles, there is consistent and emerging evidence of treatment efficacy and therapeutic outcomes demonstrated in other ways such as behavioural change, changes in attitudes towards offending, improvements in sexual knowledge and victim empathy, and self-regulation.

As Keller (2016) argued, proactive assessment and intervention planning should be undertaken in cases of ISB by persons with IDD taking the form of effective collaborations between support teams and clinical professionals, with focus maximized on individual risk factors, strengths and self-regulation skills will likely lead to improved outcomes in the assessment and intervention for people with IDD who commit ISB.

References

American Psychiatric Association (2013). *Diagnostic and Statistical Manual of Mental Disorders– V (DSM-V)*. Washington, DC: American Psychiatric Association.

Beckett, R. and Fisher, D. (1994). Victim empathy measure. In: *Community-based Treatment for Sex Offenders: an Evaluation of Seven Treatment Programmes* (eds. R. Beckett, A. Beech, D. Fisher, et al.), 136–140. London: Home Office.

Bonta, J. and Andrews, D.A. (2017). *The Psychology of Criminal Conduct*, 6e. New York: Routldge.

Bray, D. and Forshaw, N. (1996). Sex Offender's Self Appraisal Scale. Version 1.1. Preston: Lancashire Care NHS Trust / North Warwickshire NHS Trust.

Broxholme, S.L. and Lindsay, W.R. (2003). Development and preliminary evaluation of a questionnaire on cognitions related to sex offending for use with individuals who have mild intellectual disabilities. *Journal of Intellectual Disability Research* 47: 472–482.

Chambless, D. and Ollendick, T. (2001). Empirically supported psychological interventions: controversies and evidence. *Annual Review of Psychology* 52: 685–716.

Chambless, D.L., Baker, M., Baucom, D.H. et al. (1998). Update on empirically validated therapies, II. *The Clinical Psychologist* 51 (1): 3–16.

Chambless, D.L. and Hollon, S.D. (1998). Defining empirically supported therapies. *Journal of Consulting and Clinical Psychology* 66: 7–18.

Chapman, M., Hare, D., Caton, S. et al. (2013). The use of mindfulness with people with intellectual disabilities: a systematic review and narrative analysis. *Mindfulness* 4 (2): 1–12.

Cohen, G. and Harvey, J. (2016). The use of psychological interventions for adult male sex offenders with a learning disability: a systematic review. *Journal of Sexual Aggression* 22 (2): 206–223.

Coleman, E.M. and Haaven, J. (2001). Assessment and treatment of intellectual disabled sexual abusers. In: *Handbook for Sexual Abuser Assessment and Treatment* (eds. M.S. Carich and S.E. Mussack), 193–209. Vermont: Safer Society Foundation, Inc.

Craig, L.A. (2017). Working with sexual offenders with intellectual developmental disabilities. In: *Working with Sex Offenders: A Guide for Practitioners* (eds. D.T. Wilcox, M.L. Donathy, R. Gray, et al.), 136–162. Oxford: Routledge.

Craig. L. A., Dixon, L., & Gannon, T. A. (2013). *What Works in Offender Rehabilitation: An evidenced based approach to assessment and treatment*. Chichester. Wiley-Blackwell.

Craig, L.A. and Hutchinson, R. (2005). Sexual offenders with learning disabilities: risk, recidivism and treatment. *Journal of Sexual Aggression* 11 (3): 289–304.

Craig, L.A. and Lindsay, W.R. (2010a). Sexual offenders with intellectual disabilities: characteristics and prevalence. In: *Assessment and Treatment of Sexual Offenders with Intellectual Disabilities: A Handbook* (eds. L.A. Craig, W.R. Lindsay and K.D. Browne), 13–36. Chichester: Wiley-Blackwell.

Craig, L.A. and Lindsay, W.R. (2010b). Psychometric assessment of sexual deviancy in sexual offenders with intellectual disabilities. In: *Assessment and Treatment of Sexual Offenders with Intellectual Disabilities: a Handbook* (eds. L.A. Craig, K.D. Browne and W.R. Lindsay), 213–232. Chichester: Wiley-Blackwell.

Craig, L.A., Lindsay, W.R., and Browne, K.D. (2010). *Assessment and Treatment of Sexual Offenders with Intellectual Disabilities: A Handbook*. Chichester: Wiley-Blackwell.

Craig, L.A. and Rettenberger, M. (2016). A brief history of sexual offender risk assessment. In: *Treatment of Sexual Offenders: Strengths and Weaknesses in Assessment and Intervention* (eds. D.R. Laws and W. O'Donohue), 19–44. New York: Springer.

Craig, L.A. and Rettenberger, M. (2017). Risk assessment for sexual offenders: where to from here? In: *The Wiley Handbook on the Theories, Assessment and Treatment of Sexual Offending. Volume 2, Assessment* (eds. L. Craig and M. Rettenberger), 1203–1226. Chichester: Wiley-Blackwell.

Craig, L.A., Stringer, I., and Moss, T. (2006). Treating sexual offenders with learning disabilities in the community: a critical review. *International Journal of Offender Therapy and Comparative Criminology* 50: 369–390.

Craig, L.A., Stringer, I., and Sanders, C.E. (2012). Treating sexual offenders with intellectual limitations in the community. *British Journal of Forensic Practice* 14 (1): 5–20.

DoH (Department of Health) (2015). Transforming Care for People with Learning Disabilities - Next Steps. https://www.england.nhs.uk/wp-content/uploads/2015/01/transform-care-nxt-stps.pdf (accessed 14 March 2018).

Griffiths, D., Hingsburger, D., Hoath, J. et al. (2013). Counterfeit deviance revisited. *Journal of Applied Research in Intellectual Disabilities* 26: 471–480.

Griffiths, D. and Lunsky, Y. (2003). *SSKAAT-R Socio-Sexual Knowledge and Attitudes Assessment Tool–Revised manual*. Wood Dale, IL: Stoelting.

Griffiths, D.M. and Fedoroff, P. (2014). Persons with intellectual disabilities and problematic sexual behaviors. *Psychiatric Clinics of North America* 37 (2): 195–206.

Hanson, R.K., Harris, A.J.R., Scott, T.L. et al. (2007). *Assessing the Risk of Sexual Offenders on Community Supervision: The Dynamic Supervision Project (Corrections Research User Report 2007–05)*. Ottawa, ON: Public Safety Canada https://www.publicsafety.gc.ca/cnt/rsrcs/pblctns/ssssng-rsk-sxl-ffndrs/index-en.aspx (accessed 14 March 2018).

Hayes, S., Shackell, P., Mottram, P. et al. (2007). The prevalence of intellectual disability in a major UK prison. *British Journal of Learning Disabilities* 35: 162–167.

Heaton, K.M. and Murphy, G.H. (2013). Men with intellectual disabilities who have attended sex offender treatment groups: a follow-up. *Journal of Applied Research in Intellectual* 26: 489–500.

Heighway, S.M. and Webster, S.K. (2007). *STARS: Skills Training for Assertiveness, Relationships Building and Sexual Awareness*. Arlington, TX: Future Horizons.

Her Majesty's Inspectorate of Probation (2015). A joint inspection of the treatment of offenders with learning disabilities within the criminal justice system - phase two in custody and the community A Joint Inspection by HMI Probation and HMI Prisons. Manchester: Her Majesty's Inspectorate of Probation. https://www.justiceinspectorates.gov.uk/cjji/wp-content/uploads/sites/2/2015/03/Learning-Disabilities-phase-two-report.pdf (accessed 30 May 2019).

Higgins, J. and Green, S. (2011). *The Cochrane Handbook for Systematic Reviews of Interventions: Version 5.1*. London: The Cochrane Collaboration http://handbook-5-1.cochrane.org (accessed 12 June 2019).

Higgins, J.P.T., Altman, D.G., Gøtzsche, P.C. et al. (2011). The Cochrane Collaboration's tool for assessing risk of bias in randomised trials. *The BMJ*: 343. https://www.bmj.com/content/343/bmj.d5928 (accessed 12 June 2019).

Higgins, J.P.T., Sterne, J.A.C., Savović, J. et al., (2016). A revised tool for assessing risk of bias in randomized trials. In: J. Chandler, J. McKenzie, I. Boutron et al. (ed.) *Cochrane Methods. Cochrane Database of Systematic Reviews*, 10 (Suppl 1). https://sites.google.com/site/riskofbiastool/welcome/rob-2-0-tool (accessed 12 June 2019).

Hingsburger, D., Griffiths, D., and Quinsey, V. (1991). Detecting counterfeit deviance. *Habilitative Mental Healthcare* 9: 51–54.

Jones, E. and Chaplin, E. (2017). A systematic review of the effectiveness of psychological approaches in the treatment of sex offenders with intellectual disabilities. *Journal of Applied Research in Intellectual Disabilities* Published online. doi: https://doi.org/10.1111/jar.12345.

Keeling, J.A., Rose, J.L., and Beech, A.R. (2006). An investigation into the effectiveness of a custody-based cognitive-behavioural treatment for special needs sexual offenders. *Journal of Forensic Psychiatry & Psychology* 17: 372–392.

Keller, J. (2016). Improving practices of risk assessment and intervention planning for persons with intellectual disabilities who sexually offend. *Journal of Policy and Practice in Intellectual Disabilities* 13: 75–85.

Langdon, P.E. and Talbot, T.J. (2006). Locus of control and sex offenders with an intellectual disability. *International Journal of Offender Therapy and Comparative Criminology* 50 (4): 391–401.

Lindsay, W.R. (2002). Research and literature on sex offenders with intellectual and developmental disabilities. *Journal of Intellectual Disability Research* 46 (Suppl. 1): 74–85.

Lindsay, W.R. (2009). *The Treatment of Sex Offenders with Developmental Disabilities. A Practice Workbook*. Chichester: Wiley – Blackwell.

Lindsay, W.R., Law, J., Quinn, K. et al. (2001). A comparison of physical and sexual abuse: histories of sexual and non-sexual offenders with intellectual disability. *Child Abuse and Neglect* 25: 989–995.

Lindsay, W.R., Marshall, I., Neilson, C.Q. et al. (1998a). The treatment of men with a learning disability convicted of exhibitionism. *Research on Developmental Disabilities* 19: 295–316.

Lindsay, W.R. and Michie, A.M. (2013). Individuals with developmental delay and problematic sexual behaviors. *Current Psychiatry Reports* 15 (4): 1–6.

Lindsay, W.R., Michie, A.M., Haut, F. et al. (2011). Comparing offenders against women and offenders against children on treatment outcome for offenders with intellectual disability. *Journal of Applied Research in Intellectual Disability* 24 (4): 364–369.

Lindsay, W.R., Neilson, C.Q., Morrison, F. et al. (1998b). The treatment of six men with a learning disability convicted of sex offences with children. *British Journal of Clinical Psychology* 37: 83–98.

Lindsay, W.R., Olley, S., Baillie, N. et al. (1999). The treatment of adolescent sex offenders with intellectual disability. *Mental Retardation* 37: 320–333.

Lindsay, W.R., Olley, S., Jack, C. et al. (1998c). The treatment of two stalkers with intellectual disabilities using a cognitive approach. *Journal of Applied Research in Intellectual Disabilities* 11: 333–344.

Lindsay, W.R. and Smith, A.H.W. (1998). Responses to treatment for sex offenders with intellectual disability: a comparison of men with one and two-year probation sentences. *Journal of Intellectual Disability Research* 42 (5): 346–353.

Lindsay, W.R., Steptoe, L., Wallace, L. et al. (2013). An evaluation and 20-year follow-up of a community forensic intellectual disability service. *Criminal Behaviour & Mental Health* 23: 138–149.

Lindsay, W.R., Whitefield, E., and Carson, D. (2007). An assessment for attitudes consistent with sexual offending for use with offenders with intellectual disability. *Legal and Criminological Psychology* 12: 55–68.

Lunsky, Y., Frijters, J., Griffiths, D.M. et al. (2007). Sexual knowledge and attitudes of men with intellectual disabilities who sexually offend. *Journal of Intellectual and Developmental Disability* 32: 74–81.

Marotta, P.L. (2017). A systematic review of behavioral health interventions for sex offenders with intellectual disabilities. *Sexual Abuse: A Journal of Research and Treatment* 29 (2): 148–185.

McGrath, R.J., Livingston, J.A., and Falk, G. (2007). Community management of sex offenders with intellectual disabilities: characteristics, services, and outcome of a statewide program. *Intellectual and Developmental Disabilities* 45 (6): 391–398.

Michie, A.M., Lindsay, W.R., Martin, V. et al. (2006). A test of counterfeit deviance: a comparison of sexual knowledge in groups of sex offenders with intellectual disability and controls. *Sex Abuse: A Journal of Research and Treatment* 18: 271–278.

Ministry of Justice (2017). Population and Capacity Briefing for 30 September 2017. https://www.gov.uk/government/uploads/system/uploads/attachment_data/file/654646/prison-population-30-september-2017.xlsx (accessed 14 March 2018).

Moos, R.H. (1993). *Coping Response Inventory-Adult Form: Professional Manual*. Odessa, FL: Psychological Assessment Resources.

Mottram, P. G. (2007). *HMP Liverpool, Styal and Hindley study report*. https://www.choiceforum.org/docs/hmpliverpool.pdf (accessed 14 March 2018).

Murphy, G., Harnett, H., and Holland, A.J. (1995). A survey of intellectual disabilities among men on remand in prison. *Mental Handicap Research* 8: 81–98.

Murphy, G.H. (2007). Intellectual disabilities, sexual abuse and sexual offending. In: *Handbook of Intellectual Disability and Clinical Psychology Practice* (eds. A. Carr, G. OReilly, P. Noonan Walsh, et al.), 831–866. London: Routledge.

Murphy, G.H., Powell, S., Guzman, A.M. et al. (2007). Cognitive-behavioral treatment for men with intellectual disabilities and sexually abusive behavior: a pilot study. *Journal of Intellectual Disability Research* 51: 902–912.

Murphy, G.H., Sinclair, N., Hays, S.J. et al. (2010). Effectiveness of group cognitive behavioral treatment for men with intellectual disabilities at risk of sexual offending. *Journal of Applied Research in Intellectual Disabilities* 23: 537–551.

Nichols, H.R. and Molinder, I. (1984). Manual for the Multiphasic Sex Inventory. Available from, Nichols & Molinder, 437 Bowes Drive, Tacoma, WA 98466-70747 USA.

Nowicki S. (1976) *Adult Nowicki–Strickland Internal–External Locus of Control Scale*. Test manual available from S. Nowicki Jr, Department of Psychology, Emory University, Atlanta GA 30322, USA.

Prosser, H., Moss, S., Costello, H. et al. (1997). *Psychiatric Assessment for Adults 851 with a Developmental Disability (mini PASADD)*. Manchester: Hester Adrian Research Centre and the Institute of 852 Psychiatry, University of Manchester.

Rack, J. (2005). *The incidence of disabilities in the prison population*. Yorkshire and Humberside Research. Available from: The Dyslexia Institute, Park House, Wick Road, Egham, Surrey TW20 0HH.

Rose, J., Jenkins, R., O'Connor, C. et al. (2002). A group treatment for men with intellectual disabilities who sexually offend or abuse. *Journal of Applied Research in Intellectual Disabilities* 15: 138–150.

Rose, J., Rose, D., Hawkins, C. et al. (2012). A sex offender treatment group for men with intellectual disabilities in a community setting. *The British Journal of Forensic Practice* 14: 21–28.

Sherman, L.W., Gottfredson, D., Mackenzie, D. et al. (1998). *Preventing Crime: What Works, What Doesn't, What's Promising.* Washington, DC: National Institute of Justice https://www.ncjrs.gov/pdffiles/171676.PDF (accessed 12 June 2019).

Singh, N.N., Lancioni, G., Winton, A.S.W. et al. (2011). Can adult offenders with intellectual disabilities use mindfulness-based procedures to control and deviant sexual arousal? *Psychology, Crime and Law* 17: 165–179.

Sparrow, S.S., Balla, D.A., and Cicchetti, D.V. (1984). *Vineland's Adaptive Behaviour Scales; Interview Edition, Expanded Form.* Circle Pines, MN: American Guidance Service.

Stinson, J.D., Becker, J.V., and McVay, L.A. (2017). Treatment progress and behaviour following 2 years of inpatient sex offender treatment: a pilot investigation of Safe Offender Strategies. *Sexual Abuse: A Journal of Research and Treatment* 29 (1): 3–27.

Swanson, C.K. and Garwick, B. (1990). Treatment for low-functioning sex offenders: group therapy and interagency coordination. *Mental Retardation* 28: 155–161.

Talbot, J. (2008). *Prisoners' Voices: Experiences of the Criminal Justice System by Prisoners with Learning Disabilities and Difficulties.* London: Prison Reform Trust.

Talbot, T.J. and Langdon, P.E. (2006). A revised sexual knowledge assessment tool for people with intellectual disabilities: is sexual knowledge related to sexual offending behaviour? *Journal of Intellectual Disability Research* 50 (7): 523–531.

Thom, R.P., Grudzinskas, A.J., and Saleh, F.M. (2017). Sexual behavior among persons with cognitive impairments. *Current Psychiatry Reports* 19 (5): 25. https://doi.org/10.1007/s11920-017-0777-7.

Thompson, D. and Brown, H. (1997). Men with intellectual disabilities who sexually abuse: a review of the literature. *Journal of Applied Research in Intellectual Disabilities* 10: 140–158.

Thornton, D. (2002). Constructing and testing a framework for dynamic risk assessment. *Sexual Abuse: A Journal of Research and Treatment* 14: 137–151.

Walker, N. and McCabe, S. (1973). *Crime and Insanity in England.* Edinburgh: Edinburgh University Press.

Winter, N., Holland, A.J., and Collins, S. (1997). Factors predisposing to suspected offending by adults with self-report learning disabilities. *Psychological Medicine* 27: 599–607.

17

Treatment for Social Problem Solving and Criminal Thinking

Susan Hayes

Sydney Medical School, University of Sydney, Sydney, New South Wales, Australia

17.1 Introduction

Social problem solving is defined as 'the process of problem solving as it in occurs in the natural environment or real world' (D'Zurilla and Nezu 1982) and has been described as a goal-directed cognitive-behavioural process (D'Zurilla et al. 2004) which involves defining problems, generating possible solutions, making decisions, and testing solutions (Chang et al. 2004; D'Zurilla and Goldfried 1971). The process includes all aspects of adaptive functioning 'including *impersonal problems* (e.g. insufficient finances, stolen property), *personal or intrapersonal problems* (emotional, behavioural, cognitive, or health problems), *interpersonal problems* (e.g. marital conflicts, family disputes), as well as broader *community and societal problems* (e.g. crime, racial discrimination)' (D'Zurilla and Nezu 2004, p. 11).

The concept of social problem solving, therefore, is closely aligned with adaptive behaviour, including the communication skills, practical daily living skills, community, interpersonal, and socialization skills that people acquire and hone, in order to function in daily life. Research conducted in a major UK prison found that mean adaptive behaviour scores tended to be significantly lower than IQ scores, especially in the Communication domain (Hayes et al. 2007), findings which are highly relevant not only to the developmental trajectory of deficits in social problem solving, but also to the design of programmes for offenders with intellectual disabilities (ID).

17.2 Criminal Thinking

Criminal thinking is defined as 'attitudes, beliefs, and rationalizations that offenders use to justify and support their criminal behavior' (Walters 2012, p. 272), before, during, and after a criminal offence. The concept is further classified into proactive and reactive criminal thinking, with proactive thinking driving calculated criminal behaviour and

The Wiley Handbook on What Works for Offenders with Intellectual and Developmental Disabilities: An Evidence-Based Approach to Theory, Assessment, and Treatment, First Edition.
Edited by William R. Lindsay, Leam A. Craig, and Dorothy Griffiths.
© 2020 John Wiley & Sons Ltd. Published 2020 by John Wiley & Sons Ltd.

associated positive outcome expectancies on the part of the offender, and reactive thinking being associated with poor impulse control and hostile attribution biases (Walters 2007).

Whilst no research could be located on the prevalence of criminal thinking amongst individuals with ID, amongst the population of prison inmates with serious mental illness, mentally disordered offenders produced criminal thinking scores on the Psychological Inventory of Criminal Thinking Styles (PICTS) (Walters 1995) and the Criminal Sentiments Scale-Modified (CSS-M) (Simourd 1997) similar to those of non-mentally ill offenders. On the PICTS, 66% of male offenders and 49% of female participants with mental illness endorsed a reactive cognitive process and belief system consistent with a criminal lifestyle, whilst 85% of male participants and 72.4% of females had scores on the CSS-M indicating antisocial attitudes, values, and beliefs related to criminal activity. Both sets of results were comparable to non-mentally ill offenders. Specifically, mentally ill inmates present similarly to both psychiatric patients as well as non-mentally-disordered criminals, and tend to display co-occurring issues of mental illness and criminal behaviour that violates the rights and well-being of others. Hence, their offending is not principally a function of their psychiatric symptomatology, but rather is related to the attitudes, beliefs, and rationalizations that support their criminal behaviour.

Criminal thinking is strongly related to recidivism, and therefore is regarded as an important target for intervention (Folk et al. 2016). Offenders leaving prison with an inflated sense of entitlement and a cold, calculating, manipulative approach to interpersonal situations have been shown to be significantly more likely re-offend than those without these characteristics (Walters 2011; Walters et al. 2015).

17.3   The Link with Offending Behaviour

17.3.1   Social Problem Solving and Offending Behaviour

Inadequate social problem-solving skills, associated with impulsivity and aggression have been implicated in offending behaviour. However, given the possible importance of this link, there has been a dearth of research examining social problem-solving deficits in offenders (Biggam and Power 2002), and especially in the population of offenders with ID (Lindsay et al. 2011).

Cognitive skills programmes directed at changing attitudes and beliefs related to offending behaviour are being used in rehabilitation settings, and are often based on Kohlberg's six-stage model of moral reasoning (Kohlberg 1969, 1984; Lindsay et al. 2011). The aim of such programmes is to develop more sophisticated reasoning in offenders who are operating at the first two stages, that is, at the level of pre-conventional moral reasoning (Stage 1 being punishment-avoidance and obedience, and Stage 2 being self-interest and obtaining the greatest benefit for oneself). These stages are characterized by self-interest and egocentricity, whereas the intention of programmes is to encourage participants to move to Stages 3 and 4, conventional moral reasoning, developing greater social awareness, social conformity, and consciousness that individual needs may be secondary to the needs of a socially cohesive society. Some offenders may achieve Stages 5 and 6, post-conventional reasoning, that is, appreciating that there are universal principles defining conformity to shared standards, rights, or duties. The combination of egocentricity, poor social perspective taking, parenting/family environments that encourage aggression rather than prosocial behaviours, and development of the perception of the world as a hostile place can produce cognitive distortions consistent with offending behaviour (Lindsay et al. 2011).

Deficits in social problem solving have been associated with depression, suicidal ideation and behaviour, and anxiety (Nezu et al. 2002a). Individuals with depression tend to generate less effective solutions to problems. High stress and poor problem-solving ability is associated with hopelessness and suicidal intent, as well as with a tendency to produce fewer alternative relevant solutions (Biggam and Power 2002). Similarly, individuals with anxiety have a more negative problem-solving orientation, involving lower self-evaluations of one's competence in solving life problems.

A qualitative research study sought to explore the experiences of stress and the use of coping strategies from the perspective of people with ID currently residing within the forensic in-patient services of one National Health Service Trust (Burns and Lampraki 2016). Data analysis revealed three key themes: experiencing stress; sources of stress, and coping with stress. The authors emphasize the need to utilize appropriate stress assessment measures and implement effective stress reduction and management programmes to address the holistic needs of people with ID. Therefore, it is important that social problem-solving programmes address any co-existing mental disorders and sources of stress/distress in order to optimize results.

Another way of approaching the link between social problem solving and negative affect is to view psychological stress as a function of four variables, two types of stressful life events namely major negative life events and daily stressors, along with two other factors, negative emotional states and incompetency in problem solving (Nezu et al. 2002b). These authors describe the constant, dynamic interactions between these four variables as they change and influence each other. For example, major life events can be accompanied by an increase in daily problems such as financial worries or interpersonal difficulties, and deficits in effective problem solving exacerbate the intensity of both types of problems, thus increasing the likelihood of intrapersonal distress, which in turn impedes effective problem solving.

These issues are significant for offenders with ID, a group which has a higher prevalence of mental health problems than their non-offending or non-disabled counterparts, accompanied by deficits in social problem-solving capacity (Vanny et al. 2009). Social problem solving has been described as possibly 'the single most important social skill that a young person can acquire' (Frauenknecht and Black 2002).

17.3.2 Criminal Thinking and Offending Behaviour

Walters, a leader in the field of criminal thinking, stated that 'The belief that criminal thinking is central to criminal behaviour finds support in the results of several meta-analyses' (Walters 2006, p. 88). Addressing criminal thinking is, therefore, a potentially important field of study in criminology (Walters 2006). Criminal thinking tends to predict criminal behaviour, and some attitudes may be offence specific; for example, offenders who have committed violent offences tend to hold more criminal attitudes in support of violence, compared with non-violent offenders (Polaschek et al. 2004; Walters 2006). Research has demonstrated that alterations in criminal thinking are associated with changes in criminal behaviour (Walters 2006). However, Walters (2006) asserts that research on criminal thinking is an under-developed area, especially when compared with research on risk assessment, and further research into belief systems, assessment of criminal thinking and the theoretical under-pinning of measures of criminal thinking is required.

17.4 Interventions

17.4.1 Developing Social Problem-solving Skills with Offenders

Two issues will be canvassed in this section, the first being interventions to develop problem-solving skills with offenders generally, and the less researched area of interventions with offenders with ID.

Cognitive behavioural therapies (CBT) have been established as the most effective evidence-based interventions for a wide variety of disorders and have been transferred successfully to offender treatment programmes, from as early as the 1990s (Andrews et al. 1990). The elements of effective programmes include using trained therapists/ instructors who present the programme in a consistent manner, motivation on the part of participants, and programme content which is appropriate to the abilities of the participants, especially those with ID (Frauenknecht and Black 2002). As early as 1991, research with a group of participants with ID and mental illness found that problem-solving therapy decreased levels of self-reported psychiatric symptoms and facilitated improvements in adaptive behaviour (as rated by a third party) (Nezu et al. 1991). Furthermore, other early research indicated that problem-solving therapy was effective with people with ID in relation to anger management (Benson et al. 1986), decreases in maladaptive behaviours displayed in the community (Loumidis and Hill 1997), and increased social competence (Castles and Glass 1986; Nezu et al. 2002a), all factors that are relevant to offending behaviour. Given the promise of this early research it is unfortunate that comparatively few developments have taken place.

The risk-need-responsivity principles incorporated in the programmes take into account the offenders' level of risk and their criminogenic needs, and respond to other factors such as mental health, gender, ethnic background, and cognitive ability (Andrews 2001; Bonta and Andrews 2017). Lindsay et al. (2011, p. 183) state 'that cognitive interventions in general should be evaluated at an early stage as the most effective interventions is unsurprising since the theoretical underpinnings relate to the development of thinking styles and cognitive schemata'.

One example of a Social Problem-Solving Skills (SPSS) programme, developed in Florida, USA, is described as follows:

> The social problem-solving skills training program is a multiple component group behavioral intervention designed to: (a) improve incarcerated offenders' social and assertion skills; (b) broaden inmates' understanding of desirable and undesirable functions of anger as well as anger control methods; (c) develop coping skills that involve the implementation of cognitive controls (e.g., via self-instructional training and cognitive restructuring); (d) teach tension reduction techniques (e.g., progressive muscle relaxation and diaphragmatic

breathing); (e) examine behavioral responses, such as verbal hostility, indirect hostility, physical aggression, and withdrawal/avoidance and replace those responses with more adaptive problem solving-strategies; (f) increase empathic awareness and social perspective-taking; and (g) introduce verbal (voice volume, voice tone, and response latency) and nonverbal (eye contact and proximity) skills requisite to effective interpersonal responding. (Bourke and Van Hasselt 2001, p. 166)

The programme uses direct instruction, role plays, modelling, behaviour rehearsal, and positive reinforcement, therefore going beyond a CBT approach. The major goals include improved anger management skills, social skills enhancement, empathy training, and stress management. Pre-treatment and post-treatment assessments are undertaken to measure therapeutic gains, although the outcomes are not presented by the authors in this paper which describes the content of the programme.

A brief intervention consisting of five 90-minute sessions using a small group format in the Scottish Prison Service yielded promising results in reducing psychological distress and enhancing the self-perceived problem-solving abilities of young offenders in prison; some of these improvements were still evident at 3-month follow-up (Biggam and Power 2002). Symptoms of depression, anxiety, and hopelessness were reduced in the study group, compared with the non-intervention group, although impulsivity and solution implementation showed no significant alteration. The authors hypothesized that since undiagnosed Attention Deficit Hyperactivity Disorder is disproportionately high amongst offenders, and impulsivity is one aspect of this, a brief intervention may not have an impact on this long-term style of behaviour. Similar conclusions may be drawn in respect to offenders with ID, both in terms of under-diagnosis, and high levels of impulsivity which may be resistant to brief interventions. The lack of change in solution implementation skills was considered to be a result of the focus in the programme on cognitive elements of the problem-solving process, rather than an emphasis on the social skills competence of the participants, which is notably deficient in young offenders. The authors suggest that the Reasoning and Rehabilitation programme (R & R) (Ross and Fabiano 1990), used in many prisons in Britain and demonstrating efficacy with adult offenders, may be also investigated as a useful intervention with young offenders.

The R & R and Moral Reconation Therapy (MRT) (Little and Robinson 1988) are two notable approaches in the field of CBT programmes for offenders. Meta-analysis of six studies using MRT indicates reasonably strong evidence for the efficacy of this programme in reducing long-term recidivism rates by 10–20% (Wilson et al. 2005). Analysis of seven studies of R & R indicated a small effect size for effectiveness in reducing further criminal offending, although the results varied from 7 to 33% in different studies, suggesting a need for further, more rigorous assessments. Wilson et al. (2005) concluded that all the higher quality studies using CBT had moderate positive effect sizes, translating into a 16% advantage for the treatment groups (42% recidivism rate for the treated and 58% for the untreated participants). These authors raise the issue, however, of whether the integrity and effectiveness of the programmes can be sustained when implemented on a large scale, and when training of therapists is undertaken by professionals who have not been involved in the development of the programmes. Nevertheless, after reviewing a number of meta-analyses, Lindsay et al. (2011) indicate that there is evidence to conclude that cognitive skills programmes reduce recidivism in offenders in both community and custodial settings, in comparison with non-treatment participants.

Recidivism data outcomes are not the only measures used in evaluating changes in participants' problem-solving strategies and thinking styles consistent with criminal behaviour; there are a number of measures that are used to assess the outcomes of programmes. One of the most commonly used is the Social Problem-Solving Inventory – Revised (SPSI-R) (D'Zurilla et al. 2002), a 52-item, Likert-type inventory comprising five major scales reflecting the D'Zurilla et al. (2002) social problem-solving model. The five scales are Positive Problem Orientation, Negative Problem Orientation, Rational Problem Solving, Impulsivity/Carelessness Style, and Avoidance Style. However, there is relatively little information about how well the SPSI-R assesses offenders, particularly offenders with ID.

Lindsay et al. (2011) conducted a pilot study using a short, simplified form of the SPSI-R, with 132 participants, 81% male and 19% female, following either the commission of an offence or a significant incident of aggression; their IQ scores ranged from 52 to 85 (mean 67.1; SD = 7.7). The five-factor solution reached by this research was consistent with the original scales, indicating that the instrument shows psychometric integrity with this participant group. The researchers went on to use the instrument in a study evaluating the effects of a social problem-solving programme, the Social Problem Solving and Offence Related Thinking (SPORT) Programme.

The SPORT Programme uses problem-solving exercises and role plays extensively, and is designed for a client group with intellectual limitations. There are 15 sections, which take 12–15 weeks to complete. Ten men in two groups of five participated in the pilot study, five having been referred for sexual offences and five for violent offences. The SPSI-R was completed before the treatment programme commenced, halfway through the sessions, at the end of the programme, and at six-months' follow-up. Positive problem orientation and impulsive/careless style showed significant differences between the times of testing, at the 0.01 level of significance, and avoidant style differences were significant at the 0.05 level, whereas negative problem orientation and rational style showed no significant differences. There was some volatility evident in the pattern of results which the authors attributed to the small sample size. The conclusion was that assessment and treatment of social problem solving may be a useful addition to rehabilitation work with offenders with ID.

As an example of the importance of being aware of the multiple and complex problems of offenders with ID and mental disorder, depression is linked to deficits in social problem solving and unsuccessful problem solving, as well as ruminative thinking about negative feelings and memories, and inability to think about the consequences of a problem being resolved one way or another (Noreen et al. 2015). Depression was the only significant predictor for the number of relevant solutions generated and the effectiveness of the proposed resolutions. Individuals with high levels of rumination demonstrated greater difficulty in inhibiting irrelevant or inappropriate information. Hence, contemplating the possible future consequences of a problem may only be useful where the consequences generated are adaptive and appropriate, and where negative appraisals are not generated, because they may interfere with the production of effective solutions. For individuals with dual diagnoses, long-term coaching, guidance and practice in social problem solving may be needed for them to acquire the capacity to generate positive solutions and move on from maladaptive and ruminative appraisals of the future.

Retention of offenders in rehabilitation programmes, especially in prisons, is notoriously difficult, however. Offenders may not complete programmes for many reasons including their own decision to drop out, being moved to another prison, the programme being discontinued, scheduling difficulties or clashes, or their sentence ending prior to completion of the programme. A meta-analysis in the UK showed that unsurprisingly, non-completion rates are higher for community-based programmes (31.5%) than for prison programmes (19.9%) (Olver et al. 2011). Non-completers had a higher risk of reconviction and higher levels of impulsivity, but there were no significant differences for social problem solving and criminal thinking, consistent with mixed results in other research (Palmer and Humphries 2016). Palmer and Humphries (2016) suggest that further examination of the reasons for not completing and the timing of discontinuation (that is, early or later in the programme) may provide important information to attempt to prevent non-completion.

Differences have been found between mentally disordered offenders who were completers or non-completers of a programme then known as Enhanced Thinking Skills (ETS), in a forensic hospital setting (Tapp et al. 2009). Completers tended to have had a longer duration of admission in hospital prior to participating in the programme, which the authors considered may indicate higher motivation or greater preparedness for engagement in the programme. Completers rated themselves as less passive in problem solving, were less likely to have a mental illness classification, were more likely to have committed a sex offence than a violent offence, and had more previous convictions. Significant improvements were reported in the areas of reasoning, impulsiveness, justification of offending behaviour, and aggressive social problem-solving style. The ETS has been replaced by the Thinking Skills Programme (TSP), with an adapted form for offenders with ID (Adapted Thinking Skills Programme: ATSP) (Oakes et al. 2016). Evaluation of the programme suggests that ATSP is likely to deliver positive outcomes for prisoners with ID. However, the programme was evaluated in men's prisons only, and in custodial settings which were already committed to effective delivery of rehabilitation programmes, especially to prisoners with ID. ATSP will need to be implemented and assessed in a wider range of settings.

A pilot study of the revised R & R programme for 25 mentally disordered offenders with ID in two medium secure hospital units found that 92% of the participants completed the programme (Waugh et al. 2014). The programme consists of a 16-week, 90-minute group intervention provided once per week, and a manualized coaching component where patients meet with a member of staff between group sessions to help them transfer acquired skills to daily life. The researchers considered the programme to be feasible for use with offenders with ID because of its easily comprehensible content and user-friendly presentation. It was suggested that this version of the programme be compared with the parallel programme designed for use with people with Attention Deficit Hyperactivity Disorder (R&R2ADHD), to ascertain the strengths and weaknesses of both versions with offenders with ID.

Another way of examining the effectiveness of completing programmes is to consider the cost. Cost implications for treatment non-completion amongst personality disordered clients has been modelled (Sampson et al. 2013). The average 10-year follow-up cost for completers was £266 396 and for non-completers £410 526, a mean cost difference of £144 130. The authors indicated that there was a 97% chance that treatment completers, on average, would go on to incur lower costs than non-completers in the first 10 years following discharge from a forensic personality disorder service. Hence, there are not only missed treatment opportunities and personal outcomes for non-completers, but economic costs for service providers and society. Whilst data could not be located on costs for non-completion rates for offenders with ID, it is known that retaining this group in mainstream custodial behaviour programmes is difficult owing to the cognitive and adaptive deficits associated with their disability, the fact that they may be barred from entering some programmes, and the unsuitability of programmes that are heavily dependent on communication and literacy skills (Loucks 2007). The provision of appropriate programmes that will be completed by participants is undoubtedly cost effective.

If nothing else will convince justice, forensic health, and correctional administrators about the importance of identifying offenders with ID and implementing appropriate programmes, perhaps an economic argument may.

17.4.2 Interventions for Criminal Thinking

There is a great deal of overlap between criminal thinking interventions and social problem-solving approaches; for example, there is evidence that criminal thinking can be reduced through interventions that mainly focus on cognitive restructuring, social skills training and problem solving (Folk et al. 2016). Sometimes the same programmes, such as R & R, are used to reduce criminal thinking and increase social problem solving (Robinson and Porporino 2001).

Older and more educated prisoners have been found to have more significant decreases in criminal thinking (using a self-administered programme in segregated sections of the prison) than younger, less-educated prisoners (Folk et al. 2016), a finding that highlights the difficulty of changing impulsive thinking and behaviour in the population of offenders with ID with educational and literacy deficits. Given the difficulties that offenders with ID have in foreseeing the long-term consequences of their actions, maintaining motivation and concentration, and completing programmes requiring literacy skills, programmes need to be adapted for this sub-group of offenders.

The use of programmes to address criminal thinking in the population of offenders with ID has rarely moved beyond the pilot programme stage. In their small study of 10 participants, reductions in impulsiveness and increases in positive style and orientation towards social problem solving occurred (Lindsay et al. 2011), suggesting that assessment of criminal thinking and interventions directed at changing criminal thinking might offer positive avenues for treatment of this group (Lindsay et al. 2017). Supporting this view is research that indicated that offenders with serious mental illness exhibit criminal thinking styles, especially impulsivity, hostility, and emotionality, which are related to offending behaviour, and which are not solely related to their symptoms of mental illness (Wilson et al. 2014). Given the high rates of dual diagnosis of mental illness amongst offenders with ID, the authors' suggestion that it is important to develop a multi-pronged treatment approach that integrates interventions for criminal thinking and antisocial attitudes with treatment for mental illness and substance abuse issues is particularly apt.

An important aspect of assessing the efficacy of interventions for criminal thinking is accurate assessment of the concept, which can be used to identify areas to be targeted, and evaluate change. Over the years a number of scales have been developed including, but not limited to, the widely used PICTS (Walters 1995, 2002) and more recently, the Criminogenic Thinking Profile (CTP) (Mitchell and Tafrate 2012). The PICTS is an 80-item self-report measure designed to measure eight thinking styles (mollification, cut-off, entitlement, power orientation, sentimentality, super-optimism, cognitive indolence, and discontinuity) considered instrumental in protecting and maintaining a criminal lifestyle (Walters 2002). The PICTS appears to have some universality, the short form having been validated in a Japanese offender population (Kishi et al. 2015). These researchers commented that the Japanese version possesses important implications for offender rehabilitation because it identifies relevant cognitive targets and assesses offender progress. The CTP comprises eight sub-scales including concepts such as disregard for others, demand for excitement, poor judgement, emotional disengagement, parasitic/ exploitative tendencies, justifying, inability to cope, and grandiosity; the scale correlates with psychopathy and personality disorders. The use of validated measures adds significantly to evaluation of programmes which address aspects of criminal thinking, as well as indicating individual change.

17.5 Areas for Further Development

The basic question posed in this publication is 'what works?' The answer specific to this chapter is that clinicians, programme developers in corrective services, researchers, and ID specialists cannot be certain of the best interventions for social problem solving and criminal thinking for offenders with ID because there is insufficient research and evaluation of programmes. The research that has been undertaken has tended to be pilot studies, with small and select groups of participants, usually without control or comparison groups. Data about individual and group changes in attitudes and behaviour is limited, and little in the way of follow-up data have been collected. Some of these deficits in the research are difficult to overcome, given the nature of research in corrective services, in both prison and community settings. For example, the difficulties faced by ethics committees in approving research where there is a no-treatment group for a sex offender treatment trial have been the subject of comment and analysis; this may be one reason why comparison groups of convenience are often used (Sturmey et al. 2004)

The area of anger treatment has received possibly the greatest attention, with a number of studies employing wait-list control groups (Lindsay et al. 2004; Taylor et al. 2005). However, there continue to be comparatively few studies of other areas of offending and aberrant behaviour using participant groups of offenders with ID, whereas there has been burgeoning research concerning non-disabled offenders, including in the areas of moral reasoning, victim empathy, risk assessment, and staff training and support (Lindsay et al. 2007).

Another neglected area is that of interaction, knowledge exchange, and cross-fertilization between community services and forensic services for people with ID. Even basic information about an individual is seldom shared between services, making the tasks of both even more demanding. Streamlining information exchange, whilst maintaining high standards of ethics, privacy, and confidentiality, is a challenging but not impossible task, and certainly one that will benefit both consumers and staff.

Under-pinning all of the difficulties facing researchers and clinicians is the issue of identification of offenders with ID at various stages of the criminal justice system, so that they may receive appropriate programmes and interventions (Hayes 2015). It is certain that some of the research cited in this chapter regarding mentally disordered offenders will have included participants with ID who have not been identified as such. Participants with ID therefore may not have benefited to the maximum extent possible because programmes have not been tailored to their needs. Loucks' report describes in graphic detail the difficulties experienced by offenders with ID in corrective services, especially when their disabilities are not recognized, and also the problems facing correctional staff members who are not trained in the area (Loucks 2007). Until routine screening of all offenders is undertaken at a point of reception into a service, whether it be a custodial, community, or forensic secure unit, some offenders with ID will continue to be mistakenly viewed as uncooperative trouble-makers, or will be bullied and manipulated by peers, or will miss out on engagement in meaningful and change-engendering programmes.

17.6 Conclusions

Offenders with ID have multiple vulnerabilities when it comes to the areas of criminal thinking and social problem solving. Their ID and adaptive behaviour deficits render them more likely to behave in an impulsive and possibly angry or aggressive manner without consideration for long-term consequences of their actions or for the welfare of others. The high prevalence of dual diagnoses of ID and mental illness adds to the complexity, especially because deficits in social problem solving are associated with various mental disorders including depression, anxiety, and suicidality (Nezu et al. 2002b; Noreen et al. 2015). Communication limitations mean that intervention programmes need to be tailored for a group with low levels of receptive and expressive language and poor literacy skills, coupled with attenuated concentration spans and memory impairments (Hayes et al. 2007). People with ID are likely to be less effective in generating strategies for solving the range of complex daily and long-term problems (D'Zurilla and Nezu 2004) with which they are confronted.

Cognitive behaviour therapies and a range of manualized programmes appear to offer positive and effective solutions for assisting offenders with ID to improve social problem-solving skills, adaptive skills, and criminal thinking styles. Methods of evaluating these areas have been used with this group and are efficacious in demonstrating evidence-based changes in thinking and behaviour. This is a fertile area for further clinical and research endeavour with offenders with ID.

References

Andrews, D.A. (2001). Principles of effective correctional programs. In: *Compendium 2000 of Effective Correctional Programming* (eds. L.L. Motiuk and R.C. Serin), 9–17. Ottawa, ON: Correctional Service Canada.

Andrews, D.A., Zinger, I., Hoge, R. et al. (1990). Does correctional treatment work? A clinically relevant and psychologically informed meta-analysis. *Criminology* 28 (3): 369–404.

Benson, B.A., Rice, C.J., and Miranti, S.V. (1986). Effects of anger management training with mentally retarded adults in group treatment. *Journal of Consulting and Clinical Psychology* 54: 728–729.

Biggam, F.H. and Power, K.G. (2002). A controlled, problem-solving, group-based intervention with vulnerable incarcerated young offenders. *International Journal of Offender Therapy and Comparative Criminology* 46 (6): 678–698.

Bonta, J. and Andrews, D.A. (2017). The risk-need-responsivity model of offender assessment and treatment. In: *The Psychology of Criminal Conduct* (eds. J. Bonta and D.A. Andrews), 175–184. London and New York: Routledge, Taylor and Francis Group.

Bourke, M.L. and Van Hasselt, V.B. (2001). Social problem-solving skills training for incacerated offenders. *Behavior Modification* 25 (2): 163–188.

Burns, J. and Lampraki, A. (2016). Coping with stress: the experiences of service-users with intellectual disabilities in forensic services. *Journal of Intellectual Disabilities and Offending Behaviour* 7: 75–83.

Castles, E.E. and Glass, C.R. (1986). Training in social and interpersonal problem-solving skills for mildly and moderately mentally retarded adults. *American Journal of Mental Deficiency* 91: 35–42.

Chang, E.C., D'Zurilla, T.J., and Sanna, L.J. (2004). *Social Problem Solving: Theory, Research and Training*. Washington, DC: American Psychological Association.

D'Zurilla, T.J. and Goldfried, M.R. (1971). Problem solving and behavior modification. *Journal of Abnormal Psychology* 78: 107–126.

D'Zurilla, T.J. and Nezu, A.M. (1982). Social problem solving in adults. In: *Advances in Cognitive-Behavioral Research and Therapy*, vol. 1 (ed. P.C. Kendall), 201–274. New York: Academic Press.

D'Zurilla, T.J. and Nezu, A.M. (2004). Social problem solving: theory and assessment. In: *Social Problem Solving. Theory, Research and Training* (eds. E.C. Chang, T.J. D'Zurilla and L.J. Sanna), 11–27. Washington, DC: American Psychological Association.

D'Zurilla, T.J., Nezu, A.M., and Maydeu-Olivares, A. (2002). *Social Problem-Solving Inventory – Revised (SPSI-R): Technical Manual*. North Tonawanda, NY: Multi-Health Systems.

D'Zurilla, T.J., Nezu, A.M., and Maydeu-Olivares, A. (2004). Social problem solving: theory and assessment. In: *Social Problem Solving: Theory, Research and Training* (eds. E.C. Chang, T.J. D'Zurilla and L.J. Sanna), 11–27. Washington, DC: American Psychological Association.

Folk, J.B., Disabato, D.J., Daylor, J.M. et al. (2016). Effectiveness of a self-administered intervention for criminal thinking: taking a chance on change. *Psychological Services* 13 (3): 272–282.

Frauenknecht, M. and Black, D.R. (2002). Problem-solving training for children and adolescents. In: *Social Problem Solving. Theory, Research and Training* (eds. E.C. Chang, T.J. D'Zurilla and L.J. Sanna), 153–170. Washington, DC: American Psychological Association.

Hayes, S.C. (2015). Intellectual disability. In: *Expert Evidence* (eds. I. Freckelton and H. Selby). Australia: Thomson Reuters.

Hayes, S., Shackell, P., Mottram, P. et al. (2007). Prevalence of intellectual disability in a major UK prison. *British Journal of Learning Disabilities* 35 (3): 162–167.

Kishi, K., Takeda, F., Nagata, Y. et al. (2015). The Japanese criminal thinking inventory: development, reliability, and initial validation of a new scale for assessing criminal thinking in a Japanese offending population. *International Journal of Offender Therapy and Comparative Criminology* 59 (12): 1308–1321.

Kohlberg, L. (1969). Stage and sequence: the cognitive-developmental approach to socialisation. In: *Handbook of Socialisation Theory and Research* (ed. D. Goslin), 347–480. Chicago, IL: Rand McNally.

Kohlberg, L. (1984). *Essays on Moral Development: the Psychology of Moral Development.* San Francisco, CA: Harper & Row.

Lindsay, W.R., Allan, R., Parry, C.J. et al. (2004). Anger and aggression in people with intellectual disabilities: treatment and follow-up of consecutive referrals and a waiting-list comparison. *Clinical Psychology and Psychotherapy* 11: 255–264.

Lindsay, W.R., Hamilton, C., Moulton, S. et al. (2011). Assessment and treatment of social problem solving in offenders with intellectual disability. *Psychology, Crime & Law* 17 (2): 181–197.

Lindsay, W.R., Hastings, R.P., Griffiths, D.M. et al. (2007). Trends and challenges in forensic research on offenders with intellectual disability. *Journal of Intellectual and Developmental Disability* 32 (2): 55–61.

Lindsay, W.R., Michie, A.M., Finlay, C. et al. (2017). Offenders with intellectual and developmental disabilities. In: *The Routledge International Handbook of Forensic Psychology in Secure Settings* (eds. J.L. Ireland, C.A. Ireland, N. Gredecki, et al.), 40–54. London and New York: Routledge, Taylor and Francis Group.

Little, G.R. and Robinson, K.D. (1988). Moral reconation therapy: a systematic step by step treatment system for treatment resistant clients. *Psychological Reports* 62: 135–151.

Loucks, N. (2007). *No One Knows. Offenders with Learning Difficulties and Learning Disabilities - Review of Prevalence and Associated Needs.* UK: Prison Reform Trust.

Loumidis, K.S. and Hill, A. (1997). Training social problem-solving skill to reduce maladaptive behaviours in intellectual disability groups: the influence of individual difference factors. *Journal of Applied Research in Intellectual Disabilities* 10: 217–237.

Mitchell, D. and Tafrate, R.C. (2012). Conceptualization and measurement of criminal thinking: initial validation of the criminogenic thinking profile. *International Journal of Offender Therapy and Comparative Criminology* 56 (7): 1080–1102.

Nezu, A.M., D'Zurilla, T.J., Zwick, M.L. et al. (2002a). Problem solving therapy for adults. In: *Social Problem Solving. Theory, Research and Training* (eds. E.C. Chang, T.J. D'Zurilla and L.J. Sanna), 171–191. Washington, DC: American Psychological Association.

Nezu, A.M., Wilkins, V.M., and Nezu, C.M. (2002b). Social problem solving, stress, and negative affect. In: *Social Problem Solving. Theory, Research and Training* (eds. E.C. Chang, T.J. D'Zurilla and L.J. Sanna), 49–65. Washington, DC: American Psychological Association.

Nezu, C.M., Nezu, A.M., and Arean, P.A. (1991). Assertiveness and problem-solving therapy for mild mentally retarded persons with dual diagnoses. *Research in Developmental Disabilities* 12: 371–386.

Noreen, S., Whyte, K.E., and Dritschel, B. (2015). Investigating the role of future thinking in social probem solving. *Journal of Behavior Therapy and Experimental Psychiatry* 46: 78–84.

Oakes, P., Murphy, G., Giraud-Saunders, A. et al. (2016). The realistic evaluation of an adapted thinking skills programme. *Journal of Intellectual Disabilities and Offending Behaviour* 7 (1): 14–24.

Olver, M.E., Stockdale, K.C., and Wormith, J.S. (2011). A meta-analysis of predictors of offender treatment attrition and its relationship to recidivism. *Journal of Consulting and Clinical Psychology* 79: 6–21.

Palmer, E.J. and Humphries, L.M. (2016). Differences between completers and non-completers of offending behaviour programmes: impulsivity, social problem-solving, and criminal thinking. *Legal and Criminological Psychology* 21: 407–416.

Polaschek, D.L.L., Collie, R.M., and Walkey, F.H. (2004). Criminal attitudes to violence: development and preliminary validation of a scale for male prisoners. *Aggressive Behavior* 30: 484–503.

Robinson, D. and Porporino, F.J. (2001). Programming in cognitive skills: the reasoning and rehabilitation programme. In: *Handbook of Offender Assessment and Treatment* (ed. C.R. Hollin), 179–193. Chichester: Wiley.

Ross, R.R. and Fabiano, E.A. (1990). *Reasoning and Rehabilitation: Instructor's Manual*. Ottawa, ON: Cognitive Station.

Sampson, C.J., James, M., Huband, N. et al. (2013). Cost implications of treatment non-completion in a forensic personality disorder service. *Criminal Behaviour and Mental Health* 23 (5): 321–335.

Simourd, D.J. (1997). The Criminal Sentiments Scale-Modified and Pride in Delinquency scale: psychometric properties and construct validity of two measures of criminal attitudes. *Criminal Justice and Behavior* 24: 52–70.

Sturmey, P., Taylor, J.T., and Lindsay, W.R. (2004). Research and development. In: *Offenders with Developmental Disabilities* (eds. W.R. Lindsay, J.T. Taylor and P. Sturmey), 23–34. Chichester: John Wiley.

Tapp, J., Fellowes, E., Wallis, N. et al. (2009). An evaluation of the Enhanced Thinking Skills (ETS) programme with mentally disordered offenders in a high security hospital. *Legal and Criminological Psychology* 14: 201–212.

Taylor, J.T., Novaco, R.W., Gilmer, B.T. et al. (2005). Individual cognitive behavioural anger treatment for people with mild-borderline disabilities and histories of aggression: a controlled trial. *British Journal of Clinical Psychology* 44: 367–382.

Vanny, K.A., Levy, M.H., Greenberg, D.M. et al. (2009). Mental illness and intellectual disability in Magistrates Courts in New South Wales, Australia. *Journal of Intellectual Disability Research* 53 (3): 289–297.

Walters, G.D. (1995). The Psychological Inventory of Criminal Thinking Styles: I. Reliability and preliminary validity. *Criminal Justice and Behavior* 22: 307–325.

Walters, G.D. (2002). The Psychological Inventory of Criminal Thinking Styles (PICTS): a review and meta-analysis. *Assessment* 9 (3): 278–291.

Walters, G.D. (2006). Appraising, researching and conceptualizing criminal thinking. *Criminal Behaviour and Mental Health* 16: 87–99.

Walters, G.D. (2007). Measuring proactive and reactive criminal thinking with the PICTS: correlations with outcome expectancies and hostile attribution biases. *Journal of Interpersonal Violence* 22: 371–385.

Walters, G.D. (2011). Predicting recidivism with the Psychological Inventory of Criminal Thinking Styles and Level of Service Inventory-Revised: Screening Version. *Law and Human Behavior* 35: 211–220.

Walters, G.D. (2012). Criminal thinking and recidivism: meta-analytic evidence on the predictive and incremental validity of the Psychological Inventory of Criminal Thinking Styles. *Aggression and Violent Behavior* 16: 272–278.

Walters, G.D., Deming, A., and Casbon, T. (2015). Predicting recidivism in sex offenders with the Psychological Inventory of Criminal Thinking (PICTS). *Assessment* 22 (2): 167–177.

Waugh, A., Gudjonsson, G.H., Rees-Jones, A. et al. (2014). A feasibility study of the Reasoning and Rehabilitation Mental Health Programme (R&R2MHP) in male offenders with intellectual disability. *Criminal Behaviour and Mental Health* 24: 222–224.

Wilson, D.B., Bouffard, L.A., and MacKenzie, D.L. (2005). A quantitative review of structured group oriented, cognitive behavioural programmes for offenders. *Criminal Justice and Behavior* 32 (2): 172–204.

Wilson, A.B., Farkas, K., Ishler, K.J. et al. (2014). Criminal thinking styles among people with serious mental illness in jail. *Law and Human Behavior* 38 (6): 592–601.

18

Treating Substance Misuses Amongst Offenders with Intellectual and Developmental Disabilities

Danielle Newton and Jane McGillivray

School of Psychology, Deakin University, Geelong, Victoria, Australia

18.1 Introduction

The overarching objective of this chapter is to outline the literature concerning the treatment of substance misuse amongst people with intellectual and developmental disabilities (IDD), with a particular focus on individuals who have involvement with forensic services. The chapter begins with a brief overview of substance use/misuse amongst people with IDD including the prevalence in community and prison-based samples, and the reasons and risk factors for their substance use. The link between substance misuse and offending behaviour amongst this population and the few treatment programmes with evidence of effectiveness are then outlined and discussed. A list of key considerations when designing substance-use treatment programmes for this population is provided. The chapter concludes with a review of the barriers to effective assessment and treatment of substance misuse amongst people with IDD and provides a summary of further research needed in this area.

18.2 Substance Use/Misuse Amongst People with IDD

Community living has resulted in many benefits for people with IDD, such as greater community participation, enhanced adaptive behaviour, and increased quality of life (Kozma et al. 2009; Mansell 2006; Young 2003). However, greater autonomy has also resulted in increased exposure to alcohol and other drugs, heightening the potential for substance misuse amongst this population (Burgard et al. 2000; Christian and Poling 1997; Clarke and Wilson 1999). Research documenting substance use amongst people with IDD is scarce. Substance misuse (otherwise referred to as substance abuse or substance dependence) by people with IDD has been found to be as high as 14% within community-based samples (Burgard et al. 2000; Westermeyer et al. 1996), whereas the prevalence of drug and alcohol dependence in general community-based samples has been reported to range from 0.7 to 9% (McBride et al. 2009).

The Wiley Handbook on What Works for Offenders with Intellectual and Developmental Disabilities: An Evidence-Based Approach to Theory, Assessment, and Treatment, First Edition.
Edited by William R. Lindsay, Leam A. Craig, and Dorothy Griffiths.

A number of factors place people with IDD at a greater risk of substance misuse than their non-disabled peers. High impulsivity, poor self-control, low self-esteem as well as poor social and communication skills render people with IDD more vulnerable to the misuse of drugs and alcohol (Clarke and Wilson 1999; Gress and Boss 1996; Stavrakaki 2002; Sturmey et al. 2003; Taggart et al. 2007). Other risk factors include being young, male, having borderline or mild IDD, living independently, and having a concomitant mental health condition (Hassiotis et al. 2008; Taggart et al. 2006). People with IDD use drugs and alcohol for a variety of reasons including as a means of coping with social stressors (McGillicuddy and Blane 1999; Sturmey et al. 2003; Taggart et al. 2007) and as a way of socializing and 'fitting-in' with peers without IDD (Taggart et al. 2008). Moreover, people with IDD appear to 'self-medicate' with drugs or alcohol to cope with negative life experiences such as abuse, bereavement, mental health issues, loneliness, bullying, or exploitation (Taggart et al. 2007).

Studies also indicate that the risks associated with substance use may be substantially higher in people with IDD (McGillicuddy and Blane 1999; Slayter and Steenrod 2009). A substantial body of research suggests that people with IDD who engage in substance use may be at increased risk of substance misuse and associated harmful outcomes including ill health, exploitation, as well as offending behaviour (Didden et al. 2009; Jobling and Cuskelly 2006; Lindsay et al. 2013a; McGillicuddy 2006; McGillivray and Moore 2001; Slayter and Steenrod 2009; Taggart et al. 2006).

18.3   Substance Use/Misuse and Offending Behaviour

It has been increasingly recognized that many offenders with IDD have substance use issues (Chaplin et al. 2011; Chapman and Wu 2012; Didden et al. 2009; Männynsalo et al. 2009; Plant et al. 2011; To et al. 2014). Substance use has been found to be up to five times more likely amongst individuals with IDD who have a forensic history (Chaplin et al. 2011; Tenneij and Koot 2007). Furthermore, research has found that a history of convictions for violent offences is significantly more likely to be present in offenders who engage in harmful substance use or dependence (Plant et al. 2011). A number of studies have shown that offenders with IDD are frequently intoxicated at the time of their crime (Männynsalo et al. 2009; McGillivray and Moore 2001; Plant et al. 2011; Tenneij and Koot 2007; To et al. 2014). The link between substance use and offending behaviour is a critical one given the overrepresentation of people with IDD in the criminal justice system (Hayes et al. 2007; Herrington 2009), and highlights the importance of specialized treatment programmes for this population.

18.4   Evidence-Based Treatment Programmes for Substance Use/Misuse Amongst People with IDD

Despite indications that the risks associated with substance misuse are elevated amongst people with IDD (McGillicuddy and Blane 1999; Slayter and Steenrod 2009), there are surprisingly few evidence-based substance use/misuse treatment programmes targeting this population. Although the need for health interventions to be specialized or adapted for people with IDD has been recognized (Degenhardt 2000), there is little information to guide practitioners in developing and delivering these interventions (Kerr et al. 2013). Moreover, even though prisoners with IDD transitioning out of prison are a particularly vulnerable group, they receive relatively little or no support to address substance use issues, which have been linked with increased likelihood of recidivism (Baldry et al. 2013; Van Dooren et al. 2015). A systematic review of interventions aimed at reducing substance use amongst adults with IDD transitioning out of prison undertaken by Van Dooren et al. (2015), confirmed an absence of any randomized or non-randomized controlled trials of substance use interventions for this population.

Amongst the small number of interventions for substance misuse targeting people with IDD reported in the research literature, the majority are community-based programmes that do not specifically target *offenders* with IDD. These programmes have included the use of support groups and staff education, as well as educational or behavioural strategies (Mayer 2001; McGillicuddy 2006; McGillicuddy and Blane 1999; Mendel and Hipkins 2002; Stavrakaki 2002; Sturmey et al. 2003). However, a lack of evaluation and/or significant methodological limitations, make ascertaining the effectiveness of these methods problematic (Burgard et al. 2000; McGillicuddy 2006; Sturmey et al. 2003; Taggart et al. 2008). As noted by Taggart et al. (2008), many of the published treatment approaches for substance use amongst people with IDD involve small sample sizes, utilize assessment methods of questionable reliability and validity, lack control groups or follow-up, and are often conducted in settings that do not reflect the opportunities and problems of the 'real-world' (Taggart et al. 2008).

Only four published treatment programmes for substance use/misuse amongst people with IDD can be considered to have some evidence of effectiveness. As a minimum, these studies utilize a pre-post design and evaluation (see Table 18.1). In the first of these studies, conducted by McGillicuddy and Blane (1999), participants with IDD were randomly assigned to receive a prevention programme involving (i) assertiveness building, (ii) modelling and social inference, or (iii) a delayed treatment, control condition. The findings indicated that, at least in the short-term, participants demonstrated improved substance knowledge and enhanced skills following participation in both programmes (i) and (ii). However, this study utilized self-report and was designed as a substance use 'prevention' programme. It is therefore uncertain whether programme content would be effective for people with IDD already engaged in substance use/misuse. A second study utilized motivational interviewing (MI) with participants with IDD in an inpatient forensic setting to address alcohol misuse (Mendel and Hipkins 2002). Using interactive teaching methods, participants met as a group for three, one-hour sessions. Pre- and post-group testing revealed self-reported increases in participants' motivation, self-efficacy, and determination to change their drinking behaviour. However, in addition to relying on self-report, this study did not measure the impact of the programme on actual substance use behaviour change.

A third study involved an evaluation of an alcohol awareness group (AAG) (Burns et al. 2011). Thirty-four individuals with IDD residing in an inpatient forensic setting participated in 12 one-hour weekly structured and themed group sessions. The intervention was a synthesis of programmes described in previous studies (Forbat 1999; Mendel and Hipkins 2002). Pre-and post-group testing revealed an increase in level of knowledge and reported self-efficacy in relation to alcohol. Interestingly, participants with a lower IQ gained a greater level of alcohol-related knowledge compared to those

Table 18.1 Substance use programmes for people with IDD.

Author	Country	Setting	Participants (n)	Programme structure and content	Outcomes
McGillicuddy and Blane (1999)	USA	Community	84	Two prevention approaches were utilized (see McGillicuddy and Blane 1999). Each programme shared the common goals of (a) educating participants regarding the dangers of various substances, and (b) providing participants a behavioural repertoire that they could use when confronted by situations involving alcohol and other drugs. In the *Assertiveness* approach, participants were trained to refuse substances when offered if their inclination was to decline. In the *Modelling* approach, participants were trained on how to infer normative behaviour in new social situations, and how to distinguish between appropriate and inappropriate role models in various situations. Each programme was offered in hour-long sessions once-a-week for 10 weeks. Both programmes minimized didactic information and maximized experiential and interactive techniques.	Both programmes increased short-term substance knowledge (particularly in the modelling condition), but failed to impact substance-related attitudes, or substance use. Both programmes resulted in enhanced participant skills; clients receiving the assertiveness intervention improved assertiveness and refusal skills, and clients receiving the modelling/social inference intervention improved model discrimination and inferential skills.
Mendel and Hipkins (2002)	UK	Forensic learning disabilities service	7	All sessions were structured around the main elements outlined by Miller (1983) relating to motivating clients to change as summarized in the FRAMES model: *F* Feedback: to give individuals personal feedback about their drinking and the-related problems; *R* Responsibility: to emphasize their responsibility for change; *A* Advice: to give non-confrontational advice about drinking and the associated risks; *M* Menu of alternatives: to present a choice of goals and a range of methods for achieving these; *E* Empathy: to enhance their belief that they have the power to change. Motivational strategies were aimed at working on ambivalence and shifting the balance of positive and negative aspects of drinking towards the negative consequences. A total of three group sessions were held over a two-week period. The group facilitators used an interactive style of presentation with small group exercises and visual aids to illustrate themes (e.g. the Stages of Change model). Examples were used such as case vignettes involving popular media personalities.	A variety of measures (pre and post group) demonstrated increases in clients' motivation, self-efficacy, and determination to change their drinking behaviour. Findings indicated that there had been a cognitive shift in that six individuals recognized more negative than positive consequences of their behaviour as compared to their perception prior to the group.

| Burns et al. (2011) | UK | Forensic inpatient | 34 | The Alcohol Awareness Group (AAG) consisted of 12 weekly (1 hour) structured and themed group sessions. The AAG is a synthesis of the programmes described by Forbat (1999) and Mendel and Hipkins (2002). The 12 sessions are titled motivation to change; why people drink; what are we drinking?; alcohol and advertising; units/safe limits; alcohol and its effects; problem drinking (models); triggers to drinking; attitudes to drinking; saying 'no'; safer limits and alternatives to drinking and changing your lifestyle. | The AAG was successful in increasing motivation to change drinking behaviour, knowledge of problems related to alcohol, and 'safe drinking' practices. These outcomes were achieved across a wide range of cognitive abilities suggesting that those with an IQ below 60 can also benefit from this type of intervention. |
| Lindsey and Michie (2012) | UK | Forensic services | 22 | The programme comprised seven sessions outlined below (see Lindsey et al. 2014 for a more detailed overview of programme). *Sessions 1 and 2:* The programme begins with orientation, introductions, and rules generated by the group members. Simple games and quizzes that advance knowledge are typical procedures. Some examples are as follows. The group leader says a word related to alcohol or drinking and invites participants to state an associated word. Associations are discussed, leading to a general discussion about what the group knows and thinks about alcohol. *Sessions 3, 4, and 5:* These sessions introduce the differences between alcoholic and non-alcoholic drinks, the effects that alcohol has on the body and the brain, how the body gets rid of alcohol and how long it takes for this process to occur *Sessions 6 and 7:* These sessions review the risks of alcohol misuse with exercises and discussions on its relationship to violence, conflict, money problems, and stress. The theme of sensible drinking is developed with further time spent reviewing safe limits, strategies for sensible drinking in bars and at home, where there are no regulated measures. | There were no differences on alcohol-related knowledge between the groups at baseline, but after 2 months, during which the treatment group received the intervention, there was a significant improvement in alcohol knowledge in those who had participated in treatment. At 2 months' follow-up, these differences remained significant. |

with a higher IQ, suggesting that those individuals often excluded from such interventions could potentially benefit the most. In the final study, a programme aimed at increasing understanding of the effects of alcohol and the relationship between alcohol abuse and violence was evaluated with offenders with mild IDD and borderline intelligence who were at-risk of, or who were currently experiencing alcohol misuse (Lindsay and Michie 2012). Twelve individuals with IDD and evidence of alcohol abuse undertook the programme involving practical exercises, such as general role plays in alcohol-related situations and specific role-plays related to the individuals' risk situations. In comparison to 10 matched individuals who remained on a waiting-list for an equivalent period, there was a significant improvement in alcohol-related knowledge following participation in the programme, with effects maintained at a two-month follow-up (Lindsay and Michie 2012).

These studies provide some evidence of the effectiveness of treatment programmes for substance use/misuse amongst people with IDD, including those administered in forensic settings. However, to varying extents, all four studies suffer from methodological limitations. In particular, participants were assessed on variables such as knowledge of substances, self-reported intention to change behaviour, and self-efficacy; however, none explored whether participation in the programme led to actual behaviour change.

18.5   Key Considerations When Developing and Implementing Treatment Programmes for Substance Misuse Amongst People with IDD

Given the lack of a strong evidence-base for substance misuse treatment programmes for people with IDD, practitioners working with offenders with IDD have limited information to draw on when developing targeted treatment programmes. Such practitioners may benefit from a brief examination of the theoretical literature concerning the treatment of substance use amongst people with IDD. In addition, the broader literature concerning the design and implementation of treatment programmes for people with IDD, as well as the literature concerning the treatment of substance use issues amongst general population offenders, may have much to offer as it pertains to the development and implementation of treatment programmes for substance use in offenders with IDD. Some key considerations derived from this literature are now discussed.

18.6   Who Should Be the Target of Substance Use Interventions?

The effects of substance misuse might be significantly reduced or prevented entirely using prevention programmes administered to young people with IDD. As suggested by Taggart et al. (2008), health promotion programmes could go some way towards educating young people with IDD about safe drinking practices and the harms of substance use. Community programmes aimed at facilitating greater social connectedness could also assist in reducing loneliness and isolation, both known risk factors for substance use in this population (Taggart et al. 2008). Of interest, few differences have been found in the negative consequences of substance use between people with IDD who *use* and people with IDD who *misuse* substances (conceptualized as 'problems occurring in one or more life domains resulting from alcohol, psychotropic drug and illegal substance use') (To et al. 2014). This suggests that there may be benefits in providing intervention programmes to people with IDD who report substance use of any kind.

18.7 Education About Substances and the Potential for Harm

Educating people with IDD about drugs and alcohol and the potential for harm to mind, body, and relationships may be a particularly effective component of substance use/misuse treatment. Research has shown that offenders with IDD know less about the effects of taking excessive amounts of alcohol and drugs than their non-disabled counterparts (McGillivray and Moore 2001). In a subsequent study, McGillivray and Newton (2016) reported that prisoners with IDD benefited from learning about the potential harms caused by substance use and felt that this knowledge motivated them to change their behaviour. This highlights the importance of ensuring that education about the negative effects of drugs and alcohol are key components of any substance use/misuse treatment programme for this population.

18.8 Teaching Methods and Modalities

There are mixed views on which intervention modalities work best with people with IDD. However, a meta-analysis of treatment programmes for offenders with IDD determined that cognitive and behavioural approaches are more effective than other treatment approaches (Hollin 1999). Structured, concrete, goal-oriented approaches focusing on the links between beliefs, attitudes, and behaviour, and that do not require high levels of literacy, have also been proposed for this population (Hollin 1999). Offenders with IDD have reported difficulties in following the content of prison and community-based substance misuse treatment programmes (McGillivray and Newton 2016). It is, therefore, essential that treatment programmes are tailored and delivered in ways that meet the learning needs of this population. Lindsay et al. (2014) suggest that people with IDD respond best to the use of active teaching methods such as practical demonstrations and role play. Role-playing involving a problem-solving component is especially useful and helps individuals with IDD to understand how newfound knowledge and skills can be used in the 'real-world'. Role-play may involve acting out difficult or confronting situations in which participants may potentially encounter peer-pressure (Lindsay et al. 2014). See Lindsay et al. (2014) for more detailed information on appropriate learning methods and activities for this population.

18.9 Addressing Risk-Factors and Co-occurring Issues

Substance use amongst people with IDD has been associated with an array of severe emotional and behavioural problems (Didden et al. 2009; Taggart et al. 2006). It is not uncommon for people with IDD who misuse substances to experience co-occurring issues such as aggression, anger, and other mental health problems, rendering treatment of such individuals especially difficult (Degenhardt 2000; Huxley and Copello 2007; McLaughlin et al. 2007a; Sturmey et al. 2003). Loneliness, boredom, poverty, poor physical and mental health, and negative social interactions are all consequences of the social isolation experienced by many people with mild to borderline IDD who live in the community, and all constitute risk factors towards offending behaviour and substance misuse (Taggart et al. 2007). No treatment for substance misuse can be effective without attempting to address the risk factors for both substance use and offending behaviour. Interventions focused on mental health problems, abuse, unemployment, loneliness and isolation, and teaching people with IDD problem-solving and coping skills to manage these issues may help to ameliorate factors associated with substance use and offending behaviour (Taggart et al. 2008). Given that people with IDD often use drugs and alcohol as a means of coping with complex social situations and as a way of coping with negative evaluation from peers (Dagnan and Jahoda 2006; Dagnan and Waring 2004), these issues should also be a focus for treatment (Cosden 2001). Specifically, interventions should assist individuals with IDD in addressing problems of self-esteem and help them to manage perceptions of social stigma (Jahoda et al. 2006).

18.10 Treatment Goals: Abstinence Versus Controlled Usage

Whilst mainstream substance use treatment programmes often allow participants to make their own decisions about whether their goal is total abstinence or controlled usage, it has been suggested that for people with IDD, abstinence might be more appropriate (Degenhardt 2000). A controlled usage goal necessarily places a burden of assessment and decision-making on the individual and for people with IDD, this process may be too burdensome and complex (Degenhardt 2000; Van Der Nagel et al. 2011).

18.11 Motivation and Engagement

People with IDD frequently have low motivation for undertaking psychological therapies (Lindsay et al. 2013b). This is particularly the case with offenders with IDD. Research has shown, for example, that many offenders with IDD resent interference in their life and particularly resent expectations that they undertake treatment (Lindsay 2009; Taylor and Novaco 2005). Prisoners report that being 'forced' to undertake substance misuse treatment programmes either in prison or in the community are significant barriers to engagement with these programmes (McGillivray and Newton 2016). This apparent lack of willingness to engage in assessment and treatment for substance use compromises the success of such programmes (McLaughlin et al. 2007a). Addressing poor motivation is therefore an important factor in the design of any treatment programme for people with IDD, and particularly offenders with IDD.

MI may be an effective strategy in tackling resistance to changing substance use behaviours. MI is a well-established approach to the treatment of addictions, including drug and alcohol addictions (Hettema et al. 2005), and involves helping people to overcome ambivalence and better understand the barriers to change in relation to their addiction. Research with the general population has shown MI to be an effective technique for treating substance misuse, and appears to have promise for IDD populations (Mendel and Hipkins 2002). Ideally, motivation should be raised through the *consequences* of the substance misuse (Lindsay 2009). For example, violence, or abuse may be the behaviours that lead to a person with IDD being referred to substance use treatment and Lindsay (2009) suggests that these negative behaviours, as opposed to the substance addiction, should be the focus of raising motivation. Participants should be encouraged to see such scenarios as reduced contact with the police and the court system, reduced family conflict, and maintenance of their living situation as motivation for addressing their substance use.

Perceived uncooperativeness and lack of engagement may not always be the result of poor motivation. They may also be attributable to cognitive limitations associated with IDD such as problems with communication, illiteracy, memory deficits, and poor self-control/regulatory behaviour (Degenhardt 2000; Huxley and Copello 2007; McGillicuddy 2006; McGillicuddy and Blane 1999; McGillivray and Moore 2001; Sturmey et al. 2003). It is thus important that practitioners are alert to the reasons for lack of motivation and engagement and that they tailor strategies accordingly.

18.12   Treatment Follow-Up and Relapse Management

Offenders with IDD may find many substance misuse programmes to be too short to be of any real benefit, particularly when programmes are undertaken in prison settings (McGillivray and Newton 2016). Prisoners often complete these programmes with the expectation that they will likely return to substance use post-release. These findings signal the importance of long-term or ongoing community-based support for offenders with IDD. Relapse prevention (RP) strategies should be part of any ongoing treatment plan for people with IDD being treated for substance misuse. The aim of relapse management is to prevent or reduce the impact of a lapse before heavy drug or alcohol use become re-established. Developing an RP plan involves identifying high-risk situations that may lead to substance use such as feelings of anxiety, stress, or depression, isolation, loneliness, or peer-pressure, and developing coping strategies and skills to manage lapses (Lindsay et al. 2013b).

18.13   Barriers to Assessment and Treatment

Research indicates that people with IDD have a low likelihood of receiving or staying in substance abuse treatment programmes (Chapman and Wu 2012; McGillicuddy 2006; McGillivray and Newton 2016). In prison settings, although similar proportions of prisoners with and without IDD may undertake substance use programmes, substantially lower proportions of prisoners with IDD report completing these programmes (Hassiotis et al. 2011; McGillivray et al. 2016). These findings suggest that current substance-use treatment programmes administered in both community and prison settings may not be meeting the needs of people with IDD and that there may be substantial barriers to their participation in these programmes. Not only do people with IDD appear to lack opportunities to undertake such programmes, they also appear to lack the necessary support to achieve treatment completion. Barriers to treatment may arise from problems associated with recognition and assessment. Individuals with IDD and substance-misuse problems may remain unrecognized due to the characteristics of IDD masking symptoms of substance misuse (Slayter and Steenrod 2009), or a failure of some health professionals to acknowledge that people with ID use alcohol or drugs (Kalyva 2007). There is also some concern around the validity of self-report instruments used with IDD populations, particularly when used for gathering information on drug and alcohol use. A tendency in people with IDD to under-report health-related information has been demonstrated (Lennox et al. 2007), whilst prison populations in general tend to under-report substance use behaviours (McGregor and Makkai 2003).

People with IDD often report negative experiences when accessing mainstream drug and alcohol services, leading to poor engagement or opting out altogether (Degenhardt 2000; Huxley et al. 2005; Taggart et al. 2007). For example, in McGillivray and Newton (2016), offenders with IDD taking part in prison- or community-based substance-misuse treatment programmes reported that they worried about being bullied due to aspects of their disability and reported difficulties in following programme content. Difficulties coping with the cognitive demands of substance use intervention programmes due to communication difficulties, illiteracy, short attention span, memory deficits, or low self-esteem has been identified in other research (Degenhardt 2000; McGillicuddy 2006; McGillicuddy and Blane 1999; Plant et al. 2011; Sturmey et al. 2003). Cognitive limitations may lead to stigmatization, resentment, and exclusion within their treatment groups, and may be confused with noncompliance (Ruf 1999).

Several studies have indicated that people with IDD are often excluded from substance-use treatment because specialist addiction services do not have the resources and training to adequately assess and deliver treatment programmes to this population (McGillicuddy 2006; Slayter and Steenrod 2009; Sturmey et al. 2003; Taggart et al. 2008; Van Der Nagel et al. 2011). Furthermore, disability services staff, who may be better placed to provide interventions to people with IDD, commonly report that they do not have the capability or resources to provide appropriate screening, interventions, or referrals for individuals with IDD and substance-use problems (Degenhardt 2000; McLaughlin et al. 2007b; Taggart et al. 2007; Van Der Nagel et al. 2011). As a result, there is a very real possibility that people with IDD and substance misuse problems may 'slip through the cracks' of specialist addiction and disability services, and consequently, be prevented from receiving treatment (Bhandari et al. 2015).

18.14 Conclusion

Despite evidence indicating that harms associated with substance use are higher amongst IDD populations and that some offenders with IDD may obtain benefits from substance use programmes (McGillivray and Newton 2016), there is little evidence to guide practitioners in the development and implementation of such programmes for this group. In this chapter we have outlined four substance use/misuse treatment programmes that demonstrate some evidence of effectiveness (Burns et al. 2011; Lindsay and Michie 2012; McGillicuddy and Blane 1999; Mendel and Hipkins 2002).

These programmes have variously demonstrated beneficial impact on drug and alcohol knowledge and skills, motivation, and determination to change behaviour, and self-efficacy. It is not known, however, whether these changes are sustained in the long-term or whether they translate to changes in substance use behaviour. When considering the development of substance use prevention and treatment programmes for people with IDD, it is suggested that consideration be given to the following: targeted treatment modalities and teaching methods; delivery in the most effective environment; setting treatment goals appropriate to the population; including appropriate programme content; using strategies to elicit motivation and engagement with programmes; addressing risk factors for substance use; and appropriate follow-up and relapse management as part of a long-term plan.

The importance of identifying the prevalence of problematic substance use and associated treatment needs of people with IDD in prison has been highlighted as a priority research area in a recent review of the substance use and IDD literature (Chapman and Wu 2012). Ex-offenders with IDD are significantly more likely than their counterparts without IDD to report current substance dependence post-release (Dias et al. 2013). This finding is important, given evidence that the risk of recidivism is greater amongst the most disadvantaged of prisoners, including those with substance use issues (Baldry et al. 2003; Dowden and Brown 2002; Hobbs et al. 2006). Taken together this research suggests that prisoners with IDD and substance use issues may be at heightened risk of recidivism. A better understanding of the treatment and support needs of people with IDD transitioning out of prison is therefore critical. Amongst the intervention research that does exist in this area, the evidence is weak at best and suffers from a range of methodological limitations. There is a clear need for research with offenders with IDD and it should ideally utilize both objective and subjective forms of measurement, appropriate sample sizes, matched control groups, as well as community-based follow-up (Taggart et al. 2008).

It is certain that to deliver effective substance use treatment to IDD populations, a multi-system response is required (To et al. 2014). Ideally, substance-use treatment should be delivered as a collaborative effort between justice, disability, and health systems to ensure that individuals with substance-misuse problems do not 'slip through the cracks' (Bhandari et al. 2015). There is little doubt that delivering health services to people with IDD, and to even greater extent offenders with IDD, can be particularly challenging for practitioners. Staff working with these populations clearly require more training and support (Clarke and Wilson 1999). Mainstream addiction staff may require training in effective delivery of services to people with IDD and disability services staff may require training in assessing and treating substance misuse. Early identification of individuals with IDD using substances may allow for early intervention efforts, ultimately preventing later problems of substance misuse.

References

Baldry, E., Clarence, M., Dowse, L. et al. (2013). Reducing vulnerability to harm in adults with cognitive disabilities in the Australian criminal justice system. *Journal of Policy and Practice in Intellectual Disabilities* 10: 222–229.

Baldry, E., McConnell, D., Maplestone, P. et al. (2003). *Ex-Prisoners and Accommodation: What Bearing Do Different Forms of Housing Have on Social Reintegration?* Melbourne: Australian Housing and Urban Research Institute.

Bhandari, A., Van Dooren, K., Eastgate, G. et al. (2015). Comparison of social circumstances, substance use and substance-related harm in soon-to-be-released prisoners with and without intellectual disability. *Journal of Intellectual Disability Research* 59 (6): 571–579.

Burgard, J.F., Donohue, B., Azrin, N.H. et al. (2000). Prevalence and treatment of substance abuse in the mentally retarded population: an empirical review. *Journal of Psychoactive Drugs* 32 (3): 293–298.

Burns, J., Aspinall, C., and Matthews, C. (2011). An evaluation of an alcohol awareness group for learning disabled offenders in a secure setting. *Journal of Learning Disabilities and Offending Behaviour* 2: 159–166.

Chaplin, E., Gilvarry, C., and Tsakanikos, E. (2011). Recreational substance use patterns and co-morbid psychopathology in adults with intellectual disability. *Research in Developmental Disabilities* 32: 2981–2986.

Chapman, S.L.C. and Wu, L.T. (2012). Substance abuse among individuals with intellectual disabilities. *Research in Developmental Disabilities* 33 (4): 1147–1156.

Christian, L. and Poling, A. (1997). Drug abuse in persons with mental retardation: a review. *American Journal on Mental Retardation* 102: 126–136.

Clarke, J.J. and Wilson, D.N. (1999). Alcohol problems and learning disabilities. *Journal of Learning Disability Research* 43: 135–139.

Cosden, M. (2001). Risk and resilience for substance abuse among adolescents and adults with learning disabilities. *Journal of Learning Disabilities* 24: 352–358.

Dagnan, D. and Jahoda, A. (2006). Cognitive behavioural interventions for people with intellectual disability and anxiety disorders. *Journal of Applied Research and Intellectual Disabilities* 19: 91–98.

Dagnan, D. and Waring, M. (2004). Linking stigma to psychological distress: testing a social-cognitive model of the experience of people with intellectual disabilities. *Clinical Psychology and Psychotherapy* 11: 241–254.

Degenhardt, L. (2000). Interventions for people with alcohol use disorders and an intellectual disability: a review of the literature. *Journal of Intellectual & Developmental Disability* 25: 135–146.

Dias, S., Ware, R.S., Kinner, S.A. et al. (2013). Cooccurring mental disorder and intellectual disability in a large sample of Australian prisoners. *Australian & New Zealand Journal of Psychiatry* 47: 938–944.

Didden, R., Embregts, P., Van der Toorn, M. et al. (2009). Substance abuse, coping strategies, adaptive skills and behavioral and emotional problems in clients with mild to borderline intellectual disability admitted to a treatment facility: a pilot study. *Research in Developmental Disabilities* 30: 927–932.

Dowden, C. and Brown, S.L. (2002). The role of substance abuse factors in predicting recidivism: a meta-analysis. *Psychology, Crime & Law* 8: 243–264.

Forbat, L. (1999). Developing an alcohol awareness course for clients with a learning disability. *British Journal of Learning Disabilities* 27: 16–19.

Gress, J.R. and Boss, M.S. (1996). Substance abuse differences among students receiving special education school services. *Child Psychiatry and Human Development* 26: 235–246.

Hassiotis, A., Gazizova, D., Akinlonu, L. et al. (2011). Psychiatric morbidity in prisoners with intellectual disabilities: analysis of prison survey data for England and Wales. *The British Journal of Psychiatry* 199 (2): 156–157.

Hassiotis, A., Strydom, A., Hall, I. et al. (2008). Psychiatric morbidity and social functioning among adults with borderline intelligence living in private households. *Journal of Intellectual Disability Research* 52: 95–106.

Hayes, S., Shackell, P., Mottram, P. et al. (2007). The prevalence of intellectual disability in a major UK prison. *British Journal of Learning Disabilities* 35: 162–167.

Herrington, V. (2009). Assessing the prevalence of intellectual disability among young male prisoners. *Journal of Intellectual Disability Research* 53: 397–410.

Hettema, J., Steele, J., and Miller, W. (2005). Motivational interviewing. *Annual Review of Clinical Psychology* 1: 91–111.

Hobbs, M., Krazlan, K., Ridout, S. et al. (2006). *Mortality and Morbidity in Prisoners after Release from Prison in Western Australia 1995–2003*. Research and Public Policy Series No. 71. Canberra: Australian Institute of Criminology.

Hollin, C.R. (1999). Treatment programs for offenders. Metaanalysis, 'what works', and beyond. *International Journal of Law and Psychiatry* 22 (3–4): 361–372.

Huxley, A. and Copello, A. (2007). An overview of psychological interventions for addictive behaviours. In: *Clinical Topics in Addiction* (ed. E. Day), 213–228. London: RC Psych Publications.

Huxley, A., Copello, A., and Day, E. (2005). Substance misuse and the need for integrated services. *Learning Disability Practice* 8: 14–17.

Jahoda, A., Dagnan, D., Jarvie, P. et al. (2006). Depression, social context and cognitive behavioural therapy for people who have intellectual disabilities. *Journal of Applied Research in Intellectual Disabilities* 19: 81–89.

Jobling, A. and Cuskelly, M. (2006). Young people with Down syndrome: a preliminary investigation of health knowledge and associated behaviour. *Journal of Intellectual & Developmental Disability* 31: 210–218.

Kalyva, E. (2007). Prevalence and influences on self-reported smoking among adolescents with mild learning disabilities, attention deficit hyperactivity disorder, and their typically developing peers. *Journal of Intellectual Disabilities* 11: 267–279.

Kerr, S., Lawrence, M., Darbyshire, C. et al. (2013). Tobacco and alcohol-related interventions for people with mild/moderate intellectual disabilities: a systematic review of the literature. *Journal of Intellectual Disability Research* 57: 393–408.

Kozma, A., Mansell, J., and Beadle-Brown, J. (2009). Outcomes in different residential settings for people with intellectual disability: a systematic review. *American Journal on Intellectual and Developmental Disabilities* 114: 193–222.

Lennox, N., Bain, C., Rey-Conde, T. et al. (2007). Effects of a comprehensive health assessment programme for Australian adults with intellectual disability: a cluster randomized trial. *International Journal of Epidemiology* 36: 139–146.

Lindsay, W.R. (2009). Adaptations and developments in treatment programmes for offenders with developmental disabilities. *Psychiatry, Psychology and Law* 16 (Suppl 1): S18–S35.

Lindsay, W.R., Carson, D., Holland, A.J. et al. (2013a). Alcohol and its relationship to offence variables in a cohort of offenders with intellectual disability. *Journal of Intellectual and Developmental Disability* 38 (4): 325–331.

Lindsay, W.R. and Michie, A.M. (2012). What works for offenders with intellectual disabilities. In: *What Works in Offender Rehabilitation: An Evidence Based Approach to Assessment and Treatment* (eds. L.A. Craig, L. Dixon and T.A. Gannon), 285–304. Chichester: Wiley Blackwell.

Lindsay, W.R., Smith, K., Tinsley, S. et al. (2014). A programme for alcohol related violence with offenders with intellectual disability. *Journal of Intellectual Disabilities and Offending Behaviour* 5: 107–119.

Lindsay, W.R., Tinsley, S., and Emara, M. (2013b). Alcohol use and offending in people with intellectual disability. In: *Alcohol-Related Violence: Prevention and Treatment* (ed. M. McMurran), 285–302. Chichester: Wiley Blackwell.

Männynsalo, L., Putkonen, H., Lindberg, N. et al. (2009). Forensic psychiatric perspective on criminality associated with intellectual disability: a nationwide register-based study. *Journal of Intellectual Disability Research* 53 (3): 279–288.

Mansell, J. (2006). Deinstitutionalisation and community living: progress, problems and priorities. *Journal of Intellectual & Developmental Disability* 31: 65–76.

Mayer, M.A. (2001). SAMIRIS: substance abusers who have both mental illness and mental retardation. *NADD Bulletin* 4: 92–99.

McBride, O., Teesson, M., Slade, T. et al. (2009). Further evidence of differences in substance use and dependence between Australia and the United States. *Drug and Alcohol Dependence* 100: 258–264.

McGillicuddy, N.B. (2006). A review of substance use research among those with mental retardation. *Mental Retardation and Developmental Disabilities Research Reviews* 12: 41–47.

McGillicuddy, N.B. and Blane, H.T. (1999). Substance use in individuals with mental retardation. *Addictive Behaviours* 24 (6): 869–878.

McGillivray, J.A., Gaskin, C.J., Newton, D.C. et al. (2016). Substance use, offending, and participation in alcohol and drug treatment programmes: a comparison of prisoners with and without intellectual disabilities. *Journal of Applied Research in Intellectual Disabilities* 29 (3): 289–294.

McGillivray, J.A. and Moore, M.R. (2001). Substance use by offenders with mild intellectual disability. *Journal of Intellectual and Developmental Disability* 26: 297–310.

McGillivray, J.A. and Newton, D.C. (2016). Self-reported substance use and intervention experience of prisoners with intellectual disability. *Journal of Intellectual & Developmental Disability* 41: 166–176.

McGregor, K. and Makkai, T. (2003). *Self-Reported Drug Use: How Prevalent Is Under-Reporting? Trends and Issues in Crime and Criminal Justice*. Canberra, Australia: Australian Institute of Criminology.

McLaughlin, D., Taggart, L., Quinn, B. et al. (2007a). Service provision for people with intellectual disabilities who abuse substances. *Journal of Substance Use* 12: 1–11.

McLaughlin, D.F., Taggart, L., Quinn, B. et al. (2007b). The experiences of professionals who care for people with intellectual disability who have substance-related problems. *Journal of Substance Use* 12: 133–143.

Mendel, E. and Hipkins, J. (2002). Motivating learning disabled offenders with alcohol problems: a pilot study. *British Journal of Learning Disabilities* 30: 153–158.

Miller, W. (1983). Motivational interviewing with problem drinkers. *Behavioural and Cognitive Psychotherapy* 11 (2): 147–172.

Plant, A., McDermott, E., Chester, V. et al. (2011). Substance misuse among offenders in a forensic intellectual disability service. *Journal of Learning Disabilities and Offending Behaviour* 2: 127–135.

Ruf, G. (1999). *Addiction treatment for people with mental retardation and learning disabilities: Why we need specialized services.* http://thenadd.org/nadd-bulletin/archive/volume-ii (accessed 15 August 2017).

Slayter, E. and Steenrod, S.A. (2009). Addressing alcohol and drug addiction among people with mental retardation in non-addiction settings: a need for cross-system collaboration. *Journal of Social Work Practice in the Addictions* 9: 71–90.

Stavrakaki, C. (2002). Substance-related disorders in persons with a developmental disability. In: *Dual Diagnosis: An Introduction to the Mental Health Needs of Persons with Developmental Disabilities* (eds. D.M. Griffiths, C. Stavrakaki, C. Summers, et al.), 455–482. New York: NADD.

Sturmey, P., Reyer, H., Lee, R. et al. (2003). *Substance Related Disorders in Persons with Mental Retardation*. New York: NADD.

Taggart, L., Huxley, A., and Baker, G. (2008). Alcohol and illicit drug misuse in people with learning disabilities: implications for research and service development. *Advances in Mental Health and Learning Disabilities* 2 (1): 11–21.

Taggart, L., McLaughlin, D., Quinn, B. et al. (2007). Listening to people with intellectual disabilities who abuse substances. *Journal of Health and Social Health Care* 15: 360–368.

Taggart, L., McLaughlin, D., Quinn, B. et al. (2006). An exploration of substance misuse in people with intellectual disabilities. *Journal of Intellectual Disability Research* 50: 588–597.

Taylor, J.L. and Novaco, R.W. (2005). *Anger Treatment for People with Developmental Disabilities: A Theory, Evidence and Manual Based Approach*. Chichester: Wiley.

Tenneij, N.H. and Koot, H.M. (2007). A preliminary investigation into the utility of the adult behavior checklist in the assessment of psychopathology in people with low IQ. *Journal of Applied Research in Intellectual Disabilities* 20: 391–400.

To, W.T., Neirynck, S., Vanderplasschen, W. et al. (2014). Substance use and misuse in persons with intellectual disabilities (ID): results of a survey in ID and addiction services in Flanders. *Research in Developmental Disabilities* 35 (1): 1–9.

Van Der Nagel, J., Kiewik, M., Buitelaar, J. et al. (2011). Staff perspectives of substance use and misuse among adults with intellectual disabilities enrolled in Dutch disability services. *Journal of Policy and Practice in Intellectual Disabilities* 8: 143–149.

Van Dooren, K., Young, J., Blackburn, C. et al. (2015). Substance use interventions for people with intellectual disability transitioning out of prison. *Australian & New Zealand Journal of Public Health* 39: 397.

Westermeyer, J., Kemp, K., and Nugent, S. (1996). Substance disorder among persons with mild mental retardation: a comparative study. *The American Journal on Addictions* 5: 23–31.

Young, L. (2003). Residential and lifestyle changes for adults with an intellectual disability in Queensland 1960–2001. *International Journal of Disability, Development and Education* 50: 93–106.

19

Treatment for Emotional Difficulties Related to Offending for People with an Intellectual Disability

Paul Oxnam and Emma Gardner

Regional Intellectual Disability Secure Service – Mental Health, Addictions & Intellectual Disability Service 3DHB, Wellington, New Zealand

19.1   Introduction

In the past three decades, greater attention has been placed on the assessment, diagnosis, and treatment of people with an intellectual and developmental disability (IDD) who experience emotional and mental health problems (Hogue et al. 2007; O'Brien 2002a; Taylor et al. 2008). It is now well known that mental illness is two-to-four times more common in people with an IDD than in the general population (Cooper et al. 2006; Dekker et al. 2002; Emerson 2003). Less well known, is the fact that offenders with an IDD are even more likely to experience mental health difficulties than their non-offending peers (Smith and O'Brien 2004).

A number of factors are believed to contribute to the elevated rates of mental illness in people with an IDD. First, they are born with genetic, structural, and/or other biological abnormalities that may influence how they respond to, and cope with, stressors (Deb et al. 2001a; Stavrakaki and Lunsky 2007). Second, they are more likely than the general population to encounter a range of difficult life circumstances, such as, high rates of unemployment, limited social supports, stigma/discrimination, traumatizing abuse, and stressful family/carer circumstances (Deb et al. 2001a). Third, intellectual difficulties, poor memory, limited problem solving, communication difficulties, and poor judgement challenge one's ability to understand and cope with challenging life events (Deb et al. 2001b).

Despite our awareness that people with an IDD are more vulnerable to emotional difficulties, we often fail to understand their distress and misattribute mental health symptoms (e.g. head banging, social withdrawal) to the person's IDD (i.e. challenging behaviour or poor social skills, respectively) in a phenomenon known as diagnostic overshadowing (Mevissen-Renckens and de Jongh 2010). Arguably, this phenomenon may be even more prevalent in forensic IDD settings where mental health symptoms (e.g. aggression) may also be overshadowed by the assumption that the person's behaviour is antisocial in nature.

The Wiley Handbook on What Works for Offenders with Intellectual and Developmental Disabilities: An Evidence-Based Approach to Theory, Assessment, and Treatment, First Edition.
Edited by William R. Lindsay, Leam A. Craig, and Dorothy Griffiths.
© 2020 John Wiley & Sons Ltd. Published 2020 by John Wiley & Sons Ltd.

To improve the lives of offenders with an IDD and reduce their risk of reoffending, service providers must be able to determine accurately whether emotional difficulties are contributing to a person's behavioural dysregulation and subsequent offending. As such, the aim of the current chapter is to provide an overview of the three types of emotional difficulties that we encounter most frequently during the course of our work with offenders with an IDD: depression, anxiety, and trauma. We will also briefly discuss the role of group-therapy programmes in the treatment of these emotional difficulties.

19.2 Depression

Depression is the best known and most common of all emotional disorders (World Health Organisation 2018). Whilst the Diagnostic and Statistical Manual-V (DSM-V) now provides for a range of depressive disorders, the common feature of each is the presence of sad, empty, or irritable mood, accompanied by somatic and cognitive changes that significantly affect the individual's capacity to function (American Psychiatric Association 2013).

The incidence of depression amongst the general population has risen every year since the early twentieth century (Kessler et al. 2005). Internationally, the lifetime chance of a person experiencing a major depressive episode now ranges from 2 to 3% in Asian countries, such as Korea and Taiwan, to 11–16% in the UK, the USA, Canada, Australia, and New Zealand (Kessler and Bromet 2013).

Depressed mood is considered one of the most common psychiatric symptoms experienced by individuals with an IDD (Paschos and Bouras 2007), and studies indicate people with an IDD are at greater risk for depression than the general population. Marston et al. (1997), for example, found that up to 47% of people in this client group will experience depression at some point during their lifetime.

Reiss and Rojahn (1994) found that aggressive behaviour is significantly more likely when a person with an IDD is depressed than when they are well. Such aggression can be in response to frustration and minimal provocation, such as a peer changing the television channel or a telephone call not being facilitated. Because aggression (rather than the presence of a mental illness) can bring a person into contact with the law, depression should be considered a risk factor – but not a cause – for offending amongst this population (Smith and O'Brien 2004).

Most offenders with an IDD exhibit symptoms of depression similar to the general population (Lindsay and Lees 2003; Smith and O'Brien 2004). Therefore, classic DSM-V diagnostic criteria should provide a starting point for assessment. Clinicians must, however, also be mindful of the range of associated signs and symptoms specific to this population. These are captured in such publications as the Diagnostic Manual – Intellectual Disability 2 (DM-ID-2; Fletcher et al. 2017), or the Diagnostic Criteria for Learning Disability (DC-LD; Royal College of Psychiatrists 2001). For example, an offender with an IDD may spend increased amounts of time in their room and be less willing to laugh with peers and support staff. They may also need prompting to complete routines and reject opportunities to engage in pleasurable events, such as watching a favourite TV show. Physical signs to be aware of include reduced appetite, constipation, waking during the night, and poor self-care (Wells 2005).

Almost all people with an IDD are reliant on others for referral for mental health assessment and only the most cognitively able offenders with an IDD will be able to articulate the basic, concrete features of their experience (Smith and O'Brien 2004). Therefore, behavioural observations, psychometric data, and collateral information from family members and support staff are important assessment resources.

When conducting an assessment for depression, the clinician should adopt a broad psychosocial approach. Particular attention should be paid to the person's attachment and early life experiences, physical health problems, the presence or otherwise of epilepsy and autistic spectrum disorders, and previous engagement with health and support services (Stavrakaki and Lunsky 2007; Wells 2005).

Support staff can provide important observations and assist a person with a disability to share a coherent account of their presentation. Wells (2005), however, cautions that the assessing clinician should be mindful of the person's vulnerability and the potential for countertransference to be present in the support relationship. Particularly in the case of people displaying aggressive symptomology, some staff may seek an increase in behaviour control medication and not appreciate the importance of a full assessment for an emotional disorder. Alternatively, staff may report that aggressive behaviour is 'attention seeking' and fail to view the behaviour as the person's attempt to communicate their distress. Asking support staff to complete behaviour monitoring charts and seeing the person alone are ways of ensuring the completion of a balanced assessment.

Psychometric tools used for the assessment of depression in people with an IDD generally feature self-report and support staff observation scales. Popular and well-validated measures include the Psychiatric Assessment Schedules for Adults with Developmental Disabilities (PAS-ADD) Checklist (Moss et al. 1997), the Beck Depression Inventory (Powell 2003), and the Glasgow Depression Scale (Cuthill et al. 2003). The Glasgow Depression Scale features pictorial representations of symptoms and is one of the few depression-specific measures developed for this client group (Stavrakaki and Lunsky 2007).

The effective management of depression is critical to the prevention of self-injury and suicide (Smith and O'Brien 2004). More broadly, it allows the person the capacity to benefit from therapeutic, vocational, and educational opportunities that have the potential to provide a future that is both offence-free and fulfilling. Treatment approaches with this population are consistent with those used in general mental health practice. Low-dose antidepressant medications can provide symptom relief, whilst psychological interventions allow the person to gain an understanding of their presentation and its relationship to offending and other negative life outcomes (O'Brien 2002b; Paschos and Bouras 2007; Smith and O'Brien 2004).

Because people with an IDD have greater difficulty accessing their thoughts, asking the question 'what were you thinking at the time' is not always that helpful or easy to answer. Therefore, well-validated psychological treatment models, such as cognitive-behavioural therapy (CBT) and dialectical-behaviour therapy (DBT) (Linehan 1993) often need to be adapted to emphasize the *behavioural* component of the intervention. Examples of group treatment programmes that have done this effectively are described in the Group Therapy section below.

19.2.1 Case Example

Cameron is the youngest of three children. His mother and father separated when he was five and custody was shared. Cameron's father's home was characterized by a lack of structure and the presence of alcohol and violence. Although his mother provided a relatively more stable environment, she would experience bouts of deep depression approximately three times a year and be unable to provide basic care for Cameron and his siblings.

Cameron was diagnosed with a mild IDD at age seven and file information reports him as having been the victim of sexual abuse perpetrated by a neighbour at age 10. Around this time, Cameron was placed in the care of the state and he ultimately came to live in a variety of foster homes and group residences for boys.

Social workers who knew Cameron as a teenager described him as likeable, a keen fisherman, and risk-prone on a skateboard. Being socially clumsy, he struggled to make friends and was frequently bullied by more able students. As he grew taller and stronger than his peers, Cameron responded in an increasingly violent manner.

At age 17, Cameron elected to leave both school and supported accommodation. He moved back in with his father and his days lacked any structure or purpose. He started to abuse alcohol and became known to the police as a nuisance. One officer described Cameron as 'obviously lonely and sad'.

Three weeks after his 18th birthday, Cameron attempted to rob the local service station of cigarettes, candy, and a small amount of cash. During the offence, he stabbed an attendant with a steak knife, causing significant loss of blood. Although he made a getaway, Cameron was quickly identified and apprehended. He was sentenced to a six year prison term to be served in a secure hospital unit for the care and rehabilitation of offenders with an IDD.

Upon his arrival at the unit, Cameron struggled to comprehend the gravity of his situation. He claimed his life was 'over' and was frequently tearful. He rejected meals, isolated himself in his room, and engaged in superficial self-harm, using a ballpoint pen. After approximately two weeks, Cameron agreed to be seen by the hospital's psychiatrist and was placed on a low-dose antidepressant. A week later, he met with a member of the clinical psychology team to begin a comprehensive assessment of his mental health and offending needs. Through this work, which was reported through to the multidisciplinary team, a behavioural activation programme was initiated. This included opportunities to build models with the unit's occupational therapist, access to video games, and time to ride a skateboard in the unit's courtyard.

Three months after his admission, Cameron began attending the unit's emotion regulation group therapy programme, the content of which was consistent with his weekly individual psychology sessions. Through these interventions, Cameron came to identify a future 'good life' and was supported to learn about the range of emotions all people experience. A particular focus was placed on the physiological symptoms of anger, sadness, and worry. He also learned to use a structured recording tool for working through problems, and was supported to develop a series of behavioural coping strategies to use when feeling distressed. These concepts were reinforced by direct care staff, in particular Cameron's keyworker, who would spend time with him each evening reviewing the day.

Cameron has recently started working in the unit's market garden and would like a job mowing the lawns. He has opportunities for escorted leave to the local community twice a week and is excited to be able to go fishing once a fortnight with a favoured staff member.

Cameron's care team recognizes structure, recreational pursuits, meaningful vocational activities and positive peer and professional relationships are critical components to him maintaining a positive mood state.

19.3 Anxiety

In its evolutionary 'flight or fight' form, anxiety can be a healthy and helpful reaction to stress or a threatening situation. In its acute and sustained forms, however, anxiety is characterized by significant psychological and physiological distress that can impact on the wellbeing and functioning of both the individual and those around them.

Anxiety difficulties are amongst the most common mental health problems experienced by the general population. In Europe, Africa, and Asia, between 9 and 16% of people will experience an anxiety disorder (e.g. phobias, generalized anxiety, panic disorders, obsessive compulsive disorder) in their lifetime. In the USA, the lifetime prevalence of anxiety disorders is about 29% and between 11 and 18% of adults experience the condition in a given year (Kessler et al. 2005).

Anxiety difficulties are very common in people with an IDD. Emerson (2003) for example, reported the prevalence of anxiety disorders to be at least two-and-a-half times greater in children with an IDD when compared to those without a disability. Similarly, Deb et al. (2001b) found people with a disability were significantly more likely to experience phobic disorder than those without an IDD. Moreover, because of diagnostic overshadowing, anxiety disorders are likely to be even more prevalent than has been identified to date.

Although their developmental environments are typically more unsettled and traumatic than their non-offending peers, offenders with an IDD are not necessarily more anxious than people with a disability who have not offended. For example, Lindsay and Lees (2003) found that sexual offenders with an IDD experienced significantly lower levels of anxious and depressive symptomology than a control group of non-offenders who were of similar age and intellectual functioning.

In many respects, people with a mild IDD who experience anxiety difficulties present with the same symptoms as those without a disability (e.g. doubts about the future, worries about physical health needs, and the wellbeing of family members (Stavrakaki and Lunsky 2007; Wells 2005). Features of the condition that are more synonymous with the IDD population, however, include repetitive questioning, restlessness, agitation, and irritability (Wells 2005). People with an IDD who reside in inpatient care for extended periods will typically fear changes to routines, the departure of trusted staff, loss of property, and the prospect of being required to cope with reduced levels of support. Verbal abuse, property damage, and physical aggression towards care staff are symptoms very commonly seen in forensic IDD settings.

A number of psychometric assessments have been successfully adapted to account for this client group's communication limitations. These include the Glasgow Anxiety Scale for IDD (Mindham and Espie 2003), the Beck Anxiety Inventory (developed by Beck and Steer 1990; adapted by Lindsay and Lees 2003), the Zung Self-Rating Anxiety Scale (Zung 1971; adapted by Lindsay and Michie 1989), and the anxiety section of the PAS-ADD interview (Moss 1997).

Risk assessment for a person with an IDD and anxiety should occur in the context of the individual's formulation and how they communicate their distress. For example, a person who responds to overwhelming anxiety by retreating to their room and listening to soothing music, is clearly less likely to experience legal difficulties than one who reacts by abusing alcohol or punching a support person.

Medications commonly used in the treatment of anxiety difficulties include benzodiazepines, buspirone, and propranolol (Wells 2005). Benzodiazepines are often prescribed for as-required use in inpatient and forensic settings with the aim of preventing the escalation of aggressive symptomology. Long-term use is not indicated due to the potential for the person to experience dependence (Wells 2005). Buspirone and propranolol *can* be used for long-term treatment, the latter having been shown to provide relief from the somatic symptoms of anxiety. Any pharmacotherapy use must be well-monitored and potential gains evaluated alongside the presence of unwanted side-effects, which have been shown to occur at higher rates in this population (Smith and O'Brien 2004).

Psychological and environmental interventions provide the best long-term efficacy for the treatment of anxiety difficulties (Deb et al. 2001b; Paschos and Bouras 2007). Distraction techniques, relaxation, mindfulness, and graded exposure approaches have been used successfully in forensic and non-forensic settings by people with and without a disability (Stavrakaki and Lunsky 2007). Cognitive-behavioural treatment of anxiety with those who display aggressive symptomology will typically focus on helping the individual and his or her staff team to identify the physiological build-up of emotion and to modify the person's concomitant behavioural responses (Stavrakaki and Lunsky 2007). For example, the person and their team might be supported to recognize a racing heart, flushed face, and elevated tone of voice as signs the person needs support to walk away to a safe place and do a relaxation breathing exercise.

Inpatient forensic environments are often crowded buildings with large staff teams working rostered and rotating shifts. As a result, it can be challenging to provide the kind of calm, predictable, and non-threatening living environment conducive to supporting a person with anxiety difficulties.

19.3.1 Case Example

Graham is a 47-year-old man who was placed in an institution for children with an IDD in 1975. Graham left hospital care in 1998, during the deinstitutionalization era. Over the next decade, he lived in a series of different flats on an estate that housed many former hospital residents. Although support staff would drop in each day, Graham struggled to manage basic cares independently and would frequently be seen wandering the streets or scavenging for food and money. He was known to steal pornographic magazines from local bookstores and would frequently cause public disturbance by shouting at peers, bus drivers, and neighbours. Graham was described by most staff members as 'prickly' and 'an angry bloke with a short fuse'.

In 2009, at age 39, Graham was convicted of the rape of a 21-year-old woman with a disability who lived in a neighbouring flat. He received a 12-year sentence to be served in a secure hospital unit for the care and rehabilitation of offenders with an IDD.

For the first year of his admission, Graham would only converse with staff members who had worked with him in other services. He spent much of his time in his room watching television and masturbating. He resisted the unit's therapeutic programme, but would engage in individual horticulture sessions if his favourite staff member was on shift.

As occurred in the community, most of the unit's care staff experienced Graham as irritable, preoccupied, and short-tempered. He would verbally abuse staff following seemingly minor events, such as his dinner being served late, clothing going missing, staff entering his room without asking, or a car not being available to facilitate his community leave. Graham struggled to cope with the anticipation of special events and his behaviour could be particularly explosive in the days leading up to visits from his sister, who was his only family contact. Some staff speculated that Graham would purposely assault because he could no longer tolerate the anticipation of the visit and wanted to alleviate his distress by causing it to be cancelled.

Without success, the unit clinical psychologist attempted to engage Graham during the second year of his admission. She then focussed on making behavioural observations and working collaboratively with his keyworker and the team of support staff who were with Graham throughout the day. As Graham came to tolerate 15-minutes sessions with the psychologist, she was able to establish the main triggers to his irritable and aggressive behaviour and developed a sense of his physiological responses. The psychologist then constructed a formulation that helped the care team to understand that Graham was a highly anxious and fearful man whose difficulties were firmly rooted in his developmental and social-learning experiences.

To assist Graham to feel comfortable with the prospect of therapy, the psychologist asked the staff member who had known him the longest to accompany her and Graham in weekly therapy sessions. Since that time, sessions have expanded to be 40 minutes in length. Therapy usually involves processing times when Graham has felt overwhelmed, helping him to recognize physiological symptoms of anxiety, and improving his repertoire of coping skills. The psychologist and staff member often role-play problem scenarios under Graham's direction, which he appears to find very amusing. Recently, the psychologist drew on Graham's love of soft drink to help him understand that physiological tension is like a shaken bottle of pop that will cause a great mess if not able to be calmed.

Outside sessions, Graham's keyworker has worked to improve staff communication and the consistent application of support plans to address his identified triggers. The keyworker has recently initiated a relaxation breathing programme for staff to complete with Graham each shift and has been working with the unit's occupational therapist to broaden Graham's access to recreational and vocational activities. In their group supervision sessions, staff are learning not to personalize Graham's behaviour. Whilst he remains irritable and can be extremely verbally aggressive, members of staff are taking heart from the gradual reduction in Graham's level of *physical* aggression.

19.4 Trauma

Post-Traumatic Stress Disorder (PTSD) is a chronic anxiety disorder characterized by symptoms that cluster into three main areas: distressing recollections of a traumatizing event, increased arousal, and avoidance of stimuli associated with the incident (American Psychiatric Association 2013). Single episode PTSD is precipitated by a single threatening or catastrophic incident that is associated with a perceived threat of injury or death (e.g. sexual assault, natural disaster), whilst complex PTSD occurs when stressors recur over a protracted period of time (e.g. repeated sexual abuse, childhood maltreatment; Stavrakaki and Lunsky 2007).

In addition to the trauma associated with being a victim of (or witness to) a threatening event, offenders also develop trauma reactions to crimes that they have perpetrated. Evans et al. (2007), conducted semi-structured interviews with 105 young offenders convicted of serious violent offences and found that the participants experienced significant intrusive memories and ruminations relating to the offences they had committed.

Studies indicate that, for the adult population, the lifetime exposure to traumatic events ranges from 50 to 90%. Despite this, the incidence of PTSD is only approximately 5% for men and 10% for women (Ozer and Weiss 2004). Russell and Shah (2003) estimated that 25% of individuals exposed to traumatic stressors develop PTSD.

There are few studies on PTSD in people with an IDD and the studies that have been completed lack scientific rigour. When Mevissen-Renckens and de Jongh (2010) conducted a review of the literature, they found four studies that explored the prevalence of PTSD in people with an IDD and prevalence rates varied from 2.5 to 60%.

Despite the lack of data, there is evidence to suggest that people with an IDD may be more susceptible to the development of PTSD because: (i) they are more likely to experience traumatic events, such as sexual and physical abuse (Stavrakaki and Lunsky 2007), (ii) they are less able than the general population to avoid/remove themselves from the traumatic situation (Deb et al. 2001a), and (iii) their developmental and intellectual level can have an impact on their capacity to cope with traumatic events (Breslau et al. 2006).

Lindsay et al. (2001) explored patterns of sexual and physical abuse in offenders with an ID. They found that 30% of sexual offenders had experienced sexual abuse (compared to 12.7% of non-sexual offenders) and that 33% of non-sexual offenders (compared to 13% of sexual offenders) had experienced physical abuse. These elevated rates of trauma in the IDD offender population are consistent with findings from the general offender population which consistently show that offenders (both male and female) have higher rates of trauma than non-offenders. For example, Spitzer et al. (2001) found that 36% of offenders detained in a forensic psychiatric institution experience PTSD during their lifetime. This is perhaps not surprising given that offenders often come from problematic social contexts where they have been exposed to traumatic events (Garbarino 1995).

Studies in the general population have shown that trauma exposure/child abuse is closely linked to aggressive acts and criminal behaviour (Smith et al. 2005; Widom 1989). This link is unsurprising, given that PTSD is associated with impulsivity, aggression, and negative emotions (Cauffman et al. 1998; Steiner et al. 1997) which are known risk factors for offending.

Given the strong link between trauma and offending, it is important that we are able to accurately assess PTSD in offenders with an IDD. Although many of the diagnostic criteria for PTSD remain the same in both the IDD and general populations, Tomasulo and Razza (2007) made a number of adaptations to the diagnostic criteria in the DM-ID. For example, avoidance of triggers associated with the traumatic event, may present as 'non-compliance', and intrusive thoughts may present as self-injurious behaviour.

Whilst the DM-ID, and the more recent DM-ID-2, can be helpful diagnostic instruments, accurate diagnosis remains challenging: diagnostic overshadowing is common and differential diagnosis can be difficult (e.g. flashbacks may be mistaken for hallucinations, emotional numbing may be confused with depression; Mevissen-Renckens and de Jongh 2010). Moreover, deficits in receptive and expressive language make it difficult for the person to communicate their experiences and emotional states, and people who would normally provide collateral information may either not be aware that a traumatic event has occurred (Ryan 1994), or they may fail to recognize an event as traumatic (e.g. moving residence; Tomasulo and Razza 2007).

The difficulties associated with accurate assessment of PTSD in people with an IDD are compounded by the relative absence of empirically validated psychometric tools. In 2014, Hall, Jobson, and Langdon did a preliminary study adapting the Impact of Events Scale – Revised (IES-R; Weiss and Marmar 1996), a widely used measure of stress following trauma, for persons with an IDD. The Impact of Event Scale – Intellectual Disabilities (IES-IDs) was administered to 40 individuals with an IDD who had experienced at least one traumatic event along with the Lancaster and Northgate Trauma Scale (LANTS; Wigham et al. 2011), the Glasgow Depression Scale, and the Glasgow Anxiety Scale. The study showed the IES-IDs had good psychometric properties, but that further investigation with individuals who had been formally diagnosed with PTSD was required.

There is a lack of literature and empirical studies pertaining to the treatment of PTSD in people with an IDD. However, the literature that does exist has focused on three main areas: pharmacology, psychological therapies, and environmental factors. McCarthy (2001) noted that PTSD affects the hypothalamic–pituitary axis, hippocampal volume, and endogenous opioid function. Anxiolytics and antidepressants have been found to be more effective than placebo at reducing symptoms of PTSD in a small number of randomized control trials (McCarthy 2001).

Consistent with findings from the general population, psychological interventions for PTSD appear to show promise for people with an IDD. There are a small number of case studies showing a reduction in PTSD symptoms following both CBT (Kroese and Thomas 2006; Lemmon and Mizes 2002), and eye movement desensitization and reprocessing (Tharner 2006; cited by Mevissen-Renckens and de Jongh 2010).

When considering the treatment of PTSD in offenders with an IDD, one must also consider the person's environment. Being detained in a secure forensic IDD setting will inherently result in the person being exposed to stimuli that trigger their symptoms of PTSD (e.g. witnessing other clients becoming dysregulated and restricted freedom). These triggers are, in turn, likely to increase trauma-related behaviours, such as aggression and self-harm. To help address this issue, it is suggested that staff receive training and education to help them minimize frightening cues and to respond appropriately when needed (Mevissen-Renckens and de Jongh 2010).

19.4.1 Case Example

Stacy is a 35-year-old woman with a moderate intellectual disability. She was raised in a chaotic home environment by her mother and her alcoholic father. Stacy was the youngest of three children. She repeatedly witnessed physical violence being perpetrated towards her mother and was repeatedly sexually abused by a close relative.

Significant behaviour problems and aggression were apparent from early childhood and Stacy failed to thrive at school. After her father passed away, Stacy lived relatively successfully in the community with extensive support from her mother and the local church.

Stacy's ability to manage in the community deteriorated when her mother passed away. She began annoying her neighbours and regularly placed herself at risk by walking alone at night and inviting strangers into her home. She had repeated admissions to local mental health services, before she was eventually placed in a supported living environment.

Stacy's presentation continued to deteriorate; she displayed significant mood disturbance and became increasingly aggressive towards herself (i.e. cutting, head banging) and others. In 2013, Stacy violently assaulted her flat mate and received a three-year sentence to be served in a secure hospital unit for the care and rehabilitation of offenders with an IDD.

During her time in secure care, Stacy's emotional dysregulation continued. She continued to harm herself and others, she had symptoms of depression (e.g. she was often tearful), her sleep was disrupted, she engaged in sexualized behaviours and, in simple language, she described thoughts and images relating to the sexual violence perpetrated towards her.

Stacy was prescribed a range to medications to help manage her mood and behavioural disturbance. She commenced work with a clinical psychologist trained in CBT and she attended a group-based programme designed to help with emotional dysregulation. In addition, staff worked hard to minimize the number of triggers for PTSD symptoms in Stacy's environment. Over a number of years, Stacy's ability to regulate her emotions improved and the frequency of her aggressive behaviour reduced. However, she continues to struggle with intrusive thoughts and, at times, is overwhelmed with sadness and anger.

19.5 Group Therapy Programmes for the Treatment of Emotional Difficulties

Group-based interventions provide a forum for people to see that they are not the only ones with problems. This mode of treatment is essential in forensic settings where significant stigma is often attached to the acts that brought the person into secure care. Offenders are much more likely to accept both constructive feedback and encouragement from their peers than they are from staff. Crucially, they also feel safer disclosing examples of times when they have made mistakes, or committed more serious acts, if they know other people in the room have behaved similarly.

Whilst anger management and sexual offending programmes have been a prominent feature of the forensic IDD landscape for a number of years, group therapy for the treatment of specific mental health difficulties and general emotion dysregulation is a comparatively recent addition. Most programmes utilize CBT or DBT approaches and promising outcomes have been observed in both inpatient and community settings.

Group treatment for specific mental health difficulties is still relatively rare with the IDD population. However, McCabe et al. (2006) developed and evaluated a five-week CBT-based programme for the treatment of depression in non-forensic people with an IDD. The programme covered behavioural activation, the importance of relationships and social supports, cognitive restructuring, problem solving, and goal setting. Compared to the control group, the intervention group showed an improvement in levels of depression and positive feelings about the self, and a reduction in their negative automatic thoughts.

The literature also indicates that group treatment for general emotion dysregulation difficulties shows promise. Rather than focusing on a specific mental health diagnosis, these treatment programmes emphasize managing difficulties associated with any kind of overwhelming emotion (e.g. anxiety, sadness, anger).

A number of therapy programmes have been developed according to the principles of DBT. Lew et al. (2006) observed positive outcomes amongst a non-forensic sample of women with an IDD engaged in a DBT-based programme for the treatment of emotional difficulties and high-risk self-harm behaviours. This 23-week programme included specific components to develop skills for emotion regulation, interpersonal effectiveness, distress tolerance, and mindfulness. Significant improvements in wellbeing were observed, along with a reduction in self-harm behaviours that was maintained at an 18-month follow-up.

In 2010, Sakdalan, Shaw, and Collier examined the efficacy of The Adapted DBT Coping Skills Training programme for improving quality of life and reducing the risk of reoffending in a sample of violent offenders with an ID. Participants completed a 13-week programme based on an adapted version of Linehan's (1993) DBT group-therapy programme. The study conducted pre- and post-assessments of dynamic risks, relative strengths, coping skills, and global functioning. The authors observed significant decreases in the level of risks and increases in relative strengths and overall functioning.

In 2011, the current authors conducted a study examining the efficacy of a programme (Stepping Stones) developed to help offenders with an IDD manage emotional difficulties that often resulted in violence within a secure forensic service (Oxnam and Gardner 2011). The 42-week Stepping Stones programme is based on CBT and DBT principles and emphasizes recognizing and understanding emotions and learning to use a toolkit of seven core emotion regulation techniques. A chain analysis process allows participants to examine the antecedents, behaviours, and consequences of distressing events, whilst also helping them identify what they need to do to get back on track. The study showed an almost two-thirds reduction in aggression towards others, property damage, inappropriate sexual behaviour, and self-harm during the three-year period following the introduction of the Stepping Stones programme. Qualitatively, staff noted improvements in clients' ability to recognize negative emotions and respond with adaptive strategies, rather than aggression. Staff appeared more confident and were more able to respond to aggression with verbal de-escalation and prompts to 'use the toolkit', rather than resorting to restrictive practices.

The Stepping Stones programme was further evaluated using a community-based sample of offenders with an IDD. In this study, McWilliams et al. (2014) examined incident reports and administered the Profile of Anger Coping Skills (PACS; Willner et al. 2005) to staff and clients engaged in the abbreviated 22-session version of Stepping Stones. The PACS measures the frequency that individuals with an IDD use cognitive and behavioural skills to cope with emotional difficulties. The researchers found that the majority of group members demonstrated increases in self- and care-giver reported use of the strategies taught in the programme following their involvement.

19.6   Conclusions

Emotional difficulties such as depression, anxiety, and trauma are an increasingly recognized feature of the presentation of offenders with an IDD. This development is part of a broader shift within the disability community to address diagnostic overshadowing.

In assessing for emotional difficulties, the clinician must work to understand what the person is attempting to communicate through behaviours that are often concerning and offensive to staff. Utilizing assessment criteria specific to this population, collecting psychometric data, making behavioural observations, using collateral sources, and taking time to listen to those who work most closely with the person, will ensure a rich formulation that the multidisciplinary care team can invest in.

Treatment for emotional difficulties in this population must draw upon the strengths of the client and their support team and be well-organized and communicated. Creativity and perseverance is required to ensure sustained engagement and learning. Group therapy programmes provide critical opportunities for social learning, peer support and the dissemination of core concepts through the staff team.

The literature base addressing depression, anxiety, and trauma in offenders with an IDD is small in comparison with that focused on anger. Future research should further investigate the prevalence of these emotional difficulties in the offender population, describe symptoms, and discuss similarities and differences in how offenders and non-offenders present. There is also a need for the effectiveness of group therapy programmes to be evaluated in a controlled, longitudinal manner with larger sample sizes. Positive psychology, resilience, and mindfulness are examples of exciting new intervention approaches for emotional difficulties that are likely to receive closer attention and development in the coming years.

References

American Psychiatric Association (2013). *Diagnostic and Statistical Manual of Mental Disorders: DSM-5*. Washington, DC: American Psychiatric Association.

Beck, A.T. and Steer, R.A. (1990). *Manual for the Beck Anxiety Inventory*. New York: Psychological Corporation.

Breslau, N., Lucia, V.C., and Alvarado, G.F. (2006). Intelligence and other predisposing factors in exposure to trauma and posttraumatic stress disorder. *Archives of General Psychiatry* (11): 1238–1245.

Cauffman, E., Feldman, S.S., Waterman, J. et al. (1998). Posttraumatic stress disorder among female juvenile offenders. *Journal of the American Academy of Child and Adolescent Psychiatry* 37 (11): 1209–1216.

Cooper, S.-A., Smiley, E., Morrison, J. et al. (2006). Mental ill-health in adults with intellectual disabilities: prevalence and associated factors. *The British Journal of Psychiatry* 190 (1): 27–35.

Cuthill, F.M., Espie, C.A., and Cooper, S.A. (2003). Development and psychometric properties of the Glasgow depression scale for people with a learning disability. Individual and carer supplement versions. *British Journal of Psychiatry* 182: 347–353.

Deb, S., Matthews, T., Holt, G. et al. (2001a). *Practice Guidelines for the Assessment and Diagnosis of Mental Health Problems in Adults with Intellectual Disability*. Brighton: The European Association for Mental Health in Mental Retardation.

Deb, S., Thomas, M., and Bright, C. (2001b). Mental disorder in adults with intellectual disability: I: prevalence of functional psychiatric illness among a community-based population aged between 16 and 64 years. *Journal of Intellectual Disability Research* 45: 495–505.

Dekker, M.C., Koot, H.M., van der Ende, J. et al. (2002). Emotional and behavioral problems in children and adolescents with and without intellectual disability. *Journal of Child Psychology and Psychiatry, and Allied Disciplines* 43 (8): 1087–1098.

Emerson, E. (2003). Prevalence of psychiatric disorders in children and adolescents with and without intellectual disability. *Journal of Intellectual Disability Research* 47 (1): 51–58.

Evans, C., Ehlers, A., Mezey, G. et al. (2007). Intrusive memories in perpetrators of violent crime: emotions and cognitions. *Journal of Consulting and Clinical Psychology* 75 (1): 134–144.

Fletcher, R., Barnhill, J., and Cooper, S.-A. (eds.) (2017). *Diagnostic Manual-Intellectual Disability 2: A Textbook of Diagnosis of Mental Disorders in Persons with Intellectual Disability*. Kingston, NY: National Association for the Dually Diagnosed (NADD) Press.

Garbarino, J. (1995). *Raising Children in a Socially Toxic Environment*. San Francisco: Jossey-Bass.

Hall, J.C., Jobson, L., and Langdon, P.E. (2014). Measuring symptoms of post-traumatic stress disorder in people with intellectual disabilities: the development and psychometric properties of the impact of event scale-intellectual disabilities (IES-IDs). *British Journal of Clinical Psychology* 53 (3): 315–332.

Hogue, T.E., Mooney, P., Morrissey, C. et al. (2007). Emotional and behavioural problems in offenders with intellectual disability: comparative data from three forensic services. *Journal of Intellectual Disability Research* 51 (10): 778–785.

Kessler, R.C., Berglund, P., Demler, O. et al. (2005). Lifetime prevalence and age-of-onset distributions of DSM-IV disorders in the National Comorbidity Survey Replication. *Archives of General Psychiatry* 62 (6): 593–602.

Kessler, R.C. and Bromet, E.J. (2013). The epidemiology of depression across cultures. *Annual Review of Public Health* 34: 119–138.

Kroese, B.S. and Thomas, G. (2006). Treating chronic nightmares of sexual assault survivors with an intellectual disability-two descriptive case studies. *Journal of Applied Research in Intellectual Disabilities* 19: 75–80.

Lemmon, V.A. and Mizes, J.S. (2002). Effectiveness of exposure therapy: a study of posttraumatic stress disorder and mental retardation. *Cognitive and Behavioural Practice* (4): 317–323.

Lew, M., Matta, C., Tripp-Tebo, C. et al. (2006). DBT for individuals with intellectual disabilities: a programme description. *Mental Health Aspects of Developmental Disabilities* 9: 1–12.

Lindsay, W.R., Law, J., Quinn, K. et al. (2001). A comparison of physical and sexual abuse; histories of sexual and non-sexual offenders with intellectual disability. *Child Abuse & Neglect* 25 (7): 989–995.

Lindsay, W.R. and Lees, M.S. (2003). A comparison of anxiety and depression in sex offenders with intellectual disability and a control group with intellectual disability. *Sexual Abuse: Journal of Research and Treatment* 15 (4): 339–345.

Lindsay, W.R. and Michie, A.M. (1989). Adaptation of the Zung anxiety inventory for people with learning disabilities. *Journal of Mental Deficiency Research* 32: 485–490.

Linehan, M. (1993). *Cognitive-Behavioural Treatment of Borderline Personality Disorder*. New York: The Guilford Press.

Marston, G.M., Perry, D.W., and Roy, A. (1997). Manifestations of depression in people with intellectual disability. *Journal of Intellectual Disability Research* 41: 476–480.

McCabe, M.P., McGillivray, J.A., and Newton, D.C. (2006). Effectiveness of treatment programmes for depression among adults with mild/moderate intellectual disability. *Journal of Intellectual Disability Research* 50 (4): 239–247.

McCarthy, J. (2001). Post-traumatic stress disorder in people with learning disability. *Advances in Psychiatric Treatment* 7 (3): 163–169.

McWilliams, J., de Terte, I., Leathem, J. et al. (2014). An evaluation of an emotion regulation programme for people with an intellectual disability. *Therapeutic Communities: The International Journal of Therapeutic Communities* 35 (3): 105–118.

Mevissen-Renckens, E.H.M. and de Jongh, A. (2010). PTSD and its treatment in people with intellectual disabilities: a review of the literature. *Clinical Psychology Review* 30 (3): 308–316.

Mindham, J. and Espie, C.A. (2003). Glasgow anxiety scale for people with an intellectual disability (GAS-ID): development and psychometric properties of a new measure of use with people with mild intellectual disability. *Journal of Intellectual Disability Research* 47: 22–30.

Moss, S.C. (1997). *PAS-ADD Checklist*. Manchester, UK: Hester Adrian Research Centre.

Moss, S., Ibbotson, B., Prosser, H. et al. (1997). Validity of the PAS–ADD for detecting psychiatric symptoms in adults with learning disability (mental retardation). *Social Psychiatry and Psychiatric Epidemiology* 32: 344–354.

O'Brien, G. (2002a). Dual diagnosis in offenders with intellectual disability: setting research priorities: a review of research findings concerning psychiatric disorder (excluding personality disorder) among offenders with intellectual disability. *Journal of Intellectual Disability Research* 36: 169–175.

O'Brien, G. (2002b). *Behavioural Phenotypes and their Clinical Phenotypes, Clinics in Developmental Medicine*. London: MacKeith Press.

Oxnam, P. and Gardner, E. (2011). Stepping Stones – a group therapy programme for the treatment of emotion regulation difficulties in offenders with an intellectual disability. *Journal of Learning Disabilities and Offending Behaviour* 2 (4): 146–151.

Ozer, E.J. and Weiss, D.S. (2004). Who develops post-traumatic stress disorder? *Current Directions in Psychological Science* 13 (4): 169–172.

Paschos, D. and Bouras, N. (2007). Mental health supports in developmental disabilities. In: *Handbook of Developmental Disabilities* (eds. S.L. Odom, R.H. Horner, M.E. Snell, et al.), 483–500. New York: The Guilford Press.

Powell, R. (2003). Psychometric properties of the Beck depression inventory and the Zung self-rating depression scale in adults with mental retardation. *Mental Retardation* 41: 88–95.

Reiss, S. and Rojahn, J. (1994). Joint occurrence of depression and aggression in children and adults with mental retardation. *Journal of Intellectual Disability Research* 7: 287–294.

Royal College of Psychiatrists (2001). *Diagnostic Criterion for Psychiatric Disorders for Use with Adults with Learning Disabilities/Mental Retardation (DC-LD)*. Occasional paper, vol. 48. London: Gaskell.

Russell, A. and Shah, B. (2003). Posttraumatic stress disorder and abuse. *Developmental Disabilities Digest* 30 (2): 1–8.

Ryan, R. (1994). Post-traumatic stress disorder in persons with developmental disabilities. *Community Mental Health Journal* (1): 45–54.

Sakdalan, J.A., Shaw, J., and Collier, V. (2010). Staying in the here-and-now: a pilot study on the use of dialectical behaviour therapy group skills training for forensic clients with intellectual disability. *Journal of Intellectual Disability Research* 54 (6): 568–572.

Smith, A.H.W. and O'Brien, G. (2004). Offenders with dual diagnosis. In: *Offenders with Developmental Disabilities* (eds. W.R. Lindsay, J.L. Taylor and P. Sturmey), 241–263. Chichester, UK: Wiley.

Smith, C.A., Ireland, T.O., and Thornberry, T.P. (2005). Adolescent maltreatment and its impact on young adult antisocial behavior. *Child Abuse and Neglect* 29 (10): 1099–1119.

Spitzer, C., Dudeck, M., Liss, H. et al. (2001). Post-traumatic stress disorder in forensic inpatients. *The Journal of Forensic Psychiatry* 12 (1): 63–77.

Stavrakaki, C. and Lunsky, Y. (2007). Depression, anxiety and adjustment disorders in people with intellectual disabilities. In: *Psychiatric and Behavioural Disorders in Intellectual and Developmental Disabilities*, 2e (eds. N. Bouras and G. Holt), 42–61. Cambridge: Cambridge University Press.

Steiner, H., Garcia, I.G., and Matthews, Z. (1997). Posttraumatic stress disorder in incarcerated juvenile delinquents. *Journal of the American Academy of Child and Adolescent Psychiatry* 36 (3): 357–365.

Taylor, J., Lindsay, W., and Wilner, P. (2008). CBT for people with intellectual disabilities: emerging evidence, cognitive ability and IQ effects. *Behavioural and Cognitive Psychotherapy* 36 (6): 723–733.

Tharner, G. (2006). Over de toepassing van EMDR bij de behandeling van mensen met een lichteverstandelijke beperking [About the application of EMDR in the treatment of people with a mild intellectual disability]. In: *Perspectief. Gedragsproblemen, psychiatrische stoornissen en lichte verstandelijke beperking* (ed. D. Robert), 145–168. Bohn: Stafleu ven Loghum.

Tomasulo, D.J. and Razza, N.J. (2007). Posttraumatic stress disorder. In: *Diagnostic Manual-Intellectual Disability(DM-ID): A Textbook of Diagnosis of Mental Disorders in Persons with Intellectual Disability* (eds. R. Fletcher, E. Loschen, C. Stavrakaki, et al.), 365–378. Kingston, NY: NADD Press.

Weiss, D.S. and Marmar, C.R. (1996). The impact of event scale - revised. In: *Assessing Psychological Trauma and PTSD* (eds. J. Wilson and T.M. Keane), 399–411. New York: Guilford.

Wells, Y. (2005). *Management Guidelines: Developmental Disability – Version 2*. Victoria, Australia: Therapeutic Guidelines Limited.

Widom, C.S. (1989). Child abuse, neglect, and adult behavior: research design and findings on criminality, violence, and child abuse. *American Journal of Orthopsychiatry* 59 (3): 355–367.

Wigham, S., Hatton, C., and Taylor, J.L. (2011). The Lancaster and Northgate Trauma Scales (LANTS); the development and psychometric properties of a measure of trauma for people with mild to moderate intellectual disabilities. *Research in Developmental Disabilities* 32 (6): 2651–2659.

Willner, P., Brace, N., and Phillips, J. (2005). Assessment of anger coping skills in individuals with intellectual disabilities. *Journal of Intellectual Disability Research* 49 (5): 329–339.

World Health Organisation (2018). Depression Factsheet. https://www.who.int/news-room/fact-sheets/detail/depression (accessed 30 May 2019).

Zung, W.K. (1971). A rating instrument for anxiety disorders. *Psychosomatics* 12: 371–379.

20

Treatment Outcomes for People with Autistic Spectrum Disorder in Forensic Settings

Peter Sturmey

Queens College and The Graduate Center, City University of New York, New York, NY, USA

20.1 Introduction

Offending in individuals with autism spectrum disorder (ASD) has become an active area of research and practice over the last 20 years. This reflects two factors. The first is the apparent increasing prevalence of ASD in many countries. The second is the presence of many individuals with ASD with additional challenging behaviour, including offending, in community settings who previously would have been placed in institutional settings, which are no longer or much less available in many countries. These factors probably result in greater contact with the law and psychiatric services than in the past. There are already a number of reviews (e.g. Brown et al. 2016) and special issues of a journal (Woodbury-Smith 2014) of this topic. To understand this problem better, let us first consider the life of Adam Lanza, an individual with ASD who committed extreme violence.

20.2 Adam Lanza

On 14 December 2012, 20-year old Adam Lanza, shot his mother dead at home, went to Sandy Hook Elementary school in Newtown, Connecticut and shot 20 first-graders and six staff dead before taking his own life. The media feasted on the details for months; there was even a Public Broadcast Service television documentary. Following the massacre, the state of Connecticut conducted an extensive investigation into his life, family, school, and mental health services (Report of the Office of Child Advocate 2014). Adam had been diagnosed variously with Autism, Asperger syndrome, Obsessive Compulsive Disorder (OCD) (based on hand washing based on fear of contamination from germs), severe anxiety, and anorexia (he was six-feet tall and weighed only 112 pounds at the time of his death). How did this happen?

I dedicate this chapter to the late Bill Lindsay, a good friend, an outstanding researcher who made a difference and a smart man who made a career out of counting things.

The Wiley Handbook on What Works for Offenders with Intellectual and Developmental Disabilities: An Evidence-Based Approach to Theory, Assessment, and Treatment, First Edition.
Edited by William R. Lindsay, Leam A. Craig, and Dorothy Griffiths.
© 2020 John Wiley & Sons Ltd. Published 2020 by John Wiley & Sons Ltd.

The Report of the Office of Child Advocate (2014) described that Adam's developmental disabilities were evident from earliest childhood when he showed communication, sensory, and social disabilities and repetitive behaviours. He was served just before the age of three years by New Hampshire Birth to Three early intervention services. He was referred to special education preschool services and Newtown public schools provided some special education services in elementary school but did not provide services explicitly related to communication or social–emotional deficits.

His preoccupation with violence began in eighth grade when he wrote graphic violent stories. This was not apparently addressed by either his school or parents. To accommodate the wish of his mother that Adam not be distressed by school, the school district agreed to fund homebound education for a year. Homebound was a status for children 'too disabled', even with supports, to attend school. Once assigned to education in the home, the school district provided little oversight or monitoring of these services or the educational outcomes for Adam. At age 14 years Adam received a comprehensive and appropriate evaluation from the Yale Child Study Center, which both recognized the seriousness of his disabilities and his complex and extensive service needs. The evaluation noted that withdrawal from school accommodated his disabilities but did not meet his educational and other needs. Presciently, they also noted that if this continued his condition would worsen and so recommended extensive special education expert consultation, and rigorous therapy that addressed his core problems. These recommendations were ignored by the school district. Rather than respond to the assessment they continued to use inappropriate classifications which denied him help in the form of an appropriate education and mental health services. His mother halted a very brief trial of medication for OCD, perhaps because of possible medication negative side-effects. In his tenth grade, Adam made temporary progress when he was reintegrated into classes and did indeed receive and benefit from preferred activities, social support from peers, and some key preferred staff. When the school terminated a key staff member a pattern of progressive withdrawal from school and community life began again. He became isolated at school and worked alone or with tutors rather than in integrated classes. Both the school and parents regarded him as intellectually gifted, despite psychometric testing showing average intelligence.

Throughout his teenage years, Adam had continued mental health issues including OCD, extreme anxiety, low weight verging on anorexia, depression, and suicidal thoughts. These needs were often not acknowledged in medical and school records, but he received minimal and uncoordinated mental health services. During the remainder of his brief life Adam's social support network shrank. After his parents divorced, he progressively rejected social initiations from his father, withdrew from peer support at school, and spent less time with his mother. He spent long periods of time in his bedroom alone on the internet, refusing to leave the home, becoming preoccupied with extreme violence fuelled by violent media and internet groups. Remarkably and improbably, Adam graduated from school at age 17 years and completed some classes at a local college, but the school and parents continued to fail to provide service that addresses his social–emotional needs.

Throughout his life his family had access to guns and recreational use of firearms was part of his family life providing opportunities and modelling for violence and many opportunities to practise gun-related skills. A key final stressor for Adam may have been his mother's plan to move houses. The report concluded that lack of appropriate services that accommodated his needs and his mother's wishes rather than provide treatment and education, failure to recognize the gravity of his needs, availability of firearms, and progressive social isolation all contributed to this extreme violence.

20.3 Offenders with ASD: General Characteristics

Over the years a number of descriptive case reports (Chesterman and Rutter 1993; Cooper et al. 1993; Mawson et al. 1985), case series (Ghaddzuiddin et al. 1991), and reviews of this literature (Newman and Ghazuiddin 2008) have been published focusing on psychopathology and offending in individuals with ASD. Newman and Ghazuiddin (2008) reviewed studies of psychiatric co-morbidity in Asperger syndrome and identified 17 publications with 37 descriptive case studies. Of these 30% had a definite psychiatric disorder and 54% had a probable psychiatric disorder. The types of psychiatric disorders reports were quite varied and included depression, OCD, dysmorphophobia, personality disorder, schizoaffective disorder, and so on. They speculated that certain features of Asperger syndrome, such as collecting objects, sexual preoccupations, and social insensitivity, might predispose towards certain kinds of criminal behaviour. Howlin (2004) similarly noted four factors that might predispose people with ASD to offend. These were (i) they may be naïve and manipulated by others; (ii) they may become aggressive due to disruption in routines; (iii) they may have poor social skills that may result in aggression; and (iv) obsessional interest might predispose towards property offences. These studies are useful in giving detailed and vivid descriptions of the nature of offending in individuals with ASD but, since they are unsystematic, they do not give a clear answer to the questions as to what is different, if anything, about offending in individuals with ASD from offenders in the general or offenders with ID or other relevant comparison groups and what, if anything is different about their offending behaviour.

A more systematic approach that may answer some of these questions comes from studies using case control methodology. For example, Woodbury-Smith et al. (2010a, 2010b) compared 23 adults with ASD with a history of offending, 23 adults with ASD without a history of offending and 23 people without ASD on measures of recognition of emotions, theory of mind, executive functioning. The only relevant statistical difference between the groups was that offenders with ASD were less likely to recognize fear in others, but there were no differences in recognition of sadness, and all other measures. The meaning of the overall lack of differences was unclear and might merely reflect the small sample size, insensitivity of the measures, or failure to include relevant measures. Perhaps offenders with ASD might be somewhat more insensitive to emotional expression in others, which might predispose them to violence or sexual offending because they are less susceptible to punishing consequences from others when they offend.

Other studies have attempted to describe the differences between offenders with ASD and other comparison groups to elucidate if there are differences in rates or types of offences or other individual differences related to offending. For example, Lindsay et al. (2014) reported data from 477 individuals referred to a forensic disability services. There were few differences in the rates of offending between individuals with ASD and ID, but offenders with ASD were somewhat *less* likely to engage in sexually inappropriate behaviour than offenders with ID alone. Thus, to date, there is little evidence of large differences between offenders with ASD and other comparison groups.

20.4 Epidemiology

20.4.1 Prevalence

Opinions have differed as to whether ASD should make people less likely to offend (greater rigidity and rule following behaviour) or more likely to offend (insensitivity to other, obsessional features, and other forms of psychopathology). Which conclusion does the evidence favour?

King and Murphy (2014) conducted a systematic review of the epidemiology of people with ASD in the criminal justice system which identified 22 empirical papers addressing two main questions. In seven studies that investigated the prevalence of ASD amongst arrestees or offenders, the prevalence of ASD was higher than 1%, (as might be expected from general epidemiological studies) and ranged from approximately 3 to 27%. This does indeed suggest that ASD was more prevalent in the criminal justice system than the general population. The authors concluded, however, that the large variation in figures was due mainly to methodological differences in the studies. Of six studies that observed the prevalence of offending amongst individuals with ASD reported a very wide range of figures (2–26%), but those studies that included a comparison group all found *equal or lower* rates of offending in individuals with ASD than those without, although one study found higher rates of offenders amongst individuals with Asperger syndrome than autism. In terms of the type of offences committed there were seven studies which found that individuals with ASD were more likely to commit offences against people than offences against property, were involved in more school disturbances, and were less often in probation, and one study found higher rates of sexual offences in individuals with ASD than those without. The authors noted that most of the 22 studies had significant problems with case definition and assessment, definition of the population studies, measurement of offending behaviour, and dealing with the probability that in many countries individuals with ASD who commit crimes are often diverted into non-criminal justice system services.

A more recent case-controlled study of Attention Deficit Hyperactivity Disorder (ADHD), ASD, Tic Disorder, OCD, and risks of violent criminality from a cohort of 3391 children born in Stockholm between 1984 and 1994 confirmed these findings. Lundstrom et al. (2014) found individuals with these disorders on the Stockholm mental health database with the national crime register. They then matched them up with various control samples from a register of all Swedish nationals to control for possible confounding factors. Whereas individuals with ADHD and Tic Disorder had consistently elevated odds rations for violent offending, individuals with ASD and OCD did not. Thus, in a measurement system that is sensitive to detecting such differences in some disorders, they did not find evidence for increased risk of criminal violence in individuals with ASD. Thus, neither studies found empirical support of large differences between individuals with ASD and those without in terms of offending behaviour.

20.4.2 Risk Factors

There have been few empirical studies of risk factors of offending amongst individuals with ASD. Langstrom et al. (2008), reported an empirical study from Sweden conducted between 1988 and 2000 in which they matched up individuals with ASD who had been hospitalized with the national crime register. Sweden is a country of approximately 9 million people each of whom is identified with a unique identifier code. Individuals with autism were identified from International Classification of Diseases codes for child-hood autism or autistic disorder (N = 317, 69.4% male) and Asperger syndrome (N = 105, 77.1% male) for a total sample of 458 individuals (69.9% males).

When cross matched to the national crime register 31 individuals in the sample had at least one violent conviction. When offenders were compared to non-offenders, offenders were much more likely to have a history of substance abuse (adjusted OR = 74.1), have Asperger syndrome rather than autism (Adjusted OR = 5.8), personality disorder (adjusted OR = 4.8), male (Adjusted OR = 6.7), any co-morbid psychiatric disorder (adjusted OR = 4.2), and schizophrenia/other psychosis (adjusted OR = 3.6). These data broadly correspond to the descriptive case studies mentioned above and the description of Andrew Lanza. They also hint at some points of intervention for some individuals and their service needs.

20.5 What Works?

A recent review of sexual offenders with ASD by Mogavero (2016) provided a useful overview of some of the issues in this area. Early research in this area merely reported on unusual sexual and other behaviour in individuals with Asperger syndrome such as transvestitism with associated violence and inappropriate public sexual touching of others (Cooper et al. 1993). See also Chesterman and Rutter (1993), Griffin-Shelley (2010), Coskun and Mukaddes (2008), Chen et al. (2016) and Williams et al. (1996) for other examples. These studies described the possible association between signs and symptoms and the developmental and environments of individuals with ASD which might predispose some individuals to illegal sexual behaviour and contact with the law. For example, Cooper et al. (1993) noted that their individual, PM, has significant losses early in life, including two of five siblings and his mother dying when he was young, a father with Seasonal Affective Disorder-like traits, a sibling with severe intellectual disability in long-term care and a long family history contact with social services due to quarrels on the street. They described him as shy, gauche, with poor social skills, including evasive eye contact, lack of facial expressions and nonverbal communication, invading other's social space, problems initiating and terminating conversations, and insensitivity to the interests of others. He was socially isolated, had few friends, and remained a virgin in his thirties despite sexual interest in the opposite sex. He had been placed in special education at age 11, left school at age 16 with weak academic skills, and had been employed briefly but had remained mostly unemployed for years with few social bonds. Such a personal history illustrates the lack of models and typical learning opportunities for appropriate social and sexual behaviour, and models for atypical social behaviour. His inability to establish appropriate social relationships with women predisposed him to both inappropriate sexual behaviour (ISB) and violence against them.

Hellmans et al. (2007) interviewed staff working with 24 individuals with average intelligence and ASD living in institutional settings in Flanders. Generally, knowledge of self-care and socio-sexual skills such as changing underwear and knowing where it is acceptable to masturbate, were adequate. In contrast, practice was more likely to be inadequate, with nearly half touching genitals in public, and around 40% having poor or moderate knowledge of who to touch and kiss and when to talk about sex. A minority had problems masturbating to completion, masturbating with unusual objects, or sometimes injured themselves or had fetishes. Thus, the majority of these individuals were interested in sexuality, but a minority had various significant problems.

One set of potential predisposing factors mentioned in the above case reports were the judgements of adolescents with ASD of social-sexual situations. Visser et al. (2017) compared the judgements of 94 cognitively able individuals with autism, 94 typically developing adolescents, and the judgements of a panel of experts of appropriate, slightly inappropriate, and severely ISB. There were no differences between the two groups of adolescents, that is, for example, they all agreed that severely ISB was indeed inappropriate. Disagreement existed, however, between experts who were more liberal in their judgements of mildly ISB than either group of adolescents. Thus, surprisingly, there was no evidence of differences in social judgements between adolescents with ASD and adolescents with typical development, at least in this study.

Although people recognize sexual motivation and behaviour in individuals with ASD, they are often reluctant to address sexuality in individuals with ASD through embarrassment if they do address it and / or uncertainty of how to address it. This can result in failure to provide the kinds of informal and formal sex education that many children and adolescents receive, tolerating or encouraging ISB, and failure to treat problematic ISB until it becomes intolerable or dangerous. Until recently, there were only a small number of studies that have reported treatment of individuals, mostly in uncontrolled, descriptive case studies addressing problems such as public masturbation, sexual aggression, and so on, but more recently there is a growing literature on the use of Cognitive Behaviour Therapy (CBT)-type approaches, Mindfulness, and Applied Behaviour Analysis (ABA) in the assessment and treatment of ISB in offenders with ASD.

20.5.1 CBT

Melvin et al. (2017) conducted a systematic review of the treatment literature focusing specifically on treatment of offenders with ASD. The review specifically excluded treatment such as ABA for younger individuals and individuals with more severe cognitive disabilities. They identified 13 papers that were empirical, included some individuals with ASD and included some psychological or pharmacological treatments. The studies contained data on 75 individuals of whom 30 were identified as individuals with ASD. There were no randomized controlled trials but there were nine case reports and four case series. One treatment programme was represented more than once and other treatments included CBT and a range of other psychological, pharmacological, and other treatments. Outcomes were mixed. There with some positive changes on some measures including reduction in offending or offence-related behaviour and cognitions and other papers reported lack of change even after large amounts of treatment. There was little evidence for the effectiveness of non-psychological treatments such as occupational therapy and psychotropic medication was often confounded with other treatments making it difficult to judge treatment effectiveness. To illustrate these approaches let us consider the Sex Offenders Treatment Services Collaborative-Intellectual Disabilities Group (SOSTEC-ID) treatment programme.

Murphy et al. (2007) reported a pilot study of CBT for 15 men with intellectual disabilities who had histories of sexually abusive behaviour. The most common sexual offences were sexual assault and indecent exposure. Six participants also had diagnoses of ASD. CBT was delivered in a group format and covered topics such as purpose of the group, body parts, sex education, their own sexual offences, relapse prevention, and so on. Participants reported increased sexual knowledge and empathy with victims, but there was no change in attitudes and knowledge and attitudes consistent with offending. Six months after treatment none had been convicted of a re-offence, but three had engaged in inappropriate behaviour one of whom had been convicted of a re-offence just after six months. Uniquely, Heaton and Murphy (2013) reported follow up data on 34 men from seven treatment sites 44 months after treatment ended. Remarkably, improvements in knowledge, empathy, and distortions were maintained; however, one-third showed some form of sexually abusive behaviour and two had been convicted of a sexual offence.

20.5.2 ABA

ABA is a natural science approach using learning theory to change socially significant behaviour based on an understanding of the current environment's role in behaviour to guide intervention. Radical behaviourism posits that the laws of behaviour apply to both overt observable behaviour and covert behaviour – thinking, feeling, and emotions – and that both are controlled by the current environment. Thus, unlike traditional psychological models of behaviour, thoughts and feelings are behaviour to be explained, not the explanation of behaviour (Skinner 1953). ABA has characteristic methods, including use of observational data and small N experiments, and use of inductive rather than deductive philosophy of science. ABA has been used to address a very wide range of socially important behaviour including littering, teaching typical children and adults to exercise more and eat healthily, drug addiction, a wide range of psychopathology (Sturmey 2007) and autism throughout the lifespan.

20.5.2.1 Behavioural Assessment

Behavioural assessment consists of two kinds of methods. Descriptive methods include interviews, questionnaires, and naturalistic observations in which the assessor does not manipulate any independent variable. Experimental analyses are assessments in which the assessor systematically manipulates one or more independent variables to identify those that control the target behaviour of interest. Descriptive methods are commonly used by practitioners as they are often easy to implement, may result in identification of effective treatments and are often required by US Federal and State laws. Functional analyses have been highly successful for a wide range of problem behaviours such as aggression and self-injury (Hanley et al. 2003) but there is a much smaller literature on functional analysis in offenders with ASD.

In a chapter on functional assessment and analysis of ISB in men with mild intellectual disability, Vollmer et al. (2012) pointed out that conducting a functional analysis of ISB in offenders has some special challenges. These include: (i) the problem behaviour occurs infrequently or not at all if there are not opportunities to engage in the target behaviour or the behaviour only occurs when the person believes they are not being observed; (ii) it may be difficult to identify antecedents and consequences that influence ISB through functional assessment methods; (iii) state laws may prohibit the use of relevant stimulus materials, such as child pornography; (iv) it may be too dangerous to permit engagement in some ISBs under any circumstances; (v) there are ethical concerns with consent for assessment and/or treatment and possible coercion of offenders; and (vi) identifying and achieving socially valid outcomes is challenging because large reductions in the target behaviour may still result in socially unacceptable levels of the target behaviour.

Despite these challenges there is a beginning of a functional analysis of ISB in offenders with ID. The main line of evidence comes from plethysmopgraphic studies of response to different stimuli which have been combined with stimulus preference data in one study (Reyes 2009). Stimuli can vary along many dimensions – age and gender are two obvious ones but other relevant dimensions include degree of explicit sexual content, presentation format (video, pictures, slides, written text of fantasy, number, and duration of stimuli). Two studies of offenders with mild ID illustrate these methods. In Reyes et al. (2006), 10 offenders with mild ID underwent plethysmographic evaluation of their responses to visual stimuli varied by age and gender and a neutral stimulus in a multi-element design. Arousal was often relatively specific to certain categories of stimuli and varied from one participant to another. Some individuals were aroused by several categories of deviant stimuli, some were aroused by specific deviant stimuli and some were aroused only by non-deviant stimuli. In a second related study, Reyes et al. (2011) reported some preliminary data on a functional analysis of arousal in three individuals. They demonstrated that pre-session masturbation (one participant) and arousal suppression strategies such as general, non-specific instructions to not become aroused and, if necessary counting backwards from 100, suppressed arousal to preferred sexual stimuli. Reyes (2009) also reported portable plethysmographic data showing specific patterns of arousal in the natural environment. Thus, behavioural assessment of offenders with ID is possible, but has not yet been extended to individuals with ASD.

Some studies have reported functional analyses of ISB in individuals with ASD, but mostly with those who are not offenders. For example, Dozier et al. (2011) reported a functional analysis and treatment of a shoe fetish in Alex, a 36-year-old man with ASD with minimal expressive language. The problem consisted of dropping to the floor and masturbating by gyrating his pelvis against the floor near another person's feet. This problem had been going on for around 20 years and resulting in one-to-one staffing and restrictions in community access. The independent variables were gender of the other person and types of foot ware (e.g. sandals, tennis shoes, bare feet and so on). Two functional analyses showed that ISB occurred only with women with sandals or bare feet, but not other conditions. Two preliminary treatments failed. These were a pairing procedure in which women in sandals were paired with pictures of women in sandals, but after 50 pairing session no transfer of stimulus control occurred. Second, continuous snacks, leisure items, and a video of a women in sandals eliminated the ISB but was judged not to be a practical intervention. Therefore, the experimenters evaluated two treatment alternatives which were: (i) sensory extinction, which consisted of securing an athlete protector outside his pants to prevent genital stimulation; and (ii) a timeout/response interruption procedure, which consisted of using the straps of a backpack to guide Alex off the floor and to keep him in the corner of the room for one minute and fading out the straps. The experimenters used a multi-element design and response latency to evaluate the treatments. The sensory extinction procedure was ineffective, perhaps because it was not possible to completely eliminate sensory stimulation. The timeout / response interruption procedure was highly effective and programmed generalization to four novel women produced generalized improvement.

20.5.2.2 Behavioural Treatment Studies of ISB

Davis et al. (2016) reported a systematic review of ABA treatment studies in individuals with developmental disabilities, some of whom were offenders or had other legal contact. Their search identified 13 studies. Common presenting problems included public undressing, touching others inappropriately, public sexual talk, and sexual arousal to unusual objects or people. Interventions included instructional revisions, such as manipulating task difficulty, number of work tasks, task difficulty, scheduled to assignments and other aspects of the teaching environment; manipulating motivating operations; non-contingent reinforcement; differential reinforcement of alternate or zero behaviour; extinction; and punishment. In some cases, these studies have adapted functional assessment and analysis methods to identify the function of ISP. These published studies were largely effective, at least in terms of demonstrating short-term behaviour change.

Two good clinical examples, of the application of ABA comes from the ACHIEVE! Program (Pritchard et al. 2017). The ACHIEVE! Program is a multi-component residential programme for adolescents with severe behaviour problems including eloping, aggression, property damage, climbing, and harmful sexual behaviour who have been rejected by multiple previous educational, residential, and legal programmes. ACHIEVE! included seven programme elements. First, is a comprehensive data system which includes 30 minutes data on prosocial and proacademic behaviour throughout a 5 hour school day, data on severe problem behaviour 24 hour per day 7 days per week, and data on critical incidents. The critical incidents resulted in supervisory staff conducting a review within 24 hours to clarify the incident. The second element is a skill points and levels system. Points were given for five skills such as attending programming on time, engaging in safe behaviour, and individual target behaviours. Third, programme staff conduct multiple stimulus preference assessments without replacement using photographic stimuli at least monthly. Fourth, students use Amazon to identify back up reinforcers. Reminders were posted in the classroom and students could access back-up reinforcers based on daily behavioural criteria. Fifth, students had a structured activity schedule breaking the day into 10, 30 minutes periods and used goal setting, differential reinforcement, and skill-specific feedback and points. Teachers reviewed participation in the activity schedule at the end of the day with the student. Sixth, teachers used a work-reward schedule which included interspersing easy and difficult tasks. Seventh, the programme includes a graduated levels system which includes progressive access to a greater range of reinforcers and community participation. Finally, if a severe behavioural incident occurred the students was placed on a restriction of limited community access for two days. This system was developed initially with two individuals and evaluated in data-based case studies (Pritchard et al. 2011, 2013). Evaluation continued with another case study (Pritchard et al. 2016; see later) and a series of 9 cases (Pritchard et al. 2017).

An example of the application of ACHIEVE! comes from Pritchard et al. (2016) who reported treatment of ISB in Osian, a 17-year-old male with ASD who had had extensive legal contact. He had a history of possible abuse by his father and paternal uncle. He had engaged in aggressive and sexual behaviour between the ages of 8 and 11 years and was excluded from primary school following a sexual threat to another pupil. Following a confirmed allegation that he had sexually abused his eight-year-old sister, he had to live outside his family in care homes. In the care homes he continued to engage in disturbing behaviour. For example, he disclosed that he had followed two girls with a plan to sexually assault and then kill them. He further disclosed that he wanted to have children so he could teach them to have oral sex with him. Prior to the study he had eight convictions of assault against staff members and one for burglary and had been in various locked mental health and offender units where he had sexually assaulted a vulnerable boy.

At age 14 years he was admitted to a specialized residential placement. There the facility identified aggression, sexual behaviour, and self-harm as target behaviours. The first author conducted a functional behaviour assessment (FBA) using interviews with family members, Osian, and staff from previous placements and reviewed documents. The FBA revealed that some social situations, such as busy environments, were aversive to Osian and that he frequently escaped these environments through aggression to staff or kicking down doors. He also reported that he liked to shock staff with sexually explicit outbursts. He had a range of potential reinforcers such as music, internet, and black and white movies. Initially, others were kept safe by keeping him on two-on-one staffing, restricted access to the community, and placement in a classroom with two or three other children with similar needs.

Intervention consisted of a multicomponent programme which was developed in close collaboration with Osian's mother. The programme included a token economy and levels system, active support, CBT, sex and relationship education, and offence-specific training. Later, the authors added a contingency contract which included a differential reinforcement of other (DRO) behaviour contingency that if he engaged in ISB, he could not have access to community activities but could earn them back for two days of no problem behaviour. The authors collected data over a 115-week period on aggression, absconding, and ISB and community trips. The study was not an experiment. The initial treatment package was only partially effective; only following the addition of the DRO schedule did all the target behaviours decrease to 0 for the last 36 weeks of treatment and maintain at zero levels with an increase in community trips.

20.6 Psychopharmacology Studies

There has been limited research on psychopharmacological treatment of ISB and related offending in individuals with ASD. Hellmans et al. (2007) reported that 2 of 12 adolescents and young adults with high-functioning autism took psychotropic medication to reduce sexual drive – one took a neuroleptic and one took an atypical neuroleptic both without effectiveness. Coskun and Mukaddes (2008) reported a narrative case study of treatment of fetishism in a 13-year-old with ASD with mirtazapine for a clothes fetish. Although initially successful for 10 weeks, the problem reemerged when medication was stopped and had to be re-started. Subsequently, Coskun et al. (2009) reported a case series of two females and eight males with ASD aged 5–16 years treated for various ISBs, such as excessive masturbation. Retrospective data based on case notes suggested that this was effective. Others have published case studies reporting the effectiveness of propranolol for hypersexual behaviour (Deepmala 2014). In addition, there are case reports of failed multiple psychopharmacological interventions such as olanzapine and fluoxetine, buried in the detailed of some case reports (e.g. Coshway et al. 2016) or inter alia in other papers (Hellmans et al. 2007). There has also been discussion of use of hormonal treatment for ISB in some cases (Coshway et al. 2016).

At this time there is little systematic evidence supporting with the use of either psychopharmacology or hormonal treatment for ISB in individuals with ASD. Indeed, the risks of this approach may outweigh the likely benefits when alternate treatments exist and have often not been implemented to a competent degree.

20.7 Ethics

One of the main motivations to work with offenders with ASD is to protect others from the harm from further offences and to give the offender the best quality of life, whilst protecting others. Hence, effective treatment is a core ethical issue. Yet, despite the common recognition that individuals with ASD have a sexual life (Holmes and Himie 2014) which is limited and sometimes inappropriate, many people are often reluctant to address sexuality in individuals with ASD. This can include failure to provide the kinds of informal and formal education that many children and adolescents receive, tolerating or encouraging ISB, and failure to treat problematic ISB until it becomes intolerable or dangerous. One of the main ethical problems is the lack of implementing effective treatment, both to promote healthy sexuality and to prevent offending. Stokes et al. (2007), for example, found that the extent to which social skills were learned from peers predicted better successful romantic interaction.

In a seminal article on ethics of treatment, Van Houten et al. (1988) argued that recipients of behavioural treatment have 'the right to a therapeutic environment, services whose overriding goal is personal welfare, treatment by a competent behaviour analyst, programs that teach functional skills, behavioural assessment and ongoing evaluation, and the most effective treatment procedures available' (p. 381). In the context of offenders with ASD generally (and the case of Adam Lanza in particular) services fall woefully behind this standard. It behoves all of us working with individuals with ASD to work with our service organizations to strive to meet these high standards. Our failure to do so results in individuals with ASDs living more impoverished lives than they have to but it also places members of society more generally in preventable danger.

A second area of concern has been the ability of individuals with ASD to adequately participate in the legal process, having an adequate defence, and being treated fairly at all steps in the judicial process. In additional when it comes to legal processing judges must give fair summaries, explain the role of the individual's diagnoses, if any, in any alleged criminal act (Creaby-Attwood and Alley 2017; Mogavero 2016).

20.8 Adam Lanza Redux

Adam Lanza's life and death and the death of his mother, the school children and staff, was a tragedy that could have been prevented. He had poor quality services and inappropriate treatment, including lack of the right treatment, the wrong treatment, and insufficient treatment. Can we learn something from this tragedy by considering what should have happened?

In an ideal world, Adam's developmental disabilities would have been detected by a well-trained professional around the age of 18–24 months who screened children for ASD and other developmental disabilities and who could recognize even early signs of mild ASD. Instead of being placed in generic, low-intensity early intervention services, he would have received sufficient evidence-based practices from skill practitioners, namely early intensive behavioural interventions (EIBI) consisting of at least 20 hours of ABA for 2–4 years. Given his relatively mild disabilities, as reflected in average intelligence, graduating high school, and Asperger syndrome, rather than autism, there is a possibility that his ASD could have been completely prevented and that he could have functioned as a typical child and adult.

If he did not respond completely to EIBI, then a well-coordinated transition from early intervention to preschool would have resulted in a comprehensive assessment that would have identified both his academic needs, but also social and emotional needs, perhaps based on the three core domains of ASD, namely social, language, and repetitive behavioural issues. Perhaps a FBA conducted by a competent behaviour analyst or similar professional would have identified core deficits, provided teaching to address his social and language needs and may have resulted in a behaviour support plan to address his sensory and repetitive behaviours. When his social and emotional challenges and nascent interest in violence was evident after fourth grade, he would have received further evidence-based practices such as FBA and related intervention to develop alternative reinforcers, such as social reinforcers from peers, staff, and family and to encourage alternate healthy interests.

Recognizing the red flag of homebound services, the temptation to remove challenging students from schools to minimize effort on the part of school services, school staff would have made efforts to engage both parents in Adam's services whilst placing Adam's needs at the centre of their concern (Van Houten et al. 1988). That is, rather than accommodating Adam's disabilities and his mother's wishes, they would have maintained him in school and provided him with comprehensive, effective, and integrated educational and mental health services. When he began to show anxiety symptoms the school would have conducted an FBA and would have taught him relaxation, and progressively exposed him to feared stimuli and taught him the social skills to gain social support from peers, staff, and his family. When he began to show OCD, the school would have found a mental health provider to educate his mother on the benefits of exposure and response prevention for OCD and provided such evidence-based practices to reduce Adam's OCD symptoms. When Adam showed signs of depression and suicidality, his school and mental health services would have provided him with evidence-based practices, such as CBT, behavioural activation, and appropriate anti-depressants. When Adam was a teenager, his special education services, keeping an eye on his long-term adaption, would have provided him with appropriate and effective transition services by teaching him vocational and social skills necessary for a good life.

This is a fantasy, but there are plenty of other individuals like Adam Lanza out there today who still do not receive appropriate education and mental health services. We can expect this tragedy to occur again, but we can prevent it if we choose to.

References

Brown, J., Hastings, B., Cooney-Koss, L. et al. (2016). Autism spectrum disorder in the criminal justice system: a review for caregivers and professionals. *Journal of Law Enforcement* 5: 1–13.

Chen, F., Grandjean, S., and Richard, S. (2016). Psychopharmacological management of inappropriate sexual behaviors in youth with autism spectrum disorders: a case study and review of the literature. *Neuropsychiatrie de l'Enfance et de l'Adolescence* 64: 163–167.

Chesterman, P. and Rutter, S.C. (1993). Case report: Asperger's syndrome and sexual offending. *The Journal of Forensic Psychiatry* 4: 555–562.

Cooper, S.-A., Mohamed, W.N., and Collacot, R.A. (1993). Possible Asperger's syndrome in a mentally handicapped transvestite offender. *Journal of Intellectual Disability Research* 37: 189–194.

Coshway, L., Broussard, J., Acharya, K. et al. (2016). Medical therapy for inappropriate sexual behaviors in a teen with autism spectrum disorder. *Pediatrics* 137 (4) https://doi.org/10.1542/peds.2015-4366.

Coskun, M., Karakoc, S., Kircelli, F. et al. (2009). Effectiveness of mirtazapine in the treatment of inappropriate sexual behaviors in individuals autistic disorder. *Journal of Child and Adolescent Psychopharmacology* 19: 203–206.

Coskun, M. and Mukaddes, N.M. (2008). Mirtazapine treatment in a subject with autistic disorders and fetishism. *Journal of Child and Adolescent Psychopharmacology* 18: 206–209.

Creaby-Attwood, A. and Alley, C.S. (2017). A psycho-legal perspective on sexual offending in individuals with autism spectrum disorders. *International Journal of Law and Psychiatry* 55: 72–80.

Davis, T.N., Machalicek, W., Scalzo, R. et al. (2016). A review and treatment selection model for individuals with developmental disabilities who engage in inappropriate sexual behavior. *Behavior Analysis in Practice* 9: 389–402.

Deepmala, M.A. (2014). Use of propranolol for hypersexual behavior in an adolescent with autism. *Annals of Psychopharmacology* 48: 1385–1388.

Dozier, C.L., Iwata, B.A., and Worsdell, A.S. (2011). Assessment and treatment of a shoe-foot fetish displayed by a man with autism. *Journal of Applied Behavior Analysis* 44: 133–137.

Ghaddzuiddin, M., Tsai, L., and Ghaddzuiddin, M. (1991). Brief report: violence in Asperger syndrome – a critique. *Journal of Autism and Developmental Disorders* 21: 349–354.

Griffin-Shelley, E. (2010). An Asperger's adolescent sex addict, sex offender: a case study. *Sexual Addiction and Compulsivity* 17: 46–64.

Hanley, G.P., McCord, B.A., and Iwata, B.E. (2003). Functional analysis of problem, behavior: a review. *Journal of Applied Behavior Analysis* 36: 147–185.

Heaton, K. and Murphy, G.H. (2013). Men with intellectual disabilities who have attended sex offender treatment groups: a follow-up. *Journal of Intellectual Disability Research* 26: 489–500.

Hellmans, H., Colson, K., Verbracken, C. et al. (2007). Sexual behavior in high-functioning male adolescents and young adults with autism spectrum disorder. *Journal of Autism and Developmental Disorders* 37: 260–269.

Holmes, L.G. and Himie, M.B. (2014). Brief report: parent-child sexuality communication and autism spectrum disorders. *Journal of Autism and Developmental Disorders* 44: 2964–2970.

Howlin, P. (2004). *Autism: Preparing for Adulthood*, 2e. London: Routledge.

King, C. and Murphy, G.H. (2014). A systematic review of people with autism spectrum disorders and criminal justice system. *Journal of Autism and Developmental Disorders* 44: 2717–2733.

Langstrom, N., Grann, M., Ruchlin, V. et al. (2008). Risk factors for violent offending in autism spectrum disorders. *Journal of Interpersonal Violence* 24 (8): 1358–1370.

Lindsay, W.R., Carson, D., O'Brien, G. et al. (2014). A comparison of referrals with and without autism spectrum disorder to forensic intellectual disability services. *Psychiatry, Psychology and Law* 21: 957–954.

Lundstrom, S., Forsman, M., Larsson, H. et al. (2014). Childhood neurodevelopmental disorders and violent criminality. A sibling controlled study. *Journal of Autism and Developmental Disorders* 44: 2707–2716.

Mawson, D., Grounds, A., and Tantam, D. (1985). Violence and Asperger's syndrome. *British Journal of Psychiatry* 147: 566–569.

Melvin, C.L., Langdon, P.G., and Murphy, G.H. (2017). Treatment effectiveness for offenders with autism spectrum conditions: a systematic review. *Psychology, Crime & Law* 23: 748–776.

Mogavero, M.C. (2016). Autism, sexual offending, and the criminal justice system. *Journal of Intellectual Disabilities and Offending Behaviour* 7 (3): 116–126.

Murphy, G.H., Powell, S., Guzman, A.-M. et al. (2007). CBT for men with intellectual disabilities and sexually abuse behavior: a pilot study. *Journal of Intellectual Disability Research* 51: 902–912.

Newman, S.S. and Ghazuiddin, M. (2008). Violence crime in Asperger syndrome: the role of psychiatric comorbidity. *Journal of Autism and Developmental Disorders* 38: 1848–1852.

Pritchard, D., Graham, N., Ikin, A. et al. (2011). Managing sexually harmful behaviour in a residential school. *British Journal of Learning Disabilities* 40: 302–309.

Pritchard, D., Graham, N., Penney, H. et al. (2016). Multi-component behavioural intervention reduces harmful sexual behaviour in a 17-year-old make with autism spectrum disorder: a case study. *Journal of Sexual Aggression* 22: 368–378.

Pritchard, D., Hoeger, M., Dyer, T. et al. (2013). Sodium valproate withdrawal correlated with reduced aggression. *British Journal of Learning Disabilities* 42: 162–11167.

Pritchard, D., Penny, H., and Mace, F.C. (2017). The ACHIEVE! Program. A point and level system for reducing severe problem behavior. *Behavioral Interventions* 33 (1): 41–55.

Report of the Office of Child Advocate (2014). *Report: Shooting at Sandy Hook School. Report of the Office of Child Advocate*. Hartford, CT: Report of the Office of Child Advocate.

Reyes, J.R. (2009). Assessment of sex offenders with developmental disabilities. *Dissertation Abstracts International*, 69 (10), UMI Nop. 3334500.

Reyes, J.R., Vollmer, T.R., and Hall, A. (2011). The influence of presession factors in the assessment of deviant sexual arousal. *Journal of Applied Behavior Analysis* 44: 707–717.

Reyes, J.R., Vollmer, T.R., Sloman, K.N. et al. (2006). Assessment of deviant sexual arousal in adult male sex offenders with developmental disabilities. *Journal of Applied Behavior Analysis* 39 (2): 173–188.

Skinner, B.F. (1953). *Science and Human Behavior*. New York: The Free Press.

Stokes, M., Newton, N., and Kaur, A. (2007). Stalking, and social and romantic functioning among adolescents and adults with autism spectrum disorder. *Journal of Autism and Developmental Disorders* 37: 1969–1986.

Sturmey, P. (2007). *Functional Analysis in Clinical Treatment*. New York: Elsevier.

Van Houten, R., Axelrod, S., Bailey, J.S. et al. (1988). The right to effective behavioral treatment. *The Behavior Analyst* 11: 111–114.

Visser, K., Greaves-Lord, K., Tick, N.T. et al. (2017). An exploration of the judgments of sexual situations by adolescents with autism spectrum disorders versus typically developing adolescents. *Research in Autism Spectrum Disorders* 36: 35–43.

Vollmer, T.R., Reyes, J.R., and Walker, S.F. (2012). Behavioral assessment and intervention for sex offenders with intellectual and developmental disabilities. In: *The Handbook of High-Risk Challenging Behaviours in People with Intellectual and Developmental Disabilities* (ed. J.K. Luiselli), 121–144. Baltimore, MD: Paul H. Brookes.

Williams, R.G., Allard, A., and Sears, L. (1996). Case study: cross gender preoccupations in two male children with autism. *Journal of Autism and Developmental Disorders* 26: 635–642.

Woodbury-Smith, M. (2014). Editorial: ASD and illegal behaviors. *Journal of Autism and Developmental Disorders* 44: 26–79-2681.

Woodbury-Smith, M., Clare, I., Holland, A.J. et al. (2010a). A case-controlled study of offenders with high functioning autism spectrum disorders. *The Journal of Forensic Psychiatry and Psychology* 16: 747–763.

Woodbury-Smith, M., Clare, I., Holland, A.J. et al. (2010b). Circumscribed interests and 'offenders' with autism spectrum disorders: a case-controlled study. *The Journal of Forensic Psychiatry and Psychology* 21: 366–377.

21

Pharmacological Approaches for Offenders with Intellectual and Developmental Disabilities

Daniel Turner[1] and Peer Briken[2]

[1] Department of Psychiatry and Psychotherapy, University Medical Center Mainz, Mainz, Germany
[2] Institute for Sex Research and Forensic Psychiatry, University Medical Center Hamburg-Eppendorf, Hamburg, Germany

21.1 Introduction

There is no pharmacological treatment approach for offenders per se or anything like a pharmacological agent that prevents offenders from relapsing with criminal behaviours. However, different mental health conditions seem to increase the risk for offending in an individual and the pharmacological agents used in the treatment of offenders tackle the symptoms of these underlying mental disorders. This applies for offenders with an intellectual or developmental disability (IDD) as well as for those without an IDD.

Mental disorders found most frequently in general or violent offenders are antisocial personality disorders, substance use disorders, psychotic disorders, or combinations of these mental health conditions (Fazel and Danesh 2002; Fazel et al. 2008; Fazel and Grann 2006; Grann et al. 2008). In their systematic review Douglas et al. concluded that being diagnosed with a psychotic disorder increases the odds of showing violent behaviours about 49–68% (Douglas et al. 2009). In sexual offenders personality and paraphilic disorders have the highest prevalence rates (Eher et al. 2019). Furthermore, one frequent cause of IDD is traumatic brain injury (TBI) and many patients show aggressive or sexually challenging behaviours post-TBI. Mental disorders seem to occur at even higher rates in people with IDD (Cooper et al. 2007; Iverson and Fox 1989) and having a psychiatric disorder was found to be a significant factor increasing the risk of offending in individuals with IDD as well (Barron et al. 2002). As in offenders without IDD, disorders found most frequently in violent offenders with IDD are conduct or antisocial personality disorders and psychotic disorders as well as paraphilic disorders in sexual offenders with IDD (Rice et al. 2008; Riches et al. 2006). Unfortunately, there is almost no research on pharmacological interventions explicitly addressing offenders with IDD and thus most recommendations provided throughout this chapter will be based on findings with mentally disordered offenders without IDD. However, it can be assumed that those medications that have proven to work with offenders without IDD will also work in those with IDD.

The Wiley Handbook on What Works for Offenders with Intellectual and Developmental Disabilities: An Evidence-Based Approach to Theory, Assessment, and Treatment, First Edition.
Edited by William R. Lindsay, Leam A. Craig, and Dorothy Griffiths.
© 2020 John Wiley & Sons Ltd. Published 2020 by John Wiley & Sons Ltd.

21.2 Circumstances and Preconditions of Pharmacological Treatment

Before implementing pharmacological interventions in offenders with IDD a structured psychiatric examination and evaluation should be conducted in order to determine the underlying psychiatric disorder(s) and the precise symptoms the patient is presenting. This initial assessment should be performed or at least be supervised by an experienced psychiatrist and in the case of patients who have been convicted for a criminal offence it is recommendable that the diagnosing clinician has experience with forensic patients and is aware of the surrounding legal modalities. An emphasis should be placed on the evaluation of impulsive and aggressive behaviours: for example, in which situations does the patient show risk-related behaviours, are these behaviours always directed towards the same person or against the patient himself, what kind of aggressive behaviours (verbal and/or physical) does the patient show, are these behaviours criminally relevant and how high is the risk that the patient will show further aggressive behaviours in the future and of course are there any underlying disorder(s) causing the aggressive and violent behaviours. Further important points that should be assessed are the developmental history (individual level of ability, cause of intellectual disability) and the patient's capacity to give informed consent as all this information should be considered whilst making the decision about which pharmacological agent will be most appropriate. As people with IDD might have deficits in cognitive and especially verbal abilities gathering the medical history of the patient by interviewing an informant (e.g. parents, legal guardian, partner) could be necessary. Furthermore, an observation of the patient's behaviour for a longer time can be informative in some cases. Besides a thorough psychiatric assessment all patients should be physically examined as well to identify any physical exclusion criteria for a pharmacological treatment. The physical examination should include:

- Assessment of any *previous or current physical disorders*
- Intake of any *other medication* (many psychotropic drugs show diverse interactions with other medications and the risk for possible interactions should be evaluated before treatment is started)
- *Weight and blood pressure measurements* (many psychotropic drugs can lead to a considerable weight gain and high or low blood pressure)
- *Electrocardiogram* (ECG with an emphasis on the measurement of QT-interval, especially in the case of antipsychotics or selective-serotonin-reuptake-inhibitors, SSRIs, because these can lead to a prolongation of the QT-interval)
- *Electroencephalography* (EEG, to determine any anomalies concerning epileptic potentials because some anticonvulsants or antipsychotics can also trigger epileptic seizures)
- *Full blood count* (in case of antiandrogen treatment in sexual offenders this should include testosterone, LH, FSH, prolactine, calcium, phosphate, and liver enzyme levels)
- *Neurological examination* (especially in case first-generation antipsychotics are used because they have an increased risk of causing extrapyramidal motor control disabilities or dyskinesia)
- *Brain MR scans* to rule out any brain pathologies that can correlate with aggressive behaviours (especially frontal or temporal lobe tumours or injuries)
- *Osteodensitometry* in case of antiandrogen treatment

As many psychotropic drugs are accompanied by a variety of side effects and in many psychotropic medications the therapeutic dose is close to the toxic dose close monitoring of drug intake and drug serum concentrations is needed. As patients with IDD might not be able to recognize adverse effects as quickly or precisely as would individuals without IDD there is a great need to have a medical health care provider examine the patients on a regular basis – at least every three months. These regular examinations should include short psychiatric history taking with an emphasis on any behavioural changes, blood pressure measurements, ECG, and full blood counts including measurements of drug serum concentrations. As some offenders with IDD might have limited cognitive abilities or limited introspective capabilities relying solely on self-report during assessment of treatment effects and/or side effects would not be sufficient and again informants or behavioural observations could be helpful and implemented. In the case of sexual offenders, indirect measures such as penile plethysmography or viewing time could be used as well.

21.3 Gathering Informed Consent in Offenders with IDD

As pharmacological interventions are a medical procedure, informed consent has to be obtained in every case. This accounts especially for antipsychotic and antiandrogen treatment as these drugs are accompanied by a variety of side effects. Gathering informed consent is particularly delicate in offenders with IDD due to limited cognitive abilities in some patients. Although it is probably not possible in clinical practice due to time constraints it would be desirable for an offender's cognitive abilities to be assessed by two independent clinicians and to have a third clinician assessing the patient if the first two did not agree. In case the patient is not capable of completely understanding what he or she is consenting to additionally his or her legal guardian should be informed about the treatment and should be asked for written informed consent. However, this does not mean that the patient himself should not be involved in the decisional process. It is a practitioner's duty to provide all relevant information in a way that patients who might have lower cognitive abilities will understand: why they are being treated, what effects the treatment will have, and which possible side effects could occur. If a patient does not have a legal guardian and it remains questionable if the offender is able to fully understand all surrounding information, pharmacological treatment should not be provided or should be started after a legal guardianship has been implemented. In adolescent offenders the legal guardian needs to be involved in the decision as to whether or not a patient should be treated with medications in all cases.

21.4 Pharmacological Interventions for Violent Offenders with IDD

As described above mental disorders found most frequently in violent offenders with IDD are antisocial personality disorders, substance use disorders, and psychotic disorders. Thereby, one needs to differentiate between short-term and long-term treatment approaches for these mental health conditions.

In an acute situation of a sudden violent or aggressive outbreak, one would need a pharmacological agent that leads to a rapid tranquilization of the individual. Furthermore, the drug should have a rather wide therapeutic margin to prevent over dosage, should be accompanied by none or only few unpredictable side effects, and the medication should be available in formulations that can be given intramuscular (i.m.), especially in case the patient refuses a voluntary intake of the medication. Fulfilling most of these criteria, haloperidol as a first-generation antipsychotic drug or olanzapine as a second-generation antipsychotic has been recommended for the use in such emergency situations (Hockenhull et al. 2012; National Institute for Health and Clinical Excellence [NICE] 2005). In the short-term, haloperidol has primarily dampening and sedative effects and only after being applied for several weeks unfolds its antipsychotic potential. Doses of 5–10 mg i.m. or intravenous are recommended for the control of acute states of hyperarousal (Ulrich et al. 1998), whereby the dosage can be increased to up to 50 mg when given parenteral and up to 100 mg when given orally during the first 24 hours. Olanzapine can also be given orally or i.m. If olanzapine has to be administered i.m. the initial dose should be between 5–10 mg. Depending on the acute effect a second injection with 5–10 mg olanzapine i.m. could be given at the earliest two hours after the first injection, and if necessary a third injection could be given at the earliest four hours after the second injection. According to the manufacturer the maximum daily dose should not exceed 20 mg. Just recently, a new formulation of the first-generation antipsychotic loxapin has been introduced to the acute treatment of intense states of arousal or aggressive behaviour. Thereby, loxapin is the first antipsychotic agent that is available in an inhalative formulation. Loxapin should only be given in hospital settings and bronchodilatatory agents (e.g. short-acting beta-2-sympathomimetica) should be available as well, so that severe respiratory side effects that can possibly occur during inhalative loxapin treatment can be treated rapidly. Overall, loxapin usage is not recommended, however, due to its unique application form should be considered in cases where an i.m. injection is not possible.

Additionally, to the acute treatment with antipsychotics it can be recommended to also apply benzodiazepines, preferably lorazepam or diazepam in an acute state of arousal. Benzodiazepines, also have anxiety-reducing and sedative effects (Battaglia 2005), however, their depressive effect on respiratory function and their broad interaction potential with other drugs should be kept in mind (Huf et al. 2005). In acute states of arousal lorazepam (preferably 0.5–2.5 mg) and diazepam (preferably 2–10 mg) can be given orally or i.m. Benzodiazepines might loose parts of their effectiveness in patients with tolerance to alcohol or other sedating drugs (Battaglia 2005).

Despite these clear recommendations provided for emergency situations the state of research concerning long-term interventions is less clear. In the long-term, pharmacological agents should aim at increasing the controllability of violent behaviours and thereby at the best should prevent the occurrence of new criminal behaviours. Thereby, the precise long-term treatment regime should be based on the Risk-Need-Responsivity model (RNR model; Andrews and Bonta 2010). The RNR model postulates that the intensity of treatment (e.g. no specific treatment > psychotherapeutic treatment > pharmacological treatment) should take into account the individual risk for criminal recidivism, the individual criminogenic needs of the offender (e.g. empirically validated dynamic and changeable risk factors), and the individual responsivity to certain kinds of therapeutic interventions.

21.4.1 Antisocial Personality Disorder

Antidepressants, benzodiazepines, anticonvulsants, psychostimulants, antipsychotics, mood stabilizers, lithium, and divalproex sodium have all been used in the treatment of people with an antisocial personality disorder (Khalifa et al. 2010; Warren et al. 2003), however, their application was not necessarily based on strong scientific evidence. It was suggested that neurochemical changes could play an important role in the aetiology of the disorder (Skodol et al. 2002) and pharmacotherapy could be able to modulate the neurotransmitter function and/or concentration leading to improved self-control and less violent and aggressive acts (Khalifa et al. 2010; Markovitz 2004). Thereby, especially alterations in the serotonin system have been associated with impulsive and aggressive behaviours in individuals with an antisocial personality disorder (Khalifa et al. 2010; Sugden et al. 2006).

One open and uncontrolled study with 34 violent offenders has indeed shown that SSRIs lead to a reduction in impulsive and aggressive behaviours after a three-month treatment period (Butler et al. 2010). Similarly, Cherek et al. (2002) found reductions in aggressive behaviours after SSRI treatment in 12 male subjects with an antisocial personality disorder and who were currently on parole. SSRIs are primarily used in the treatment of depressive, anxiety, or obsessive–compulsive disorders. The advantage of SSRIs is that they are well tolerable and are accompanied by only a few side effects, indicating that their application could be continued for several years. Frequently occurring side effects are nervousness, sleeping disorders, fatigue, headache, sexual dysfunctions, dizziness, increased appetite and weight gain, oliguria and hyponatremia (Damsa et al. 2004; Guay 2009). Despite these promising first findings, two recent meta-analyses could not identify any high-quality studies concerning the use of SSRIs in antisocial personality disorder and have thus argued against their use at least on a regular basis. (Khalifa et al. 2010; NICE 2005).

Altogether Khalifa et al. (2010), identified only eight randomized controlled trials to be included in their meta-analysis, and only four of these reported findings explicitly addressing individuals with an antisocial personality disorder and only one was con-ducted in an offender sample. Of the studied pharmacological agents only phenytoin (Barratt et al. 1997; Stanford et al. 2001, 2005), carbamazepine, and valproate (Stanford et al. 2005) when compared to placebo treatment led to a significant reduc-tion in impulsive aggression in persons diagnosed with an antisocial personality disorder. The anticonvulsants phenytoin and carbamazepine are approved for short- and long-term treatment of epileptic seizures and carbamazepine is additionally used for phase prophylaxis in bipolar disorders. In both agents the therapeutic dose is near the toxic dose and thus taking the medication requires close monitoring of plasma levels, speaking against an application in antisocial individuals. Intoxication can lead to bradycardia, tremor, ataxia, nystagmus, anaemia, and many other adverse effects. Valproat, also an anticonvulsant, has a wider therapeutic index and intoxica-tions occur at a much lesser rate making its use for individuals with an antisocial personality disorder more preferable. Intoxications with valproat are characterized by drowsiness, delir, cardiovascular depression, and muscular hypotension. As all of the above-named agents are rather old medications and some of them are not longer used in clinical practice on a regular basis due to their frequent and severe side effects, the authors of the Cochrane Review concluded that the current state of research for all agents appears to be too weak to provide any evidence-based recommendations for the pharmacological treatment of violent or aggressive behaviours in individuals or offenders with an antisocial personality disorder (Khalifa et al. 2010). However, in need for any pharmacological interventions medical health care providers can still consider the above-described agents (SSRIs, carbamazepine, valproate, and phenytoin) in an individualized treatment approach. Furthermore, the National Institute for Health and Clinical Excellence (NICE) guidelines suggested to treat in any case co-morbid conditions, e.g. psychosis, substance use problems, or paraphilic disorders because in some antisocial patients treatment of these co-morbid conditions can already lead to a considerable reduction of aggressive and violent behaviours (NICE 2005).

21.4.2   Substance Use Disorders

Most interventions for drug using offenders aim at reducing addictive behaviours and craving and by lowering these symptoms lead to a reduction of drug related crimes in the long run. However, many illegal drugs, e.g. heroin, cocaine, methamphetamines but also alcohol can trigger violent and aggressive behaviours detached from the addictive potential (Tomlinson et al. 2016). Most pharmacological intervention studies aiming at a reduction of violent and aggressive behaviours in patients with substance use disorders who have come into conflict with the law have been conducted with opioid dependent patients, primarily those addicted to heroine. Internationally, methadone treatment has been the primary treatment choice for heroin addiction in prison (Moller et al. 2007; Perry et al. 2013; Stallwitz and Stover 2007). Methadone is a synthetic opioid and a pure agonist at the μ-opioid receptor. In contrast to heroin methadone does not lead to a feeling of being high and therefore has a lower addictive potential than heroin. In an approach to provide an overview about current treatment settings Amato et al. (2013) concluded that settings are too diverse to be analysed meta-analytically. Another agent frequently used in drug replacement therapy is buprenorphine. Buprenorphine is used in the treatment of most severe pain disorders as well as in heroin withdrawal treatment. Due to its high potency there are less overdoses as compared to methadone. In a recent meta-analysis Fareed et al. (2012) found that a daily dose of 16–32 mg showed the best effects in heroin withdrawal treatment (Fareed et al. 2012; Perry et al. 2013). Although both agents have been used for many years and also in many different settings the most recent Cochrane review came to the conclusion that although both drugs are effective in withdrawal treatment, they are not more effective than placebo in reducing criminal behaviours in offenders with a substance use disorder. There was only one study included in that review that found a reduced criminal activity in drug-using offenders being treated with methadone as compared to those not being treated with any pharmacological agents (Kinlock et al. 2005; Perry et al. 2013). Studies comparing methadone and buprenorphine found no differences between the drugs concerning the frequency of new incarcerations or general criminal activities.

Although antagonistic treatment with naltrexone revealed no positive effects in terms of reduced drug use, there was strong evidence that naltrexone treatment leads to a significant reduction in criminal activity (Perry et al. 2013). It has to be noted though that increased mortality rates were found under naltrexone treatment (Gibson and Degenhardt 2007; Perry et al. 2013), indicating that naltrexone treatment needs close monitoring during application especially when given orally (Gibson and Degenhardt

2007; Perry et al. 2013). As mentioned earlier close monitoring of drug intake is not always possible and this accounts especially for offenders in prisons and even more in the community. Taken together it can be recommended to use methadone during drug withdrawal treatment in offenders if one of the main treatment goals is a reduction of criminal behaviours.

21.4.3 Psychotic Offenders

Antipsychotic medications are used for a reduction of psychotic symptoms and to increase psychosocial functioning. Systematic reviews have shown that antipsychotic agents lead to a reduced rate of aggressive acts as well, especially in schizophrenic patients and related disorders (Fazel et al. 2014; Leucht et al. 2012). First-generation or typical antipsychotics are to be differentiated from second-generation or atypical antipsychotics. Both classes interact with dopamine receptors in the brain whereby atypical antipsychotics additionally interact with the serotonin system. Whether first-generation or second-generation antipsychotics are more effective concerning the reduction of psychotic symptoms or concerning the reduction of violent and aggressive behaviours is currently still unclear and debated (Hockenhull et al. 2012; Swanson et al. 2008). Dyskinesia and extrapyramidal-motoric symptoms as adverse effects seem to occur less frequently in atypical antipsychotics and thus it is widely accepted to recommend atypical antipsychotics as first-line treatment. In 2014, Fazel and colleagues assessed the effectiveness of antipsychotic agents to reduce violent and aggressive criminal behaviours in a sample of over 80 000 Swedish adults (Fazel et al. 2014). Thereby, the authors chose a within-subject design and compared periods where individuals were taking antipsychotic medications to periods where the same individual did not take any antipsychotic agents. They found a 64% reduced violent crime conviction rate in periods during which individuals were taking any antipsychotic medications. This accounted for any crimes, drug-related crimes, and violent crimes. Although not as strong as the effect observed in antipsychotic agents, mood stabilizers also led to a clear reduction in the conviction rate and when adding antipsychotics to mood stabilizers this effect was even more pronounced. Interestingly, adding mood stabilizers to antipsychotics did not make any difference and likewise adding SSRIs also had no additional protective effect (Fazel et al. 2014). Furthermore, higher doses of antipsychotics displayed more protective effects (Fazel et al. 2014). In a meta-analysis conducted by Leucht et al. (2012) analysing data of 403 patients, an absolute reduction of aggression and violence in schizophrenic patients from 12 to 2% in a two-year follow-up period was found after antipsychotic treatment. The one antipsychotic drug with the most pronounced anti-aggressive or anti-violent effect seems to be clozapine. In this context Mela and Depiang (2016) found a significantly longer survival time until the first reconviction with a violent offence after release from a forensic-psychiatric hospital in the clozapine group as compared to the group taking another antipsychotic drug (Mela and Depiang 2016). The authors argued that this effect would go beyond a mere improvement of positive, negative, and cognitive psychotic symptoms, because other studies as well have found a reduction in violent and aggressive behaviours during clozapine treatment even in the absence of a reduction in psychotic symptoms (Balbuena et al. 2010) and have found clozapine to be superior compared to olanzapine and haloperidol in lowering aggressive behaviours in the long-term (Krakowski et al. 2008). Mela and Depiang suggested that since patients being treated with clozapine need closer and more precise monitoring of blood values and heart function, they are more strongly connected to the medical system. More frequent contacts with their medical health care provider require a higher patient compliance and could enhance socio-cultural and prosocial functioning and behaviours. The same effect was found in patients taking depot antipsychotic medications as compared to oral medication intake (Kane et al. 1998; Kane and Garcia-Ribera 2009). However, it has to be noted that due to the severe side effects that can occur under clozapine treatment, especially agranulocytosis, and cardiac toxicity, clozapine should not be used as a first-line treatment and should be reserved for patients in whom multiple treatment approaches with second-generation antipsychotics have not significantly improved psychotic and aggressive symptomatology.

Antipsychotics are also frequently used to control aggressive behaviours in patients with IDD without a psychotic disorder. McDougle et al. (1998) compared 14 adults with autistic or pervasive developmental disorder who were treated with risperidone, a second-generation antipsychotic agent, for 12 weeks with 10 autistic patients who were treated with placebo and found a significantly reduced rate of aggressive behaviours in the risperidone group (McDougle et al. 1998). However, in the last years a lot of criticism has come up about treating patients with IDD without a psychotic disorder with antipsychotic medications to lower aggressive behaviours. In a large randomized controlled trial Tyrer and colleagues compared 86 non-psychotic patients with IDD of whom 28 were treated with haloperidol, 29 with risperidone and 29 with placebo for aggressive behaviours. The authors found reduced rates of aggression after four weeks of treatment in all groups, whereby the reduction was most pronounced in the placebo group (Tyrer et al. 2008). This finding led the authors to the conclusion that antipsychotic drugs should no longer be used in the treatment of aggressive behaviours in patients with IDD without a psychotic disorder (Tyrer et al. 2008). Matson and Neal (2009) in their systematic review could confirm this view and recommended that it is advisable to consider psychotherapeutic interventions instead of antipsychotic or other medications in the treatment of aggressive behaviours in individuals with IDD without a psychotic disorder (Matson and Neal 2009).

21.4.4 Offenders with IDD Following TBI or Organic Brain Disease

TBI is one of the most frequent causes of disability, including intellectual disability in young adults. Following TBI, many patients show challenging behaviours, including aggressive and violent behaviours as well as challenging sexual behaviours (Chew and Zafonte 2009; Turner et al. 2015). These behavioural changes can also set an individual at increased risk of committing criminal behaviours. A recent systematic review found a prevalence between 10 and 20% for severe TBI in young offenders (Hughes et al. 2015). Patients with IDD due to organic brain diseases can be found with a prevalence of about 5% within the prison population (Diamond et al. 2001). The treatment of violent and criminal behaviours in both groups seems to be comparable.

Current treatment guidelines for the treatment of aggressive behaviours following TBI suggest using antiepileptic drugs or mood stabilizers as first line pharmacological treatment (Plantier and Luauté 2016). Preferably, treatment providers should use carbamazepine or valproate. It has to be noted though that there exist no randomized controlled trials assessing the effectiveness of these pharmacological agents. However, due to their antiepileptic potential and their well-known and controllable side effects, these agents hold some advantages compared to other medications.

In the 1980s beta-blockers were introduced to the treatment of violent and aggressive behaviours in individuals with severe organic or traumatic brain disease (Greendyke et al. 1986; Greendyke and Kanter 1986). A Cochrane review identified four randomized controlled trials evaluating beta-blockers (propranolol and pindolol) with two of them (both performed with propranolol) showing that treatment with beta-blockers led to a significant reduction of aggressive behaviours compared to placebo treatment (Fleminger et al. 2006). However, it has to be noted that in these studies doses up to 520 mg/d propranolol were given, pointing out that adverse effects could limit the use of beta-blockers in the treatment of aggressive behaviours (Chew and Zafonte 2009). Current guidelines recommend the use of propranolol at a dosage of 40–80 mg/d (Plantier and Luauté 2016). Antipsychotics are also commonly used in the treatment of aggressive behaviours in individuals post-TBI, however, there are no randomized controlled trials proving their effectiveness. Furthermore, patients post-TBI are at an increased risk of developing neuroleptic malignant syndrome and epileptic seizures (Plantier and Luauté 2016). Thus, antipsychotics should only be used in those patients who were being treated with antipsychotics before suffering from TBI or other brain damage. Further drugs that have been studied in the context of aggressive behaviours in patients post-TBI are methylphenidate, amantadine, SSRIs, and lithium. However, none of these agents was able to significantly reduce aggressive and violent behaviours and thus their use cannot be recommended (Chew and Zafonte 2009).

21.5   Treatment of Sexual Offenders with IDD

The state of research concerning pharmacological interventions for sexual offenders with IDD is also rather scarce and high-quality studies are completely missing. In their attempt to summarize the current state of research Ashman and Duggan found no randomized controlled trials addressing sexual offender therapy in individuals with IDD, neither concerning pharmacological nor psychological interventions (Ashman and Duggan 2008). Again it was suggested that research findings concerning the effectiveness of pharmacological agents that were derived from sexual offender samples without IDD could be transferred to those with IDD (Sajith et al. 2008).

Pharmacological treatment should be used in sexual offenders who were diagnosed with a paraphilic disorder or comparable mental health conditions only (e.g. hypersexual disorder or obsessive–compulsive sexual behaviour disorder) (Turner et al. 2017). The first treatment approaches with pharmacological agents in sexual offenders were undertaken in the 1950s. Today SSRIs, steroidal antiandrogens (cyproterone acetate; CPA, medroxyprogesterone acetate; MPA), and Gonadotropin-Releasing-Hormone-agonists (GnRH-agonists) are recommended for the use in sexual offenders to decrease paraphilic fantasies and urges. It is estimated that around 15–20% of sexual offenders are treated with medications (McGrath et al. 2010; Turner et al. 2013). It has to be noted though that all recommended agents act via a general reduction of sexual drive and none of the agents may actually have an influence on the paraphilic disorder itself (Turner and Briken 2018). However, a reduction in the intensity of paraphilic fantasies can help some sexual offenders to be more open for psychotherapeutic interventions that can then teach the offender to achieve higher self-control over his paraphilic urges. Furthermore, it can be suggested that especially for sexual offenders with IDD pharmacological interventions seem to be useful as their limited cognitive abilities might make them less accessible for psychotherapeutic interventions (Turner & Briken, 2018).

Several treatment guidelines have been published assisting practitioners in making the decision whether or not a certain patient should be treated with pharmacological agents due to paraphilic fantasies or behaviours. Currently, the most extensive and probably also most widely used and accepted treatment guidelines are those published by the World Federation of Societies of Biological Psychiatry (WFSBP) (Thibaut et al. 2010). Based on the intensity of the paraphilic fantasies and urges and on the personal risk for future sexually violent behaviours the WFSBP guidelines suggest a six-step treatment algorithm, whereby the main treatment goal on every level is to achieve control over paraphilic fantasies, compulsions, and behaviours. On every level specific risk-reducing psychotherapy should be provided as well.

Patients with rather mild forms of paraphilic disorders, e.g. exhibitionism and a low risk for sexually violent behaviours should be treated with SSRIs at a similar dose as would be applicable in the treatment of obsessive–compulsive disorders (e.g. Fluoxetin 40–60 mg/d or Paroxetin 40 mg/d). If SSRI treatment alone does not lead to the desired improvements in paraphilic symptomatology low dose CPA (50–100 mg/d) should be given additionally. On the next level the CPA dose should be increased to 200–300 mg/day given orally or 200–400 mg/week via i.m. injections. In high-risk patients or those with an exceptionally high risk therapy should be escalated to GnRH-agonists or to a combination of GnRH-agonists and CPA or MPA, respectively. However, it has to be noted that the combination of GnRH-agonists and CPA or MPA will lead to a complete suppression of all sexual activities including non-paraphilic sexual fantasies and behaviours.

In 2016, the WFSBP working group published guidelines on the biological treatment of paraphilic disorders in adolescent sexual offenders (Thibaut et al. 2016). Comparably, to the adult treatment guidelines psychotherapeutic interventions are considered to be first-line treatment in all cases. In adolescent patients with a low to moderate risk of sexually violent behaviours (e.g. indecent exposure, touching the body or genitals of others) SSRIs can be given additionally to psychotherapy at the same dosage as they would be used in obsessive–compulsive disorders (e.g. fluoxetine up to 40 mg/d). Pharmacological treatment should be escalated to the additional application of antiandrogens in adolescents with a high risk of sexually violent behaviours that are associated with coercive sexual sadism in fantasies or behaviours, whereby the treatment provider can choose between CPA (100–200 mg/d), MPA (50–300 mg/d) or GnRH-agonists (11.25 mg i.m./3-month). It has to be noted that antiandrogen treatment requires adolescents to be at least in Tanner stage V (meaning fully developed genitalia and a testes volume >20 ml) as well as completed bone development. Whilst treatment should be restricted to 6 months in patients under 17 years, there is no time restriction in older patients.

21.6 Conclusions

As has been shown throughout this chapter the current state of research concerning pharmacological interventions in offenders with IDD is almost non-existent and there are almost no high-quality studies in terms of randomized controlled trials. Nevertheless, in the short-term practitioners should use haloperidol or second-generation antipsychotics, such as olanzapine, because there seems to be much experience with these drugs and they have proven to be effective in emergency situations. So far, antipsychotics have been used most frequently in the long-term treatment of patients with IDD displaying aggressive or violent behaviour, however, current studies have shown that these agents seem to be no more effective than placebo. Therefore, in offenders with IDD without any co-morbid mental health conditions only psychotherapy should be provided, and practitioners should refrain from pharmacological interventions. Antipsychotics should only be used in patients with a co-morbid psychotic disorder. In violent offenders with IDD and an underlying antisocial personality or conduct disorder a first-treatment approach with SSRIs could be started, which could be escalated to anticonvulsants. In opioid-dependent offenders methadone should be considered as first-line treatment, although this will probably have only a limited effect on the prevention of criminal behaviours. Offenders with IDD following traumatic or organic brain disease should preferably be treated with anticonvulsants, however, some studies have also found that beta-blockers could be a useful alternative. In sexual offenders, clinicians should turn to the WFSBP guidelines for the treatment of paraphilic disorders in adults and adolescents, which provide clear recommendations concerning the selection of the most suitable agent. Nevertheless, it becomes clear that much more research, especially high-quality studies comparing single agents with each other or against placebo treatment is needed to provide clearer recommendations for the pharmacological treatment of offenders with IDD.

References

Amato, L., Davoli, M., Minozzi, S. et al. (2013). Methadone at tapered doses for the management of opioid withdrawal. *Cochrane Database of Systematic Reviews* (2): CD003409.

Andrews, D.A. and Bonta, J. (2010). Rehabilitating criminal justice policy and practice. *Psychology, Public Policy, and Law* 16 (1): 39–55. http://doi.org/10.1037/a0018362.

Ashman, L.L.M. and Duggan, L. (2008). Interventions for learning disabled sex offenders. *Cochrane Database of Systematic Reviews* (1): CD003682.

Balbuena, L., Mela, M., Wong, S. et al. (2010). Does clozapine promote employability and reduce offending among mentally disordered offenders? *Canadian Journal of Psychiatry* 55 (1): 50–56.

Barratt, E.S., Stanford, M.S., Felthous, A.R. et al. (1997). The effects of phenytoin on impulsive and premeditated aggression: a controlled study. *Journal of Clinical Psychopharmacology* 17 (5): 341–349.

Barron, P., Hassiotis, A., and Banes, J. (2002). Offenders with intellectual disability: the size of the problem and therapeutic outcomes. *Journal of Intellectual Disability Research* 46 (6): 454–463.

Battaglia, J. (2005). Pharmacologcial management of acute agitation. *Drugs* 65 (9): 1207–1222.

Butler, T., Schofield, P.W., Greenberg, D. et al. (2010). Reducing impulsivity in repeat violent offenders: an open label trial of a selective serotonin reuptake inhibitor. *Australian and New Zealand Journal of Psychiatry* 44 (12): 1137–1143.

Cherek, D.R., Lane, S.D., Pietras, C.J. et al. (2002). Effects of chronic paroxetine administration on measures of aggressive and impulsive responses of adult males with a history of conduct disorder. *Psychopharmacology* 159 (3): 266–274.

Chew, E. and Zafonte, R.D. (2009). Pharmacological management of neurobehavioral disorders following traumatic brain injury: a state-of the-art review. *The Journal of Rehabilitation Research and Development* 46 (6): 851. http://doi.org/10.1682/JRRD.2008.09.0120.

Cooper, S.-A., Smiley, E., Morrison, J. et al. (2007). Mental ill-health in adults with intellectual disabilities: prevalence and associated factors. *British Journal of Psychiatry* 190: 27–35.

Damsa, C., Bumb, A., Bianchi-Demicheli, F. et al. (2004). 'Dopamine-dependent' side effects of selective serotonin reuptake inhibitors: a clinical review. *The Journal of Clinical Psychiatry* 65 (8): 1064–1068.

Diamond, P.M., Wang, E.W., Holzer, C.E. et al. (2001). The prevalence of mental illness in prison. *Administration and Policy in Mental Health* 29 (1): 21–40. http://doi.org/10.1023/a:1013164814732.

Douglas, K.S., Guy, L.S., and Hart, S.D. (2009). Psychosis as a risk factor for violence to others: a meta-analysis. *Psychological Bulletin* 135 (5): 679–706.

Eher, R., Rettenberger, M., and Turner, D. (2019). The prevalence of mental disorders in incarcerated contact sexual offenders. *Acta Psychiatrica Scandinavica* 139 (6): 572-581.

Fareed, A., Vayalapalli, S., Casarella, J. et al. (2012). Effect of buprenorphine dose on treatment outcome. *Journal of Addiction Disorders* 31 (1): 8–18.

Fazel, S. and Danesh, J. (2002). Serious mental disorder in 23 000 prisoners: a systematic review of 62 surveys. *Lancet* 359: 545–550.

Fazel, S., Doll, H., and Långström, N. (2008). Mental disorders among adolescents in juvenile detention and correctional facilities. *Journal of the American Academy of Child & Adolescent Psychiatry* 47 (9): 1010–1019. http://doi.org/10.1097/CHI.0b013e31817eecf3.

Fazel, S. and Grann, M. (2006). The population impact of severe mental illness on violent crime. *The American Journal of Psychiatry* 163 (8): 1397–1403.

Fazel, S., Zetterqvist, J., Larsson, H. et al. (2014). Antipsychotics, mood stabilisers, and risk of violent crime. *Lancet* 384: 1206–1214.

Fleminger, S., Greenwood, R.R., and Oliver, D.L. (2006). Pharmacological management for agitation and aggression in people with acquired brain injury. *Cochrane Database of Systematic Reviews* (4): CD003299.

Gibson, A. and Degenhardt, L.J. (2007). Mortality related to pharmacotherapies for opioid dependence: a comparative analysis of coronial records. *Drug and Alcohol Review* 26: 405–410.

Grann, M., Danesh, J., and Fazel, S. (2008). The association between psychiatric diagnosis and violent re-offending in adult offenders in the community. *BMC Psychiatry* 8: 92.

Greendyke, R.M. and Kanter, D.R. (1986). Therapeutic effects of pindolol on behavioral disturbances associated with organic brain disease: a double-blind study. *Journal of Clinical Psychiatry* 47 (8): 423–426.

Greendyke, R.M., Kanter, D.R., Schuster, D.B. et al. (1986). Propranolol treatment of assaultive patients with organic brain disease. A double-blind crossover, placebo-controlled study. *Journal of Nervous and Mental Disease* 174 (5): 290–294.

Guay, D.R.P. (2009). Drug treatment of paraphilic and nonparaphilic sexual disorders. *Clinical Therapeutics* 31 (1): 1–31. http://doi.org/10.1016/S0149-2918(09)00023-X.

Hockenhull, J.A., Whittington, R., Leitner, M. et al. (2012). A systematic review of prevention and intervention strategies for populations at high risk of engaging in violent behaviour: update 2002–8. *Health Technology Assessment* 16 (3): 1–152.

Huf, G., Alexander, J., and Allen, M.H. (2005). Haloperidol plus promethazine for psychosis induced aggression. *Cochrane Database of Systematic Reviews* 1: CD005146.

Hughes, N., Williams, W.H., Chitsabesan, P. et al. (2015). The prevalence of traumatic brain injury among young offenders in custody: a systematic review. *Journal of Head Trauma Rehabilitation* 30 (2): 94–105. http://doi.org/10.1097/HTR.0000000000000124.

Iverson, J.C. and Fox, R.A. (1989). Prevalence of psychopathology among mentally retarded adults. *Research in Developmental Disabilities* 10 (1): 77–83.

Kane, J.M., Aguglia, E., Altamura, A.C. et al. (1998). Guidelines for depot antipsychotic treatment in schizophrenia. *European Neuropsychopharmacology* 8 (1): 55–66.

Kane, J.M. and Garcia-Ribera, C. (2009). Clinical guideline recommendations for antipsychotic long-acting injections. *British Journal of Psychiatry* 195: S63–S67.

Khalifa, N., Duggan, C., Stoffers, J. et al. (2010). Pharmacological interventions for antisocial personality disorder. *Cochrane Database of Systematic Reviews* 8: CD007667.

Kinlock, T.W., Battjes, R.J., Schwartz, R.P. et al. (2005). A novel opioid maintenance program for prisoners: report of post-release outcomes. *The American Journal of Drug and Alcohol Abuse* 31 (3): 433–454.

Krakowski, M.I., Czobor, P., and Nolan, K.A. (2008). Atypical antipsychotics, neurocognitive deficits, and aggression in schizophrenic patients. *Journal of Clinical Psychopharmacology* 28: 485–493.

Leucht, S., Tardy, M., Komossa, K. et al. (2012). Antipsychotic drugs versus placebo for relapse prevention in schizophrenia: a systematic review and meta-analysis. *The Lancet* 379 (9831): 2063–2071.

Markovitz, P.J. (2004). Recent trends in the pharmacotherapy of personality disorders. *Journal of Personality Disorders* 18 (1): 90–101.

Matson, J.L. and Neal, D. (2009). Psychotropic medication use for challenging behaviors in persons with intellectual disabilities: an overview. *Research in Developmental Disabilities* 30 (3): 572–586.

McDougle, C.J., Holmes, J.P., Carlson, D.C. et al. (1998). A double-blind, placebo-controlled study of risperidone in adults with autistic disorder and other pervasive developmental disorders. *Archives of General Psychiatry* 55 (7): 633–641.

McGrath, R.J., Cumming, G.F., Burchard, B.L. et al. (2010). *Current Practices and Emerging Trends in Sexual Abuser Management: The Safer Society 2009 North American Survey*. Brandon, VT: Safer Society Press.

Mela, M. and Depiang, G. (2016). Clozapine's effect on recidivism among offenders with mental disorders. *The Journal of the American Academy of Psychiatry and the Law* 44: 82–90.

Moller, L., Gathere, A., Juergens, R. et al. (2007). *Health in Prisons. A WHO Guide to the Essentials in Prison Health*. Copenhagen: World Health Organization.

National Institute for Health and Clinical Excellence (NICE) (2005). *Violence: The Short-term Management of Disturbed/Violent Behaviour in In-patient Psychiatric Settings and Emergency Departments*. London: NICE.

Perry, A.E., Neilson, M., Martyn-St. James, M. et al. (2013). Pharmacological interventions for drug-using offenders (review). *Cochrane Database of Systematic Reviews* 12: CD010862.

Plantier, D. and Luauté, J. (2016). Drugs for behavior disorders after traumatic brain injury: systematic review and expert consensus leading to French recommendations for good practice. *Annals of Physical and Rehabilitation Medicine* 59 (1): 42–57. http://doi.org/10.1016/j.rehab.2015.10.003.

Rice, M.E., Harris, G.T., Lang, C. et al. (2008). Sexual preferences and recidivism of sex offenders with mental retardation. *Sexual Abuse: A Journal of Research and Treatment* 20 (4): 409–425.

Riches, V.C., Parmenter, T.R., Wiese, M. et al. (2006). Intellectual disability and mental illness in the NSW criminal justice system. *International Journal of Law and Psychiatry* 29 (5): 386–396.

Sajith, S.G., Morgan, C., and Clarke, D. (2008). Pharmacological management of inappropriate sexual behaviours: a review of its evidence, rationale and scope in relation to men with intellectual disabilities. *Journal of Intellectual Disabilities Research* 52 (12): 1078–1090. http://doi.org/10.1111/j.1365-2788.2008.01097.x.

Skodol, A.E., Siever, L.J., Livesley, W.J. et al. (2002). The borderline diagnosis II: biology, genetics and clinical course. *Biological Psychiatry* 51: 951–963.

Stallwitz, A. and Stover, H. (2007). The impact of substitution treatment in prisons - a literature review. *International Journal of Drug Policy* 18: 464–474.

Stanford, M.S., Helfritz, L.E., and Conklin, S.M. (2005). A comparison of anticonvulsants in the treatment of impulsive aggression. *Experimental and Clinical Psychopharmacology* 13 (1): 72–77.

Stanford, M.S., Houston, R.J., Mathias, C.W. et al. (2001). A double-blind placebo-controlled crossover study of phenytoin in individuals with impulsive aggression. *Psychiatry Research* 103 (2–3): 193–203.

Sugden, S.G., Kile, S.J., and Hendren, R. (2006). Neurodevelopmental pathways to aggression: a model to understand and target treatment in youth. *Journal of Neuropsychiatry and Clinical Neurosciences* 18 (3): 302–317.

Swanson, J., Swartz, M.S., Van Dorn, R.A. et al. (2008). Comparison of antipsychotic medication effects on reducing violence in people with schizophrenia. *The British Journal of Psychiatry* 193 (1): 37–43.

Thibaut, F., Bradford, J.M.W., Briken, P. et al. (2016). The World Federation of Societies of Biological Psychiatry (WFSBP) guidelines for the treatment of adolescent sexual offenders with paraphilic disorders. *The World Journal of Biological Psychiatry* 17 (1): 2–38. http://doi.org/10.3109/15622975.2015.1085598.

Thibaut, F., De La Barra, F., Gordon, H. et al. (2010). The World Federation of Societies of Biological Psychiatry (WFSBP) guidelines for the biological treatment of paraphilias. *The World Journal of Biological Psychiatry: The Official Journal of the World Federation of Societies of Biological Psychiatry* 11 (4): 604–655. http://doi.org/10.3109/15622971003671628.

Tomlinson, M.F., Brown, M., and Hoaken, P.N.S. (2016). Recreational drug use and human aggressive behavior: a comprehensive review since 2003. *Aggression and Violent Behavior* 27: 9–29.

Turner, D. and Briken, P. (2018). Treatment of paraphilic disorders in sexual offenders or men with a risk of sexual offending with luteinizing-hormone-releasing-hormone-agonists: an updated systematic review. *Journal of Sexual Medicine* 15 (1): 77–93.

Turner, D., Basdekis-Jozsa, R., and Briken, P. (2013). Prescription of testosterone-lowering medications for sex offender treatment in German forensic-psychiatric institutions. *The Journal of Sexual Medicine* 10 (2): 570–578. http://doi.org/10.1111/j.1743-6109.2012.02958.x.

Turner, D., Petermann, J., Harrison, K. et al. (2017). Pharmacological treatment of patients with paraphilic disorders and risk of sexual offending: an international perspective. *World Journal of Biological Psychiatry* epub ahead of print. doi:https://doi.org/10.1080/15622975.2017.1395069.

Turner, D., Schottle, D., Krueger, R. et al. (2015). Sexual behavior and its correlates after traumatic brain injury. *Current Opinion in Psychiatry* 28 (2): 180–187. http://doi.org/10.1097/YCO.0000000000000144.

Tyrer, P., Oliver-Africano, P.C., Ahmed, Z. et al. (2008). Risperidone, haloperidol, and placebo in the treatment of aggressive challenging behaviour in patients with intellectual disability: a randomised controlled trial. *The Lancet* 371: 57–63.

Ulrich, S., Neuhof, S., Braun, V. et al. (1998). Therapeutic window of serum haloperidol concentration in acute schizophrenia and schizoaffective disorder. *Pharmacopsychiatry* 31 (5): 163–169.

Warren, F., Preedy-Fayers, K., McGauley, G. et al. (2003). *Review of treatments for severe personality disorder*. Home Office Online Report 30/03. London: Home Office. http://citeseerx.ist.psu.edu/viewdoc/download?doi=10.1.1.614.6986&rep=rep1&type=pdf (accessed 30 May 2019).

Part V

Conclusions

22

Future Directions for What Works for Offenders with Intellectual and Developmental Disabilities

Dorothy Griffiths[1] and Leam A. Craig[2,3,4]

[1] *Brock University, St. Catharines, Ontario, Canada*
[2] *Forensic Psychology Practice Ltd, The Willows Clinic, Sutton Coldfield, UK*
[3] *Centre for Applied Psychology, University of Birmingham, Birmingham, UK*
[4] *School of Social Sciences, Birmingham City University, Birmingham, UK*

22.1 Introduction

> Evidence-based practice (EBP) is a process in which the practitioner combines well-researched interventions with clinical experience and ethics, and client preferences and culture to guide and inform the delivery of treatments and services. The practitioner, researcher, and client must work together in order to identify what works, for whom, and under what conditions. This approach ensures that the treatments and services, when used as intended, will have the most effective outcomes as demonstrated by the research. It will also ensure that programmes with proven success will be more widely disseminated and will benefit a greater number of people. (Social Work Policy Institute n.d., paragraph 1)

In reviewing the relevant issues addressed in this volume, three major shifts appear to be emerging. First, there was a strong trend towards a holistic approach to the assessment and treatment of people with intellectual and developmental disabilities (IDD) who offend that is multimodal. Second, there was prominent emphasis on habilitation, directed at reducing vulnerabilities that put the offender at risk of future offences and that affect treatment outcomes. Third, there was a recognition of the importance of comprehensive planning and support to achieve long-term effects and provide the offender with the elements of a quality of life that could prevent relapse.

22.2 A Multimodal Approach to Offender Treatment

Compared to earlier approaches that treated offenders as a homogeneous group and elements of treatment as discrete variables, research, and practice appears to be more recently directed at examining a more complex multifactorial methodology to integrated assessment, intervention and follow-up. The assumption appears to be that although there are some actuarial factors that provide static predictors of offenders as a whole, an integrated biopsychosocial assessment and treatment approach is showing promise for empirically evaluated outcomes that will enhance generalization and maintenance over follow-up.

In recent decades scientifically based methods to evaluate the risk related to recidivism have emerged. Commonly used static tools are the Static-99R (Hanson and Thornton 2000; Brouillette-Alarie et al. 2017), the Violence-VRAG-R (Harris et al. 2015), the Sexual Offender Risk Appraisal Guide-SORAG (Quinsey et al. 1998), and Risk Matrix-2000 (Thornton et al. 2003) (for review see Craig and Rettenberger 2016; Rettenberger and Craig 2017). Whilst the risk assessment scales noted above were designed for offenders without IDD, both the VRAG (Camilleri and Quinsey 2011) and the Static-99R (Tough 2001; Harris and Tough 2004; Hanson et al. 2013) have reported promising validity for use with persons with intellectual disabilities. Evaluation of static factors have been suggested to be valuable in deciding the nature of support and supervision required in keeping with the principle of risk, as described by Bonta and Andrews (2017) as an element of their Risk–Need–Responsivity (RNR) model. Additionally, for the purpose of therapeutic outcomes, dynamic risk factors represent contributing conditions that provide critical factors for intervention.

Some actuarial risk assessment instruments only evaluated static factors (e.g. Static-99R; Risk Matrix 2000), which did not allow for evaluation of changes in risk as a result of intervention or other changeable factors. More recently there has been an emphasis on assessing risk for recidivism as a means to determine the nature of supports, environmental setting, and intensity of intervention a person might need to live safely in the community (Keeling et al. 2009; Willis and Grace 2008, 2009). As a result, assessments have shifted to include aggregate ratings of risk based on both static and dynamic risk factors. Dynamic factors denote potentially changeable factors that have been linked to the offending behaviour, such as lack of self-management or self-regulation strategies (see Hanson et al. 2007; McGrath et al. 2012). These factors have come to be referred to as criminogenic needs (see Bonta and Andrews 2017) and have formed the basis of treatment focus.

Since static indicators are unchangeable, noted researchers have questioned their value in determining treatment for persons with intellectual disabilities (Harris and Tough 2004; Hanson et al. 2013; Wilson et al. 2014). As a result, dynamic risk assessment has gained distinction as an important method of evaluating factors that should be addressed in treatment and in long-term support and transition plans. Dynamic factors are changeable factors that have been determined to have contributed to the individual's offence and which Mann et al. (2010) noted represent psychologically meaningful risks. To assess for these dynamic factors in persons with intellectual disabilities, Steptoe et al. (2008) developed the Dynamic Risk Assessment and Management System (DRAMS) as a tool to examine these dynamic factors for persons with IDD. Preliminary results indicated that the items of the scale were predictive of events that preceded an offence for a person and as a result provided not only information regarding the prediction of recidivism but as a foundation to establish a programme to prevent a relapse. Lindsay (2011) noted that risk assessment research has developed quickly in the past decade, demonstrating promising studies treatment of issues related to offending.

Ellem et al., in Chapter 13 of this book, noted that research has moved 'beyond a purely psychological and clinical focus that is often found in the "What Works" (WW) literature, to a non-linear and non-reductionist way of understanding multiplicity of need (Pycroft 2014)'. They further pointed to the importance of examining offending through complexity theory in which specific social issues are examined relative to both the specific population and context (Whitehead 2010; Pycroft 2014).

This shift in focus has been evident in the offender field in general but may have even greater significance when discussing persons with IDD. As Snoyman et al. (Chapter 14) noted when discussing community supports, it is vital to consider persons with IDD holistically, not only addressing their criminogenic needs but their disability needs as well. They however cautioned that in regard to community supports, such a hypothesis has yet to be tested empirically.

This more holistic approach is noted in the range of assessment and treatment areas addressed in this volume, that includes anger and violence (Willner et al., Chapter 6; Didden et al., Chapter 15), social problem solving and criminal thinking (Langdon, Chapter 8; Hayes, Chapter 17), alcohol related violence (VanDerNagel et al., Chapter 9; Newton and McGillivray, Chapter 18), emotional difficulties related to offending (Richards et al., Chapter 11; Oxnam and Gardner, Chapter 19), and co-morbidities such as personality disorder (Beail, Chapter 5). Within the range of potential therapeutic areas there is also consideration given to the behavioural and cognitive phenotypes in genetic disorders related to offending (Rice et al., Chapter 4) and to other diagnoses such autism (Sturmey, Chapter 20). This emergent theme is perhaps best summed up by Ellem et al. (Chapter 13) who noted that:

> successful reintegration and abstinence from criminal activity is regarded as a process that is influenced by a myriad of psychological, developmental, and sociological factors (Maruna 2001; Pycroft 2014). It is argued that successful reintegration is best supported by the cumulative effect of a wide spectrum of interventions with attention given to a prosocial identity in ex-prisoners with IDD (Ward and Gannon 2006; Lewis 2014).

22.3 Habilitative Emphasis

The core of intervention for problematic behaviour in the IDD field involves systematic individualized analysis that would lead to a programme uniquely designed to the needs of the individual. In the IDD field, Ted Carr (1977) was one of the first researchers to introduce a systematic method of individualized analysis. His work identified the specific functions that behaviour served (positive reinforcement, negative reinforcement, and automatic reinforcement) from which individualized intervention plans were derived based on the functional determination. As a result of the analysis, habilitative programmes are designed to provide the individual with the functional replacement skills needed to change their circumstances in an appropriate way or to cope differently with circumstances that cannot be changed. It often involves communication skill development, social skills training, social problem solving, and so on.

Carr's work has been reported to be an important step in the evolution of functional analysis (Sturmey and Bernstein 2004). Functional behavioural assessment was originally described by Iwata et al. (1982) as an experimental analogue assessment but was later adapted for descriptive methods of analysis (Durand and Crimmins 1988; O'Neill et al. 1997).

Prior to the emergence of functional assessment, treatment for highly challenging behaviours had focused primarily on the use of aversive approaches, which included Faradic (electrical) stimulation. A huge debate emerged in the field throughout the next decade as illustrated in the classic text edited by Repp and Singh (1990), in which various perspectives on the use of non-aversive and aversive interventions for persons with developmental disabilities were expounded by leading experts in the field. Topics including the role of the environment, the role of skill building, least restrictive use of reductive procedures, treatment acceptability, and quality of life were explored. As a result, the field of Applied Behaviour Analysis (ABA) experienced a divergence within the discipline (Jacobson and Holburn 2004) in which Positive Behaviour Support (PBS) emerged.

Carr and Sidener (2002) suggested that the defining features of PBS are person-centred planning, functional assessment, positive strategies, multicomponent intervention, environmental focus, meaningful outcomes, ecological validity, and systems-level analysis. PBS provided a link between empirical approaches to behaviour such as functional assessment, and application to achieve socially valid changes in behaviour (Sugai et al. 2000). 'Of significance is the adoption of system-wide models of behavior support, which are geared toward "real world" settings, and implemented by relevant stakeholders' (Luiselli 2004, p. 48).

Although based solidly on behavioural principles, PBS integrated the philosophy of normalization and the process of person-centred planning (Wacker and Berg 2002). Person-centred planning approaches were introduced as a way of reconceptualizing service systems to meet individual needs. Although variations have been called by various names (e.g. essential plans, lifestyle plans, personal futures plans) they share some core principles. Holburn et al. (2000) suggested that the person-centred planning involves the person, those closest to the person, and natural community supports. It is a process that is collaborative and involves long-term commitment. Plans are based on personal preferences, involving real choice and decisions, and focused on incorporating natural community supports and creative opportunities to provide a life that is satisfying to the person. The marriage of person-centred planning with a positive behavioural approach results in what Risley (1996) has described as 'getting a life'.

The development of PBS from the foundation of ABA has been discussed extensively (e.g. Carr 1997) and has not been without its detractors (Johnston et al. 2006). Whether PBS represents a different form of ABA or whether it just encompasses ABA, has been debated in the field (Carr and Sidener 2002). Nonetheless, this debate has been an important influence on how persons with intellectual disabilities who present with challenging behaviour are provided with support and treatment.

Although there has been significant interest and research focused on forensic issues related to persons with intellectual disabilities in the last 20 years, the field has relied on adaptation of advances in work with nondisabled offenders. Current practice in working with persons with intellectual disabilities who have mental health challenges also takes a holistic, strength-based, and multifactorial approach. To date, there remains a lack of consensus in the field about which tools are most effective in determining the appropriate intervention path for a particular person; although we are certainly getting closer to agreement. The value of comprehensive assessment in that process cannot be underestimated. A comprehensive behavioural assessment is vital in understanding the conditions under which the behaviours are more or less likely to occur (i.e. the antecedent events that may occasion the behaviour), and the function that the behaviours serve for the person (i.e. the consequences that maintain the behaviour). Although traditionally, these events were approached as only observable events, Baker et al. (2002) and others now highlight the importance of evaluating the role that biomedical issues may play in presenting a behavioural symptom. They suggested, for example, that physiological arousal can be seen an antecedent event for certain problem behaviours. Gardner (2002) cautioned, however, that physical, psychiatric, or physiological challenges are not necessarily the direct cause of many challenging behaviours but serve as contributing factors in combination with other environmental or social circumstances. Notwithstanding, current best practice as outlined by the Code of Ethics for Applied Behaviour Analysts requires that these biomedical considerations should be addressed prior to behavioural intervention.

Mental health issues that may underlay or contribute to the offending behaviour have historically been unrecognized in the population of persons with IDD. Their offending behaviours have more typically been linked to their poor judgement or lack of moral development related to their disability, that Reiss et al. (1982) identified as diagnostic overshadowing. However, since the 1980s there has been a growing awareness of the high rates of dual diagnosis amongst persons with IDD and a strong emergence of research in this area. Since the 1980s, the field also began to recognize the role that biological factors could play in the presentation of challenging behaviour. Behavioural medicine began (e.g. Luiselli 1989) a recognition of the role that mental health (e.g. Reiss 1994), and genetics could play in the presentation of challenging behaviour (e.g. Griffiths et al. 2014), and the importance of using an integrated biopsychosocial approach (Gardner et al. 1996, 2012).

In Chapter 19, Oxnam and Gardner noted the importance, in assessment of emotional difficulties of offenders, that clinicians understand from the perspective of the individual what the function their behaviour serves. They identified the importance of using a variety of methods to identify the motivation surrounding the behaviour as a basis for case formulation. Oxnam and Gardner suggested that:

> The literature base addressing depression, anxiety and trauma in offenders with an ID is small in comparison with that focused on anger. Future research should further investigate the prevalence of these emotional difficulties in the offender population, describe symptoms, and discuss similarities and differences in how offenders and non-offenders present. There is also a need for the effectiveness of group therapy programmes to be evaluated in a controlled, longitudinal manner with larger sample sizes. Positive psychology, resilience and mindfulness are examples of exciting new intervention approaches for emotional difficulties that are likely to receive closer attention and development in the coming years.

In addition, VanDerNagel et al. (Chapter 9, this text), show the importance of examining the role that substance abuse may play in an offender's history, noting that offenders with IDD are more likely than neurotypical offenders to report substance abuse following incarceration, and that such abuse may be a critical factor in recidivism.

22.4 Comprehensive Long-Term Planning and Follow-Through

This shift in emphasis in the treatment of criminal behaviour of persons with IDD reflects the changes that have been simultaneously occurring in the disability field in recent decades. Scotti et al. (1996) summed this up when discussing what works in the field of behavioural intervention for persons with IDD:

> The time is well past for the behavioural intervention literature to merely focus on demonstrating the effects on circumscribed target behaviours of certain procedures implemented in carefully controlled (and often segregated) settings. Broader effects must not only be assessed but actively sought. These include not only assessing the effects of intervention on collateral behaviors but determining changes in lifestyle and quality of life that occur as a result of intervention (e.g., level of independence, choice making, living in typical homes in the community, meaningful employment and social roles, friendships and social networks), Furthermore, enhancing lifestyle and quality of life should be a crucial intervention component rather than simply an outcome of target behavior reduction (p. 133).

This shift towards more individualized treatment coincides with the concept that was promoted by Andrews and Bonta (2010). Their model, based on assessment and intervention for RNR, proposed that interventions are more likely to be successful when the intensity of intervention matches the level of risk posed, and where interventions specifically target known criminogenic needs in a manner that considers client characteristics (e.g. motivation, intellectual ability, learning styles). Their model however has been criticized for a lack of attention to the entire picture of treatment needs, specifically related to issues of responsivity (Ward et al. 2007). Alternatively, the Good Lives Model (GLM; Ward and Gannon 2006) for sex offenders in the typically developing population proposed a more holistic approach that includes building a goal-oriented life focused on achieving common human goals that will improve well-being. A third perspective was suggested by Wilson and Yates (2009) who opined that the seeming divide between the two approaches of Risk/Need/Responsibility and the GLM is a red herring. In examining the two models, Wilson and Yates (2009) suggested that RNR is the overarching framework in which successful interventions are likely to succeed and that GLM is one curriculum that could possibly ensure appropriate attention is paid to need and responsivity in that overarching framework. This would ultimately lead to the development of 'an integrated strategy [that] would further assist in reducing offender recidivism, while increasing offender self-efficacy, re-integration potential, and community safety' (Wilson and Yates 2009, p. 60).

This shift in how offender assessment and treatment has developed in recent years points to the overarching direction away from generic treatment to one that is individualized. Fundamental to this change is the premise that there are many variables that impact on the commission of an offence by a given individual and that effective treatment requires a holistic assessment of the individual variables and consequent treatment to address those individual factors. Although logically sound, this shift creates some dilemma for researchers who might find it more parsimonious to use manualized approaches to treatment that are tightly standardized to ensure replicability. The arguments posed against manualized approaches to treatment were elaborated in Chapter 2 by Griffiths.

In contrast to manualized treatment approaches, research based on an individualized and holistic method would follow a person-oriented approach that is both dynamic and holistic (Magnusson and Bergman 1988). In such an approach to research, the individual would be studied as a whole, based on the patterns of individual characteristics that are relevant to the problem under consideration. This type of treatment calls for models of treatment that can be individualized and tailored to the needs of the individual whilst still following a common protocol.

There are five advantages of this type of research in the study of offenders that speaks to the heart of ethical practice, namely it: (i) allows for treatment to be specific to the individual, (ii) integrates multiple and complex factors, (iii) allows for a logical and functionally organized protocol, (iv) ensures that the same operating procedures are followed, thereby (v) allowing for replication and validation of the same process to be followed for all, despite the fact that each individual receives an individualized intervention plan.

Although at the time of the writing of this book little evidence of the outcome of this type of research existed, this chapter is posed to address future directions. However, such a direction must be based on expanding what has currently been determined to work. As such, the use of this model within treatment and research must be grounded in what we already know.

What we know is that there has emerged a confluence of research that has demonstrated that the use of these strategies for other challenging behaviours has resulted in enhanced changes in quality of life (i.e. Feldman et al. 2002) and that the application of person-centred approaches in planning for persons with intellectual disabilities results in enhanced achievement of personal goals and escalation of the supports needed to achieve these goals in the future (Gosse et al. 2017). Whilst neither of these studies focused on offenders, the emerging research points to the benefits of a person-centred planning and the use of an integrated multimodal approach to working with persons with intellectual disabilities who present with challenging behaviours.

Previously, the direction for treatment of offenders with IDD was largely a reflection of the work that was being conducted with the general offender population. However, advancements in the field of assessment and treatment of a range of behaviours with persons with IDD have advanced greatly in recent decades. This work may hold promise for future work with offenders with IDD.

22.5 Implications for the Future of What Works with Offenders with IDD

The What Works (WW) systems of evaluation were designed to identify which assessment methodologies and intervention approaches meet the empirical rigour of the WW principles. Although the three systems of evaluation (Cochrane Collaboration [Higgins et al. 2011, 2016; Cochrane Library www.cochranelibrary.com]; Sherman et al. 1998; Chambless et al. 1998; Chambless and Hollon 1998; Chambless and Ollendick 2001) have a slightly different emphasis, they share a commonality in underscoring the importance of the highest quality of evidence from clinical research and from systematic reviews in order to identify which approaches are the most effective in having a long-term impact on reducing offending behaviour. Collectively, these systems emphasize that offender assessment and intervention approaches should follow manualized approaches, use psychometrically sound assessment measures, be based on multi-site comparisons, using control groups and have participants who have been randomly assigned to treatment, or alternatively include cohort studies and waiting list-controlled trials. However, the WW systems of evaluation have been criticized for emphasizing long-term recidivism outcomes typically as the sole or primary outcome measure of success for offender intervention programmes (Spiranovic et al. 2015). As discussed throughout this book, WW principles are not easily translated when considering the assessment and treatment of people with IDD who offend and there are significant limitations in using rates of recidivism as the primary outcome measure of programme success.

We have seen in this volume that practitioners and researchers have gone beyond a purely mechanical focus, emphasizing an understanding of multiplicity of need. Studies described here have incorporated comprehensive evaluative frameworks into programme designs, and rather than relying on recidivism data, adopted well designed observational studies and well controlled case studies to demonstrate psychological change and attitudinal shift in offenders with IDD.

We offer some suggestions as to where the future direction of WW research in this client group should go.

- *Theory and assessment development*: Unlike the non-IDD offender literature where several theories of offending behaviour have been postulated, within the IDD offender literature only a handful of theories have been developed, most of which focus on sexual offending behaviour, with the Counterfeit Deviance Hypothesis being the most researched theory. As well as the development of theory, it follows that evaluators need to develop tools that are able to measure the extent to which users are achieving intermediate outcomes that can capture progress (or lack of progress) over time and combine this with other research methods that can highlight factors that either support or inhibit the achievement of outcomes.
- *Evaluations to incorporate user feedback*. Unlike the desistance literature for non-intellectually disabled offenders (Maruna 2001; Weaver and McNeill 2007; Healy 2010; Laws and Ward 2011; McDermott 2012; McNeill et al. 2012; Willis and Ward 2013; Farmer et al. 2015) there is comparatively little in the way of desistance research specific to offenders with IDD. As elucidated throughout this volume, the theory, assessment, and treatment of people with IDD who offend is highly idiosyncratic and assumes a holistic multimodal approach. Others have observed that desistance is an individualized process (McAlinden et al. 2017) and desistance can be reached through a number of different paths. The engagement and desistance evidence base for this client group is still developing, but a number of studies have found that behavioural and attitudinal change can be achieved using cognitive behavioural therapy (CBT) approaches. However, what is less clear is how these changes are maintained and reinforced over time. There are likely to be a number of individual factors that are associated with reduced reoffending in this client group, but crucially, how people with IDD are processed by the criminal justice system and partner agencies may alter their likelihood of reoffending. To better understand how offenders with IDD engage and demonstrate attitudinal change, and remain offence free, practitioners and researchers can better support and accelerate the

desistance process, it is important to incorporate user feedback into research designs and get offenders' views on what helped or hindered them in, during, and following, the intervention. The wider use of observational research would also help to map the nuances of the desistance journey and the experience of interventions, providing richer data on what helps and what hinders desistance.

- *Diversity of outcome success:* Others have argued that focusing on a single indicator of success (e.g. reoffending) as an outcome may be inappropriate to measure the process of desistance (Armstrong and McNeill 2012), particularly in this client group as many individuals are held in secure forensic services beyond the end of the intervention. Hedderman et al. (2011) have suggested that by taking a wider conception of the process and indicators of desistance may allow a better understanding of the interventions that are successful in reducing re-offending. Such indicators may be attitudinal change as measured using appropriate and psychometrically robust assessment measures. Rather than focusing on 'what works', the emphasis would be on '*how it works*', '*why it works*' and '*how change can be sustained*'.
- *Diversity of programme modality and implementation*: Across the non-IDD offender treatment literature, group-based CBT approaches are often highlighted as the interventions of choice over other types of interventions, and whilst the same is true for the majority of treatment programmes for offenders with IDD, some studies have reported positive results using other techniques such as self-control methods (e.g. Meditation on the Soles of the Feet, and the Mindful Observation of Thoughts meditation procedure) (Singh et al. 2011) and dialectical behaviour therapy (Verhoeven 2010). Interactive programmes are likely to have greater impact than using didactic method. The reasons why this may be, and the factors affecting active participation, particularly for this client group, are important areas for further research.
- *Strengths-based programmes*: Within the non-IDD offender rehabilitation literature, there is growing emphasis on strength-based psychology and interventions citing models such as the GLM (Ward 2002; Ward and Gannon 2006). Here, the focus is on positively orientated interventions centred on the ideas of the GLM targeting criminogenic needs, poor problem solving, poor self-regulation, and relationship difficulties (see Craig and Rettenberger 2018). However, whilst the desire to acquire primary human goods and key pathways to desistance will be a preferred outcome for many offenders, the instrumental means and available resources by which they can achieve these goods vary considerably (Hilder and Kemshall 2013). Nevertheless, whilst the interventions based on GLM principles for non-IDD offenders are yet to be fully evaluated, there are no studies using strengths-based approaches with offenders with IDD. Given the current emphasis of the relative merits of strengths-based interventions, further work is necessary to evaluate the impact of strength-based programmes in practice for offenders with IDD.

References

Andrews, D.A. and Bonta, J. (2010). *The Psychology of Criminal Conduct*, 5e. Cincinnati, OH: Anderson.

Armstrong, S. and McNeill, F. (2012). *Reducing reoffending: review of selected countries*, SCCJR Research Report No: 04/2012. www.sccjr.ac.uk/publications/reducing-reoffending-in-scotland (accessed 26 June 2018).

Baker, D.J., Blumberg, R., and Freeman, R. (2002). Considerations for functional assessment of problem behavior among persons with developmental disabilities and mental illness. In: *Programs and Services for People with Dual Developmental and Psychiatric Disabilities* (eds. J. Jacobson, J. Mulick and S. Holburn), 51–66. Kingston, NY: National Association for Dual Diagnosis.

Bonta, J. and Andrews, D.A. (2017). *The Psychology of Criminal Conduct*, 6e. Cincinnati, OH: Anderson.

Brouillette-Alarie, S., Proulx, J., and Hanson, K. (2017). Three central dimensions of sexual recidivism risk: understanding the latent constructs of Static-99R and Static-2002R. *Sexual Abuse: A Journal of Research & Treatment* https://doi. org/10.1177/1079063217691965.

Camilleri, J.A. and Quinsey, V.L. (2011). Appraising the risk of sexual and violent recidivism among intellectually disabled offenders. *Psychology, Crime & Law* 17 (1): 59–74.

Carr, E.G. (1977). The motivation of self-injurious behavior: a review of some hypotheses. *Psychological Bulletin* 84: 800–816.

Carr, E.G. (1997). The evolution of applied behaviour analysis into positive behavior support. *Journal of the Association for Persons with Severe Handicaps* 22: 208–209.

Carr, J.E. and Sidener, T.M. (2002). On the relation between applied behavior analysis and positive behavioral support. *The Behavior Analyst* 25: 245–253.

Chambless, D. and Ollendick, T. (2001). Empirically supported psychological interventions: controversies and evidence. *Annual Review of Psychology* 52: 685–716.

Chambless, D.L., Baker, M., Baucom, D.H. et al. (1998). Update on empirically validated therapies, II. *The Clinical Psychologist* 51 (1): 3–16.

Chambless, D.L. and Hollon, S.D. (1998). Defining empirically supported therapies. *Journal of Consulting and Clinical Psychology* 66: 7–18.

Craig, L.A. and Rettenberger, M. (2016). A brief history of sexual offender risk assessment. In: *Treatment of Sexual Offenders: Strengths and Weaknesses in Assessment and Intervention* (eds. D.R. Laws and W. O'Donohue), 19–44. New York: Springer.

Craig, L.A. and Rettenberger, M. (2018). An etiological approach to sexual offender assessment: CAse Formulation Incorporating Risk Assessment (CAFIRA). *Current Psychiatry Reports* 20 (6): 20–43.

Durand, V.M. and Crimmins, D.B. (1988). Identifying the variables maintaining self-injurious behavior. *Journal of Autism and Developmental Disorders* 18: 99–117.

Farmer, M., McAlinden, A.-M., and Maruna, S. (2015). Understanding desistance from sexual offending: a thematic review of researc findings. *Probation Journal* 62 (4): 320–335.

Feldman, M., Condillac, R.A., Tough, S. et al. (2002). Effectiveness of community positive behavioral intervention for persons with developmental disabilities and severe behavior disorders. *Behavior Therapy* 33 (3): 377–399.

Gardner, W.I. (2002). *Aggression and Other Disruptive Behavioral Challenges: Biomedical and Psychosocial Assessment and Treatment*. New York: National Association for Dual Diagnosis.

Gardner, W.I., Graeber, J.L., and Cole, C.L. (1996). Behavior therapies: a multimodal diagnostic intervention model. In: *Manual of Diagnosis and Professional Practice in Mental Retardation* (eds. J. Jacobson and J. Mulick), 355–369. Washington, DC: American Psychiatric Press.

Gardner, W.I., Griffiths, D.M., and Hamelin, J. (2012). Biopsychosocial treatment of aggression. In: *The Handbook of High-risk Challenging Behaviors: Assessment and Intervention* (ed. J.K. Luiselli), 83–102. Baltimore: Paul H Brookes Publishing Co.

Gosse, L., Griffiths, D., Owen, F. et al. (2017). Impact of individualized planning approach on personal outcomes and supports for persons with intellectual disabilities. *Journal of Policy and Practice in Intellectual Disabilities* 14 (3): 198–204.

Griffiths, D.M., Condillac, R., and Legree, M. (2014). *Genetic Syndromes and Applied Behaviour Analysis*. London: Jessica Kingsley Publishing.

Hanson, R.K., Harris, A.J.R., Scott, T.L. et al. (2007). *Assessing the Risk of Sex Offenders on Community Supervision: The Dynamic Supervision Project (User Report 2007–05)*. Ottawa, ON: Public Safety Canada.

Hanson, R.K., Sheahan, C.L., and VanZuylen, H. (2013). *STATIC-99 and RRASOR Predict Recidivism Among Developmentally Delayed Sexual Offenders: A Cumulative Meta-analysis*. Public Safety Canada http://www.sexual-offender-treatment.org/119.html (accessed 12 March 2018).

Hanson, R.K. and Thornton, D. (2000). Improving risk assessments for sex offenders: a comparison of three actuarial scales. *Law and Human Behavior* 24: 119–136.

Harris, A.J.R. and Tough, S. (2004). Should actuarial risk assessments be used for sex offenders who are intellectually disabled? *Journal of Applied Research in Intellectual Disabilities* 17: 235–241.

Harris, G.T., Rice, M.E., Quinsey, V.L. et al. (2015). *Violent Offenders: Appraising and Managing Risk*, 3e. Washington, DC: American Psychological Association.

Healy, D. (2010). *The Dynamics of Desistance: Charting Pathways Through Change*. Cullompton: Willan.

Hedderman, C., Gunby, C., and Shelton, N. (2011). What women want: the importance of qualitative approaches in evaluating work with women offenders. *Criminology and Criminal Justice* 11 (1): 3–19.

Higgins, J.P.T., Altman, D.G., Gøtzsche, P.C. et al. (2011). The Cochrane Collaboration's tool for assessing risk of bias in randomised trials. *The BMJ*: 343. https://www.bmj.com/content/343/bmj.d5928 (accessed 12 June 2019).

Higgins, J.P.T., Sterne, J.A.C., Savović, J. et al., (2016). A revised tool for assessing risk of bias in randomized trials. In J. Chandler, J. McKenzie, I. Boutron et al. (ed.).*Cochrane Methods. Cochrane Database of Systematic Reviews*, 10 (Suppl 1). https://sites.google.com/site/riskofbiastool/welcome/rob-2-0-tool (accessed 12 June 2019).

Hilder, S. and Kemshall, H. (2013). Multi-agency approaches to effective risk management in the community in England and Wales. In: *What Works in Offender Rehabilitation: An Evidence-based Approach to Assessment and Treatment* (eds. L.A. Craig, L. Dixon and T.A. Gannon), 436–451. Chichester: Wiley-Blackwell.

Holburn, S., Jacobson, J.W., Vietze, P.M. et al. (2000). Quantifying the process and outcomes of person-centred planning. *American Journal of Mental Retardation* 105: 402–416.

Iwata, B.A., Dorsey, M.F., Slifer, K.J. et al. (1982). Toward a functional analysis of self-injury. *Analysis and Intervention in Developmental Disabilities* 2: 3–20.

Jacobson, J.W. and Holburn, S. (2004). History and current status of applied behavior analysis in developmental disabilities. In: *Behavior Modification for Persons with Developmental Disabilities: Treatments and Supports*, vol. 1 (eds. J.L. Matson, R.B. Laud and M.L. Matson), 1–32. Kingston, NY: NADD Press.

Johnston, J.M., Foxx, R.M., Jacobson, J.W. et al. (2006). Positive behavior support and applied behavior analysis. *Behavior Analysis* 29: 51–74.

Keeling, J.A., Rose, J.L., and Beech, A.R. (2009). Sexual offending theories and offenders with intellectual disabilities. *Journal of Applied Research in Intellectual Disabilities* 22: 468–476.

Laws, D.R. and Ward, T. (2011). *Desistance from sex offending: alternatives to throwing away the keys*. New York: The Guilford Press.

Lindsay, W.R. (2011). People with intellectual disability who offend or are involved with the criminal justice system. *Current Opinion in Psychiatry* 24 (5): 377–381.

Luiselli, J.K. (1989). Behavioral treatment of pediatric feeding disorders in developmental disabilities. In: *Progress in Behaviour Modification* (eds. M. Hersen, R. Eisler and P.M. Miller), 91–131. Newbury Park, CA: Sage.

Luiselli, J.K. (2004). Behavior support and intervention: current issues and practices in developmental disabilities. In: *Behavior Modification for Persons with Developmental Disabilities: Treatments and Supports*, vol. 1 (eds. J.L. Matson, R.B. Laud and M.L. Matson), 33–53. Kingston, NY: NADD Press.

Magnusson, D. and Bergman, L.R. (1988). Individual and variable-based approaches to longitudinal research on early risk factors. In: *Studies of Psychosocial Risk: The Power of Longitudinal Data* (ed. M. Rutter), 45–61. New York: Cambridge University Press.

Mann, R.E., Hanson, R.K., and Thornton, D. (2010). Assessing risk for sexual recidivism: some proposals on the nature of psychologically meaningful risk factors. *Sexual Abuse* 22: 191–217.

Maruna, S. (2001). *Making Good: How Ex-convicts Reform and Rebuild Their Lives*. Washington, DC: American Psychological Association Books.

McAlinden, A.-M., Farmer, M., and Maruna, S. (2017). Desistance from sexual offending: do the mainstream theories apply? *Criminology and Criminal Justice* 17 (3): 266–283.

McDermott, S. (2012). Moving forward: Empowering women to desist from offending. *Research Paper 2012/2*: The Griffins Society. https://www.thegriffinssociety.org/moving-forward-empowering-women-desist-offending (accessed 8 April 2014).

McGrath, R.J., Lasher, M.P., and Cumming, G.F. (2012). The sex offender treatment intervention and progress scale (SOTIPS): psychometric properties and incremental predictive validity with Static-99R. *Sex Abuse* 24 (5): 431–458. https://doi.org/10.1177/1079063211432475.

McNeill, F., Farrall, S., Lightowler, C. et al. (2012). How and why people stop offending: discovering desistance. *Insights: evidence summaries to support social services in Scotland, 15*. Glasgow: IRISS. www.iriss.org.uk/sites/default/files/iriss-insight-15.pdf (accessed 11 April 2014).

O'Neill, R.E., Horner, R.H., Albin, R.W. et al. (1997). *Functional Assessment and Program Development for Problem Behaviour: A Practical Handbook*. Pacific Grove, CA: Brookes/Cole.

Pycroft, A. (2014). Probation practice and creativity in England and Wales: a complex system analysis. In: *Applying Complexity Theory: Whole Systems Approaches to Criminal Justice and Social Work* (eds. A. Pycroft and C. Bartollas), 199–220. Bristol: The Policy Press.

Quinsey, V.L., Harris, G.T., Rice, M. et al. (1998). *Violent Offenders: Appraising and Managing Risk*. Washington, DC: American Psychological Association.

Reiss, S. (1994). *Handbook of Challenging Behavior: Mental Health Aspects of Mental Retardation*. Worthington, OH: IDS Publication.

Reiss, S., Levitan, G.W., and Szyszko, J. (1982). Emotional disturbance and mental retardation: diagnostic overshadowing. *American Journal of Mental Deficiency* 8 (6): 567–574.

Repp, A.C. and Singh, N.N. (1990). *Perspectives on the Use of Nonaversive and Aversive Intervention for Persons with Developmental Disabilities.* Sycamore, IL: Sycamore Publishing.

Rettenberger, M. and Craig, L.A. (2017). Actuarial risk assessment of sexual offenders. In: *The Wiley Handbook on the Theories, Assessment and Treatment of Sexual Offending. Volume 2, Assessment* (eds. L.A. Craig and M. Rettenberger), 609–642. Chichester: Wiley-Blackwell.

Risley, T. (1996). Get a life! Positive behavioral intervention for challenging behavior through life arrangement and life coaching. In: *Community, School, Family and Social Inclusion Through Positive Behavioral Support* (eds. L.K. Koegel, R.L. Koegel and G. Dunlap), 425–437. Baltimore, MD: Brookes.

Scotti, J.R., Ujcich, K.J., Weigle, K.L. et al. (1996). Interventions with challenging behaviour of persons with developmental disabilities: a review of current research practices. *Journal of the Association for Persons with Severe Handicaps* 21: 123–134.

Sherman, L.W., Gottfredson, D., Mackenzie, D. et al. (1998). *Preventing Crime: What Works, What Doesn't, What's Promising.* Washington, DC: National Institute of Justice https://www.ncjrs.gov/pdffiles/171676.PDF (accessed 12 June 2019).

Singh, N.N., Lancioni, G.E., Winton, S.W. et al. (2011). Can adult offenders with intellectual disabilities use mindfulness-based procedures to control their deviant sexual arousal? *Psychology, Crime & Law* 17 (2): 165–179.

Social Work Policy Institute (n.d.), *Evidence Based Practice.* http://www.socialworkpolicy.org/research/evidence-based-practice-2.html (accessed 12 March 2018).

Spiranovic, C., Cockburn, H., Bartels, L. et al. (2015). Outcome measures for evaluating the effectiveness of juvenile justice programs. *Victoria University Law and Justice Journal* 5: 23–33.

Steptoe, L., Lindsay, W.R., Murphy, L. et al. (2008). Construct validity, reliability and predictive validity of the dynamic risk assessment and management system (DRAMS) in offenders with intellectual disability. *Legal and Criminological Psychology* 13: 309–321.

Sturmey, P. and Bernstein, H. (2004). Functional analysis of maladaptive behaviors: current status and future directions. In: *Behavior Modification for Persons with Developmental Disabilities: Treatments and Supports*, vol. 1 (eds. J.L. Matson, R.B. Laud and M.L. Matson), 1–32. Kingston, NY: NADD Press.

Sugai, G., Horner, R.H., Dunlap, G. et al. (2000). Applying positive behavior support and functional assessment in schools. *Journal of Positive Behavior Interventions* 2: 131–143.

Thornton, D., Mann, R., Webster, S. et al. (2003). Distinguishing and combining risks for sexual and violent recidivism. In: *Understanding and Managing Sexually Coercive Behavior*, vol. 989 (eds. R.A. Prentky, E.S. Janus and M.C. Seto), 225–235. New York: Annals of the New York Academy of Sciences.

Tough, S.E. (2001, November). Validation of two standard risk assessments (Rapid Risk Assessment for Sex Offense Recidivism, 1997; Static–99, 1999) on a sample of adult males who are developmentally disabled with significant cognitive deficits. Paper presented at the Association for the Treatment of Sexual Abusers 20th Annual Research and Treatment Conference, San Antonio.

Verhoeven, M. (2010). Journeying to the wise mind: dialectical behaviour therapy and offenders with an intellectual disability. In: *Assessment and Treatment of Sexual*

Offenders with Intellectual Disabilities: A Handbook (eds. L.A. Craig, W.R. Lindsay and K.D. Browne), 317–340. Chichester: Wiley-Blackwell.

Wacker, D.P. and Berg, W.K. (2002). PBS as a service delivery system. *Journal of Positive Behavior Interventions* 4: 25–28.

Ward, T. (2002). Good lives and the rehabilitation of offenders: promises and problems. *Aggression and Violent Behavior* 7: 513–528.

Ward, T. and Gannon, T.A. (2006). Rehabilitation, etiology, and self-regulation: the comprehensive good lives model of treatment for sexual offenders. *Aggression and Violent Behavior* 11: 77–94.

Ward, T., Melser, J., and Yates, P.M. (2007). Reconstructing the risk need responsivity model: a theoretical elaboration and evaluation. *Aggression and Violent Behavior* 12: 208–228.

Weaver, B. and McNeill, F. (2007). Desistance. In: *Dictionary of Probation and Offender Management* (eds. R. Canton and D. Hancock), 90–92. Cullompton: Willan.

Whitehead, P. (2010). *Exploring Modern Probation: Social Theory and Organisational Complexity*. Bristol: Policy Press.

Willis, G.M. and Grace, R.C. (2008). The quality of community reintegration planning for child molesters: effects on sexual recidivism. *Sexual Abuse: A Journal of Research and Treatment* 20: 218–240.

Willis, G.M. and Grace, R.C. (2009). Assessment of community reintegration planning for sex offenders: poor planning predicts recidivism. *Criminal Justice and Behavior* 36 (5): 494–512.

Willis, G.M. and Ward, T. (2013). The good lives model: does it work? Preliminary evidence. In: *What Works in Offender Rehabilitation: An Evidence-Based Approach to Assessment and Treatment* (eds. L.A. Craig, L. Dixon and T.A. Gannon), 305–318. Chichester: Wiley-Blackwell.

Wilson, R.J., Prescott, D.S., and Burns, M. (2014). People with special needs and sexual behaviour problems: balancing community and client interests while ensuring effective risk management. *Journal of Sexual Aggression* 21: 86–99.

Wilson, R.J. and Yates, P.M. (2009). Effective interventions and the good lives model: maximizing treatment gains for sexual offenders. *Aggression and Violent Behavior* 14: 157–161.

Index

Tables are followed by the letter 't'.

*The Wiley Handbook on What Works for Offenders with Intellectual and Developmental Disabilities:
An Evidence-Based Approach to Theory, Assessment, and Treatment*, First Edition.
Edited by William R. Lindsay, Leam A. Craig, and Dorothy Griffiths.
© 2020 John Wiley & Sons Ltd. Published 2020 by John Wiley & Sons Ltd.